ENVIRONMENTAL LAW

THE LAW AND POLICY RELATING TO THE PROTECTION OF THE ENVIRONMENT

This book is printed on recycled paper

ENVIRONMENTAL LAW

THE LAW AND POLICY RELATING TO THE PROTECTION OF THE ENVIRONMENT

Third Edition

Simon Ball BA, BCL
Stuart Bell LLB Hons, Barrister

BLACKSTONE PRESS LIMITED

First published in Great Britain 1991 by Blackstone Press Limited,
9–15 Aldine Street, London W12 8AW. Telephone: 0181–740 1173

First edition 1991
Second edition 1994
Reprinted 1994
Third edition 1995

ISBN: 1 85431 443 2

British Library Cataloguing in Publication Data
A CIP catalogue record for this book is available from the British Library

Typeset by Style Photosetting Ltd, Mayfield, East Sussex
Printed by Ashford Colour Press, Gosport, Hants

This book is printed on recycled paper

Contents

Preface   xi

Abbreviations   xv

Table of Cases   xvii

Table of Statutes   xxiii

Table of Statutory Instruments   xxxv

Part I   General Principles of Environmental Law   1

1 What is environmental law?   3

The scope of this book — Some themes of the book — The shape of the book — The history of environmental law — The modern age of environmental law — The future of environmental policy — The future of environmental law — The costs of compliance — The costs of non-compliance — Policy and environmental law

2 Sources of environmental law   24

Some major features of environmental legislation — Informal sources of law and practice — European Communities (EC) law — International law — Judicial review — Remedies — Procedure — Restrictions on judicial review — The Ombudsman

3 Environmental protection agencies   36

Department of the Environment (DoE) — Other parts of Central Government — Parliamentary Select Committees — Royal Commission on Environmental Pollution (RCEP) — Other advisory bodies — The Environment Agency — Her Majesty's Inspectorate of Pollution (HMIP) — National

Rivers Authority (NRA) — Sewerage undertakers — General environmental
duties and the water industry — Countryside bodies — Local authorities —
Decision-making in local authorities

4 The European Community and the environment   55

The nature of the EC — The institutions of the EC — The European
Commission — The Council of Ministers — The European Parliament —
The European Court of Justice — The European Environment Agency —
Sources of EC law — Validity of EC legislation — Compliance by Member
States with EC law — Remedies for non-compliance — The common market
— The EC's environmental policy — The constitutional basis of the EC's
environmental policy — Articles 100 and 100A — Articles 130R, 130S and
130T — Article 235 — Qualified majority voting — Which Article? — Is
uniformity required? — The *Danish Bottles* case — The scope of EC
environmental policy — The range of environmental Directives — The types
of mechanism used — The future of EC environmental policy — Subsidiarity
— EC environmental law and Britain

5 The regulation of environmental protection   89

Administrative regulation — The processes of regulatory decision-making —
Anticipatory and continuing controls — Planning and prevention — Standards in environmental law — Interrelationship of standards — Other
characteristics of standards — Strengths and weaknesses of different types of
standard — Locally set and centrally set standards: Britain versus the EC —
Why Britain and the EC differ — The 'British approach' to regulation —
Decentralisation — Discretion — Gradualism and reliance on scientific
evidence — The importance of context — Are things changing? — Deregulation — Market mechanisms or the use of economic tools — Future uses of
economic instruments — The polluter pays principle — Eco-auditing and
environmental management systems — The civil law as a tool for environmental protection — The criminal law as a tool for environmental protection

6 The enforcement of environmental law   121

The British approach to enforcement — The nature of enforcement mechanisms in environmental protection — The legal context — The attitude
towards the offence — Attitudes towards the offender — The use of sanctions
other than prosecution — The process of enforcement — Lack of public
confidence in the enforcement system — Differing levels of enforcement —
Administrative difficulties — Staffing and funding levels — Changes in
attitudes to enforcement — The redefinition of the regulatory role — The
redefinition of the enforcement agencies' relationship with industry — The
redefinition of the importance of environmental protection — The development of enforcement policy — Enforcement and deregulation — Public
participation in the enforcement process

7   Access to environmental information   140

The development of a general environmental secrecy policy — Mechanisms of secrecy — Commercial confidentiality — 'Green nutters' — Administration costs — The Royal Commission's approach — The effect of secrecy upon risk perception — Environmental rights — The recommendations of the Royal Commission — Water pollution — Other registers in the water industry — Waste disposal — Registers in relation to contaminated land — Integrated pollution control — The Chemical Releases Inventory — Air pollution — Access to information held by local government — The Environmental Information Regulations 1992 — The public's utilisation of registers

8   The common law and the protection of the environment   167

The characteristics of the common law as a mechanism of environmental protection — Is the common law as a protection mechanism dead? — Civil liability in statutes — The law of tort and environmental protection — The law of nuisance — Defences to a claim for nuisance — Private rights under the common law and the grant of planning permission — An assessment of nuisance as a tool for environmental protection — Public nuisance — Trespass — Negligence — The rule in *Rylands* v *Fletcher* — Defences — The usefulness of the rule in *Rylands* v *Fletcher* — The protection of riparian rights — Civil law remedies — Statutory nuisance — The control of statutory nuisances — The categories of statutory nuisance — What is required to satisfy the local authority? — Who is the 'person responsible'? — The abatement notice — Defences — The right of appeal against an abatement notice — Individual actions by any person — Sentencing powers for contravention of an abatement notice — The use of injunctions and proceedings in the High Court.

Part II   Sectoral Coverage of Environmental Law   203

9   Town and country planning   205

The main features of town and country planning — Town and country planning as a tool of environmental policy — Town and country planning and some themes of this book — The planning legislation — What is town and country planning? — Planning policy — Deregulation — Local planning authorities — Forward planning: development plans — The history and future of development plans — Local plans — Unitary development plans — Development plans and development control — Non-statutory plans and guidance — Development control: definition of development — Material change of use — Use Classes Order — Existing uses — The General Development Orders — Is planning permission required? — Applying for planning permission — Decisions by the local planning authority — Alternative and special procedures — Special areas — The Secretary of State's powers — Summary of rights of third parties — The local planning authority's discretion — The presumption in favour of the development plan — Other material considerations — Conditions — Legal tests for the validity of conditions — Conditions and policy — Planning conditions and pollution control — Planning obligations — Planning appeals — Procedure on appeals — Challenging the decision of the Secretary of State — Enforcement of planning law — Enforcement notices — Stop notices — Injunctions — Other enforcement powers — Enforcement where there is no breach of planning law — Planning and hazardous substances

10   Environmental assessment   262

What is environmental assessment? — Environmental Assessment Directive — Environmental Assessment Directive and direct effect — Is the project subject to environmental assessment? — Environmental assessment and permitted development — Pre-application procedures for establishing the need for environmental assessment — Pre-application directions from the Secretary of State — Challenges to the decisions of the Secretary of State or local planning authority — Other procedures for determining the need for environmental assessment — The environmental statement — Undertaking the process of environmental assessment — Environmental assessment in simplified planning zones and enterprise zones — Environmental assessment in practice — The case for reform?

11   Integrated pollution control   282

Pollution of the atmosphere — Pollution on land — Control of water pollution — The administrative jungle and the mechanisms of protection — Consequences of the fragmented approach — Time for a change — Best practicable environmental option — The EC's role in change — *Vorsorgeprinzip:* anticipation through foresight — HMIP – a unified body — The Environment Agency and IPC — The introduction of integrated pollution control — Organisation and administration of the system of integrated pollution control — The requirement for authorisation — Determination of the need for an authorisation — Prescribed processes — Meaning of process — Release of prescribed substances — Exceptions — Overlapping controls — Planning permission — Applications for authorisation — Fees — Public participation and other consultation procedures — Call-in procedure — Commercial confidentiality and national security — The determination of an application — BATNEEC — Integrated pollution control notes — Implementation of the IPC system — Transfer of authorisations — Enforcement powers — Offences and remedies — Corporate liability — Crown immunity — Appeals — The European approach to integrated pollution prevention and control

12 Atmospheric pollution   322

Local atmospheric pollution — International difficulties: acid rain — Global
issues: ozone depletion and global warming — Global issues — Air pollution
policy — Air quality strategy — Monitoring of air pollution — The EC and
air pollution — The Air Quality Standards Regulations 1989 — The control
of smoke under the Clean Air Act 1993 — The control of grit, dust and
fumes — The control of height of chimneys — Miscellaneous controls —
Smoke control areas — The control of noxious emissions to the atmosphere
other than smoke, dust, grit and fumes — The scope of air pollution control
— Applications — The determination of the application — Air pollution
guidance notes — The control of emissions from motor vehicles — European
policy on motor vehicles

13 Waste management   346

Waste policy — The use of economic instruments and waste management —
The landfill tax — Recycling — Legislative history — Transitional provisions
— Waste disposal and town planning — EC Directives on waste — Waste
disposal under the Control of Pollution Act 1974 — The failings of COPA
1974 — The Environmental Protection Act 1990, Part II — Waste authorities
under the EPA 1990 — What is waste? — What is controlled waste? —
Exemptions — Waste plans — Waste management licensing — Environment
powers — Fees and charges — Public registers — The powers of the Secretary
of State — Appeals — Offences — Defences — Dangerous disposal of waste
— Overlap with EPA 1990, Part I — Clean-up powers — Contaminated land
— Other statutory provisions for the clean-up of contaminated land —
Statutory powers to clean up contaminated land — Duty of care — Carriage of
waste — Waste brokers — General powers of WRAs — Special waste — Civil
liability for unlawful disposal of waste

14 Water pollution   411

Water pollution — The water industry — The Water Act 1989 and the Water
Resources Act 1991 — Water pollution controls — Scotland — Pollution
policy — The EC and water pollution — Future of EC water pollution policy
— Water supply — Consents for the discharge of trade or sewage effluents —
General pollution offence — Penalties — Defences — Meaning of 'cause or
knowingly permit' — The consent system — Revocation and variation —
Transitional provisions — Annual charges for discharge consents — The role
of the Secretary of State — Appeals — How are consents set? — Water
quality objectives — Public registers — Integrated pollution control —
Sewage discharges — Radioactive discharges — Sampling and enforcement
powers — Enforcement policy — Preventative and remedial powers —
Precautions against pollution — Water protection zones — Nitrate sensitive
areas — Planning controls — Other water pollution offences — Statutory
nuisances — Water pollution and the common law

15   Disposal of waste to sewers   461

Trade effluent discharges — Applying for a trade effluent consent — How are consents set? — Trade effluent charges — Public participation — 'Red List' substances — Enforcement — Discharges from sewage works — Domestic sewage discharges

16   The conservation of nature   468

History — Types of legal protection — The nature conservation agencies — The protection of individual animals and plants — Habitat protection— Sites of special scientific interest (SSSIs) — Duties on owners and occupiers — Specific duties in the water industry — Nature conservation orders — National nature reserves (NNRs) — Local nature reserves — Marine nature reserves (MNRs) — Limestone pavements — Management agreements — Planning permission — Loss and damage to SSSIs — The international perspective — EC Wild Birds Directive 79/409 — EC Habitats Directive 92/43 — The 1994 Regulations — European marine sites — European sites and other regulatory systems — The Ramsar Convention — Summary of protection of internationally important sites

17   The protection of the countryside   499

Town and country planning — Extra protections — The Countryside Commission — Landscape protection and management agreements — Agriculture and landscape

18   The protection of trees and woodlands   510

Trees and planning permission — Tree preservation orders (TPOs) — Conservation areas — Compensation — Felling licences — Proposals for change — Hedgerows

Bibliography   518

Index   530

Preface

Once again, in the short period since the second edition of this book was published, there have been some important changes in environmental law. Without a doubt, the most significant development has been the enactment of the Environment Act 1995, which has as its central feature the creation of two environmental protection agencies, the Environment Agency (for England and Wales) and the Scottish Environment Protection Agency (SEPA). However, the 1995 Act also includes the following: some important provisions on the remediation of contaminated land, which proved controversial during the passage through Parliament; the prospective repeal of the partial immunity that abandoned mines currently enjoy in relation to water pollution; the repeal of the provisions on tripartite, or 'legal', samples; changes to the structure of national park authorities and to the purposes of national parks; important new powers on the management of air quality; a new system of producer responsibility for certain products and materials; authorisation for the production of a national waste strategy; some complex provisions relating to existing mineral planning permissions; new powers for the protection of important hedgerows; provisions on the removal of Crown immunity from environmental legislation; and a whole host of minor and consequential amendments.

Part I of the Act, which concerns the two new environment agencies, merits closer attention, since it affects most aspects of the book. In England and Wales, the Environment Agency brings together the National Rivers Authority with Her Majesty's Inspectorate of Pollution and the waste regulation authorities. In essence, the Act transfers all the various functions carried on by these bodies to the new Agency. One result is that the Agency has a number of water resource functions that are not directly connected with environmental protection — indeed, in terms of numbers of employees, those concerned with the control of pollution will be in a minority.

It is also important to understand what the Act does *not* do. It does not bring all pollution control functions within the Agency, since air pollution control remains the responsibility of local authorities (although this is not the position in Scotland, where SEPA takes over these functions). Nature conservation and countryside protection also stay outside the remit of the

Agency, as do planning and environmental assessment functions. Also, the Act does not unify the legislation — for example, in relation to its water pollution functions the Agency will have the powers set out in the Water Resources Act 1991, whilst in relation to integrated pollution control it will have the different powers and duties in the Environmental Protection Act 1990. It is disappointing that the opportunity has not been taken to unify the law in these areas. At the time of writing it is hoped that the agencies will be operational from 1 April 1996 to coincide with local government reorganisation, but that is not entirely certain since there is a great deal of work to be done in preparation for the change.

Apart from the provisions on national parks, the Environment Act 1995 is to come into force by commencement order. At the time of writing only one such order has been made (SI 1995 No. 1983) and that deals mainly with matters that are preparatory to the transfer of powers to the Environment Agency and the creation of the new system of liability for contaminated land. Accordingly, in the book we have explained the position as it is at 1 August 1995, although with reference to what will happen when the Act comes into force. However, two important qualifications must be made. One is that schedule 22 to the Act made a large number of detailed changes to the existing legislation. Since these changes will only come into force when a commencement order to that effect is made, in order to avoid undue confusion over minor points we cannot guarantee that in all cases we have set out the future law as well as the current situation. The other is that in some cases the exact details of the changes made by the Act are as yet unknown, since so much has been left to the Secretary of State to fill in by statutory instrument.

In addition to the Environment Act 1995, other major changes in the last couple of years which are included in this edition for the first time are the Deregulation and Contracting Out Act 1994, the Conservation (Natural Habitats etc) Regulations 1994 (which purportedly implement the EC Habitats Directive), the Waste Management Licensing Regulations 1994 (which finally introduced the system of waste management licensing on 1 May 1994), the Urban Waste Water Treatment (England and Wales) Regulations 1994 and the Surface Waters (River Ecosystem) (Classification) Regulations 1994 (which move statutory water quality objectives one stage nearer, although the rate of movement on this issue is glacial).

In terms of cases, there has been a number of important cases on water pollution offences which are discussed in Chapter 14. Other significant decisions are *Wheeler* v *JJ Saunders Ltd* and *Gateshead MBC* v *Secretary of State* (both, in their own ways, on the relationship between planning and pollution control), *R* v *Secretary of State for Trade and Industry ex parte Duddridge* (on the precautionary principle), *R* v *Her Majesty's Inspectorate of Pollution ex parte Greenpeace Ltd (No. 2)* (concerning the standing of environmental groups), *Wychavon DC* v *Secretary of State for the Environment & Velcourt Ltd* (on environmental assessment), and *Tesco Stores Ltd* v *Secretary of State* (which provides guidelines on the controversial issue of planning gain).

On the EC front there has been the eventual agreement of Directive 94/62 on packaging and packaging waste, although the proposed Directives on integrated pollution prevention and control, the ecological quality of water and landfill are still the subject of negotiation.

As we have pointed out before, policy in the environmental field is as important as law. Is it possible to discern any important trends? To some extent this is difficult, since little has changed from the last edition when we commented that it was difficult to discern with any degree of clarity exactly what the current Government's policy on the environment was. What legislative changes there have been have either been required by EC Directives or have been delayed for so long that they can hardly be said to represent a firm and enthusiastic policy. This ambivalence comes over in the drafting of the Environment Act 1995. Whilst the creation of two environment agencies is to be applauded, the most controversial section in Part I of the Act is undoubtedly s. 39, which requires the agencies to take into account the likely costs and benefits of their decisions. At one level this could be justified as increasing the accountability of the Agency and merely making explicit the sorts of considerations any public body will take into account anyway. However, at another level this section could be seen as part of a concerted campaign by the Government to reduce the effectiveness of the environmental protection agencies. The same thoughts are triggered by the deregulation initiative. Whilst this has not yet led to any major casualties in the area of environmental protection, the extremely wide powers in the Deregulation and Contracting Out Act 1994 are a constant threat to proper environmental protection. These two Acts also illustrate a clear shift in power from Parliament to the executive Government, because they leave so much (including even the definition of statutory concepts such as contamination) to be defined in centrally produced guidance notes and circulars.

There is one other trend that transcends environmental law. This is that it is increasingly being accepted that environmental issues are 'lifestyle' issues in the sense that the protection of the environment is intimately tied up with the way that people live and is not a marginal issue, of relevance only to polluting industries and those who live next door to them. The emphasis in environmental policy has shifted to looking at such things as transport policy and car use, recycling and usage of raw materials, ethical issues relating to the environment, and patterns of usage of water. In short, the emphasis has shifted to issues of sustainability. Even the Government has caught on, with the publication of the rather bland, but useful, *Sustainable Development: The UK Strategy* (Cm. 2426) in January 1994 and some tentative steps towards sustainable planning in the town and country planning system.

In this context, it needs to be explained that we do not seek to discuss all of these disparate issues in this book. This is not a book about environmental policy as such, but a book about the law, albeit one that takes the policy context as being of central importance. Accordingly, whilst we recognise the great importance of ethical consumerism, recycling initiatives, environmental audit, environmental management systems and the greening of the supply chain, the full discussion of these issues is for another book (although we look at market mechanisms in general and at BS 7750 on Environmental Management Systems, the producer responsibility provisions in the 1995 Act and the proposed landfill tax in particular). So is discussion of direct action, although the Brent Spar story illustrates graphically that litigation and legal action are not necessarily the best way to achieve a favourable result.

We also need to re-emphasise that this is not a book about environmental liability. As a result, many of the more commercially relevant topics are not dealt with in the depth that would otherwise be the case; nor is the important and growing topic of 'toxic torts', which justifies a book to itself because of the overlaps between environmental and personal injury litigation. It is also worth repeating that this is a book that seeks to provide a general introduction to the central issues within *domestic* environmental law and does not seek to look at the laws of other countries or at international law. There are also some areas which cannot be covered for reasons of space, such as marine pollution, the protection of the cultural heritage, and the environmental release of genetically modified organisms.

The law is stated as at 1 August 1995.

Simon Ball
Stuart Bell
October 1995

Abbreviations

AONB	area of outstanding natural beauty
APC	air pollution control
AQMA	air quality management area
AQS	air quality standards
BATNEEC	best available techniques not entailing excessive cost
BOD	biochemical oxygen demand
BPEO	best practicable environmental option
BPM	best practicable means
COPA 1974	Control of Pollution Act 1974
COSHH	Control of Substances Hazardous to Health
CRI	Chemical Releases Inventory
DoE	Department of the Environment
EA	Environment Agency
EC	European Community
EPA 1990	Environmental Protection Act 1990
ESA	environmentally sensitive area
HMIP	Her Majesty's Inspectorate of Pollution
HSA	hazardous substances authorities
HSC	hazardous substances consent
HSE	Health and Safety Executive
IPC	integrated pollution control
LAAPC	local authority air pollution control
MAFF	Ministry of Agriculture, Fisheries and Food
MHLG	Ministry of Housing and Local Government
MNR	marine nature reserve
NCC	Nature Conservancy Council
NNR	national nature reserve
NRA	National Rivers Authority
RCEP	Royal Commission on Environmental Pollution
SEPA	Scottish Environment Protection Agency
SSSI	site of special scientific interest
TPO	tree preservation order
WDA	waste disposal authority
WRA	waste regulation authority

Table of Cases

Aitken v South Hams DC [1994] 3 All ER 400 197
Alderson v Secretary of State [1984] 49 P&CR 307 241
Allen v Gulf Oil Refining Limited [1981] 1 All ER 353 178
Alphacell Ltd v Woodward [1972] AC 824 16, 430, 433
Anderson v Oppenheimer (1880) 5 QBD 602 189
Arlington Securities Ltd v Secretary of State [1989] JPL 166 239
Ashcroft v Cambro Waste Products Ltd [1981] 3 All ER 699 385
Associated Provincial Picture Houses Limited v Wednesbury Corporation
 [1948] 1 KB 223 30, 271, 432
Attorney General's Reference (No. 1 of 1994) [1995] 2 All ER 1007 431, 432, 433
Attorney General's Reference (No. 2 of 1988) [1990] JEL 80 361, 376
Attorney General's Reference (No. 2 of 1994) [1995] Env LR 143 448
Attorney-General v Cory Brothers & Co [1921] 1 AC 521 189
Attorney-General v Gastonia Coaches Limited [1977] RTR 219 174
Attorney-General v PYA Quarries [1957] 2 QB 169 183, 184

Ballard v Tomlinson (1885) 29 ChD 115 182, 183, 458, 459
Barvis v SSE [1971] 22 P&CR 710 221
Beju Bop Ltd v Home Farm (Iwerne Minister) Ltd [1990] Water Law 90 457
Bell v Canterbury CC [1989] 1 JEL 90 515
Bellew v Cement Co. [1948] Ir.R 61 172, 174
Bishop Auckland Local Board v Bishop Auckland Iron and Steel Company
 (1882) 10 QBD 138 195
Bliss v Hall (1838) 4 Bing NC 183 176
Bolton MBC v Secretary of State for the Environment [1995] JPL 581 213
Bradford MBC v Secretary of State [1986] JPL 598 241
Bradley (E) & Sons v Secretary of State for the Environment [1983] 47 P&CR 375 217
Bricket Wood case [1989] JPL 629 248
British Railways Board v Secretary of State (1990) *The Times*, 29 October 241
Bruton and National Rivers Authority v Clarke [1994] Water Law 145 451, 459
Bullock v Secretary of State [1980] 40 P&CR 246 513
Burdle v Secretary of State [1972] 3 All ER 240 223

Cambridge CC v Secretary of State [1991] JPL 428 221
Cambridge Water Co. Ltd v Eastern Counties Leather plc [1994] 1 All ER 53
 18, 19, 170, 182, 186, 188, 190, 399, 458
Carr v London Borough of Hackney [1995] Env LR D37 197
Chapman v Gosberton Farm Produce [1993] Env LR 191 198
Chasemore v Richards [1859] 7 HLC 349 457

Cheshire CC v Armstrong's Transport (Wigan) Ltd [1995] Env LR 62   368
City of London Corpn v Secretary of State [1971] 23 P&CR 169   224, 226, 241
Clifford v Holt [1899] 1 Ch 698   333
Clyde & Co. v Secretary of State [1977] JPL 521   239
Coleshill Investments v MHLG [1969] 2 All ER 525   221
Collis Radio Ltd v Secretary of State [1975] 29 P&CR 390   239
Comitato di Coordinamento per la Difesa della Cava v Regione Lombardia
   [1994] Water Law 147   81
Commission v Belgium [1993] 1 CMLR 365, [1993] JEL 273   77
Commission v Belgium [1982] CMLR 627   64, 441
Commission v Council [1993] ECR I-939   74
Commission v Council [1992] JEL 109   74
Commission v Council [1993] Water Law 109   356
Commission v Denmark [1989] 54 CMLR 619   57, 63, 65, 77, 456
Commission v Germany [1991] ECR 883   490
Commission v Germany [1991] Water Law 179   66, 493
Commission v Italy [1981] 1 CMLR 331   69
Commission v Spain [1993] Water Law 209   87, 490, 491, 498
Commission v United Kingdom [1993] Water Law 168   85, 87, 421
Commission v United Kingdom [1994] Water Law 59   64, 85, 87, 422
Cooke v Adatia [1989] LGR 32   197
Coventry City Council v Cartwright [1975] 1 WLR 845   193, 195
CPC (UK) Ltd v National Rivers Authority [1995] Env LR 131   137, 448
Crossley v Lightowler [1866] 11 Ch App Cas 478   458

Danish Bottles see Commission v Denmark
Draper v Sperring (1869) 10 CB 113   195
Duke v GEC Reliance Ltd [1988] AC 618   86
Durham CC v Peter Connors Industrial Services Ltd [1993] Env LR 197   386

East Northants DC v Fossett [1994] Env LR 388   197
Elliott v Islington LBC [1990] 4/4 Env Law 9   513
Enfield LBC v Secretary of State [1975] JPL 155   236
Esso v Southport Corporation [1956] AC 218   185
Evans v Godber [1974] 3 All ER 341   484

Faccini Dori v Recreb Srl [1995] All ER (EC) 1   62
Fawcett Properties Ltd v Bucks CC [1961] AC 636   240
Forestry Commission v Frost [1990] JPL 929   516
Foster v British Gas plc [1990] 3 All ER 897   62
France v Commission [1994] Water Law 120   75
Francovich v Italy (Case C6/90 [1993] 2 CMLR 66   20, 66, 67, 86

Gateshead MBC v Secretary of State for the Environment [1995] JPL 432   94
Gateshead MBC v Secretary of State for the Environment and Northumbrian
   Water Group [1995] Env LR 37   300
Gertsen v Municipality of Toronto [1973] 41 DLR (3d) 646   409
Gibbons v SW Water [1993] Env LR 244   191
Gillingham BC v Medway (Chatham) Dock Company [1992] Env LR 98   174, 179
Givaudan v MHLG [1966] 3 All ER 696   248
Goldman v Hargrave [1967] 1 AC 645   459
Goldsmith v Tunbridge Wells Improvement Commission (1866) 1 Ch App 349   191, 201
Grampian RC v Aberdeen DC [1984] 47 P&CR 633   241
Gransden (E.C.) v Secretary of State [1986] JPL 519   235
Great Portland Estates Ltd v Westminster CC [1984] 3 All ER 744   178, 209, 219, 239
Greater London Council v Secretary of State [1986] JPL 193   239
Greater London Council v The London Borough of Tower Hamlets (1983) 15 HLR 57   194

Griffin v South West Water Services Ltd [1995] Water Law 5   62

Hall v Shoreham UDC [1964] 1 WLR 240   241
Halsey v Esso Petroleum Company [1961] 1 WLR 683   181
Hammersmith London Borough Council v Magnum Automated Forecourts Ltd
   [1978] 1 WLR 50   200
Harrison v Southwark and Vauxhall Water Company [1891] 2 Ch 409   175, 184
Hartley v MHLG [1970] 1 QB 413   225
Harvey v Secretary of State for Wales [1990] JPL 420   251
Herbert v Lambeth LBC [1992] LG Rev 421   113

Impress (Worcester) Ltd v Rees [1971] 2 All ER 357   432
IRC v National Federation of Self Employed and Small Businesses Ltd [1982] AC 617   32

JB and M Motor Haulage Ltd v LWRA [1993] Env LR 243   405
Jennings Motors v Secretary of State [1982] 1 All ER 471   225
Jones v Llanrwst UDC [1908] All ER 922   185, 459

Kent CC v Batchelor [1976] 33 P&CR 185   512
Kent CC v Beaney [1991] 5 Env Law 89   385
Kent CC v Queenborough Rolling Mill Co. Ltd [1990] JEL 257   367
Kincardine and Deeside DC v The Forestry Commissioners [1992] 1 Env LR 151   87, 265
Kirklees MBC v Wickes Building Supplies Ltd [1992] 3 All ER 717   255

Ladbrokes Ltd v Secretary of State [1981] JPL 427)   241
Lambert (A) Flat Management v Lomas [1981] 2 All ER 280   198
Lappel Bank case (unreported, 18 August 1994)   87
Leigh Land Reclamation Ltd v Walsall MBC [1991] 191 ENDS Report 37   360, 370, 385
Lemmon v Webb [1895] AC 1   192
Litster v Forth Dry Dock & Engineering Co. Ltd [1989] 2 WLR 634   86
Lloyds Bank v Guardian Assurance (1987) 35 Build LR 34   200
Lockhart v National Coal Board [1981] SLT 161   430
London Borough of Southwark v Ince (1989) 21 HLR 504   194
London Residuary Body v Lambeth BC [1990] 2 All ER 309   105, 237
Long v Brook [1980] Crim LR 109   367

Maidstone BC v Mortimer [1980] 3 All ER 552   511
Main v Swansea CC [1985] 49 P&CR 26   228, 230
Malton Board of Health v Malton Manure Company (1879) 4 ExD 302   195
Malvern Hills DC v Secretary of State [1983] 81 LGR 13   222
Mansi v Elstree RDC [1964] 16 P&CR 153   253
Marleasing SA v La Commercial International de Alimentatión SA [1992] 1 CMLR 305
                                                                 61, 65, 66, 86
Marquis of Granby v Bakewell UDC (1923) 87 JP 105   191
Marshall v Southampton and South West Hampshire Area Health Authority
   [1986] 2 WLR 780   62
McDonald v Associated Fuels [1954] 3 DLR 713   184
McKinnon Industries Limited v Walker [1951] 3 DLR 577   176
Merlin v British Nuclear Fuels plc [1990] 3 All ER 711   19
Meston Technical Services Ltd and Wright v Warwickshire County Council
   [1995] Env LR D36   368
Miller-Mead v MHLG [1963] 2 QB 196   253
Murphy v Brentwood DC [1990] 2 All ER 908   459

National Coal Board v Thorne [1976] 1 WLR 543   194
National Rivers Authority v Alfred McAlpine Homes (East) Ltd [1995] JEL 60 433
National Rivers Authority v Alfred McAlpine Homes (South) Ltd [1994] Env LR 198   386

National Rivers Authority v Harcros Timber and Building Supplies Ltd
  [1992] Env LR 172   448
National Rivers Authority v Shell (UK) [1990] Water Law 40   450, 451
National Rivers Authority v Welsh Development Agency [1993] Env LR 407   432
National Rivers Authority v Wright Engineering Co. Ltd [1994] Env LR 186   432
National Rivers Authority v Yorkshire Water Services Ltd [1995] 1 All ER 225
                                                 430, 431, 433, 446, 466
Network Housing Association v Westminster CC [1994] *The Times*, 8 November 1994   197
Nicholls v Ely Sugar Factory Ltd [1936] Ch 343   458
North Uist Fisheries Ltd v Secretary of State for Scotland [1991] SLT 333   480
North Western Utilities Limited v London Guarantee and Accident Co. Ltd
  [1936] AC 108   189

Parliament v Council [1995] Env LR D14   74
Pepper v Hart [1993] 1 All ER 42   481
Petition of the Kincardine and Deeside DC [1992] JEL 289   87
Pilkington v Secretary of State [1973] 1 WLR 1527   231
Pioneer Aggregates (UK) v Secretary of State [1984] 3 WLR 32   208, 225, 231
Polymeric Treatments v Walsall MBC [1993] Env LR 427   405
Price v Cromack [1995] 1 WLR 988   432, 433
Pride of Derby Angling Association v British Celanese Ltd [1952] Ch 149   460
Pye (J.A.) Ltd v West Oxfordshire DC [1982] 47 P&CR 125   236
Pyx Granite Ltd v MHLG [1958] 1 QB 554   240

R v Amber Valley DC ex parte Jackson [1985] 1 WLR 298   231
R v Boal [1992] 3 All ER 177   375, 386
R v Chambers and others [1989] JPL 229   135
R v Dovermoss Ltd [1995] ELM 106   428
R v Exeter CC ex parte J L Thomas & Co Ltd [1990] 1 All ER 413   177, 239
R v Folkestone Magistrates' Court ex parte Kibble [1993] Env LR 400   197
R v Gillingham BC ex parte Parham Ltd [1988] JPL 336   244
R v Hammersmith LBC ex parte People Before Profit (1982) 80 LGR 322   33
R v Her Majesty's Inspectorate of Pollution ex parte Greenpeace Ltd (No. 2)
  [1994] 4 All ER 329   19, 33
R v Hillingdon BC ex parte Royco Homes [1974] 2 QB 720   240
R v HMIP ex parte Greenpeace Ltd (1994) Env LR 76   150
R v Jenner [1983] 2 All ER 46   254
R v Kuxhaus [1988] 2 All ER 705   252
R v Lloyd (1802) 4 Esp 200   183
R v London Borough Transport Committee ex parte Freight Transport Association Ltd
  (1990) *The Times*, 4 October   75, 77, 87
R v Metropolitan Stipendiary Magistrate ex parte London Waste Regulation Authority
  [1993] 3 All ER 113   370
R v Nature Conservancy Council ex parte London Brick Property Ltd [1995] ELM 95   479
R v Plymouth CC ex parte Plymouth and South Devon Co-operative Society Ltd
  [1993] JPL B81   244, 246
R v Poole BC ex parte Beebee [1991] JPL 643   33, 256, 272, 488
R v Poole Borough Council ex parte Beebee and others [1991] JPL 643   272
R v Rotherham MBC ex parte Rankin [1990] JEL 503   228
R v Secretary of State ex parte Friends of the Earth
  [1995] 245 ENDS Report 44   85, 87, 422
R v Secretary of State for Foreign Affairs ex parte World Development Movement Ltd
  [1995] 1 All ER 611   19, 34
R v Secretary of State for the Environment ex parte Rose Theatre Trust Company
  [1990] 1 All ER 754   19, 33, 83, 105
R v Secretary of State for Trade and Industry ex parte Duddridge [1995] Env LR 151   19, 88
R v Secretary of State for Transport ex parte Factortame [1990] 3 CMLR 1   67

R v Sheffield CC ex parte Mansfield [1978] 37 P&CR 1   247
R v Smith [1985] JPL 183   253
R v St Edmundsbury BC ex parte Investors in Industry Commercial Properties Ltd
  [1985] 1 WLR 1168   230
R v Swale Borough Council and Medway Ports Authority ex parte The Royal Society
  for the Protection of Birds [1991] JPL 39   32, 268, 271
R v Tower Hamlets LBC ex parte Ahern (London) Ltd [1989] JPL 757   253
R v Wealden DC ex parte Charles Church (South East) Ltd [1989] JPL 837   244
R v Westminster CC ex parte Monahan [1988] JPL 557   239
Rainham Chemicals v Belvedere Fish Guano Company [1921] 2 AC 465   188
Read v Croydon Corporation [1938] 4 All ER 631   426
Read v Lyons [1947] AC 156   188
Reynolds v Clarke (1725) 1 Stra 643   184
Rickards v Lothian [1913] AC 263   187
Robinson v Kilvert (1889) 41 ChD 88   175
Rookes v Barnard [1964] AC 1129   191
Rossall v London Borough of Southwark, (unreported)   197
Rushmer v Polsue and Alfieri [1906] Ch 234   173
Rylands v Fletcher (1865) 3 H&C 774   182, 183, 187, 189, 190, 398, 409, 459

Saunders Clark v Grosvenor Mansion Company Limited & D'Alles-Sandry
  [1900] 2 Ch 373   172
Save Britain's Heritage v Secretary of State [1991] 2 All ER 10   33
Schulmans Incorporated Ltd v National Rivers Authority [1993] Env LR D1   433
Scott-Whitehead v National Coal Board (1987) 53 P&CR 263   186, 459
Shanley (M J) Ltd v Secretary of State [1982] JPL 380   241
Sheffield CC v ADH Demolition (1984) 82 LGR 177   335
Short v Poole Corporation   30
Smeaton v Ilford Corporation [1954] 1 Ch 450   177, 189, 467
Smith v East Elloe RDC [1956] AC 736   249
Snook v Secretary of State [1977] 33 P&CR 1   222
Southern Water Authority v Nature Conservancy Council [1992] 3 All ER 481   19, 481
Southern Water Authority v Pegrum [1989] Local Government Review 672   431
St Albans DC v Secretary of State [1993] JPL 374   237
St Helens Smelting Co. v Tipping (1865) 11 HLC 642   168, 173, 174, 181
Steeples v Derbyshire CC [1984] 3 All ER 468   231
Stevenage BC v Wilson [1993] Env LR 214   194
Stoke on Trent CC v B & Q Retail Ltd [1984] AC 754   254
Stringer v MHLG [1970] 1 WLR 1281   235, 239
Sturges v Bridgman (1879) 11 ChD 852   173, 174, 176, 177
Sweet v Secretary of State and Nature Conservancy Council [1989] JEL 245   479, 483

Tameside MBC v Secretary of State [1984] JPL 180   239
Tandridge DC v P&S Civil Engineering Ltd [1995] Env LR 67   298
Taylor Woodrow Property Management Ltd v National Rivers Authority [1995] JEL 55 433
Tesco Stores Limited v Secretary of State for the Environment and others
  [1995] JPL 581   245, 246
Thanet DC v Kent CC [1993] Env LR 391   369
The Wagon Mound (No. 2) [1967] 1 AC 617   459
Times Investments Ltd v Secretary of State [1990] JPL 433   242
Trent River Authority v F. H. Drabble & Sons Ltd [1970] 1 WLR 98   436
Turner v Secretary of State [1973] 28 P&CR 123   249
Tutton v A D Walter [1985] 3 WLR 797   186
Twyford Parish Council v Secretary of State for Transport [1992] 1 Env LR 37;
  [1992] JEL 273   87, 265

Vessoso and Zanetti ([1990] 2 LMELR 133   59, 368

Von Colson [1986] 2 CMLR 430   61, 65, 66

Wales v Thames Water Authority [1987] 1/3 Environmental Law 3   444
Wallington v Secretary of State [1991] JPL 942   195, 223
Waste Incineration Services Ltd v Dudley MBC [1992] Env LR 29   387
Wellingborough BC v Gordon [1993] Env LR 218   198
Welsh Water Authority v Williams Motors (Cwmdu) Ltd, *The Times*, 5 December 1988   432
Westminster CC v Jones [1981] JPL 750   254
Wheatcroft (Bernard) Ltd v Secretary of State [1981] 257 EG 934   230
Wheeler v JJ Saunders [1995] 2 All ER 697; [1995] Env LR 286   170, 173, 179, 460
Woodhouse v Walsall MBC [1994] Env LR 30   375, 386
Wrothwell Ltd v Yorkshire Water Authority [1984] Crim LR 43   431
Wychavon DC v NRA [1993] JEL 121   87, 432, 433
Wychavon DC v Secretary of State for the Environment & Velcourt Ltd
    [1994] JEL 351   87, 265
Wycombe DC v Secretary of State [1988] JPL 111   235
Wyre Forest DC v Bostock [1991] Env LR 235   201

Young & Co. v Bankier Distillery Co. [1893] AC 698   457, 458
Young v Secretary of State [1983] 47 P&CR 165   225

Table of Statutes

Agriculture Act 1986
  s.17 50, 508
  s.18 508
Alkali Act 1863 9, 141, 180, 323, 324
Alkali Act 1874 323, 324
Alkali Acts 94, 282, 283, 285, 324
Alkali Etc. Works Regulation Act 1906 47, 284, 292, 300, 324
Ancient Monuments and Archaeological Areas Act 1979 33

Channel Tunnel Act 1987 232
Clean Air Act 1956 142, 324, 333, 339
  s.16 194
Clean Air Act 1968 142, 324, 333, 336, 338
Clean Air Act 1993 33, 119, 161, 282, 300, 332, 333, 335, 339, 369
  Part I-III 333
  s.1 333, 334, 335, 336
  s.1(1) 334
  s.1(3)-(5) 334
  s.2 334, 335
  s.2(2)(b) 335
  s.2(3)-(6) 335
  s.3(1)-(2) 333
  s.4 336
  s.4(1) 336
  s.4(4) 336
  s.6 336
  s.6(3) 342
  s.7 336, 342
  s.7(5) 341
  s.7(7) 341
  s.10 336, 338
  s.14 337
  s.15 337, 339
  s.15(2)-(3) 338
  s.15(6) 338
  s.16 338

Clean Air Act 1993 – *continued*
  s.17 195
  s.18 339
  s.18(2) 339
  s.20 334, 339
  s.34(1)-(2) 161
  s.41 333
  Sch.1 339
    para.1(3) 341
Clean Air Acts 52, 283
Clean Rivers (Estuaries and Tidal Waters) Act 1960 415
Climate Treaty 1994 326
Comprehensive Environmental Response Compensation and Liability Act 1981 410
Conservation of Seals Act 1970 474
Control of Pollution Act 1974 10, 12, 25, 106, 120, 136, 139, 142, 150, 151, 163, 164, 165, 200, 201, 283, 313, 352, 353, 354, 358, 359, 360, 361, 362, 367, 368, 370, 376, 377, 378, 379, 385, 386, 415, 416, 420, 427, 428, 429, 430, 434, 436, 437, 443, 444, 447, 452, 456
  Part I 352, 358, 361
  Part II 25, 145, 150, 151, 423
  Part III 196
  Part IV 142
  s.2 358, 360
  s.3 359, 367
  s.3(4) 386
  s.5 358, 361
  s.5(1) 404
  s.5(2)-(4) 358
  s.6 358
  s.6(4) 358
  s.7-s.8 358
  s.8(4) 358
  s.9-s.10 358
  s.13 358

Control of Pollution Act 1974 – *continued*
  s.16 359
  s.30 364
  s.31 431
  s.31(2)(e) 428
  s.31(4)-(5) 25
  s.40 447
  s.40(4) 437
  s.46(1)-(3) 25
  s.51(1) 358
  s.58(4) 198
  s.60 198
  s.61 198, 201
  s.65-s.67 198
  s.72 285
  s.88 359, 408
  s.100 456
Control of Pollution (Amendment) Act
  1989 10, 362, 401, 403, 404
  s.1(1) 403
  s.6 404
Countryside Act 1968 503
  s.11 39
  s.15 486
  s.15(4) 487
Criminal Justice Act 1988
  s.24 448

Deposit of Poisonous Wastes Act 1972 9,
  282, 352
Deregulation and Contracting Out Act
  1994 xii, xiii, 22, 26, 109, 110, 138,
  139
  s.5 109

Electricity Act 1989 232
Environment Act 1995 xi, xii, xiii, 11, 13,
  18, 24, 25, 27, 36, 38, 39, 41, 42, 44,
  45, 46, 48, 49, 52, 104, 110, 112, 128,
  139, 150, 151, 155, 160, 306, 327, 328,
  331, 363, 389, 392, 396, 412, 417, 426,
  430, 434, 436, 437, 448, 450, 462, 504,
  505, 516
  Part I xi, xiii
  Part II 26
  Part III 503, 504
  s.1(1) 41
  s.1(5) 42
  s.4 42
  s.4(1) 45
  s.4(5)-(7) 43
  s.5 42, 43
  s.5(3) 42, 45
  s.6 42, 43, 482
  s.7 43, 482
  s.7(1) 43
  s.7(3) 46

Environment Act 1995 – *continued*
  s.8 43, 46, 482
  s.9 43, 482
  s.39 xiii, 27, 44, 45
  s.40 438
  s.41-s.44 42
  s.55 136
  s.60 413, 430, 450, 451
  s.61 503
  s.63 214, 504
  s.66 505
  s.71 505
  s.72 505
  s.75 348
  s.76-s.78 357
  s.93-s.95 25
  s.97 517
  s.98 509
  s.108 45
  s.110 45
  s.111 110, 448, 466
  Sch.7 504
  Sch.22 46
Environmental Protection Act 1990 xii, 4,
  8, 10, 11, 12, 13, 20, 24, 25, 26, 31, 39,
  42, 46, 50, 51, 52, 104, 106, 107, 113,
  122, 132, 135, 136, 137, 138, 139, 149,
  157, 158, 193, 194, 198, 201, 291, 292,
  293, 307, 312, 316, 340, 348, 353, 354,
  361, 362, 363, 364, 368, 369, 370, 376,
  377, 378, 379, 380, 386, 389, 394, 399,
  404, 407, 412, 416, 445, 450, 466, 472,
  473, 478
  Part I 26, 52, 91, 97, 106, 107, 108,
  109, 156, 157, 159, 292, 299, 317, 318,
  331, 332, 333, 340, 347, 353, 357, 369,
  387, 388, 429, 445, 482
  Part II 33, 133, 136, 156, 298, 352, 353,
  361, 362, 364, 365, 375, 376, 383, 386,
  389
  Part III 52, 192, 376, 397, 456
  Part IV 52, 362
  s.1 4, 8
  s.1(2) 316
  s.2(1) 293
  s.3(5) 115, 308, 331
  s.4(2) 293
  s.4(9) 314
  s.6 24
  s.6(1) 301
  s.6(2) 304
  s.6(3)-(5) 307
  s.7 132, 293, 307
  s.7(1) 308
  s.7(2) 307-8
  s.7(2)(c) 443
  s.7(3) 308

Environmental Protection Act 1990 –
  continued
s.7(7)   308, 311
s.7(10)   308
s.8   304
s.8(8)   305
s.8K(1)   395
s.8K(3)   395
s.9   313
s.10   299, 314, 445
s.10(3)   314
s.10(5)   156
s.11   314, 315, 343
s.11(4)(b)   156
s.11(5)   314
s.11(6)   314, 315
s.11(11)   314
s.12   315, 343
s.12(1)-(3)   315
s.13   315, 343
s.13(2)-(3)   315
s.14   316, 343
s.14(1)   316
s.14(3)   316
s.15   157, 319, 343
s.15(5)(a)-(b)   319
s.17   316, 317
s.19   159
s.19(2)   157
s.20   156, 343
s.20(7)   157
s.21   156, 157, 158, 307, 343
s.21(2)   157
s.22   156, 157, 307, 319, 343, 344
s.22(2)   158
s.22(2)(a)   307
s.22(3)   158, 307
s.22(4)   158
s.22(5)   158, 307
s.23   313, 317
s.23(1)   157, 301
s.23(2)   317
s.23(5)   317
s.24   318
s.25(1)   317
s.26   140, 318
s.27   394
s.27(1)   318
s.28   445, 446
s.28(1)   298, 388
s.28(3)(a)-(b)   445
s.28(4)   445
s.29   374, 387
s.30-s.31   363
s.33   364, 370, 371, 372, 384, 389, 400,
        403, 404, 409
s.33(1)   384, 388, 398, 408

Environmental Protection Act 1990 –
  continued
s.33(1)(c)   372, 373, 387, 388, 398, 408
s.33(2)   372
s.33(3)   298, 387
s.33(5)-(6)   385
s.33(7)(a)   386
s.33(7)(b)-(c)   387
s.34   399, 400, 404
s.34(2)   400
s.34(7)   400
s.34(10)   400
s.35   377
s.35(2)   373
s.35(3)   376, 377
s.35(4)   377
s.35(6)   377
s.35(7)   383
s.35(8)   374, 378
s.35(11)   381
s.36   373, 380
s.36(2)   374
s.36(3)   374, 376
s.36(5)   373
s.37(1)(a)-(b)   380
s.37(2)   380
s.37(3)   383
s.37(4)   380
s.38(1)   380, 381
s.38(2)   381
s.38(6)   380
s.38(7)   383
s.38(9)-(10)   381
s.39   377, 378
s.39(6)-(7)   378
s.40   377
s.41   382
s.41(5)   382
s.41(7)   382
s.42   379, 380, 382
s.42(2)-(3)   379
s.42(6)   380, 381, 382
s.42(8)   383
s.43   383
s.43(2)(c)   384
s.43(4)-(6)   384
s.43(7)   381, 384
s.44   373
s.44A   348
s.45(1)-(2)   363
s.46(2)   352
s.48   352
s.49   352, 363
s.50   215, 348, 354, 370
s.50(4)   370
s.51   363
s.51(3)   334

Environmental Protection Act 1990 –
  continued
  s.52   114, 352
  s.52(3)   352
  s.55   333, 352
  s.55(2)   334
  s.59   113, 388
  s.59(3)-(8)   388
  s.61   381, 391, 398
  s.61(1)   398
  s.61(3)   339, 398
  s.61(7)   398
  s.61(9)   379
  s.61(10)   398
  s.62   406
  s.63(1)   370
  s.63(2)   370, 398, 408, 409
  s.64   153, 333, 335, 336, 382, 407
  s.64(6)   154
  s.65   153, 154, 383
  s.66   153, 154, 383
  s.66(2)-(5)   154
  s.66(7)   154
  s.66(8)   155
  s.66(11)   155
  s.67   363
  s.69   404, 405
  s.70   154, 404, 405
  s.70(1)   198
  s.71   404, 405
  s.72   383
  s.73   171, 398
  s.73(6)   171, 408, 409
  s.74   374
  s.74(3)-(4)   375
  s.74(7)   375
  s.75   364, 371
  s.75(2)   365
  s.75(4)   368
  s.75(7)   369
  s.77   379
  s.78A   395
  s.78A(2)   392
  s.78A(6)   392
  s.78B   393
  s.78B(2)   392
  s.78C(10)   393
  s.78E   393, 394
  s.78E(1)-(2)   394
  s.78E(4)   394
  s.78F(4)   395
  s.78F(7)   395
  s.78F(9)   394
  s.78H(1)   393, 394
  s.78H(5)   393, 394
  s.78H(6)-(16)   393
  s.78J   395

Environmental Protection Act 1990 –
  continued
  s.78J(2)   395
  s.78K(4)   395
  s.78L-s.78N   396
  s.78P(8)   396
  s.78Q   392
  s.78Q(4)   392
  s.78R   155, 396
  s.78S-s.78T   156
  s.78U   392
  s.78X   393, 395
  s.79   192, 193, 344, 397
  s.79(1)(a)-(b)   194
  s.79(1)(c)   198
  s.79(1)(e)   195
  s.79(1)(f)   196
  s.79(1)(h)   193, 198
  s.79(3)   194
  s.79(4)   195
  s.79(7)   193, 195, 197
  s.79(9)   198
  s.79(10)   344
  s.80   193, 199, 200, 397
  s.80(1)   196
  s.80(2)   200
  s.80(2)(c)   197
  s.80(4)   197
  s.80(5)-(6)   200
  s.80(7)   198
  s.80(9)   198
  s.81   113
  s.81(3)   397
  s.81(5)   200, 201
  s.82   199
  s.82(2)   200
  s.87   119
  s.132   472
  s.140   456
  s.143   155, 391
  s.145(1)   429
  s.151   196
  s.156   29
  s.157   318, 386
  s.158-s.159   318
  s.159(2)   318
  Sch.1   306
    para.1(3)   156, 301
    para.2   156
    para.3(5)   306
    para.5(1)   306
    para.5(3)   306
    para.6-para.7   156
  Sch.2   363
  Sch.3   199
    para.3(1)   306
    para.4   193

Environmental Protection Act 1990 –
continued
Sch.6 472
Sch.9 486
Sch.15 300
European Communities Act 1972 28, 161,
262
s.2 86
s.2(1) 28
s.2(2) 28, 454, 493
Explosives Act 1875 370

Finance Act 1995 350
Fire Precautions Act 1971 386
Food and Environment Protection Act
1985 372, 429
Forestry Act 1967 515, 516
s.1(3A) 516
s.9(2) 516
Forestry Act 1986 516

Gulf Oil Refining Act 1965 178

Health and Safety at Work etc. Act
1974 42, 47, 142, 150, 156, 258, 292,
295, 300, 370
s.28(7) 142, 156
Housing and Planning Act 1986 212, 233
Housing, Town Planning etc. Act 1909 9

Land Drainage Act 1991 42
s.61A–61E 482
Law of Property Act 1925
s.84 246
Local Government (Access to Information)
Act 1985 53, 161, 234
Local Government Act 1972
s.100 53
s.100A–s.100K 53
s.101 53
s.222 201, 254
Local Government Act 1985 212, 214, 218
s.12–s.28 218
Local Government etc. (Scotland) Act
1995 417
Local Government (Miscellaneous
Provisions) Act 1982 243
Local Government, Planning and Land Act
1980 51, 212, 215, 232, 233
s.134 232
s.148 233

Medicines Act 1968
s.130 406
Merchant Shipping (Oil Pollution) Act
1971 171
s.1–s.2 171

Mines and Quarries Act 1954 196
Mines and Quarries (Tips) Act 1969 369

National Health Service and Community
Care Act 1990 232
National Parks and Access to the
Countryside Act 1949 477, 503
s.5 503
s.11A(1)-(2) 503
s.15 484
s.16 484, 486
s.17 484
s.20 484
s.21 485
s.87 506
s.106 484
Natural Heritage (Scotland) Act 1991 50,
472
Nature Conservancy Council Act
1973 471
Noise and Statutory Nuisance Act
1993 193
Norfolk and Suffolk Broads Act 1988 214,
504
Nuclear Installations Act 1965 171
s.7–s.10 171
s.47 19

Official Secrets Act 1911 141
s.2 141
Official Secrets Act 1989 141

Planning Acts 219, 237
Planning and Compensation Act 1991 12,
135, 209, 215, 217, 218, 221, 224, 227,
233, 237, 243, 244, 249, 251, 252, 253,
254, 255, 354, 505, 511
s.15 28, 262
s.26 219
Sch.4 215
Planning (Hazardous Substances) Act
1990 12, 256, 257, 258, 260
s.1 256
s.3 256
s.9 257, 260
s.9(1) 257
s.9(2)(d) 257
s.9(5) 257
s.10(2) 258
s.11 260
s.11(7)(a) 260
s.11(8) 260
s.13 259
s.14 260
s.23 259
s.23(4A) 259
s.24 259

Planning (Hazardous Substances) Act
    1990 – *continued*
    s.26   259
    s.28   260
    s.29   258
    s.36   259
Planning (Listed Buildings and
    Conservation Areas) Act 1990   12,
    135, 221
Police and Criminal Evidence Act 1984
    s.76   449
    s.78   448
    s.82   449
Powers of Criminal Courts Act 1973
    s.35   113
Protection of Badgers Act 1992   474, 476
    s.1(1)   476
    s.1(3)   476
    s.2-s.5   476
    s.8   476
    s.10   476
Protection of Birds Act 1954   10, 469
Public Bodies (Admission to Meetings) Act
    1960   53
Public Health Act 1848   192
Public Health Act 1855   192
Public Health Act 1860   192
Public Health Act 1875   9, 10, 192, 324
Public Health Act 1936   192, 194, 285, 324
    s.81(2)   196
    s.259   456
    s.259(1)(a)-(b)   456
Public Health Acts   52, 200
Public Health (Smoke Abatement) Act
    1926   324, 333

Radioactive Substances Act 1993   48, 369,
    447, 482
Rehabilitation of Offenders Act 1974   404
River Boards Act 1948   284, 414
Rivers Pollution Prevention Act 1876   9,
    415
Rivers (Prevention of Pollution) Act
    1951   120, 415, 430
Rivers (Prevention of Pollution) Act
    1961   120, 142, 415
    s.12   142

Salmon and Fresh Water Fisheries Act 1975
    s.4(1)   455
Sea Birds Protection Act 1869   469
Sea Birds Protection Act 1872   469
Sea Birds Protection Act 1880   469

Single European Act 1986   56, 58, 68, 69,
    70, 73, 74, 75, 78
Supreme Court Act 1981
    s.31   32
    s.31(3)   32

Territorial Sea Act 1987   428, 485
Theft Act 1968
    s.4(3)   474
Town and Country Planning Act
    1947   206, 208, 214, 222, 232
Town and Country Planning Act 1968   215
Town and Country Planning Act 1971   215
Town and Country Planning Act 1990   11,
    24, 25, 26, 122, 195, 209, 220, 223,
    228, 243, 246, 294, 467, 480, 481
    Part II   215
    s.7   233
    s.30   216
    s.31   216
    s.31(3)   216
    s.32-s.35   216
    s.35A-C   216
    s.36-s.37   216
    s.38   216, 354
    s.39-s.41   216
    s.42   216, 218
    s.43   216
    s.44-s.46   216, 218
    s.47   216
    s.48   216, 218
    s.49-s.52   216
    s.54A   108, 209, 219, 236, 237, 238, 257
    s.55   25, 221, 488
    s.55(1)   219
    s.55(2)(a)   221
    s.55(2)(d)   223
    s.55(2)(e)   223, 500, 510
    s.55(2)(g)   221
    s.55(3)(a)   223
    s.55(3)(b)   223, 355
    s.55(5)   223
    s.56   222
    s.57   224
    s.57(1)   219
    s.59   232
    s.63(2)   228
    s.69   231
    s.70   94
    s.70(1)   240
    s.70(2)   218, 219, 234–5, 244, 245
    s.71A   262
    s.72   240
    s.73   228, 242, 246, 247
    s.75   240
    s.75(1)   231
    s.75(3)   240

Town and Country Planning Act 1990 –
   continued
s.77   234
s.78   225, 234, 246
s.82   233
s.88   233
s.90   231
s.91   222
s.92   228
s.92(2)   228
s.97   225, 231, 256
s.98-s.99   225, 231
s.100   225, 231, 488
s.102   225, 256
s.106   171, 243, 244, 246, 256
s.106(1)   244
s.106(3)   244
s.106(5)-(6)   244
s.106(11)   244
s.106AB   246
s.171B(1)-(3)   251
s.171C   255
s.171D   255
s.172   250
s.173   253
s.174(2)   252
s.178   252, 259
s.179   252
s.181   252
s.182   250
s.183   254
s.187A   255
s.187B   254
s.188   231, 252
s.191   251, 374
s.191(2)   225
s.192   227, 251
s.193-s.194   251
s.196A-C   255
s.197   510
s.198   510, 511
s.198(6)   513
s.199   510, 512
s.200   510
s.201   510, 512
s.202   510
s.203   510, 515
s.204-s.205   510
s.206   510, 514
s.206(4)   513
s.207-s.209   510, 514
s.210   510
s.210(1)   511
s.210(4)   511
s.211-s.212   510, 515
s.213-s.214   510
s.214A   511

Town and Country Planning Act 1990 –
   continued
s.215   397
s.284   249
s.285   253
s.287   216, 218
s.288   234, 249, 512
s.289   254
s.294   232, 251
s.294(3)   251
s.316   231
s.320-s.321   247
s.336   220, 257, 500
Sch.1   355
Sch.7   233
Town and Country Planning Acts   267, 354

Water Act 1973   284, 414
Water Act 1989   48, 132, 163, 164, 165,
   284, 414, 416, 420, 427, 437, 464
Sch.23   416
Water Consolidation (Consequential
   Provisions) Act 1991
Sch.1   455
Water Industry Act 1991   11, 24, 49, 369,
   415, 425, 447, 462
s.3   43, 49
s.4   482
s.67   426
s.70   426
s.72   424
s.98   467
s.106   467
s.111   467
s.118   299, 430, 462, 466
s.121   462, 466
s.122   464
s.124-s.126   464
s.129   464
s.141   462
s.143   464
s.171   466
s.189   152
s.195   152
s.196   152, 465
s.206   465
Water Resources Act 1963   284, 414, 415
Water Resources Act 1991   xii, 11, 24, 30,
   42, 49, 127, 132, 136, 137, 138, 171,
   369, 372, 385, 386, 411, 414, 415, 416,
   427, 436, 437, 440, 443, 444, 445, 446,
   447, 450, 451, 452, 453, 466
Part III   429
s.5   438, 439, 442
s.6-s.7   48
s.16   42, 43, 48, 49, 482
s.17   440, 482

Water Resources Act 1991 – *continued*
s.18   482
s.28   483
s.28(3)(a)-(b)   299
s.28(4)   299
s.29   482, 483
s.30   483
s.31   483
s.49A   46
s.51   483
s.82   441
s.83   440, 441, 442, 444
s.83(4)   442
s.84   108, 440, 441, 443
s.85   119, 120, 299, 426, 429, 430, 433,
   434, 445, 446, 451, 455
s.85(1)(a)   428
s.85(5)   429
s.85(6)   428, 433
s.87   430
s.87(1)   430
s.87(2)   430, 431, 446, 466
s.88   299, 429, 436
s.89   429
s.89(3)   429
s.90(1)-(2)   455
s.91   439
s.92   451, 452
s.93   452
s.93(3)   453
s.94   453
s.95   172
s.100(b)   460
s.101   429
s.104   427
s.131   437
s.161   113, 136, 389, 397, 450, 451
s.161B   450
s.169-s.174   48, 447
s.190   151, 434, 444
s.190(1)(c)   151
s.196   438
s.202   48, 438
s.204   444, 445
s.206   435
s.209   151, 448
s.209(1)   448
s.213   443
s.217   434
s.221   427
Sch.1   48
Sch.10   110, 434, 439
  para.1(7)   435, 444
  para.2(5)   435
  para.2(6)   436
  para.4   439
  para.5-para.6   436

Water Resources Act 1991 – *continued*
Sch.11   452, 483
Sch.12   453
Sch.20   447
Sch.25   455
Wildlife and Countryside Act 1981   10, 11,
   13, 19, 22, 468, 470, 471, 474, 475,
   476, 477, 478, 480, 481, 482, 485, 487,
   488, 489, 490
Part I   474
Part II   39, 477
s.1(1)-(2)   474
s.1(4)-(5)   474
s.2(1)-(2)   475
s.3   474
s.4   475
s.5-s.6   474
s.9(1)-(2)   475
s.9(4)-(5)   475
s.10   475
s.11(1)-(2)   475
s.13   476
s.14   477
s.16   475
s.22   474
s.27   475
s.28   93, 481, 489, 494
s.28(1)   478–9
s.28(2)   479
s.28(4A)   479
s.28(8)   481, 488
s.28(11)   481
s.29   479, 494
s.34   486
s.34(1)-(2)   486
s.35   484
s.36   485
s.37   485, 495
s.37(3)   486
s.39   503, 508
s.41(3)   501
s.41(4)   508
s.42-s.43   506
s.50   487, 503
Sch.1   474
Sch.2
   Part I-Part II   475
Sch.5   474, 475, 476
Sch.6   475
Sch.8   474, 476
Sch.9   477
Sch.11   486
Sch.12   485
Sch.13   502
Wildlife and Countryside (Amendment) Act
   1985   478, 479, 506
s.4   516

Wildlife and Countryside (Service of
     Notices) Act 1985   478

European legislation
   Bern Convention on the Conservation of
     European Wildlife and Natural
     Habitats   490
   EC Directive 67/548   68
   EC Directive 70/157 (Approximation of
     Exhaust Systems)   75, 87
   EC Directive 70/220 (Vehicle
     Emissions)   79, 345
   EC Directive 73/404 (Detergents)   423
   EC Directive 75/439 (Waste Oils)   69,
     377
   EC Directive 75/440 (Surface Water for
     Drinking)   286, 421, 424, 425, 442
   EC Directive 75/442 (Waste)   59, 74, 79,
     81, 352, 356, 360, 364, 368, 369
     Art.1   365
     Art.4   81
     Art.11   372
   EC Directive 76/160 (Bathing
     Waters)   79, 84, 85, 87, 421, 423,
     442
   EC Directive 76/403 (Disposal of PCBs)
     79
   EC Directive 76/464 (Dangerous
     Substances in Water)   79, 80, 85, 86,
     101, 290, 418, 419, 420, 440, 442,
     465
   EC Directive 78/176 (Titanium Dioxide
     Industry)   79, 423
   EC Directive 78/319 (Toxic and
     Dangerous Waste)   79, 356, 405
   EC Directive 78/659 (Water Standards for
     Freshwater Fish)   79, 421, 424
   EC Directive 79/409 (Wild Birds)
     13, 69,
     78, 80, 87, 470, 474, 490, 491, 493,
     494, 495, 497, 498
     Annex I   490
     Art.1-Art.3   490
     Art.4   490, 491
     Art.4(4)   490, 491, 498
   EC Directive 79/831 (Classification,
     Packaging and Labelling of
     Dangerous Substances)   79
   EC Directive 79/869 (Sampling Surface
     Water for Drinking)   420
   EC Directive 79/923 (Shellfish
     Waters)   79, 421, 424
   EC Directive 80/68 (Groundwater)   79,
     374, 420, 424

European legislation – *continued*
   EC Directive 80/778 (Drinking
     Water)   64, 66, 67, 79, 85, 87, 286,
     421, 422, 423, 426, 453
     Art.9   421
   EC Directive 80/779 (Smoke and Sulphur
     Dioxide)   79, 330, 331, 332, 339,
     340
   EC Directive 82/176 (Mercury)   419
   EC Directive 82/501 (Major Accidents
     Hazards)   79
   EC Directive 82/884 (Lead)   79, 331,
     332
   EC Directive 83/513 (Cadmium)   79,
     419
   EC Directive 84/156 (Mercury)   79, 419
   EC Directive 84/360 (Emissions from
     Industrial Plants)   79, 81, 290, 291,
     330, 331, 357
   EC Directive 84/491
     (Hexachlorocyclohexane)   79, 419
   EC Directive 84/532 (Noise from
     Construction Plant)   79
   EC Directive 84/631   77
   EC Directive 85/203 (Nitrogen Dioxide)
     79, 331, 332
   EC Directive 85/210 (lead in petrol)   331
   EC Directive 85/337 (Assessment of the
     Effects of Certain Private and Public
     Projects in the Environment)   262,
     264, 265, 266, 269, 278, 279, 281
     Annex I   264
     Annex II   264
     Annex III
       Art.3   274
       Art.5   274
       Art.4.2   265
   EC Directive 85/337 (Environmental
     Impact Assessment)   28, 73, 80, 82,
     86, 87, 161
     Annex I-Annex II   87
   EC Directive 86/118 (Noise in the
     Workplace)   79
   EC Directive 86/278 (Sewage
     Sludge)   79, 357
   EC Directive 86/280 (Carbon
     tetrachloride, pentachlorophenol and
     DDT   419, 420
   EC Directive 86/609 (Emissions from
     Large Combustion Plants)   290
   EC Directive 87/217 (Asbestos)   79
   EC Directive 87/219 (Sulphur content of
     gas oil)   332
   EC Directive 88/76 (Emissions from
     Vehicles)   73, 332
   EC Directive 88/195 (Lead in Petrol)   79

European legislation – *continued*
 EC Directive 88/347 (Chloroform,
  hexachlorobenzene,
  hexachlorobutadiene, aldrin, dieldrin,
  endrin ,isodrin 419
 EC Directive 88/609 (Emissions from
  Large Combustion Plants) 73, 79,
  331
 EC Directive 89/369 (New Municipal
  Waste Incinerators) 79, 357
 EC Directive 89/428 (Titanium Dioxide
  Industry) 74
 EC Directive 89/429 (Existing Municipal
  Waste Incinerators) 79, 357
 EC Directive 89/458 (Emissions from
  Vehicles) 58, 332
 EC Directive 90/219 (Genetically
  Modified Organisms) 80
 EC Directive 90/220 (Genetically
  Modified Organisms) 80
 EC Directive 90/313 (Access to
  Information on the Environment)
  14, 66, 78, 80, 82, 86, 116, 161
 EC Directive 90/415 (1, 2-dichloroethane,
  trichloroethylene,
  tetrachloroethylene,
  trichlorobenzene 419
 EC Directive 91/156 (Waste) 74, 79, 81,
  351, 353, 356, 368
 EC Directive 91/238 (Roadworthiness of
  Private Cars and Light Vehicles)
  345
 EC Directive 91/271 (Urban Waste Water
  Treatment) 20, 79, 84, 265, 422,
  425
 EC Directive 91/441 (Vehicle
  emissions) 79, 332
 EC Directive 91/542 (Emission from
  heavy duty vehicles) 345
 EC Directive 91/676 (Nitrates) 79, 422,
  423, 454
 EC Directive 91/689 (Hazardous
  Waste) 73, 79, 356, 405, 407
 EC Directive 92/43 (Habitats) xii, 78,
  80, 86, 265, 470, 474, 475, 476, 477,
  490, 491, 492, 493, 495, 497
  Annex I-Annex III 492
  Art.4(4) 492
  Art.5 492, 494
  Art.6 494
  Art.6(1) 492
  Art.6(2) 493, 494, 4982
  Art.6(3) 493, 498
  Art.6(4) 491, 493, 495, 496, 498
  Art.10 492, 493
  Art.11 492, 494
  Art.12-Art.13 494

European legislation – *continued*
 EC Directive 92/55 (Catalytic Converters)
  345
 EC Directive 92/72 (Air Pollution by
  Ozone) 330
 EC Directive 92/75 (Energy Labelling for
  Domestic Appliances) 83
 EC Directive 92/313 (Access to
  Information) 265
 EC Directive 93/59 (Emission from larger
  vans) 345
 EC Directive 94/12 345
 EC Directive 94/15 (Genetically Modified
  Organisms, amended) 80
 EC Directive 94/62 (Packaging and
  Packaging Waste) 75, 80, 81, 82,
  357
 EC Directive 94/67 (Hazardous Waste
  Incinerators) 79
 EC Directive (draft) (Air Quality
  Standards) 332
 EC Directive (draft) (civil liability for
  damage caused by waste) 82, 119,
  409
 EC Directive (draft) (integrated pollution
  prevention and control) 81, 320,
  321
 EC Directive (draft) (landfill) 39
 EC Directive (proposed) (Air Quality
  Assessment and Management) 331
 EC Treaty 56, 68, 69, 71, 72, 73, 292
  Art.2 67, 70
  Art.3 67, 70
  Art.3B 72
  Art.5 63, 67
  Art.8A 68
  Art.30 76
  Art.36 76
  Art.100 69, 70, 71, 73, 78
  Art.100A 69, 70, 71, 72, 73, 74, 75,
   76, 78
  Art.100A(3) 70, 76
  Art.100A(4) 70, 75
  Art.119 61
  Art.130R 69, 71, 73
  Art.130R(1) 71
  Art.130R(2) 19, 71, 72, 77, 81, 88
  Art.130R(3) 71
  Art.130R(4) 71, 72
  Art.130R(5) 71
  Art.130S 69, 71, 72, 73, 74, 75, 78
  Art.130S(5) 72, 73
  Art.130T 69, 71, 75
  Art.169 65, 67
  Art.170-Art.171 65
  Art.173 63
  Art.177 59, 65, 87, 498

European legislation – *continued*
  Art.189B-Art.189C   58, 70, 74
  Art.235   69, 73, 78
  European Convention on Human Rights
    59
  Treaty on European Union (Maastricht
    Treaty)   56, 58, 65, 70, 72, 73, 74
  Art.3B   83
International legislation
  Basel Convention on Control of
    Transboundary Movement of
    Hazardous Wastes and their Disposal
    1989   357

International legislation – *continued*
  Bonn Convention on the Conservation of
    Migratory Species of Wild Animals
    1979   490
  Montreal Protocol   29
  Ramsar Convention on Wetlands of
    International Importance Especially
    as Waterfowl Habitat 1971   29, 473,
    490, 491, 496, 497
  Vienna Convention for the Protection of
    the Ozone Layer   29, 332
  Washington Convention on International
    Trade in Endangered Species of Wild
    Fauna and Flora   490

Table of Statutory Instruments

Air Quality Standards Regulations 1989
(SI 1989 No.317)   84, 96, 331, 332
Animal By-Products Order 1992
(SI 1992 No.3303)   369

Bathing Waters (Classification) Regulations
1991 (SI 1991 No.1597)   442
Building Regulations 1991 (SI 1991
No.2768)   339

Chemical Hazard Information and
Packaging Regulations 1993 (SI 1993
No.1746)   407
Clean Air (Arrestment Plant) (Exemption)
Regulations 1969 (SI 1969
No.1262)   336
Clean Air (Emission of Grit and Dust from
Furnaces) Regulations 1971 (SI 1971
No.162)   335, 336
Clean Air (Height of Chimneys)
(Exemption) Regulations 1969 (SI 1969
No.411)   338
Clean Air (Height of Chimneys) (Prescribed
Form) Regulations 1969
(SI No.412)   337
Clean Air (Measurement of Grit and Dust)
Regulations 1971 (SI 1971
No.616)   337
Clean Air (Units of Measurement)
Regulations 1992 (SI 1992
No.35)   337
Conservation (Natural Habitats etc.)
Regulations 1994 (SI 1994
No.2716)   xii, 84, 474, 477, 491, 493
r.3(2)   495
r.7-r.8   494
r.18   494
r.20-r.22   494
r.24   494

Conservation (Natural Habitats etc.)
Regulations 1994 – continued
r.28   494
r.33-r.36   495
r.48-r.49   496
r.53   496
r.60-r.64   496
Sch.2   475
Control of Explosives Regulations 1991
(SI 1991 No.1531)   370
Control of Pollution (Anglers' Lead
Weights) Regulations 1986 (SI 1986
No.1992)   456
Control of Pollution (Anglers' Lead
Weights) (Amendment) Regulations
1993 (SI 1993 No.49)   456
Control of Pollution (Anti-Fouling Paints
and Treatments) Regulations 1987 (SI
1987 No.783)   456
Control of Pollution (Collection and
Disposal) Regulations 1988 (SI 1988
No.819)   358
Control of Pollution (Consents for
Discharges etc.) (Secretary of State's
Functions) Regulations 1989 (SI 1989
No.1151)   439
Control of Pollution (Discharges by the
NRA) Regulations 1989 (SI 1989
No.1157)   439
Control of Pollution (Radioactive Waste)
Regulations 1989 (SI 1989
No.1158)   447
Control of Pollution (Registers) Regulations
1989 (SI 1989 No.1160)   151, 444
r.7(3)(b)   151
r.7   151
Control of Pollution (Silage, Slurry and
Agricultural Fuel Oil) Regulations 1991
(SI 1991 No.324)   451

Control of Pollution (Supply and Use of
    Injurious Substances) Regulations 1986
    (SI 1986 No.902)   456
Controlled Waste (Registration of Carriers
    and Seizure of Vehicles) Regulations
    1991 (SI 1991 No.1624)   403
Controlled Waste Regulations 1992 (SI 1992
    No.588)   365, 369
Controlled Waters (Lakes and Ponds) Order
    1989 (SI 1989 No.1149)   428

Dark Smoke (Permitted Periods)
    Regulations 1958 (SI 1958
    No.498)   334

Environmental Information Regulations
    1992 (SI 1992 No.3240)   14, 84, 149,
    154, 161
Environmental Protection (Applications,
    Appeals and Registers) Regulations
    1991 (SI 1991 No.507)   156, 159,
    293, 301, 305, 307, 315, 319, 341
    r.4(1)   156
    r.9(2)(a)   156
    r.9(2)(d)-(e)   157
    r.15   156
Environmental Protection (Authorisation of
    Processes) (Determination Periods)
    Order 1991 (SI 1991 No.513)   293,
    306, 341
Environmental Protection (Duty of Care)
    Regulations 1991 (SI 1991
    No.2839)   400, 402
Environmental Protection (Prescribed
    Processes and Substances) Regulations
    1991 (SI 1991 No.472)   293, 294,
    313, 340
Environmental Protection (Prescribed
    Processes and Substances)
    (Amendment) Regulations 1992 (SI
    1992 No.614)   294

Habitat (Former Set-Aside Land)
    Regulations 1994 (SI 1994
    No.1292)   509
Habitat (Salt-Marsh) Regulations 1994 (SI
    1994 No.1293)   509
Habitat (Water Fringe) Regulations 1994
    (SI 1994 No.1291)   509

Inquiries Rules   249

Motor Vehicles (Type Approval) (Great
    Britain) Regulations 1994 (SI 1994
    No.981   344, 345

Nitrate Sensitive Areas (Designation) Order
    1990 (SI 1990 No.1013)   454
Nitrate Sensitive Areas Regulations 1994
    (SI 1994 No.1729)   454
Notification of Installations Handling
    Hazardous Substances Regulations
    1982 (SI 1982 No.1357)   260

Ozone Monitoring and Information
    Regulations 1994 (SI 1994
    No.440)   330

Planning (Hazardous Substances)
    Regulations 1992 (SI 1992
    No.656)   256
    r.4   7
    r.24-r.25   261
Prescribed Processes etc. Regulations 1991
    (SI 1991 No.472)   388

Road Traffic (Carriage of Explosives)
    Regulations 1989 (SI 1989
    No.615)   370
Road Vehicle (Construction and Use)
    Regulations   344, 345
Rules of the Supreme Court
    Order 53   32, 249
    r.4   32
    r.4(3)   32

Smoke Control Areas (Authorised Fuels)
    Regulations 1991 (SI 1991
    No.1282)   339
Smoke Control (Exempted Fireplaces)
    Orders   339
Special Development Order   232, 233
Special Waste Regulations   405, 407
Statutory Nuisance (Appeals) Regulations
    1990 (SI 1990 No.2276)   199
Statutory Nuisance (Appeals) (Amendment)
    Regulations 1990 (SI 1990
    No.2483)   199
Surface Waters (Classification) Regulations
    1989 (SI 1989 No.1148)   424, 442
Surface Waters (Dangerous Substances)
    (Classification) Regulations 1989 (SI
    1989 No.2286)   442
Surface Waters (Dangerous Substances)
    (Classification) Regulations 1992 (SI
    1992 No.337)   442, 443
Surface Waters (River Ecosystem)
    (Classification) Regulations 1994 (SI
    1994 No.1057)   xii, 442

Town and Country Planning (Assessment of
  Environmental Effects) Regulations
  1988 (SI 1988 No.1199) 262, 263,
  266
  r.3 271
  r.5(1) 270
  r.5(3)-(6) 270
  r.6 271
  r.6(5) 271
  Sched.1 269
  Sched.2 267
Town and Country Planning (Assessment of
  Environmental Effects) (Amendment)
  Regulations 1992 (SI 1992
  No.1494) 278
Town and Country Planning (Assessment of
  Environmental Effects) (Amendment)
  Regulations 1994 (SI 1994
  No.677) 262-3
Town and Country Planning (Determination
  by Inspectors) (Inquiries Procedure)
  Rules 1992 (SI 1992 No.2039) 247-8
Town and Country Planning (Development
  Plan) Regulations 1991 (SI 1991
  No.2794) 216, 217
Town and Country Planning (Enforcement)
  (Inquiries Procedure) Rules 1992 (SI
  1992 No.1903) 253
Town and Country Planning (Enforcement
  Notices and Appeals) Regulations 1991
  (SI 1991 No.2804) 253
Town and Country Planning (Environmental
  Assessment and Permitted
  Development) Regulations 1995
  (SI 1995 No.417) 226, 269
Town and Country Planning (Fees for
  Applications and Deemed Applications)
  Regulations 1989 (SI 1989
  No.193) 238
Town and Country Planning (Fees for
  Applications and Deemed Applications)
  (Amendment) (No.2) Regulations 1992
  (SI 1992 No.3052) 229
Town and Country Planning (General
  Development) Order 1988 (SI 1988
  No.813) 209, 277
  Art.18 277
  r.8 277
  r.14 278
  r.16 278
  r.18 278
  r.20 277, 278
  r.21 278
  r.22 277
Town and Country Planning (General
  Development) Order 1988 (SI 1988
  No.1813) (as amended) 278

Town and Country Planning (General
  Development) Order 1988 – continued
  Part A 295
  Schedule 4-Schedule 6 296
Town and Country Planning (General
  Development Procedure) Order 1995
  (SI 1995 No.419) 209, 226, 227, 458
  Art.4 226
  Art.10 488
Town and Country Planning (General
  Permitted Development) Order 1995
  (SI 1995 No.418) 209, 219, 221, 230,
  241, 269, 481, 500, 501
  Art.3 228
  Art.4 228, 502
  Art.6-Art.8 229
  Art.18 229
  Art.20 231
  Sched.2
    part 6-part 7 500, 501
Town and Country Planning (General
  Regulations) 1992 (SI 1992
  No.1492) 231
Town and Country Planning (Inquiries
  Procedure) Rules 1992 (SI 1992
  No.2038) 34, 247
Town and Country Planning (Modification
  and Discharge of Planning Obligations)
  Regulations 1992 (SI 1992
  No.2832) 246
Town and Country Planning (Tree
  Preservation Order) Regulations 1969
  (SI 1969 No.17) 512
Town and Country Planning (Use Classes)
  Order 1987 (SI 1987 No.764) 219,
  223, 241
Town and Country Planning (Windscale and
  Calder Works) Special Development
  Order 232
Town and Country Planning (Written
  Representations Procedure) Regulations
  1987 (SI 1987 No.701) 247
Trade Effluent (Prescribed Processes and
  Substances) Regulations 1992 (SI 1992
  No.339) 466
Trade Effluents (Prescribed Processes and
  Substances) Regulations 1989 (SI 1989
  No.1156) 465

Urban Waste Water Treatment (England and
  Wales) Regulations 1994 (SI 1994
  No.2841) xii, 422

Waste Management Licensing Regulations
  1994 (SI 1994 No.1056) xii, 84, 353,
  356, 364, 365, 371, 374-5, 382, 385,
  404

Waste Management Licensing Regulations
    1994 – *continued*
  r.1(3)   369
  r.3-r.4   375
  r.10   153
  r.11(1)   154
  r.12   377
  r.16   387
  r.16(1)(a)   387
  r.17   371
  r.18(1)   372
  r.18(3)   372
  r.18(4)   375

Waste Management Licensing Regulations
    1994 – *continued*
  r.24(8)   369
  Sched.3   371
  Sched.4   384
    Part II   366
    Part III   371
    Part IV   366, 371
  Sched.5   405
Water Supply (Water Quality) Regulations
    1989 (SI 1989 No.1147)   84, 421,
    425, 426
  r.29   153

PART I   GENERAL PRINCIPLES OF ENVIRONMENTAL LAW

ONE
What is environmental law?

In the 1980s some commentators doubted whether the issue of 'the environment' would last. They have been proved wrong, since it is clearly one of the big issues, perhaps the biggest issue, of the 1990s.

It is a big issue in political terms, since protection of the environment is high on most people's priorities for the 1990s. As a result political parties and governments are falling over each other in their eagerness to appear green, even if as yet their actions rarely match their rhetoric. It is big in terms of the size of the problems faced and the solutions required; global warming, the destruction of the ozone layer, acid rain, deforestation, overpopulation and toxic waste are all global issues which require an appropriately global response. It is big in terms of the range of problems and issues—air pollution, water pollution, noise pollution, waste disposal, radioactivity, pesticides, countryside protection, conservation of wildlife—the list is virtually endless. In the words of the White Paper on the Environment, *This Common Inheritance* (Cm. 1200, 1990) the issues range 'from the street corner to the stratosphere'. Finally, it is big in terms of the knowledge and skills required to understand a particular issue. Law is only one element in what is a major cross-disciplinary topic. Lawyers need some understanding of the scientific, political and economic processes involved in environmental degradation. Equally, all those whose activities and interests relate to the environment need to acquire an understanding of the structure and content of environmental law, since it has a large and increasing role to play in environmental protection.

The scope of this book

Faced with all these elements of 'bigness', authors of books on environmental law have to make many choices, otherwise each book would become unmanageably large. Inevitably what is included in this book reflects the personal interests and prejudices of the authors. The shape and structure of this book—what is included, what is omitted, what is covered in detail, what is covered in outline, how it is put together—must therefore be explained.

The book is entitled 'Environmental Law' and an explanation of these two words will clarify some preliminary points about its content.

Environmental

This is a difficult word to define. Its normal meaning relates to 'surroundings', but obviously that is a concept that is relative to whatever object it is which is surrounded. Used in that sense environmental law could include virtually anything; indeed, as Einstein once remarked, 'The environment is everything that isn't me'. However, 'the environment' has now taken on a rather more specific meaning, though still a very vague and general one, and may be treated as covering the physical surroundings that are common to all of us, including air, space, waters, land, plants and wildlife.

A definition of this nature is used in the Environmental Protection Act 1990 (EPA 1990), s. 1, which defines the environment as consisting of 'all, or any, of the following media, namely, the air, water and land'. Rather than offering a hostage to fortune by attempting to lay down some impossibly precise definition, we propose to adopt this one for the general description of the book's content. A more precise description can be given simply by stating what is and what is not covered by the book. We intend to concentrate on those laws and practices which relate primarily to the protection of the whole or part of the general surroundings, as opposed to those where the true objective is the protection of public health, or individual people such as workers or consumers.

Obviously, it is not possible to consign some areas of law with certainty to one category or another and, as a result, the exact dividing line between what is and what is not included is rather artificial. But a line has to be drawn somewhere. Accordingly, we cover the law and practice on the protection of air, water and land against pollution, and the protection of the ecosystem, together with those ancillary issues which help to explain these areas, such as public participation, access to information, remedies and procedures.

Such things as consumer protection laws, product liability laws, health and safety legislation and animal protection laws are not covered, although they can often be relevant to solving environmental problems. There are also a number of areas of what is undeniably environmental law which are omitted on grounds of space. The growing package of legislation on the protection of the cultural heritage is omitted. Little will be said about radioactivity, where the law is very complex indeed and where there is a large overlap between the environmental and human protection parts of the law. The provisions in the EPA 1990 on the introduction of genetically modified organisms into the environment and on litter are also omitted.

Law

This book is not intended to be merely a description of the various rules and regulations, although obviously that is a part of any useful book on the law. Such a description would give little clue to what happens in practice. Whether, and how, the law is enforced is just as important as what the law is. Indeed, given the discretionary nature of many of the powers and duties imposed on environmental decision-makers, it is unreal to draw a hard and fast distinction between what the law is and how it is used. This book will therefore seek to emphasise policy as much as law, and practice as much as principle.

There are some other general limitations on the subject matter of the book in addition to the ones mentioned above. It is not about all those laws which 'relate to' the environment, since that too could cover virtually anything. We intend to concentrate on those laws and practices which have as their object or effect the *protection* of the environment. Those things which merely have an indirect impact on the state of the environment, such as tax levels, grants and incentives, are thus excluded from full coverage, although their relevance is referred to in passing and they may frequently be of crucial importance to the policy-maker.

In addition, for reasons of space, we intend to concentrate on domestic laws and practices. We will not attempt to deal with truly international problems in any detail, a choice which is justified by the publication of the excellent and comprehensive *International Law and the Environment* (Birnie and Boyle, 1992). Even so, the importance of international agreements in influencing and moulding our domestic law should be recognised.

The crucial relevance of European Communities (EC) law must be emphasised. We adopt the attitude that EC law *is* domestic law in the sense that it cannot be ignored even though it does not always give rise to enforceable obligations and remedies. Therefore EC controls, both current and proposed, will be integrated into each part of the book where relevant. In addition, there is a separate chapter on the basic constitutional rules of the EC and on the history, philosophy and current direction of its environmental policy. It is hard to overestimate the central importance of EC law and policy to British environmental law. This importance is often masked by the fact that in the environmental field EC law tends to require some form of implementation in this country before it is formally recognised. Once implemented, the EC derivation of the rule is then frequently forgotten because the domestic law is cited as the applicable law.

Some themes of the book

This description of the scope of the book highlights a number of important themes. One is that there is a great deal of interaction between rules which have as their main objective the protection of the environment and those which aim to protect people. Just as in nature conservation it has become accepted in the last 30 years that there is no use in protecting individual animals or species unless you also protect their habitats, in all matters we now accept that protection of human beings involves protection of their environment. The converse is also true in that many rules originally aimed at protection of people end up protecting the environment. For example, standards in relation to radioactivity are often set with the protection of humans in mind, but have an important impact on environmental levels of radiation. Similarly, the presence or absence of laws on cruelty to animals has a significant impact on nature conservation even though that is not their primary motive.

A related theme is that the rules are simply the tools of the trade of law-makers, environmental protection agencies and environmentalists. A rule which has as its objective one goal is frequently of enormous use in an entirely different way. For example, the law of nuisance owes its existence and shape to the objective of protecting property rights, but it still has an important, though often unpredictable, part to play in regulating environmental standards in the interests of the community. This is one of the major themes of this book: that there is often more than one way of tackling a problem and that the environmental lawyer must be seen as a problem-solver who chooses the most appropriate tool for the particular problem encountered. Often this will involve using a combination of different tools. As an example, many rules of property law may be used to further environmental ends: the Royal Society for the Protection of Birds follows a policy of buying land for nature reserve purposes on the principle that the exercise of ownership rights will often provide a better method of protection than many statutory designations or protections. This is not to say that the whole of property law must be somehow annexed as a part of environmental law, but that environmental lawyers should make use of any piece of law which has a relevance to the problem in hand.

A further issue relates to the nature of law. It is often stated that law is not constructive; that it does not build houses or plant trees. We regard this as an inaccurate notion. There is no doubt that many laws do lay down straightforward negative rules restricting specified forms of behaviour. But many laws lay down rights as well as wrongs. Much of environmental law consists of setting out a framework for behaviour—who should make decisions, how they should make them, what procedures must be followed. Such law is clearly not just negative.

In *Countryside Conflicts* (Lowe et al, 1986), the authors state that, 'planning control is no more than an essentially negative power; a device for stopping objectionable proposals'. This pessimistic view, which is undoubtedly widespread (especially amongst non-lawyers), seems to miss the point that planning law, like much of environmental law, is also about positive concepts, as expressed in the word 'planning' and illustrated by the production of development plans as an integral part of the process. In relation to pollution control, a similar point can be made by noting that the regulatory agencies spend a far greater proportion of their time providing positive advice on how to reach the standards they set than on enforcing those standards through legal threats and remedies.

This distinction between negative and positive tools links to a division in the subject matter of environmental law. It is common to equate environmental protection with pollution control. However, whilst pollution control undoubtedly represents a major part of environmental law, there are many other issues, such as the retention of biological diversity and the preservation of landscape, which also make up the subject. These issues often require slightly different legal mechanisms.

Finally, and perhaps most importantly, the law provides remedies. To many people, whether they are environmentalists or industrialists or lawyers giving advice, this is the most central aspect of law, since they want to know what they can do about a situation. One of the interesting developments of recent years has been the search for adequate remedies for environmental problems. Legal tools have been accepted as legitimate devices for helping to solve environmental problems. Law plays an often underrated but enormously important role, alongside scientific, technological, social and economic solutions, in helping to combat environmental degradation. In this role, many novel legal concepts have been developed.

The shape of the book

A major aim of this book is to illustrate the proposition that there is developing such a thing as environmental law. Most lawyers are brought up on the idea that there are a number of core, or basic, subjects which are essentially about techniques and in which a set of central organising principles can be distilled from the law. Criminal law, constitutional law, public law, contract law, torts, equity and property law would be good examples. The traditional view would then be that, alongside those basic subjects, are as many areas of law as there are areas of life, in each of which the techniques of the basic subjects are used; for example, the law relating to family relationships, the law relating to housing. But over a period of time, there is no doubt that these topic-related areas build up their own principles and reasoning processes. A good example of this process would be the development of the principles of public law over the last 40 years.

We would argue that environmental law is starting to acquire its own conceptual apparatus, in the sense that there is being built up a set of principles and concepts which can be said to exist across the range of the subjects covered. This is very much at an early stage, but the process of establishing environmental law as a separate discipline has begun. This makes it important to explain some general concepts, such as the 'polluter pays' principle, near the beginning of the book (see p. 116). It also explains the division of the book into two parts, one on the general themes of environmental law and the other on specific environmental issues. As suggested above, an environmental lawyer ideally needs to understand both parts in order to possess the tools required to carry out the task of solving particular problems properly.

Part I of the book looks at those general issues which cut across all issues of environmental protection, but which are in practice an essential part of any understanding of the law. The discussion in this part should also provide a form of vocabulary to help with an understanding of the context of the specific laws and practices which are dealt with in Part II.

Part I thus covers the nature of the regulatory systems adopted for environmental protection, the sources of the law, the institutions and agencies involved in environmental protection, the process of setting environmental standards and the different types of standard that may be adopted, the role of the EC, secrecy and freedom of access to information, the role of the common law and the important question of how environmental laws are actually enforced.

In *Part II* the specific laws relating to particular environmental issues are treated on a chapter by chapter basis. However, there is a significant problem of organisation here. Should the law be divided up according to the medium in which the environmental threat manifests itself (i.e. air, water, land etc.)? Should it be divided according to the identity of the polluter (e.g. cars, factories, power stations etc.)? Should it be divided according to the nature of the pollutant (e.g. radiation, lead, pesticides, CFCs etc.)? Or should it even be divided according to the nature of the target which is being protected (e.g. people, animals, ecosystems, the atmosphere)?

There is no single answer. The laws are not designed on any one of these four axes, but on all four at once. The best that can be done is to select groupings of laws that more or less hang together in a way that makes sense to someone faced with a problem. It must then be remembered that in reality all these things interrelate, so that a problem on the disposal of waste to land cannot be considered without some consideration of the law on incineration, or discharges to water, or recycling. Integrated pollution control and the adoption of the related concept of best practicable environmental option in the EPA 1990 are explicit recognitions of this interrelation.

Certain issues also play a role which it is impossible to explain in terms of any one of the four axes set out above. The law on town and country planning is an example. It clearly has a central role in protecting against threats to amenity and is in other ways an important part of the law on environmental protection. For example, hazardous or undesirable developments can be prevented or subjected to conditions, making the need for planning permission an essential part of most systems of pollution control. But it also has a role in organising economic development which is outside environmental law in its strict sense.

As a result the chapter divisions in Part II may be seen as artificial in a number of ways. We try to cover the protection of the major environmental media—air, land and water—from pollution, at the same time as considering the various means of disposing of waste—sewage disposal, incineration, landfill, discharge to rivers, discharge to the sea, reuse and recycling.

Environmental protection law is undoubtedly undergoing a period of unprecedentedly rapid change (see below). It is therefore intended to give special prominence to those areas where there have been recent changes and to refer to potential future developments wherever possible. In a subject area such as this, where activities have to be planned reasonably far in advance, it is always best to know what is likely to happen in the future as well as what is actually the law at the time. In this sense environmental law is forward-looking law.

The history of environmental law

An understanding of the current state of environmental law requires some understanding of its history. Not surprisingly for such a densely populated country, environmental controls have a long history, going back to medieval statutes on small-scale pollution and the development of private law principles to deal with threats to communal assets such as water. Of course, until recently, few would have thought of these laws as part of something called 'environmental law', since their main focus was on the protection of private and common property.

Britain's position as the cradle of the Industrial Revolution led to the very early development of public controls specifically related to environmental protection. The most significant provisions were developed in response to public health problems in the mid-nineteenth century, culminating in the landmark Public Health Act 1875.

Britain can boast what is normally considered the world's first national public pollution control agency, the Alkali Inspectorate, which was established by the Alkali Act 1863 to control atmospheric emissions primarily from the caustic soda industry. Water pollution controls followed in the Rivers Pollution Prevention Act 1876, although these proved to be virtually unenforceable in practice. Britain also introduced some of the earliest provisions on town planning. The first legislation to cover this subject was the Housing, Town Planning etc. Act 1909, which again derived from public health pressures and which vested controls in local authorities, at this stage on a non-obligatory basis. Obligatory town and country planning controls were introduced on a nationwide scale in 1947—again early in world terms.

In addition to these public controls, the law of nuisance was developed (especially in the nineteenth century) as a means of providing private redress for environmental harm, although on a very selective basis. Britain also had some of the earliest voluntary bodies concerned with environmental protection.

National, centralised control of problems (such as through the Alkali Inspectorate) was very much the exception in this period of development, and most public health and environmental protection was carried out at a local level by a vast array of local boards and, at a later stage, local authorities. Some uniformity was effected by the Public Health Act 1875, which produced model by-laws for such things as the design and layout of housing, but most of the early provisions reflect a tendency (which is still apparent) to regulate only the most dangerous or sensitive matters at a central level.

In these formative years, law-making tended to be ad hoc in the extreme. This is self-evident with case law, which by its very nature must react to the facts of cases brought. But legislative changes were also reactive, with Parliament tending to legislate for problems on an individual basis, in isolation from other areas and without any thought for wider development or consolidation of the law. For example, one effect of the early Alkali Acts and the controls over atmospheric emissions is reputed to have been an immediate worsening of water quality as industries chose liquid discharge as a replacement method for the disposal of their wastes. The same reactive tendency can be seen more recently. A good modern example is the enactment of the Deposit of Poisonous Wastes Act 1972, which passed through Parliament in only a few days in response to a much-publicised discovery of the fly-tipping of poisonous waste near a school playground.

As a result, environmental law has traditionally been split amongst a number of statutes, many of them covering much other material with little to do with environmental protection. Grandiose titles have often concealed the fact that an Act only covers part of the law on a particular area. For example, the Wildlife and Countryside Act 1981 did not really have much to offer for the protection of the wider countryside outside sites protected for nature conservation and landscape purposes, and even the Control of Pollution Act 1974, which was the first of the modern breed of large statutes concerned exclusively with pollution control, had very little to say about air pollution.

One reason for this fragmentation was often lack of Parliamentary time provided by the Government of the day, fuelled by the perceived lack of importance of environmental issues. This is undoubtedly changing rapidly as the political importance of environmental protection has grown immensely in recent years. But many environmental measures in the past have resulted from single issue campaigns, or from Private Member's Bills. For example, one of the reasons why the protection of birds has always been at a greater level than the protection of animals and plants is the passage of the Protection of Birds Act 1954 as a Private Member's Bill sponsored by the Royal Society for the Protection of Birds. A further example to show that this still happens is the Control of Pollution (Amendment) Act 1989, a Private Member's Bill to require the registration of carriers of controlled waste, passed in response to fly-tipping in London.

One effect of this long, and unplanned, history is that modern Britain has inherited a far less coherent system of pollution control than many other countries. The same historical factors also explain the relatively large number of agencies dealing with environmental matters, although recent changes in institutional responsibility have significantly improved matters in this respect.

A further effect is the survival of anachronisms. The name 'Alkali Inspectorate' lasted until the 1980s (when it became part of Her Majesty's Inspectorate of Pollution) and, although there have been changes in the EPA 1990, we still have laws on statutory nuisances which retain the essential shape they were given in the Public Health Act 1875. Anachronisms may also be seen in the limitations on access to environmental information and public participation in environmental decision-making (see Chapter 7) and in the still widespread immunity of the Crown in relation to environmental regulation (although this is being removed gradually).

Of course, as well as a long history of pollution control, Britain has a long history of pollution. This has left a legacy of problems that require urgent action, such as abandoned waste tips, derelict land, discharges of toxic wastes and untreated sewage into estuaries and the sea, and a host of other matters. There are other problems, stemming from the fact that many matters were not perceived as problems in the past, or that lower standards were accepted then. For example, perpetual planning permissions for peat extraction or gravel extraction were commonly granted in the 1940s and 1950s. Many of these are in areas now accepted as sensitive and worthy of protection, but under the current law the permission may only be removed by the payment of compensation for the loss of development rights.

Britain's ageing industrial base also creates difficulties when new, improved controls and standards are introduced. Fairness requires that existing producers are given some time to adapt to new standards, yet there is at the same time a problem of unfairness if controls are introduced so as to produce an inequality between new and existing producers.

The modern age of environmental law

Environmental law has changed rapidly in the last few years, and further change can be expected in the future to reflect the vastly increased prominence of environmental issues. Although it is not possible to specify a precise date or event, the modern age of environmental law can tentatively be said to have begun some time in the early 1970s.

There has been an obvious shift in the emphasis of the law since then to reflect newer environmental concerns. Many problems were simply not perceived as such in the 1960s, or were subordinated to other more pressing matters, such as the raising of living standards or the provision of full employment. The emphasis at that stage was on health and safety matters, a point well illustrated by the placing of the Alkali and Clean Air Inspectorate within the Health and Safety Executive when it was established in 1974. Land use was also emphasised; indeed, it could be argued that the very fact that Britain had (and still has) what is probably the world's most advanced system of land use planning led to the concentration of controls at that stage rather than to encouraging the development of adequate continuing pollution controls.

By comparison, the focus of modern legislation is on the control of pollution, and growing concern is being expressed about global and transfrontier problems, the control of hazardous substances and processes, the minimisation and management of waste, and the conservation of natural resources and protection of ecosystems. In short, current concerns tend to reflect the need to control the almost inevitable by-products of the modern, technological, industrial age.

In terms of legislation, the law is becoming more concentrated in a smaller number of Acts. The *EPA 1990* contains the main bulk of provisions on air pollution from stationary sources, waste management and disposal, the integrated control of the most potentially polluting processes, litter, the environmental impact of genetically modified organisms, noise and statutory control of environmental nuisances. The *Water Resources Act 1991* contains the law on water pollution and water resources, whilst the *Water Industry Act 1991* covers matters relating to water supply and sewerage. The *Wildlife and Countryside Act 1981* includes much of the relevant law on nature conservation in Parts I and II. The *Environment Act 1995* introduces new legal provisions in relation to liability for contaminated land. It also creates the Environment Agency, which will take over functions related to integrated pollution control, waste regulation, water pollution and water resources, and radioactive substances, although without any major changes in the substance of the law. The *Town and Country Planning Act 1990* includes in consolidated

form most of the relevant statutory law on town and country planning and
tree protection, though the related Planning (Listed Buildings and Conservation Areas) Act 1990 and Planning (Hazardous Substances) Act 1990 now
include separate treatment of listed buildings and hazardous substances
consents. There is also the Planning and Compensation Act 1991, which
made some significant amendments to the 1990 Acts.

None of these Acts is a full code in relation to the relevant subject matter.
There are numerous individual issues which are dealt with by separate pieces
of legislation, such as on mobile sources of pollution, or on pesticides. There
are other issues where the controls are still spread amongst a large number of
Acts, such as in relation to landscape protection. It is also necessary to point
out that much of the detailed law in any area is actually provided in statutory
instruments and a wide range of other documents made under the relevant
Acts. The process of producing a coherent body of environmental law, begun
in the Control of Pollution Act 1974 (which put most of the law on water
pollution and waste disposal in one place, but which is now virtually fully
replaced by later legislation in England and Wales), has certainly moved
forward some distance.

One of the important features of this process is that the development and
direction of the statutory controls is more planned than before. The main
Acts referred to above are all Government-sponsored Acts, illustrating an
increasing tendency to plan and interlink legislation properly, although there
is still a habit of including unrelated matters in legislation just in case no other
opportunity arises in a packed Parliamentary timetable. For example, the
EPA 1990 includes miscellaneous provisions on the control of dogs, the
dismantling of the Nature Conservancy Council and the prohibition of straw
and stubble burning. The publication of the wide-ranging White Paper on the
environment, *This Common Inheritance* (Cm. 1200, 1990), underlined this
commitment to a planned development of environmental policy. The important aspect of the White Paper was not the new policies it included (these were
very limited and many of the proposals had a distinctly recycled feel to them),
but its mere existence as a declaration of the importance of the environment
and of having a definite set of policies towards its protection.

There is also an increasing institutional coherence, although the process is
not yet complete (see Chapter 3). The National Rivers Authority was
established in 1989 as a national body regulating water pollution and a
number of other activities affecting water quality. Her Majesty's Inspectorate
of Pollution was established in 1987 to bring together a number of sectoral
Inspectorates and was given integrated powers over the most hazardous
industrial processes in the EPA 1990, an Act which also created greater
coherence in relation to the control of air pollution by local authorities and
the management of waste and waste disposal. Once again it is clear that
controls over stationary sources of pollution are more coherent than those
over mobile or non-point sources. The next few years will see the creation of
a unified Environment Agency for England and Wales with responsibility for
integrated pollution control, the regulation of waste, the control of radioactivity and the regulation of water pollution. There is also the possibility that

the European Environment Agency, the creation of which became a reality in 1993, will expand its role from that of information broker to that of European environmental police force.

A different aspect of developments in relation to institutional responsibilities is the Government's policy of splitting production from regulation. This may be termed the need to differentiate the poachers from the gamekeepers. In recent years this has been achieved by the creation of the National Rivers Authority. Prior to that the regulation of water pollution was the responsibility of the regional water authorities, who were also responsible for causing pollution from sewage works which they operated. A more recent example is the enforced separation of waste regulation functions from waste disposal functions in the EPA 1990 (see Chapter 13), a process that has been taken further in the Environment Act 1995.

A final change, which may be seen from the examples referred to, is that environmental protection is becoming increasingly centralised, although this must be seen against the perspective that, as stated above, the system inherited from earlier years was particularly decentralised. There are many reasons for this—the increasing technological and scientific demands on pollution controllers, Central Government antipathy towards local government, increased emphasis on uniform and integrated planning of solutions to problems, and the impact of EC membership. This issue is considered further in Chapter 5.

A most important factor in all of these changes has been the influence of the European Communities (EC). The EC has a well-developed environmental policy and has passed numerous pieces of environmental law. At a general level, membership of the EC has led to the consideration and adoption of new methods of control and to the need to confront environmental issues in an organised way at Central Government level. More specifically, EC legislation and pressure has led to many actual and proposed changes in the law (often after British resistance), for example, on sulphur dioxide emissions, the dumping of sewage sludge in the sea and reductions in emissions from vehicles. Other changes have been more indirect; for example, the Wildlife and Countryside Act 1981 was necessary to comply with EC Directive 79/409 on Wild Birds, and the opportunity was taken to modify other areas of the law at the same time. Without the EC obligation there must be some doubt whether any legislation would have been brought forward at that time—and even greater doubt as to whether it would have been persevered with in the light of the widespread opposition to the Government's original proposals, which were significantly altered as the Bill passed through Parliament.

The future of environmental policy

In the light of EC membership, and the pressure now brought to bear by the whole international community on environmental issues, it is difficult to disentangle British policies from global and regional ones. It is also difficult to predict the future accurately in this area because environmental policy is currently a highly political area. For example, it is difficult to imagine many issues that could raise a greater number of separate, highly-charged, political issues than the proposals for some form of 'carbon tax'. Nevertheless, a number of key directions for future policy present themselves:

(a) The emphasis is shifting away from the more traditional reactive methods of solving environmental problems towards the prevention of harm. This is illustrated by the progressive adoption of laws that set standards for products or the processes by which they are made, rather than for discharges or emissions. The introduction of integrated pollution control, a process-based control, is an important step in this direction.

(b) The importance of the market in controlling environmental problems is being stressed. Partly this stems from the philosophical obsessions of the Conservative Government, but it is also related to the preference for preventative mechanisms, since market mechanisms (often referred to as 'economic instruments') may help to prevent pollution occurring by sending signals to consumers as to the true environmental cost of their activities. Examples can be seen in the proliferation of schemes for charging for environmentally harmful activities, in the frequent references nowadays to the 'polluter pays' principle, and in proposals for a 'landfill tax'. In *This Common Inheritance: The Second Year Report* (1992), the Government puts forward the policy that there should be a presumption in favour of using economic instruments as opposed to direct regulation, though it must be commented that, as yet, rhetoric outweighs performance on this point.

(c) The EC also stresses the role that mechanisms other than administrative regulation have to play in the protection of the environment. The key concept in its fifth Action Programme on the Environment, covering the period 1993 to 2000 and entitled *Towards Sustainability,* is that of 'shared responsibility'. This means that responsibility for environmental problems is shared between government, producers and consumers. By suggesting that producers and consumers should be empowered to make decisions that have an impact on environmental performance, it heralds the development of a wider range of legal and policy responses to environmental problems.

(d) A further matter that links all of the above together is the provision of information about the environment. It is obvious that increased interest in environmental issues has led to a political need for greater access to information. But there is a further reason why freedom of information is a central issue. This is that market mechanisms do not work, and concepts such as shared responsibility mean nothing, unless there is access to accurate information. As a result, wide-ranging provisions on access to information have been enacted at both EC and domestic levels—see Directive 90/313 and the Environmental Information Regulations 1992 (SI 1992 No. 3240).

(e) An important issue is the internationalisation of many problems. A number of high-profile issues, such as global warming, depletion of the ozone layer, the protection of the rainforest, and attempts to save the whales, have galvanised interest in environmental issues, and there is no doubt that the future agenda will increasingly be set on the international stage. This point has not been lost on the Government, which sought to rescue its tattered environmental reputation (which in the 1980s led to Britain being called 'the Dirty Man of Europe' as a result of obstructiveness in relation to such things as acid rain, controls over CFCs and the dumping of wastes at sea) by devoting a significant proportion of *This Common Inheritance* to international issues.

Of course, the clearest expression of this process was the United Nations Conference on Environment and Development (UNCED), held in Rio de Janeiro in June 1992. Although this was rightly criticised for failing to produce anything of enormous immediate significance, it did produce agreement on a number of things. These included a framework convention on climate change, a convention on biological diversity, a declaration on the sustainable development of forests, and Agenda 21, which is effectively a very wide-ranging environmental action plan for the next century. The implications of these commitments are currently being fed through into domestic policies, so Rio is probably most accurately seen as the beginning of a process rather than the end of one.

(f) A central strand of policy at Rio was the emphasis on the conservation of natural resources. The key concept was that of 'sustainable development', an idea that was originally developed by the World Commission on Environment and Development (the Brundtland Commission) in its report, *Our Common Future*, in 1987. *Our Common Future* defined sustainable development in general terms as 'development that meets the needs of today whilst not affecting the ability of future generations to meet their own needs', thus suggesting that global resources (including environmental resources) should be measured, with the objective of ensuring that they are not depleted over time. Clearly, this idea requires some further development itself, in particular in relation to how one goes about measuring intangible global assets and whether it is permissible to substitute one type of asset for another. One thing that is clear is that sustainable development still represents a commitment to growth. In *This Common Inheritance* the Government stresses the view that continued growth is a necessary (although not a sufficient) condition for maintaining the quality of life, and this view is reiterated in *Sustainable Development: The UK Strategy* (Cm. 2426, 1994), the Government's strategy document on the matter. The idea of sustainable development should therefore be distinguished from the concept of sustainability, which merely reflects the state of something being sustainable in the long term.

(g) At a national level the implications of sustainability are most obvious in relation to the steps that are being taken to reduce waste (of both materials and energy) by tackling the problem at source. The policy is now that waste reduction is to be preferred to recycling, and recycling to disposal. The minimisation of waste is clearly going to be an important feature of future production methods, not least because of the spiralling cost of waste disposal. A further, tentative shift in favour of sustainability can be seen in town planning policies. It is now suggested that such things as the energy implications of locational decisions (e.g. how far people have to travel to get to new developments) ought to be taken into account in planning decisions, which represents quite a remarkable 'U turn' by the Government from its past unbridled approval of out-of-town shopping centres and the 'Great British car economy'. At least, however, the most important message of sustainability appears to be getting across. This is that there is not some remote category of people called 'polluters' and everything will be all right if they can be controlled, but that environmental protection is a matter for everyone and involves everyone making informed choices about their own lifestyles.

The future of environmental law

An introductory chapter may seem a strange place to consider the future of the law, since any such discussion must inevitably involve an understanding of the present position. However, it is useful to sketch out some general ideas about the direction in which environmental law might be going at this stage so as to set the rest of the book in context.

The starting point is to repeat the proposition that environmental law has not been developed as a self-contained discipline, but has simply borrowed concepts from other areas of law. One result is undoubtedly a degree of incoherence, but another is that the objective of the protection of the environment is not always best served by the legal mechanisms available, because these other areas were not developed with the particular problems of environmental protection in mind. For example, the private law concentrates on the protection of private interests and has difficulties when it comes to protecting common or public interests in the unowned environment. No damages are payable for harm to the environment as such, and only those with personal or property rights may bring an action (thus excluding animals, trees, rivers etc). No value is placed on the environment itself and environmental protection is simply an incidental by-product of the protection of other interests. As Lord Scarman pointed out in 1974 in *English Law—The New Dimension*:

> For 'environment' a traditional lawyer reads 'property': English law reduces environmental problems to questions of property . . .. The judicial development of the law, vigorous and imaginative though it has been, has been found wanting.

Public law does recognise the public interest, but difficulties arise out of a lack of acceptance of the idea that the environment has some independent status or value, as distinct from rights conferred on individuals and communities. Even the criminal law struggles with environmental 'crimes', since it has often been pointed out in the courts that many of the offences created are not criminal in the 'true' sense (see the acceptance by the House of Lords in *Alphacell Ltd* v *Woodward* [1972] AC 824 that water pollution offences are in the category of 'acts which in the public interest are prohibited under a penalty'). Finally, the structure of the judicial system (with its emphasis on adversarial and backward-looking two-party litigation and with its procedural rules which are not user-friendly to those wishing to bring environmental cases and which fail to give the public interest a separate voice) is not particularly well-suited to consideration of environmental disputes, because typically they have multiple causes, give rise to complex scientific arguments, involve a complex interplay between public, private and criminal law, and require the balancing of difficult political or policy questions.

With these current defects in mind, the following thoughts can be put forward about the future development of environmental law.

(a)   In terms of civil law, there may well be a development of some sort of redress for purely environmental harm. For example, current EC proposals on civil liability envisage damages being payable for impairment of the environment (see, for example, the EC Commission Green Paper, *Remedying Environmental Damage*, 1993).

(b)   At a wider level, the work of environmental philosophers may be adopted so as to establish a legal concept which accords the environment some status in its own right (one hesitates to use the unclear phrase 'environmental rights', which might be better used to describe procedural rights possessed by individuals, such as rights to information, rights to be consulted, rights to have reasons provided for a decision and rights to make a complaint). This could be achieved by the recognition that, in line with the discussion about sustainability above, the planet is effectively held in trust for future generations. It could thus lead to the development of some sort of public trust doctrine. However, the development of such a concept is fraught with problems, since there is an all too obvious potential conflict between the precautionary and restrictive measures that are often required for sensible action on the environment and the traditional legal emphases on personal freedom and protection of property. This conflict can only really be resolved by the development of some sort of 'environmental constitution' that sits alongside other constitutional protections.

(c)   With regard to the criminal law, one reason that is often given for the failure to enforce against environmental laws is that a criminal remedy is inappropriate. Consideration may, therefore, be given to the 'decriminalisation' of whole areas of environmental law, so that a distinction could be drawn between, on the one hand, infringements that are properly characterised as administrative in nature and, on the other, truly criminal breaches, such as blatant cases of environmental vandalism. One advantage of this may be to encourage stiffer penalties for those in the second category. In similar vein, consideration should be given to the idea that fines imposed for environmental offences (of either type) should be paid into special funds for the enhancement or protection of the environment. This is not currently possible owing to the Treasury's insistence that all fines go into central funds—an attitude which does not fit easily with the 'polluter pays' principle. (Indeed, many of the market mechanisms favoured by the current Government simply do not work—in the sense of providing an appropriate incentive to act in a particular manner—without an element of earmarking of funds.)

(d)   There is, perhaps, a growing realisation that the different areas of law—public law, private law, criminal law—merely provide, in the environmental context, a set of different tools to achieve a specified objective, in this case the protection of the environment. For example, in relation to contaminated land it is clear that someone has to 'pay' for the contamination, either by cleaning it up, or by living with the consequences. There are essentially four possible options: the polluter could be made liable; the current owner or occupier could be liable; the State could pay (i.e. through some public clean-up mechanism)—this really means that the the public pays through some form of taxation; or, finally, the loss could lie where it falls, meaning that the environment and the local community effectively 'pay'. For a policy-maker the issue is how to come up with a solution that is effective, efficient and fair, whilst the tools that are available include, but are not limited to, legal mechanisms. The interesting thing about the solution provided in the Environment Act 1995 is that it combines the various tools in quite a sophisticated fashion and produces a situation where the public interest is protected by a combination of mechanisms that borrow from public, private and criminal law (see Chapter 13).

(e)   The above example raises the question of whether the development of the law is a matter for the courts or for Parliament. In *Cambridge Water Co. Ltd* v *Eastern Counties Leather plc* [1994] 1 All ER 53, Lord Goff stated in respect of environmental protection:

> . . . given that so much well-informed and carefully structured legislation is now being put in place for this purpose, there is less need for the courts to develop a common law principle to achieve the same end, and indeed it may well be undesirable that they should do so.

This can be interpreted as a reflection of the fact that Parliament is able to create a coherent and structured system, rather than one developed on an ad hoc, case-by-case basis; but it also reflects the point that Parliament has a greater democratic legitimacy than the courts when it comes to allocating responsibility for environmental harm. In the same passage Lord Goff also stated:

> As a general rule, it is more appropriate for strict liability in respect of operations of high risk to be imposed by Parliament, than by the courts.

This raises a different point about the *nature* of the liability that should be imposed. At present there is a clear division between those, such as the Government and most industrial organisations, who see the imposition of strict liability as unfair and punitive and therefore wish to retain a fault-based system as far as possible, and those, including the EC Commission in its Green Paper, *Remedying Environmental Damage*, who see strict liability as the most efficient and effective method of allocating responsibility for environmental harm. This issue is likely to remain a controversial one for many years.

(f)   Notwithstanding the above points, there is a very live debate about whether a separate environmental court or tribunal should be established (see the articles referred to in the bibliography). It is quite easy to establish a prima facie case that the current legal system does not work too well when confronted with environmental disputes, and that a new structure and set of procedures could work better. However, it must also be borne in mind that in many ways it is the substance of the law that is the problem, not the procedures, although the two are related.

(g) What, then, is the current approach of the British courts? In the *Cambridge Water* case the House of Lords was wary of extending liability for environmental harm and, indeed, imposed severe restrictions on liability for historic pollution. In *Merlin* v *British Nuclear Fuels plc* [1990] 3 All ER 711, the High Court decided that the entry of radiation into a house did not amount to 'injury to any person or damage to any property' within the meaning of the Nuclear Installations Act 1965, s. 47. In *Southern Water Authority* v *Nature Conservancy Council* [1992] 3 All ER 481, the House of Lords adopted a very literal interpretation of the Wildlife and Countryside Act 1981 in finding against the NCC (see p. 481). Many other examples could be given, but these cases illustrate that, in the main, the courts have been very cautious when it comes to developing new ideas on environmental protection. The situation is repeated in relation to EC law, an issue which is discussed in greater detail in Chapter 4. A final example is *R* v *Secretary of State for Trade and Industry ex parte Duddridge* [1995] Env LR 151, where the Divisional Court refused in very clear terms even to consider the application of the precautionary principle set out in Article 130R(2) of the EC Treaty as part of English law. One exceptional set of cases, however, concerns water pollution offences, where the interpretation that successive courts have been willing to place on the word 'cause' has been very wide (see p. 430) and clearly stems from the desire of the judges to provide a law that is effective in terms of environmental protection.

(h) There is another area where the courts have proved active. In recent years, there has been an increased willingness to develop judicial review mechanisms to provide for openness in decision-making and accountability to the public for decisions made in its name. For example, the courts are now accepting a wider role for environmental and other public interest groups in litigation. In *R* v *Her Majesty's Inspectorate of Pollution ex parte Greenpeace Ltd (No. 2)* [1994] 4 All ER 329, Otton J decided that Greenpeace had *locus standi* to challenge the decision to allow the thermal oxide reprocessing plant at Sellafield to start operating. He pointed in particular to the campaigning group's genuine interest in the issues raised and to its expertise and resources, and even referred to it as 'eminently respectable and responsible'. In *R* v *Secretary of State for Foreign Affairs ex parte World Development Movement Ltd* [1995] 1 All ER 611 (the *Pergau Dam* case) a similarly wide approach was also adopted, leading to the suggestion that the very restrictive ruling in *R* v *Secretary of State for the Environment ex parte Rose Theatre Trust Ltd* [1990] QB 504 is unlikely to be followed in future. This widening of *locus standi* will be encouraged by the recommendations of the Law Commission in *Administrative Law: Judicial Review and Statutory Appeals* (Law Comm No. 226, 1994) that *locus standi* should be found where the application is in the 'public interest', that unincorporated associations should be enabled to make applications in their own name, and that costs should be awarded from central funds where there is a public interest challenge.

(i)   Despite the negative points that have emerged in the previous discussion, there will certainly be a continuing increase in environmental litigation. The increased formality of many areas of environmental policy increases the possibility of a successful public law challenge; practising lawyers are increasingly aware of the possibilities thrown up by legal action; environmental interest groups have learnt the usefulness of the legal process in making political points as well as in winning cases; and EC law throws up a whole new area of litigation arising out of the doctrines of direct effects and indirect effects and the decision in the *Francovich* case (see Chapter 4).

(j)   Finally, whatever happens in relation to these major issues, there will continue to be some fine-tuning of the mechanisms that already exist. One of the defects of the law has been its piecemeal development, and it is clear that measures that have proved successful in one area are likely to be adopted in others. For example, there seems very little reason why the enforcement remedies available to Her Majesty's Inspectorate of Pollution under the EPA 1990 should not be available in relation to water pollution control, especially when the same matters come to be regulated by one body, the Environment Agency.

The costs of compliance

Whatever the exact direction that the law takes, one thing is clear about the future; the cost of compliance with the law is going to rise sharply, both for polluters and for society in general. This is mainly because regulatory standards are getting stricter and are being enforced more rigorously. But there are other factors, such as a heightened perception of the true environmental cost of many activities and the greatly increased pressure that is being brought to bear by the public, environmental groups and green consumers and investors.

The cost of sewage disposal illustrates the point. Disposal to the sewers has traditionally been thought of as a fairly cheap and efficient way of disposing of wastes. But the introduction of integrated pollution control means that increased controls will be applied to discharges of prescribed substances to the sewers. The costs of sewage treatment are also increasing because of changes relating to the disposal of their own wastes by sewage works. For example, the standards set for discharges to controlled waters are being tightened as the National Rivers Authority reviews existing consents, and this will carry a new urgency in the light of the need to meet the requirements of EC Directive 91/271 on Urban Waste Water Treatment. The cost of disposal of sewage sludge will also rise. Not only is the cheap option of dumping sewage sludge in the sea being phased out, after strong international pressure, but the cost of disposal on land is likely to rise significantly. Incineration is another possibility for disposal of sludge, but that too is coming under increasingly tight regulation. The privatised nature of the sewerage undertakers emphasises the need to take these factors into account. At the moment these sewerage undertakers are reviewing existing trade effluent consents for discharges to the sewers, and it is clear that in the next few years conditions restricting the discharge of certain substances will increasingly be imposed and that charges for discharges to sewers will rise.

The costs of non-compliance

Apart from the direct cost to business of complying with stricter regulatory controls, the potential liabilities for non-compliance are also increasing. These liabilities fall into five general categories:

(a) *Criminal liabilities.* The number of criminal offences for non-compliance with environmental legislation is immense, and in recent years the regulatory agencies have shown an increased willingness to resort to prosecution. Private prosecution is also a possibility. Fines will be the normal penalty, though in a number of cases sentences of imprisonment have been imposed (there is normally a potential personal liability for directors and senior managers). Maximum fine levels have risen in recent years, as have actual levels of fines imposed.

(b) *Administrative sanctions.* In most regulatory systems there is a range of options available to the regulator, including variation, suspension or revocation of a licence. Since these steps may lead to the closure of a plant, they are obviously of great importance.

(c) *Clean-up costs.* In most environmental legislation there is a power to clean up after a pollution incident and recover the cost from the polluter or (in some cases) the occupier.

(d) *Civil liability.* There is growing interest in the 'toxic torts', although many of the actions have in fact been around for a long time. Many environmental actions rest upon strict liability. Although liability may often be difficult to establish, the size of claims may be very high indeed.

(e) *Adverse publicity.* In practice the publicity attracted as a result of infringements of the law may be as costly as any direct costs.

In the light of all these risks, not to mention the increased costs of waste disposal and of complying with stricter standards, some of the most significant recent developments in the environmental field relate to management issues. For example, a British Standard on Environmental Management Systems (BS 7750), relating to the adoption of an appropriate management system, was introduced in 1994. The EC has agreed a Regulation on Eco-Management and Auditing (Regulation 1836/93), which goes further in some respects by requiring a public statement of environmental performance, external verification procedures, and a commitment to continuing improvements in environmental performance. Both these schemes are voluntary in the sense that there is no compulsion to join them. However, it appears that the pressures from supply chains and from the public may well be such that in practice many firms will be forced to introduce some form of environmental auditing of their business.

Policy and environmental law

A final introductory thought, but a most important one, is that environmental law is a political discipline. It is political in the narrow sense that major differences can be discerned between political parties as to the correct policy to apply. These differences do not normally relate to the ends to be achieved, but to the methods to be adopted in doing so, and the costs to be incurred. A clear example is the controversy provoked by the passage of the Wildlife and Countryside Act 1981 over whether voluntary or compulsory controls should be adopted in relation to the protection of important natural sites (see Chapter 16). A further example relates to the whole history of town and country planning in the 1980s, when the very dramatic changes to planning policy led to disagreement and dispute. These are clear examples of the application of 'Thatcherism' to the environment, as a Government with a deep suspicion of planning and regulation sought to grapple with a system based on coherent planning for the future. However, there are others which relate to such things as privatisation and deregulation. The Deregulation and Contracting Out Act 1994 shows that little has really changed since the 1980s and also emphasises the point that the whole context of environmental law may well change if a different administration is elected.

Environmental law is also political in the wide sense that it involves the making of policy decisions about the best way to achieve certain objectives. This is emphasised in this book by looking at law as being about techniques or tools for solving problems. It is not just lawyers and environmentalists who have a choice of tools they may use to achieve a particular objective. Legislators and policy-makers also have a range of tools available to them. The law is one tool alongside such things as fiscal policy, education, research, and voluntary solutions. There are different types of legal mechanism that may be used, such as the setting of environmental quality objectives, or of strict limits on emissions, or controls attached to processes or products. These various possibilities are discussed in detail in Chapter 5, but it ought to be recognised that, in order to combat complex problems of pollution and environmental harm, a combination of methods is often required.

It is impossible to say that Britain always adopts one method rather than another, but it is clear that the tendency has been to adopt flexible mechanisms of control, where what is permitted is judged by reference to its effect on the receiving environment. As a result, the British approach to pollution control tends to be fairly pragmatic, and involves a great deal of discretion. This discretion is normally exercised by specialist regulatory agencies, although local authorities also have very significant environmental protection functions. An important point is that this discretion is exercised on grounds that are not restricted to environmental factors. There is a traditionally close connection in British environmental regulation between social, political and economic factors and decisions on environmental protection.

This emphasis on taking into account a wide range of factors before making a decision links to a fundamental point about the way that 'pollution' and 'environmental harm' are defined. Once again, it is difficult to formulate precise definitions, but a general guide would be to say that they cover situations where there is an excess of something over what is desirable. There is no doubt that they are relative concepts; one person's waste is another's raw materials. As a result, Nicholas Ridley's famous comment that 'Housing is not a form of environmental pollution' can be seen as inaccurate in some cases.

The level of pollution is also relative. For example, because of the self-cleansing properties of the environment, it may well be said to be less polluting to discharge into a large fast-flowing river than into a small sluggish one, and higher levels of pollution from industrial sources may be tolerated in one area than in another because of the corresponding advantages of the economic prosperity that the industries bring. It is nonsensical to talk of getting rid of pollution. It only makes sense to consider how to reduce it and the levels which are acceptable.

Everything therefore depends on what is considered acceptable. This involves economic, political, social and cultural criteria as well as scientific and environmental ones. It is therefore important to understand that, in implementing environmental protection policies, regulatory agencies are effectively carrying out a political balancing process. As Hawkins puts it in *Environment and Enforcement* (1984), 'The power to define and enforce consents is ultimately a power to put people out of business, to deter the introduction of new business or to drive away a going concern'.

TWO

Sources of environmental law

Most of the formal sources of environmental law are statutory. Compared with subjects such as contract or tort there is very little judge-made law, and most of what there is consists of interpretations of statutory provisions. Obviously there are areas of the common law which can be used to promote environmental protection, such as the law of nuisance, or the rules on restrictive covenants, but the environmental advantages they bring tend to be incidental to the main purpose of the law concerned. For a discussion of the common law's contribution to environmental protection see Chapter 8.

Some major features of environmental legislation

Environmental statutes tend to exhibit a number of features:

(a) they are often framework Acts, requiring delegated legislation to be made to make them effective;
(b) their commencement is often delayed or staged;
(c) they include unclear definitions;
(d) they confer wide discretions.

Delegated legislation

Much of the detail of environmental statutes is left to be worked out in various forms of delegated legislation, such as regulations, rules, orders and schemes. This is particularly true of some of the main pieces of legislation in environmental law—the EPA 1990, the Water Resources Act 1991 and the Water Industry Act 1991, the Environment Act 1995 and the Town and Country Planning Act 1990. In each case a person who read the Act on its own would get a very limited view of the law. For example, the general requirement that an authorisation must be obtained from Her Majesty's Inspectorate of Pollution before 'prescribed processes' are carried on is laid down in the EPA 1990, s. 6, but the list of processes is prescribed in

Regulations, as are the detailed procedures for acquiring an authorisation. In the Town and Country Planning Act 1990, the central definition of what requires planning permission owes just as much to statutory instruments—the General Development Order and the Use Classes Order—as to the general definition laid down in s. 55 (see Chapter 9).

Delegated legislation may take a number of forms. In most cases, it is made by the Secretary of State or some other member of the Government (such as the Minister of Agriculture). But this is not necessarily the case, and it does not always involve the use of statutory instruments laid before Parliament. For example, the National Rivers Authority's Scheme for Charges in Respect of Applications and Consents for Discharges to Controlled Waters is made by the Authority, although it does require certain publicity procedures and the approval of the Secretary of State.

Very wide powers are often granted in relation to matters that are delegated. In some cases, such as the General Development Order and the Use Classes Order and the producer responsibility provisions in the Environment Act 1995, ss. 93–95, this virtually amounts to giving the Secretary of State a power to rewrite the Act. There are obvious problems of accountability with such an approach, since far less Parliamentary scrutiny is given to delegated legislation than to Acts of Parliament. There is also the prospect that the powers may not be used. For example, under the Control of Pollution Act 1974, powers were given to the Secretary of State to make regulations on precautions to be taken over the control of potentially polluting matter, and on water protection zones (s. 31(4) and s. 31(5) respectively), yet none were ever made.

Commencement

Legislation often requires implementation by statutory instrument before it comes into force. The Control of Pollution Act was enacted in 1974, yet Part II relating to water pollution was not brought into force until 1986, and then only in a piecemeal and gradual manner. Some parts of the Act were never brought into force (e.g. ss. 46(1)–(3) on the powers of water authorities to vary consents after an act of pollution). Apart from the suspicion that such delays are used for political purposes, this gradualist approach obscures what the law is and brings it into disrepute by creating uncertainty for the public, regulatory bodies and industry alike.

The EPA 1990 included a provision for most of it to be brought into force by commencement order. This led to the provisions on waste management licensing not being brought into force until May 1994. As far as integrated pollution control is concerned, the provisions of the Act have been brought into force, but are not applicable to individual processes until the commencement date published in Regulations has passed (see p. 313). It seems contrary to the rule of law that the decision on whether, and how far, to implement enacted legislation should be left entirely to the discretion of the Secretary of State. However, that is the position and the same approach has been adopted for the Environment Act 1995, virtually all of which requires a commencement order before it comes into force.

Definitions

Definitions are often left unclear in the legislation. Normally this is to preserve flexibility in the application of the law. For example, until the enactment of the EPA 1990, the central concept in the law on air pollution was that of 'best practicable means' (BPM). This phrase was never statutorily defined. Instead, it was explained in relation to different processes in BPM Notes published by Her Majesty's Inspectorate of Pollution (HMIP) and its predecessors. Even these were not comprehensive, since an important feature of BPM is that it allows flexibility to cater for local and individual circumstances. Interestingly, the BPM Notes were often drawn up in consultation with interested parties, including representatives of the industry concerned.

The same approach is adopted for the definition of the key phrase in Part I of the EPA 1990—'best available techniques not entailing excessive cost' (BATNEEC). Integrated pollution control (IPC) and local authority air pollution control (APC) Guidance Notes explaining the content of BATNEEC have been published for each prescribed process, although with less reliance on the industries concerned.

A similar process can be seen in the Town and Country Planning Act 1990, where fundamental concepts such as development and material change of use have deliberately been left as open as possible in the legislation. In this case, they have been further defined by the courts in numerous cases, but the original flexibility has been retained by the courts' insistence that the application of the law to the facts of any individual case is a matter for the relevant decision-maker (the so-called 'fact and degree' test). If anything, this approach is becoming more common. In the Environment Act 1995, Part II, a new system providing for remediation of contaminated land is established, yet the fundamental question of whether land is 'contaminated' will owe as much to guidance issued by the Secretary of State which local authorities must follow, as it does to the partial definition set out in the Act. What should be determined as a matter of law is thus relegated to a matter of administrative discretion. An even more remarkable example is provided by the Deregulation and Contracting Out Act 1994, which includes a general power for any Minister to amend or repeal existing legislation by means of a statutory instrument if it appears that the measure imposes a burden on any trade, business or profession, and that the amendment or repeal will reduce that burden. These examples illustrate a clear shift in power away from Parliament and the courts to the executive Government.

Discretions

Wide discretions are frequently given in the legislation. This is a particularly clear feature of British environmental law (see p. 105). There are many examples, ranging from the discretion given to the Secretary of State on the form of delegated legislation, through discretion as to whether an area should be designated for special protection, discretion on the setting of standards (e.g. in the permitted level of a pollutant discharged or emitted), to discretion over the enforcement of the law. In all areas of environmental law it is hard to get away from discretionary decision-making.

However, two important trends must be pointed out at this stage—the increased structuring of the discretions and the increased role of Central Government. In the past, it has been normal for environmental legislation to grant public agencies and bodies a large amount of discretion, often in the form of a subjective power which is then regulated by the courts. Over the last few years, the agencies have themselves structured the exercise of their discretions through such things as internal agency guidelines and strategies, and have thus made the whole system more formalised (a good example is the adoption by the NRA of a formal policy on prosecution and other enforcement action). This gives the courts a greater potential role in environmental decisions. However, the effect is arguably limited by the other trend which, as pointed out above, is that ever greater powers are being given to Central Government to dictate the sorts of considerations that must be taken into account in any exercise of a discretion. This process is seen very clearly in the Environment Act 1995. As a specific example, s. 39 imposes a requirement that the Environment Agency take into account the likely costs and benefits before making decisions; but, more generally, the whole way in which the Environment Agency will operate will be decided by guidance and directions issued by Central Government.

These features of environmental legislation help to explain some of the essential characteristics of the 'British approach' to environmental protection, such as flexibility and pragmatism (see p. 101). The width of the discretions given also militates against uniformity in either the definition or the application of the law.

Informal sources of law and practice

One particular result of giving wide discretion to decision-makers is that the concept of environmental 'law' expands to include a wide range of matters. For example, the IPC and APC Guidance Notes mentioned above are crucial to any understanding of what is actually required of industry in relation to pollution, even though they have no formal legal effect other than as matters to be taken into account by the appropriate enforcing body. Similarly, in areas of the law that depend on the discretionary balancing of policy factors, an understanding of the sources of policy is central. In many cases, prevailing policies effectively make or change the law. One of the most famous of policies in town planning—the Green Belt—has no statutory foundation at all (apart from around London). It stems entirely from a Central Government restraint policy dating back to the 1950s, which has been applied on a local basis in many areas. In theory, the whole idea of Green Belt could be amended, or even scrapped, tomorrow merely by a change in Government policy.

The story of town planning in the 1980s illustrates this point graphically, since what amounted virtually to a revolution in town planning law took place with very few changes to the legislation and delegated legislation. The main vehicle of change was Central Government Circular guidance on policy, which could be imposed on local authorities through the appeal system. It is arguable that a student of current planning law would learn more about what will happen in practice by reading Government policy documents than by reading the legislation.

The range of what must be considered as law is also widened by some of the features of environmental law. It is law in action rather than law for lawyers. It involves the solving of practical problems, so everything which is likely to have an impact on the solution of a problem should be understood, including policy and evidence of practice. It is also a forward-looking law; because of the need to plan for the future, it is desirable to know what the law is going to be as well as what it is.

Thus, the sources of environmental law are far wider than Acts of Parliament, delegated legislation and cases. Much of what constitutes law in its wider sense is in Circulars and policy documents issued by Central Government or the regulatory agencies. (It should be noted that there are normally different Circulars issued by the Department of the Environment and the Welsh Office, but these normally say the same things. In this book references to Circular numbers are to those issued by the Department of the Environment.)

It may also be argued that 'law' should include the actual practice of agencies with responsibilities in the environmental field; an argument which is at its strongest when dealing with enforcement. This makes it desirable that as much as possible about the practice and policy actually relied upon by decision-makers is published officially, an aim which (sadly for writers of environmental law books) is not yet met in practice.

European Communities (EC) law

It would not be proper to conclude a discussion of the sources of the law without a reference to EC law, which is of enormous importance in the environmental field. Membership of the EC has clearly involved a distinct loss of sovereignty for Member States, and in this country this is given constitutional force by the European Communities Act 1972. Section 2(1) provides that EC legislation is recognised as law in Britain, although by no means all EC environmental legislation is directly effective in the sense that it can be relied upon by individuals before it is implemented by domestic measures (see p. 65).

By virtue of the European Communities Act 1972, s. 2(2), EC legislation can be transposed into domestic law by delegated legislation even if there is no parent statute authorising it. For example, Directive 85/337 on Environmental Impact Assessment was implemented in British law through the passage of regulations by reference to that subsection. This power has a technical limitation, since no provisions extra to the EC legislation may be added without a new piece of enabling legislation. For example, this explains why the domestic regulations on environmental assessment originally went no further than required by the Directive (some would argue that they did not actually go as far as that), but that limitation has now been removed by a new statutory power to make regulations on environmental assessment under the Planning and Compensation Act 1991, s. 15.

EC law is explained in greater detail in Chapter 4, but an important point to establish here is that, as with the position in domestic law, EC environmental law consists of far more than legal rules. It is as necessary to understand the policies, principles and future direction of EC law as it is to understand its current legal content.

International law

International law governs relations between states. Unlike EC law, it has no direct effect on domestic law or on individuals. However, it will often have an indirect effect, for example by publicising a particular issue, by laying down generally accepted standards, or by imposing political pressure on states to change their laws or practices. Thus the North Sea Conferences have had an important impact on British domestic policies in relation to the dumping of sewage sludge in the North Sea, which will now cease. Many pieces of legislation include powers for the Government to introduce changes into domestic law in order to comply with international obligations. For example, the EPA 1990, s. 156 enables the Secretary of State to make regulations to modify other parts of the Act in order to comply with EC or international obligations.

For the most part, international environmental law consists of Conventions agreed by signatory states, such as the Ramsar Convention on Wetlands of International Importance (see p. 496), or the Vienna Convention for the Protection of the Ozone Layer. These may provide general guidance on activities or they may lay down precise standards and requirements (for example, the Montreal Protocol to the Vienna Convention does this). The important point is that such law is not ultimately binding, except in a political sense, because of the lack of sanctions available for non-compliance. However, it is often implemented by domestic or EC legislation, a process which has happened to the Montreal Protocol. It is anticipated, by analogy with the development of international law in other spheres, that it will develop some generally agreed principles to cover such things as trans-boundary pollution, that will apply even without the need for a treaty.

Judicial review

Environmental enforcement authorities are public bodies exercising public powers. Mostly, these powers are exercised under statute and consequential delegated legislation. However, in exercising these powers, it may be that such bodies do not follow statutory procedures, that they arrive at decisions unfairly, or that they attempt to make decisions which they have no power to make. The High Court oversees the exercise of these powers by administrative bodies by means of judicial review. The main ground for judicial review is that an administrative body has made a decision which was outside the statutory powers given to it (i.e. *ultra vires*). This may happen in one of three ways.

(a) No power to make the decision itself

If the National Rivers Authority decided to issue a trade effluent discharge consent for a discharge made to a sewer, a matter which is controlled by the privatised water services company, then the decision would be subject to judicial review because it could not be made within the National Rivers Authority's powers under the Water Resources Act 1991.

(b) The improper exercise of discretion

This principle was first expounded by Lord Greene MR in the case of *Associated Provincial Picture Houses Limited* v *Wednesbury Corporation* [1948] 1 KB 223:

> . . . a person entrusted with a discretion must, so to speak, direct himself properly in law. He must call his own attention to the matters which he is bound to consider. He must exclude from his consideration matters which are irrelevant to what he has to consider. If he does not obey those rules, he may truly be said, and often is said, to be acting 'unreasonably'. Similarly there may be something so absurd that no sensible person could ever dream that it lay within the powers of the authority. Warrington LJ in *Short* v *Poole Corporation* gave the example of the red-haired teacher, dismissed because she had red hair. That is unreasonable in one sense. In another it is taking into account extraneous matters. It is so unreasonable that it might almost be described as being done in bad faith; and, in fact, all these things run into one another.

Therefore, the improper exercise of discretion can be subdivided into a number of different categories: taking into account irrelevant considerations, failing to take into account relevant considerations, and acting so irrationally that the decision could only have been made in bad faith. Examples include taking into account the political party that an applicant supported when deciding an application for a waste disposal licence, and failing to consider the special attention to be paid to the provisions of the development plan on a planning application.

(c) Procedural unfairness

Although, in theory, the review of decisions made with procedural impropriety falls within the unreasonableness ground above, it is distinct enough to form its own head of review. There are two elements making up procedural fairness. These are that every person has a right to a fair hearing and that there should be no bias in a decision-making process. The right to a fair hearing includes the right to meet any case put against an applicant and the right to present cogent and coherent evidence in support of a case. The prohibition against bias covers such situations as local authority planning committee members participating in decisions to grant planning applications on land which they own. In such circumstances it is impossible for the decision-maker to reach a fair decision.

When a decision is made in any of the above circumstances, an aggrieved person has the right to apply to the High Court for judicial review. Such a right should not be confused with any statutory right of appeal, which may give rise to a reconsideration of the merits of a case, rather than consideration of questions of law. Indeed, theoretically, a court exercising its power of judicial review is not entitled to substitute its own decision for that of the administrative body.

Remedies

The High Court has several remedies available to it to overturn a decision made unlawfully.

(a) Certiorari
An order of certiorari is used to quash an administrative decision made unlawfully. Thus, where a noise abatement order has not been made correctly because of procedural defects, the order itself would be declared null and void.

(b) Prohibition
Where there is a threat that a statutory power will be unlawfully exercised then a prohibition forbids a statutory body from exercising its power in the threatened way.

(c) Mandamus
An order for mandamus forces a statutory body to carry out its statutory duty. For example, where a waste disposal authority is under a statutory duty to supervise sites governed by a waste management licence under the EPA 1990, such an order would force them to carry out this supervision properly. This is perhaps the remedy which is most obviously concerned with the control of environmental bodies. Many authorities are under a duty to carry out activities which have a consequential effect on environmental protection. A failure to carry out these duties may be due to the 'unreasonableness' of the body making the decision. Thus, the rights of people aggrieved by such a lack of activity are considerably enhanced.

(d) Declaration
The reform of judicial review procedures in 1977 added the remedies of declaration and injunction to the other remedies. When a declaration is sought the court seeks to give a statement as to the legal relations between the parties, but that is all it does and the declaration cannot be enforced. A declaration seeks no more than to state the legal position and does not seek to change the respective legal positions of the parties. Thus, a declaration is suitable for a situation where there are uncertainties over whether or not a certain set of facts falls within a category of law.

(e) Injunctions

Although an injunction is available as a remedy under the judicial review procedure, it is the least used remedy, since it is not available against the Crown. As much of environmental protection is carried out by Crown bodies, such a remedy is limited.

Procedure

The procedure for judicial review is contained within the Rules of the Supreme Court, Order 53. An application has to be made within three months from the date when the grounds of the application first arose, unless the court considers that there is good reason for extending the period (Ord. 53, r. 4). This time limit does not apply where there is any other statutory provision which has the effect of limiting the time within which an application for judicial review may be made (Ord. 53, r. 4(3)). In addition, the court may refuse to hear an application if there has been undue delay in bringing it, even if it is brought within the three months period (see, for example, *R* v *Swale BC ex parte Royal Society for the Protection of Birds* [1991] JPL 40).

However, in order to bring a claim for judicial review, the applicant must show a 'sufficient interest' in the decision or power to which the application relates (Supreme Court Act 1981, s. 31(3)). There has been some suggestion that this interest has to be greater where the application is for the remedies of prohibition or certiorari, but it is generally accepted that the only test is to show a sufficient interest for remedies. The phrase 'sufficient interest' is of tremendous importance in matters of environmental protection. As will be shown in Chapter 8, the protection of private law rights is contained within the common law and thus anyone seeking to protect their own private interests in land may resort to the common law rather than going through the even more expensive procedure of judicial review. But it is clear that somebody with a private interest in land affected by an administrative decision would have 'sufficient interest' or *locus standi*. It is more difficult to show that a person has the necessary standing by virtue of an interest in the environment as a whole, as it is not generally accepted that there are 'environmental rights' available to the public at large. The basis of the law on standing is contained in *IRC* v *National Federation of Self Employed and Small Businesses Ltd* [1982] AC 617, where Lord Wilberforce said that the decision as to who had a 'sufficient interest' under the Supreme Court Act 1981, s. 31 had to be considered with the known merits of a case:

> It will be necessary to consider the powers or the duties of those against whom the relief is asked, the position of the applicant in relation to those powers or duties, and to the breach of those duties said to have been committed. In other words, the question of sufficient interest cannot, in such cases, be considered in the abstract, or as an isolated point: it must be taken together with the legal and factual context.

In the planning system many actions have been brought by interest groups, where sufficient interest can be demonstrated by objecting to proposals or giving evidence at a local inquiry (see *Save Britain's Heritage* v *Secretary of State* [1991] 2 All ER 10 or *R* v *Hammersmith LBC ex parte People Before Profit* (1982) 80 LGR 322). In purely environmental matters, however, it is suggested that such an interest would be more difficult to show. In *R* v *Secretary of State for the Environment ex parte Rose Theatre Trust Company* [1990] 1 All ER 754, Schiemann J considered an application made by the Theatre Trust Company in relation to the Secretary of State's refusal to schedule the site of the Rose Theatre in Southwark (which was being developed) as an ancient monument under the Ancient Monuments and Archaeological Areas Act 1979. In deciding whether or not the company had any standing to bring an action in judicial review, he decided that, although it was not necessary for an applicant to demonstrate a financial or legal interest in the matter complained of, the statute giving rise to the power or duty had to be examined and the question asked as to whether or not the construction of that statute gave the applicant a right to have a duty performed. As the power confirmed by the Act in that case was specifically to be exercised by the Secretary of State in the public interest, on the construction of the Act the judge decided that no individual citizen or company had the right to challenge the decision in any event.

This decision is perhaps not as wide-ranging as it would seem. In many environmental regulations the purpose of the legislation is to protect certain groups or certain areas. For instance, under the Clean Air Act, it is clear that protection is to extend to a local authority's area and therefore a resident within that area would be entitled to expect that the statutory obligations would be carried out properly under that Act. Similarly, the waste disposal regime contained within Part II of the EPA 1990 seeks to control the disposal of waste so that it does not cause harm to the environment or to human health. This may be given a broad construction by the courts and it would, it is suggested, give wide rights of standing to all those who were intended to be protected. Guidance on this matter was given more recently in another decision of Schiemann J, *R* v *Poole BC ex parte Beebee* [1991] JPL 643. In this case he considered whether various environmental groups had sufficient standing to challenge a decision by Poole BC to grant itself planning permission for housing on a site of special scientific interest. The British Herpetological Society was held to have standing because of its long association with the site (indeed, one of the conditions of the planning permission was that the Society would be allowed to mount a rescue of reptiles and amphibians from the site). The World Wide Fund for Nature, which was involved mainly to fund the action, was stated not to have standing. It was made clear, however, that the Nature Conservancy Council would also have standing in such a case because of its official responsibilities for nature conservation.

In any case, the authority of the *Rose Theatre* case has been challenged in two recent decisions, and it is, perhaps, unlikely to be followed in the future. In *R* v *Her Majesty's Inspectorate of Pollution ex parte Greenpeace Ltd (No. 2)* [1994] 4 All ER 329, Greenpeace challenged the decision to allow the thermal oxide reprocessing plant at Sellafield (THORP) to commence operations. Pointing to Greenpeace's genuine interest in the issues raised and to its expertise and resources, Otton J decided that the group had sufficient interest, although he did note that it also had many members in the region who may be affected. In *R v Secretary of State for Foreign Affairs ex parte World Development Movement Ltd* [1995] 1 All ER 611 (the *Pergau Dam* case), the court, if anything, went even further in allowing a pure public interest claim to proceed, since there were clearly no local residents involved. In particular, it was emphasised that if the applicants were not granted *locus standi* then a clear illegality would not be subject to challenge. It is clear that the courts are now accepting a wider role for environmental and other public interest groups in bringing cases to court. This development will be carried further if the recommendations of the Law Commission are accepted. In *Administrative Law: Judicial Review and Statutory Appeals* (Law Comm No. 226, 1994) it recommended that *locus standi* should be found where the application is in the 'public interest', unincorporated associations should be enabled to make applications in their own name, and costs should be awarded from central funds where there is a public interest challenge.

It should be noted that there is one exception to all of this. The Attorney-General, as guardian of the public interest, always has *locus standi*. An applicant without 'sufficient interest' could therefore ask the Attorney-General to bring an action on their behalf. This is called a 'relator' action. The shadow applicant pays the costs but manages to side-step the rules on standing. However, the Attorney-General has an unchallengeable discretion whether to bring an action in this manner.

Restrictions on judicial review

There are a number of restrictions on the use of judicial review as a method of controlling the activities of enforcement bodies. First, as stated previously, the matter is not a hearing of the merits of a case. Thus, when a decision is quashed or a duty is enforced, it does not necessarily mean that the final decision of the administrative body will be to the liking of the person seeking judicial review. A good example of this is in the case of the judicial review of planning decisions. If an Inspector, on appeal, makes a decision which is contrary to the Inquiries Procedure Rules (for instance by not taking into account written representations from objectors), the resulting decision may be challenged. The Inspector's decision in those circumstances could be overturned by the High Court, but the final decision would be referred back to a fresh Inspector, who could very well arrive at the same decision as the first Inspector, even though taking into account the representations made.

Furthermore, where individuals with 'sufficient interest' apply for judicial review of a decision they have to be able to show that they have suffered prejudice. Therefore, although the court is not entitled to make a judgment on the merits of the individual case, it may well be that the substance of the point raised by the interested party shows an unlawful act, but, on the facts of the individual case, the applicant did not suffer any prejudice from the decision itself. Thus, where an interested party was not entitled to put its views across at a planning inquiry, there may well be a breach of the right to a fair hearing. However, where it could be shown that other people had put over a similar case, a judicial review remedy may be refused.

Where there are other remedies available, the court has a discretion to refuse an application for judicial review. Therefore, in the situation where an applicant is seeking an injunction and also has private rights which could give rise to a similar remedy under the common law, a court can refuse to exercise its discretion in relation to the public law remedy.

Overall, the role of judicial review in controlling administrative actions has grown in importance over the past 20 years. The introduction of new concepts to govern the full breadth of administrative action gives rise to an important avenue of redress to the private individual.

The Ombudsman

There may be instances where, although there is no abuse of the statutory power which would render a decision reviewable, there is some maladministration which could give rise to a public complaint. In such cases a complaint can be made to the Ombudsman in control of those activities. In the case of Central Government activities (e.g. the Department of the Environment) the investigating Ombudsman is the Parliamentary Commissioner for Administration, whereas in the case of complaints against a local authority or the National Rivers Authority, the matter is dealt with by the Commissioner for Local Administration. The governing factor in such complaints is whether or not the authority concerned have acted within appropriate standards of administrative conduct, rather than whether or not they have acted lawfully.

Complaints to the Ombudsman normally go through either a local councillor or an MP (depending upon the level of authority concerned), although they need not do so in all cases. The nature of the Ombudsman remedy is both singular and advisory. Therefore, an aggrieved party who has other rights of action, whether under the common law or by means of judicial review, must pursue that particular avenue, as long as it is realistic to do so. Secondly, an Ombudsman has no statutory power to impose an award of damages, or to alter the legal position (e.g. by quashing a decision). Normally, the Ombudsman will make a recommendation for compensation which, although having no statutory backing, is accepted by the statutory body concerned in over 95% of cases. The role of the Ombudsman should not be underestimated. The incidence of complaints to the Ombudsman has risen in recent years because it is a quick, cheap, and often effective mechanism for channelling complaints about public authorities. It is a mechanism which the public are happy to utilise because of its informal nature and simple procedure. It is perhaps worthwhile to point out that the stages of a complaint are relatively straightforward and provide an adequate opportunity for the proper presentation of grievances. It is also important that the Ombudsman has significant investigatory powers: these will have an impact on the practices of the public bodies over which jurisdiction is exercised.

THREE
Environmental protection agencies

For many years the number of different agencies involved in environmental protection reflected the fragmented nature of policy and law enforcement in this area. Some rationalisation was brought about with the establishment of the National Rivers Authority (NRA) and Her Majesty's Inspectorate of Pollution (HMIP). Until the establishment of the Environment Agency (EA) by the Environment Act 1995, however, the spread of responsibilities remained wide. It is anticipated that the EA will come into being in April 1996, although there is still much work to be done in attempting to unify all the differing powers and responsibilities. At the time of writing, therefore, the pre-environment agencies still exist and will only be abolished or amalgamated on the appointed date. Thus, references to the old agencies will remain in this book. Naturally, when the EA comes into being all references to enforcement agencies will have to be read accordingly.

The introduction of the EA has seen an amalgamation of three of four main regulatory agencies—the NRA, the WRAs and HMIP (local authorities being the fourth). It should also be borne in mind that the increase of guidance on both technical and policy matters has meant that the role of local authorities may change. There are, however, a range of other bodies with powers and responsibilities for environmental protection. Some of these bodies exercise purely policy-making functions, whilst others carry out specific regulatory agencies.

One of the notable changes brought about by the EA will be the implicit recentralisation (in one sense) of many regulatory powers. In particular, the Environment Act 1995 has seen the move towards centralised strategies in relation to air quality and waste. In addition, local authorities are under a duty to have regard to guidance from the DoE and the EA when operating the provisions in relation to contaminated land. Whereas most powers will be exercised by local offices with regard to local conditions, the overall emphasis is on central guidance to improve the consistency and quality of decision-making.

A side-effect of this recentralisation is the consequential loss of accountability. A distinction needs to be drawn between those bodies which are elected and those which are not. The EA has no direct accountability and, in the light of the wide discretionary powers which it will exercise and the policy which it will be responsible for, this is a central issue.

Department of the Environment (DoE)

As its name suggests, the DoE has the major responsibility within Central Government for environmental matters. This is mainly manifested at the level of policy, but since environmental law is essentially about the taking of discretionary, political decisions, this means that the DoE has an enormous impact, even if this is not always apparent from a bare statement of the law. However, three important qualifications must be made about the role of the DoE.

First, it is not the only part of Central Government which sets policy in relation to environmental matters. Indeed, it is arguable whether there is such a thing as a national environmental policy, as opposed to a set of individual policies for individual issues. Other Government Departments, such as the Ministry of Agriculture, Fisheries and Food (MAFF), the Department of Trade and Industry and the Department of Transport, exercise enormous influence in their own fields. The Welsh, Scottish and Northern Ireland Offices also exercise responsibility within their own geographical areas. It is clear that the DoE is not a particularly strong Department within Central Government, even in relation to environmental matters.

Secondly, it has few operational powers relating to environmental protection. Those that it does have are often delegated to others. For example, although planning appeals are made to the Secretary of State, in the vast majority of cases they are decided by members of the Planning Inspectorate, which has been an executive agency of the DoE and the Welsh Office since April 1992.

Thirdly, it is not concerned simply with environmental protection. It has a very wide portfolio which includes responsibility for local government (including the vexed question of local government finance), housing and the water industry. It is fairly clear that some of these areas take priority over environmental protection at present.

Some of these points require amplification. The Secretary of State has very wide legislative and quasi-legislative powers which stem from the framework nature of the main environmental protection legislation, and also from the need to update legislation in the light of EC requirements. Very wide discretionary powers are also granted: for example, the decision whether to declare an area an urban development area is virtually an unfettered discretion given to the Secretary of State.

There are also very wide powers in relation to appeals against decisions made by the regulatory bodies. This is most obvious in the planning area, but an appeal to the Secretary of State is a common feature of many of the regulatory systems covered in this book. This reflects the political (i.e. policy-based) nature of much of this area of law. For example, it is significant that the Planning Inspectorate has always been kept within the DoE, rather than being moved to the Lord Chancellor's Department. This reflects the fact that the important feature of its decisions is that they are based on policy rather than on any notion of judicial fairness, despite the increasing formality of planning procedures.

The DoE may impose its policies in a number of ways. One is by changing the law (a feature of the British system of Government is that the Government is rarely defeated in Parliament). Another is through exercising powers granted under the legislation. This may include the making of directions, the power to approve actions of regulatory bodies, the power to make appointments to the various regulatory bodies, or the power to hear appeals. Interference has been at its clearest in town planning, where there is the greatest opportunity to disagree over matters of policy. Although the DoE has reserved the main legislative powers in the Environment Act 1995, the transfer of a variety of powers to the EA has been viewed suspiciously by some observers. A third method is by the manipulation of available resources. The DoE and the Treasury have complete responsibility for the budgets of a number of the regulatory agencies (e.g. HMIP, the Countryside Commission and the Nature Conservancy Councils). They also control local government finances very tightly. One avenue for future development here is the way that regulatory agencies, such as the NRA, are being encouraged to acquire some financial independence by charging for parts of their work. For example, the NRA, with over 8,000 permanent staff, receives over 75% of its income from various charging schemes. This theme has been developed strongly in the Environment Act 1995, with a range of revenue-raising measures.

Given the importance of independent regulatory agencies in environmental law, it is also significant that the DoE is the channel through which Parliamentary accountability of a number of these agencies, such as the NRA and the Countryside Commission, is provided.

Internally, the DoE has four Directorates in its Environmental Protection Group (see Burr, The Department of the Environment, in *Environmental Challenges: The Institutional Dimension*, ICCET, 1990). These are the Directorate of Rural Affairs, with responsibility for the countryside, conservation and rural development, the Directorate of Air, Noise and Wastes, the Central Directorate of Environmental Protection, and Her Majesty's Inspectorate of Pollution, although this will change with the birth of the EA.

Other parts of Central Government

Important roles are played by other government departments in particular sectors. For example, control of pollution from vehicles is largely the responsibility of the Department of Transport, whilst many policy decisions of central importance to global warming and acid rain are made by the Department of Trade and Industry. The Department of National Heritage, created in April 1992, has responsibilities in relation to ancient monuments and the listing of historic buildings.

An important aspect of decisions is how far they take into account environmental considerations. A number of pieces of legislation now include general requirements to take the environment into account. For example, there is a very vague, but potentially useful, duty imposed on all public bodies in the Countryside Act 1968, s. 11. This states, 'In the exercise of their functions relating to land under any enactment every Minister, government department and public body shall have regard to the desirability of conserving the natural beauty and amenity of the countryside'.

This has perhaps been overtaken by a more significant development arising out of the White Paper, *This Common Inheritance* (Cm. 1200, 1990). This is that each government department now has a nominated Minister responsible for considering the environmental implications of its policies and programmes. There is a strong link with a second proposal that there should be an appraisal of the policies of each department in the light of their environmental implications, although progress in this respect has been slow.

Parliamentary Select Committees

Parliamentary Select Committees may be said to perform the functions of scrutinising the day-to-day activities of Government. They also, in the environmental field, help to inform public debate outside Parliament. In the House of Lords, the European Communities Sub-Committee was especially important in analysing the potential impact of proposed EC legislation. However, the Sub-Committee has now been abolished as part of a general review of Lords Committees. In the House of Commons, the Select Committees are organised so as to mirror government departments. There is thus a House of Commons Select Committee on the Environment. This body has had a large impact on the direction of environmental policy, and can be said to be very influential in this area. Sir Hugh Rossi was the Chairman between 1983 and 1992, and in that time the Committee concentrated on environmental (as opposed to local government or housing) issues, conducting inquiries into such matters as Acid Rain (1984), the Operation and Effectiveness of Part II of the Wildlife and Countryside Act 1981 (1985), Pollution of Rivers and Estuaries (1987), Air Pollution (1988), Toxic Waste (1989), Pollution of Beaches (1990), the Draft EC Directive on Landfill (1991), and the Government's Proposals for an Environmental Agency (1992).

There is little doubt that the reports of these inquiries, all of which have been unanimous on a cross-party basis, have an influence on Government. As an example, the Report on Contaminated Land (January 1990) recommended the creation of public registers of contaminated land, a recommendation that was introduced into the EPA 1990, although the Government rescinded the commitment to introduce these registers. Nevertheless, the introduction of the new contaminated land provisions in the Environment Act 1995 owes a lot to the early recommendations of the Select Committee.

Royal Commission on Environmental Pollution (RCEP)

This is a rather rare beast, a standing Royal Commission with its own Secretariat. It has been in existence since 1970 and has produced 18 Reports on a variety of matters. These Reports have enormous authority in relation to the subject matter discussed and exert a significant influence on the direction of future policy, although by no means all the recommendations of the Royal Commission are implemented. The Royal Commission has been a particularly strong supporter of the widening of access to environmental information, and can also claim to have popularised the concept of 'Best Practicable Environmental Option'. Important Reports have been the Fifth Report, *Air Pollution Control: An Integrated Approach* (Cmnd. 6371, 1976), the Tenth Report, *Tackling Pollution—Experiences and Prospects* (Cmnd. 9149, 1984), the Eleventh Report, *Managing Waste: The Duty of Care* (Cmnd. 9675, 1985) and the Twelfth Report, *Best Practicable Environmental Option* (Cm. 310, 1988). The most recent Reports are the Sixteenth Report, *Freshwater Quality* (Cm. 1966, 1992), which has a wealth of technical information on water pollution, the Seventeenth Report, *Incineration of Waste* (Cm. 2181, 1993), which supports the development of incineration linked to energy recovery, and the Eighteenth Report, *Transport and the Environment* (Cm. 2674, 1994). After reporting on soil, the next issue to be studied by the Royal Commission is the difficult question of the definition of 'Best Practicable Environmental Option'.

Other advisory bodies

In addition to the RCEP, the Government has established a number of non-statutory advisory bodies with various roles. In particular, three bodies established as a result of the publication of the UK's Strategy on Sustainable Development assist with the consideration and implementation of environmental policy and the strategy for sustainable development. The UK Round Table on Sustainable Development consists of 30 members from a selection of bodies, including non-governmental organisations, business, local government and the Church. Unfortunately, it received a set-back when the first of its recommendations—to insert a duty on OFGAS to have regard to sustainability in the Gas Bill—was rejected. It has set aside five main issues for discussion, including sustainable transport, energy policy and environmental auditing.

Secondly, there is a five person panel of advisors known as the Government's Panel on Sustainable Development. This Panel reports directly to the Prime Minister and advises upon issues arising from the strategy. Some critics of the Round Table group (who have suggested that it is a cosmetic exercise) think that the panel will have much more influence over policy. It has a number of topics on its agenda, including the use of economic instruments in environmental policy and environmental education and training.

Finally, the Government launched its 'Going for Green' initiative, which is intended to involve voluntary groups within the community to promote sustainable development.

The Environment Agency

The history of the Environment Agency (EA) is long and tortuous. In 1989 the House of Commons Select Committee on the Environment, in its Report on Toxic Waste, recommended that an Environmental Protection Commission should be established with responsibility for the whole range of pollution control matters. This recommendation was rejected by the Government, a stance that was reiterated in the White Paper *This Common Inheritance* (Cm. 1200, 1990). One reason given was that there had been many changes in relation to environmental protection in recent years, and that such a major change might have to wait until things had settled down. The White Paper did suggest, however, that consideration would be given to the establishment of an umbrella body overseeing the work of HMIP and the NRA. It also proposed that HMIP should become a separate executive agency within the Government (i.e., a 'Next Steps' agency) 'as soon as possible', although it would still remain part of the DoE. This mechanism has been popular with the current Government as a means of providing regulatory agencies with a degree of independence, whilst at the same time injecting some basic management principles and subjecting the agencies to some of the rigours of the market-place.

However, in an important reversal of policy, in July 1991 the Prime Minister, John Major, announced the Government's intention to create a unified environmental protection agency, a move that had already gained the support of all other political parties. Details of what was intended gradually emerged. There were two main points of argument which led to a significant period of delay. One was whether the waste regulation duties of the local authorities should be included within the agency's ambit—to do so would create a uniformity of practice that is currently lacking, but would obviously reduce local accountability. The other was whether the NRA should be brought within the agency *en bloc,* or whether only its pollution control functions properly belonged there. The Minister of Agriculture argued strongly for the NRA's non-pollution control functions to be devolved to the Ministry of Agriculture, Fisheries and Food, but that was strongly opposed by environmentalists and the NRA itself, who argued that the need to retain integrated catchment management was at the heart of everything the NRA does.

After some discussion and consultation the Government accepted that the EA would take over all the powers and functions of HMIP and the NRA, together with the waste regulation duties of the local authorities. Despite earlier promises, the Drinking Water Inspectorate (which is currently part of the DoE) is not included; neither are any direct functions relating to nature conservation (although there are a number of general duties relating to sites which are of nature conservation interest), illustrating the somewhat limited scope of the EA and the continued marginalisation of nature conservation matters. The EA is, effectively, a pollution control agency with a large number of additional water-related functions, such as land drainage and flood defence (interestingly, staff involved in these other functions will probably outnumber those involved in pollution control).

The EA is an independent corporate body, covering England and Wales (s. 1(1)). It is run by an an executive board of not less than eight and not more than 15 members, all of whom are appointed by the Secretary of State.

It is not a Crown body and does not have Crown immunity (s. 1(5)). Scotland has a separate agency (SEPA).

The Environment Act 1995 contains a large number of provisions dealing with the raising of funds by way of fees and charges and it is expected that the EA will be self-funding (ss. 41–44).

The functions of the EA

Generally, the functions of the EA are reflected in existing statutes (e.g. the Water Resources Act 1991 and the EPA 1990). For a brief overview of the powers which will be transferred, please see the individual sections on the powers of the NRA, HMIP and waste regulation authorities set out below. In addition to the transfer of duties from pre-existing legislation, the Environment Act 1995 creates a raft of new duties, objectives and aims. Many of these are vague and some will continue to be meaningless until such time as further detailed guidance is drafted by the Secretary of State. They have their origin in some of the general duties which applied to the NRA (see p. 49). As such it will be interesting to see how the approaches of each of the separate 'arms' of the EA puts the aims and objectives into practice. The EA is therefore responsible for (amongst other things):

(a) *Water resources* This includes water resources management, pollution control and flood defence under the Land Drainage Act 1991. Under s. 6 of the Environment Act 1995 the EA has a duty to promote the conservation and enhancement of the amenity of waters and water flora and fauna. These general duties reflect those under s. 16 of the Water Resources Act 1991 (see general duties below). When the EA comes into existence and s. 6 is brought into force, the existing provision will be revoked.

(b) *Pollution control* This includes waste management licensing, control over the transport of waste, control over IPC processes, investigation and clean up of heavily contaminated land (special sites) and the control of processes under the Health and Safety at Work Act 1974. The EA has to exercise its pollution control powers for the purpose of preventing or minimising, or remedying or mitigating the effects of, pollution of the environment (s. 5). Included in this general duty is a duty to carry out assessments on existing or potential levels of pollution in the environment with options for preventing, minimising, remedying or mitigating the effects of that pollution (s. 5(3)). This is notable as it is the first time that such general duties have been applied to the areas of waste management and IPC.

(c) *Research and technical information* This includes the production of process guidance notes, technical advice and information in relation to contaminated land, the provision of information on the environment and consultees in relation to the strategies for waste and air quality.

The relevant chapters in Part II of this book contain further details of specific duties (and see below).

General powers and duties

The principal aim of the EA is set out in s. 4 of the Environment Act 1995 which provides that in discharging its functions 'so to protect or enhance the environment, taken as a whole, as to make a contribution to the objective of attaining sustainable development'. As an objective it has little meaning without some guidance as to the definitions of the key phrases within it. Therefore, the Secretary of State is under a duty to provide guidance to the EA on how this general aim should be fulfilled. One of the inherent dangers in such a provision is that it is capable of change without recourse to legislation. This could give rise to environmental policy being downgraded by a pro-economic development policy. There is a duty on the Secretary of State to consult before issuing such guidance and a draft has to be put before both Houses of Parliament with rights of veto available if either House resolves to do so (s. 4(5)–(7)).

In addition to the duties in relation to pollution control (s. 5) and water (s. 6) the EA has general environmental and recreational duties under ss 7–8. These general duties reflect those under the Water Resources Act, s. 16, and s. 3 of the Water Industry Act 1991 (see below). An important distinguishing feature, however, is that these duties apply to *all* of the functions, powers and duties exercised by the Agency. These are all positive duties and include the furthering (and, in respect of pollution control functions, having regard to) the conservation and enhancement of natural beauty and the conservation of flora, fauna, geological or physiographical features of special interest (s. 7(1)). When exercising its functions the EA must *have regard to*:

(a)   the desirability of protecting and conserving buildings, sites and objects of archaeological, architectural, engineering or historic interest;

(b)   any effect which the proposals would have on the economic and social well-being of local communities in rural areas;

(c)   the desirability of preserving for the public any freedom of access to areas of woodland, mountains, moor, heath, down, cliff or foreshore and other places of natural beauty;

(d)   the desirability of maintaining the availability to the public of any facility for visiting or inspecting any building, site or object of archaeological, architectural, engineering or historic interest.

In addition the EA has to *take into account*:

(e)   any effect upon the beauty or amenity of any area or on any flora, fauna, features, buildings, sites or objects;

(f)   any effect on freedom of access to facilities set out in (d) above.

These are the most comprehensive set of duties imposed upon any environmental regulator. Whilst it is easy to see that they could be little more than outlines of the overall functions of the EA, the general duties should have an impact in relation to strategy and policy-making. It is, perhaps, a little more difficult to argue that the duties will have a significant influence over individual decisions.

The Secretary of State has the power to issue statutory codes of practice covering the exercise of the general duties (s. 9).

The cost-benefit duty
Probably the most controversial duty imposed upon the EA is the duty to take
into account the costs and benefits of exercising its powers. Section 39 of the
Environment Act 1995 provides:

[The EA]—

(a) in considering whether or not to exercise any power . . . or
(b) in deciding the manner in which to exercise any such power,
shall, unless and to the extent that it is unreasonable for it to do so in view
of the nature or purpose of the power or in the circumstances of the
particular case, take into account the likely costs and benefits of the
exercise or non-exercise of the power or its exercise in the manner in
question.

The consequences of this provision could be tremendously wide-ranging.
The exercise of discretionary powers to investigate, prosecute, or seek a clean
up of pollution could all be affected by the uncertainty of determining
whether the severity of the pollution outbalances the potential costs in
exercising statutory powers—in cases where the polluter might not be
identified. It is also easy to see that the section could give rise to challenges
by way of judicial review from polluters. Although such challenges would be
given short shrift where they were based upon technical arguments concerning the accuracy of the balancing exercise (at least if the recent judgments of
the High Court are a guide), a challenge might be successful where the
cost-benefit exercise had not been undertaken or only partially carried out.
Indeed, when the Environment Act 1995 was passing through Parliament the
supporters of the clause (e.g. the CBI and the Institute of Directors) reflected
industrial interests who could be expected to be the beneficiaries of any
successful judicial review exercise.
The objectors to the clause (including most of the well-known environmental action groups) argued that the section could have an impact on *all* of the
powers exercised by the EA from major policy decisions to minor enforcement
action, thus rendering day-to-day running of the Agency unworkable. The
RCEP also expressed concern that the general view of the section was that it
would give rise to legal challenges to powers exercised by the Agency.
What, then, does this duty actually entail? A part of the answer will lie in
the publication of central guidance from the DoE. At the time of writing a
draft version of the guidance has been produced which suggests that it will
become a primary part of the Agency's decision-making process. In particular, the only express circumstance where it would be 'unreasonable' to carry
out the duty would be where there was 'imminent danger of serious harm'.
As this phrase has a particularly narrow meaning in relation to enforcement
action taken in respect of IPC/LAAPC and contaminated land (see pp. 316
and 393–4), it is clear that the duty will cover a vast array of decisions made
by the Agency. The duty is intended to be applied both to strategy and to
individual cases with the object of avoiding disproportionately large costs.

Athough the guidance will give an indication of the nature of the cost-benefit duty it cannot provide the full picture. As with planning policy, the courts are likely to be compelled to give a view on the nature of the duty. Unlike planning policy, however, the questions involved in exercising the cost-benefit duty will involve the specific balancing of technical, environmental and economic considerations which are unfamiliar territory for the courts. It is difficult to see the High Court making inquiries into the accuracy of the Agency's determinations (unless it is so unreasonable that no reasonable authority could have come to that determination).

In addition to the main duty under s. 39, there are also residual cost-benefit duties in the Environment Act 1995. The EA is under a duty to consider costs when seeking to achieve its general aim (s. 4(1) (see above)) and it has to set out the costs and benefits when setting out options for exercising its general pollution control functions (s. 5(3) and see above).

Assimilation of enforcement and entry powers
Under existing legislation each enforcement agency has a variety of enforcement inspection and entry powers. When the Agency comes into being it will have a unified set of enforcement powers. These powers will be exercised for the purpose of:

(a)   determining whether any environmental legislation is being complied with;

(b)   exercising or performing any of the Agency's pollution control functions;

(c)   determining whether or how a pollution control function should be exercised.

Section 108 of the Act provides that an officer appointed by the Agency can, when there is no emergency:

(a)   enter premises at any reasonable time,

(b)   be accompanied on to premises by a police constable should the officer apprehend that they will be obstructed in their duty;

(c)   make any investigation as necessary including: measurements, taking samples, photographs and questioning individuals (answers given to such questions will not be admissible in any prosecution brought against *that person*);

(d)   carry out experimental borings and install and maintain monitoring equipment (with at least seven days notice):

Where occupants are likely to refuse the officer can seek a warrant prior to entry onto premises. Documents which are subject to legal professional privilege are exempt from the above requirements. In cases of emergency entry can be gained at any time, with force if necessary. In such circumstances no prior notification is required when setting up monitoring equipment or carrying out experimental borings. Under s. 110 it is an offence to intentionally obstruct an authorised officer in the exercise of their duties.

In addition to inspection and entry powers, enforcement powers are also amended to bring the different powers in to some sort of unified whole. Schedule 22 of the Act inserts s. 49A into the Water Resources Act which allows the Agency to serve an Enforcement Notice where there has been, or is likely to be a breach of a condition of a discharge consent. This is a new power which widens the range of enforcement options in relation to water pollution. There is a right of appeal against such a notice and it will be a criminal offence to fail to comply. It will be interesting to see if the use of the new enforcement power will lead to a decrease in prosecutions. HMIP has used the enforcement notice procedure on a relatively high number of occasions (in comparison to the number of prosecutions).

Overlap with other agencies

Although the EA will assume responsibility for the majority of powers in relation to pollution control, there are still a number of other bodies with direct responsibility for environmental protection. In particular, local authorities will play an important role in regulating contaminated land, statutory nuisances, noise, air quality and planning. In addition, the water service companies' control over discharges to sewers remains unaffected by the Environment Act 1995 (although there is a power for the EA to apply its general environmental duty to any proposals relating either to the functions or land-holdings of the water companies (s. 7(3)).

There are, however, some overlaps between the EA and nature conservation bodies. English Nature, the Countryside Commission for Wales, the National Parks Authorities and the Broads Authority are under a duty to inform the EA of the identity of any land which may be affected by the Agency which is of special nature conservation interest because of its flora, fauna or geological or physiographical features (s. 8). Where the EA has been notified of the identity of such land, it is under a duty to consult with the relevant body before carrying out or authorising works which would destroy, damage or significantly prejudice those features notified. This applies to all authorisations which are regulated by the EA. Although nature conservation bodies have always been consultees on applications for regulatory consents previously, this duty to consult is considerably wider and would include not only actions carried out by the EA itself but enforcement actions which would require remedial measures to be taken by third parties.

Her Majesty's Inspectorate of Pollution (HMIP)

HMIP has responsibility in England and Wales for operating the system of integrated pollution control introduced by the EPA 1990, the control of scheduled processes under air pollution legislation (until this system is replaced by integrated pollution control), the control of radioactive substances and the monitoring of waste disposal. It therefore has effective responsibility for the regulation of pollution from the most hazardous activities. It also has planning and research functions in relation to these tasks. Despite its name, it has few operational responsibilities for most types of water pollution, waste disposal to land or other polluting activities such as noise. For HMIP's specific powers in relation to integrated pollution control (IPC), see Chapter 11.

HMIP was established in 1987 with the intention of providing a more integrated and coherent approach to pollution control, particularly through the introduction of such concepts as best practicable environmental option. It brought together the Industrial Air Pollution Inspectorate of the Health and Safety Executive (previously called the Alkali and Clean Air Inspectorate), and the Radiochemical, Hazardous Waste and embryonic Water Inspectorates of the DoE. It is a part of the DoE.

In its short existence it has been dominated by the air pollution and radioactivity functions, though this is changing as the integrated nature of its new responsibilities has an effect on its operation. This domination is important in view of the history of controls in those areas, where the tradition has been for a somewhat secretive and conciliatory approach to be taken to polluters.

A problem for HMIP since its creation has been a shortage of resources, particularly staff. This was a major reason for the introduction of IPC being delayed to April 1991. It was reported as having a staff complement of 223 in January 1991, with approval given for an expansion to over 300 by the end of 1991/2 and over 400 when IPC is fully operational. However, in September 1990, HMIP reported vacancies for 24 Inspectors out of a total complement of 135. One reason was thought to be the low pay relative to equivalent jobs in industry, so pay increases were introduced in an attempt to rectify the problem. The adequate funding of HMIP remains one of its major difficulties, although recent reports by the Comptroller and Auditor General and the Public Accounts Committee have suggested that HMIP's activities are now on a firmer footing than in the past.

Until October 1989, HMIP was organised into four divisions, dealing with air, water, radioactivity and hazardous wastes. In preparation for IPC, it was reorganised into three Regions (East, based in Bedford; West, based in Bristol; and North, based in Leeds), which deal with all aspects of pollution in their areas. These regional offices are supported by a central Regulatory Standards Division, which coordinates guidance and technical standards. There are also five industry groups which cover the main sectors within IPC.

The current responsibilities of HMIP are as follows:

(a) In relation to air pollution, it has a residual responsibility for works operating scheduled processes under the provisions of the Health and Safety at Work etc. Act 1974 and the Alkali etc. Works Regulation Act 1906. This has largely been replaced by responsibility for around 5,000 works under the IPC system. The remaining air pollution matters are the responsibility of local authorities.

(b) In relation to water pollution, HMIP exercises control over discharges from processes covered by IPC, though it is subject to a degree of interference from the National Rivers Authority (NRA). It also licences aqueous radioactive discharges. All other discharges are the responsibility of the NRA (for controlled waters) and the relevant sewerage undertaker (for discharges to sewers). Prior to the Water Act 1989, HMIP was responsible for granting discharge consents to water authorities; this function has been taken over by the NRA.

(c)   In relation to radioactive emissions, HMIP operates the authorisation procedures under the Radioactive Substances Act 1993. These cover the registration of 6,000 premises and the authorisation of over 1,000 waste disposal processes.

(d)   On waste disposal, HMIP has a largely supervisory and research role. Its functions include monitoring the management of hazardous wastes, publishing waste management papers and giving advice to waste disposal authorities.

When the EA is established it is envisaged that HMIP will continue as a semi-autonomous group within the Agency.

National Rivers Authority (NRA)

The NRA is an independent, non-departmental public agency which has been in existence since 1 September 1989, when it was established under the Water Act 1989. It took over many of the regulatory powers of the old regional water authorities and has responsibility in England and Wales for a wide range of water matters. Included within this is primary responsibility for dealing with pollution of inland, underground and coastal waters, although HMIP takes over whenever a process is subject to IPC.

The other functions of the NRA relate to flood defence and land drainage, water resources and the licensing of abstractions, salmon and freshwater fisheries, navigation, conservancy and harbour authority functions. In addition, it has environmental duties set out in the Water Resources Act 1991, s. 16 and a number of ancillary powers (which are replaced in the Environment Act 1995). These relate to such things as the acquisition of information (s. 202), and powers of entry and taking of samples (ss. 169–174).

The NRA must have a minimum of eight and a maximum of 15 members, who are to be appointed by the Secretary of State for the Environment, the Secretary of State for Wales and the Minister of Agriculture, Fisheries and Food. At present there are 15 members. Other provisions relating to its structure, including its powers to employ people and a wide power to delegate, are set out in the Water Resources Act 1991, sch. 1. It is not a Crown body and therefore does not benefit from Crown immunity.

The NRA has a regional structure, based on the old regional water authority regions, though in early 1993 it announced that the existing 10 regions would be reduced to eight. Each of these regions has a consultative Regional Rivers Advisory Committee established under the Water Resources Act 1991, s. 7. There is a further Advisory Committee for Wales established under s. 6. Nevertheless, one of the strengths of the NRA is its national status and it is striving to build up a uniform system of pollution control throughout the country. This is to be achieved by the establishment of uniform policies and practices on setting discharge consents and on enforcement, and this will be continued after the establishment of the EA.

The financing of the NRA is quite complex, since it varies for each of its functions. For flood defence, money is raised by a levy on county and metropolitan councils, who will recoup this through drainage charges. For water resources, the cost of the system is recovered through charges for abstractions. The NRA is also undergoing a period of change as far as the financing of water pollution control is concerned. In relation to pollution control, the main source of money in the first year of operation was Treasury grant, but a scheme for charging for discharges to controlled waters was introduced in 1991. This is expected to cover a large proportion of the NRA's expenditure on pollution control in the future. Further cost recovery measures were introduced in the Environment Act 1995.

Sewerage undertakers

In relation to discharges to sewers, the licensing body is the privatised sewerage undertaker, which grants what are called trade effluent consents. This is an unusual example of a private body undertaking an environmental regulation function, although it is arguable that a sewerage undertaker is in reality doing little different from a private waste disposal contractor in providing a method of waste disposal through privately owned facilities. Appeals against trade effluent consent decisions go to the Director General of Water Services (OFWAT), who is appointed under the Water Industry Act 1991 and whose main functions relate to the regulatory control of the newly privatised water industry. The sewerage undertakers are largely unaffected by the introduction of the EA. For a further explanation of the water industry see Chapter 14.

General environmental duties and the water industry

These general duties are contained in the Water Resources Act 1991 and are mirrored and extended in the Environment Act 1995.

Under the Water Resources Act 1991, s. 16 and the Water Industry Act 1991, s. 3, all bodies with responsibilities in relation to water (i.e. the NRA, water and sewerage undertakers, the Director General of Water Services, internal drainage boards, and the Secretary of State and Minister of Agriculture, Fisheries and Food when carrying out water-related functions) are placed under some general environmental duties. These include *furthering* the conservation and enhancement of natural beauty and the conservation of flora, fauna and geological and physiographical features of special interest, and *having regard to* such things as matters of archaeological, architectural and historic interest, the beauty and amenity of an area, the nature conservation interest of an area, and public access to natural and other features.

In addition, the NRA is placed under a duty to *promote* the conservation and enhancement of the natural beauty and amenity of inland and coastal waters and associated lands, the conservation of flora and fauna dependent on an aquatic environment, and the use of such waters and lands for recreational purposes. Further specific duties are laid down in relation to specially protected sites, such as sites of special scientific interest (SSSIs) (see p. 478). A *Code of Practice on Conservation, Access and Recreation* has been issued jointly by the Secretaries of State and the Minister of Agriculture, Fisheries and Food after consultation with a large range of interested bodies. Contravention does not give rise to any criminal offence or civil right of action, but will be taken into account by relevant bodies in deciding whether to use any powers available to them.

These general duties are couched in fairly positive terms. Whilst they may not give rise to direct legal rights they are of enormous importance in internal decision-making within these bodies and as political levers for environmentally sensitive decisions. They are certainly stronger than in other legislation and may act as a model for other systems.

Countryside bodies

Within the countryside, the absence of a controlling 'Department of Rural Affairs', such as many other countries possess, is crucial. In the past the dominant force has tended to be MAFF, simply by virtue of the weight of resources available to it. This has traditionally been a very insular Ministry, although under the Agriculture Act 1986, s. 17, the Agriculture Ministers are now required to seek to achieve a balance between the interests of agriculture, the economic and social needs of rural areas, and conservation and recreation.

There are, however, other independent agencies within the Government responsible for specific matters. In England there is a Nature Conservancy Council for England (known as English Nature) and a Countryside Commission, which have responsibilities for nature conservation and for recreation, landscape and amenity respectively. This division of responsibility reflects a split in functions decided upon as long ago as 1949 and some reasons behind this are explained in Chapter 16. The Nature Conservancy Council was organised on a Great Britain basis until 1 April 1991 when, for largely political reasons, it was split into three separate national bodies by the EPA 1990. (In this book, for ease of reference, these are referred to generically as the Nature Conservancy Councils.) In Wales, the nature conservation functions were amalgamated with the amenity functions in a new Countryside Council for Wales. In Scotland, a similar body called Scottish Natural Heritage has been established under the Natural Heritage (Scotland) Act 1991, which also combines the two functions. There is no intention at present to combine English Nature and the Countryside Commission for England.

Local authorities

Since the abolition of the metropolitan county councils in 1986, there have been two separate structures for local government in England and Wales. There are three if the system within London is counted separately, although it is similar to the one that applies in the metropolitan areas. In metropolitan areas, there is a one-tier system, the metropolitan district councils. These obviously have responsibility for all matters, although some functions (police, fire, transport and, in most metropolitan areas, waste management) are run by joint boards of the Councils. In non-metropolitan areas, there is a two-tier system of county and district councils. In constitutional terms these two tiers are equal, but they have differing responsibilities. County councils have responsibility for the police, fire services, personal social services, transport, highways, education, libraries, waste management and strategic planning. District councils have responsibility for housing, development control, recreation, and environmental and public health.

This split causes problems for the public, which often finds it difficult to identify which tier is responsible for any particular matter. The problem is particularly acute in the environmental sphere because of the overlapping powers of the two tiers (e.g. in town planning). In April 1991, the Government issued a consultation paper on the future of local government which suggests that the two-tier system will be abolished in some counties, citing the confusion over who is responsible for what as one factor which clouds democratic and financial accountability in these areas.

The conclusions of this consultation exercise will lead to an increase in the number of unitary authorities. They have yet to be implemented. Until they are, there are 36 metropolitan district councils, 33 London borough councils (including the City of London), 47 county councils and 373 district councils, all of which undertake a wide variety of tasks in relation to environmental protection. There are, at present, six main areas to consider:

(a) Town and country planning
The local authority is normally the local planning authority. This means that it is responsible for the making of development plans and for the control of development. The powers also incorporate responsibility for related matters, such as tree preservation orders, listed building protection, conservation areas, hazardous substances consents, the control of derelict land, and the protection of the countryside. As explained above, planning functions are split between county and district councils, with county councils being responsible for strategic planning and for national parks, minerals and waste disposal matters, whilst district councils have responsibility for other development control decisions. The scope for conflict between the two tiers was lessened slightly by the reduction in the range of county functions in the Local Government, Planning and Land Act 1980.

(b) Waste regulation and disposal
The EPA 1990 defines three types of authority with responsibility for waste. The *waste collection authority* is normally the district council and has duties relating to the collection and recycling of household and commercial waste. The *waste regulation authority* is normally the county council, though it is the district council in Wales and in metropolitan areas, unless a joint body has been established. It is responsible for the operation of the waste management licensing system and for the duty of care in respect of controlled waste. The same authority will be the local planning authority for waste disposal matters.

It will also normally be the *waste disposal authority,* with responsibility for the actual disposal of waste. However, in line with the Government's preference for competitive tendering, waste disposal carried out by local authorities has to be done by an arm's-length local authority waste disposal company, which will be in competition with private waste contractors. The powers of the waste regulation authority will, of course, be amalgamated into the EA.

(c) Public health matters
Local authorities have always had responsibility for a very wide range of matters under the Public Health Acts. In particular, this involves duties in relation to the control of statutory nuisances, the law on which it has been remodelled in the EPA 1990, Part III (see Chapter 8). Local authorities also have powers as principal litter authorities in relation to the duties and offences laid out in the EPA 1990, Part IV.

(d) The control of noise
Local authorities have primary responsibility for the control of noise from premises. In the past these provisions have been separate from those relating to statutory nuisance, but in the EPA 1990 the two sets of powers are treated together (see Chapter 8).

(e) Air pollution
Local authorities have long had responsibility for the control of smoke, dust, grit and fumes under the Clean Air Acts and related legislation. In the EPA 1990, Part I, they are given more complete powers to control air pollution from plants which are not the responsibility of HMIP under integrated pollution control.

(f) Contaminated land
Perhaps the biggest change for local authorities brought about by the Environment Act 1995 is the shift away from waste management (which will be absorbed, minus the waste collection authorities by the EA) to the regulation of contaminated land. In a role which echoes the position of local authorities in respect of statutory nuisances, there is a duty to inspect local authority areas for the presence of contaminated land and to take action against the person responsible for the contamination or the owner/occupier of the land in question. Unfortunately, little has been said about the resources available to some of the smaller authorities to actually carry out such a change of role. A more detailed explanation of the old and new roles is given in Chapter 13. One of the difficulties with this range of powers is that, when faced with a local pollution problem, people are frequently confused as to whether it is the responsibility of the local planning authority, the environmental health department, or the waste regulation authority. The problem is compounded by the range of other agencies with environmental powers and duties. The result is that the majority of complaints are directed in the first instance to the environmental health department, even if that is not the appropriate body.

Decision-making in local authorities

Local authorities are elected bodies. In theory it is the elected councillors who make the ultimate decisions, usually through the appropriate committee. However, in practice, most actual decisions are taken by officers, with the committee rubber stamping them. The councillors are always free to disagree with the recommendation of an officer, but, in so doing, they must be careful to act only on grounds permitted in the relevant legislation, otherwise their decision will be capable of being challenged as *ultra vires*. The constitutional monopoly of the elected councillors has also been removed. The Local Government Act 1972, s. 101, provides that the local authority may delegate any of its powers (apart from a few that must be exercised by a resolution of the whole council, such as the adoption of a local plan) to committees, or to specified officers.

This structure makes councils accountable to the electorate. But it also means that the range of considerations taken into account by local authorities is necessarily wider than those which relate simply to environmental protection. Local authorities, because of their elected status, have a democratic right to balance the advantages of conflicting courses of action which is arguably lacking in many other bodies, even if it does occasionally mean that strange decisions are reached.

In addition, all local authorities are subject to rules on the ability of the public to attend meetings and to receive information about the council's activities. Originally, the Public Bodies (Admission to Meetings) Act 1960 gave members of the public a right of admission to meetings of local authorities. This was extended in the Local Government Act 1972, s. 100, to cover all committee meetings. That provision was itself greatly expanded in the Local Government (Access to Information) Act 1985, which added new ss. 100A–100K to the 1972 Act. In essence, a member of the public has a right not only to attend meetings of the council and its committees and sub-committees, but also to have access to agendas, minutes, and background reports. This enables information to be obtained on such things as the grounds for a decision, or whether the councillors have diverged from the recommendation of an officer. This written information must be available at all reasonable hours at the offices of the council, and members of the public may make copies of it.

There are limitations. There is a list of exempt information, and the council may resolve to exclude the public if publicity would be prejudicial to the public interest. This may cover meetings such as those to consider whether to recommend that enforcement action is taken on a particular issue, since it may be rendered useless if prior warning is obtained. However, in practice, many local authorities not only allow access to meetings, but permit objectors to address the meeting.

Unlike the questions of secrecy and access to environmental information covered in Chapter 7, the purpose of these powers is to show openness in decision-making and to give an impression of public accountability in what is accepted to be a political system. These powers should therefore be compared with the restrictions on access to meetings of most of the other regulatory bodies discussed.

Mention of local authorities would not be complete without a reference to their current finances. It is quite clear that with restrictions on spending they are unable to carry out properly many of the tasks entrusted to them in the environmental area, thus calling into question the effective enforcement of parts of environmental law.

FOUR

The European Community and the environment

Notwithstanding its economic basis, the EC is a major and increasing source of British environmental protection law. It also has a central and profound influence on the direction of environmental policy, both at a Community level and within each Member State. As a result, every subject covered by this book is affected, either directly or indirectly, by the activities of the EC.

There are four main ways in which the EC plays a role in shaping British environmental law and policy:

(a)   Some pieces of EC legislation lay down rules and standards that are directly enforceable in Member States without any need for further implementation. In these cases EC law is British law.

(b)   Other pieces of EC legislation are addressed to Member States and require changes in British law or administrative practice. This is normally the situation in relation to environmental legislation, because of the predominant use of Directives, which are not necessarily directly effective within Member States (see p. 65). British law is therefore not the same as EC law until the EC law has been implemented. In such cases the precise role of the EC in initiating the change is often forgotten, since the domestic legislation resulting from the EC requirements will constitute the law which is applied in practice. An important point to note is that EC law and British law often differ in such circumstances, because EC law frequently consists of aims and goals and procedural frameworks rather than precise legal rules, and allows for some discretion in the Member States as to how and when to implement it.

(c)   The third role is somewhat wider and rests upon the constitutional position that Britain now occupies as a Member State of the EC. The EC not only passes environmental laws, it has an environmental policy. This policy and the general economic and environmental principles which underpin it exert an important influence on British policy-making and on British attitudes towards environmental law and its enforcement. The direction in which environmental protection will go therefore depends as much on wider

European attitudes as it does on ingrained British ideas, although of course British ideas will in turn help to mould the general EC view and to affect the attitudes of the other Member States.

(d)   Finally, the economic policies of the EC have a profound effect on the direction of both EC and domestic environmental law. Environmental protection cannot be isolated from economic policy and the substantial completion of the single internal market by the end of 1992 has had significant spin-off effects on the environment. Indeed, many 'green' commentators would argue that the economic policies of the EC, based as they are on economic growth and on economies of scale in industrial and agricultural production, are themselves antithetical to the achievement of the aims of a clean environment and conservation of natural resources.

The specific pieces of EC law and policy that have an influence on British law will be integrated into the relevant chapters of the rest of the book. This chapter will concentrate on more general matters, such as the place of environmental policy within the EC, the history and principles of that policy, the institutions of the EC and their law-making and enforcement powers, and the way in which the policies and laws are implemented in Britain. However, it must be stressed that all the nuances of EC law cannot be covered in one chapter; accordingly, this chapter will concentrate on those issues which are of relevance to environmental protection and will not seek to provide an exhaustive account of general EC law principles.

The nature of the EC

The EC is more than just a free trade agreement between 15 fairly similar Western European states. It has institutions and law-making powers of its own, making it a form of supranational state in which the Member States have limited their sovereign rights, albeit within limited fields (although for political reasons the extent of this is often denied).

The activities over which the EC has powers are set out in the Treaties which establish the EC, which are effectively the EC's constitution. In the past there have been three Treaties and three linked Communities, the European Economic Community (EEC), the European Coal and Steel Community (ECSC) and the European Atomic Energy Community (Euratom). It has been the EEC, established by the Treaty of Rome, which has been the central Community and to which environmental policy relates. The Treaty of Rome was amended by the Single European Act 1986, which first introduced references to the environment, and all the Treaties were further amended by the Treaty on European Union, signed on 7 February 1992 at Maastricht. Rather confusingly, this Treaty, which came into force on 1 November 1993, altered the name of the EEC Treaty to the EC Treaty. In this book all references to Treaty Articles are to the EC Treaty, as amended. The formal title of the EC has also altered to the European Union (EU), but in this book we will retain the more familiar initials 'EC'.

The institutions of the EC

The four main EC institutions are the Commission, the Council, the Parliament, and the European Court of Justice. Each has powers and duties specified in the Treaty and an obligation to further the aims of the EC. There is also an advisory Economic and Social Committee and the European Environment Agency.

The European Commission

The Commission is the executive of the EC. It consists of 20 independent members appointed by the Member States (two each from the five larger states—Germany, France, Britain, Italy and Spain—and one each from the others), serviced by a large number of officials. It has responsibility for implementing EC policies and initiates and draws up proposals for legislation for the Council to approve. It also has a major responsibility for policing and enforcing EC law, in which role it has extensive investigatory powers.

It is the Commission which draws up the environment action programmes and drafts proposed EC legislation. By means of information agreements with the Member States, the Commission is informed of proposals for domestic legislation and these often give rise to a Commission proposal for a common policy across the EC. However, the ambivalent nature of the Commission must be appreciated. On the one hand it is often the driving force behind new environmental policies: on the other it is responsible for enforcing the economic aims of the EC (see its position in the *Danish Bottles* case—p. 76).

Internally the Commission is divided into a number of Directorates. Directorate General XI (DG XI) deals with Environment and Nuclear Safety. As a result of the formal adoption of the principle that environmental policies should form a component of the EC's other policies, DG XI has had its hand strengthened slightly in relation to its dealings with other Directorates, such as those with responsibility for transport and energy policy, which have traditionally tended to have greater influence.

The Council of Ministers

The Council is a political body made up of one representative of each Member State. The identity of this representative alters according to the nature of the business. Thus, transport ministers normally agree transport measures, environment ministers normally agree environmental measures and so on. As a body it has a duty to ensure the attainment of the Treaty objectives, but clearly national interests play a central role in the Council's decisions.

As a result the Council's voting procedures are crucial. There are some differences in the procedures to be adopted for different matters. Some pieces of legislation have to be passed unanimously by the Council, acting on a proposal from the Commission, and after consultation with Parliament and the Economic and Social Committee. Others can be passed by a qualified majority of the Council, a system of weighted voting in which Member States can be outvoted (see p. 73).

The European Parliament

The European Parliament is mainly a consultative and advisory body, although it does have some supervisory powers over the Commission and the budget. The advent of direct elections in 1979 revitalised the European Parliament and it has been a significant mouthpiece of concern over environmental issues ever since. For example, it set in motion a ban on imports of sealskin products. It also has an important role in ensuring a certain amount of openness in EC decision-making, particularly through its Committee on the Environment, Public Health and Consumer Protection which scrutinises legislative proposals. The deliberations of the Council and the Commission are secret, and debates on proposals for legislation in Parliament are the only truly open part of the EC's decision-making process.

Consultation with Parliament has always been a mandatory requirement, in the absence of which a piece of EC legislation will be void. The Single European Act 1986 increased Parliament's powers over legislation in a significant way by introducing the 'co-operation procedure', which empowers it to reject or propose amendments to legislation subject to qualified majority voting. The procedures are complex, but in essence the Council will adopt a 'common position' based on the Commission's proposals. If Parliament rejects this 'common position', the Council may only adopt the measure if it does so unanimously. If Parliament proposes amendments, the Commission must reconsider the matter. It may choose to insert Parliament's amendments and, if it does so, the Council has a choice: it can either agree the amended proposal by a qualified majority, or it can agree some other formula unanimously, or it can allow the proposal to lapse. This procedure was used in relation to Directive 89/458 on Emissions from Small Cars, when Parliament inserted a stricter test than that wanted by the majority of the Council or originally proposed by the Commission. The Commission agreed with the stricter test and amended the proposal, thus effectively forcing the Council to agree also, or face not having a Directive at all (see Haigh and Baldock, *Environmental Policy and 1992*, 1989).

The co-operation procedure is now set out in Article 189C, which was added by the Maastricht Treaty. However, as a further complication, it also introduced a new 'co-decision procedure' in Article 189B, which involves the resolution of disputes through a Conciliation Committee, made up of representatives of the Council and the Parliament, and which provides an enhanced role for the Parliament. Of greater practical importance to environmental law is the fact that the Maastricht Treaty also extends the scope of qualified majority voting so that it will cover most pieces of proposed environmental legislation (see p. 73). As a result, though in future there will be three different procedures through which environmental legislation can be passed (under Articles 189C, 189B, and where unanimity is still required), in most cases Parliament will have a significant involvement, thus going some limited way towards tackling the problems of secrecy and lack of democratic accountability inherent in EC legislative procedures.

The European Court of Justice

The European Court of Justice consists of judges appointed by common agreement of the Member States. It is assisted by Advocates-General, one of whom makes reasoned submissions to the Court in each case. It has supreme authority on matters of EC law. This means that it has ultimate power to interpret the meaning of the Treaties and of any legislation made by the other institutions. The Court can thus, if asked, review the legitimacy of the actions of the other institutions, provide answers on matters of EC law to Member States' courts and declare whether Member States are implementing EC law properly.

Article 177 plays a major role here. Under Article 177, any court or tribunal in a Member State can refer any matter of EC law to the European Court of Justice for its interpretation of the law. This procedure aims to ensure uniformity between Member States in their application of the law. It also provides a method of obtaining an authoritative ruling. Since the Court is the ultimate arbiter of any law having an EC input, Article 177 references should be made where there is any doubt as to the meaning of EC law, or the compatibility of domestic law with it. However, one drawback is that national courts effectively have a discretion whether to make a reference or not.

In carrying out its functions the European Court of Justice has been exceptionally activist and creative. It has developed several novel principles, including the doctrines of the supremacy of EC law and of direct effects, and has been responsible for extending the scope of the powers of all the institutions (including itself). It has done this by adopting a purposive approach to interpretation in which it looks as much at the spirit as at the letter of the law. On matters of EC law, therefore, the Court's view is central to any discussion of the law. For example, in Cases 206 and 207/88 *Vessoso and Zanetti* ([1990] 2 LMELR 133), it ruled that the definition of waste in the framework Directive on Waste 75/442 included waste which was to be recycled, since it was waste as far as the disposer was concerned irrespective of the intentions of the recipient.

The Court gives one agreed judgment. These are often very brief and formal and for the full reasoning the opinion of the Advocate-General must be read, although sometimes the Court and the Advocate-General do not agree. The European Court of Justice should not be confused with the European Court of Human Rights, which exists to police the European Convention on Human Rights.

The European Environment Agency

The European Environment Agency is a new body provided for in Regulation 1210/90. However, the Regulation only came into force when it was agreed in October 1993 that the headquarters of the Agency would be in Copenhagen. The Agency has been established with the limited role of gathering information and data on the state of the environment in the EC. A report on the state of the environment must be published every three years. It also has functions relating to the dissemination of that information and the harmonisation of methods of measurement of data throughout the EC. This will include such things as the development of adequate forecasting and cost-benefit techniques. In order to help with these tasks, the European Environment Information and Observation Network will be established, under which Member States must inform the Agency of their main national environmental information networks, which the Agency will then integrate into an EC Network. In recognition of the international nature of environmental pollution, the Agency is open to non-EC members.

The Agency has not been given any enforcement or policing powers in relation to environmental legislation, despite a determined attempt by the European Parliament to introduce such powers by proposing amendments to the Regulation. However, there is a provision in the Regulation that requires the Council to reconsider the scope of the Agency's powers within two years of the Regulation coming into force, in particular specifying a possible role in the monitoring of the implementation of EC environmental legislation. In time, therefore, the Agency may well evolve into a European Environment Inspectorate.

As a separate, complementary, development, in 1992 the various national agencies (including HMIP) established a network of environmental enforcement authorities. Known as the 'Chester group' after its first meeting place, this network will facilitate the exchange of information and experience on common problems relating to standard-setting and enforcement.

Sources of EC law

EC law is contained in the Treaties, legislation passed by the institutions, international treaties to which the EC is a party, and the judgments and principles of the European Court of Justice.

To understand the relevance of these sources, an explanation of the concepts of the supremacy of EC law and direct effects is required. The doctrine of the supremacy of EC law is that, where there is a conflict between EC law and national law, EC law prevails, even if the national law is later in time; national courts should thus apply EC law rather than national law which does not comply with EC law. This is, however, intimately linked with the idea of direct effects. A law has direct effects if it gives rise to rights and obligations which can be enforced by individuals and companies before national courts. If an EC law is directly effective in this sense, the doctrine of supremacy means that the non-conforming national law can simply be ignored.

Not all EC law is directly effective in this sense. For any provision to be directly effective it must be sufficiently clear and precise to form a cause of action. It must also be unconditional and must not require further definition at the discretion of the Member State. There are also limitations on direct effects related to the source of the EC law. Treaty Articles and Regulations are capable of having direct effects, as long as they fulfil the above tests. For Directives, the Treaty suggested that they would not be capable of having direct effects. However, the European Court of Justice has indulged in some significant judicial legislation and has decided that Directives may have direct effects if the action is against the State or an emanation of the State, but not if against another private body. Since most environmental legislation is in the form of Directives, this is of great importance.

Even if not directly effective, EC law may have some effect in domestic courts. The European Court of Justice held in *Von Colson* [1986] 2 CMLR 430 that domestic legislation must be interpreted so as to comply with EC law if the domestic law was passed to implement it. Since then, the European Court of Justice has decided in *Marleasing* [1992] 1 CMLR 305 that national courts should interpret national legal provisions in accordance with EC law, irrespective of whether they pre-date or post-date it. However, it appears that national courts may decline to adopt this approach in circumstances where to do so would breach the legitimate expectations of parties to the action.

Treaty provisions
The provisions of the EC Treaties lay down the powers of the EC institutions and the procedures for decision-making as well as laying down certain substantive legal requirements. They are of enormous importance in actions before the Court relating to the legality of EC actions. In addition, some Treaty provisions are directly effective (e.g. Article 119 on equal pay), but this is not the case for the Articles concerned with the environment.

Regulations
Regulations are legislative acts of general application. They are normally directly effective, as long as they are sufficiently precise. However, there are few Regulations in the environmental sphere, except those relating to the process of giving effect to international treaties, agricultural policy and administrative matters, such as the European Environment Agency and the eco-auditing and eco-labelling schemes.

Directives
Directives are addressed to Member States and are binding as to the result to be achieved. They are well-suited to environmental measures, since they leave the choice of how to implement them to the Member States, which will each have different methods for setting environmental laws. Most EC environmental legislation is in the form of Directives.

Normally implementation is required within a specified time period (often two years). This will be done by the Member State changing its domestic law and it will be in breach if it has not *fully and correctly* implemented the Directive within the time limit. In Britain, once the Directive is implemented the domestic rule will constitute the relevant law.

A distinction must be drawn here between formal and actual compliance. Changing the law to comply with EC law constitutes formal compliance. However, this is no guarantee that the law is complied with in practice since, for example, a regulatory agency may exercise its discretion not to enforce the law. Increasingly the Commission is looking for evidence of both formal and actual compliance, although its lack of resources for monitoring developments in all the Member States hampers this. The creation of the European Environment Agency may well help here in the future.

A Directive cannot be relied upon in the courts of a Member State unless it is directly effective. Originally it was assumed that Directives could not be directly effective, since discretion was given to the Member States on the method of their implementation. But, the European Court of Justice has held that Directives which are sufficiently precise as to the ends to be achieved are directly effective once the time limit has expired. However, even then, Directives have direct effect *only* against a Member State or an emanation of the State (this is known as vertical direct effect), not against another private body or person (horizontal direct effect). The reason for this distinction is that the State itself cannot plead a failure to implement the Directive properly as a defence—a form of estoppel principle (see the European Court of Justice decision in *Marshall* v *Southampton and South West Hampshire Area Health Authority* [1986] 2 WLR 780). The continuing existence of the distinction was re-asserted in *Faccini Dori* v *Recreb Srl* [1995] All ER (EC) 1.

An 'emanation of the State' has been defined widely by the European Court of Justice in *Foster* v *British Gas plc* [1990] 3 All ER 897, where it was stated that:

a body, whatever its legal form, which has been made responsible pursuant to a measure adopted by the State, for providing a public service under the control of the State, and has for that purpose special powers beyond those which resulted from the normal rules applicable in relations between individuals, is included among the bodies against which the provisions of a Directive capable of having direct effect might be relied upon.

One limitation is that it is up to the national courts to apply this test. However, in *Griffin* v *South West Water Services Ltd* [1995] *Water Law* 5, it was decided, in the context of employment law, that a privatised water company is an emanation of the State. The judge made it clear that it is the functions that the body carries out, rather than its precise legal ownership and structure, which determine the point. It is thus likely that all the privatised utilities will be treated as emanations of the State, at least as far as their 'public' functions are concerned.

The effect of these cases is that some environmental Directives will be directly effective in some circumstances. If that is the case, an incompatible domestic law can be ignored and the Directive applied instead by the national court. A number of environmental Directives have now been held to be directly effective in British courts (see p. 87). Other remedies for failure to implement a Directive are also discussed below.

Decisions, Recommendations and Opinions
Decisions are binding on the individual or group to whom they are addressed, and may also be directly effective. They are again rare in environmental law,

being limited mainly to matters of monitoring and information gathering, but precautionary steps in relation to CFCs were taken in the 1980s by means of Decisions. The institutions may also issue Recommendations and Opinions. These are not binding and only have a persuasive effect.

Court decisions

The decisions of the European Court of Justice give rise to law and this has been a particularly fertile area. The Court has borrowed and developed general principles of law from the jurisprudence of the Member States, such as the principles of natural justice, proportionality, certainty, equality and the protection of legitimate expectations. The concept of proportionality is a particularly important one in environmental law and was applied in the *Danish Bottles* case (*Commission* v *Denmark* [1989] 54 CMLR 619 (see p. 76)).

Validity of EC legislation

The validity of Regulations, Directives and Decisions can be challenged within two months under Article 173. This Article sets out grounds which are slightly wider than the English *ultra vires* rules. As a judicial review action it also requires the applicant to have *locus standi*. Member States, the Commission, the Council and Parliament have it, whilst an individual has to show direct and individual concern. Such a requirement virtually restricts individuals to challenging Decisions addressed to them.

Compliance by Member States with EC law

Under Article 5, Member States are required to 'take all appropriate measures, whether general or particular, to ensure fulfilment of the obligations arising out of this Treaty or resulting from action taken by institutions of the Community'. A further requirement is to 'abstain from any measure which could jeopardise the attainment of the objectives of the Treaty'. Abiding by EC law therefore entails a positive and a negative obligation: implementation of relevant Directives, and not doing anything contrary to EC law. Since environmental law consists mainly of Directives, compliance will be discussed in terms of them.

In order to comply with a Directive, a Member State must implement it fully and within the time limit. Any incompatible law must be repealed. It is irrelevant whether other States have also failed to comply.

It thus appears that there are a number of ways in which there may be non-compliance with a Directive:

(a) failure to implement at all within the time allowed (the case law is clear that there is no real excuse for this, since the Member State will have agreed the time limit in the first place);

(b) failure to implement all the requirements of the Directive;

(c) implementation by adopting an incorrect interpretation of the Directive, the European Court of Justice being the ultimate arbiter of this point;

(d)   attempting to implement by mere changes in administrative practice; *Commission* v *Belgium* [1982] CMLR 627 makes it clear that a change in the law is required, because administrative measures may be altered at any time by the administration;

(e)   inadequate implementation in practice.

This last type of non-compliance arises where a Member State has passed all the legislation required to implement a Directive, but there is no compliance in fact. For example, it could arise where a Member State fails to enforce the provisions of a law, or where standards laid down in a Directive are not adhered to in practice. In Case C337/89 *Commission* v *United Kingdom* [1994] *Water Law* 59, the European Court of Justice effectively equated non-compliance in fact with non-compliance in law. It decided that, by failing to comply with the maximum admissible concentration of nitrate in drinking water in some supply zones, the British Government was in breach of Directive 80/778 on Drinking Water. This raises some important points, because in a decentralised country the national Government is not necessarily the body that was actually responsible for the breach and, indeed, may not, in some cases, be in a very strong position to rectify matters. Nevertheless, it appears that the national Government will be held responsible as a matter of EC law.

Each Member State will normally be required to send a 'compliance letter' to the Commission explaining the measures that have been taken to ensure compliance with a Directive. These provisions are often stated in each individual Directive, but have not always been adhered to rigorously in the past. Accordingly, a Directive relating to the harmonisation of provisions on reports on the implementation of environmental Directives was passed in 1991. This will no doubt increase the Commission's ability to identify non-compliance, as will the creation of the European Environment Agency, though at present it is quite clear that complaints from environmental groups and individuals in Member States are the most significant sources of information on non-implementation.

Remedies for non-compliance

If a Member State does not implement a Directive properly, or maintains in force a law which is contrary to EC law, there are only a limited number of options. The main responsibility for ensuring compliance rests with the Commission, which has a discretion to start infringement proceedings. Its current policy is to start these automatically in cases where any failure to comply is alleged.

These infringement proceedings have various stages. The Commission will write to the State informally, asking it to explain its position. If a satisfactory answer is not received, a formal letter will be sent, and the State's observations will be formally required. If the Commission is still not satisfied that the matter can be settled, it will issue a Reasoned Opinion, explaining what it thinks are the main features of the non-compliance. Most cases are resolved at these preliminary stages, and there are obvious parallels with the graded procedures adopted in practice by most regulatory agencies when dealing with breaches of domestic environmental law.

Under Article 169, the Commission then has a discretion to bring the Member State before the European Court of Justice. Another Member State may join in Article 169 proceedings as a third party to argue for one side or the other (for example, Britain did this to support the Commission in the *Danish Bottles* case). If the Commission does not bring infringement proceedings, another Member State may bring them under Article 170, although this is very rare. An individual has no *locus standi* to bring infringement proceedings, or to compel the Commission to do so, but is limited to drawing an alleged non-compliance to the attention of the Commission.

The European Court of Justice is the ultimate arbiter of whether there has been compliance in law, and will give a decision on whether the State is in breach of EC law, but in the past it had few powers to enforce its ruling. Nevertheless, States normally have complied as a matter of political necessity. Otherwise the Commission or another Member State can reinstitute the infringement proceedings (again this is rare). The Maastricht Treaty has changed matters considerably. Under a new Article 171, the Commission may issue a Reasoned Opinion if it considers that a Member State has not complied with a judgment of the Court. If the Member State then continues to fail to comply, the Commission can bring the case back before the Court, which may impose a penalty. The wording of the Article leaves it unclear how the size of the penalty will be calculated and who the recipient will be, but there is potential for these penalties to be very large indeed. The Commission has also discussed the possibility of withholding EC funds provided for environmental matters in the event of non-compliance.

In addition to these formal infringement procedures, the Court of Justice has used the concept of the supremacy of Community law to develop various strands of case law which relate to the question of compliance with EC law. Two of these—the doctrine of direct effects and the interpretation principle established by *von Colson* and *Marleasing* (known as 'indirect effects')—have already been mentioned above. But it is worth summarising them again because, when these judicial developments are all taken together, they ensure that a lot of pressure can be exerted on Member States to implement Directives properly and in full.

(a) The doctrine of direct effects is of great importance, since directly effective EC laws can be relied upon in the courts of Member States without the need for implementation: any incompatible national law can simply be ignored. If a national court is unwilling to accept that a Directive is directly effective, the applicant may ask it to refer the question to the European Court of Justice under the Article 177 procedure. The main drawback of the direct effects doctrine is that for Directives it only applies vertically against emanations of the State. Not only does this restrict its application in the environmental sphere, because many potential claims will be horizontal ones against private companies for failing to meet specified standards, it also creates problems of fairness, since public and private bodies are treated differently. Two other limitations of the direct effects doctrine are that framework Directives will not normally lay down sufficiently precise standards, and that many potential claimants will lack the appropriate standing to launch a claim in national law.

(b) The indirect effects doctrine established in *von Colson* and *Marleasing* (that national laws should be interpreted so as to comply with EC law) avoids one of the limitations of direct effects by allowing horizontal actions. But it can be criticised for imposing unfair burdens on private bodies, since they will often have relied on the provisions of British law in carrying out their activities, only to find that their expectations are not met when the law is interpreted in a wider manner. It remains to be seen how far this doctrine will have an impact in British law, since it ultimately depends on the willingness of British judges to adopt the EC interpretation and on the existence of some national law that can plausibly be 'interpreted' in the appropriate manner.

(c) The third development stems from the decision of the European Court of Justice in *Francovich* v *Italy* (Case C6/90 [1993] 2 CMLR 66). The case concerned the rights of employees in the event of their employer's insolvency, but it laid down the important general principle that a Member State could in some circumstances be liable to an individual for harm caused by a failure to implement a Directive. In effect, the decision created a new tort. The Court laid down three requirements:

(i)   that the result pursued by the Directive involved the conferring of rights for the benefit of individuals;

(ii)   the content of those rights could be determined by reference to the Directive; and

(iii)   there was a causal link between the failure to implement the Directive and the harm suffered by the individual.

Requirement (i) creates a possible difficulty in relation to some environmental laws. Whilst it is clear that Directives such as the Drinking Water Directive (80/778), or the Directive on Freedom of Access to Information on the Environment (90/313), give rights to individuals, in many cases the Directive is primarily directed towards protection of the environment. However, it is suggested that most Directives laying down standards can be interpreted as conferring implied rights on individuals. This conclusion is supported by decisions of the European Court of Justice, such as in Case 131/88 *Commission* v *Germany* [1991] *Water Law* 179. Requirement (ii) lays down a clarity requirement that must be determined on a case by case basis. Requirement (iii) emphasises that there must be some harm caused to the plaintiff—the action cannot be used to make a general point about non-implementation. However, the causation issue is also tricky, since in most situations the harm will be caused by an operational failure rather than by the Government's non-implementation.

The decision in *Francovich* gives rise to many questions that will have to be answered by the courts in the next few years. One point of particular importance is what needs to be proved to show a failure to comply. *Francovich* itself concerned the straightforward situation where there was a decision of the European Court of Justice under Article 169 establishing Italy's failure to comply with the relevant Directive. Situations where the Member State knows that it must be in breach (e.g. where there is a failure to pass any implementing legislation) are clearly covered. But the interesting case for environmental law is about non-implementation in practice (e.g. through non-enforcement of the law). If this is covered, the *Francovich* doctrine becomes a very significant weapon for the indirect enforcement of EC law.

(d) The fourth development that is of significance arises out of Case 213/89 *R* v *Secretary of State for Transport ex parte Factortame* [1990] 3 CMLR 1, which decides that a national court must set aside national procedural laws that represent an obstacle to the implementation of EC law. Since an important limitation of the doctrines explained above is that there needs to be a cause of action in national law in order to raise the EC issue, this raises some interesting possibilities. In many typical environmental cases the applicant will either fail to establish *locus standi* for a judicial review action, or will be unable to bring an action in tort because it has no interest that the law recognises (for example, the plaintiff may be an amenity group, or may have suffered only economic loss). The judgment in *Factortame*, relying on Article 5 of the Treaty, suggests it is strongly arguable that such restrictive national laws should be dispensed with where a matter of EC law is concerned.

These various developments give rise to a range of propositions. For example, if a consumer were to become ill as a result of drinking water from the public supply that did not comply with the standards laid down in the Drinking Water Directive (80/778), it would seem that there is a claim either directly in tort, relying on the direct effect of the Directive, or under the *Francovich* doctrine, even if the water did comply with national standards. A more far-reaching example might be where an environmental group wished to challenge the non-implementation of a Directive (or even a failure to enforce it, since the two are arguably the same thing in practice). In addition to making a complaint to the Commission, it could seek a declaration claiming that directly effective standards were not being enforced, and argue on the basis of *Factortame* that the rules on *locus standi* should not be used to deny it access to the courts. It might even carry out a clean-up operation and claim its expenses under *Francovich*, even though such a claim would be bound to fail if only national laws were used. Many of these very interesting propositions are likely to be tested in the courts over the next few years.

The common market

The fundamental basis of the EC has always been economic. The primary aims were originally set out in Articles 2 and 3 of the Treaty of Rome, which established the EEC in 1957. These are the creation of a 'common market' (i.e. a fully integrated single internal market within the boundaries of the Member States) in 'goods, persons, services and capital', together with the progressive harmonisation of the economic policies of the Member States. In order to achieve these primary aims, internal barriers to trade and competition need to be dismantled, so that there are no internal frontiers to hamper the free movement of goods, persons, services and capital, and no discrimination between people or firms on the grounds of nationality. This policy of free competition may be referred to as the provision of a level playing-field for producers across the EC. Common tariff barriers against the outside world are also to be erected and common policies developed in relation to certain key sectors of the economy, such as agriculture, transport, coal and steel, and energy.

This fundamental economic basis remains. In 1985, the Member States agreed to push for the completion of a fully integrated internal market by the end of 1992, and this requirement was incorporated into the Treaty as Article 8A by the Single European Act 1986. There is little doubt that this led to fresh impetus towards economic integration, although there is equally little doubt that full integration will have to wait for some time after 1992 in some sectors (e.g. fiscal policy).

It is clear that there is a fundamental conflict between some of these aims and the protection of the environment. This problem has been tackled by the creation of an environmental policy.

The EC's environmental policy

There was no mention of the environment in the original Treaty of Rome. To some extent this was because the primary aims of the EEC were, as explained above, economic, but it was mainly because the potential environmental impact of the expansionist, growth-related economic policies adopted at the time was not perceived. By the early 1970s, however, the need for some form of policy on the protection of the environment was accepted. There were two reasons for this. One was the acceptance of the interrelationship between economic growth and environmental degradation. The other was that the environment was then emerging as a significant political issue. Environmental protection thus fits into the activities of the EC in two overlapping ways: first as an adjunct to economic policy, and secondly as a positive end in itself.

In October 1972, declaring that 'economic expansion is not an end in itself', the Heads of State of the Member States accordingly requested the Commission to draw up an EC environmental policy. It responded by formulating the first Action Programme on the Environment. (This has been followed by four further Action Programmes in 1977, 1982, 1987 and 1992. This was the effective beginning of what is now a very wide-ranging environmental strategy. (Even so, it was not actually the beginning of EC involvement in environmental matters—as long ago as 1967, Directive 67/548 provided specifically for the classification, packaging and labelling of dangerous substances.) Well over 200 items of environmental legislation have now been agreed as part of this policy, ranging across the whole spectrum of matters covered by this book.

The constitutional basis of the EC's environmental policy

The constitutional basis for an environmental policy must be considered in two distinct phases: before and after the Single European Act 1986. The history of the development of the EC's environmental policy will be considered first, because it is a good illustration of the way that the institutions have in practice widened the scope of what the EC deals with by a generous reading of the Treaty.

Before 1986 the legal justification for the policy was not entirely clear. In practice, two Articles of the Treaty, Articles 100 and 235 (the former relating to the harmonisation of national laws in order to further the establishment of the common market, the latter relating to the EC's general and residual powers), were used as justification. Directives relating to pollution control and common standards tended to be justified on the basis of Article 100, whilst those where the content was almost purely environmental, such as Directive 79/409 on Wild Birds, were justified on the basis of Article 235. It was quite common for both Articles to be cited, just in case of a challenge.

In cases that did come to the European Court of Justice, the environmental policy was supported, which is not surprising since it had been formulated with the agreement of all the Member States. In *Commission v Italy* [1981] 1 CMLR 331, the Court held quite clearly that environmental matters may fall within Article 100. It stated:

Provisions which are made necessary by considerations relating to the environment and health may be a burden on the undertakings to which they apply, and if there is no harmonisation of national provisions on the matter, competition may be appreciably distorted.

Then, in a case 240/83, on the legitimacy of Directive 75/439 on Waste Oils, the European Court of Justice stated that environmental protection was 'one of the Community's essential objectives', and as such it justified some restrictions on the operation of the common market (see [1985] ECR 531). In a sense this amounted to a rewriting of the Treaty by the European Court of Justice as a matter of political reality.

In 1986, the Single European Act went some way towards reflecting the reality of the situation by amending the Treaty to add a whole new title relating to the protection of the environment. (It also added some express social aims, such as protection of the health and safety of workers, consumer protection, and research and technological development, to reflect a similar expansion of activity in those fields.) By adding new Articles 130R, 130S and 130T, the Act introduced explicit law-making powers in relation to environmental matters. In addition, it effectively amended Article 100 by adding a new Article 100A, which has been of great importance for the development of environmental policy, even though it is primarily aimed at speeding up the completion of the single internal market. These changes not only regularised the existing *de facto* position, they also established some clearer constitutional rules than there had been in the past on the extent of the law-making powers and on how decisions were to be made.

The Maastricht Treaty continued the process of integrating environmental matters into the heart of the EC's activities by making further amendments to the Articles mentioned above. It also recognised for the first time that the development of 'a policy in the sphere of the environment' is one of the EC's main activities (see Article 3), and replaced Article 2, which sets out the objectives of the EC, with a new version that includes the tasks of promoting throughout the Community 'a harmonious and balanced development of economic activities' and 'sustainable and non-inflationary growth respecting the environment'. Article 2 thus acknowledges that there is a balance to be struck between economic and environmental factors. Of course, there remains a very live political debate about how far this widening of the aims of the EC has moved it away from a strictly economic union towards political union. Environmental policy is perhaps a good indicator of this process, since the more that explicit environmental objectives are adopted, the more it looks as if the EC is moving towards full political union.

Articles 100 and 100A

Article 100 enables Directives to be made that seek to harmonise laws and administrative practices of Member States which directly affect the establishment or functioning of the common market. The normal methods of achieving this are to lay down uniform, common standards or to outlaw specified discriminatory practices.

The relationship with the environment here is that a unified internal market depends upon trade and competition not being distorted by Member States applying different rules and standards. The EC therefore tries to harmonise laws in all the Member States so that a producer in one country does not have an unfair advantage over one in another. A law permitting producers in one country to pollute more than an equivalent producer in another country is seen as anti-competitive, since it amounts to a form of disguised subsidy. In this sense environmental policy is little more than incidental to the central economic policy.

By inserting Article 100A, the Single European Act introduced qualified majority voting for many proposals of this nature. However, as a safeguard, it also required as an objective that, if action is taken under Article 100A concerning health, safety, environmental or consumer protection, a high level of protection should be taken for those standards (Article 100A(3)). In addition, it added a power for Member States to derogate from the common standards in certain limited ways (Article 100A(4)—see p. 75).

The Maastricht Treaty made little change to these Articles, except that Directives proposed under Article 100A will in future be subject to the 'co-decision procedure' established in Article 189B, rather than the 'co-operation procedure' of Article 189C, thus extending the role of the European Parliament for Directives agreed under Article 100A.

Articles 130R, 130S and 130T

These Articles provide a specific justification for environmental protection laws, even where there is no direct link to the economic aims of the EC. Article 130S provides the mechanics by setting out the voting procedures in the Council (see below). In contrast with Articles 100 and 100A, either Directives or Regulations are possible, although few environmental Regulations have been made. A further contrast is that, whilst Articles 100 and 100A require the uniform application of standards, under these Articles that is not always required, since the motivating force behind them is the improvement of environmental standards rather than the creation of the common market. Accordingly, Article 130T specifically provides for the possibility that stricter measures than those agreed under Article 130S may be employed by Member States, as long as they are compatible with the rest of the Treaty (for fuller discussion of the need for uniformity, see p. 75).

Article 130R(1) lists as *objectives* of the EC's environmental activities the preservation, protection and improvement of the quality of the environment, the protection of human health, and the prudent and rational utilisation of resources. Article 130R(2) sets out four central *principles* of EC environmental policy, which should be taken into account when framing policy and legislation:

(a) preventative action should be preferred to remedial measures;
(b) environmental damage should be rectified at source;
(c) the 'polluter pays' principle; and
(d) environmental policies should form a component of the EC's other policies.

These principles are discussed further on p. 77.

Under Article 130R(3), the EC institutions are required to *take account of* available scientific and technical data, environmental conditions in the various regions of the EC, and the balanced development of those regions when preparing any proposals. In addition, some form of cost-benefit analysis should be performed before environmental measures are agreed—another example of the close interrelationship between environmental and economic matters.

The international dimension is covered by Article 130R(5). Many pollution, conservation and environmental matters, such as acid rain, the protection of migratory species, or pollution of the North Sea, are international in scope. A supranational body such as the EC is well-placed to tackle them by having a common internal environmental policy with uniform standards. It may also act by putting forward a common platform in dealings with the rest of the world. Article 130R(5) specifically permits the negotiation and conclusion of international agreements, a power which justifies the EC's independent involvement in international treaties and dealings with Eastern Europe.

There is one rather unclear limitation on these powers. Article 130R(4) stated that the EC should take environmental measures which can be better attained at an EC level than at a domestic level. This has always been known as the principle of subsidiarity, and it suggested that the true purpose of EC environmental legislation should be the establishment of common policies and standards rather than any interference in local issues. But there was some disagreement over its exact meaning. Some argued that it was a competency clause, which prevented the EC from interfering in matters which are better attained at a national level. But it specifically did not say that the EC may *only* take decisions which can more effectively be taken at Community level, and an alternative (and preferable) view is that it was only a guideline (see Krämer, *EEC Treaty and Environmental Protection*, 1990, p. 70).

The Maastricht Treaty appears to resolve this argument. It deleted Article 130R(4) and inserted a general principle of subsidiarity in Article 3B, which applies to all EC activities. This states:

> In areas which do not fall within its exclusive competence, the Community shall take action, in accordance with the principle of subsidiarity, only if and in so far as the objectives of the proposed action cannot be sufficiently achieved by the Member States and can therefore, by reason of the scale or effects of the proposed action, be better achieved by the Community. Any action by the Community shall not go beyond what is necessary to achieve the objectives of this Treaty.

This is clearly a competency clause, but it remains to be seen how far it will restrict the development of EC environmental policy, since as a matter of law (as opposed to policy) it would seem that nearly all current EC environmental law could be justified under this test (see p. 83 for a discussion of what has happened on this point).

The Maastricht Treaty made a number of other amendments, including renumbering some of the existing provisions. The amended version of Article 130R(2) states that EC action on the environment must aim at a high level of protection, thus bringing it into line with Article 100A. More significantly, the Treaty also added to the list of basic principles in Article 130R(2) 'the precautionary principle'. This principle is normally taken to mean that measures should be taken even before a causal link has been established between pollution and environmental harm. As such, it adopts a far more cautious and proactive approach to possible environmental harm than a principle based on prevention of harm and it could therefore have very far-reaching effects on the scope of EC environmental law in the future.

A new Article 130S(5) provides that if a measure agreed under Article 130S involves disproportionate costs for a particular Member State, the Council may allow for temporary derogations and/or for financial support to meet those costs out of the special Cohesion Fund. This provision was inserted to buy off complaints from a number of the less-developed Member States that the burden of EC environmental policy fell unfairly on them since it hindered their industrial and economic development. They perceive this to be unfair because the other Member States have arguably reached their current level of development only by taking advantage of the absence in the past of the standards now imposed by modern environmental laws.

Article 235

Article 235 is a catch-all power which permits the institutions of the EC to take appropriate measures to attain any of the objectives of the EC that cannot be achieved through other powers. It has frequently been cited in the past as a justification for environmental actions, especially those relating to international action, although there is no longer any great need to do so in the light of Articles 130R and 130S.

Qualified majority voting

The system of qualified majority voting in the Council in theory allows environmental policy to be pushed forward at a faster rate than where unanimity is required. One obvious reason is that the possibility of a national veto is reduced. For example, the objections of the Danish Government (which wanted stricter standards than those proposed) to Directive 88/76 on Emissions from Large Cars resulted in it being outvoted in the Council. More recently, the British Government was outvoted on the EC list of hazardous wastes adopted pursuant to Directive 91/689 on Hazardous Waste. However, another reason is that the system encourages the Member States to reach a compromise position within the Council. The combined effect may enable some proposed Directives to avoid the fate of, for example, Directives 88/609 on Emissions from Large Combustion Plants (which deals with the causes of acid rain) and 85/337 on Environmental Impact Assessment, both of which were delayed for many years by the opposition of one or two Member States. However, this does not mean that Directives will always be agreed swiftly, even with qualified majority voting, because there are also complex political considerations to take into account, although less-developed Member States may now be bought off by concessions based on Article 130S(5). The increasing involvement of the European Parliament is also relevant to whether a compromise position can be reached.

Prior to the Single European Act 1986, unanimity was required for all environmental legislation, whether agreed under Article 100 or Article 235. This was changed by the Act, so that, in order to move more quickly to the single internal market, a qualified majority would suffice for Directives agreed under Article 100A. Unanimity was still required under Article 130S, although a little-used exception was introduced in the second subparagraph to cover situations where a unanimous Council had agreed in advance that a qualified majority would apply.

This was changed again by the Maastricht Treaty, which amended Article 130S so that most environmental legislation agreed under it is subject to qualified majority voting. The only types of environmental legislation where unanimity is still required are those primarily of a fiscal nature (for example, the proposed carbon tax), measures relating to town and country planning or land use (unless they are concerned with waste management), measures concerning the management of water resources, and measures affecting national policies on energy supply (for example, a proposal restricting the use of coal on environmental grounds).

Which Article?

The difference in the voting procedure in the Council has been one reason why, since the Single European Act, the Article that is used in adopting a Directive is important. Another reason relates to the involvement of the European Parliament. The Single European Act introduced the 'co-operation procedure' for Directives adopted under Article 100A, thus giving the Parliament a greater input (as to which, see p. 58) than it had for Directives agreed under Article 130S. Once again, the Maastricht Treaty changed things by applying the new 'co-decision procedure' set out in Article 189B, which gives Parliament even greater influence, to Directives agreed under Article 100A. For Directives agreed under Article 130S (apart from the exceptional cases where unanimity is still required), the 'co-operation procedure' as set out in Article 189C applies.

The question of which Article is appropriate in any given case has been tested on a number of occasions in the European Court of Justice. In Case 300/89 *Commission* v *Council* [1992] JEL 109, the Court annulled Directive 89/428 on the Titanium Dioxide Industry on the grounds that the wrong Article (and thus the wrong voting procedures) had been used. The Commission, in proposing the Directive, had argued that it could be adopted under Article 100A, because it related to the harmonisation of rules relating to an industrial process. The Council, however, unanimously agreed that it should be adopted under Article 130S, since the content of the Directive related to environmental protection. The Court of Justice decided that the Commission's argument was essentially correct. It stated that where environmental measures also contributed to the establishment of the internal market they fell within Article 100A, thus suggesting that most environmental Directives could be based on Article 100A. It also noted that, where there was a choice between alternative Articles, Article 100A should be chosen because it allowed greater input from Parliament through the co-operation procedure. This decision opened the way at the time for the wider use of qualified majority voting on environmental matters.

However, in a later case, C155/91 *Commission* v *Council* [1993] ECR I-939, which concerned the correct legal basis of Directive 91/156 amending the framework Directive on Waste 75/442, the Court of Justice altered its view and adopted instead a test based on the centre of gravity of the Directive. In this case it decided that the principal objective of the Directive, which was the protection of the environment, was the crucial factor, and not any ancillary effect on the functioning of the internal market. Directive 91/156 could thus be distinguished from Directive 89/428. This centre of gravity approach has now been further supported in *Parliament* v *Council* [1995] Env LR D14, where the Court of Justice refused an application by the Parliament for the annulment of Regulation 259/93 on transfrontier shipments of hazardous waste because, even though it had obvious effects on free movement of goods, the Regulation fell within the framework of the Community's environmental policy. The conclusion is probably that most environmental Directives should now be based on Article 130S, although it remains possible to adopt harmonisation Directives having some environmental elements under Article 100A.

Is uniformity required?

There is a difference between Articles 130S and 100A over whether Member States may diverge from the standards laid down. Article 130T allows Member States to apply more stringent environmental measures than those agreed under Article 130S, as long as they do not distort trade between Member States. But, for Directives agreed under Article 100A, uniformity is required throughout the EC: the standards that are set must be common, otherwise the objective of a common market is not achieved. Article 130T cannot be used to justify a derogation from a Directive agreed under Article 100A. For example, in *R v London Borough Transport Committee ex parte Freight Transport Association Ltd, The Times,* 4 October 1990, the Court of Appeal held that the Committee's requirement that silencers be fitted to air brakes in certain London streets was illegal because it contravened Directive 70/157 on the approximation of exhaust systems (which was held to be directly effective). The Directive had been agreed under Article 100A and therefore stricter standards were an infringement of the common market. This decision was overturned by the House of Lords on appeal, though without challenging the point in issue here (see [1992] JEL 121).

There is one exception under Article 100A(4). National provisions may be stricter than the Directive if the Directive was adopted by a qualified majority, the national provision is justified by the need to protect the environment or the working environment, and the Commission verifies this. This exception was intended to cover the situation where a Directive was agreed under Article 100A despite the opposition of a Member State. It was central to the political balance agreed in the Single European Act because it provided a palliative to qualified majority voting. Article 100A(4) has been invoked successfully by the German Government in relation to what effectively amounts to a ban on the use of pentachlorophenol in Germany, although not before the original decision by the Commission to accept the ban was annulled by the European Court of Justice (see Case C-41/93, *France v Commission* [1994] *Water Law* 120). The Court did not address the scope of Article 100A(4) directly, but it did state that the exception should be interpreted restrictively because it derogates from the single internal market and therefore suggests that it applies only where a Member State has an *existing* piece of legislation that is more stringent than the Directive at the time the Directive is adopted.

However, this interpretation is somewhat at odds with Directive 94/62 on Packaging and Packaging Waste. As well as imposing requirements on the composition and recoverability of packaging, this controversial Directive imposes a duty on Member States to establish national systems to provide for the collection and recovery of packaging (many Member States already have such schemes). It then provides for recovery and recycling targets, in relation to which it is interesting to note that, whilst the Directive was adopted as a harmonisation Directive under Article 100A, Member States were allowed to set higher targets if they wished. In addition, three Member States (Portugal, Greece and Ireland) were allowed to meet lower targets. It is clear that these differences were agreed because of the political difficulties that arose in the negotiation of the Directive, but it is hard to see how this fits in with the normal requirement of uniformity under Article 100A (see London and Llamas, 'EC Packaging Directive' [1995] NLJ 221).

The *Danish Bottles* case

The interests of environmental protection may also be used as a defence in other ways. For example, Article 36 permits national laws which are effectively restrictions on imports (under Article 30), if there is a genuine need to protect, amongst other things, the environment, public health or national treasures.

The very important decision of the European Court of Justice in the *Danish Bottles* case (*Commission* v *Denmark* [1989] 54 CMLR 619) amplifies this point into a more general rule. The Court concluded that the protection of the environment is one of the EC's so-called 'mandatory requirements'. As such it can justify an interference with the operation of the common market, as long as the method adopted is proportionate to the aim which is being protected. However, it will not justify derogation from a Directive agreed under Article 100A.

The case arose from a Commission challenge to Danish laws which required beer and soft drink containers to be returnable, arguing they were a form of disguised discrimination against foreign manufacturers and hence an impediment to free trade under Article 30. The European Court of Justice held in clear terms that it was permissible to use environmental protection as an excuse for such discrimination. It went on to hold that such a derogation from the free market must be proportionate to the end to be achieved. Since a returnability requirement was clearly more environment-friendly than a recycling one, this requirement was acceptable. But a further licensing requirement, whereby only a limited number of container shapes was permitted, was disproportionate and thus illegal in EC law.

This decision has an obvious impact on the ability of Member States to pass environmental legislation that is stricter than in other Member States and which thus interferes with the common market. But it also has an impact on the attitude of the Commission, since in order to re-establish the single internal market, it will seek to lay down common standards by proposing EC legislation. There is an incentive to move towards common standards based on the stricter environmental protection legislation of the non-conforming State, using Article 100A(3) as a justification.

Some extension of the *Danish Bottles* principle can be seen in the *Wallonian Waste* case, Case C2/90 *Commission* v *Belgium* [1993] JEL 133. This case concerned what was effectively a ban on waste imports imposed by the Walloon Regional Executive. The European Court of Justice decided that waste constituted goods for the purposes of the Treaty and thus there was a clear infringement of the provisions on free movement of goods. However, it went on to decide that the ban was justified on environmental grounds. In so doing, it held that wastes are goods of a special character. Accordingly, the general principle set out in Article 130R(2), that pollution should be rectified at source, was called into play to suggest that wastes should be disposed of as close to their place of origin as possible. This enabled the Court to avoid the otherwise inevitable conclusion that the ban was discriminatory and is an important example of how these general principles can be used so as to have an impact on the development of the law. A further interesting feature of the case was the rather bizarre (but logical) result that the ban was legal as far as it applied to ordinary wastes, but not as far as hazardous wastes were concerned, because Directive 84/631 laid down an exhaustive system for the transfrontier shipment of hazardous waste. Therefore, in accordance with the argument accepted by the Court of Appeal in the *London Borough Transport Committee* case (see above), the ban on hazardous waste was illegal because it contravened the provisions of the Directive.

Some attempt to formalise these decisions has been made by the Maastricht Treaty, which added a new paragraph to Article 130R(2). This allows Directives seeking to harmonise EC laws to include a safeguard clause permitting a Member State to take *provisional* measures for environmental reasons. This does not appear to alter anything decided by *Danish Bottles,* but the Article does add a further requirement that such measures are subject to inspection by the Commission.

The scope of EC environmental policy

The Action Programmes on the Environment have laid down certain basic principles of EC environmental policy. The most important are set out in Article 130R(2). They are that:

(a)   preventative action is to be preferred to remedial measures;
(b)   environmental damage should be rectified at source;
(c)   the polluter should pay for the costs of the measures taken to protect the environment (the 'polluter pays' principle, see p. 116); and
(d)   environmental policies should form a component of the EC's other policies.

These are not directly enforceable obligations, but they will be taken into account in drawing up environmental and other EC legislation. They also influence domestic pronouncements and policies and, as illustrated above, can be used in the development of EC environmental law. The Maastricht Treaty added an important new principle, the precautionary principle.

The Action Programmes also plan future action in relation to the environment. The first two Action Programmes were reactive in nature and concentrated on pollution control and on remedial measures. This fitted in with the economic justification of environmental policy under Article 100, but was also designed to tackle the most obvious and pressing problems first. The third and fourth Action Programmes emphasised preventative measures at the same time as continuing the work on pollution control. For example, a number of Directives were agreed on product standards and on the design of industrial plant and processes. They also stressed the need to integrate environmental protection into other EC policies. Whilst there are not too many clear examples where this has happened as yet (the designation of environmentally sensitive areas for agricultural grant purposes is one of the few direct examples), the importance of this principle for the shape of future policy should not be underestimated. However, perhaps the most significant feature of the third and fourth Action Programmes was that attention was increasingly paid to structural, or 'horizontal', measures that laid down procedures or ancillary administrative matters. For example, legislation was passed on the assessment of the environmental impact of major projects (85/337), eco-labelling (Regulation 880/92), freedom of access to environmental information held by public bodies (90/313), and eco-management and audit (Regulation 1836/93).

There is no doubt that the amendments made by the Single European Act aided this shift in emphasis by encouraging more wide-ranging measures. For example, because of Danish objections to the use of Article 235, it was accepted after the passage of the Wild Birds Directive 79/409 that no further legislation would be passed on wildlife unless it related to trade. Such a limitation is now clearly removed, as the passage of the Habitats Directive 92/43 illustrated. As a further example, Directive 90/313 on Freedom of Access to Information on the Environment was made under Article 130S and there is little doubt that it would have been difficult to justify such a measure under Articles 100 or 100A.

The fifth Action Programme, entitled *Towards Sustainability*, was agreed at the end of 1992. It will cover the period 1993 to 2000. As its title suggests, it stresses the sustainable management of natural resources and provides a more wide-ranging environmental policy than before. It further switches the emphasis away from grouping environmental controls by reference to environmental media, such as air, water or land, to looking horizontally at all the environmental implications of various sectors of the economy. In particular, as part of the principle of integrating environmental policies within the EC's other policies, it concentrates on the following sectors: industry, transport, agriculture, energy and tourism.

A central concept in the scheme of the fifth Action Programme is that of 'shared responsibility'. This is the idea that responsibility for solving environmental problems is shared between government, industry and consumers. This heralds a movement away from using legislation and regulation to solve problems towards a greater use of financial and other market mechanisms. It also suggests a more inventive use of legal instruments, including civil liability and voluntary mechanisms, and the provision of more information on the state of the environment.

The range of environmental Directives

It is not possible in the space available to list all EC Directives that relate to the environment. What follows is a selective list intended to illustrate the major areas of EC involvement. Greater detail on individual Directives is given in the relevant chapters of Part II of this book and in Haigh, *Manual of Environmental Policy: the EC and Britain* (Longman, looseleaf), which explains each Directive in turn. Where the number of a Directive is given below, it normally refers to the original piece of legislation, which may subsequently have been amended. In some cases, such as in relation to the use and production of CFCs or emissions from vehicles, no number is given simply because the amount of legislation is very great.

EC Directives have been made in relation to the following:

(a)   setting quality standards for water (e.g. Surface Waters for Drinking 75/440; Drinking Water 80/778; Bathing Waters 76/160; Water Standards for Freshwater Fish 78/659; Shellfish Waters 79/923; Nitrates 91/676);

(b)   setting emission standards for discharges to water (e.g. Dangerous Substances in Water 76/464; Groundwater 80/68);

(c)   setting quality standards for air (e.g. Smoke and Sulphur Dioxide 80/779; Nitrogen Dioxide 85/203; Lead in Air 82/884);

(d)   setting emission standards for emissions to the atmosphere (e.g. various Directives on Emissions from Vehicles such as 70/220, 88/76, 89/548 and 91/441; Emissions from Industrial Plants 84/360; Emissions from Large Combustion Plants 88/609; New and Existing Municipal Waste Incinerators 89/369 and 89/429; Hazardous Waste Incinerators 94/67);

(e)   setting noise standards (e.g. Noise in the Workplace 86/188; various Directives on Noise from Vehicles; Noise from Construction Plant 84/532);

(f)   controlling emissions of dangerous pollutants (e.g. Dangerous Substances in Water 76/464; Toxic Waste 78/319 as amended by 91/689; Mercury 84/ 156; Lindane 84/491; Cadmium 83/513; Disposal of PCBs 76/403 and various Directives on CFCs, Lead and Pesticides);

(g)   controlling the disposal of waste (e.g. Framework Directive on Waste 75/442 as amended by 91/156; Toxic Waste 78/319 as amended by 91/689; Sewage Sludge 86/278; Urban Waste Water Treatment 91/271);

(h)   controlling the storage and use of hazardous materials (e.g. Major Accident Hazards 82/501 (the 'Seveso' Directive); Asbestos 87/217);

(i)   controlling dangerous activities (e.g. Transfrontier Shipment of Toxic Waste Regulation 259/93);

(j)   setting product standards (e.g. Lead in Petrol 88/195; the various Directives on Noise and Emissions from Vehicles; Classification, Packaging and Labelling of Dangerous Substances 79/831);

(k)   setting standards for the operation of certain industries (e.g. Emissions from Industrial Plants 84/360; Titanium Dioxide Industry 78/176 and 89/ 428; Emissions from Large Combustion Plants 88/609);

(l)   procedures for the planning of development (e.g. Environmental Impact Assessment 85/337);

(m) protection of wildlife (e.g. Wild Birds 79/409; Habitats 92/43; Trade in Endangered Species Regulation 3626/82);

(n) protection of the countryside (e.g. the Agri-Environment Regulation 2078/92);

(o) the use and release of genetically modified organisms (e.g. 90/219 and 90/220, as amended by 94/15);

(p) recycling and waste reduction (e.g. Packaging and Packaging Waste 94/62).

There are also important Directives and Regulations on an ever-widening range of ancillary matters. Regulation 1210/90 establishes the European Environment Agency. In addition, it replaces the current programme on the collation of information on the environment (CORINE) with new regimes of environmental monitoring and dissemination of information. Directive 90/313 on Freedom of Access to Information on the Environment is another essential part of the process of providing accurate information, which is so important if responsibility for environmental improvement is to be shared between regulators, industry and the public. Regulation 880/92 on Eco-Labelling and Regulation 1836/93 on Eco-Management and Audit further emphasise the role that voluntary initiatives by business will play in future policy. Lastly, there is the Financial Instrument for the Environment (LIFE), contained within Regulation 1973/92, which provided financial support for environmental matters, especially on the promotion of sustainable development and nature conservation, up to a total of 400 million ECUs by the end of 1994.

The types of mechanism used

It is very difficult to draw any firm conclusions from such a wide range of Directives. As one would expect, they utilise a wide range of techniques, selecting different tools for different jobs. Some of these issues are covered in Chapter 5, where, in particular, the differences between Britain and the other Member States over the types of standard to be adopted in relation to Directive 76/464 on Dangerous Substances in Water are discussed.

Two mechanisms that require some consideration at this stage are limit values and framework Directives. Limit values relate to a process whereby standards are set that require a certain minimum or maximum threshold level to be reached, but allow Member States to impose more stringent standards if circumstances require. They are thus of great use for creating general uniformity throughout the EC whilst retaining some flexibility on the ground.

Framework Directives lay down a general framework or structure of controls and come in two general types. The first type is illustrated by Directive 76/464 on Dangerous Substances in Water, which sets out a framework of controls and principles that could be applied in the future by further Directives. These Directives (sometimes called 'daughter Directives') are used to set limit values for particular dangerous substances. The second type is illustrated by Directives 75/442 and 91/156 on Waste, which set out general requirements and procedures, but leave it to Member States to set specific standards. This second type is becoming very common, in part as a recognition of the doctrine of subsidiarity, but also because of the EC's increasing emphasis on structural and procedural measures. For example, the proposed Directives on integrated pollution prevention and control and on the ecological quality of water are both of this general type. This has one important impact on the enforcement of EC environmental law—framework Directives are far less likely to be directly effective than the more specific 'regulation-style' Directives that were often used to set EC standards in the past. For example, in Case C236/92 *Comitato di Coordinamento per la Difesa della Cava* v *Regione Lombardia* [1994] *Water Law* 147, the European Court of Justice decided that Article 4 of Directive 75/442 (as amended by Directive 91/156), which requires Member States to take the necessary measures to ensure that waste is disposed of without harming human health or the environment, was not sufficiently precise to be directly effective because of its essentially programmatic nature.

The future of EC environmental policy

There are a number of trends in relation to the future of the EC's environmental policy which may be picked out.

(a) Future policies are increasingly likely to be preventative in nature. The focus of attention in environmental and safety matters is shifting from straight regulation of activities to precautionary measures, such as the fixing of product standards (e.g. on lead content in petrol), or plant design standards (e.g. Directive 84/360 on Emissions from Industrial Plants), or the avoidance of problems through waste reduction and recycling (e.g. Directive 94/62 on Packaging and Packaging Waste). In particular, the existence of the single internal market demands that emphasis is placed on products and processes so that free competition does not lead to a lessening of standards and to environmental degradation.

(b) Cross-media approaches to pollution control are likely to be encouraged, along the lines of integrated pollution control in this country. Most of the existing Directives have tended to concentrate on one particular sector, whether an industry, a substance or an environmental medium. The Commission has drafted a proposal for a Directive on integrated pollution prevention and control (see COM(93)423 final).

(c) The integration of environmental matters into other policies, as required by Article 130R(2), is likely to increase, especially since this is essential for pursuing effective preventative measures. In this respect, Green Papers have been issued on such things as the urban environment and the impact of transport on the environment.

(d) One of the impacts of the single internal market is likely to be a concentration of economic activity in the geographical centre of Europe. The potential effects of this on more marginal areas have already been recognised through the EC's Regional Policy and the environmental effects will require tackling. One way of doing this will be through the Cohesion Fund and the support available under the LIFE programme.

(e)   Ancillary measures, such as freedom of information, the encouragement of public participation in decision-making, and the creation of environmental rights are likely to be stressed, following the lead of Directive 90/313 on Freedom of Access to Information on the Environment and Directive 85/337 on Environmental Impact Assessment, which encouraged openness in the planning of environmentally significant developments. This is crucial to the success of many of the EC's programmes, since consumers can only take responsibility for environmental affairs if they are given sufficient and accurate information on the environment and the environmental performance of polluters.

(f)   This previous point links to the need for an increased democratisation of the EC's decision-making processes. At present, efforts in this regard are effectively channelled into the granting of greater powers to the European Parliament.

(g)   Action on international problems, such as global warming, acid rain, ozone depletion and oil pollution, will continue to be taken, since the EC is well placed to tackle these problems. This book has not dealt in detail with these issues, but the role of the EC has been significant in coordinating a European-wide response and this will continue. In particular, the EC has stressed in *Towards Sustainability* the role that it can play in combating climate change. It may well be that the main contribution that the EC will make in this area is the development of some form of 'carbon tax', although this is a matter which is currently fraught with political difficulties.

(h)   As on the domestic scene, economic and fiscal instruments can be expected to be developed. The Environment Council accepted the idea in principle at its meeting in October 1990. This commitment to financial instruments is reiterated in *Towards Sustainability*. Included within the category is the use of civil liability, and it is significant that the EC published a Green Paper on environmental liability in 1993 entitled *Remedying Environmental Damage* (COM(93)47 final). This expressed a preference for the use of strict civil liability, coupled with a clean-up fund where liability could not be established. There is no doubt that this will prove to be very controversial, as was the Commission's draft Directive on strict civil liability for damage caused by waste when it was published (see p. 409), but it can be anticipated that the civil law will play an increased role in EC law in the future.

(i)   The Commission has also stated an intention to concentrate on the enforcement of existing legislation. Environmental law is one of the areas where Member States have been weakest in implementing EC legislation (see the Ninth Annual Report on Commission Monitoring of the Application of Community Law, 1991, COM(92) 126 final). Over 200 infringement proceedings are pending on environmental matters, and given the limited monitoring that is done of compliance, this is clearly an underestimate of the number of Directives that remain unimplemented. Increased numbers of infringement proceedings may be expected, particularly if the European Environment Agency does gain monitoring powers. Of special importance will be those situations where a Member State has not implemented EC law in practice, despite having formally complied by passing the required laws.

(j) A final theme relates to the concept of sustainability. It is clear that the EC will emphasise the minimisation of waste and the recycling of waste that is produced. One example of this is a proposed framework Directive on energy efficiency (the SAVE programme), which has already given rise to Directive 92/75 on Energy Labelling for Domestic Appliances. But perhaps the most important steps here relate to packaging, where Directive 94/62 on Packaging and Packaging Waste sets recovery and recycling targets and seeks to reduce the excessive amount of packaging that is used.

In summary, the main agenda for the EC until the turn of the century has been set by the fifth Action Programme, *Towards Sustainability*. This reflects the shift in emphasis in all Member States towards considering the use of financial and other instruments as a means of ensuring environmental improvement, rather than always using methods connected with regulation by a public body. The Regulations on Eco-Labelling and Eco-Management and Audit are important examples of such methods, since they create voluntary schemes which industry can choose whether to join or not. But that is not to say that mandatory regulatory schemes will no longer be used, as current proposals for Directives on integrated pollution prevention and control and the extension of environmental assessment illustrate.

Subsidiarity

One doubt attached to the future direction of environmental policy relates to the concept of subsidiarity (i.e. the requirement added by Article 3B of the Maastricht Treaty that the EC should only make laws that are best made at that level, leaving Member States to take measures that are better taken at a national level). This could be used to slow down progress on EC measures, or even to repeal existing legislation. The concept was discussed at the Edinburgh Summit in December 1992, which reached such conclusions as that the Community should only legislate to the extent that is necessary, that framework Directives should be preferred to detailed ones and that voluntary codes should be considered where appropriate. In the event, the hit-list of Directives that were candidates for amendment or repeal did not include any environmental measures. However, the threat posed by subsidiarity was shown by the British Government's action in bringing forward a list of Directives it wished to see amended and a further list of proposals it wished to see discontinued. The first category included the various Directives on air quality standards, drinking water, bathing waters and hazardous waste, whilst the second included the proposed Directives on landfill, packaging waste and ecological quality of water, as well as the proposal to extend the Directive on environmental impact assessment to plans, policies and general programmes in addition to specific applications for development. It appears that this threat has been resisted by the EC institutions and that the most that will happen is that some Directives, especially those on water quality, will be re-assessed in the light of current scientific knowledge and that future Directives are more likely to take the form of framework Directives, leaving precise standards to the Member States.

EC environmental law and Britain

There is little doubt that the EC's environmental policy and the various Directives and Regulations adopted in pursuance of it have had an important influence on British environmental law. They have led directly to new legislation, new standards being adopted, significant changes in Government policy, and also a general reassessment of the whole British approach to pollution control. It is not practical to provide an exhaustive list, but the following examples should give a flavour of the impact of EC environmental law. Further examples are covered at relevant places elsewhere in the book.

(a)   New domestic legislation has been passed in relation to: environmental assessment (see the various regulations explained in detail in Chapter 10); drinking water quality (see the Water Supply (Water Quality) Regulations 1989 (SI 1989 No. 1147)); the protection of important natural habitats (see the Conservation (Natural Habitats etc.) Regulations 1994 (SI 1994 No. 2716)); the definition of waste (see the Waste Management Licensing Regulations 1994 (SI 1994 No. 1056), sch. 4); and access to environmental information (see the Environmental Information Regulations 1992 (SI 1992 No. 3240)).

(b)   New standards have been adopted for such things as air quality (see the Air Quality Standards Regulations 1989 (SI 1989 No. 317)), emissions from cars (e.g. in relation to lead and carbon dioxide) and bathing waters (in order to reflect the standards laid down in Directive 76/160). In addition, consents for discharges to controlled waters incorporate standards laid down in EC Directives, as do the water quality objectives which underpin many decisions on the control of water pollution.

(c)   The impact on policy can be seen clearly in the case of the privatisation of the water industry. The Government originally intended to privatise the whole industry, including the regulatory aspects, but was forced to create a public regulatory agency (in the form of the National Rivers Authority) when it became clear that a private regulator would not fulfil the requirement for a 'competent authority' to have responsibility for overseeing the Directives on water pollution. A different example is that Directives 91/271 on Urban Waste Water Treatment and 76/160 on Bathing Waters have led to important changes in capital spending programmes in the water industry. It is also arguable that the partial shift in British policy from basing controls on the impact on the receiving environment to using concepts based on best available techniques has been strongly influenced by the EC. Finally, the existence of EC standards has been of great importance for environmental groups, who have something with which to compare British practice when publicising alleged deficiencies in environmental performance.

As noted earlier, the influence has not all been in one direction, although it is clear that in the past Britain has often been in a minority over particular measures (for example, the problems encountered in the drafting of Directive 76/464 on Dangerous Substances in Water are discussed in Chapter 5). As far as the future is concerned, it is significant that the ability to veto measures is now restricted by the qualified majority voting procedures used for most EC environmental legislation and that the EC has recently been extended by the accession of three new Member States, each of which could be said to have fairly strong environmental credentials. A further issue is that the role of the UK Parliament in agreeing EC legislation is minimal, apart from the House of Lords Select Committee on the European Communities, which issues reports on proposed legislation frequently (for example, its comments on the EC Commission Green Paper, *Remedying Environmental Damage*, are a very constructive contribution to the debate on strict liability for environmental harm).

As with all Member States, not all Directives have been implemented fully, although the British record is actually better than most. There has been a particular problem in Britain with implementing on time. Britain has now formally been found to be in breach of EC Directives on two occasions. In Case C56/90 *Commission* v *United Kingdom* [1993] *Water Law* 168, the European Court of Justice held that Britain was in breach of Directive 76/160 on Bathing Waters in relation to standards at Blackpool and Southport beaches. In Case C337/89 *Commission* v *United Kingdom* [1993] *Water Law* 59, the European Court of Justice decided that there had been a failure to implement Directive 80/778 on Drinking Water by (i) failing to ensure that water used for food production purposes was covered by the implementing regulations (a failure now rectified), and (ii) failing to comply with the maximum admissible concentration of nitrate in some supply zones. This second part of the decision is very important, because the Court decided that the duty to comply with maximum admissible concentrations is an absolute one, thus effectively treating non-compliance in practice in the same way as formal non-compliance and opening the way for future infringement proceedings based on a failure to enforce EC standards properly in practice. In Britain this is of importance because of the way that much of the practical implementation of the law is delegated to independent agencies and quangos.

In this context, the Court of Appeal decision in *R* v *Secretary of State ex parte Friends of the Earth* [1995] 245 *ENDS Report* 44 is instructive. The case arose out of the European Court of Justice decision on Directive 80/778 on Drinking Water referred to above. The Court of Justice had decided that the duty to comply with the standards laid down in the Directive is absolute, rather than simply to take all practicable steps to comply, as had been argued by the British Government. When it later transpired that certain water companies were supplying water that was in breach of the pesticide standards set out in the Directive, the Secretary of State had accepted undertakings from them about their plans to remedy the situation, rather than making an enforcement order. This was challenged by Friends of the Earth, but the Court of Appeal accepted that, whilst the *primary* duty imposed by the

Directive on the Government was absolute, this then gave rise to a *secondary* duty to comply with the judgment. It appears that this secondary duty is not absolute in the same way, but is capable of being qualified by practical considerations.

Further infringement proceedings against the British Government are possible over Directive 76/464 on Dangerous Substances in Water (although it appears that all the Member States are in the same position over failures to introduce pollution reduction programmes for 'black list' substances) and Directive 85/337 on Environmental Impact Assessment, where infringement proceedings were started over the failure to carry out an environmental assessment of the East London River Crossing (the route of which was to have cut through Oxleas Wood site of special scientific interest), although this project has now been abandoned by the Department of Transport.

It is also possible that actions will be commenced in relation to the actual implementation of a number of Directives in practice, including Directives 90/313 on Freedom of Access to Information on the Environment and 92/43 on Habitats. This is related to the way in which Directives are now being implemented. In response to worries about the formal transposition of Directives into British legislation, the tendency nowadays is for implementing regulations to repeat the wording of the relevant Directive and to make little attempt to 'translate' what are often unclear terms into the sort of precise language that is normal in British legislation. The regulations implementing both of the above Directives illustrate this point perfectly. The result is that the meaning of the regulations remains unclear and that fuller enlightenment must await either administrative guidance (which gives undesirably wide powers to the administration and is, in any case, not conclusive), or a decision by the courts (normally this would involve a judicial review action, with all the difficulties and expense that entails). For example, it is unclear exactly which bodies and what categories of information are covered by the Environmental Information Regulations 1992, but conclusive answers to these points will only be given should an aggrieved party bring a challenge against a body which it believes has failed to comply with the Regulations. Such a roundabout method of discovering the scope of the law is most undesirable.

This raises the issue of the attitude that the British courts have adopted towards EC environmental law. At a general level they have come to terms with the supremacy of EC law, although this has come about indirectly through the European Communities Act 1972, s. 2, which provides the constitutional basis for the application of EC law in Britain. One result is that they have been willing to construe domestic legislation to comply with EC law if it was passed in order to implement it. The clearest example is provided by *Lister* v *Forth Dry Dock & Engineering Co. Ltd* [1989] 2 WLR 634, where the House of Lords adopted a purposive interpretation of the Transfer of Undertakings Regulations in accordance with the relevant Directive. However, it is not yet clear whether the British courts will be willing to follow the *Marleasing* case and apply the doctrine of indirect effect where no intention to implement EC law can be discerned (see the House of Lords' decision in *Duke* v *GEC Reliance Ltd* [1988] AC 618). In addition, the *Francovich* principle has not yet been tested in the British courts.

As far as the doctrine of direct effects is concerned, the position is equivocal. In *R* v *London Borough Transport Committee ex parte Freight Transport Association Ltd* (1990) *The Times*, 4 October, the Court of Appeal held that a requirement in Directive 70/157 on Noise from Vehicles was directly effective; in *Twyford Parish Council* v *Secretary of State for Transport* [1992] JEL 273, it was held that the requirement to carry out an environmental assessment was directly effective in relation to projects covered by Annex I of Directive 85/337; and in *R* v *Secretary of State ex parte Friends of the Earth* [1995] 245 *ENDS Report* 44, the Court of Appeal accepted implicitly that the standards laid down in Directive 80/778 on Drinking Water were directly effective (as, indeed, was clear from the European Court of Justice decision in Case C337/89 *Commission* v *United Kingdom* [1993] *Water Law* 59). On the other hand, in the *Petition of the Kincardine and Deeside DC* [1992] JEL 289, the Scottish Court of Session decided that the requirement to carry out an environmental assessment was not directly effective in relation to projects covered by Annex II of Directive 85/337 because of the discretion given to Member States, and in *Wychavon DC* v *Secretary of State for the Environment & Velcourt Ltd* [1994] JEL 351, Tucker J appeared to hold that *none* of the provisions of Directive 85/337 has direct effects. In addition, in the *Twyford* case, the judge refused relief to the applicants on the ground that they had not suffered substantial prejudice, whilst in both the *Twyford* and *Wychavon* cases, the judges stated that they would have exercised their discretion not to grant relief to the applicants, even if they had agreed with their legal arguments. It is hard to reconcile the reasoning in these cases with accepted principles of EC law.

It is also significant that the courts have shown a marked reluctance to refer matters to the European Court of Justice under Article 177. A clear example is the Court of Appeal's decision in the *Lappel Bank* case (unreported, 18 August 1994) where, although the judges were split on the interpretation of Directive 79/409 on Wild Birds, they declined to make a reference, although the House of Lords later rectified the position by making a reference (see p. 497 for a fuller explanation of this case). It may also be asked why no reference was made in the *Twyford*, *Kincardine* and *Wychavon* cases, where the EC law issue was demonstrably unclear from the fact that different decisions were reached on it.

It can be argued that, compared with the willingness that the European Court of Justice displays to adopt robust interpretations of the law, the performance of the British courts is far from impressive. For example, whilst the Court of Justice has been willing on a number of occasions to interpret the somewhat vague provisions of environmental Directives as laying down clear objective criteria (see, for example, Case C56/90 *Commission* v *United Kingdom* [1993] *Water Law* 168, where it stated that the criteria for designation as a traditional bathing water were objectively clear from Directive 76/160, and Case C355/90 *Commission* v *Spain* [1993] *Water Law* 209, where it held that the requirements for classification as a special protection area for birds were objectively clear from Directive 79/409), the British courts have always managed to find some hurdle to explain why the applicant should not succeed.

As a final example, in *R* v *Secretary of State for Trade and Industry ex parte Duddridge* [1995] Env LR 151, the Divisional Court refused to apply the precautionary principle as part of English law. This principle is now enshrined within Article 130R(2) of the EC Treaty, as amended at Maastricht, but the court decided that it only laid down a general principle upon which EC policy on the environment should be based and did not impose any immediate obligations on Member States. Whilst this is not entirely surprising, the fact that the court also described the proposition that the principle should be adopted as part of British law as a matter of commonsense as 'startling' does, perhaps, illustrate that British judges may struggle when it comes to developing new principles to cope with the peculiarities of environmental litigation.

FIVE

The regulation of environmental protection

Despite the current vogue for suggesting economic or fiscal mechanisms for combating environmental problems, the system of regulation by public bodies remains the prime tool for environmental protection in this country. This commitment to regulation was reiterated in the White Paper *This Common Inheritance* (Cm. 1200, 1990), which stated that 'administrative controls will for the foreseeable future remain at the heart of Britain's system of environmental control—just as they are in many other countries in the world', even at the same time as the possibility of using economic mechanisms is suggested as a future, additional, tool. More equivocally in *This Common Inheritance—The Second Year Report* (1992), the Government states that there should in future be a presumption in favour of using economic instruments as opposed to direct regulation.

What does regulation mean in this context? At one level all the word means is the use of rules to control activities. These could be criminal law rules, or civil law rules, or private non-legal rules operated by a body such as a trade association, or maybe even the 'rules' of the free market. In this book, however, the word regulation is used to mean administrative or bureaucratic regulation (i.e. the application of rules and procedures by public bodies so as to achieve a measure of control over activities carried on by individuals and firms).

Other means of controlling activities, such as the criminal law, the civil law and the use of the market, will be considered later, but since these are often subsidiary to administrative regulation, this will be explained first.

Administrative regulation

Administrative regulation is far more than just the setting of rules on what can and cannot be done. It denotes a coherent *system* of control in which the regulating body sets a framework for activities on an ongoing basis, with a view to conditioning and policing behaviour as well as laying down straight rules.

The advantages of such a system include the ability to provide uniformity, rationality and fairness between those who are regulated. Some form of public accountability is also produced by having a public body responsible for regulation. In particular, one advantage over the criminal law is that a coherent link can be made with other policies, so as to balance all relevant factors. This is often seen as an important part of the British approach to regulation: that it involves an explicit balancing of environmental factors with such things as economic and social considerations.

British regulatory systems can be said to exhibit a pragmatic and flexible approach. The same mechanism is not used for each situation. In some cases the reason is simply that it is recognised that a control mechanism that works for one problem is unlikely to work for a different one. This is a good illustration of the use of law as a tool or a technique to help to solve particular problems. In other cases, there are historical reasons, since one of the features of having a long history of environmental control is that the administrative structures have built up piecemeal and in response to problems as they arise. For example, many controls have in the past been given to local authorities purely because they happened to be dealing with similar matters already, or because there was no other relevant body around at the time.

The processes of regulatory decision-making

Before looking at the main features of regulation in this country, it is necessary to summarise the main processes or stages in regulatory decision-making. These are:

(a)   the establishment of general policies;

(b)   the setting of standards or specific policies in relation to the environmental issue concerned;

(c)   the application of these standards and policies to individual situations;

(d)   the enforcement of standards and permissions;

(e)   the provision of information about the environment and the regulatory process.

(a)   The establishment of general policies

The process of establishing general policies is not really part of the regulatory system, but a necessary precondition for any system of environmental control. Having said that, one of the most obvious features of the British political system is the absence of formal national policies in many areas. Even where there are local or sectoral plans, there is often no national plan, or, if there is, it is made up of somewhat imprecise and flexible policies laid down in a variety of documents. A good illustration of the flexible nature of policy-making in Britain is provided by the town and country planning system, where the 'national plan' is to be found scattered amongst numerous Circulars, Planning Policy Guidance Notes, Ministerial decisions, White Papers and other assorted policy statements.

Given the essentially political nature of much of environmental law, the general tenor of the policies tends to be decided by Central Government. The presumption in favour of development in town planning is one example, but general decisions on energy and transport policy, such as the favouring of road transport over rail, or the retention of a nuclear power programme, are others. Certain political philosophies may also be imposed by Central Government; good examples are the principle of voluntariness in relation to controlling agricultural activities, or the policy of privatisation. However, because of the decentralised nature of much of pollution control, some general policies are effectively decided by bodies other than the elected Central Government. Other policies stem from general assumptions about the nature of the regulatory system itself—which we later refer to as the 'British approach' to environmental regulation (see p. 101).

A final factor is that the shape of many policies is now decided, or at least affected, by the EC. Arguably some of the most significant impacts on the environment in the next few years will follow from the establishment of the single European market and the countervailing powers adopted by the EC in terms of such things as regional and social policy.

(b) The setting of standards or specific policies in relation to the environmental issue concerned

Any system of control must have some objectives that are set for it, otherwise it runs the risk of ceasing to be rational, uniform or fair. These may be fairly explicit objectives, such as air quality standards with specific maximum concentrations for a range of pollutants, or they may be far more vague, such as a water quality objective to the effect that a river should be capable of supporting fish.

In the past reliance has usually been placed on rather vague standards, such as the test of nuisance at common law, or the idea that best practicable means should be used to reduce gaseous emissions to the atmosphere. In addition, standards were often set in an informal manner, as used to happen with non-statutory water quality objectives. More specific and more formal standards are becoming far more common, a good example being the publication of Process Guidance Notes for processes covered by Part I of the EPA 1990. In the development control system, policies of this type are set out in development plans and in Planning Policy Guidance Notes. There is often overlap between this stage and stage (a) above.

(c) The application of these standards and policies to individual situations

This is often seen as the central part of the regulatory process. There are numerous examples where a permission, authorisation, consent or licence is required from a public body. (Different pieces of legislation use different words but they all mean essentially the same thing.) Whether one is granted, and the nature of any conditions attached, will normally be a discretionary decision, but one that is made by reference to the general standards established at stage (b). The application of standards may also be seen in such processes as court actions for nuisance and the specific application of whether best practicable means or best available techniques are being used.

(d) The enforcement of standards and permissions

In practice, one of the most important areas of environmental law is whether the legal instruments that are available are used, since there is often considerable discretion given to the regulatory body. 'Enforcement' covers a far wider range of matters than the single question whether to prosecute for breaches of the law. In any regulatory system, there is normally a whole range of administrative and other remedies available in addition to prosecution. The question of which remedy to use is also tied up with how the regulator should proceed. There is a wealth of evidence to show that informal methods of enforcement are often preferred, and that regulators normally adopt a 'compliance strategy' towards enforcement, rather than a 'sanctioning strategy' (i.e. one based on confrontation, see Chapter 6). Questions of inspection and monitoring also arise as part of the enforcement process.

(e) The provision of information about the environment and the regulatory process.

A theme which runs through the regulatory process concerns the openness of the system. This includes such questions as the production of official information on the state of the environment, the availability of public registers, and the publication of information about how the regulatory system itself works. Britain's traditionally secretive administrative processes are slowly becoming more open. This is most obvious in relation to stage (c), but is also apparent in the extension of public registers, enabling more information to be available for enforcement purposes. It may also be seen in the increased willingness of the Government to issue consultation papers before changes in the law and practice are adopted.

Anticipatory and continuing controls

Regulatory mechanisms may be divided into two general types, anticipatory controls and continuing controls.

Anticipatory controls

These are measures in which controls are imposed on an activity at its commencement in order to forestall potential environmental problems. Usually the objective is to prevent the activity unless certain requirements or conditions are met. The category includes a wide range of licensing-type controls, where permission of some sort is required before an activity may be started or carried on. These are normally complemented by a combination of criminal and administrative sanctions if the activity starts without permission, or if the permission is contravened.

The range of possible anticipatory controls is quite wide. It includes:

(a) An outright ban (e.g. the intended ban on the use of CFCs in products, or the prospective ban on the dumping of sewage sludge at sea). Of course, there is no *necessity* for a public regulatory body to be involved here, but someone will need to police the ban.

(b) A prohibition on an activity unless a particular body is notified in advance (e.g. the requirement under the Wildlife and Countryside Act 1981, s. 28 that owners and occupiers of a site of special scientific interest notify the relevant Nature Conservancy Council of any intention to carry out a potentially damaging operation, thus forewarning the Council of a possible need to take further protective steps).

(c) A prohibition on an activity unless it is registered, registration being something that cannot normally be refused by the registering body (e.g. there is a requirement that carriers of controlled waste register with the waste regulation authority).

(d) A prohibition on an activity until a licence, permission, authorisation or consent is obtained, where the granting of the permission is at the discretion of the regulating body.

In relation to this last type, there are two distinct categories of permission or consent. Some are one-off permissions which, once granted, create what are in effect permanent rights because it is difficult to vary or revoke them. A good example is the granting of planning permission, where revocation entails the payment of compensation. Others provide for variation or revocation in the light of future circumstances. Most pollution control consents fall into this category, examples being the requirements to obtain an authorisation from HMIP for carrying on a prescribed process, or a consent from the National Rivers Authority for a discharge to controlled waters.

Continuing controls

These are measures where the carrying out of an activity is controlled on a continuing basis. Typically they relate to the way an activity is carried on, so another way of referring to them would be as *operational* controls. An obvious example is the ongoing duty to comply with the terms of a consent, licence, authorisation, or permission granted by a pollution control authority, which will normally be combined with a range of other regulatory controls relating to monitoring and enforcement. The distinction between anticipatory controls and continuing controls is thus that one relates to *whether* an activity should be carried on in the first place, whilst the other relates to *how* it is carried on once it has started.

Of course, anticipatory and continuing controls are mutually supportive and most regulatory systems combine the two types of mechanism. Anticipatory controls still require some monitoring to ensure that the prohibited activity is not being carried on. Conversely, most continuing controls rest on the need for some initial permission before an activity may be started; indeed, the threat of withdrawal of the initial permission may well constitute the strongest inducement to comply with continuing regulatory requirements. For example, planning permission is required before a new activity is started, but that permission will often include conditions that require some adherence to defined standards over a period of time, such as permitted working hours or noise limits. Similarly, consents, authorisations and licences obtained from pollution control authorities normally combine the initial need for a consent with an ability to vary the requirements as the situation changes. This mutually supportive position is reinforced by the fact that many activities are subject to the requirements of more than one regulatory system.

Planning and prevention

The town and country planning system is the major system of anticipatory control in environmental law. To a large extent this stems from the very nature of planning control. It involves the preparation of plans, which may then guide future behaviour. The controls are necessarily imposed at the outset, whilst most pollution control mechanisms basically assume a continuing activity. Planning also mainly concerns land use, siting and locational issues that logically pre-date the operational controls.

A further reason results from practice. In these other systems, it is rare for the initial consent to be refused or revoked (although this power does remain as a threat for those who contravene the continuing controls). For example, it appears that no instance was ever recorded of a certificate of registration being refused under the Alkali Acts, either at the outset or on renewal (see Wood, *Planning Pollution Prevention*, 1989). In other areas of pollution control, the record may be slightly different, but there are still few examples of a consent from a pollution control authority actually being refused where there is already a planning permission.

One result is that the main burden of deciding whether a particular plant should go ahead normally falls upon the local planning authority. By way of example, a new factory will require planning permission as well as consents for emissions from HMIP or the NRA, and maybe the sewerage undertaker and local authority (in its capacity as regulator of air pollution) as well. It will be the local planning authority that decides whether to have the factory in that particular place. The pollution control authorities tend to see their task as setting limits on what is acceptable in terms of pollution from the site proposed rather than as stopping the development going ahead at all. Traditionally, these authorities have had little scope for saying, 'this development would be better somewhere else', though that is a matter they could raise when consulted by the local planning authority over the development proposal. (For an analysis of the relationship between the systems of planning and pollution control, see *Gateshead MBC* v *Secretary of State for the Environment* [1995] JPL 432.)

This is perhaps inevitable given the differences in nature between local planning authorities and other regulatory bodies. A local planning authority has a specific remit under the Town and Country Planning Act 1990, s. 70 to consider *all* material factors relating to a development, whilst other bodies often have a more limited range of relevant factors to consider in making their decision. It is also an elected body, where ultimate power resides with elected members, and therefore has greater legitimacy in terms of making a balanced policy decision to refuse a development.

Standards in environmental law

Most environmental controls rely on some form of measurable standard. This standard may be used as a guideline (i.e. an objective) or it may be used as a means of defining what an individual or firm may do. Indeed, one of the distinctive features of environmental regulation is that the regulatory body often has responsibility for defining the standard as well as enforcing its application.

There are a number of different types of standard, but a crude division can be made into those which are set by reference to the *target* which is being protected and those which are set by reference to the *source* of the pollution. Source-related standards may be further divided into emission standards, process standards and product standards. There are other factors that have a significant impact on the nature of a standard, such as whether it is centrally or locally set, uniform or flexible, precise or imprecise.

The following summary is not intended to be an exhaustive list of the various types of standard (from the list of variables above obviously the number of potential types is very great), but is an attempt to introduce a basic vocabulary of terms. It also aims to illustrate some of the more common methods used, together with some thoughts on their relative strengths and weaknesses. In a sense, these are the tools available to the legislator in deciding how a regulatory system is to work.

(a)   Environmental quality standards (target standards)
Some standards concentrate on the effect on a particular target. In many cases, the protected target may be human beings and the standard is accordingly set by reference to the effect on them (e.g. the effect of radiation on workers). However, since this is a book about environmental protection, it will concentrate on situations where the protected target is the environment, or part of it. The phrases 'target standards' and 'environmental quality standards' will therefore be treated as interchangeable.

The effect on the target may be measured in different ways. It may relate to a biological effect, thus channelling all information directly into a consideration of the actual impact of a pollutant (e.g. a standard requiring that a discharge to water is not harmful to fish or aquatic animals). Alternatively, it may relate to the exposure of the target, from which certain biological or other effects may be presumed. In the environmental field, however, it will more usually relate simply to some measurable quality of the receiving environment, such as the level of a particular pollutant.

An environmental quality standard can therefore be defined as a standard where conformity is measured by reference to the effect of a pollutant on the receiving environment. It is unusual for the selected target to be the whole environment. More commonly a particular medium will be chosen as the reference point, such as air or water. In order to retain flexibility, there will frequently also be a geographical limitation: the standard may thus be set by reference to a particular river or area, or may be even more specific, such as where air quality or noise levels are fixed within factories or any other enclosed area.

Examples of environmental quality standards include:

(a)   setting air quality standards for the maximum or minimum concentration of any specified substance in air (e.g. the Air Quality Standards Regulations 1989 (SI 1989 No. 317) set mandatory standards for sulphur dioxide, nitrogen dioxide, lead and smoke);
(b)   setting water quality standards for the concentration of specified pollutants in 'controlled waters' (see p. 440, where the establishment of statutory water quality objectives is discussed);
(c)   the nuisance test at common law, under which property owners are entitled to the enjoyment of their property without unreasonable interference from neighbours.

It will be clear that these standards may be set by reference to any number of parameters. For example, a water quality standard could be set specifically for the maximum concentration of zinc, or a whole range of parameters may be used, as is the case for drinking water. It will also be clear that the standard can be precise or imprecise—the nuisance standard is a good example of an imprecise standard.

(b) Emission standards
An emission standard can be defined as a standard where conformity is measured by reference to what is emitted rather than the effect on the receiving environment. Emission standards thus tend to concentrate on wastes produced. For example, the content of a discharge from a pipe or chimney could be controlled by reference to an emission standard.
Examples of emission standards include:

(a)   the maximum content of a particular substance in a liquid discharge from a pipe to a sewer or 'controlled waters';
(b)   the noise level measured as it emanates from a building;
(c)   the maximum content of a particular substance in an emission from chimney or exhaust pipe.

(c) Process standards
A standard may be imposed on a process either by stipulating precisely the process which must be carried on, or by setting performance requirements that the process must reach. In the second case there would be a choice as to how to reach these requirements. These standards may relate to the whole of the process or, alternatively, to a part of it, such as the way that a product is made or the way effluent is treated. They may include requirements about the technology that is used, the raw materials, or operational factors such as whether the process is being carried out properly.
Examples of process standards include:

(a)   a requirement that a particular pre-treatment plant for effluent be used;
(b)   a stipulation on the height of a factory chimney;

(c)   a stipulation about the use of a particular grade or quality of fuel;

(d)   a requirement that the 'best available techniques not entailing excess-ive cost (BATNEEC) are used (see p. 308), though the general requirement is often translated into a set of emission standards in practice;

(e)   conditions attached to the operation of a landfill site or incinerator.

It is clear that current practice is to emphasise the use of process standards, and this is illustrated by their use in Part I of the EPA 1990. They are a good means of preventing harm to the environment arising in the first place.

(d)   Product standards

Product standards may be defined as where the characteristics of an item that is being produced are controlled. This may be done with the aim of protecting against damage the product may cause whilst it is being used, or when it is disposed of, or even during its manufacture. Examples include:

(a)   a requirement that all new cars are capable of running on unleaded petrol;

(b)   a requirement that cars are fitted with catalytic converters;

(c)   it may even be thought that requirements on the labelling of goods are a type of product standard.

Interrelationship of standards

Of course, these four types of standard are not exclusive of each other. An emission standard will often be set so as to achieve an environmental quality standard. Product standards for a car will include many matters relating to the emissions from it, such as lead, carbon dioxide or noise. In addition, the cumulative effect of these emissions will have an impact on the attainment or otherwise of any environmental quality standard.

Taking one particular, toxic pollutant, lead, environmental concentrations may be controlled in a number of ways:

(a)   Environmental quality standards may be set, stating that levels of lead should not rise above a certain level in the air, in water, or in the soil.

(b)   Emissions of lead may be controlled, so that any emission, whether into air or water or on to land, should not include more than a specified concentration of lead, to be set in some form of permission or consent.

(c)   Processes may be regulated to reduce the use of lead, or to reduce by good design possible emissions and escapes of lead into the environment.

(d)   Products likely to include lead may be regulated, either to ban its use (e.g. lead fishing weights) or to limit the use of lead (e.g. setting maximum amounts of lead in leaded petrol).

Other characteristics of standards

As stated earlier, a number of other matters are also important in relation to the nature of a standard. The standard may be a precise one, such as one set by reference to a scientifically provable maximum or minimum—often a numerical value. Alternatively, it may be an imprecise one, such as a requirement that 'best practicable means' (BPM) or BATNEEC are used, or one applying the common law test of nuisance.

The standard may be a uniform one across the country (or the EC), or it may vary from area to area. Indeed, it may be set on an individual basis. Certain matters demand uniform standards. For example, uniformity is normally desirable for emissions from mobile sources such as cars, otherwise problems are caused at boundaries. For similar reasons, most product standards are set on a uniform basis. It is strongly argued by some that uniformity creates equality, a particularly important consideration in the context of the EC and the single internal market. Limit values, as used by the EC in a number of Directives, create a special form of uniformity. They require that a certain standard is reached, but allow Member States to impose more stringent standards if circumstances require.

The standard may be set centrally or locally. This distinction tends to reflect the same division as that between uniform and individualised standards, since centrally set standards will usually be uniform whilst locally set ones will vary with the discretion given to the decision-maker. In this context, it must be remembered that few standards in Britain are set by legislation. Often this exercise is left to local bodies, although this is changing as EC standards permeate domestic environmental law.

Strengths and weaknesses of different types of standard

Obviously it is not possible to cover all types of standard, but it is possible to see the relative strengths and weaknesses of the more commonly used examples.

Environmental quality standards, by concentrating on what it is that requires protection, are able to deal with inputs to the environment from all sources and via all potential pathways, whilst the other mechanisms, used on their own, tend to permit cumulation of any particular pollutant. For the same reason, environmental quality standards can also cater for potentially harmful combinations of substances on the environment. They can thus enable a policy-maker to identify areas where work is needed, and channel resources effectively. They can also be tailored for particular circumstances, for example by being more stringent in sensitive areas than in others.

However, there are a number of limitations to environmental quality standards. They require constant monitoring of the environment, which may prove to be impractical or expensive. Enforcement poses difficulties, since failure to reach a standard may alert us to the existence of a problem, but does not necessarily tell us the cause or how to remedy it. For example, in order to clean up a river which is chronically contaminated with organic wastes, a regulator would first have to identify the causes of the pollution and then find some method of restricting inputs that was fair and enforceable. A further problem of environmental quality standards is that they may give no incentive to polluters to improve their performance in areas where the standard is already being met.

The very nature of environmental quality standards is that they tend to be set as *objectives* rather than as legal requirements, except in those situations where there is a limited number of sources and targets, such as enclosed work environments. This use as objectives makes them useful at the strategic and planning stages of the regulatory process (see p. 90). For example, development plans often set environmental quality standards, even if they are frequently very imprecise, such as a policy that developments liable to cause a nuisance should not be permitted in a defined area.

By contrast, the strength of emission standards is that they are relatively easy to control and monitor by sampling at the point of emission. Enforcement is also easier because of the simplicity of the causation requirements where there is a point of discharge. In addition, an emission standard may be tightened progressively to encourage a discharger to improve the process, whilst still retaining choice as to how this is done.

A main drawback of emission standards relates to the difficulty of controlling diffuse (or non-point) emissions, such as fertiliser or pesticide run-off, by these means. There is also the difficulty (shared with process standards and product standards) of organising a system that can cope with an accumulation of similar emissions in one area, such as car exhausts in Los Angeles or similar industrial concerns in one water catchment area. This second difficulty is not an insoluble problem, however. It may be tackled by setting very strict local emission standards, by linking them explicitly to an environmental quality standard, or by applying the 'bubble' approach (i.e. by aggregating together all emissions in a particular area and permitting a total amount of emissions for that area).

Process standards are obviously limited to where there is a process to control and thus tend to apply mainly to the manufacturing industry. Their main strength is that they may be set so as to prevent a problem arising in the first place. They may also help to pool resources for research at a central level. There is a potential disincentive for producers to find more effective ways of reducing pollution, unless the standards are made progressively stricter, or are periodically altered, or are set at levels that force the producer to develop the technology so as to reach the standard (so-called 'technology forcing' rules).

Product standards are similarly limited to where there is a product and have similar strengths and weaknesses as process standards. As stated above, both categories also have difficulty in catering for the cumulative effect of pollutants on their own.

Locally set and centrally set standards: Britain versus the EC

It has often been noted that Britain and the rest of the EC do not seem to see eye to eye on pollution control. This is sometimes translated into a conflict between a British preference for locally set and variable (i.e. non-uniform) emission standards, set by reference to local environmental quality, and an EC preference for centrally set uniform emission standards. Haigh (in *EEC Environmental Policy and Britain*) points out that any conflict on these grounds has been much exaggerated (see below).

Nevertheless, these two types of standard provide an excellent opportunity for a case study on their relative strengths and weaknesses.

Locally set and variable emission standards set by reference to local environmental quality

Each of the features of this combination of ideas merits some mention. Referring everything to environmental quality can be said to target controls where they are needed—at the protection of the environment. In this way, the impact of non-point emissions and background levels of pollution may be taken into account, as well as discharges from pipes and chimneys. The fact that neither the emission standards nor the environmental quality standards are uniform provides flexibility. This enables more sensitive areas to be protected more strictly, or polluters who are seen as more useful to the community to be treated more leniently. In all cases, a great deal of discretion is granted to decision-makers. It is also argued that, since standards can be varied to take account of local circumstances, the mechanism is economically efficient. For example, greater pollutant loads could be permitted in remote, unpopulated areas or where the self-cleansing properties of the local environment are greater.

Centrally set uniform emission standards

These have obvious advantages. Uniform standards are easily imposed, easily implemented and easily monitored. They are fair between polluters since all are treated the same, and they avoid difficult problems about allocating the right to pollute amongst different polluters. As a result they may be relatively cheap for the regulator to operate, because they involve less administrative discretion than variable standards. They also fit in well with the economic principles of the EC's common market.

On the other hand, they can be said not to allow local conditions to be taken into account, because there is no flexibility (although this can be provided at the enforcement stage). They are meant to be unable to deal with the situation where there is a number of polluters in one area, since there is no jurisdiction to reduce the emission standard to fit local conditions. They are also sometimes said to lead to the possibility of a uniformly polluted country if there is one relevant discharge in every area. These last two criticisms are rather too general, since good use of preventative controls would help in both cases.

Why Britain and the EC differ

It is not difficult to think of reasons why Britain may differ from other Member States within the EC. As an island, Britain has no frontiers. Thus, the argument about fairness has never had the impact that it has in France and Germany, which share the Rhine as a border, and where the inequality of one factory being allowed to discharge more than another on the other bank is obvious. Other factors stem from the 'British approach' to pollution control, such as that Britain has a tradition of discretionary, local decision-making and a system based on pragmatism, in which the effects on the environment are balanced with social, economic and political factors.

But the main argument for the British position probably stems from self-interest. With its rainy climate, fast-running streams, ample coastline and relative remoteness, Britain can claim a comparative advantage when it comes to pollution. Put very crudely, the same discharge is supposed to cause less pollution in Britain than in other countries, because of its lesser effect on the environment. When it comes to setting standards, some people in Britain do not see why stringent uniform standards should apply across the EC if they have no justification in terms of environmental protection in the British context, even if they provide that protection elsewhere.

As stated earlier, the differences have been exaggerated. Even discounting the influence of EC legislation, there are many examples of uniform emission standards applying in Britain, although this is sometimes hidden by being the product of administrative practice rather than legislative action. This is especially the case in relation to dangerous substances, where no amount of discretionary balancing with other factors will make them safe. Also the differences set out above relate mainly to water pollution, which is, arguably, the area where Britain has the greatest comparative advantage. Even in relation to water pollution, the differences have mainly surfaced over one particular Directive—the framework Directive 76/464 on Dangerous Substances in Water. It was in relation to this Directive that Britain's position led to alternative regimes being adopted for the control of dangerous substances (see p. 48). But, as Haigh points out, it seems that what the other EC Member States saw as cause for concern was not the use of environmental quality objectives to define the context for the setting of variable discharge consents, but the fact that these quality standards were, at the time, informal, unpublished, and set by regional authorities. It is not hard to imagine that other Member States thought they were being told that the British approach to controlling dangerous substances was that 'it all depends on the circumstances'.

As a final point, it should be noted that in any case Directive 76/464 did *not* lay down uniform emission standards. It laid down limit values, and many of the arguments against uniform emission standards do not apply to these, because there is the flexibility to have a stricter standard if desirable.

The 'British approach' to regulation

Since administrative regulation can take many forms, it is important to establish the distinctive features of the British style or approach. In other words, what types of rules and standards are employed? How are they set and by whom? How are they enforced and by whom? What role does the public play in these processes?

In *National Styles of Regulation* (1986), Vogel identifies a number of characteristics of the British style. The book claims to be 'an examination of British environmental policy as seen through the eyes of a student of American politics', and consists of a comparison of approaches to environmental regulation in Britain and the USA. Vogel writes that Britain's regulatory style is characterised by flexibility and informality, and summarises the system as involving:

> An absence of statutory standards, minimal use of prosecution, a flexible enforcement strategy, considerable administrative discretion, decentralised implementation, close co-operation between regulators and the regulated, and restrictions on the ability of non-industry constituents to participate in the regulatory process.

At the risk of producing an unmanageable list, to these points could be added others, such as delegation of decision-making to autonomous quasi-governmental and non-governmental bodies, extensive use of industrial self-regulation, a limited availability of legislative and judicial scrutiny of regulators, a gradualist approach to change, reliance on scientific knowledge for decision-making and habitual reference to economic factors before decisions are made.

Vogel compares this approach with that of the USA, which he characterises as rule-oriented, normally employing rigid and uniform standards, and making little use of industrial self-regulation. In addition, less use is made there of administrative discretion, prosecution is much more common, there is great executive and judicial scrutiny of regulators and technology-forcing rules are favoured. All of these features lead to conflict between regulator and regulated and to an adversary mentality.

Of course many of these differences are not unique to environmental regulation in the two countries, but are a matter of general political culture. They probably stem from different attitudes towards regulation engendered by different population densities and degrees of cultural homogeneity. In Britain the need for a balancing process is all too clear, whilst in the USA the 'frontier mentality' is understandably more prevalent.

At this point a warning should be given. Since the 1960s the situation in the USA has changed dramatically, and what Vogel describes in the 1980s is quite different from what happened before. Similarly, the British approach is currently changing quite rapidly. The informal and flexible basis remains, but the approach has undoubtedly got more open, more centralised, more legalistic and more contentious, especially in the last 10 years or so. The changes in legislation have been substantial, but there have also been more disguised internal changes of practice by regulators. As a result, Vogel's analysis is beginning to look outdated.

One crucial factor in this change is the attitude of the EC. The British approach has tended to conflict with that adopted by other Member States and has had to be modified to fit in with that. At the same time, the increased profile of environmental issues, particularly international ones requiring common responses, has led to some changes of style out of political necessity. A further factor lies in the political preferences of the current Government, which has after all been in power for a long time, and has adopted some radical, if controversial, policies in that period. It is clear that such major features of policy as the rejection of long-term planning in favour of market forces, deregulation of unnecessary bureaucratic controls, privatisation of public services, imposition of strict spending controls on public bodies, the general weakening of local authority power, and the use of voluntary controls allowing choice wherever possible have all had an impact on the nature of regulation in this country.

The following sections will explore some of the manifestations and implications of the British approach, and will seek to illustrate just how it is changing and in what direction. However, it must be stressed that this is only a general approach. No-one would suggest that all these symptoms are displayed by each of the various regulatory processes in the country, merely that these are recognisable general features.

The implications of the British approach also vary at the different stages identified earlier, with the result that, for example, general policy-making remains mainly a central function, rather than being particularly decentralised (although many of these general policies are now in practice agreed at international or EC level). Nevertheless, the general features of the regulatory system can be illustrated by considering a number of key issues.

Decentralisation

Decision-making is decentralised in three ways: by being given to a wide range of bodies, by significant use of delegation, and by geographical decentralisation.

There are numerous bodies exercising environmental responsibilities (see Chapter 3). Unlike countries with a unified environmental protection agency, Britain has a large number of autonomous or semi-autonomous environmental agencies, such as the National Rivers Authority, Her Majesty's Inspectorate of Pollution, the Nature Conservancy Councils, the Health and Safety Executive, the Nuclear Installations Inspectorate, and the Countryside Commission. Local authorities also have wide-ranging environmental protection powers in relation to such things as air pollution, waste regulation and disposal, noise control, town and country planning and environmental health. There is also decentralisation within Central Government. Although the Department of the Environment is nominally responsible for much of environmental policy, many decisions and policies which have important environmental effects are made by the Department of Trade and Industry (e.g. on power stations), or the Department of Transport (e.g. on emissions from vehicles), or the Ministry of Agriculture, Fisheries and Food (e.g. on agricultural support schemes). The diversity is compounded by the tendency to have separate bodies in Wales and Scotland.

Even within the Department of the Environment, matters are often delegated. For example, appeals against refusals of planning permission are normally dealt with by the Planning Inspectorate Executive Agency, although this remains formally part of the Department of the Environment.

Over the years this decentralisation of power has tended to result in a rather incoherent environmental policy, with very little uniformity across the country. Even such a central function as the monitoring of the environment has tended to be done in an uncoordinated way. There have been a number of changes in recent years which have altered matters. For example, the regulation of water pollution was organised on a regional basis until 1989, when the NRA was established as a national body covering England and Wales. HMIP was created in 1987 to draw together a number of inspectorates at that time operating separately within the Department of the Environment and the Health and Safety Executive. Both these institutional changes clearly fostered uniformity in decision-making. The Environment Act 1995 creates the Environment Agency for England and Wales, thus continuing the process of producing a more coherent and uniform institutional structure.

Decisions are also commonly made locally. Local authorities have the wide powers referred to above, whilst many of the inspectorates and other agencies operate on a regional basis, granting some discretion to local decision-makers. There is a philosophy underpinning this, of course. The British approach is geared pragmatically towards the protection of the receiving environment, so it is sensible that decisions are taken by people or bodies with a knowledge of local conditions, whether environmental, social or economic.

An important change has been the centralisation of policy decisions in recent years. This has been most marked in relation to matters where there is conflict between central and local government. For example, in the town and country planning system, increased intervention in local decisions by Central Government was the major issue of the 1980s. It was manifested mainly through hard-hitting and directory Circulars, which were applied on appeal so as to alter the policy context of most planning decisions, though there were also changes to the law and in institutional structure designed to reduce local control, through such creations as urban development corporations. However, centralisation is also a reality in relation to pollution control. For example, local authorities have lost a significant amount of discretion in relation to air pollution as a result of the EPA 1990 and the Environment Agency, when established, will take over the waste regulation functions previously carried out by local authorities.

Centralisation may also be seen at work in the control of public spending. The regional water authorities were severely limited for many years in their ability to make capital expenditure decisions, and the same is true for local authorities. For bodies such as the Countryside Commission which rely almost entirely on Government grant, the position is even clearer.

Finally there is a very significant element of centralisation involved in the relationship between Britain and the EC. Not only is EC decision-making essentially secret, but there is little input to it by local or regional bodies in Britain. However, the crucial point is that EC law is binding on Member States. The requirement to conform with it, coupled with the policy goal of uniformity throughout the EC, means that power is taken away from local and non-governmental bodies and given to central bodies. This is clearly true in relation to the first two stages of the regulatory processes identified earlier (the policy-making and objective-setting stages), and it is becoming increasingly true for the third stage (the operational stage of setting individual consents) as well.

Discretion

The amount of discretion is great at all the stages of regulatory decision-making. Parliament rarely sets firm policies and standards in legislation, allowing for these to be defined in delegated legislation or through administrative guidance. For example, in the town and country planning system the nature of central guidance is nowhere dictated in the legislation, but is set out in Government Circulars and Planning Policy Guidance Notes, which may be altered at any time.

At the standard-setting and consent-setting levels the discretion is usually given to the relevant regulatory body. As examples, local planning authorities have the ability to grant or refuse planning permission as they think fit (subject mainly to the Secretary of State's control over policy on appeal), the NRA has discretion over the setting of standards for discharges to water, and HMIP has wide discretion in the definition of 'best available techniques not entailing excessive cost' (BATNEEC).

A similar wide discretion can be seen at the enforcement stage. There are few statutes which lay down duties to enforce the legislation, or which set out statutory factors to take into account, and usually the decision whether to take action is taken by the regulatory body on the basis of practical and political factors which are not mentioned in the legislation. Since many of the most important remedies are administrative remedies which are unavailable to individuals, this discretion is of enormous practical importance. Enforcement is discussed in greater detail in Chapter 6.

Judicial interference is frequently limited by the width of discretions given in legislation. This is best illustrated in the town and country planning legislation, where there is a clear policy of judicial non-intervention in decisions about the weight to be attached to material considerations. A recent reiteration of this policy is shown in *London Residuary Body* v *Lambeth BC* [1990] 2 All ER 309, where the Secretary of State's decision to grant planning permission for office development in London County Hall was held to be unchallengeable by the House of Lords. This was so even though he had accorded overriding weight to the presumption in favour of development where there was nothing else in favour of the development and some grounds against. A different example is the decision in *R* v *Secretary of State for the Environment ex parte Rose Theatre Trust Ltd* [1990] 1 All ER 754, where a decision by the Secretary of State not to make the site and remains of the Rose Theatre a scheduled ancient monument was held to be unchallengeable because of the width of the discretion given in the legislation. There are few cases on the extent of the discretion given to pollution control authorities, but it can be expected that the courts would adopt a similar non-interventionist stance there.

As a result of all these factors, and also the general British preference for variable rather than uniform standards, the British system of environmental control has become characterised by flexibility and lack of uniformity.

Gradualism and reliance on scientific evidence

The place of these ideas as two of the key tenets of British pollution control is emphasised in Department of the Environment Pollution Paper No. 11, *Environmental Standards—The UK Practice*. This very readable document was published in 1975 and is now somewhat out-of-date, but it has great significance in terms of explaining the British approach to pollution control, since it is effectively a justification of that approach in the face of alternatives being put forward within the EC.

The philosophy of gradualism is that pollution controls should be strengthened gradually as economic circumstances, the goodwill of producers and scientific abilities allow. This links very strongly with the related idea that decisions should be taken on the basis of a reliable scientific base, although it should be recognised that science does not necessarily produce facts in the environmental sphere, but estimates of risks or probabilities. There is accordingly always a political factor involved in whether to accept a risk or not (see below).

One major effect of these two ideas has been that environmental controls have tended to be reactive rather than anticipatory. They have rarely been concerned with laying down a framework in advance, leading to the fragmentation of the system and to its lack of uniformity. A more specific effect is that time is normally given for changes to be made in order to give industry time to adjust capital programmes and work methods. In relation to the requirement that best practicable means be used, it has been normal practice to allow any process to continue for its operational life (often 10 years) before declaring it in contravention of the requirement, even though it may have been superseded before then. A similar discretion is provided for in relation to BATNEEC under the EPA 1990, but the time allowed for changes is typically much shorter.

The extended time scale for implementing the 1990 Act (full implementation is not planned until 1996), apart from being a comment on the complexity of the new requirements, is a further example of the gradualist approach. Interestingly, the timetable for the introduction of Part I of the Act was laid down after an undertaking was given in Parliament to do so, and thus avoid a re-run of the non-implementation of the Control of Pollution Act 1974. At the EC level, this approach is also reflected in the time scale allowed for implementation of Directives, which is normally at least two years, and often five years. A final example is that the British have frequently rejected the use of 'technology-forcing' rules. These represent the setting of a rule which is stricter than currently achievable, though with a time scale for its achievement. The theory is that producers will thus be forced to adapt their current technology to meet the requirements. This concept is much used in the USA, but in Britain the potential cost to industry is more frequently used to argue for a gradual change.

The importance of context

In establishing environmental controls, importance is nearly always attached to economic and other factors. As Pollution Paper No. 11 puts it:

The tendency in setting standards in the UK is less to seek an absolute scientific base than to use scientific principles and all relevant and reliable evidence, then to try and progressively reduce emissions in a way that is consistent with economic and technological feasibility and with what at any one time is thought to be an acceptable ultimate objective.

It is difficult to separate the reasons for this policy from its effects. One reason is undoubtedly the historical influence that the town and country planning system, with its explicit requirement to balance all material considerations, has had on the development of the law, but a major reason must relate to the definition of pollution and the objectives of environmental controls.

Pollution has been defined as a relative concept, in the sense that there is no absolute rule about what amounts to pollution. The same applies to other forms of environmental change, such as urban or agricultural development. It is not possible to eradicate pollution, merely to reduce it. It follows that, at some stage, a choice has to be made about what is, and what is not, permissible. This is ultimately a political question, and involves a balancing of various factors. However, there are two possible objectives of pollution control. One is to aim to reduce pollution to 'acceptable' levels. An alternative is to aim to reduce pollution as far as possible. In Britain the first approach is implicitly adopted in relation to most substances. This explains the inevitability of a political balancing process, and also the preference for variable environmental quality standards. The second approach tends to lead to a reduction in discretion and to greater reliance on uniform standards, because if one producer can reduce to a particular level others should be able to do so as well.

The contextual approach accepts, therefore, that there is always going to be a trade-off between environmental protection and other factors, such as cost. This is fundamental to most British environmental controls. For example, it is reflected in the phrase 'best available techniques not entailing excessive cost' (BATNEEC) which is the cornerstone of Part I of the EPA 1990. The best available techniques part of the formula suggests that every step should be taken to protect the environment, but the not entailing excessive cost part qualifies it by reference to economic factors. One of the most interesting features of the interpretation of the 1990 Act is proving to be the way that the balance is being struck in practice between the two parts.

This philosophy of balancing environmental protection with material welfare is apparent in most areas of the law. It explains the wide discretions given to decision-makers, the emphasis on decisions being taken by reference to local factors, and the practice of defining some concepts after consultation with the industry involved. The emphasis on balance also explains such fundamental features of British law as the preference for flexible environmental standards rather than uniform ones, and the flexible and cooperative enforcement strategies that are employed by regulatory agencies.

Are things changing?

As the previous section suggests, a number of things appear to be changing in relation to the traditional British approach to regulation. In particular, there is an increasing tendency for standards to be set centrally (which often goes hand in hand with more uniform standards), and a related tendency for them to be set out more explicitly in legislative instruments or formal policy documents. This has been referred to as 'the new formalism' by Macrory (see 'Environmental Law: Shifting Discretions and the New Formalism' in *Frontiers of Environmental Law*, ed. Lomas, 1991).

A number of examples could be used to illustrate the point. Perhaps the clearest relates to the way that EC standards are imposed through Directives, thus effectively replacing local discretion with central prescription, but there are also examples from domestic legislation. In relation to water pollution, a major change over the next few years will be the setting of statutory water quality objectives by the Secretary of State for stretches of controlled waters. The NRA will be under a duty (under the Water Resources Act 1991, s. 84) to exercise its powers so as to ensure, as far as it is practicable to do so, that the statutory water quality objective is achieved at all times. This will cover, amongst other things, its powers in relation to setting discharge consents and will clearly entail the whole process becoming more open and predictable (see p. 440). A similar process can be seen at work in the town planning requirement (in the Town and Country Planning Act 1990, s. 54A) that decisions are to be made in accordance with the provisions of the development plan, unless material considerations indicate otherwise (see p. 237). A third example can be taken from Part I of the EPA 1990. The very full, clear and precise advice provided in Process Guidance Notes as to the meaning of BATNEEC in relation to each process has in practice reduced the discretion of individual inspectors quite significantly. As a result, the in-built conflict between the two parts of the BATNEEC definition that is referred to above seems to be being decided very much in favour of BAT, particularly as far as local authority air pollution control is concerned. This is because individual inspectors, who have to cope with a very wide range of different processes, are likely to impose the standards in the relevant Process Guidance Notes in full unless the operator can come up with a good reason why they should not.

As well as centralising decisions and reducing discretions, this new formalism also increases the potential role of the courts. It has already been noted how the courts have played a lesser role in the development of environmental policy in this country than in, for example, Germany or the USA. This is probably because of the wider discretions provided in the legislation, which are often unchallengeable. However, the development of more explicit standards, coupled with clear operational duties imposed on the regulatory agencies, means that a greater number of decisions may potentially be challenged through judicial review. A good example is the duty imposed on the NRA under the Water Resources Act 1991, s. 84, referred to above: it is quite possible that this could be used in the future to compel the NRA to adopt a certain course of action. The likelihood of the courts playing an increasing role in the development of environmental law is further increased by recent developments in relation to judicial review and EC law. For example, the concept of the supremacy of EC law has been used to develop various doctrines with the aim of ensuring not only that legislation is passed to implement EC Directives, but also that the laws that are passed are implemented and enforced in practice.

Of course, much of this discussion is only of real relevance to regulatory systems. If, as may be the case in the future, market mechanisms are preferred to regulation, they may represent a force moving in the opposite direction. One of the potential results of deregulation and a shift towards the use of market mechanisms is a decentralisation of decisions from Government to consumers and industry.

There is another general change that can be identified, which is that there is a discernible shift away from reliance on flexible standards based on the impact on the receiving environment towards standards based on the use of the best available techniques. This is seen at its clearest in relation to Part I of the EPA 1990, where the conditions attached to authorisations are set by reference to BATNEEC, but it is also an inevitable by-product of a more centralised and formal system. It also follows from the increased involvement of lenders, insurers and other stakeholders in decisions on environmental management, since they are likely to insist on the use of the best available techniques as a protection against liability or loss of their stake.

Deregulation

This term appears to carry three separate, but overlapping, meanings. One refers to the so-called 'war on red tape', which the Government has pursued over the last few years: in other words, that excessively bureaucratic procedures and practices should be removed or simplified. A second meaning relates to the general disinclination to use regulatory mechanisms unless they are necessary, which often translates into favouring voluntary and market-style mechanisms. A third meaning can be discerned in terms of a policy not to interfere with the operations of business. It is clear that the current Government has carried out deregulatory policies in each of these senses for many years, but since the announcement in 1993 of a 'deregulation initiative' the process has become more formal and has actively involved Government Departments and others searching out examples of perceived over-regulation.

The Deregulation and Contracting Out Act 1994 is the main manifestation of this process. It includes a general power for any Minister to amend or repeal existing legislation by means of a statutory instrument if they are of the opinion that the measure imposes a burden on any trade, business or profession, and that the amendment or repeal will reduce that burden. There are some limited consultation and procedural requirements that temper this very wide power, but it is clear that it could be used in the future to attack a number of environmental protections. In addition, s. 5 of the 1994 Act empowers Ministers to 'improve' various enforcement procedures (a term which includes such things as revocation and variation of a licence, as well as criminal prosecution) by statutory instrument. For example, the Minister may, in relation to any specific enforcement regime, require that a business be notified in advance of any intention to take enforcement action and afforded an opportunity to make representations and be entitled to a written statement explaining why remedial action is being taken. The Act also provides some very vaguely worded provisions allowing Ministers to provide for appeals against enforcement action. Whilst it is arguable that these provisions, if used, would create greater accountability in terms of enforcement decisions taken by regulatory agencies, it is difficult to see how these two new powers remove 'red tape' in the first sense used above, since they appear to impose extra requirements. The real justification behind them appears to be in accordance with the third meaning of deregulation used above.

As yet, none of the powers in the 1994 Act has been used in relation to environmental matters, although some candidates for deregulation have been identified. The real impact of the deregulation initiative on environmental law thus remains to be seen, and is no doubt inextricably bound up with the whole question of the political balance of the current Government and whether it continues in office.

Meanwhile, it has resulted in some limited changes in the Environment Act 1995. Schedule 10 to the Water Resources Act 1991 has been altered so as to reduce the amount of public involvement in the setting of discharge consents. The schedule also extends the period within which consents may not be varied from two years to four. However, somewhat ironically, the other matter in the 1995 Act which could be said to be deregulatory in the first sense used above actually has the effect of increasing environmental protection, since s. 111 repeals the requirement for a tripartite sample in certain legal proceedings, thus making it easier for the NRA to bring prosecutions.

Market mechanisms or the use of economic tools

These rather general phrases are meant to encompass all approaches which seek to use prices or economic incentives and deterrents to achieve environmental objectives. This could be done, for example, by encouraging pricing systems that signal the true environmental costs of products to consumers, thereby making environment-friendly items cheaper than those that pollute or waste natural resources. In a sense, therefore, these economic tools or instruments are the exact opposite of using the free market, since they normally involve an interference or intervention in the free market for the purpose of environmental protection. However, they do involve the use of the market in the sense that they are normally designed to allow consumers and industry to make choices about their actions. By way of contrast, many people would argue that most, though certainly not all, regulatory systems tend to operate so as to remove choice.

There is thus a potential confusion in referring simply to 'using the market' for environmental protection ends, since that runs together the policy of allowing an unrestricted free market to allocate resources on the assumption that that is somehow more efficient, and the separate policy of intervention in the market for protective purposes. As Nicholas Ridley, a devoted free marketeer, wrote in an explanation of the Government's environment policy whilst Secretary of State for the Environment: 'It is an essential part of the free market philosophy that regulation by Government is necessary to secure the public interest in environmental protection' (*Politics Against Pollution: The Conservative Record and Principles,* Centre for Policy Studies, 1989).

Annex A to the White Paper *This Common Inheritance* (Cm. 1200, 1990) discusses a range of different ways in which economic instruments may be used to further environmental protection. These build on five general categories identified by the Organisation for Economic Cooperation and Development, namely, charges, subsidies, deposit or refund schemes, the creation of a market in pollution credits and enforcement incentives. It is accepted in the White Paper that charges and subsidies have constituted the main uses of economic instruments so far. It also becomes clear that some of the mechanisms are self-standing whilst others, such as most charging schemes, require a regulatory framework and proper policing, so they must be seen as additional to, rather than separate from, regulatory systems.

The following types of economic tool or instrument may be used.

(a) Charges for the administrative cost of operating the regulatory system

This now goes under the title of 'cost recovery charging' and has been adopted in relation to a number of regulatory activities. The idea is to recover the regulatory costs that are incurred in granting applications or consents, or in such things as inspecting, monitoring or policing those consents. The current policy is not to charge for the general costs of operating the whole regulatory system, but to limit the charge to the amount which can be referable to each consent or discharge. In the interests of administrative simplicity, the charges are normally arranged in bands, rather than being worked out individually.

For example, in relation to water pollution, a scheme of charging for applications for consent was introduced in October 1990. This was intended to recoup the costs of administering the application procedures for discharge consents. More significantly, annual charges to recover the cost to the NRA of policing any discharges to controlled waters were introduced on 1 July 1991 (see the *Scheme of Charges in Respect of Applications and Consents for Discharges to Controlled Waters*). These are set so as to recoup the costs associated with inspecting and monitoring discharges, not the full cost of monitoring water quality, which will still be paid for by the taxpayer (see p. 437).

Similar schemes were introduced from 1 April 1991 for applications and authorisations for operating a process subject to integrated pollution control (*HMIP Integrated Pollution Control Fees and Charges Scheme (England and Wales)*) and for local authority air pollution control (*Local Enforcing Authorities Air Pollution Fees and Charges Scheme (England and Wales)*). In the Integrated Pollution Control Scheme, the various processes subject to integrated pollution control have been divided into components and a flat rate is payable for each component. This is an attempt to cover the approximate cost to HMIP of granting and monitoring an authorisation. A further scheme has been introduced for waste management licences.

Cost recovery charging systems may be progressive and thus have a beneficial environmental effect. For example, the charging schemes referred to involve higher charges for discharges which cost more to monitor, and these are often those which cause more pollution.

Fees for planning applications were introduced in the early 1980s. At present there are standard fees set according to the size and nature of the proposed development and they do not reflect the full cost to the local planning authority of processing the application, much less the cost of policing the system of planning controls. However, it is proposed to increase these fees over the next few years so that more of the full cost of the system is recovered.

There always has been a rather different system of charging for discharges to sewers. This involves a rate for domestic consumers which is linked to property value, and a variable rate for trade dischargers linked to the volume and strength of the discharge as measured by Chemical Oxygen Demand. This produces a relatively unsophisticated method of charging for the cost of sewage treatment according to the demands made upon the system by the discharge. An incidental effect of concentrating on volume is, however, to reduce the level of water used and the level of waste, and thus to encourage both conservation of resources and recycling.

(b) Charges reflecting the full environmental cost of an activity

The system of charging for sewage discharges shows the potential for use of charging systems which aim to charge for the full environmental cost of an activity. Such systems may be seen as the true environmental or pollution taxes referred to by Pearce, Markandya and Barbier in *Blueprint for a Green Economy*, 1989. The most topical example is the so-called 'carbon tax'. The objective behind this idea is to raise the price of fossil fuels to reflect their true (and hitherto uncosted) environmental effect, thus curtailing their use and reducing the greenhouse effect. There are distinct problems with such an idea. One is obtaining sufficient information about the discharge or process to make the taxes work properly. This would seem to demand a strong regulatory structure to police the system, although self-monitoring methods may have a large part to play in this respect. Another is the problem of obtaining accurate information about environmental effects on which to base the tax levels.

There is no doubt that this is an idea which is going to be greatly used in the future, and the Government has, on a number of occasions, promised to consider it for discharges to 'controlled waters'. However, despite the recommendation of the Royal Commission on Environmental Pollution in its Sixteenth Report, *Freshwater Quality* (Cm. 1966, 1992), that a system of charges reflecting impact on the environment should replace the present system of cost-recovery charges in order to act as an incentive to clean up environmentally harmful discharges, little has yet happened. It is significant that powers to introduce such environmental charges were not included in the Environment Act 1995.

(c)   Charges to finance environmental or pollution control measures

A number of examples may be given here. The NRA may, under the Water Resources Act 1991, s. 161, pass costs incurred in preventing or remedying water pollution back to the person who caused it. The waste regulation authority may recover costs incurred in cleaning up unlawful deposits of waste from the occupier or the person who made the deposit (EPA 1990, s. 59). In relation to statutory nuisances, there are similar clean-up and cost-recovery powers in EPA 1990, s. 81.

Fines levied in court for offences may also be seen as a form of environmental charge. Indeed, given the nature of environmental offences and the limited moral blame often attached to them, many people treat fines as administrative penalties rather than as true criminal sanctions. The typically low level of fines means that their economic effect is limited, though levels are rising steadily, for example, the maximum fine for many environmental offences was raised to £20,000 on summary conviction by the EPA 1990. In the Crown Court, Shell (UK) was fined £1m for polluting the River Mersey, in addition to which it paid a reported £6m in clean-up and other costs. However, at present there is no way of ensuring that fines are actually used for the benefit of the environment or that part of it which is damaged. One interesting development in this respect is the decision in *Herbert* v *Lambeth LBC* [1992] LG Rev 421, that a compensation order may be made under the Powers of Criminal Courts Act 1973, s. 35, where damage has been caused by a statutory nuisance.

Civil law remedies may also be seen as achieving the same objectives. Many statutes now include civil liability for damage to people or their property, and the creation of a remedy of breach of statutory duty may act as a potent method of reallocating costs. The drawback at present is that few civil actions recognise fully the costs involved in environmental damage. The law has never developed any concept of 'environmental rights', with the result that the only possible civil law claimants are people with private rights. Put more simply, animals, birds and plants do not have civil law rights. However, the draft EC Directive on Civil Liability for Damage Caused by Waste (COM (91) 219 final) introduces the concept of 'impairment of the environment' and provides that any plaintiff should be entitled to recover for costs incurred in preventing or remedying harm to the environment (in addition to damages for injury to persons or property), as well as obtaining injunctive remedies. This may signal a new development of environmental rights.

(d)   Charges levied on polluting materials or processes

Instead of a charge being levied on the results of pollution, it could be levied on a process or a product. The best example is the landfill tax that was announced by the Chancellor of the Exchequer in November 1994 and which it is intended to introduce in October 1996. The idea is that a tax will be payable on all waste that is disposed of to landfill. It is then anticipated that the amount of the tax will be passed back by the operators of the landfill site to the originators of the waste, thus increasing the cost of landfill and acting as an incentive to reduce the amount of waste produced. The potency of the incentive will relate to the level of the tax. Originally, it was proposed by the Government that the tax should be based on the value of the waste, but it was pointed out by many commentators that this may lead to cost-sensitive producers of waste sending it to cheaper sites, which are likely to be precisely those sites where environmental standards are lowest, and lead to undesirable transportation of wastes in an attempt to find a cheaper site. It has now been announced that the tax will be based on the weight of the waste, with inert wastes (such as demolition wastes) subject to a lower rate to reflect their lesser environmental impact. It is also proposed that landfill operators will be able to obtain rebates from the tax by setting up environmental trusts which promote sustainable waste management practices.

The proposed tax is somewhat of a breakthrough since, although it has been appreciated for some time that taxes could be used to combat pollution and contamination problems, little has been achieved. However, the Treasury has always vigorously opposed any attempt to earmark taxes and charges for specific spending purposes (a process known as 'hypothecation') and, without that, a subsidiary aim of environmental taxes, which is that they should be linked directly to environmental spending, will not be achieved. For example, the proceeds from the landfill tax could be used to fund the clean-up of 'orphaned' closed landfill sites (i.e. those where the original operator cannot be found or does not have the resources to afford the clean-up), although the proposed environmental trust funds may also be used in the same way. Nevertheless, the introduction of a landfill tax may well herald a faster development of environmental taxes in the future.

An alternative is that a charge may be reduced for relatively environment-friendly activities. The most obvious example is the reduced tax payable on unleaded petrol compared with leaded petrol. This has led to a significant rise in the use of unleaded petrol over the last few years. A further example is the EPA 1990, s. 52, which introduced the concept of waste recycling credits for authorities or others who retain waste for the purpose of recycling it.

(e) Subsidies and grants

These are commonly used for environmental ends, although their use within the EC is restricted by the rules on illegal state aids. For example, subsidies are available for the construction of facilities for the improvement of the treatment of agricultural water and silage effluent—both particularly potent, and increasingly common, causes of pollution. Care has to be taken that the subsidies achieve the result intended. Some subsidies on forestry and agriculture, for example, have been accused of having detrimental environmental effects because of their inability to select between beneficial and non-beneficial projects.

Compensation payments for environmentally sensitive activities may also be seen in this category. The prevailing policy in relation to countryside protection has tended to be one of voluntariness, whereby farmers and landowners are compensated for agreeing to forgo certain advantages in the interests of the environment. Sometimes this is through the payment of direct compensation and sometimes through the negotiation of management agreements. For example, management agreements may be agreed in relation to the protection of national nature reserves or sites of special scientific interest, and similar methods are being used in other designated areas such as environmentally sensitive areas and nitrate sensitive areas.

(f)   The creation of a market in pollution credits
A further instrument is the use of tradeable quotas, or emissions trading. These are methods of creating a market in the right to pollute. For example, a total for emissions of a specified substance may be set for a particular area. Firms may then bid for the right to take up a part of that total. Prospective or new polluters would have to buy the rights of existing holders if there was no spare capacity. By restricting the available emissions, prices would be driven up, providing an incentive to reduce emissions or to develop alternatives.

The idea is most developed in the USA, but the groundwork for its use in Britain is laid in the EPA 1990, s. 3(5), which allows the Secretary of State to establish total emissions of any substance either nationally or for a limited area, and to allocate quotas, with power progressively to reduce the total allowed. This idea is designed for use in relation to the commitment to cut carbon dioxide emissions by specified dates (currently the EC commitment is to stabilise emissions at 1990 levels by 2000), as agreed internationally as a method of combating global warming. Once again, a regulatory structure would be needed to police the system.

(g)   Deposit and refund schemes
Although deposit and refund schemes are clearly severe interferences with a free market, it is also clear that they may have an enormous impact on the amount of waste produced. The current Government favours voluntary mechanisms here, rather than ones imposed by law, and seeks to get them introduced by the industries concerned. By way of example, the British Government intervened in the *Danish Bottles case* (*Commission* v *Denmark* [1989] 54 CMLR 619) in the European Court of Justice, supporting the EC Commission's argument that a Danish law requiring drinks containers to be returnable was contrary to the free market principles of the EC. The Court of Justice upheld most of the Danish scheme despite its clear anti-competitive effect, on the grounds that the aim of environmental protection justified some interference with the operation of the single internal market within the EC.

Future uses of economic instruments

The above summary is not intended to be an exhaustive list of those mechanisms which might be tried, or even of those which are already in use, but to give an idea of the type of instrument that may be available. As stated before, there is little doubt that market-related instruments will increasingly be used in the future. Indeed, they could currently be said to be 'flavour of the month' as far as environmental regulation is concerned.

One reason for this is undoubtedly that market mechanisms appeal to the political philosophy of the current Government. There is a strong link with the principle of choice, the idea that people should be given a choice of how to act, as long as their actions do not breach some generally accepted limits. This idea is seen most strongly in the realm of town and country planning where the importance attached to market forces is made explicit in much of Central Government policy advice. The principle is also seen in relation to such things as the adoption of voluntary methods of protection in the countryside (see p. 477) and the preference for pollution control systems which set objectives whilst leaving producers to work out for themselves how to achieve them. There is also a strong link with the related policy of deregulation pursued throughout the 1980s and 1990s and explained in White Papers such as *Lifting the Burden* (Cmnd 9571, 1985) and *Building Businesses, Not Barriers* (Cmnd 9794, 1986). Amongst other things, this policy amounts to a rejection of imposed restrictions in favour of agreed ones and a removal of unnecessary state powers.

Within the EC, the Commission has also suggested a shift in EC environmental policy towards the greater use of economic instruments rather than the administrative regulation approach. Appropriately enough, this suggestion was originally linked to the EC-wide system of environment-friendly labelling for goods, recognising that in order for any of these market-based methods to work there needs to be accurate information available to consumers and regulators. It is significant that EC action has been concentrated in this area in the 1990s. For example, 1990 saw the agreement of Directive 90/313 on Freedom of Access to Information on the Environment and Regulation 1210/90 on the establishment of the European Environment Agency, which will initially have a role in acquiring and disseminating information about the state of the environment in the EC.

The polluter pays principle

The EC can claim another important contribution to the development of economic instruments; its environmental policy has always included the adoption of the 'polluter pays' principle, although it was probably the Organisation for Economic Cooperation and Development (OECD) which first popularised the idea in the early 1970s (see OECD, *The Polluter Pays Principle*, 1975). The principle basically means that the producer of goods or other items should be responsible for the costs of preventing or dealing with any pollution which the process causes. This includes environmental costs as well as direct costs to people or property. It also covers costs incurred in avoiding pollution, and not just those related to remedying any damage. There is a very strong link between the principle and the idea that prevention is better than cure. It will also be clear from the foregoing discussion that these costs should include the full environmental costs, not just those which are immediately tangible.

The relevance of this principle to the discussion of economic instruments is obvious, since a producer will have to pass on any costs in the price of goods to the ultimate consumer. However, this is only a principle, it has no legal force and there is no agreed definition that has anything approaching the precision of a statute. On the contrary, there has frequently been dispute over its exact scope, especially over the limits on payments for damage caused. It is essentially a guide to desirable courses of action, but it is fairly clear that it has rarely been fully satisfied in either EC or British environmental legislation.

As a result the principle has sometimes seemed to be all things to all people, and has even been used to justify views with which it has little connection, for example the suggestion that producers may pollute as long as they pay for it. That is a complete misunderstanding of the principle's true meaning, and the potential abuse of such an imprecise phrase should be appreciated.

Eco-auditing and environmental management systems

Within the context of economic instruments, it is appropriate to consider briefly the development of environmental management systems and environmental auditing, a rare area where Britain can claim to lead the world in the development of an environmental concept. Many firms are now tackling the increased pressures and potential liabilities imposed by environmental law by adopting some form of environmental management system. Indeed, it is likely that compliance with a recognised system will soon become a requirement of the purchasing policies of some major purchasers, or be required by a firm's lenders or insurers. Some form of environmental reporting in company accounts is also likely to be required in the future.

There are two main systems currently being put forward, though there are other industry-based systems as well:

(a) The British Standards Institute has developed a British Standard 7750 on Environmental Management Systems, which was launched in 1994 following a pilot programme. BS 7750 is a voluntary system in the sense that a firm can choose whether to adopt it or not. It is based on a quality management approach similar to BS 5750 on Quality Management, with the result that no specific levels of environmental performance are stipulated, the setting of the firm's environmental objectives being a matter for the firm itself. However, the firm must have a publicly available environmental policy, which must include at a minimum a commitment to meeting legal standards and a commitment to improved environmental performance. Having established an environmental policy, the firm should carry out an initial review of its position, including the compilation of a register of relevant legislation and policy requirements and a separate register of environmental effects. It should then set environmental objectives and targets, establish a management programme so that these targets can be met, and set up the appropriate operational controls and records systems. Finally, the company should audit its activities to check conformity with the programme, and review the policy and objectives in the light of that audit.

(b) EC Regulation 1836/93 on Eco-Management and Audit came into force in April 1995, having been agreed in 1993. Since a Regulation is directly applicable in Member States, it will become part of British law automatically without the need for implementing legislation and will thus lay down a uniform EC-wide system.

The objectives of the EC Eco-Management and Audit Scheme (EMAS) are similar to those behind BS 7750, in that they are to promote improvements in industry's environmental performance by the establishment and implementation of environmental management systems by companies, and the systematic, objective and periodic evaluation of the environmental performance of these systems. One area where the EC Regulation goes further than BS 7750 is in requiring the provision of information on a firm's environmental performance to the public. For example, an environmental statement, which must include such things as a summary of the relevant figures on pollutant emissions, waste generation, raw material usage and energy and water consumption, must be published every year. This statement has to be validated by an independent, accredited verifier, who will also verify the company's policy, objectives and audit programme for conformity with the Regulation.

Mention should also be made of eco-labelling. There is an EC Regulation on the subject (880/92), which was implemented in Britain through the establishment of an Eco-labelling Board in November 1992. The essence of the scheme is that criteria are developed to enable the environmental impact of a product to be analysed by taking into account the whole of its life cycle. Criteria are currently being developed for a limited range of products, with the intention that a proportion of the products within the range can be awarded an eco-label. Despite delays caused by methodological problems, the first eco-labels for washing machines and a small range of other products have now been agreed.

The civil law as a tool for environmental protection

The detailed role of the civil law is considered in Chapter 8. However, as pointed out in the section on charges (see p. 110), the civil law can be seen as a form of market mechanism, so it is worth making a few general comments about civil liability in this chapter. There is little doubt that the last few years have seen a great increase in interest in the use that can be made of civil law mechanisms—by policy-makers as well as by lawyers. Recognising that civil liability appears to fit in well with the basic principles of EC environmental policy, such as the polluter pays principle, the EC issued a Green Paper on civil liability in 1993 entitled *Remedying Environmental Damage* (COM(93)47 final). This comes down generally in favour of the development of regimes based on strict liability, where causation rather than fault would be the dominant factor behind a finding of liability. Where no liability could be shown, or where the person liable has gone bankrupt or is untraceable, some form of fund paid for by relevant industries or activities would be established to compensate plaintiffs. One unresolved issue relates to whether all activities should be subject to strict liability, or whether it should be limited (as it has generally been in Britain) to specific, more hazardous activities. The proposed EC Directive on Civil Liability for Damage Caused by Waste envisages a wide-ranging liability for all waste, whilst the Council of Europe Convention on Civil Liability for Damage Resulting from Activities Dangerous to the Environment, 1993, as its name suggests, proposes strict liability for only a limited range of activities.

The imposition of civil liability has other effects as well as simply sorting out the question of liability for specific incidents. It acts as an incentive to act in a particular way, because of the high possible risks. In so doing, it fulfils the precautionary principle and fits in well with the current EC emphasis on shared responsibility, since producers will act so as to reduce and manage risks themselves. It thus acts as a stimulus to integrate risk management principles into all levels of business decision-making, as there is little doubt that the threat of civil action is a potent one, especially in an age when insurance against such risks is hard to obtain.

The criminal law as a tool for environmental protection

The criminal law can be used either to provide direct criminal sanctions for environmental harm, or in a subsidiary and complementary role within a regulatory system. It tends to be of greater use in the second way. This is because the main purpose of the criminal law is to punish clearly identified wrongs. Yet, in relation to many environmental matters, it is often impossible to identify wrong without reference to other factors. For example, it is clearly desirable to have industry and many other activities which may cause pollution. The question is not a simple one of whether to have them, but a more difficult one of how much pollution is acceptable (see also the definition of pollution on p. 22). That requires a balancing of the various factors involved against what is reasonable—a discretionary, political process, for which the regulatory system is well-suited. The criminal law is rather inadequate for such a balancing process, and thus tends to be used mainly to deal either with clear acts of environmental vandalism, or to support the regulatory system once it has decided what is and what is not acceptable.

There are a number of examples of offences which stem directly from environmental harm. Under the EPA 1990, s. 87, it is an offence to drop or deposit litter in a public or other specified place. In the Water Resources Act 1991, s. 85, there is a general offence of causing or knowingly permitting any poisonous, noxious or polluting matter to enter controlled waters. It is not always necessary to show actual harm to the environment: in some cases an activity may be prohibited because harm can be assumed to follow or because the risk of harm is too great to take. For example, under the Clean Air Act 1993 it is an offence to emit dark smoke from premises.

However, even in these cases, enforcement is often left to a public body. One reason for this is practical, given the difficulty in some situations of identifying and proving environmental harm. Another reason is that the right of prosecution has often been restricted in English law. This is becoming less common, but a good example is the restriction in relation to water pollution.

Under the Rivers (Prevention of Pollution) Acts 1951 and 1961, which established a system of consents for discharges to water for the first time and also a general pollution offence in similar terms to the Water Resources Act 1991, s. 85, it was provided that a prosecution could only be brought by a water authority, or with the consent of the Attorney-General. This restriction was removed by the Control of Pollution Act 1974, with the result that there is now a right of private prosecution for all the basic water pollution offences.

A third reason for enforcement being left to public bodies is the lack of available public information relating to pollution. Under the Rivers (Prevention of Pollution) Acts, there was no public register of consents, samples taken of water quality, or samples taken of discharges; indeed it was an offence for water authority officers to disclose such information gained in the course of their duties. Under the Control of Pollution Act 1974, a system of public registers was first established, which is starting to remove the secrecy of earlier years. Similar limitations on private prosecution and access to information have been present in most areas of environmental law over the years.

The most frequent use of the criminal law is therefore in a subsidiary capacity to administrative controls (i.e. to the regulatory system). Many criminal offences consist not of committing a direct act of pollution, but instead of ignoring the dictates of the regulatory body. Under the Water Resources Act 1991, s. 85, it is a criminal offence to discharge trade or sewage effluent without, or in breach of, a consent from the NRA. In relation to town and country planning, the offence consists not of breaching planning control but of ignoring an enforcement notice. This makes the criminal offence truly subsidiary to the regulatory process, since only the local planning authority may issue an enforcement notice, thus taking the possibility of enforcement away from the public.

All of these matters have an effect in decriminalising the law. The offence is not directly linked to the environmental harm, but to an administrative process. Enforcement is normally by an administrative body and often for breach of an administrative requirement. The message that is given is that these things are truly related to administrative processes rather than the criminal law. In addition, the low sentences that are imposed (sometimes because only low sentences are available), the marked reluctance to prosecute, the limited amount of moral censure that has traditionally been attached to environmental offences, the lowly status of many who are selected for prosecution and the escape of many major industrial polluters from prosecution (all factors which are discussed elsewhere in this book) tend to emphasise the decriminalisation of the laws. Once again, however, there is no doubt that things are changing very rapidly as a result of changes in the perception of the general public. One development in the future may well be the making of an overt distinction between 'administrative' offences against the regulatory system and true environmental offences, with higher personal penalties being available in the latter category.

SIX

The enforcement of environmental law

The British approach to enforcement

Essentially, enforcement is carried out by regulatory bodies. Although there are supplementary powers available to those with private rights under the common law, there are inherent disadvantages in relying upon extra-statutory powers to control the protection of the environment (see Chapter 8).

The identity of the enforcement model exercised by those regulatory bodies is strongly underscored by the themes which dominate Part I of this book. For instance, flexibility in both the setting of standards and the methodology of pollution abatement, use of non-statutory 'guidance' to control emission standards, large degrees of open texture within statutory definitions to enable enforcement bodies to utilise discretionary powers and the reliance upon self-policing based upon the mutual self-interest of industrialists and enforcement officers are characteristic of the British approach to enforcement.

It is possible to identify two different models which are utilised in the enforcement process: first, the cooperative (or conciliatory) model and, secondly, the confrontational approach. The cooperative approach is characterised by the development of a continuing relationship between enforcer and polluter. Thus, mutual respect and trust develop which can be utilised to ensure that there is compliance with a system of law, or, in the case of environmental protection, of quality standards. The confrontational approach involves the penalising of activities. At its extreme, such an approach can result in the punishment of every breach.

The nature of enforcement mechanisms in environmental protection

Regulatory enforcement is concerned with the use of tools or mechanisms to achieve an objective. It is not *only* concerned with punishment but also with bringing about compliance.

At one end of the enforcement spectrum, powers of prosecution enable regulatory bodies to punish one-off incidents, but the use of the criminal sanction is only one in a variety of mechanisms used to control activities. Formal statutory/ regulatory enforcement tools are also available. For instance, the EPA 1990 contains provisions which allow for authorisations to be varied or revoked and for activities to be prohibited or to be subject to enforcement procedures without any reference to the criminal courts.

Furthermore, there are 'informal' tools. The word 'informal' here does not necessarily indicate that such controls are not serious. There are stages in all enforcement procedures which can be identified as being the 'last warning' or penultimate step before 'formal' action. These are not formal sanctions in the true sense. For example, the service of an abatement notice or a notice for the requisition of ownership details under the Town and Country Planning Act 1990 are 'formal' steps which can lead to prosecution although there is no element of punishment explicit in such action when taken in isolation.

Further down the severity scale of regulatory enforcement lie such informal mechanisms as threats or an increased number of visits from an enforcement officer. Such tools will be used at an initial stage in an enforcement procedure, but do not constitute sanctions.

Lastly, there are informal problem-solving mechanisms. The idea that the regulatory bodies can be viewed as consultants or educators underpins the cooperative approach so prevalent in Britain.

Throughout any discussion of the legal context of the practical enforcement of pollution control, it must be borne in mind that those bodies who regulate activities often do so with an 'active' discretion; that is to say a discretion which actually defines the limits of what is permissible in any case. Such an approach is clearly evidenced by the use of non-statutory guidance notes to set emission standards. Moreover, there is further discretion over and above this 'active' discretion; when enforcement bodies decide whether or not to seek a sanction for the breach of these standards.

The legal context

The vast majority of pollution offences are defined as offences of strict liability. That is to say there does not need to be proof of any negligence or fault on behalf of the defendant/offender for liability to attach. Indeed, most pollution offences tend to be accidental in the sense that there is no premeditation on behalf of the person responsible. However, with offences of strict liability, theoretically every breach should amount to an offence as there is no element of fault, the absence of which can be offered as a defence. Nevertheless, when the figures are examined, the incidence of prosecution for environmental pollution offences is remarkably low. By way of example the South-West and Southern Water Authorities brought no prosecutions for water pollution offences in 1988 and 1989. Other authorities were also relatively reluctant to prosecute. This should be viewed against a background where figures show that in certain areas as few as 35% of discharges of trade effluents are made at levels which are in compliance with their consents. Thus, there is an apparent dichotomy between the theory of strict liability and the exercise of the discretion as to enforcement. How has this situation arisen?

The pollution control system in Britain has all the characteristics of an administrative and bureaucratic regulatory system. Within the wider definition of regulatory systems it falls into the same class as many other analogous systems, including the system of the criminal law.

However, one of the major differences between the regulatory system of pollution control and the criminal regulatory system is that the central aim of the pollution system is to *prevent* harm to the environment and/or human health rather than to detect and then punish harm. Often, under environmental legislation, enforcement agencies utilise regulations to control continuing activity rather than to penalise single offences. The basis of this mechanism of control is the fostering of an ongoing relationship between the enforcers and those who pollute. By encouraging the use of a system which controls activities rather than punishes, this relationship is cultivated.

This relationship can only exist because of the wide amount of discretion used in interpreting regulations; this allows 'technically' guilty offenders in breach of regulations to avoid liability. The methods that the enforcement authorities use are largely peculiar to the pollution control system. The enforcement agencies will normally carry out specific statutory enforcement activities only when there is a belief (on behalf of the individual officer of the agency concerned) that the continuing relationship between the enforcers and the polluters is being ignored. The breakdown is characterised by an increasing unpleasantness and a move away from a cooperative approach for as long as an unauthorised activity is carried on.

There have been three studies carried out examining the activities of enforcement bodies in England. The first and second, *Environment and Enforcement* (Hawkins) and *Policing Pollution* (Richardson, Ogus & Burrows) investigated the enforcement mechanisms utilised under the old-style water authorities. The third, *The Reasonable Arm of the Law* (Hutter) looked at the role of local authority environmental health officers. By questioning officers at length about their attitudes to enforcement in relation to both 'offenders' and the offence itself, all three studies provide an in-depth study of the themes of environmental enforcement. Further studies carried out in Scotland gave similar findings (see Watchman, Barker and Rowan-Robinson 'River Pollution: A Case for a Pragmatic Approach to Enforcement' [1988] JPL 764).

The evidence presented in these three studies demonstrates that the enforcement agencies often walk a tight-rope between a co-operative approach and the effective enforcement of environmental legislation. *Policing Pollution* indicated that out in the 'real world' of environmental enforcement the final sanction of prosecution for the breach of a regulation was very rarely used. In the study it was shown that officers believed that prosecutions tended to upset offenders to such an extent that any co-operation or continuing relationship built up between the two parties was quickly and effectively demolished. Moreover, officers tended to utilise a quasi-enforcement system based upon 'informal' mechanisms of enforcement as perceived by individual officers rather than as provided for in regulations.

It was shown that prosecution was used only in approximately 10 cases out of every 3,000 breaches of the trade effluent discharge consent system. These statistics raised an obvious question—why was there such a reluctance to prosecute on behalf of the enforcement authorities?

The attitude towards the offence

One of the main reasons for encouraging a co-operative, continuing relationship rather than a confrontational approach is the moral ambivalence surrounding regulatory offences. For a long time pollution offences were regarded as morally neutral. Research suggested that although the enforcement agencies were enforcing the same standards for all polluters they were not necessarily concerned with the standards themselves. Instead they tended to look at the intent behind the act of pollution.

The discretion used in enforcing the strict regulations were identified as being within a 'doughnut-ring' of decision-making. Enforcement officers used this discretion to attach moral blame to a particular incident by altering the level of a particular sanction involved with the moral opprobrium which they felt towards the activity. This was one explanation of the extremely low prosecution rate, as the enforcing authorities were reluctant to use the ultimate sanction of prosecution unless the level of moral blame was at the top end of the scale, which could be equated with gross criminal negligence or actual intent on behalf of the offender. Most accidents were and are not viewed as being morally offensive as 'they could have happened to anyone'. Secondly, the enforcement agencies tended to have grave doubts about the level of criminal penalties involved for breach of the regulatory system. The fines were notoriously low and therefore were not always seen as an effective sanction when compared to the profits which were often generated from the polluting activities. Additionally, the low level of punishment tended to reinforce the view that it was not only the enforcers who had morally ambivalent views of the offence, but the judiciary as well.

Moreover, the typical attitude to 'white collar crimes' suggested that offences committed as a result of industrial activity were less heinous than normal offences. It was often said that pollution was a natural consequence of industrial activity which also created jobs. For the balance to be weighted in favour of protecting against harm to the environment therefore, the need to protect had to outweigh significantly the utility of the process in creating jobs.

Traditionally, those who have polluted have been of a high status in society and those affected by pollution of low status. Pollution was more commonplace in working-class areas of high industrial activity. Indeed, many of those living in the area were working in the factory which was polluting the area. It was often seen as a way of life rather than a matter for complaint.

Commentators have also identified the existence of the so-called capture theory in the relationship between the polluters and enforcement agencies. The capture theory testifies to the belief that large corporations (as the traditional polluters) have a large degree of control over the enforcers by using the traditional power-relationship model. Thus, the smaller enforcement agencies are traditionally in awe of the larger powerful corporations who not only are worth many millions of pounds but also have tremendous influence.

Attitudes towards the offender

The attitude towards the offender was not necessarily based upon the actual cause of the pollution incident but what the enforcement agencies believed to be the cause of the pollution incident. Research has shown that where there were problems with trade effluent discharges, offenders were far more likely to be prosecuted if they made their relationship with the enforcement agency more difficult. The reverse was also true: if the offender had a good relationship with the enforcement agency then it was less likely that a prosecution would ensue. This brought an element of 'just deserts' into the enforcement process; moral blame was more likely to attach to an offender where previous warnings had been given of a particular danger. The work of the enforcement agencies was technically and scientifically based rather than based on the sanctions available under the law. They had perceived that their relationship with the offender was designed to help to achieve a particular solution rather than enforcing the regulations by the letter of the law. Co-operation with the polluters to achieve a better quality environment rather than confrontation was always seen to be their objective.

Enforcement agencies tended to view offenders in three different groups:

(a)   Business firms seen as amoral calculators. The view of the enforcement agencies was that certain businesses are motivated entirely by profit and would disobey the law when they calculated that it was in their interest to do so. The enforcement agencies tended to view this type of operation with considerable disdain and were far more likely to want to prosecute every breach.

(b)   Firms seen as political citizens. The operators of these businesses were perceived as going about their business properly and any breach of the regulation was likely to be on the basis that the operators felt that the regulation was unreasonable and was requiring them to carry out actions which were unnecessary in a purely commercial sense.

(c)   Firms seen as organisationally incompetent. These firms could be characterised as ignorant and beset by organisational difficulties rather than possessing any particular moral attitude. In practice, non-compliance by them was perceived by the enforcement agencies as bad housekeeping derived from a lack of understanding or a lack of responsibility on behalf of the individuals in charge of industrial processes. Enforcement agencies were unwilling to identify such firms as amoral calculators because of their perception of the individuals within them.

In the last type of case, the enforcement agencies utilised a cooperative approach which gave them the role of educator/consultant rather than policeman. Another underlying reason or justification for this co-operative approach was shown perversely in the enforcement agencies' attitude to those who they viewed as being amoral calculators. It has been said that where an amoral calculator is identified it was quite clear that they would enforce the regulations strongly and severe punishment would result. However, it was argued that the understaffing of the enforcement agencies meant that prosecutions in all cases of breach would be impossible and therefore it was imperative that the co-operative approach be taken. It was felt that industry could 'pull out the plug' if a confrontational approach were taken. Indeed, one officer was quoted as saying 'if we lose co-operation we lose control'. Thus, the need for co-operation was mutual.

The use of sanctions other than prosecution

As the regulatory system of pollution control was and is concerned with the continuing prevention of harm, the availability of sanctions other than prosecution could be considered to be an influential factor in deciding whether or not to prosecute.

Many contraventions are of a chronic nature rather than an acute, one-off accident. In such circumstances, the use of non-criminal sanctions may be more appropriate. Variation and enforcement notices etc. permit a continuation of the co-operational approach as they allow for a remedy without any explicit punishment. As such, they offer an opportunity for a greater flexibility for negotiation and co-operation. However, where there is a one-off pollution incident the use of such sanctions is limited.

Even where non-criminal sanctions are used there is still scope to punish the unco-operative offender as most of the non-criminal sanctions have as their ultimate step the prosecution for breach.

The process of enforcement

Having examined some of the attitudes that the enforcement agencies have towards both the offender and the offence, how do they translate these attitudes into the process of enforcement?

In *Policing Pollution*, Richardson suggested that there was often a pattern of enforcement which was adopted by the old-style water authorities to underpin the co-operational approach. A six-fold process was identified:

    (a)   presenting the problem;
    (b)   problem solving;
    (c)   presence;
    (d)   threats;
    (e)   taking a legal sample;
    (f)   prosecution.

(a) Presenting the problem

The first stage in the process of enforcement was identified as the setting up of a reasonable image of the enforcers. The idea being that they wished to present themselves as reasonable people making reasonable demands.

This was achieved by appearing authoritative and stating the problems that a company faced. This approach was strongly linked to the view of the firm as a political citizen. By appearing authoritative but reasonable it was hoped that a solid base could be established on which to build a relationship of mutual trust.

(b) Problem solving

After a problem had been presented, the next phase of this quasi-enforcement system involved an investigation to find a reasonable solution. Sometimes, in complicated cases, the attempt to find a solution using the co-operational method obscured the fact that standards were being breached. There was often a perception amongst enforcement bodies that where a problem was complex then it was only to be expected that there would be a failure to attain the required standard.

(c) Presence

Policing Pollution suggested that not all traders responded to these first two steps in the enforcement process. If there was little effort made to co-operate, enforcement officers would become more assertive. This attitude was founded upon a belief that the longer an offender failed to comply, the more likely it was that the business could be identified as an amoral calculator. Consequently, it was less important to follow a strategy of co-operation because a greater degree of moral blame could attach to the offender. In an attempt to increase the severity of the pressure upon an offender, the next 'step' in this process was an increase in presence. Any offender persisting in non-compliance was visited regularly and constant check-ups were made. This was hoped to have the effect that 'big brother was watching' and firms would recognise the futility of continuing to confront the enforcement agencies.

(d) Threats

Although a heightened degree of presence carried with it an implied threat, continuing non-compliance often resulted in explicit threats. Even here, there were grades of threatening behaviour. For example, at one end of the spectrum there were verbal warnings, whereas at the other formal letters on headed notepaper signed by the Chief Inspector/Head of Committee/Chief Executive etc. Throughout this process, officers could also assure themselves of the reasonableness of their actions, which reinforced their view that they were still attempting to seek compliance rather than punishment.

(e) Taking a legal sample

The penultimate step before prosecution was the taking of a formal legal sample. Such samples form the essential evidence on which a prosecution can be founded. Indeed, in the case of the Water Resources Act 1991, such a sample has to be taken to be admissible. This was seen to be a very serious step and one which was not taken lightly. As a serious step, officers were wary of utilising such powers regularly. As a 'last chance' mechanism, the value of such a procedure would be lost if samples were taken regularly without any consequential prosecution in the case of continuing non-compliance. Although the nature of the formal sample procedures will be abolished under the Environment Act 1995, the formal step of 'taking a sample' could still continue.

(f)   The prosecution

Within the system of enforcement for water pollution the final step was and is prosecution. *Policing Pollution and The Reasonable Arm of the Law* indicated that there were no particular objective factors which determined the incidence of prosecution. Thus, it made little difference that one area was heavily populated and another more rural, or one industrialised and another residential. Even within regions figures varied.

Although these steps of enforcement characterised the water authorities' operations prior to privatisation under the Water Act 1989, other enforcement agencies have also been identified as using a similar framework. Indeed, in *The Reasonable Arm of the Law,* Hutter puts it thus:

> 'Enforcing the law' to an environmental health officer means securing compliance with the law through persuasion and advice, rather than the apprehension and subsequent punishment of offenders. The law is regarded as a means to an end rather than an end in itself and officers consider themselves to be delivering a service both to the local community—by promoting and maintaining a required standard of public health—and, in some respects, to the regulated—by advising them on how best to attain these standards, rather than being members of an 'industrial police force'.

This methodology of compliance rather than sanction is unusual in that, in a heavily regulated system, those outside the enforcement agencies would assume that the regulations are being enforced properly. What effects does this have?

Lack of public confidence in the enforcement system

The public are often the main source of primary information regarding pollution incidents. Enforcement agencies are often understaffed and overworked. Not all pollution occurs between 9.00 am and 5.00 pm and certainly not when an officer happens to be on site. Many prosecutions are instigated by vigilant members of the public.

Often third parties are viewed with mistrust by both enforcers and polluters. Complaints from the public can put a co-operational relationship in jeopardy. The enforcers are faced with a dilemma, should they proceed against an activity to the detriment of the trust built up or should they continue to seek the co-operation of an offender but risk the wrath of a disappointed third party?

An argument has been put forward by Hawkins that the enforcement bodies often choose a third way. In *Environment and Enforcement* he suggests that selective enforcement *enhances* the public's view of the enforcers. By choosing 'high profile' cases the agencies could attempt to draw attention to their own effectiveness:

> A policy of fuller enforcement expressed in a swelling prosecution rate cannot be employed as an indicator of efficiency, for in an environment of ambivalence this risks being treated as evidence of agency harassment. It is rather in the careful and sparing selection of cases for prosecution that the agency is best able to protect its own interest by showing that 'something is being done'.

However, the Tenth Report of the Royal Commission of Environmental Pollution quoted a poll commissioned by the EC which found that 93% of interviewees agreed with the proposition that stronger measures should be taken to protect the environment against pollution. This led later on in the Report to the comment that 'The success of our regulatory authorities needs to be judged on their performance rather than their methods'. This reiterated their finding in the Sixth Report in 1976 that the public lacked confidence in the Industrial Air Pollution Inspectorate because there was a view that the interests of the Inspectorate were too closely linked with those of industry. The point being made stressed the public's misunderstanding of the conciliatory approach. In traditional regulatory systems, there may be a degree of discretion, but this would normally stem from a desire to police effectively by means of not over-loading the system. It is difficult for the public to understand that using a conciliatory approach is, by its very nature, helping to secure compliance.

The close links between industry and their enforcers can be directly attributed to this non-confrontational approach. In an era of increasing environmental awareness the public need to *see* that the law is being used effectively. It is difficult to explain to a member of the public that the co-operational strategy will secure environmental quality improvements where a company is clearly breaking the law. Actual proof of the breach of a regulation would normally result in enforcement and thus the public perceive that the enforcement of statutory regulations in the environmental field is not a worthwhile process.

Differing levels of enforcement

One of the findings of the different research projects carried out in the 1980s was that there were various levels of enforcement in different geographical locations. For instance, in *Policing Pollution*, it was shown that in a three-year period 48 prosecutions were brought by a 'northern water authority' for the contravention of trade effluent consents. In a 'southern water authority' not a single prosecution was brought over the same period. Indeed, officers within that authority only had 'a very hazy impression of the prescribed route that the decision [about whether to proceed with the prosecution] would take'. Secondly, the figures for the northern water authority for prosecution stemmed mainly (some 90%) from one division of that authority.

This lack of uniformity could be a consequence of the 'doughnut-ring' model of decision-making. Many different factors need to be taken into account when considering whether or not to bring enforcement action, and clearly within one authority more factors would preclude a prosecution than promote it. Put another way, the many different factors, including the personalities of the officers themselves, alter the width of the 'doughnut-ring' when deciding whether or not to prosecute. The wider the discretion, the more uncertain a system becomes.

The counterbalance to discretion is certainty, and, depending upon the width of the discretion used, there will be varying degrees of certainty as to whether or not a particular regulation will be enforced. Uncertainty detracts from the power of the regulatory framework. Some officers were disturbed by this lack of uniformity. They favoured a more explicit policy applicable at least throughout the whole authority, if not nationwide. They were evidently anxious to ensure procedural reasonableness and the application of predetermined rules to guide the exercise of their discretion.

The concern expressed stems from the need for a degree of certainty to ensure that both enforcers and industry know where they stand in relation to any breach. Certainty brings fairness of a different sort from that in a system where there is a wide discretion. If all those controlled by the regulatory system know the parameters within which they can work, and that such parameters are applied equitably throughout the system, then clearly there are greater degrees of moral and legal authority. When the enforcement agencies express concern over the uniformity of regulatory enforcement, it is quite clear that the system itself cannot be operating with total efficiency.

Administrative difficulties

Aside from the attitudes that enforcement agencies have towards the offence and the offender, other external factors have had a marked effect upon the efficient enforcement of environmental regulations. These can properly be related to all the usual problems facing administrative and bureaucratic systems.

As was seen in Chapter 3, the traditional model for environmental regulation in Britain has been to set up large administrative bodies charged with both organisational and regulatory responsibilities. Thus, agencies have been both poacher and gamekeeper. This of course can lead to fundamental difficulties because of the contradictory nature of these two functions. The two main examples of this dual role were in the control of water pollution under the regional water authorities and the control of the disposal of waste to land through the county-wide waste disposal authorities. Both these authorities carried out activities which were the subject of control which had to be policed by themselves. The water authorities operated sewage treatment plants, and the waste disposal authorities were site operators disposing of waste within their own area. Additionally, these two bodies possessed the regulatory powers for the supervision of private sector activities. The failure to separate the two contradictory roles created great problems. Often the gravest breach of regulations came from the operational arm of the regulatory authorities. For instance, pollution from the water authorities' sewage treatment plants was perhaps the most significant factor in the deterioration of water quality. In the waste disposal sector, the Commons Environment Committee stated:

> . . . many local authorities appear to have concentrated on their operational activities to the detriment of their regulatory duties . . . [some waste disposal authorities] regard keeping consignment notes in a box in the corner as adequately discharging their record-keeping responsibilities.

This dual role led to two difficulties in enforcement. First, the private sector argued that it was inequitable for the enforcement agencies to prosecute when their own operations were also in breach. Secondly, it led to a desire to use the conciliatory approach because many officers within the enforcement agency empathised with those in the private sector as to the problems faced in pollution avoidance. Their officers had experienced difficulties within their own agency and thus were far more likely to be sympathetic in enforcing the law generally.

Staffing and funding levels

To maintain a proper level of enforcement, adequate manpower and funding has to be available. If there were only 500 police officers covering the whole of England and Wales we would undoubtedly see a dramatic increase in the levels of crime. Environmental enforcement has, however, been the poor relation in terms both of staff on the ground and funds available to those staff.

The crisis in local government is well documented. Cuts in funding and low morale has led to a smaller complement of staff attempting to deal with a large number of complaints. However, the other enforcement agencies fare little better. HMIP currently has 427 staff against a preferred number of 434.5. This obscures the true picture however, as the number of staff has been cut significantly as a result of an efficiency drive.

In the past, the Inspectorate did not meet its targets for enforcement visits or for the number of samples taken. For example, the numbers for site visits fell from 7,350 in 1989/90 to a figure of 3,867 in 1990/91. More recently figures for inspections have risen to the highest level for some years. When seen in the context of an annual inspection rate of over 10,000 in the early 1980s, however, the figures are poor, especially in the light of the increase in staff. In particular, HMIP has conceded that even with the increase in inspection visits the organisation is only carrying out about 60% of the necessary inspections. In a situation such as this it is difficult to maintain a confrontational stance. The enforcement agencies expect to rely upon industry co-operating by keeping within the emission limits.

Changes in attitudes to enforcement

Most of the research referred to so far in this chapter dates back to empirical studies in the mid 1970s to the early 1980s. Perceptions of environmental difficulties have changed dramatically since that time. New environmental quality objectives imposed by the EC have meant that the enforcement agencies are being placed under increasing pressure to take a proactive approach to enforcement and to use prosecution as the short term weapon to bring industry into line in the long term. For instance, the EPA 1990, s. 7, provides for such objectives to be taken into account when authorising processes subject to integrated pollution control and air pollution control. Similarly the Water Resources Act 1991 makes water quality objectives a statutory consideration. The evidence of this fundamental change in the control of pollution in Britain can also be seen with the introduction of the Air Quality Standards Regulations 1989 (SI 1989 No. 317). This move towards fixed standards and away from individualised flexible enforcement requires the redefinition of the enforcement of environmental protection.

The redefinition of the regulatory role

With the creation of the National Rivers Authority under the Water Act 1989 and the formation of the new system of regulation in the waste disposal industry under the EPA 1990, there has been a move away from the dual-function approach of the 1970s and 1980s. The NRA and the new waste regulation authorities have had almost total regulatory control without the problems of operational complications to blunt their effectiveness. This, in turn, has allowed the NRA to become the self-styled 'Water Guardian' and to concentrate on the policing side of its role in order to achieve compliance by confrontation. This has been evidenced by an increase in the incidence of prosecution since its creation. Figures show that the number of prosecutions for water pollution has risen at least 25% each year in the initial years of its life.

The incidence of prosecution is only one piece of evidence of a changing attitude to enforcement. In the first of a series of water quality papers, the NRA outlined its approach to enforcement. In addition to the conciliatory model, there was a desire to prosecute where a discharger had shown little care in attempting to comply with consent obligations. Informal, internal guidelines offer guidance as to when prosecution should be pursued. These guidelines, which are used on a national basis, attempt to class incidents by reference to objective standards such as numbers of fish killed or repetitious breaches. Theoretically this should ensure consistency of decision-making and avoid previous concerns about the unreasonable exercise of discretion. Although at first glance this may not be far away from the previous attempts at moral judgment in exercising enforcement discretion, it does however demonstrate that the NRA is far more likely to consider accidents as requiring enforcement action even where moral opprobrium is low. Furthermore, the NRA has brought a number of prosecutions against the privatised water services companies. According to prosecution figures, four of the 10 most prosecuted companies are from the water industry. This will have indirect effects upon those who discharge into sewers controlled by the companies. Where levels of prosecutions against the private water companies rise, they in turn have to enforce trade discharge standards, thus increasing the enforcement pressure considerably.

Finally, the waste regulation authorities do not have the same difficulties that faced officers under the waste disposal authority of policing sites which are in a better condition than those run by their own authority. The arm's-length local authority waste disposal companies are subject to the same degree of control as private operations, and therefore will undoubtedly face different pressures as Part II of the EPA 1990 settles down after the upheaval of the introduction of the Waste Management Licensing Regulations.

The redefinition of the enforcement agencies' relationship with industry

The traditional image of the enforcement agencies collaborating with industry over a table in a room at the factory with a cup of tea while 'problem-solving' is fast disappearing. Most enforcement agencies were renowned in the past for their ability to be sympathetic in suggesting ways to abate pollution. Indeed most guidance notes controlling the processes within an industry were drafted with close assistance from those who operated the processes themselves.

HMIP took a different stance when drawing up the guidance notes to govern integrated pollution control and air pollution control. The Inspectorate specifically rejected the Chemical Industry Association's claims that it should be involved throughout the process of drawing up the guidelines. The dismay expressed by the association emphasised the about-turn in this traditional relationship. It was suggested by some within the association that, in the absence of representations from industry, the system would be unworkable as a large number of appeals against unreasonable authorisations would overload the Inspectorate.

HMIP stressed the advisory capacity of all consultees. The then Director, Frank Feates, pointed out that he would be happy to take into account the views of the Chemical Industry Association but that these views would not be the overriding consideration. Other bodies would also be entitled to make representations.

Furthermore, the Inspectorate has made it clear that it sees its role as having four main strands:

(a)   a preventative approach;
(b)   a positive but structured relationship with operators;
(c)   the provision of information and guidance to industry on an arm's length basis; and
(d)   a systematic targeting of resources towards the highest priorities.

These strands include a possible suggestion that those producers supplying high quality pollution technology will be the proper people to advise HMIP as to what constitutes the 'best available techniques'. This move indicates that the Inspectorate will take into account a much wider sample of opinions when deciding the framework which it governs. Thus, the 'active' discretion in standard-setting and methods of abatement will have an objective basis.

There are other more far-reaching changes, however, which go beyond formal enforcement to more proactive issues, such as the setting of consent levels. In its first water quality paper, *Discharge Consent and Compliance Policy: A Blueprint for the Future,* the NRA made a number of recommendations stressing the importance of tighter numeric consents with percentile limits for 'environmentally significant discharges'.

This confrontational style has also spread into the way in which prosecutions are presented. When the facts of a pollution incident are put before the court, an assessment is made of the damage caused by the pollution in ecological as well as scientific terms. Photographs are often used to display vividly to a court what is meant by the dry, and often incomprehensible, scientific evidence. Attempts are made to explain to the court in lay terms both the short- and the long-term effects of the pollution caused. These sometimes emotive prosecutions are bound to have a confrontational effect and will undoubtedly undermine any continuing relationship to some extent.

Unfortunately, the size and complexity of the task facing the enforcement agencies has undermined the attempt to move away from the co-operative approach. The number and poor quality of IPC applications, for instance, has led to disproportionate amounts of time being spent upon administering the system of authorisations. In local authorities an acknowledged shortfall in the number of APC applications has largely been overlooked, whilst monitoring and enforcement visits have fallen.

The redefinition of the importance of environmental protection

The changes in emphasis in the regulatory system are not solely ones of detail and are more than superficial. Underlying the changes is a fundamental shift in the way that environmental problems are perceived, not only by the public but also by the enforcement agencies themselves. The concept of the environment having rights of its own is increasing in importance, and generally the desire to protect the environment has begun to undermine previous assumptions made as to the benefits of industrial activities which cause pollution. As environmental issues have become more important in the public eye, the desire to ensure that environmental standards are maintained has increased generally. These changes have brought about a retreat from the co-operational approach to a new, more ambivalent standard. That is not to say that the enforcing agencies are ambivalent as to the difficulties faced by industrialists. However, they are now balancing the co-operational and the confrontational approaches in order to achieve environmental quality improvements.

When public interest in the environment increases, the moral opprobrium attaching to pollution increases. Incidents such as the Camelford disaster, where aluminium sulphate was put into the drinking water supply, have supported the view that the public is now ready to perceive incidents of environmental pollution as being more than mere administrative difficulties. The distinction between this particular branch of white collar crime and other more recognisably 'criminal' activities is becoming blurred.

This change in emphasis has had a consequential effect upon areas of environmental regulation. First, there has been an increase in the fines and penalties for pollution offences. Historically, it was unusual for a prosecution for environmental pollution to be heard anywhere other than the magistrates' court. The level of fines imposed by the magistrates tended to reflect the public opinion of white collar crime being a morally neutral offence. Although many environmental pollution offences are triable either in the magistrates' court or the Crown Court, the option to try the matter in the Crown Court, with the opportunity to seek an unlimited fine and even imprisonment, was not often taken.

It is now becoming more usual for matters to be committed to the Crown Court. Perhaps the most celebrated Crown Court prosecution, of Shell (UK) in February 1990 for an oil spillage into the River Mersey, reflects the latent powers of the Crown Court which have not been very much in evidence. In that case the total of the fine and compensation costs amounted to several million pounds, which cancelled out much of the annual profit derived from the process which caused the pollution. In that particular situation, it was clear that the Crown Court judge not only viewed the offence with the seriousness that it required but also took into account (perhaps subconsciously) the need to make the polluter pay. Moreover, the judge specifically pointed out that the level of fine was 'lenient' taking into account all the mitigating factors.

The notoriously low levels of fine, which have traditionally undermined the use of prosecutions, have been increased to take into account the need for the magistrates to have wider powers to reflect the seriousness of offences which do not merit being heard in the Crown Court. As a consequence, most of the offences of environmental pollution under the EPA 1990 have had the maximum fine level in the magistrates' court increased from £2,000 to £20,000. This is also mirrored in the increased penalties in the Planning and Compensation Act 1991. Furthermore, there are explicit references in some Acts to the financial benefit which has accrued or is likely to accrue to an offender (for example, see the Planning (Listed Building and Conservation Areas) Act 1990 and *R v Chambers and others* [1989] JPL 229). Finally, the demand for increased fines to take into account the potential profits from pollution was made explicit by the Government in the White Paper, *Crime, Justice and Protecting the Public,* which said:

Companies which see commercial advantage in creating pollution or neglecting safety precautions cannot be punished effectively by fines at the level given to most offenders.

It then goes on to say that higher levels of fines should be imposed to take into account both the means and the resources of the offenders.

Although there are still difficulties in ensuring that there are sufficient funds and sufficient manpower to meet the increasing work in detection, these difficulties are being addressed. Furthermore, charging schemes to cover the cost of administering applications for authorisations under the IPC and APC systems and under the Water Resources Act 1991 ensure that the levels of funding for the administrative side of the regulatory function can be properly balanced to take into account the complexity of the work required.

The development of enforcement policy

The overhaul of the Control of Pollution Act 1974 with the introduction of the EPA 1990 and the Water Resources Act 1991 was intended to herald a new era for environmental law. The Government expressed its aim of enforcing environmental standards rigorously in 1990 in the White Paper, *This Common Inheritance*, and sufficient time has passed since the implementation of these Acts for the enforcement policy of the main agencies (i.e. the NRA and HMIP) to be reappraised. The fact that water regulation authorities (WRAs) have been decentralised (and thus have no truly consistent policy) and the relative unfamiliarity with Part II of the EPA 1990 mean that it is impossible to gain any accurate picture of the enforcement of the law on waste management.

The NRA has of course, formulated a specific policy, with prosecution as an active component (see further p. 449). The use of prosecution however, has largely been aimed at unforeseen circumstances where accidents have resulted in major pollution incidents. In the cases of chronic pollution and persistent breaches of consent the NRA is more likely still to employ conciliatory tactics to resolve the issue. Compliance levels are still poor, with industrial operators achieving levels of 65% in the year 1993–4. This may largely be due to the fact that there are few administrative powers (e.g. enforcement notices) to deal with water pollution.

In addition, there has been relatively little use of the preventative or remedial powers provided in s. 161, although there is some evidence that the use of the cost-recovery provisions may become more widespread. Indeed, it is understood that along with the introduction of s. 55 of the Environment Act 1995 the Government has encouraged the NRA to make more concerted efforts to recover the costs incurred on all investigation works. The primary reason for any previous reluctance to carry out preventative works has been the inherent uncertainty surrounding the expenditure of money which may not be recovered from the party responsible for the pollution.

HMIP has adopted a slightly different policy to the NRA. Prosecution is still seen somwhat as a last resort—with an average of 14 prosecutions per year between 1993–95 (although this is a dramatic percentage increase over historic rates of a two to three-year period). Other formal enforcement action has doubled on a year-on-year basis, with some 103 enforcement notices served in 1994/95. Many of these enforcement notices have required the updating of old equipment or the installation of additional equipment to deal with a specific problem. Compliance rates are more difficult to judge than with discharge consents, but the levels of 'justifiable' complaints from the public in relation to releases from prescribed processes has risen to the highest levels since the 1970s, and the Director of HMIP accepted that the levels of complaint probably reflected a deterioration in the level of performance of industry. HMIP's enforcement policy, whilst not explicit, has developed with the use of administrative sanctions being the most obvious policy strand.

There is a marked contrast between the powers available to HMIP and the NRA (although the major differences will disappear with the assimilation of enforcement powers under the Agency (see pp. 45–6)). The variety of powers open to HMIP have been used to 'soften' the confrontation between Agency and industry. The use of enforcement notices after a pollution incident gives the 'offender' some time to correct any situation without the ignominy of a prosecution. HMIP publicises the service of the notice and the public is reassured that action is being taken. On the surface, every party would appear to have found a satisfactory solution. The critical flaw in the process is that the enforcement notice has value only when and if it is complied with. If an operator does not comply, HMIP has a further discretion in deciding whether to prosecute. Clearly, where there has been flagrant disregard paid to the notice the decision should be straightforward. Difficulties arise, however, when an unsuccessful attempt has been made to comply with the notice and HMIP is faced with the traditional dilemma of whether the operator should be morally blamed for the non-compliance. In addition the public has little notification of the outcome of the enforcement process because actual compliance with the original notice is not publicised.

Although there have been significant changes in enforcement policy and practice since the introduction of the EPA 1990 and Water Resources Act 1991 the figures for non-compliance and complaints suggest that there is still a reluctance to prosecute for breach of statutory authorisations. Do the explanations set out earlier in this chapter still apply? One thing is certain—the factors governing any decision to enforce are still complex and differ on a case-to-case basis. It is possible, however, to identify a slight shift away from the traditional views of the offender and the offence which bears out the redefinition of many of the critical factors as set out above. The creation of national bodies with centralised policies has encouraged a much more uniform application of enforcement powers (but some mild regional differences can still be identified).

Athough decisions to prosecute are still discretionary there is much more public scrutiny of individual incidents and it would be very unlikely for the moral blameworthiness of an offender to be a material factor in the determination. Environmental harm is now often the most relevant factor in determining whether to prosecute and serious incidents rarely escape some form of sanction. Indeed, there has been a number of NRA prosecutions which have been brought with a general acknowledgement that although the defendant was guilty on the basis of the strictness of liability in the 1991 Act they were not in the 'wrong' in the traditional, moral sense (e.g. *CPC* v *NRA* [1995] Env LR 131 (see p. 432).

The true picture is that although there has been some movement away from the traditional conciliatory approach, co-operation between industry and the regulators has not broken down. Indeed, HMIP has taken an active role in advising industry on improving its performance (with subsequent financial savings for the company involved (see *ENDS Report* 242, p. 6)). In reality the general consensus between the two sides of the enforcement system is never likely to break down fully as detection and prosecution of every breach would be impracticable and undesirable. The introduction of the Environment Agency may see some cultural changes (particularly in respect of waste management) but the real indicator of the success of any new enforcement policies—a general improvement in environmental quality standards—is probably some way off. It is interesting to note that in the water sector, the prosecution rates are now falling, yet water quality has improved in some instances. Some (in particular the NRA) have argued that both are a direct consequence of a more confrontational policy.

Enforcement and deregulation

Perhaps the biggest general influence over the enforcement policies of all enforcement agencies (especially local government) is Central Government's commitment to removing what is viewed as unnecessary and interfering regulation. Since the introduction of the new statutory regime under the EPA 1990 and the Water Resources Act 1991, industry has argued that the legislation is too complex and compliance involves excessive amounts of both expenditure and other resources. This complaint has found a sympathetic response with the introduction of the framework of the Deregulation and Contracting Out Act 1994 (see p. 109 for an explanation of the provisions of the Act). Although the full impact of the Act upon environmental legislation has yet to be determined, the potential implications of the provisions were demonstrated with the publication of the proposals of the seven Business Deregulation Task Forces (organised into industry sectors) which were appointed by the Government to examine opportunities for reform.

The Task Forces chose to emphasise the gap between the intention of Central Government when making law and policy and the manner in which that intention was implemented by enforcement authorities on the ground. The proposals from the Task Forces ranged from planning (including the extension of permitted development rights and a requirement for local planning authorities to accept the recommendations of a Development Plan Inspector) and waste management to IPC, LAAPC and water pollution. Some of the recommendations were accepted and implemented in subsequent legislation. The clear danger of the 'Task Force' approach is that it tackles the perceived problems of over-regulation from only one perspective. Although some environmental legislation is complex, there are often legitimate reasons for having such requirements. Whilst removing such hurdles means that business can operate without interference, it should only be necessary where the environmental impact of the change can be accurately predicted to be insignificant.

Although the 1994 Act has not implemented any of the other recommendations of the Task Force, the new power is available to enable any future proposals to be enacted. It is not possible to predict accurately the future role of the Act but the passage of the Environment Act 1995 through Parliament may give some indication of the Government's attitude to the administrative approach to enforcement. For example, the contaminated land provisions were weakened considerably during the Bill's passage and a number of preconditions to the serving of a remediation notice were imposed (see p. 393). Other examples include the cost benefit duty under s. 39 and other similar provisions (see p. 44). Ironically, the deregulation initiative which started out as a 'war on red tape' has now developed (particularly in relation to enforcement) into a situation where the enforcement agencies have to carry out numerous theoretical and practical exercises before commencing any enforcement action.

Public participation in the enforcement process

Having examined closely the way in which regulatory bodies enforce the law, it must be pointed out that there are residual powers providing for direct action to be taken by members of the public. It is likely that the next phase of environmental enforcement will be supplemented by a greater degree of public participation in the enforcement process. Generally, there is a constitutional right to bring private prosecutions for statutory offences. However, in environmental matters, this right has often been specifically limited by the statute concerned (e.g. in air pollution legislation). The Control of Pollution Act 1974 did not have any prohibition on prosecutions for offences of water pollution and anglers' associations and others took action themselves against water authorities. This trend has continued under the EPA 1990. Unfortunately, such powers are often overlooked. Indeed, as the Environmental Protection Bill passed through Parliament, the Labour Party proposed an amendment in order to include a clear reference to the public right to prosecute. This was rejected as unnecessary. As the public become aware of their rights, any action on the part of the regulatory bodies may become superfluous.

In order for non-statutory enforcement bodies or individuals to take enforcement action, members of the general public need to have proper access to environmental data. To bring a prosecution, information is required so as to identify properly the breaches of any regulation. Of course, a major weakness in the environmental regulatory system in Britain is the difficulty of achieving access to environmental information.

SEVEN

Access to environmental information

As we have seen in Chapter 3, the system of the enforcement of pollution control is exercised in the main by statutory enforcement agencies. These enforcement agencies do not necessarily, however, engender public confidence. As restrictions on the right to take action by private prosecution are removed, the general public is able to enforce the law where, for instance, an enforcement agency fails to prosecute for a regulatory breach. These powers of prosecution have significant powers connected which can require further remedial action. For example, under the EPA 1990, s. 26, where a prosecution is successful a court can order action to be taken within a certain time-limit to ensure that any breach complained of is remedied. These powers potentially allow the general public to have a degree of control over the enforcement of pollution control.

Why then do the public not take more action? There are a variety of reasons which include high cost, apathy, ignorance of the powers available and a fear of the legal system. However, even if these difficulties could be overcome, access to the information which could form the basis of an enforcement action has traditionally been limited.

Most environmental offences involve the carrying out of unauthorised activities. These may arise from the breach of a condition in an authorisation or they may be entirely unauthorised actions. To assess levels of compliance, the public require access not only to information concerning the details of an authorisation but also to monitoring data which can provide an assessment of the success of the controls.

The enforcement agencies, of course, have specific and wide-ranging powers to enable them to obtain information. These powers are not available to the general public, but the information obtained by the appropriate agency is crucial in assessing whether or not enforcement action should take place. It is this information which, if it were accessible, could be utilised by those outside the statutory enforcement system to bring an action themselves. Moreover, the public have additional rights of enforcement both through resort to the common law for a private remedy (see Chapter 8) and in the case of the abuse of statutory powers by an enforcement body by an application for judicial review.

Without adequate information, public rights such as these have little value. Although documents containing general information about environmental pollution are freely available, specific information is far more difficult to obtain. For instance, basic information as to who is polluting, where they are polluting, with what they are polluting and how much is being emitted, can be elusive. This chapter examines some of the reasons for this secrecy, in addition to putting forward the possible dangers of keeping environmental information from the general public.

The development of a general environmental secrecy policy

The roots of environmental secrecy can be traced back to the mid-nineteenth century and the age of industrialisation when, in 1864, the Alkali Inspectorate, which was then empowered to regulate atmospheric pollution, commenced its enforcement activities under the Alkali Act 1863 with a policy of keeping any information regarding the alkali industry private unless publication was demanded by a particular statute or was permitted by the owner. Naturally, the alkali industry itself was concerned to keep the information secret in order to ensure that the public did not know of the dangers and consequences of the pollutants emitted into the atmosphere. This, coupled with the beginning of a co-operational approach between enforcers and the polluters, ensured that the Inspectorate was very unlikely to make such information available to members of the public unless specifically required to do so.

Central Government holds important information about the environment. As central policy makers and legislators, its ability to make fundamental changes in the nature of environmental protection heightens the need for proper public accountability. Until recently, the disclosure of information in these areas, when unauthorised, would have resulted in the commission of a criminal offence under the Official Secrets Act 191 1, s. 2. Although Central Government has very little detailed information which would be of help to the public, the unamended Official Secrets Act 1911 gave rise to situations which could only be described as bizarre.

The Draconian nature of the restrictions placed upon Central Government organisations led to the reform of the Official Secrets Act in 1989. This Act narrowly protects a certain limited class of information, which does not now include environmental information. However, the time taken to respond to the proposals made by the Franks Committee in 1972 and by a White Paper in 1978 reflects the reluctance of Central Government to take action upon not only general information held by themselves, but also more detailed environmental information held by others.

Mechanisms of secrecy

Historically, secrecy has been endemic in environmental legislation. Many statutes contained specific sections explicitly forbidding the disclosure of information relating to environmental discharges. Even if there were no specific sanctions for disclosure, access to information was prohibited unless another statute specifically required that it be made available to the general public.

Water pollution

The Rivers (Prevention of Pollution) Act 1961 restricted the public right of access to information concerning applications, discharge consents, or effluent samples taken by the enforcing authority, unless the person/company making the discharge permitted its disclosure, or there was a further statutory requirement to disclose. In *The Secrets File*, Maurice Frankel gives an illustration of the type of situation which arose under this old legislation. In a case where a pigment manufacturer was discharging highly polluting substances into the Humber Estuary he says:

> On three occasions the company has been asked for the results of its monitoring—and it has refused on each occasion. Although the water authority has copies of data it is prevented by law from passing it on; an official releasing the information without the company's consent could, under Section 12 of the Rivers (Prevention of Pollution) Act, be jailed for three months. The water authority also carries out its own monitoring of the effluent discharge; again, it is prevented by law from releasing the results without the company's permission.

Such a situation seems inconceivable in a time where access to such information is much more widespread.

Air pollution

The Alkali Inspectorate maintained a policy of secrecy from its inception and, in its very first report in 1864, stressed the importance of keeping information from the public, 'Of course, all information regarding any work must be considered private unless publication is demanded by the Act or permitted by the owner'. This policy was maintained on an informal basis until the introduction of the Health and Safety at Work etc. Act 1974. Under s. 28(7), the Alkali Inspectorate was subject to an unqualified prohibition to ensure that no information was publicised regarding any details of recordings or measurements taken whilst exercising their duties.

Under the Clean Air Acts 1956 and 1968, a local authority's power to publish information could be said to have been somewhat wider than that contained under the Health and Safety at Work etc. Act. Under Part IV of the Control of Pollution Act 1974, local authorities were allowed to publish information on emissions to air from premises other than private dwellings if that information was not information that could be required by the Alkali Inspectorate. Unfortunately, this power was restricted in three ways. First, before publicising information a committee had to be created to involve business/industry and local amenity groups to discuss the proposals to make information public. Secondly, the powers under the Act were directory rather than mandatory, that is to say that the local authorities were not under any legal duty to publish the information. Thirdly, there was an appeal mechanism available to those operators affected by any disclosure if the collection of the information required would have been too expensive, a trade secret or not in the public interest. With these hurdles to overcome and no positive incentive, the expenditure required to set the system in motion would prove to be greater than the benefits received. Additionally, with an enforcement regime based upon the co-operational approach, any attempt to impose discretionary powers upon industry would have fractured the fragile basis of local authority control. As evidence of this, it was reported in 1982 that in the whole country only eight premises had been made the subject of local authority registers and only five local authorities had cut their way through the administrative jungle in order to set up the registers.

Miscellaneous controls

Other examples of the restrictions on the free availability of information can be found in the legislation covering a variety of environmental issues, such as pollution at sea, radioactive substances and hazardous sites. One of the major reasons for such strenuous efforts to keep information away from the public eye stems largely from the views of industry about the free availability of information. This was best characterised in a statement made by the CBI in 1979 entitled 'The Release of Environmental and Technical Information' which stated:

> greater release of data enhances the risk of their misinterpretation and the likelihood of unwarranted alarm or ill-founded 'remedial' actions . . . Data are often highly detailed and technical, requiring interpretation by trained toxicologists; hence the capacity for correct interpretation is limited. This restricts further the amount and type of information which could usefully be released without problems of misinterpretation . . . The threat of legal proceedings would be enhanced by increasing disclosure of data. Applications for injunctions at common law could become more likely, putting industry at greater risk of additional costs and penalties even when it satisfies the requirements of the competent control authorities.

This feeling was amplified when the CBI again attacked existing legislation allowing public access to information on effluent discharges under Part II of the Control of Pollution Act 1974 as 'one of the worst bits of legislation on the statute book'. It was against this background that attempts were made to defend the formal and informal 'cloak of secrecy'.

Commercial confidentiality

Industry's main argument in favour of secrecy was outlined in the evidence submitted by the CBI for the Tenth Report of the Royal Commission on Environmental Pollution. It was suggested that free public access to environmental information could affect the viability of industrial operations:

General disclosure of data about the content of discharges to the environment causes industry concern because it could involve highly sensitive data
which may be of commercial advantage to a competitor. Such data are first
and foremost the property of the discharger and their disclosure should not
be expected or demanded without good reason. In practice, industry often
discloses information which relates to the quality of the environment, as a
responsible neighbour and part of society; but this disclosure cannot be
assumed to be a public right nor can refusal to disclose be taken to mean
that there is 'something to hide'. On the contrary, it normally means that
the firm believes it right to keep to itself its own property disclosure of
which could damage it commercially.

Concern stemmed from the belief that competitors will be able to investigate public registers to gain access to secrets. This could be done in one of
two ways. First, by checking the data relating to discharges, it would be open
to competitors to calculate the composition of effluents in terms of the types
or amounts of raw materials used in a process. This would help in the
assessment of the output of a particular factory and thus give competitors a
commercial advantage. Secondly, it was often claimed by industrialists that
keeping information relating to applications for environmental authorisations
on public registers would allow free access to information governing the
composition of complex products. These products would often have taken a
number of years to research and develop and the costs involved in that
process could only be recovered if the information was kept confidential.

In reality, these fears have been overstressed. Any commercial operation
intent upon finding out about a rival's business can use far more sophisticated
methods of commercial espionage than relying on public information. Even
complex compounds can be analysed using fairly simple procedures. Additionally, the constituents of a compound are often widely used within an
industry, and the idea that information is commercially confidential only truly
applies to those outside the industry.

Moreover the protection of intellectual property is well provided for in the
patent and trade mark legislation. The need for additional secrecy is often
unwarranted. The situations where this protection is not available seem
particularly limited.

Evidence from other countries with free access to environmental information suggested that there were few occasions on which the availability of the
information led to the breach of commercial confidentiality. When the CBI
were asked to give examples, they were able to point to only three cases which
justified these concerns.

The Royal Commission on Environmental Pollution considered the question of trade secrets over a number of reports during the 1970s and 1980s.
Their conclusion was always the same, that the reliance upon the concept of
confidentiality did not reflect the true nature of the risk involved with greater
disclosure. In the Commission's Second Report in 1972 (Cmnd. 4894) it was
stated that there was:

a need for an increased flow of information to persons of responsibility who can use it for the ultimate benefit of the environment, e.g. MPs, research workers in universities and persons with similar interests in pollution.

In the Commission's Seventh Report in 1979 (Cmnd. 7644), this stance was reiterated. Referring to industry's refusal to disclose information on 'trade secret' grounds, it was stated that commercial confidentiality was often a 'reflex action' which did not reflect the commercial risk involved. The Tenth Report of the Commission in 1984 (Cmnd. 9149) concluded that the emphasis given to commercial confidentiality was disproportionate and misconceived. Even so, in oral evidence to the House of Lords Select Committee in 1989, the CBI reiterated their view that there was always a risk that technical information taken out of context can be misinterpreted by non-scientists.

In determining applications for commercial confidentiality in IPC applications, both HMIP and the Secretary of State have taken a pragmatic view. Although there has been a large number of applications for the exclusion of information from the public register only a minority have been successful. Moreover, some of the information has been excluded on the basis of its irrelevance to the determination of an application, as opposed to any confidentiality.

'Green nutters'

The second justification for the maintenance of secrecy often put forward by industry was that open access would lead to mischief-making and an unacceptable level of interference by fanatics. *The Secrets File* gives the example of comments made by an environmental health officer in 1977:

> Action groups, civic societies and pseudo environmental organisations persistently petitioned and pressured local authorities to implement those provisions . . . action groups frequently composed of university research workers, lecturers, people who had failed election through the ballot box and including many cranks, persisted in twisting the truth concerning emissions to atmosphere and their predictions of doom were made to the delight of an ever-waiting national press . . .

This sort of view is not just historical. In 1984 the CBI called Part II of the Control of Pollution Act a 'busybody's charter' and during the passage of the Environmental Protection Bill through the House of Commons, Andrew Hunt, MP for Basingstoke, said that widened rights of prosecution available to the public would 'allow the "green nutters" to get on parade and have a field day of litigation against industry on entirely inconsequential grounds'. Further MPs warned of dire consequences. The chemicals industry would 'disappear from this country', there would be an 'endless stream of prosecutions', and environmental groups would use the information and prosecutions merely as a media tool rather than a means of securing environmental improvements.

The underlying factor in this concern does not stem from misinterpretation of the data. Rather it emphasises the conciliatory strategy employed by the statutory enforcement agencies. If the information supplied on the public register raises issues of non-compliance where industrial operations are breaching their consents, then clearly it serves as evidence that there are difficulties in pursuing a non-confrontational enforcement strategy. In answer to the issues raised in the debate, a junior minister put it thus:

> If an individual has the necessary evidence to mount a case, he should be free to do so . . . we must rely on the courts to deliver justice. The commitment of industry to pollution controls is the surest defence against such litigation.

In other words, if the enforcement agencies are not willing or able to prosecute an offender then an individual should, if there is a proper case to be answered, be allowed to act.

It is not altogether clear who these 'fanatics' would be. It has been alleged that 'they' are amateurs and are unable to analyse properly the data available. In the words of the CBI expressed earlier in the chapter, 'only trained toxicologists' could interpret this information.

The reality is somewhat at odds with this view. Many environmental pressure groups employ specialists as full-time technicians. Others have members who can interpret data perfectly adequately because of many years of experience. The Royal Commission's Tenth Report said that they had seen a growing professionalism in such groups. This had led to high quality reports which compared favourably to those drawn up by trained toxicologists. It is also interesting to note that the Second Report identifies 'research workers' and 'others' as receiving the ultimate benefit of greater disclosure. In the intervening period, the pressure groups have increased in both number and size. Greenpeace and Friends of the Earth often carry out monitoring exercises supplementing statutory enforcement bodies. Clearly, the definition of 'extremists' depends upon which side of the enforcement fence you are. To industrialists, such groups are causing trouble; on the other hand, the pressure groups see themselves as demonstrating the authority that the enforcement agencies lack.

The House of Lords Select Committee did not consider this to be a problem. They said:

> The Committee most emphatically do not subscribe to the public need to be 'protected' on the grounds that raw data may be unintelligible or misleading; many members of non-governmental organisations which may wish to utilise the raw data are familiar with the processes of interpretation. There is inevitably the risk that some raw data may be used mischievously to suit a particular purpose, but that must be accepted as part of the price of openness.

In any event, experience has demonstrated that the fears of industrialists were not justified. Although the numbers of prosecutions brought by enforcement agencies is still relatively small, the proportion of private prosecutions is minute.

Administration costs

In setting up any system of public registration for environmental consents, the CBI pointed out that the administration costs of such an exercise would not be proportionate to the public benefit which would accrue. No doubt this was in the hope of appealing to a political ideology which wanted to cut down on administration and bureaucracy and considered that the creation of a further burden upon an understaffed, over-worked administration would be inadvisable. However, it is clear that records are required to be kept in any event to maintain the proper running of any system and therefore the additional burden would be minimal.

There is, of course, another interpretation to be put upon this argument in favour of non-disclosure. The ability of the public to monitor the success or failure of the enforcement agencies in controlling pollution problems could add to the workload of the agencies in more than a mere administrative fashion. The most likely avenue for complaint once non-compliance is discovered on the register by a member of the public will be to the enforcement agencies. The investigation of these complaints over and above the more general monitoring will amount to an increase in the activity of the agency and therefore increase costs. This underlying argument—that secrecy would be cheaper than openness—cannot be doubted. However, whether 'cheaper' means 'more effective' is perhaps more contentious. The House of Lords Select Committee put it simply, 'The fundamental principle to which the Committee adhere is that information should in no circumstances be protected by price'.

The ability of enforcement agencies to maintain registers in a number of different formats, including the more usual paper records, but also extending to information held on computer, microfiche or photographic record, enables cheaper updating of the information and also cheaper storage and easier access. Whether or not the public interest in the registers is sufficient to justify the expenditure incurred is a different matter.

The Royal Commission's approach

Having had the arguments for restriction of access to environmental information put to them on a number of occasions, the Royal Commission on Environmental Pollution consistently denied their strength. They considered that the public were entitled to know of the risks that they faced from environmental pollution. Furthermore, they took the view that the only way to re-establish public confidence in the enforcement system was to allow the public access to the information which would allow them to take enforcement action themselves, and that the public had a 'beneficial interest' in the environment, and therefore were entitled to know how much it was being polluted. Thus, whilst finding that these concepts held great weight, the

Royal Commission rejected the justifications for secrecy and recommended that the public should be:

> . . . entitled to the fullest possible amount of information on all forms of environmental pollution, with the onus placed on the polluter to substantiate a claim for exceptional treatment. Accordingly, we recommend that a guiding principle behind all legislative and administrative controls relating to environmental pollution should be a presumption in favour of unrestricted access for the public to information which the pollution control authorities obtain or receive by virtue of their statutory powers, with protection for secrecy only in those circumstances where a genuine case can be substantiated.

This was to form the 'guiding principle' for áll legislative and administrative control relating to environmental pollution.

The effect of secrecy upon risk perception

Where information is difficult to obtain, the perception of the risk involved in an activity may well be misconceived. The Royal Commission said that 'Secrecy—particularly the half kept secret—fuels fear'. The reality is that there is no widespread conspiracy to keep the public from finding out about environmental pollution. However, when the public is not allowed to judge for itself the incidence of pollution within the environment, the true picture may never be known. It is necessary to disclose such information to enable informed debate not only about the risks to the public and the environment but also as to what steps might be taken to minimise those risks. In their Eleventh Report the Royal Commission commented further on the assessment of risk:

> A proper evaluation of the risk requires access to the relevant information and its interpretation, and the public will not be reassured by interpretations provided by the putative polluter who has an interest. In the absence of public confidence in the role of bodies that are both authoritative and independent, interpretations by the press or pressure groups are often accepted even if they go beyond what an informed expert would regard as justified by the evidence.

There are those who believe, however, in a paternalistic form of government. Thus, it could be argued that where there is legislation in place and enforcement agencies are empowered to take action against pollution, there is no need for members of the public to be involved in such activities. However, in Chapter 6 we have seen that, in terms of prosecution rates and compliance with existing standards, the formal enforcement agencies have had limited success. The need to supplement the official enforcement agencies is still required.

The ability to detect environmental pollution is not solely the responsibility of the enforcement agencies. Many incidents are reported first by members of the public, and the availability of information would enable them to assess whether or not criminal activities are taking place. For legislation to be effective, the public will need to have confidence both in the enforcement agencies and their willingness to take action once they have been notified of any pollution.

Environmental rights

Industry does not have a general authorisation to pollute the environment. Although individuals do have private rights over the environment (e.g. landowners), the environment is not owned by any one individual. The general public has an interest over all elements of the environment and, as a consequence, that interest should be balanced with the competing interests of industry and its right to pollute. Where there are such competing interests, there should be a facility whereby each party has full access to information which allows decisions to be made as to which of the competing interests should take precedence. In the words of the Royal Commission 'the public must be considered to have a right, analogous to a beneficial interest, in the condition of the air and water and to be able to obtain information on how far they are being degraded'.

It may be argued by those in industry that these very people who have a beneficial interest in the environment are also the people who are employed in the factories which compete with that right. The right to pollute is essentially a utilitarian right, which has been expressed by those who defend such a right on the basis that the need to maintain a certain standard of living more than outweighs the need to ensure that there is long-term protection of the environment. This view is being increasingly challenged. The need to maintain natural resources and to ensure a proper environmental quality requires that the full extent of any particular problem should be assessed.

The recommendations of the Royal Commission

The history of the Royal Commission, and particularly of the recommendations regarding confidentiality, has been an interesting study of the way in which industry and government have joined together to block at every available opportunity the introduction of a concept which in industry's view could jeopardise the successful and profitable operations of its members. In total, five Royal Commission Reports address the issue of access to environmental information in one way or another, but it was not until the mid 1980s that initial steps were taken to make disclosure more widespread. Furthermore, it was only with the introduction of the EPA 1990 and the Environmental Information Regulations 1992 that disclosure of environmental information in all sectors of control is becoming a reality.

The Royal Commission's tune has hardly changed since 1974 when in its Second Report it stated:

> as a rule . . . the legislation which protects secrecy over industrial effluents and wastes no longer safeguards genuine trade secrets . . . it is in the public

interest that information about waste should be available not only to the statutory bodies which have a right to demand it but to research workers and others who make use of it to improve the environment . . .

As a consequence, the Control of Pollution Act 1974 introduced a system of access to public registers of information on water for the first time. The implementation of Part II of the Control of Pollution Act was delayed for more than 10 years until mid 1985, amidst pressure by the CBI to delay disclosure even further. Other areas either remained secret or, in the case of the Health and Safety at Work etc. Act 1974, moved away from informal agreements to more formal statutory non-disclosure powers. In 1986, the Government departed from its previous standpoint when urging the EC to pass a Directive requiring all Member States to allow free access to environmental information. This new-found enthusiasm was short-lived. In 1986, in Pollution Paper No. 23, an inter-departmental Working Party responded to the Royal Commission's criticisms in the Tenth Report by embracing the 'guiding principle' but rejecting the recommendations to move towards a uniform regime of public access to all environmental information. Thus the Working Party charted a difficult course between appeasing the critics and political pragmatism by supporting minimal changes designed to avoid upsetting the system. When in 1989 the first drafts of the Environmental Protection Bill were published, it showed that there were to be no general obligations of disclosure introduced by the new Act. However, when Chris Patten was appointed Secretary of State for the Environment there was a further change in policy and, by January 1990, it was accepted that the public should have free access to information about industry's compliance with environmental authorisations which had been obtained under statutory powers. Clearly there were to be safeguards, but the underlying concept of free access was agreed.

This move towards openness has broadened with the introduction of the Environment Act 1995. Increasingly, access to environmental information is moving into areas such as the provision of general information on the state of the environment (e.g. see the Chemical Release Inventory) and wider consultation on issues of importance (although, for another view, see *R v HMIP ex parte Greenpeace Ltd* (1994) Env LR 76 and p. 19).

Water pollution

In many ways the provisions on public registers of water pollution have been the model for the introduction of other controls. After much pressure from the Royal Commission, Part II of the Control of Pollution Act 1974 introduced a system of public registration which would contain not only information on the consents granted to a company to allow it to discharge effluent into water, but also the frequency with which the limits of the consent were not complied with. Despite an 11-year gap between the publication of the Act and the implementation of the information requirements, the principles of the register were seen to be a model for other areas of environmental control.

The provisions of Part II of the Control of Pollution Act were re-enacted in the Water Resources Act 1991, s. 190. The public registers contain a wide variety of information. The Act requires that the contents of the register must be available at all reasonable times for inspection by the public free of charge. Copies of the entries can be taken by anybody on payment of a reasonable charge. The information contained on the register is prescribed in detail by the Control of Pollution (Registers) Regulations 1989 (SI 1989 No. 1160).

Where an application for a discharge consent is made, the NRA is obliged to enter the details of the application within 28 days under reg. 3(2). The details contained within the register cover such things as the name of the applicant and any additional information which has been supplied in order to amplify the application. If the application is granted, details of the consent, plus any conditions attached to that consent, also have to be entered within the 28-day limit (s. 190(1)(c)). These must include the name of the person/company to whom consent is given, where the discharge will take place and when the consent will take effect. If there is any notice served on the holder of the discharge consent, that fact must also be registered on the register (this includes revocation or variation notices). Furthermore, the register must show the time limit within which no variation may be made to the consent.

Normally, the format for recording the information will show the maximum levels of substances to be contained in the effluent as laid down by the original consent alongside a figure showing the content of the effluent as taken on the sample date. The particulars contained in the registers should normally indicate where the sample was taken from, the date and time of day it was taken and whether or not any action was required to be taken on behalf of the NRA. Where the sample was taken by or on behalf of the NRA, the information must be placed on the register within two months of the sampling date (reg. 7). There are facilities for people other than the NRA to take samples (e.g. self-monitored samples). In such a case, the sample information should contain reference to the fact that it was taken by a different person. Such information has to be placed on the register not more than 28 days from the receipt of the information by the NRA (reg. 7(3)(b)).

Similar provisions apply where a formal legal sample has been taken under the Water Resources Act 1991, s. 209. These are samples which are taken prior to prosecutions. Indeed, there is evidence to suggest that the taking of formal samples as a mechanism in the co-operational strategy for pollution enforcement is often seen to be a last resort. Where a formal sample has been taken this will alert a member of the public to the seriousness of the situation within the plant. The process of formal samples is, however, prospectively repealed in the Environment Act 1995.

Previously, under the Control of Pollution Act 1974, the time limit for placing information on the register did not start to run until the information was given to the 'registrar' within the water authority. This led to practical difficulties of enforcement. In 1988, Derbyshire County Council prosecuted the North West Water Authority for pollution from a sewage works situated at Whaley Bridge. There was evidence of samples being taken which showed a massive breach of the consent levels set for the works. Previously, there had been breaches of up to four times the consent limit, but the figures which showed that there had been a breach of up to 20 times the consent limit were not put on the public register until some five months after they were taken.

The regulations currently exempt certain information which it would be contrary to the public interest to make public or which is a trade secret. In such circumstances, the Secretary of State is entitled to issue a certificate (under sch. 10, para. 1(7)) to exclude it. When the Environment Agency comes into existence these provisions will be assimilated with other confidentiality provisions, with exclusion of information on the grounds of commercial confidentiality and/or that inclusion of the information would be contrary to the interests of national security (see s. 191A–B WRA 1991).

Any entry in the register has to be kept there for a period of five years only; thereafter it would be maintained on the register only if it is necessary for the exercise of the NRA's pollution control functions.

The register system has been criticised by a number of bodies. It is considered that the 'raw data' showing the results of single samples does not provide lay people with an adequate picture of compliance. There is, as yet, no information relating to environmental quality standards or a summary of any cumulative effects of the discharge. Moreover, some of the samples taken are defined as 'operational' and thus do not fall within the definition of 'samples to be taken as a result of pollution control'.

Other registers in the water industry

There are a range of registers covering different areas in the water industry. Under the Water Industry Act 1991, s. 196, water service companies (in their role as sewerage undertakers) maintain registers containing details of all consents, variations, agreements and directions. Unfortunately, no monitoring data is placed on the register so it is impossible for third parties to check levels of compliance. This has been criticised by a number of environmental groups as there is some conflict between the commercial nature of trade effluent agreements and the discretionary nature of enforcement for breaches. It has been estimated that over £100m is paid by industry to the water services companies and all are negotiated in secret. Where there is no access to levels of compliance it is difficult to see the adequacy (or otherwise) of the system.

Details of private water and sewerage undertakers are maintained on a register by the Director General of Water Services (Water Industry Act 1991, s. 195). This contains details of all directions, consents and enforcement orders.

A register containing details of abstraction and impounding licences is maintained by the NRA (s. 189). The register contains details of the holder, the location of the abstraction point, the volume of water abstracted, the provision and location of metering and expiry date. Once again, no metering data are required to be entered on the register and there is no way of checking compliance levels.

Information on drinking water quality is maintained in a register kept under the Water Supply (Water Quality) Regulations 1989 (SI 1989 No. 1147 as amended). Regulation 29 provides for a range of informatiom to be kept on the register including information on any emergency relaxation of standards, sampling results, compliance levels, particulars of action taken to comply with undertakings, and general information on general water quality.

Waste disposal

Section 64 of the EPA 1990 places a duty upon each WRA to maintain a register containing details of information in relation to the waste management licensing system. This duty is subject to ss. 65–66 which exclude information on the grounds of confidentiality (see below). There is an additional duty upon all English waste collection authorities, which are not WRAs, to maintain a register of information relating to current or recently current licences and copies of notices affecting the scope or status of the licences (e.g. modification, suspension or revocation notices).

The Waste Management Licensing Regulations 1994 (SI 1994 No 1056) flesh out the details of the registers. Regulation 10 prescribes the information to be included in the registers which includes:

(a)   full particulars of current or recentiy current (i.e. in force at any time within the previous 12 months) waste management licences. This should include copies of the licences and working plans;

(b)   full particulars of any application, including a full copy of the application with supporting documentation and copies of consultation responses;

(c)   details of applications for modification and transfer of licences;

(d)   details of suspension, variation or enforcement notices;

(e)   details of convictions for any waste management offence (not necessarily in connection with any licence in the area) and any details of convictions for 'relevant offences' under the 'fit and proper persons' provision;

(f)   copies of any reports produced by the WRA in the exercise of its supervisory duties (whether formal or informal), including correspondence with the NRA in relation to water pollution emanating from waste sites and information obtained on investigations and examinations;

(g)   details of monitoring information from either the applicant or the WRA;

(h)   details of directions from the Secretary of State which relate to pollution control and environment rather than administrative matters;

(i)   detaiis of site records in relation to 'special waste' and summary information on arisings of special waste in the WRA's area;

(j)   full particulars in relation to the surrender of a waste management licence, including copies of all the documents submitted with the application, any information obtained as a result of any site inspection, a copy of consultation responses and a copy of the determination and certificate of completion in cases where the surrender is accepted;

(k)   details of exempt establishments.

The WRA is required to keep the register open to the public at all reasonable times, free of charge, at its principal office and provide copies of all documents on request with the payment of a reasonable charge (s. 64(6)). Although there is no time limit for the provision of information on the register after receipt, Circular 11/94 suggests that it should be entered 'as soon as is reasonably practicable' with a warning that a delay of longer than two months could render the WRA liable to be in breach of the Environmental Information Regulations.

Information on licences is to be kept on the register for the lifetime of the licence plus an additional 12 months (i.e. when it is still 'current'). With regard to other information which is not related to the licence, including inspection data or the exercise of emergency powers under s. 70, it is anticipated that it will be kept on the register for a period of four years.

Exclusions

Regulation 11(1) of the Waste Management Licensing Regulations 1994 provides a general exception to the requirements set out above where the information relates to actual or prospective legal proceedings. Thus, where a WRA has information which might be used as evidence in a prosecution or even civil proceedings, there is no requirement to disclose the information to the public. Once the case has been heard the requirement to disclose reapplies.

Under EPA 1990, s. 65, information which would, in the Secretary of State's opinion, be contrary to the interests of national security, is to be excluded. This will allow for a fairly limited body of information to be excluded owing to its sensitive nature. There will be no indication on the register that such information has been excluded, as it has been suggested by the Government that even the acknowledgement that there was such information would be contrary to national security itself.

Under EPA 1990, s. 66, there is the traditional exemption for information which is commercially confidential. However, it is for the Secretary of State to decide whether or not something is commercially confidential, and the Department of the Environment has made it very clear that there will be only a limited number of instances where such an exclusion will apply. There is an additional power under s. 66(7) to allow for an outline description of the process notwithstanding that it is commercially confidential. This aims to provide a general view of a waste disposal site where supplying details would give rise to problems of confidentiality.

Where an application is made for a waste management licence, it is open to the person applying to ask for the information to be excluded from the register because of its commercial confidentiality (s. 66(2)). The waste regulation authority has 14 days to make a determination, and if it fails to do so then the information is treated as being commercially confidential (s. 66(3)). Where the waste regulation authority is to include the information on the register on the grounds that it is not confidential, it has to allow the applicant an opportunity to make representations on that particular issue and the authority must take into account the representations made (s. 66(4)). If, after this somewhat complicated procedure, the authority still decides to publish the information, there is a period of 21 days in which information is not to be published and an appeal is allowed to the Secretary of State (s. 66(5)).

As mentioned earlier, the confidentiality of information depends to a large extent upon whether or not it would prejudice to an unreasonable degree the commercial interests of the person concerned (s. 66(11)). Clearly one of the areas of difficulty will be whether or not this is to be determined by a subjective or an objective test. If it were to be subjective, then clearly any applicant for a waste management licence would be quick to assert that the information would prejudice them to an unreasonable degree and therefore it should be excluded. On the other hand, if objectivity is sought, the waste regulation authority would be able to balance the effect upon an individual with the desirability of making the information public. The Department of the Environment has made it clear that it is for the person opposing the disclosure to substantiate that the disclosure would prejudice to an unreasonable degree some person's commercial interest. There is a need to demonstrate that this disclosure of information would negate or significantly diminish the commercial advantage that one operator has over another. Where information is treated as commercially confidential, under s. 66(8), the information will only be excluded from the register for a period of four years. This allows for the fact that commercial confidentiality endures only for a finite period and after a certain length of time the need to disclose such information to the public will outweigh the harm created to the commercial interests of the individual. There is, however, a right to apply for continuation of the exclusion (s. 66(8)).

Registers in relation to contaminated land

After the withdrawal of the registers of contaminative uses under s. 143 of the EPA 1990, the Environment Act 1995 has introduced a set of registers which reflects those found in other areas of environmental law. Section 78R of the EPA 1990 now provides for each enforcing authority (the EA and local authorities) to maintain a register containing information on the following:

(a) remediation notices served and remediation statements published by the relevant authority;

(b) appeals against remediation notices and charging notices;

(c) notices designating land as a special site and any subsequent notice terminating the designation;

(d) any notification of remedial steps taken (although the presence of such information on the register is not conclusive proof of either the adequacy of the works nor even that the works have been carried out);

(e) convictions.

The Secretary of State is expected to make Regulations giving further details of the content of the register. There is the traditional exclusion of information where it would be contrary to national security (s. 78S) or if it is commercially confidential (s. 78T). The provisions in relation to confidentiality reflect those under the IPC register, with the question of determining confidentiality remaining with the enforcing authority and the Secretary of State. They include the right of appeal to the Secretary of State and exclusion of information from the register pending determination.

Integrated pollution control

Under the Health and Safety at Work etc. Act 1974, s. 28(7), all information relating to the works covered by that Act were forbidden to be disclosed by the Industrial Air Pollution Inspectorate. This was criticised on many occasions. The Royal Commission said that these restrictions should be removed as they were an obsolete and unnecessary bar on the disclosure of information. The introduction of the system of integrated pollution control and air pollution control under Part I of the EPA 1990 has now seen the removal of those restrictions and far more open access to information of an environmentally-sensitive type.

The controls are contained in EPA 1990, ss. 20 to 22, and govern both Part A processes controlled by HMIP and Part B processes controlled by local authorities. Local authorities will hold information relating to processes they control and processes controlled by HMIP. There are further controls contained within the Environmental Protection (Applications, Appeals and Registers) Regulations 1991 (SI 1991 No. 507). The format of the registers closely follows those of the waste management licence registers under Part II of the Act.

The register contains details of (reg. 15):

(a)   all particulars of any application of an authorisation made to the authority;

(b)   all particulars of any notice served on the applicant by the authority under paragraph 1(3) of sch. 1 to that Act and of any information furnished in response to such a notice;

(c)   all particulars of any representations made by any person required to be consulted under paragraph 2, 6 or 7 of sch. 1 to the EPA 1990 pursuant to reg. 4(1);

(d)   all particulars of any authorisation granted by the authority;

(e)   all particulars of any variation notice, enforcement notice or prohibition notice issued by the authority;

(f)   all particulars of any notice issued by the authority withdrawing a prohibition notice;

(g)   all particulars of any notification given to the holder of an authorisation by the authority under s. 10(5) of the Act;

(h)   all particulars of any application for the variation of the conditions of an authorisation under s. 11(4)(b) of the Act;

(i)   all particulars of any revocation of an authorisation effected by the authority;

(j)   all particulars of any notice of appeal under s. 15 of the Act against a decision by the authority, the documents relating to the appeal mentioned in reg. 9(2)(a), (d) and (e), any written notification of the Secretary of State's determination of such an appeal and any report accompanying any such written notification;

(k)   details of any conviction of any person for any offence under s. 23(1) of the Act which relates to the carrying on of a prescribed process under an authorisation granted by the authority, including the name of the offender, the date of conviction, the penalty imposed and the name of the court;

(l)   all particulars of any monitoring information relating to the carrying on of a prescribed process under an authorisation granted by the authority obtained by the authority as a result of its own monitoring or furnished to the authority in writing by virtue of a condition of the authorisation or s. 19(2) of the Act;

(m)   in a case where any such monitoring information is omitted from the register by virtue of s. 22 of that Act, a statement by the authority, based on the monitoring information from time to time obtained by or furnished to them, indicating whether or not there has been compliance with any relevant condition of the authorisation;

(n)   all particulars of any report published by an enforcing authority relating to an assessment of the environmental consequences of the carrying on of a prescribed process in the locality of premises where the prescribed process is carried on under an authorisation granted by the authority; and

(o)   all particulars of any direction (other than a direction under s. 21(2) of the Act) given to the authority by the Secretary of State under any provision of Part I of the Act.

Again, these registers have to be freely available at all reasonable times for inspection by the public free of charge and copies are allowed to be taken of the documentation on the payment of a reasonable charge (s. 20(7)).

The EPA 1990 acknowledges the introduction of more sophisticated methods of information retrieval and allows the registers to be kept in any form, which would include computer retrieval, microfiches or photographic storage.

There are two exceptions to the normal rule that information should be freely available. First, there are safeguards against the disclosure of information which is contrary to the interests of national security. Section 21 allows the Secretary of State to direct that information should be excluded if its disclosure would be contrary to national security. This power is also available if a person makes an application to exclude the information on the grounds that it is contrary to national security; they must notify the Secretary of State specifying the information and its apparent nature and then they must notify the enforcing authority of what they have done. There will be no reference to such information on the face of the register because of the chance that any harm might arise out of the disclosure of such sensitive information.

The second exclusion applies to information which is commercially confidential. Section 22 forbids disclosure of information which 'would prejudice to an unreasonable degree the commercial interests' of a person. Unlike s. 21, the determination of what is commercially confidential lies at first with the enforcing authority and then on appeal with the Secretary of State. It is open to a company applying for an authorisation to apply at the same time for information related to that authorisation to be treated as commercially confidential. This also applies when there is an application for a variation of an authorisation, or information is supplied to the authority which concerns compliance with a condition of the authorisation, or which is in response to a formal request by the authority (s. 22(2)). Where a company applies for information to be treated as commercially confidential, the enforcing authority has 14 days to decide whether or not to exclude the information. If the authority fails to make a determination after 14 days it is deemed to have excluded the information (s. 22(3)).

An enforcing authority is permitted to notify an applicant that the information the company has supplied might be commercially confidential. In these particular circumstances, the applicant is then allowed to object to the information being put on the register and to make representations to the authority justifying that objection (s. 22(4)). It is difficult to envisage when this provision will be applied. It seems quite clear that any company wishing to protect its own trade secrets will try to do so from the outset. Moreover, it is not easy to understand quite how an enforcing authority will know that certain information is commercially confidential.

Where the enforcing authority decides that the information supplied is not commercially confidential, it is nevertheless not permitted to enter the information on the register for 21 days, giving time for the company to appeal to the Secretary of State to determine whether or not the information is confidential (s. 22(5)).

The Secretary of State does have an overriding power to direct that information be included on the registers even though it is commercially confidential if it is in the public interest for it to be so included. This may well apply to particularly sensitive operations which cause great public concern and which have been the subject of a large amount of lobbying from members of the public. It is in circumstances where particular concern is expressed to the local authority or to HMIP by community groups or local residents that the Secretary of State may find a political bonus in releasing the information required. A good example of when this power could be used would be where there was a large disaster. The then Environment Minister, David Trippier, when explaining this particular section of the EPA 1990 said:

After the Chernobyl disaster, commercial confidentiality affected the amount of information that we could release. The lack of public information served only to increase public disquiet.

Naturally the right to overrule commercial confidentiality is a draconian one and will only be used in limited circumstances.

The time limit for the exclusion of information from the register is four years from the original exclusion. This obviously takes into account the fact that the confidentiality of information may well have decreased somewhat over that time period and therefore the exclusion of the information from the register is no longer justified. However, it is open to the applicant to apply to the authority for a further exclusion on the grounds that the information is still commercially confidential.

The Environmental Protection (Applications, Appeals and Registers) Regulations 1991 (SI 1991 No. 507) make detailed provision for the maintenance of the registers. There are a number of areas for concern. First, only data obtained by the enforcement agencies as a result of their own monitoring, or as supplied to them in exercise of their powers of information gathering under EPA 1990, s. 19, or under a condition of an authorisation, are to be included.

Secondly, in relation to information concerning 'the assessment of the environmental consequences of a prescribed process', the only requirement is to release 'all particulars of any reports published'. Clearly, the enforcing authority will have a discretion as to whether or not it publishes such 'data'. Once again there is evidence to suggest that informal non-disclosure agreements may preclude the provision of access to environmental information. Lastly, there is no deadline for the entry of information after it has been received.

The first decisions on the commercial confidentiality rules related to appeals by the power generating utilities. Both appeals involved applications for authorisations for power stations under Part I of EPA 1990.

In the first case, PowerGen argued that the disclosure of emission levels from its power stations would prove to be valuable to either a competitor or a supplier of fuel. This claim was rejected by the Secretary of State as it was considered that the figures would not unreasonably prejudice PowerGen's interests and should therefore be disclosed.

In the other decision, on an application by National Power, the Secretary of State thought that the relevant information was unnecessary to enable the public to comment on the applications and was information which would not normally be required to assess whether or not to grant an authorisation.

These decisions would tend to suggest that the test for commercial confidentiality depends just as much on the relevance of the information to the application as on the effect of disclosure on commercial interests.

The Chemical Releases Inventory

The information kept on the IPC registers does not, however, provide enough information to enable a proper assessment to be made of the total effects of releases upon the environment as a whole. Whilst it enables individuals to appraise an individual operator and its performance as set against its authorisation conditions, it does not provide an adequate measure of compliance with general environmental quality objectives.

Therefore, in addition to the registers kept under Part I of the EPA 1990, HMIP also publishes a database of aggregated information taken from the registers, which is known as the Chemical Release Inventory (CRI).

Information from the database forms the basis of an annual report, which sets out figures for releases from prescribed processes to all environmental media in tabular form.

The main purpose of the CRI is to fulfil part of the Government's commitment to increase access to environmental information, as set out in *This Common Inhentance*. Secondly, it is intended to clarify the scale and nature of releases from IPC processes and to facilitate an informed analysis of the sources and effects of pollution which should enable priorities for action to be identified. Finally, it is hoped that the CRI will provide a useful resource to enable industry to identify opportunities for waste minimisation. The model for the CRI is taken from the Toxic Release Inventory (TRI) in the US. Since the publication of the TRI in 1987 the so-called 33/50 programme (which was based upon information contained in the TRI) has resulted in over 600 US companies reducing emissions by 33% by the end of 1992 and 50% by the end of 1995.

Although the database was established in 1991, the first printed annual report was published at the end of 1994, with information gathered in the calendar years 1992 and 1993. As IPC was introduced over a number of years for different processes the first report included only a relatively small proportion of information on releases.

The data which forms the database is gathered from individual operators as a normal part of the requirement to provide monitoring information. When completed it will cover over 360 substances (and 125 isotopes). The individual monitoring information is then aggregated by HMIP using formulae agreed with the operator so that an overall picture can be gained. This is then incorporated with other information so that regional and sectoral information can be presented. The annual report gives information on the releases of substances released from all processes to all media. It also provides tables that show releases of substances to each media, by country (the database covers England and Wales), by county and by district council, with separate tables covering industry sectors, industry types and process types.

In addition to the annual report, individuals can search the database itself. Searches can be made by reference to HMIP region, operator details, location, substance, media and authorisation number.

Although the CRI is the first attempt to take environmental information onto a broader scale, it has been the subject of criticism. First, it does not give a completely accurate picture of all releases. For example, it does not include non-point sources such as motor vehicles. This has led to a vast understatement of the quantities of certain chemicals. In the case of methane, where most releases arise from livestock or landfill operations, it is estimated that less than 1% of the total releases are to be found in the database. Secondly, there is no information kept in relation to LAAPC consents and/or discharge consents. HMIP has expressed the intention to incorporate such information as soon as practicable and it is expected that the amalgamation of the enforcement agencies under the Environment Act 1995 should help facilitate this.

Air pollution

In the majority of cases, access to information relating to air pollution will be covered under the registers discussed above. However, there are further controls under a number of different statutes. Primarily, smoke pollution is dealt with under the Clean Air Act 1993. There are no specific directions for disclosure, although under s. 34(1) local authorities have vague powers to arrange for research and publicity with regard to air pollution. However, these vague powers are then virtually nullified by s. 34(2), which makes it a criminal offence to disclose any information obtained under the Clean Air Act provisions which relates to a trade secret.

Access to information held by local government

Environmental information held by local authorities is available to the general public under the Local Government (Access to Information) Act 1985 and the Environmental Information Regulations 1992.

Under the 1985 Act all regulatory powers exercised by local authorities can be the subject of public scrutiny where those powers are exercised by way of committee. This would include areas such as planning, waste disposal, environmental health (e.g. statutory nuisances), air pollution and mineral matters. This information is normally available in the form of reports made by officers to committee, which would include any accompanying documentation (for further details, see p. 53).

The Environmental Information Regulations 1992

The pace of moves towards free access to environmental information has quickened with the introduction and adoption of the EC Directive on Freedom of Access to Environmental Information (90/313).

The implementation of the Directive into domestic legislation has seen a move away from the traditional register-based access to environmental information into a broader system. The Environmental Information Regulations (SI 1992 No. 3240), which were brought into force on 31 December 1992, extended the availability of information held by public bodies. The regulations were made under the European Communities Act 1972 and thus follow the terms of the Directive closely. As in the case of the Environmental Assessment Directive 85/337, however, there are some variations, and arguably some exclusions.

Under the regulations, public authorities with responsibilities for the environment must make environmental information available to any person who requests it. 'Environmental information' is defined widely and includes information on the quality and state of air, water, soil, flora, fauna, natural sites and other land. It also covers activities which adversely affect these areas and the measures which are used to protect them.

The regulations apply to all public authorities which have responsibilities for the environment. The Department of the Environment, local authorities, waste regulation authorities and other public bodies carrying out regulatory functions would come within the definition. There is, however, a whole range of private bodies which carry out public functions in relation to the environment. For instance, the water services companies and the local authority waste disposal companies both carry out roles which are semi-public. It is assumed that such bodies would be subject to the regulations, at least in relation to some of their functions, although the picture is far from clear.

Where a request is made to a public body it has to be responded to as soon as possible, and in any event not more than two months from the date of the request. If the request is refused then any refusal must be in writing and reasons given. The reasons for rejecting the request may vary. The body to whom the request is addressed may consider that it is not subject to the regulations, there may be no information which can usefully be given, or the information requested does not fall within the terms of the regulations. Lastly, the information may be exempt or, where a request is vague, formulated in too general a manner or manifestly unreasonable. In these circumstances the public body is entitled to reject the request.

Exceptions

There is a long list of categories of information which are exempt from the regulations. Certain of these categories are considered to be strictly confidential, whereas others are subject to the discretion of the relevant authority:

(a) *Mandatory confidentiality.* Certain categories of information are always viewed as being confidential:

(i)   Personal information where an individual has not given consent to its disclosure.
(ii)   Material disclosed voluntarily by a third party.
(iii) Information which would increase the likelihood of damage to the environment if disclosed.

(b) *Discretionary confidentiality.* Certain categories of information are considered to be confidential only if the authority determines them to be so:

(i)   Information affecting national security, public defence, or international relations.
(ii)   Information which is or has previously been *sub judice* or the subject of an inquiry.
(iii) Information from internal communications or unfinished documents.
(iv)   Commercially confidential information.

The availability of information

The information which is available includes anything contained in any records, registers, reports, returns and computer records.

A charge can be made in respect of the costs attributable to the supply of the information, and such a charge can be levied as a condition of the supply of the information. As is usual, the information only has to be available in such a form and at such times and places as is reasonable.

Remedies for failure to supply information

There is no right of appeal against the refusal to supply the information. Central guidance suggests that the only available remedy is that of judicial review. It is, however, difficult to envisage the situation where an individual would be prepared to mount such an action without a firm idea of the type of information which is required.

Although the regulations would appear to make a wider range of information available to members of the general public, they are not without criticism. Clearly, the wide range of mandatory and discretionary exceptions makes the categories of information which are available particularly narrow. Moreover, without any right of appeal it is unlikely to be utilised frequently. Lastly, the ability to refuse a request on the grounds of unreasonableness or vagueness precludes the use of the regulations for anything but a specific request about information which is known to be held by the public body. In such circumstances the regulations may be superfluous.

The public's utilisation of registers

One of the major difficulties undermining the system of easier access to information within Britain is that research has shown that, even where there is information which can easily be obtained, public participation in the system is said to be low. In their Fourth Report, the Royal Commission stated:

> certainly experience in the local government field has shown that 'public participation'—often consisting of little more than one way provision of information at meagrely attended public meetings—can be an unrewarding ritual for those charged with the task of organising it. However, the essential requirement is that information should be *available*, not that it should be forcefully fed to the public.

It is clear, though, that the basis upon which the system is founded is that the public should have a desire to receive information from the register for themselves. The empirical evidence suggests otherwise. A research project carried out on the utilisation of the registers kept under the Control of Pollution Act 1974 and then the Water Act 1989 has shown that there are relatively few people who are particularly interested in the registers. In the period August 1985 to December 1986, when the registers were first opened, a survey showed that there were 75 enquiries made to Severn Trent Water Authority, 85 to Anglian Water and 70 to Yorkshire Water, making up a total of some 230 requests to look at the register as compared with the millions of people who were resident in each of those areas. Furthermore, when the figures were broken down, by far and away the majority of enquiries were from sellers of septic tank equipment who used the registers as a database from which to sell their wares. Other enquiries came from environmental protection groups who used the registers to check up on information regularly.

The system of registers has received general approval from most parties. The difficulties with the previous systems under COPA 1974 and the Water Act 1989 have, however, underlined some practical problems. In evidence submitted to the House of Lords European Select Committee, Friends of the Earth pointed out that many samples collected were not entered on to the register because they were 'operational' samples rather than samples taken for the purposes of monitoring compliance and legislation. Thus, it was argued that too great a discretion was given to the enforcement agency, which allowed the system to be abused.

Moreover, Friends of the Earth argued that the effectiveness of the register was governed by five factors. They suggested that a system of registers should be:

(a)   conveniently located;
(b)   user friendly;
(c)   not excessively expensive;
(d)   interactive;
(e)   adequately resourced.

The Select Committee regarded it as '. . . of paramount importance that any system of registers should both be accessible geographically and "user friendly". These features should be possible with modern data-processing techniques'.

It was suggested that a two-tier system be utilised. The first tier would contain basic data in a register form with an indication of any further information available at the second tier. The second tier itself might contain the more complicated information which would explain some of the references on the simpler level.

Even so, the registers as they exist have a low level of interest for the members of the general public. Figures available from the NRA's Annual Report in 1989/90 disclosed a marked increase in the utilisation of the registers and this has increased substantially in the 1990s. However, as percentages of the overall population of each individual authority, the use of the registers is still remarkably low. Tim Burton, who has carried out detailed research into access to environmental information in water registers, identified three areas of possible explanation for the low level of utilisation of these registers. These were awareness, accessibility and difficulty with interpreting the data itself.

Awareness
Many members of the public are uncertain as to who controls the different areas of pollution control. As has been seen in Chapter 3, there is a plethora of environmental enforcement agencies each with their own individual responsibilities. It is often difficult for those closely involved in the field to understand such a complex administrative structure. For the lay person it is sometimes impossible to differentiate between the various local and national

agencies. Furthermore, the presence of registers containing public information is perhaps even less well known. Initially, there were delays in the implementation of the Control of Pollution Act 1974 and the 11-year gap between the passing of the Act and the introduction of the registers tended to obscure their value. One of the suggested reasons for the increase in the utilisation of the registers after the Water Act 1989 was the redefinition of the regulatory role and the media attention given to the newly created NRA. However, the information available to members of the public to inform them of the existence of the registers is still particularly low. In Appendix 6 of the NRA Annual Report and Accounts for 1989/90, there is a list of the publicity material published by each regional authority. It is interesting to note that of the ten regional offices, only two, Yorkshire and Anglian, have specific publicity material relating to the public registers. It may be no coincidence then that, when looking at the figures for the utilisation of the registers, both Anglian and Yorkshire have consistently been two out of the top three for numbers of enquiries, only being overtaken by the Thames region, which has a far higher population level. Clearly, a national policy is required on the production of materials to make the public more aware of the registers. National initiatives rather than just publicity on a region-by-region basis would iron out any disparity between different areas.

Access

The policy governing the location of the registers has differed from region to region. The geographical area of each regional authority is very large and that could mean that people would have to travel a long way in order to view the registers. Certain regions use their powers under the regulations to set up duplicate copies of the registers at different regional offices. For instance, Yorkshire NRA set up their registers at York, Bradford, Leeds and Sheffield. However, two regions, Thames and Anglian, established only one register. In the case of Anglian, where the register was set up at their head office in Peterborough, some people who lived within the area of the water authority were almost 150 miles away from the registers. Clearly, there was very little incentive for many people to go and check the registers.

Also, in most legislation the registers are required to be open only for 'reasonable hours'. This term has received a number of interpretations, including a view that 'reasonable' could take into account the fact that there were insufficient staff to keep the registers open for significant periods of the day. It has been assumed that 'reasonable' is to be viewed from the perspective of the person coming to view the registers. However, most are open only during working hours and there is no effort made to make one evening a week or a month available to people who wish to view the registers, but do not have the ability to leave work early. One suggestion is that there should be some form of 'travelling road show' set up by the NRA which could visit towns within the region other than the central office, informing and educating the public of their right to come and view the register. This would facilitate public participation and, in addition, increase public awareness of the separation of the water services companies from the regulatory body.

Additionally, charges can be made for copies taken from the register. Charging differentials between the regions is high. Some regions charged nothing for a small amount of copying, whereas others inflicted relatively high charges. When all these facts are taken together a visit to see the register can amount to a rather daunting experience. As two officials from the old Severn Trent Water Authority put it, 'the obstacles to the man in the street are quite formidable'. Moreover, these formidable obstacles make life particularly unpleasant for those people who are not normally used to dealing with officialdom. This will not act as an incentive for them to use the register again. Tim Burton points out:

> If a first time enquirer finds the enquiry an 'unpleasant' experience not only will he be unlikely to return, but he may dissuade other potential enquirers from taking their first step towards utilisation of the registers.

HMIP has made a number of changes to the availability of information by increasing the number of centres where the public can make enquiries.

Difficulties with the information on the registers themselves

One of the issues constantly raised about the interpretation of data contained on the register has been that the information would be too complicated for the lay person to understand. There can be a distinction drawn here between the 'semi-professional' amenity groups and the person off the street who is looking at the registers for the first time. In the latter case, to enable the proper interpretation of the data there should always be staff readily available to assist enquirers. The provision of expert help to enable the data to be properly understood is essential to ensure that the registers are utilised by 'newcomers' to the regulatory system. If it is intended that the registers should receive a wider recognition, education as to the manner of use of the registers, together with expert advice on interpretation, will enable the private individual to assess the data in an informed manner. Although the registers have been under-utilised in the past, reasons for this are being dealt with. The desire of the public to visit these registers will undoubtedly increase as further information becomes available and there is an increased awareness of environmental issues.

There is one final point. The registers will enable individuals to check and see the slow but steady progress towards the improvement of environmental quality standards in Britain. With the issue of the environment being high on the political agenda the pressure on any Government to 'produce the goods' will only be heightened when there is a national 'auditing' facility contained within the system of registers.

EIGHT

The common law and the protection of the environment

The development of the law relating to the protection of the environment is not solely governed by the realm of public and administrative law. Although the spread of administrative and bureaucratic controls has accelerated within the last 50 years, traditionally, at first glance anyway, private law has attempted to serve a similar function in controlling damage caused to the environment. This similarity has caused confusion. Private law, essentially the law of tort and contract, serves as a mechanism of environmental protection primarily through the control of competing uses of land rather than the protection of the environment.

The system of common law developed from the time of the Norman conquest in an attempt to cope with new disputes over use and abuse of land. As the system developed, it incidentally became a mechanism for environmental protection. The hybrid nature of the common law's role in environmental protection can be demonstrated by looking at the characteristics which distinguish it from the more usual methods of public law control.

The characteristics of the common law as a mechanism of environmental protection

The common law acts only as a protector of private interest

The primary function of private law actions is to protect interests in land rather than the more nebulous concept of 'environmental rights'. Consequently, the factors governing the decision to take action against polluters are mainly personal. Potential plaintiffs are more concerned about balancing their own interests against the loss suffered, be that financial or the loss of enjoyment of their property. The protection of the environment demands that other factors have to be taken into account. Sometimes it is clear that human interests are contrary to the interests of the environment. For example, it is possible to acquire an easement to pollute a river. It is arguable whether such activity could ever be in the interests of the environment. However, in certain circumstances, the private law seeks to protect the private interests of individuals.

The protection of private rights is based upon imprecise standards

We have already seen in Chapter 5 that the public law controls protecting the environment are based primarily upon standards of environmental quality. Such standards regulate activities specifically by attempting to impose definite limits upon substances which can be emitted into the environment. These levels are often expressed as quantitative limits. These limits allow for relatively simple enforcement as the detection of breaches can be effectively monitored and proper assessments can be made of any discharge.

The monitoring of such discharges involves scientific and technical skills. Without those skills, the accumulation of devastating substances can affect the environment on a long-term basis.

It is this type of pollution which can only be dealt with effectively by quantitative standards and scientific monitoring. Private law mechanisms meet neither criteria. Generally, the common law is based upon imprecise standards unrelated to specified levels. In attempting to balance competing private interests, the common law looks to the reasonableness of actions rather than restricting conduct to specific levels. What is reasonable depends upon the circumstances of each case. Maintaining this balance means that the same result will not be guaranteed from any two cases.

The main mechanism of control, the tort of private nuisance, can broadly be defined as the unreasonable interference with the reasonable use and enjoyment of land. This implies that there are areas which require further analysis. What is a reasonable use? What would be unreasonable? These questions underline the large degree of uncertainty involved in bringing an action in private nuisance. An illustration of the types of uncertainty surrounding private law actions in nuisance and how there can be a detrimental effect to the environment can be found in the so-called locality doctrine in private nuisance.

This doctrine asserts the need to take into account 'the circumstances of the place where the thing complained of actually occurs' (*St Helens Smelting Co.* v *Tipping* (1865) 11 HLC 642). Putting it simply, those who live in towns or close to factories have to expect a dirtier, smellier environment than those who live in the countryside. The flaws in this doctrine are clear. In terms of environmental protection, those areas which require the greatest degree of control are often the same as those to which the most damage has to occur before an action can be founded. The accumulation of polluting substances, be they dust, noise or fumes, actually raises the degree of nuisance required. As one commentator puts it 'Those who suffer most from the ravages of pollution are the least worthy of protection' (McLaren (1972) *10 Osgoode Hall Law Journal* 505).

The right of action is limited

As the common law seeks to balance competing individual rights, the right to take action is normally vested only in those who are directly harmed. Generally, this means the individual in possession of land which suffers damage. Although there are narrow rights for groups to take action in public nuisance, the basis of an action in common law still remains the protection of land and its ownership rather than the environment. The concept of 'environmental rights' is as yet undeveloped in the United Kingdom. The idea that there should be an ability to bring an action on behalf of flora and fauna rather as children bring actions through a guardian *ad litem* seems strange. The private law seeks to compensate one landowner by granting compensation from another. A move away from this system would be difficult. The private law does not properly seek to compensate for environmental damage where there are no rights of ownership to protect or an owner does not wish to pursue an action.

Problems of proof

Whereas, in public law, the proof of the breach of a regulation involves scientific evidence that is more or less irrefutable, there is great difficulty in showing a cause of action for environmental pollution in the common law.

First, there are often problems surrounding the establishment of a causal link between the origins of pollution and the damage. For instance, it is the nature of airborne deposits that they could have originated from a site many miles from the area of damage. Seeking to show that the damage emanates from a particular site in these circumstances is particularly difficult. Moreover, in areas of heavy industrialised activity these difficulties become even more complex. For instance there could be five factories within a two mile radius, all producing and dispersing similar acidic emissions into the atmosphere. Trying to differentiate between each emission requires highly technical evidence. The expense of carrying out investigations such as these will often militate against individuals taking action and it may be that no definite culprit can be identified.

Secondly, there is a large degree of subjectivity involved in assessing the reasonableness of activities. Unfortunately, what would be acceptable to some in terms of environmental damage would not be acceptable to others. Some find the smells of certain fumes offensive whereas others have a high tolerance level. Again, this uncertainty prevents any proper guidelines being laid down as to when activities will incur liability.

Private law as a fault-based system

In certain circumstances, the bringing of an action under common law requires there to be some fault on behalf of the person creating the damage. Very few pollution incidents occur because of deliberate actions by careless and unthinking individuals. Mostly incidents arise because of a number of circumstances which would not normally be foreseeable but which give rise to damage. The common law does not always seek to redress any damage caused by such accidents. It is only in situations where the pollution is foreseeable that an action will normally be founded.

Reactive controls

Private law controls are only reactive and compensatory rather than preventative. It is only very rarely that private law can be used to prevent environmental damage. Although it is possible in certain circumstances to seek anticipatory injunctions, on the whole the controls tend to be post-damage, that is to say, after the harm is discovered. Private law offers no continuing control, nor does it necessarily seek to remedy harm. When compensation is paid there are no rules governing the manner in which the money has to be spent. Damages are often assessed as being the difference in value between the land as it was before an act of damage and the value afterwards. This does not necessarily include clean-up costs although those can form a part of any claim.

Controls are not purely environmental

The wide range of activities covered by civil remedies extends far beyond those activities covered under the umbrella of the environment. As an incidental effect, the common law provides for the prevention of pollution or the protection of the public but the protection spreads much wider to the coverage of a whole range of civil rights. The effect of this is to ensure that the system has built up in an unsystematic way and in some ways mirrors the piecemeal nature of the statutory controls.

Is the common law as a protection mechanism dead?

The criticisms of the private law as being too expensive, too long-winded and too uncertain have led to its low utilisation as a tool for environmental protection. The roots of its weaknesses can be traced back to the nineteenth century when industrial pollution was in its infancy. With no statutory regulations to control the growth of polluting processes it might be thought that the common law would serve as the primary mechanism for protection. However, McLaren presented very cogent arguments that other factors, including institutional, social and economic matters, outweighed the importance of the environmental benefit to be procured from such control (see pp. 154 and 168).

The courts have consistently struggled with the use of the common law for environmental protection. Indeed, the judiciary have often sought to separate the system of administrative regulatory protection from private law remedies where, in fact, there is often a significant overlap. In *Wheeler* v *JJ Saunders* (see below at p. 179) the court took the view that the planning system (with the emphasis upon the public interest) was entirely different to the exercise of private rights which protect property interests. In addition, the House of Lords' judgment in the *Cambridge Water* decision (see below at p. 182) suggested that the courts would prefer the relative 'safety' of the growth of administrative mechanisms to developing the common law. Taken together, these strands of judicial thinking would appear to make the development of the common law for environmental protection unlikely. This would be more acceptable if administrative controls were adapted to provide substitutes for private rights, such as compensation.

Civil liability in statutes

In addition to the common law, there is a number of statutes which impose liability by means of private law remedies, rather than the more usual public law methods.

(a) Nuclear Installations Act 1965
The individual problems of nuclear installations are not adequately dealt with by the law of tort. As the incident in Chernobyl demonstrated, the damage caused by nuclear actions can be widespread and not confined to a specific period of time. There are also difficulties of proving a causal link between the injury caused and exposure to radiation. Many diseases that are caused by radiation also occur naturally, and trying to establish whether or not there is an epidemiological link is frequently fraught with difficulties. Therefore, to avoid these difficulties, the Nuclear Installations Act 1965 introduced absolute civil liability for all damage caused from certain occurrences (ss. 7–10).

(b) Merchant Shipping (Oil Pollution) Act 1971
In the wake of numerous oil disasters in the mid- to late 1960s, international concern led to the introduction of this Act to compensate for damage from oil. It is specific in that liability under the Act only arises from pollution from oil tankers. The implementation of this statute again deals with the inadequacies of tort in trying to cope with transfrontier contamination. The intention of the Act is to impose strict liability on owners of ships in relation to physical damage to property and personal injury from oil pollution (s. 1). The financing of the majority of losses stemming from the Act is covered by a compulsory insurance scheme, although there is a further international fund for compensation which pays out in situations where a shipowner cannot afford to pay the damages. There are a number of statutory defences which cover circumstances such as war, intentional acts of damage by third parties, or poor governmental control of navigation or lighting (s. 2).

(c) Environmental Protection Act 1990, s. 73
Section 73(6) of EPA 1990 imposes civil liability for the unlawful deposit of waste (see p. 408).

(d) Other private law remedies
The most common application of private law remedies as used for environmental protection is that of the law of tort (see below). However, there are other private law mechanisms which are useful in this context. Restrictive covenants, for instance, govern the activities which can be carried out upon land. A further example can be seen where local planning authorities and/or developers enter into planning obligations under the Town and Country Planning Act 1990, s. 106. Such obligations may be used for a whole variety of purposes, including to restrict the class of occupants of premises or to restrict the type of operation that can be carried out from those premises. These mechanisms have the advantage of maintaining a fairly tight degree of control over the use of land, which can only be varied in a few circumstances.

A mechanism which is being used more frequently is the ability to enter into contractual agreements to restrict the use of land. Management agreements made in nitrate sensitive areas under the Water Resources Act 1991 are essentially contracts between the Minister of Agriculture, Fisheries and Food and an individual to restrict the use of certain agricultural activities so that the nitrates used in farming will not pollute the waters in the area. Under s. 95 of the Act, a voluntary arrangement can be agreed whereby certain agricultural practices will not be carried out on the land and in return compensation will be paid for the restrictions. These types of management agreement are not as wide-ranging as freehold or leasehold covenants as they are not necessarily binding on third parties (unless of course statute makes them so).

The law of tort and environmental protection

This book does not aim to deal specifically with the law of tort as it is more than adequately covered in other textbooks. However, the general principles can, in certain circumstances, be used to protect the environment and these are outlined below.

The law of nuisance

As stated earlier, the law of nuisance is concerned with the unlawful interference with a person's use or enjoyment of land, or of some right over or in connection with it. This definition illustrates one of the primary distinctions between nuisance and other torts in that the protection afforded is directed towards controlling proprietary interests rather than the control of an individual's conduct. As has already been pointed out, the protection of proprietary rights can have the incidental effect of providing a general benefit to the wider community by achieving improvements in environmental quality. There have been occasions where the effect upon the community has been a negative one. In *Bellew* v *Cement Co.* [1948] Ir.R 61, an interlocutory injunction was granted to restrain the noisy blasting at a quarry. This remained effective for several months. The effect of this stoppage upon the supply of cement in Ireland was devastating as 80% of the cement used in Ireland was created by materials from the quarry. Thus the court upheld the protection of the private right involved at the expense of employment and construction.

The basis for a claim in nuisance is founded upon a balancing exercise centred around the question of reasonableness. As was stated in *Saunders Clark* v *Grosvenor Mansion Company Limited & D'Alles-Sandry* [1900] 2 Ch 373:

the Court must consider whether the defendant is using his property reasonably or not. If he is using it reasonably, there is nothing which at law can be considered a nuisance; but if he is not using it reasonably . . . then the plaintiff is entitled to relief.

Thus, in attempting to assess liability in a nuisance action, a balance is made between the reasonableness of the defendant's activity and its impact upon the plaintiff's proprietary rights.

In assessing the balance, a court will take into account a number of specific factors including the locality of the nuisance, the duration of the nuisance, and any hypersensitivity on the part of the plaintiff.

The locality doctrine

The case of *St Helens Smelting Co.* v *Tipping* (1865) 11 HLC 642 illustrates the workings of the doctrine particularly well. In the mid-nineteenth century, St Helens was the centre of the alkali industry. The average life expectancy was well under 25 and it had built up a reputation as one of the dirtiest towns in Britain. The physical impact of the works had left most vegetation in the area dead and adversely affected the health of cattle. Mr Tipping brought an action in private nuisance. The court drew the distinction between actual physical damage to property and a nuisance which would only cause 'personal discomfort'. In the latter situation, the locality of the nuisance would be a material factor in assessing the balancing exercise. In a famous quote in the case of *Sturges* v *Bridgman* (1879) 11 ChD 852, Thesiger LJ stated, 'What would be a nuisance in Belgrave Square would not necessarily be so in Bermondsey'.

The unfortunate consequences of this approach have already been outlined. Although there is a distinction drawn between actual damage done to property and interference with the enjoyment of property, in practice there is often an overlap. It has been alleged that the economic effect of nuisance can be just as detrimental as physical damage to an interest in land. If, for instance, a house is situated by a pig farm, the smells emanating from that may well make the house less attractive to potential buyers, but under the locality doctrine it could be argued that in an agricultural area an owner has to expect such farmyard smells (see, however, *Wheeler* v *JJ Saunders* below at p. 179).

However, even in the most heavily industrialised areas, there is not an absolute freedom to produce polluting materials. An illustration was given in the case of *Rushmer* v *Polsue and Alfieri* [1906] Ch 234, where Cozens-Hardy LJ said:

> It does not follow that because I live, say, in the manufacturing part of Sheffield I cannot complain if a steam-hammer is introduced next door, and so worked as to render sleep at night almost impossible, although previously to its introduction my house was a reasonably comfortable abode, having regard to the local standard; and it would be no answer to say that the steam-hammer is of the most modern approved pattern and is reasonably worked. In short, if a substantial addition is found as a fact in any particular case, it is no answer to say that the neighbourhood is noisy and that the defendant's machinery is of first-class character.

In that case, there was an injunction sought against a printing press being operated in Fleet Street, even though there were many other printing presses in the area and others also operated at night. The House of Lords affirmed the decision of the Court of Appeal and granted the injunction.

When viewing the case law on the locality doctrine, two main strands of judicial thinking can be identified. McLaren in his article on the foundation of the law of private nuisance suggests that there are two contradictory judicial views. The first is based upon property rights and is essentially a natural rights theory. Basically, where there is any interference with property rights which is not trivial then there should be a right of action to take steps to prevent such interference (e.g. *Bellew* v *Cement Company*). The second judicial view takes a more rational approach to the problem of environmental pollution and nuisance claims. This could be described as the view of social utility. In this view there tends to be a balance taken between the social utility of the action complained of as weighed against the environmental harm caused (see *St. Helens Smelting Co.* v *Tipping* and *Sturges* v *Bridgman*). A third view could be that in the cases involving physical damage it is much easier to be influenced by the natural rights argument as the extent of the damage is easily quantified. With the uncertainty of the assessment of damages for interference with the reasonable enjoyment of land there is a far greater demand for a counterbalance to be taken.

There can, however, be situations where the grant of planning permission has such a significant effect upon the locality that a nuisance will not arise (see *Gillingham BC* v *Medway (Chatham Dock Co.) Ltd* below at p. 179).

Sensibility

One of the balancing factors to be taken into account is the amount to which the nuisance can be 'sensed'. The law does not take into account mere trivial unpleasantness.

Unlike other forms of tort, nuisance is not actionable without proof of damage. The inconvenience has to be able to be 'sensed' by reasonable members of the public. It has to be capable of being seen, smelt or tasted by persons other than the defendant. However, that does not mean to say that where one person senses the nuisance that is sufficient for an action to be founded.

A good example of this rule of *de minimis* can be found in the case of *Attorney-General* v *Gastonia Coaches Limited* [1977] RTR 219. This case involved a nuisance emanating from a company which was operating a large number of coaches from a residential area. The activities on the site included general maintenance as well as the storage of the vehicles overnight. The judge in the case made a distinction between the two different elements of nuisance. First he said that the nuisance from the smell of the fumes from the engines and the noise from the engines as they were revved could amount to a nuisance. However, he also said that the noise emanating from the vehicles as they were cleaned and repaired did not amount to 'serious interference'.

The duration of nuisance

For a nuisance to be actionable it must be something which is more than temporary. Isolated incidents can give rise to a nuisance only where the use which gives rise to the risk of that isolated nuisance is of itself a continuing use. For example, a factory which produces fumes does not necessarily have to produce those fumes continuously over a period of years for there to be a nuisance. However, where there are isolated incidents occurring regularly then the use of the land for that purpose is of itself a nuisance. The more isolated the occurrence, however, the less the likelihood that the use being carried out is a nuisance. In *Harrison* v *Southwark and Vauxhall Water Company* [1891] 2 Ch 409, the defendant was a water company which had dug a shaft to pump water from land adjacent to the plaintiffs. As the shaft was being sunk the pumps that were being used created a continuous noise. Mr Harrison brought an action in nuisance to stop the noise. In finding against Mr Harrison the court held that the works were not actionable because they were temporary and that such temporary works would only be actionable if unreasonable methods were used, unless physical damage was caused. Vaughan Williams J said:

> For instance, a man who pulls down his house for the purpose of building a new one no doubt causes considerable inconvenience to his next door neighbours during the process of demolition; but he is not responsible as for a nuisance if he uses all reasonable skill and care to avoid annoyance to his neighbour by the works of demolition. Nor is he liable to an action, even though the noise and dust and the consequent annoyance be such as would constitute a nuisance if the same . . . had been created in sheer wantonness, or in the execution of works for a purpose involving a permanent continuance of the noise and dust.

Again, judicial thinking seems to have been affected by taking a realistic balance of the number and type of occurrences as against the utility involved in the operation itself.

The hypersensitive plaintiff

The test for assessing a nuisance has two elements. Not only must the use of land which is complained of be unreasonable, but also the use of the land to which the nuisance applies must be a reasonable use. If a potential plaintiff is particularly sensitive to one type of nuisance then it will not be actionable unless that nuisance would have affected a 'reasonable' person. In *Robinson* v *Kilvert* (1889) 41 ChD 88, the defendant let out part of his building to the plaintiff to be used as a paper warehouse. The defendant himself kept some of the space in the building for a particular use which required the air within the building to be kept hot and dry. This use had consequently heated the floor of the paper warehouse and damaged the paper kept there. Unfortunately, the paper stored in the upper rooms was of a particularly sensitive nature. Normal paper would not have been affected to such an extent. The defendant argued that the plaintiff had not told him of the intended use of the premises and in the particular circumstances the Court of Appeal held that there was no nuisance:

> A man who carries on an exceptionally delicate trade cannot complain because it is injured by his neighbour doing something which would not injure anything but an exceptionally delicate trade.

The effect of the rule laid down in that case is perhaps not as wide as first imagined. The principle only applies when the unreasonableness of the conduct is specifically the result of the hypersensitivity of the plaintiff. If there is an independent cause of action brought because of the inherent unreasonableness of the nuisance, then action can still be taken. In the Canadian case of *McKinnon Industries Limited* v *Walker* [1951] 3 DLR 577, the defendants operated a motor car plant which emitted poisonous gases. The plaintiff grew orchids for sale and the gases unfortunately killed off his stock. He brought an action in nuisance. The defendants argued that the growing of orchids was a hypersensitive activity and therefore any damage suffered was not as a result of the unreasonable use of land. The court disagreed and held that the nuisance was independent of the special sensitivity of the plaintiff.

Thus, in pollution cases, there will be very few occasions where this particular factor will be taken into account. Normally, the type of pollution complained of will be itself a cause of action which can cancel out any arguments put forward about hypersensitivity.

Defences to a claim for nuisance

There are a number of defences which attempt to restrict the ambit of the law of nuisance. However, in practice, they are either so difficult to prove as to be useless, or of dubious merit.

The defence of prescription
Although it is possible in principle to acquire a right to pollute as an easement through 20 years continuous use, there are so many caveats that the practical use of the defence is very restricted. For the defence to apply, the right to pollute must be exercised openly, continuously and not with any specific permission of the person against whom it is so acquired. It must also be the result of a lawful act, so a discharge in breach of a consent would not suffice. For example, in the case of *Sturges* v *Bridgman* (1879) 11 ChD 852, the defendant, a confectioner, had used a noisy pestle and mortar in his premises in Wimpole Street for more than 20 years. There had not been any complaints over that period but a doctor residing at the back of the site built a new consulting room close to the defendant's operational area. Consequently, the noise became a problem. The Court of Appeal held that the defendant in this case had not acquired a right to pollute by prescription. In the court's opinion, the nuisance had commenced only after the consulting room had been constructed, because previously the activities complained of did not give rise to any interference. When the consulting room was occupied, however, such interference began. Thus, the period of 20 years did not start to run until the construction of the consulting rooms.

No defence to say that the plaintiff came to the nuisance
In *Bliss* v *Hall* (1838) 4 Bing NC 183, the defendant operated a business as a tallow chandler. This business had been operated for at least three years when the plaintiff moved in nearby. Unfortunately, the defendant's business

created highly toxic fumes which were blown over the plaintiff's land. The defendant argued that, as he had been on the site before the plaintiff, the plaintiff should have realised the state of the premises nearby and should therefore not be able to bring an action in nuisance. Tindal CJ said:

> The Plaintiff came to the house he occupies with all the rights which the common law affords, and one of them is the right to wholesome air. Unless the Defendant shows a prescriptive right to carry on his business in the particular the Plaintiff is entitled to judgement.

When this principle is combined with the principle contained in *Sturges* v *Bridgman,* it is clear that whenever an individual moves into an area there could be the creation of a new 'nuisance history' which negates the prescriptive rights principle because of the need to allow a further 20 years before a prescriptive right attaches.

In practical terms, the principle that it is no defence for a defendant to allege that the plaintiff has come to the nuisance is very important. Many old factories constructed in early Victorian times have now been surrounded by new housing. These potentially antagonistic uses can give rise to conflict. On the one hand, industrialists argue that they have been carrying out polluting activities for a large number of years without complaint and anyone who moved into the area would fully know of any problems. However, in law, the creation of a new right to take action effectively renders the process liable to be brought before the civil courts.

The courts have also held that a planning authority can grant planning permission for a new development even though this is likely to give rise to complaints from the new occupiers as a result of an existing incompatible use (see *R* v *Exeter CC ex parte JL Thomas and Co. Ltd* [1990] 1 All ER 413).

Statutory authority

There may be occasions where nuisances are caused by statutory or non-statutory bodies exercising their statutory authority. Where a body can point to such authority then this will amount to a defence if an action is brought against them for any consequential nuisance.

For example, in *Smeaton* v *Ilford Corporation* [1954] 1 Ch 450, there were particular problems with the Corporation's sewers. The nuisance complained of arose because the sewers in the area were overloaded as a consequence of many new houses in the area utilising their right to be connected to the existing sewer system. Unfortunately, the sewers were not able to cope properly with the amount of sewage. Furthermore, the local authority did not have powers to refuse to connect the houses to the existing sewer system. Upjohn J held that the overloaded sewers were not a nuisance, since the local authority had a statutory duty to take domestic sewage and could not refuse the amount that was causing an overflow. There is, of course, a degree of control over such difficulties by restricting the grant of planning permission for development of housing, or restricting housing development without proper provision being made for discharges to sewers.

Although most statutory obligations are expressly contained within the body of the statute itself, it is also clear that a defendant could claim the defence of statutory authority where there is a clear implication that such activities have been authorised by an Act. In *Allen* v *Gulf Oil Refining Limited* [1981] 1 All ER 353, the Gulf Oil Refining Act 1965 (a private Act of Parliament) gave the defendants power to acquire land for an oil refinery at Milford Haven. The oil refinery emitted smells, noise and vibration and a local resident brought an action against Gulf Oil in nuisance. The plaintiff argued in that case that although the Act gave the defendant the power to acquire land for the construction of the refinery, it did not give any guidelines as to how the refinery should be operated. Therefore, when the defendant sought to rely upon the defence of statutory authority it was suggested that, as the Act did not specifically allow for the operating of the plant in a manner which gave rise to a nuisance, the defence was unavailable. The House of Lords held that the statute implicitly gave the defendant an immunity to every act inevitably flowing from the construction of the refinery. The only possible exception to this would be where the nuisance complained of was of a greater degree than was necessary or where such activities were carried out in a negligent manner.

It should be pointed out that, where private rights are interfered with, it is often the case that statutes themselves provide for compensation. For example, where a new road is being built, statutory compensation is payable where there is injurious affection to the enjoyment of property which is the direct result of the works carried out. There are, however, situations where the interference with private rights is not compensated.

Private rights under the common law and the grant of planning permission

There is often a conflict between private rights under the common law of nuisance (i.e. the right to have the use of one's property without unreasonable interference) and the public law nature of the grant of planning permission (i.e. development granted in the public interest). Many uses of land which give rise to nuisances have the benefit of planning permission. In determining the grant of permission it must be assumed that the local planning authority has balanced the impact of the development upon private interests (e.g. neighbours) with any competing public interest and has concluded that the public interest in allowing the development to proceed outweighs any detriment (this assumption could be questionable in some cases). There is, however, still some overlap between the two systems as both environmental considerations and private interests are part of the decision-making process and they are, in certain circumstances, concerned with land-use (see *Great Portland Estates* v *Westminster CC* [1984] 3 All ER 744).

Difficulty arises when considering the nature of the overlap between these two considerations. The question arises, does the grant of planning permission extinguish the private rights of an individual to take action against an inevitable consequence of that which has been allowed to be developed (by virtue of the grant of planning permission)? In *Gillingham BC* v *Medway (Chatham) Dock Company* [1992] Env LR 98, Buckley J decided that the grant of planning permission for a commercial port was analogous to the defence of statutory authority (see above) and that it acted as a defence to a public noise nuisance from lorries travelling to and from the port. This case was criticised by a number of commentators (see Crawford [1992] JEL 262 and Waite [1992] 4 LMELR 119) because a broad interpretation of Buckley J's judgment suggested that the grant of planning permission could negate any action in nuisance. This would, if followed, have serious implications for those seeking to protect their private rights in nuisance. Effectively, it would mean that private rights would be extinguished without any redress or compensation which would be contrary to established principles of English law.

A narrow interpretation of the decision in *Gillingham*, and one adopted in the last edition of this book (see pp. 147–8) suggested that planning permission did not act as a *defence* to an action in nuisance. Instead, Buckley J's decision went to the heart of the *defnition* of a nuisance and the locality doctrine in particular. Under this interpretation the case could only be viewed as supporting the proposition that the grant of planning permission may act to change the nature of the area for the purposes of the locality test. Thus, the presence of lorries on the roads leading to and from the port was reasonable in the context of a commercial area.

The Court of Appeal clarified the situation in *Wheeler* v *JJ Saunders* [1995] Env LR 286 where the narrow interpretation of the *Gillingham* decision was preferred. The case concerned the grant of planning permission for pig-weaning units and allegations of a smell nuisance which occurred after the development was implemented. The court decided that the grant of planning permission could not act as a defence to a nuisance action and did not deprive the plaintiffs of the right to bring an action in nuisance. Moreover, the court sought to distinguish the *Gillingham* decision and redefined the narrow interpretation (to an even narrower definition). First, Gibson LJ sought to apply the *Gillingham* principle only to those developments which demand a consideration of 'strategic' planning issues which necessitated an explicit consideration of the public interest. Thus, in the case of, for example, a commercial port, it was clear that the interference with private rights had been balanced against the public interest and the development was found to be acceptable. This begs the question of what the dividing line is between 'strategic' decisions such as a commercial port, and secondary developments such as pig units; but Gibson LJ left this issue undetermined with the comment that 'it may be—and I express no concluded opinion—that some planning decisions will authorise some nuisances'.

Secondly, the *Gillingham* decision is restricted to those situations where the effects of the development make a specific change to the nature of the locality. In *Wheeler* the pig unit was situated in a rural area and did not bring about such a radical change. Finally, Buckley J in the *Gillingham* case suggested that the mere grant of permission could be sufficient enough to change the nature of the locality and implied that the allocation of land in a development plan could have the same effect. Sir John May made it clear in *Wheeler* that it is the implementation of the development rather than the grant of permission which could change the character of the area. This would appear to be the correct approach as the implementation of a development could have different consequences from that envisaged at the date of grant of planning permission.

The Court of Appeal, therefore, has truly dissected the *Gillingham* principle with the consequence that the decision has little practical effect, although it would still be true to say that major strategic developments can change the character of a locality (which is probably a view which would have been held before the *Gillingham* case). Both decisions demonstrate, however, that the judiciary is uncomfortable with the overlap between the exercise of rights conferred by public law powers and private law remedies. This, perhaps, reflects the essential problem which faces a court when adjudicating between the exercise of a right which has been determined to be acceptable in the public interest, and private rights which have been unreasonably interfered with. Both can be correct (in the court's eyes), yet one must lose. In *Wheeler* Gibson LJ accepted that there can be no assumption that the local planning authority can take away private rights, but suggested that there might be occasions where the regulatory body can legitimately override private rights. There are, of course, situations where the exercise of public powers can override private rights (e.g. the exercise of compulsory purchase powers), but compensation is normally payable to offset the loss. In relation to concepts like environmental harm this is difficult to envisage.

An assessment of nuisance as a tool for environmental protection

The common law principles of nuisance were available to counteract the problems of industrial pollution a long time before industrial growth started to bring about an increase in noxious emissions. However, it was still felt necessary to introduce statutory regulations under the Alkali Acts of 1863 to counteract the problems caused. This was not the only example of statutory intervention. There has been much argument amongst academics as to why, given the availability of common law remedies, it was felt necessary to introduce the supplementary administrative/public law controls.

Essentially, the reasons that have been identified for suggesting that the common law was under-utilised echo many of the weaknesses of the other mechanisms in environmental control. Environmental law was not, and is not, in a legal vacuum. The social and political context of pollution and the law neutralised attempts to deal with the environmental issues of increased industrialisation.

Resort to the law in the nineteenth century was always a rich person's prerogative. Taking an action to law was both lengthy and ultimately outside the reach of the vast majority of the population. Until 1854 an action to prevent a nuisance through an injunction required two actions to be taken, one through the common law, and one through the Court of Chancery.

Secondly, as we have seen, to bring an action in nuisance required a proprietary interest. In the mid-nineteenth century it has been estimated that only somewhere in the region of 15% of the population were owner/ occupiers. Thus, the vast majority of the population would have great difficulty in even founding an action. When coupled with the level of damages, notoriously low for interference with the enjoyment of land, there was an inevitable reluctance to take action.

Moreover, what has subsequently been identified as a complex system of power relationships ensured that in the social context there was tremendous pressure not to 'cause trouble'. Few workers would wish to proceed against their bosses and it was also clear that there was a certain degree of class solidarity amongst the industrialists themselves. Many factory owners bought up large areas of land surrounding their own sites and constructed low cost, high density housing to house their workers. This, coupled with the fact that it was often the case that the presence of an industry lowered surrounding land prices, meant that a factory owner could purchase the right to pollute the surrounding area very cheaply. Furthermore, although society has become inherently more litigious over the last 50 to 100 years, bringing environmental actions was, and has always been, somewhat different to the norm.

One of the few recorded cases, *St Helens Smelting* v *Tipping* (referred to above), illustrates these points well. Mr Tipping was a rich cotton magnate who owned 1300 acres of land. He could afford to risk the backlash of industrialists because of the well-documented conflict between the cotton and the chemical industries. The damages received in his case and also in other nuisance cases were appallingly low. In *Halsey* v *Esso Petroleum Company* [1961] 1 WLR 683, there had been constant noise, dirt and commotion which had caused great difficulties and misery to the plaintiff for some five years. Finding for the plaintiff, the court awarded the derisory sum of £200 damages.

Although the physical effects of pollution could often be seen, the long-term effects of exposure to noxious fumes and hazardous chemicals were not fully understood. In an era where so many preconditions were placed upon the bringing of an action, the ignorance of many of those subjected to a high level of pollution ensured that no action would ever be taken. Lack of technical knowledge often led to practical difficulties of proving the source of pollution. Without scientific instruments, and without a right to enter onto land and take samples, individuals were restricted in their ability to monitor problems.

The power of industrialists at legislative, local government and magisterial level was too great for the 'person in the street'. Thus, a climate was set in which pollution control received a low priority. Local authorities were most reluctant to use their powers to prosecute for public nuisances, and indeed were often responsible for much pollution themselves. The law of nuisance was just one aspect of a legal regime which included as its other elements political, social, economic and philosophical responses to pollution. The limitations of the civil law in general, which apply more particularly to the law of nuisance, were commented on in the Third Report of the Royal Commission on the Pollution of Rivers in 1867:

It [bringing a common law action] is an expensive remedy. For the same money which is spent over a hard fought litigation against a single manufacturer, a Conservancy Board armed with proper powers, might for years keep safe from all abuse, a long extensive river with hundreds of manufactories situated on its banks.

The law of nuisance and its relationship with environmental protection was discussed in *Cambridge Water Company* v *Eastern Counties Leather* [1994] 1 All ER 53. In that case, the Cambridge Water Company purchased a borehole at Sawston near Cambridge for the purpose of supplying drinking water to the surrounding inhabitants. ECL operated their business in Sawston and used a number of solvents in their processes. They had been established on their site for over 100 years, and until 1976 solvent had been delivered to their premises in 40 gallon drums. During that time fork-lift trucks were used to transport the solvent drums from storage. Over time, there were frequent spillages of solvent which found its way into the underground aquifer.

In 1985, as a result of an earlier EC Directive, regulations were introduced in the UK which restricted the maximum allowable concentration of particular solvents in drinking water. As a matter of chance, the drinking water abstracted from the borehole near Sawston was found to contain high levels of solvent. Further tests identified the tannery as being the main source of the solvent. The water company had to shut down that particular borehole and seek a supply from elsewhere. As a consequence, they brought an action in nuisance (see *Rylands* v *Fletcher* below) and negligence against ECL for the monetary losses involved in locating a new supply of ground water.

At first instance, the water company's claims were rejected. The claims in nuisance and negligence were said to depend upon whether or not the consequences of the spillages were reasonably foreseeable. Kennedy J stated that the correct test was: 'What would the reasonable supervisor overseeing the operating of the plant have foreseen to be the possible consequences of repeated spillages over perhaps 10 years?' The judge went on to hold that the supervisors could not have foreseen any environmental hazard from spillages of a mundane and regular nature. For nuisance to be established proof of actual damage was required. The damage suffered arose only upon the introduction of the regulations, and that post-dated the spillage by a number of years. Thus the claims in nuisance and negligence were rejected.

When considering the case under the rule in *Rylands* v *Fletcher*, the main issue was whether the storage of the solvents as an adjunct to a manufacturing process was a non-natural use of land. In determining that point, consideration had to be given to the question of whether the storage created special risks for adjacent occupiers and whether the activity had a general utility for the surrounding community. The court decided that, as the location of the factory was in an industrial village, the storage of solvents did not amount to a non-natural use of land.

The Water Company appealed and the Court of Appeal overturned the decision of the High Court. The court followed the decision in *Ballard* v *Tomlinson* (1885) 29 ChD 115 and decided that the nuisance complained of was an interference with a natural right incidental of the ownership of land (ie the right to abstract uncontaminated ground water), liability was therefore strict and the only effective issue was causation which had been adequately demonstrated by the plaintiff.

The defendants appealed to the House of Lords. The Law Lords allowed the appeal on the basis that liability in private nuisance depended upon the foreseeability of the relevant type of damage occurring (i.e. the pollution of ground-water). On the facts of the case, it was held to be unforeseeable that repeated spillages of solvent before 1976 would lead to any environmental hazard or damage. *Ballard* v *Tomlinson* could be distinguished as the issue of foreseeability had not arisen in that case.

The court stated that the rule in *Rylands* v *Fletcher* was historically linked to the law of nuisance. Indeed, Lord Goff made it clear that the rule was to be regarded as an extension of the law of nuisance to cases of isolated escapes from land (see the discussion of the rule on p. 187).

Two points arise from this decision. First, the activities which gave rise to the damage took place some time before the introduction of statutory controls over ground-water quality. It is arguable that after the introduction of such controls, the foreseeability of damage would increase. Certainly, in recent times with the introduction of environmental management systems and increased corporate attention to environmental compliance, it would be foreseeable that repeated spillages of toxic material would give rise to environmental damage. Thus, although there is only a small chance of retrospective liability for pollution, damage caused relatively recently or from continuing activities should still be actionable.

Secondly, and perhaps more importantly, the court displayed a marked reluctance to expand or develop the principles of nuisance. Lord Goff made it clear that recent legislation was being put in place to provide for liability in respect of pollution and it was undesirable to develop a common law principle to achieve the same end. If this strand of judicial thinking is followed it would seem as if the future growth of the common law as a mechanism of environmental protection is uncertain.

Public nuisance

Although seemingly a close relative of private nuisance, the law relating to public nuisances contains both similar elements and distinguishing features. Public nuisance can be defined as a nuisance which affects a wide class of the public in general. It is a criminal offence to cause a public nuisance, though damages can also be claimed as a civil remedy by anyone who suffers special damage over and above that suffered by the rest of the public.

An illustration is the case of *R* v *Lloyd* (1802) 4 Esp 200. A number of people living in Cliffords Inn complained of a noise nuisance which was disturbing their work. Although the court did not rule out the possibility that it might have amounted to a private nuisance it was held that the inhabitants of only three chambers did not constitute a wide class of the public in general. The case of *Attorney-General* v *PYA Quarries* [1957] 2 QB 169 demonstrates the width of class required. The defendants operated a quarry. During operations they carried out various blasting activities. These activities caused vibration and noise over a wide area. In attempting to lay down guidelines, Denning LJ declined to specify what numbers would be required to show that a particular nuisance was public rather than private. He did however say:

> I prefer to look to the reason of the thing and to say that a public nuisance is a nuisance which is so widespread in its range or so indiscriminate in its effect that it would not be reasonable to expect one person to take proceedings on his own responsibility to put a stop to it, but that it should be taken on the responsibility of the community at large.

If the need to show an effect over a wide class of the public is set aside, there is a good degree of overlap with the factors that are taken into account when deciding whether or not there is a private nuisance. For an example, in the *PYA Quarries* case above, if there had only been intermittent blasting then it may have arguably fallen foul of the rule in *Harrison* v *Southwark and Vauxhall Water Company,* which would have negated any liability not only in private but also in public nuisance.

Trespass

One of the simplest of the torts, trespass, involves direct interference with personal or proprietary rights without lawful excuse. Trespass to the person has never been properly developed in pollution cases, although in theory making someone inhale toxic fumes could give rise to an action in trespass. The main reason for this restriction lies in the requirement of directness. The interference with the personal or proprietary right must be direct rather than consequential. As an example, in *Reynolds* v *Clarke* (1725) 1 Stra 643, Fortescue J said, 'if a man throws a log into the highway and it hits me I may maintain trespass because it is an immediate wrong; but if, as it lies there, I tumble over it and receive an injury, I must bring an action upon the case because it is only prejudicial in consequence'. In relation to trespass onto land a good illustration would be that throwing stones onto someone's property would be a direct trespass, whereas allowing tiles to fall off a badly repaired chimney would not be.

Furthermore, an act of trespass has to be intentional or negligent. *McDonald* v *Associated Fuels* [1954] 3 DLR 713 illustrates the distinction well. Although in this Canadian case an action was successfully brought in negligence, the court also decided that a trespass action would have succeeded. The case involved the supply of sawdust fuel to the plaintiff's house. The delivery method was somewhat unusual in that the defendants parked their truck and blew the sawdust into a bin inside the house by means of a blower unit. Unfortunately, the intake mechanism for the sawdust was too close to the exhaust system of the truck. Consequently, as well as sawdust, carbon monoxide was blown into the house, the occupants were overcome and one of the occupants broke a hip when she collapsed. It is clear here that the trespass itself (i.e. the entrance of the carbon monoxide directly into the house) was not intentional. However, the act which caused the trespass was.

A major disadvantage with an action in trespass is that a causal link between the directness of an act and the inevitability of its consequences has to be established. In *Jones* v *Llanrwst UDC* [1908] All ER 922, faecal matter from sewage had collected in the local authority's drains and was passed untreated into the River Conway. As a consequence, it collected on the gravel banks of a river owned by the plaintiff. The question that the court was asked to answer was whether or not this deposit could amount to a trespass as it was not intended to pass onto the plaintiff's land. The court held that it was a trespass as it was intentional in the sense that the sewage was intentionally passed into the river; it was also direct in the sense that it inevitably came onto the plaintiff's land. Thus, even though it may have appeared that the matter was some way away from the plaintiff's land when it first entered the river, it was still both intentional and direct.

Jones v *Llanrwst UDC* was distinguished in the case of *Esso* v *Southport Corporation* [1956] AC 218, which at first glance would seem to fail on similar facts. A 680 tonne tanker was grounded in the Ribble Estuary. In order to lighten the ship, the master discharged much of the cargo of oil. This was then carried by the wind and the tide onto Southport's beach. The beach was under the ownership of the Corporation and they claimed against the company for the clean up costs involved. The case largely concerned the question of negligence as there was more than a suggestion that the cause of the pollution was bad navigation. That case failed, but views were expressed in the House of Lords on the possibility that the output of the oil onto the beach was a trespass. Lords Radcliffe and Tucker expressed the view that this could not be a trespass and sought to distinguish it from the *Llanrwst* case by looking at questions of inevitability. Unlike the river which inevitably flowed downstream, there was no inevitability about the deposit of the oil onto the foreshore, which depended on the action of the wind, waves and tide.

This principle would make it almost impossible to bring an action in trespass for air pollution. In a situation where air currents and wind could throw the pollution in any particular direction, the element of directness required for trespass would be difficult to show.

One of the main advantages of bringing an action in trespass is that there is no need to show damage. Trespass is actionable *per se*, therefore all that needs to be shown is some interference. Whereas most environmental pollution actions will involve some form of damage, the need to show only that trespass has occurred as a matter of fact enables an injunction to be obtained far more easily than with any other common law mechanism (see **Remedies** below).

Negligence

To attempt a full coverage of the law of negligence in a book on environmental protection is unnecessary. There are many other texts which contain a considered study of the principles. Moreover, the utility of the principles of negligence in bringing an action for environmental protection is somewhat limited.

The law of negligence is a fault based system; in order to succeed in negligence there has to be some fault on behalf of the defendant. Thus negligence would only really be utilised where other remedies under the common law (e.g. nuisance and trespass) are not available. Furthermore, proving negligence owes much to the state of technology at the time; where a polluting factory meets the standard expected of other factories of that type at that time, then any action in negligence will fail.

It is also necessary to foresee the type of harm which will result from an activity. In *Cambridge Water Co* v *Eastern Counties Leather* (above), an action in negligence was dismissed at first instance because at the time when the incident giving rise to damage occurred it would not have been reasonably foreseeable that the particular type of damage (i.e. pollution of ground water above levels laid down under an EC Directive) would have been the consequence of routine spillages of solvent. It is not sufficient to show that 'pollution' would have been foreseen as that would be too wide a category of damage.

The three main principles of negligence are that the plaintiff must establish that (a) a duty of care is owed by the defendant to the plaintiff; (b) that the defendant has breached that duty; and (c) that there has been foreseeable damage resulting from the breach. Notably, there is no need to establish a proprietary interest prior to making a claim in negligence. Thus anyone who has suffered damage from the negligence can bring an action. This widens the class of possible claimants.

Considering how often negligence is used to provide a cause of action in other areas of life, it is perhaps surprising to find how little it has been used to control environmental problems. There have historically been fairly few examples, although in recent years there has been an upsurge in the use of the mechanism. Examples include the case of *Tutton* v *A D Walter* [1985] 3 WLR 797, which involved the use of insecticide. Farmers had been advised by the manufacturers and Central Government that using a particular insecticide when oil rape was flowering could lead to the death of insects such as bees. Furthermore, they were told that the insecticide was actually most effective when used after the flowering period. Unfortunately, the defendant sprayed his crop whilst the oil rape was in flower and a number of bees owned by the plaintiff were killed. The court held that the farmer was liable for using the insecticide in a negligent manner.

More importantly perhaps, the case of *Scott-Whitehead* v *National Coal Board* (1987) 53 P&CR 263 showed the court's approach to statutory bodies and the advice they should give concerning environmental matters. The defendants discharged an emission of a chlorinated solution into a river. The river was in drought and therefore there was insufficient water to dilute the strength of the pollutant. The plaintiff was farming down stream and abstracting water to irrigate his crops. The water abstracted from the river contained a high level of pollutant and damage was caused to his crops. The second defendant in this case, the regional water authority, was held to be liable in negligence for not advising the farmer of the potential danger from the condition of the water he was abstracting. Extending the principle in this case, it may well be possible to bring an action against other environmental bodies in negligence if it can be shown that their failure to give adequate warnings of pollution contributed to damage.

The rule in *Rylands* v *Fletcher*

The principle known as 'the rule in *Rylands* v *Fletcher*' was first established in the case of that name reported in 1865 ((1865) H&C 774). It involved the construction of a reservoir on the defendant's land. The contractors failed to block off mine shafts with the result that when the reservoir was filled up, water went into the shafts and flooded a mine belonging to the plaintiff. Although there was no negligence on behalf of the defendant, the House of Lords held that he should be liable. In the lower court, Blackburn J first expounded the principle:

> . . . that the person who for his own purposes brings onto his land and collects and keeps there anything likely to do mischief if it escapes, must keep it in at his peril, and, if he does not do so, is *prima facie* answerable for all the damage which is the natural consequence of its escape.

Thus, the principle imposes strict liability (but not absolute liability) if something brought onto land or collected there escapes.

The implications as far as environmental protection is concerned are clear. Many acts of pollution are caused by materials and/or substances which are brought onto land escaping from that land. Over the years the rule has been applied in relation to water, fire, gases, electricity, oil, chemicals, colliery spoil, poisonous vegetation and even a chair-o-plane at a fairground! The sheer simplicity of the principle would seem to cover many potentially hazardous situations. However, the limitations of the principle are such that it is rarely successful nowadays.

Non-natural user

By far and away the most important restriction upon the principle is that where a substance is kept on land it must have been kept by means of a 'non-natural user'. Originally, this may have meant only that there is no liability if the water (in the case of *Rylands* v *Fletcher*) had been a natural lake or naturally flooded area rather than a man-made reservoir. In time, it came to mean that the use had to be 'some special use bringing with it increased danger to others and must not merely be the ordinary use of the land or such a use as is proper for the general benefit of the community' (*Rickards* v *Lothian* [1913] AC 263).

Thus a slightly different interpretation to the word natural came about. Instead of meaning 'artificial' the courts began to interpret the phrase as meaning an 'abnormal' use of land. Consequently, some rather strange things have been held to be a natural use of land and a flexible test of what is an *especially* or *unduly* hazardous activity has evolved which has attempted to import some element of public utility.

In *Rainham Chemicals* v *Belvedere Fish Guano Company* [1921] 2 AC 465, a factory which manufactured high explosives for the Ministry of Munitions exploded, killing a number of people and damaging the respondent's factory. The House of Lords held it to be a non-natural user and also found that the effects of the explosion amounted to an escape even though it was actually bits of the factory which had escaped rather than the substance stored, i.e. the explosives. However, in a similar case, *Read* v *Lyons* [1947] AC 156, the defendants managed the Elstow Ordnance Factory where they made high explosive shells for the Government. Ms Read was an inspector in the factory in 1942 when there was an explosion in which she was injured. There was no negligence in their activities, but she argued that the defendants were manufacturing high explosive shells and they knew them to be dangerous, and therefore the rule in *Rylands* v *Fletcher* ought to be applied. In the House of Lords, Lord MacMillan said:

> Every activity in which man engages is fraught with some possible element of danger to others. Experience shows that even from acts apparently innocuous, injury to others may result. The more dangerous the act the greater is the care that must be taken in performing it . . . . one who engages in obviously dangerous operations must be taken to know that if he does not take special precautions, injury to others may very well result. In my opinion it would be impracticable to frame a legal classification of things as things dangerous and things not dangerous, attaching absolute liability in the case of the former but not in the case of the latter . . . . accordingly I am unable to accept the proposition that in law the manufacture of high-explosive shells is a dangerous operation which imposes on the manufacturer an absolute liability . . . .

This decision may well have had something to do with the fact that in war time it would clearly be a natural use of industrial land to make explosives. However, it is now common for a court to find that an ordinary industrial use is a natural use if it is sited with due care and consideration. To that extent, where a factory is given a planning permission, that would, it is suggested, amount to prima facie evidence that consideration had been given as to its suitability as a use. The definition of 'non-natural' user was further discussed in *Cambridge Water Co.* v *Eastern Counties Leather* (above), where it appeared, at least in the High Court, as if the extension of the non-natural use exception was so great as to extinguish the rule altogether.

Other restrictions on the use of the rule
Further limitations on the principle do not have the same restrictive nature as the non-natural user principle. However, they are still important in seeking to restrict the introduction of a strict liability concept into the common law. First, there is a requirement that the substance escapes from the land where it is kept. Therefore, in *Read* v *Lyons,* the workers in the ammunition factory

could have no action under the rule in *Rylands* v *Fletcher*. Furthermore, the principle applies specifically to protect landowners and therefore it is generally accepted that no actions for personal injuries received from the escape of substances from a non-natural user of land can lie.

There is also a requirement that the relevant damage be foreseeable. In *Cambridge Water Co.* v *Eastern Counties Leather,* the House of Lords allowed an appeal by Eastern Counties Leather on the ground that foreseeability of damage was a prerequisite of liability under the rule in *Rylands* v *Fletcher.* In allowing the appeal, the court took the view that the rule should form a natural extension of the law of nuisance to cover isolated escapes from land and should not be developed further.

Although there have been a number of restrictions placed upon the rule in *Rylands* v *Fletcher,* this does not necessarily condemn an action based on an escape of hazardous substances from land to failure; it merely means that negligence, nuisance or trespass must be shown for liability to accrue. In many circumstances, fault will be able to be shown fairly easily.

Defences

There are a number of defences to an action brought under the rule in *Rylands* v *Fletcher*. It has been suggested that there is a defence where the plaintiff benefits from the harmful activity. Therefore, where gas, electricity or water supplies have caused damage on the plaintiff s property, no liability should accrue. The concept behind this defence perhaps takes the desire to restrict absolute liability too far (see *North Western Utilities Limited* v *London Guarantee and Accident Co. Ltd* [1936] AC 108). The thinking behind the development of this principle has been somewhat confused (e.g. the decision in *Anderson* v *Oppenheimer* (1880) 5 QBD 602). Some have seen the use of this defence as an extension of the defence of consent, which can be simply stated, as in *Attorney-General* v *Cory Brothers & Co* [1921] 1 AC 521—if the plaintiff has allowed the defendant to accumulate the matter or thing which is being complained of, then they are unable to sue if it escapes. Secondly, as in the case of private nuisance, it is a defence that a statute authorises the activity complained of (see *Smeaton* v *Ilford Corporation* [1954] Ch 454).

Finally, although it is a defence to plead an Act of God (i.e. the nuisance was brought about by a set of extreme circumstances) the relevance of this defence is somewhat restricted. As one commentator has put it (*Street on Torts*, 9th ed):

> The defence has received in connection with this tort a prominence out of all proportion to its practical importance. If an escape is caused, through natural causes without human intervention, in 'circumstances which no human foresight can provide against, and which human prudence is not bound to recognise the possibility', there is then said to exist the defence of Act of God.

The only things which fall under this defence would be escapes caused by such things as earthquakes, tornadoes or freak acts of nature.

The usefulness of the rule in *Rylands* v *Fletcher*

After the decision of the House of Lords in *Cambridge Water Co.* v *Eastern Counties Leather* it could be argued that the effectiveness of the rule in *Rylands* v *Fletcher* has been diluted to such an extent that it is virtually useless. It is perhaps more appropriate to call the rule an extension of the law of private nuisance rather than a specific class on its own. The Court also stated, obiter, that in the light of 'carefully structured legislation' designed for environmental protection there was less need to develop the rule to provide for liability in respect of pollution. Consequently, the future of the rule looks uncertain.

The protection of riparian rights

There is a separate action for interference with the rights of owners of riparian land. Although this action has some similarities with private nuisance, it is in practice used far more frequently owing to the strength of riparian owners' natural rights to water. For further explanation of the law on riparian rights see p. 395.

Civil law remedies

Of course, the use of the common law as a mechanism for environmental protection would be useless unless there were effective remedies once a cause of action had been established. There are three main types of remedies which can be sought: compensatory and preventative remedies, and abatement. Monetary damages act as compensation for any damage suffered but also can pay for any clean up costs involved in rectifying pollution. On the other hand, an injunction allows for actions which are creating an environmental problem to be stopped by order of the court. Lastly, there are certain limited circumstances where plaintiffs can take individual action and abate the activity causing environmental damage.

The utility of the common law in dealing with environmental pollution depends upon the nature of the problem. An isolated occurrence could cause tremendous environmental damage and, where a problem is not likely to recur, it may well be an adequate remedy to pay for the restoration of the environment to its prior state. However, in cases where the pollution is perhaps of a lower level but more persistent, it may be necessary to prevent an accumulation of potentially hazardous substances which cannot be properly compensated through damages alone. Therefore, in certain cases, an injunction may be the only suitable remedy. There are, however, many instances where the remedies available through the common law will give a far wider range of options to potential plaintiffs than are available through seeking to have statutory bodies act on their behalf.

Damages
The aim of awarding damages at common law is to place the plaintiff as far as possible in the position they would have been in had the wrongful act not

occurred. This could be calculated in two ways; on the cost of clean-up operations necessary to restore the property to its previous state, or the difference between the value of the property as it was after the pollution had affected it, and before. It is a principle which is not particularly clear. In *Marquis of Granby* v *Bakewell UDC* (1923) 87 JP 105, the defendant operated a gas works which discharged poisonous effluent into a river over which the plaintiff had fishing rights. The effluent killed all the plaintiff's fish and thus he claimed damages against the defendant for the interference with his fishing rights. He received compensation equalling the costs of restocking the river in addition to the loss of a large amount of the food supply for other stocks. The court also took into account the effects of the pollution on higher quality areas of the river and considered that the damages would be higher where environmental pollution was greater.

Damages for all *future* loss are only available in lieu of an injunction. This remedy is used only sparingly because of the ready availability of the more usual injunction procedure.

Lastly, exemplary or punitive damages can be awarded in specific instances. The basis of such an award is to deter the defendant and others from committing torts which may result in financial benefit to the person responsible. The scope for these damages is, however, limited to classes of tort which were the subject of an award of exemplary damages before 1964 (*Gibbons* v *SW Water* [1993] Env LR 244) and cases where there has been oppressive, arbitrary or unconstitutional action by servants of the government, or where the defendant's conduct was calculated to make a profit which would exceed the damages payable (*Rookes* v *Barnard* [1964] AC 1129). Thus a claim for exemplary damages in public nuisance after the public water supply was polluted was rejected on the ground that public nuisance fell outside the above categories (*Gibbons* v *SW Water*, above).

Injunctions

The granting of an injunction is a discretionary remedy which can prohibit a defendant from carrying on an activity which is causing pollution. The principles for the granting of an injunction are well established. Normally, either the activity complained of has to be continuing at the date of action, or there has to be a threat that the activity will continue. Even though the activity may have ceased at the time of trial, an injunction can still be sought if it existed when the action was brought.

When exercising its discretion, the court will take a number of factors into consideration. First, it will not grant an injunction if the activity complained of is not of sufficient gravity or duration to justify stopping the defendant's activities. Turner LJ in *Goldsmith* v *Tunbridge Wells Improvement Commissioners* (1866) 1 Ch App 349 said:

it is not in every case of nuisance that this Court should interfere. I think that it ought not to do so in cases in which the injury is merely temporary or trifling; but I think that it ought to do so in cases in which the injury is permanent and serious: and in determining whether the injury is serious or not, regard must be had to all the consequences which may flow from it.

The court attempts to balance the competing interests of the plaintiff and defendant by assessing the balance of convenience between the parties. Where all things are equal, an attempt will be made to assess the social utility of the activity by comparing its public importance with the interference to the private rights of the plaintiff. Basically, the harm suffered to the plaintiff has to be balanced against the effect that granting of an injunction would have upon the defendant.

There are situations where it is possible to obtain an injunction before the occurrence of the event causing injury or damage. A *quia timet* injunction, as it is known, does not require proof of environmental damage at all. However, there must be sufficient proof of imminent damage and it must be demonstrated that if the activity were to continue the damage accruing would be substantial and of such degree that it would be difficult to rectify.

Injunctions are rarely specific in nature; the court merely sets the standard for the defendant to meet and this standard can be achieved in any way possible. For example, it may be met either by closing down a particular plant which is causing environmental difficulties or by fitting new arrestment equipment. Even where an injunction is granted it is often on the basis that a certain amount of time is given for compliance.

Abatement

The remedy of abatement tends to be more of historic interest than it is useful. The remedy involves the removal of a nuisance by the injured party without recourse to legal proceedings. The courts view this remedy unfavourably as it is extra-judicial in nature and therefore open to abuse. An example of the use of abatement can be found in *Lemmon* v *Webb* [1895] AC 1, where action was taken to trim back the branch of a tree which encroached on land from a neighbouring site. Any damages subsequent to an abatement action are restricted to damages in respect of harm prior to the abatement.

Statutory nuisance

The law of statutory nuisance represents a bridge between the common law controls of environmental protection and the more characteristic statutory mechanisms. The law on statutory nuisance was consolidated in the Public Health Act 1936, following previous Acts of 1848, 1855, 1860 and 1875. Originally, the purpose of the Act was to attempt to control matters which, although nuisances in the common law sense, affected sanitation levels and thus public health in Victorian times. The law has been updated yet again and consolidated in Part III of the EPA 1990. The main aim of the statutory nuisance provisions is to provide a quick and easy remedy to abate nuisances with which the common law is too slow or too expensive to deal.

The control of statutory nuisances

District councils and London borough councils are under a duty to inspect their areas for statutory nuisances (EPA 1990, s. 79). The consequence of this is that if an individual within an area complains of a statutory nuisance emanating from within that area then a district council is obliged to investigate. The EPA 1990 implies that the level of such an obligation is only to take such steps as are reasonably practicable. Although the duty imposed is only that inspection be periodic, it is clear that if there is strong evidence to suggest that a statutory nuisance exists within an area, and a local authority refuse to inspect, then it is possible that the remedy of judicial review will lie to any aggrieved applicant. It is important, therefore, for any individual wishing to complain to a local authority to ensure that proper evidence is gathered (e.g. dates, times and length of the nuisance if it has already occurred, or strong evidence to show that the statutory nuisance is about to occur). There are default powers under EPA 1990, sch. 3, para. 4 which allow the Secretary of State to take action if local authorities are not carrying out their duty.

The general control of statutory nuisance is contained in EPA 1990, s. 80. This provides that where a local authority is satisfied that a statutory nuisance exists, or is likely to occur or recur, it is under a mandatory duty to serve an abatement notice on the person responsible for the nuisance or, if that person cannot be found, the owner or occupier of the premises on which the statutory nuisance is present.

The categories of statutory nuisance

There are a number of categories of statutory nuisance contained in the EPA 1990, s. 79. These are supplemented by other statutes which declare specific categories to be a statutory nuisance and thus controlled under the provisions of the Act (EPA 1990, s. 79(1)(h)). Much of the language used in s. 79 is somewhat antiquated and difficult to reconcile with modern technology. The categories of statutory nuisance are listed in the headings below. The Act lays down certain activities or states of affairs which will amount to a statutory nuisance if 'prejudicial to health or a nuisance'.

The scope of statutory nuisances has been widened under the Noise and Statutory Nuisance Act 1993, which reinforces local authorities' powers and enables them to take action against noise in the street. This includes noise from vehicles, equipment, machinery or loudspeakers. Another part of the Act deals with powers to take action against faulty burglar alarms.

'Prejudicial to health or a nuisance'
The main criterion for the existence of a statutory nuisance is that anything complained of must be either 'prejudicial to health or a nuisance'. These are not to be read conjunctively.

'Prejudicial to health' is defined under EPA 1990, s. 79(7), as meaning injurious, or likely to cause injury, to health. In *Coventry City Council* v *Cartwright* [1975] 1 WLR 845, the Council owned a vacant site within a residential area on which they allowed people to dump all sorts of materials. These included not only normal household refuse, but also building and construction materials. Occasionally, the Council would move household materials. A nearby resident complained of a statutory nuisance under the

Public Health Act 1936. The Divisional Court held that, where the accumulation complained of was inert rather than putrescible, there was no likelihood of disease or that vermin would be attracted which could spread disease. Although there was a chance that physical injury could be caused to people who walked on the site, that did not amount to being prejudicial to health.

In defining the word 'nuisance', it is generally accepted that the word contained within the EPA 1990 has the same definition as that under the common law. In *National Coal Board* v *Thorne* [1976] 1 WLR 543, the nuisance complained of amounted to defective guttering and windows within premises. The complainant argued that the physical condition of the building amounted to a nuisance under the Public Health Act. Watkins J said that a 'nuisance coming within the meaning of the Public Health Act 1936 must be either a public or private nuisance as understood by common law'. Thus, when deciding on the point of whether or not a statutory nuisance could arise when it was the inhabitants of premises who were suffering, such a state of affairs could not amount to nuisance because it was not an interference with the use or enjoyment of neighbouring property. There has to be more than just mere discomfort to the occupier's enjoyment of property unless such a state of affairs would be prejudicial to health.

Any premises in such a state as to be prejudicial to health or a nuisance

Section 79(1)(a) provides that where premises are kept in a state which is prejudicial to health or a nuisance then this will amount to a statutory nuisance. 'Premises' includes land and any vessel not powered by steam-reciprocating machinery. The physical extent of the premises must be viewed in context. In *Stevenage BC* v *Wilson* [1993] Env LR 214, premises extended to the garden of a house where an abatement notice had included only the word 'dwelling'. The provision covers the physical state of premises rather than any use to which those premises are put. Therefore, where noise or dust etc. is emitted from those premises from a use, this is not covered. The aim is to prevent situations where there are physical elements which are either prejudicial to health or a nuisance. Such things would cover the lack of proper insulation of council-owned flats against noise (see *London Borough of Southwark* v *Ince* (1989) 21 HLR 504) and dwellings which are subject to heavy condensation from poor heating and ventilation (see *Greater London Council* v *The London Borough of Tower Hamlets* (1983) 15 HLR 57).

Smoke emitted from premises so as to be prejudicial to health or a nuisance

Section 79(1)(b) replaced the Clean Air Act 1956, s. 16, which previously made separate provision for the control of smoke from premises. There are exemptions contained within s. 79(3) so that:

(a) smoke emitted from a chimney of a private dwelling within a smoke control area;

(b)   dark smoke emitted from a chimney of a building, or a chimney serving the furnace of a boiler or industrial plant attached to a building, or for the time being installed on any land;
(c)   smoke emitted from a railway locomotive steam engine;
(d)   dark smoke emitted, otherwise than as mentioned above, from industrial or trade premises

will not be statutory nuisances. Section 17 of the Clean Air Act 1993 deals with smoke nuisances in Scotland.

Fumes or gases emitted from premises so as to be prejudicial to health or a nuisance
Section 79(4) controls fumes or gases emitted from private dwellings. Fumes are defined as 'any airborne solid matter smaller than dust, gases including vapour and moisture precipitating from vapour' (EPA 1990, s. 79(7)).

Any dust, steam, smell or other effluvia arising on industrial, trade or business premises and being prejudicial to health or a nuisance
The meanings of dust, steam and smell are fairly well established. However, the term 'effluvia' was defined in *Malton Board of Health* v *Malton Manure Company* (1879) 4 ExD 302. This case involved the production of manure by the defendant company which produced vapours. It could not be conclusively demonstrated that these vapours were prejudicial to healthy people in the locality, although the Board of Health did demonstrate that it had the effect of making people who were ill more ill. The court held that this effect could amount to effluvia which were prejudicial to health. It is suggested that the meaning of effluvia covers the outflow of harmful or unpleasant substances.

Any accumulation or deposit which is prejudicial to health or a nuisance
To come within s. 79(1)(e), the accumulation or deposit has to be capable of causing disease rather than injury (see *Coventry City Council* v *Cartwright*, above). The wide range of accumulations or deposits covered by this section have included sheep dung (*Draper* v *Sperring* (1869) 10 CB 113) and cinders which emitted offensive smells (*Bishop Auckland Local Board* v *Bishop Auckland Iron and Steel Company* (1882) 10 QBD 138).

Any animal kept in such a place or manner as to be prejudicial to health or a nuisance
The keeping of a large number of animals on premises can give rise to a number of different enforcement actions. First, the keeping of a large number of animals may amount to sufficient intensification of a use to give rise to a change of use, which could result in enforcement action under the Town and Country Planning Act 1990 (see *Wallington* v *Secretary of State* [1991] JPL 942). Secondly, there may be common law actions which could be brought for nuisance. Thirdly, there could be action taken by the local authority under

by-laws passed under the Public Health Act 1936, s. 81(2), and finally, there could be action taken under the statutory nuisance provisions of s. 79(1)(f).

Noise emitted from premises so as to be prejudicial to health or a nuisance

This provision replaces Part III of the Control of Pollution Act 1974 dealing with noise from premises. There is an exemption for noise from model aircraft.

Any other matter declared by any enactment to be a statutory nuisance

This provision is to include any statutory nuisance provided for under future statutes. it also includes nuisances from mines, shafts and quarries under the Mines and Quarries Act 1954 (EPA 1990, s. 151).

What is required to satisfy the local authority?

In practice, it is the responsibility of the local environmental health officer to decide upon whether or not a statutory nuisance is occurring or is likely to occur. As has been stated, the test is whether or not a statutory nuisance is prejudicial to health or a nuisance. An environmental health officer will visit the premises and make a subjective decision as to whether or not the state of the premises or anything on those premises amounts to a nuisance. When reverting to the common law for the definition of nuisance, it is up to the environmental health officer to balance the many different factors used when deciding on whether or not a common law nuisance exists. The most important of these factors are:

(a) the nature and the location of the nuisance;
(b) the time and duration of the nuisance; and
(c) the utility of the activity concerned.

Balancing all these factors together is the only way in which an environmental health officer can make an adjudication between respective neighbours' rights, because it is quite clear that a statutory nuisance will only apply to affected neighbours' properties.

Section 80(1) provides that for a local authority to act, the statutory nuisance must exist or be likely to occur or recur. Thus this procedure can be used to prevent a nuisance before it actually occurs, although there has to be evidence that a forthcoming activity is likely to give rise to a statutory nuisance and the standard of evidence required is particularly high. However, where these problems can be overcome, such as in the case of a party where there is more than a suggestion that powerful audio equipment will be used, this may well be the only method of prohibiting certain types of nuisances in advance. Where a local authority has delegated enforcement powers to individual officers then those officers are able to carry out the enforcement procedures on behalf of the local authority.

Who is the 'person responsible'?

The enforcement of a statutory nuisance is normally against the 'person responsible', which is defined in EPA 1990, s. 79(7) as being 'the person to whose act, default or sufferance the nuisance is attributable'. This is a particularly wide definition and can include a local authority (see *Rossall* v *London Borough of Southwark*, unreported), or a landlord who has allowed a tenant to carry on offensive activities. It can also include a tenant who has denied access to a landlord who wished to carry out works to abate a nuisance (see *Carr* v *London Borough of Hackney* [1995] Env LR D37).

If there are any difficulties in locating the 'person responsible' for the existence of a statutory nuisance, EPA 1990, s. 80(2)(c), states that the definition of the person responsible can be extended to include the owner or occupier of the premises in question.

The abatement notice

Once the local authority, through its environmental health officesr, is satisfied that a statutory nuisance exists, it is under a duty to serve an abatement notice which must require any or all of the following:

(a)   the abatement of the nuisance or the prohibiting or restricting of its occurrence or recurrence;

(b)   the execution of works or other steps necessary to comply with the notice.

The wording of an abatement notice needs to be clear and precise. The recipient of the notice needs to know what must be done to comply because criminal sanctions would be imposed if the notice were to be breached see *Network Housing Association* v *Westminster CC* [1994] *The Times*, 8 November 1994). In the case of a noise nuisance, however, it is not necessary to specify maximum noise levels (see *East Northants DC* v *Fossett* [1994] Env LR 388). In addition, there is no requirement that the notice be corroborated by evidence of a particular occupier who has suffered unreasonable interference with the enjoyment of property (see *Cooke* v *Adatia* [1989] LGR 32). The notice should specify the time within which compliance is required.

Where an individual has been served with an abatement notice, the contravention of that notice, without reasonable excuse renders that person guilty of a criminal offence under the EPA 1990, s. 80(4). Once a notice is served it takes effect in perpetuity even in the case of a notice served under the old Control of Pollution Act powers (see *Aitken* v *South Hams DC* [1994] 3 All ER 400 overruling *R* v *Folkestone Magistrates' Court ex parte Kibble* [1993] Env LR 400).

Defences

Where an offence has been committed under s. 80(4) there are a number of defences.

Reasonable excuse

It is a defence to a prosecution for the contravention of an abatement notice to show that there was a reasonable excuse for carrying out the activity which resulted in the contravention. The test laid down for this would seem to be an objective one, i.e. 'would a reasonable person think that the excuse given was consistent with a reasonable standard of conduct?'. The defence is not available where an abatement notice has been contravened deliberately and intentionally in circumstances wholly under the control of the defendant. Thus, a defendant could not argue that because there had been a three year gap between the service of an abatement notice and its breach and no one had complained about the breach as it was of minimum inconvenience, there was a 'reasonable excuse' (*Wellingborough BC* v *Gordon* [1993] Env LR 218). It is not sufficient to say that there would be a defence to a private law action in nuisance. Indeed, in *Lambert (A) Flat Management* v *Lomas* [1981] 2 All ER 280, it was said that COPA 1974, s. 58(4) was designed to provide a defence to a criminal charge where an individual had some reasonable excuse, such as some special difficulty in relation to compliance with the abatement notice. It was not an opportunity to challenge the notice; that should only properly be done on an appeal.

Best practicable means

Where an abatement notice is served on trade or business premises and the nuisance complained of is caused in the course of the trade or business, it is a defence under certain heads of EPA 1990, s. 70(1), to show that the best practicable means have been used to prevent or counteract the nuisance (s. 80(7)). This does not apply to fumes or gases emitted from premises (s. 79(1)(c)), or the catch-all provision under s. 79(1)(h). Although there is not any complete definition contained within the EPA 1990, certain elements are required to be taken into account under s. 79(9). These include local conditions and circumstances, the current state of technical knowledge, the financial implications, and the design, installation, maintenance, manner and periods of operation of plant and machinery.

The defence has to be established on a balance of probabilities, and the burden of proof lies on the defendant to show that it had taken reasonable steps to prevent or counteract the nuisance. Thus, where a defendant had submitted a planning application for noise reducing bunding to counteract a noise nuisance, but failed to answer the local planning authority's request for further information, it failed to discharge the burden of proof that it was using best practicable means to prevent or counteract the nuisance (*Chapman* v *Gosberton Farm Produce* [1993] Env LR 191).

Special defences

There are specific defences available in relation to noise and nuisances on construction sites and in areas where there are registered noise levels under the noise abatement zone procedure (see EPA 1990, s. 80(9) and COPA, ss. 60, 61 and 65–67).

The right of appeal against an abatement notice

Where an individual is served with an abatement notice there is a right of appeal against the notice to a magistrates' court. One advantage of the appeal system over a defence to a prosecution under contravention proceedings is that it allows for a far greater range of appeal grounds and therefore provides a greater scope for disputing the nuisance. An appeal normally lies within 21 days of the service of the notice. The grounds of appeal are set down in regulations made under EPA 1990, sch. 3. The Statutory Nuisance (Appeals) Regulations 1990 (SI 1990 No. 2276) and the Statutory Nuisance (Appeals) (Amendment) Regulations 1990 (SI 1990 No. 2483) set out the grounds of appeal against an abatement notice, which include:

(a)   that the abatement notice is not justified in the terms of s. 80;
(b)   that there has been a substantive or procedural error in the service of the notice;
(c)   that the authority have unreasonably refused to accept compliance with alternative requirements, or that their requirements are unreasonable or unnecessary;
(d)   that the period for compliance is unreasonable;
(e)   that the best practicable means were used to counteract the effect of a nuisance from trade or business premises.

Furthermore, the regulations allow for the suspension of an abatement notice pending the court's decision, unless the local authority override the suspension in the abatement notice with a statement to the effect that the notice is to have effect regardless, and that:

(a)   the nuisance is prejudicial to health;
(b)   suspension would render the notice of no practical effect (e.g. where nuisances are to cease before the action can be heard in court); or
(c)   any expenditure incurred before an appeal would be disproportionate to the public benefit.

Individual actions by any person

It is often the case that local authorities' environmental health departments are overworked and understaffed and have neither the resources nor sometimes the inclination to deal with disputes regarding statutory nuisances. Section 82 of the Act allows a complaint to be made to a local magistrates' court by any person who is aggrieved by the existence of a statutory nuisance. This procedure allows for any person within an area to bring a more affordable and expeditious proceeding than a private law action. One particular limitation upon this procedure is that the nuisance must be in existence and therefore cannot be used to anticipate problems. Therefore, a person has no right of action under this section to stop a nuisance which is likely to occur in the future (e.g. loud parties). If the person can satisfy the magistrates that there is an existing nuisance, or that there is likely to be a recurring nuisance, they are under a duty to issue an abatement notice requiring the defendant to abate the nuisance within a specified time, and to execute any works necessary for that purpose and/or prohibiting a recurrence of the nuisance, and requiring the defendant, within a specified time, to carry out any works necessary to prevent the recurrence. The magistrates may fine a defendant at a level not exceeding level 5 on the standard scale (s. 82(2)). There is a notice procedure, which differs slightly from that which governs local authority actions, in that s. 80(6) provides that where an individual is bringing an action they must give not less than three days' notice in relation to a noise nuisance and, in relation to other statutory nuisances, 21 days' notice, before the bringing of proceedings under s. 80(2).

Sentencing powers for contravention of an abatement notice

Section 80(5) and (6) of the EPA 1990 provide for penalties for a person who is guilty of an offence of contravening an abatement notice. The matter is triable only in the magistrates' court and, if found guilty, a private offender is liable to a fine not exceeding level 5 on the standard scale (£5,000). If the offence continues after the conviction they are liable to a further fine not exceeding one-tenth of that level for each day on which the offence continues. The previous levels of fine included under the Public Health Act and Control of Pollution Act indicated that for major industrial uses there were no real disincentives to carry out works to improve premises. Indeed, it was often cost effective to pay fines at a low level in order to ensure that a particular activity could be carried on rather than abated. Section 80(6) closes this particular loophole by imposing a maximum fine of £20,000 on industrial, trade or business offenders.

The use of injunctions and proceedings in the High Court

In many cases the provisions of s. 80 would not provide an adequate remedy in terms of either gravity or speed. Under s. 81(5), a local authority may take action in the High Court for the purpose of securing the abatement, prohibition or restriction of any statutory nuisance where it is of the opinion that proceedings for an offence of contravening an abatement notice would not provide a sufficient remedy. The usual method for doing this would be by seeking an injunction in the High Court. In *Hammersmith London Borough Council* v *Magnum Automated Forecourts Ltd* [1978] 1 WLR 50, the Court of Appeal decided that this was an additional power to that contained under the statutory noise nuisance provisions contained within COPA 1974. Thus, the right to take proceedings in the High Court could be used after an abatement notice had been served, but before the prosecution for contravention had been heard, in order to expedite the cessation of the nuisance.

The scope for injunctions has widened considerably with the decision in *Lloyds Bank* v *Guardian Assurance* (1987) 35 Build LR 34, which stated that the jurisdiction of the High Court was not affected by any proceedings under the statutory nuisance provisions of COPA 1974. The real effect of this decision has been to suggest that it will not be open to any individual to apply for an injunction under the common law which is in stricter terms than any abatement notice which has already been served under COPA 1974 or the EPA 1990. However, it is open to the local authority to tighten up on a weak abatement notice by applying for an injunction in the High Court under s. 81(5). In such proceedings it will be a defence to prove that noise was authorised by a construction site consent under COPA 1974, s. 61.

Injunctions are a discretionary remedy and will not be granted lightly. The activity complained of must be of sufficient gravity and/or duration to justify stopping it (*Goldsmith* v *Tunbridge Wells Improvement Commission* (1866) 1 Ch App 349).

The powers available to local authorities may flow from the primary statute (e.g. EPA 1990), or from s. 222 of the Local Government Act 1972. These powers are available concurrently (*Wyre Forest DC* v *Bostock* [1991] Env LR 235).

PART II SECTORAL COVERAGE OF ENVIRONMENTAL LAW

NINE
Town and country planning

The British system of town and country planning is undoubtedly one of the most sophisticated systems of land use control in the world. It is virtually unique in incorporating controls over the use of land as well as over the design and form of the built environment. Accordingly, it plays a central role in environmental law because of its enormous importance in relation to locational and siting issues. It is, as stated earlier (see p. 94), perhaps the pre-eminent example in this country of an anticipatory system of control. However, town and country planning is not just about environmental protection. It has a wider role in organising economic development, and in balancing economic, political, social and environmental factors to do with development in a democratic context. This wider role is outside environmental law in the sense in which the term is used in this book, so this chapter is restricted to summarising those parts of planning law which have the greatest importance for environmental protection.

This chapter is written in the firm belief that planning law can be reduced to a number of central principles, and that once the structure of the system is understood, many of the details become self-explanatory. As a result, many matters of detail are omitted, but there are many excellent specialist books and encyclopaedias which readers are urged to consult (see Bibliography).

In particular, it should be noted that, for reasons of space, the specific provisions on listed buildings and conservation areas are not covered in this chapter. Pieces of planning law relevant to other chapters within Part II of the book are summarised at the appropriate places.

The main features of town and country planning

These are as follows:

(a) The local planning authority draws up a development plan, which sets out the strategy for development in the area. This involves a measure of public participation. Development plans are permissive (i.e. they do not guarantee what is going to happen, but act as guides to future development) and must be taken into account in any decision.

(b) All 'development', which is widely construed and includes changes of use as well as physical development, requires planning permission from the local planning authority before it may be carried out.

(c) Procedures are laid down for applications for planning permission. These involve consultation with other public bodies and some limited public involvement.

(d) The local planning authority decides on grounds of planning policy whether to grant permission or refuse it, taking into account the development plans, Central Government policies and any other material considerations.

(e) Unlike most other systems of town planning, which rely heavily on zoning of areas within which certain generalised rules will apply, in this country each case must be considered on its merits.

(f) If permission is granted, it may be subject to conditions; indeed, this is the normal position. If permission is refused, no compensation is normally payable—the right to develop land was effectively nationalised in the Town and Country Planning Act 1947.

(g) The applicant has a right of appeal to the Secretary of State against any refusal or conditions. This is a complete rehearing of the whole matter, including the policy issues, and thus enables the Secretary of State to exercise a stranglehold on policy by having the final say on it.

(h) There is no right of appeal for third parties and no right to appeal against a grant of planning permission.

(i) There is a further right of appeal from the decision of the Secretary of State to the High Court on what are essentially the same grounds as for judicial review. The courts thus exercise a supervisory jurisdiction over the procedures and the decisions taken. However, the courts will not intervene on grounds of fact or policy.

(j) Enforcement of the law is through another discretionary procedure in which the local planning authority may serve an enforcement notice requiring specified steps to be taken. It is an offence to fail to comply with an enforcement notice. Once again, a right of appeal to the Secretary of State is provided and, as this may involve consideration of policy issues, it is in most cases deemed a retrospective application for planning permission.

(k) Planning permission effectively gives a right to develop. Unlike most systems of pollution control, there is no power to vary a planning permission in the future (unless compensation is paid).

Town and country planning as a tool of environmental policy

There are thus three main areas with relevance to environmental law:

(a) The system of development plans, which ensures that environmental protection is considered at the level of policy-making. These plans often set the basic ground rules for action on the environment in any particular area,

although they must be read in conjunction with the policy guidance emanating from Central Government.

(b)   The development control process, in which planning permission is
required from the local planning authority for acts of development. This is a
good example of a 'mixed economy' solution to environmental control (i.e.
the initiative for development is normally taken by private developers, but
permission to go ahead is required from a public authority). This ensures a
strict anticipatory control over many activities before they start and normally
involves liaison with the relevant pollution control and environmental agencies.

(c)   The power to impose conditions relating to environmental protection
on a grant of planning permission. These are capable of creating some form
of continuing control over activities.

The traditional conflictual model of a regulatory body regulating the applicant by granting or refusing permission is currently breaking down. Modern
town planning may be seen as a negotiative process in which consultation
between the prospective developer and the local planning authority in
advance of the application is the norm, and in which proposals are both made
and considered in the light of local and national policies. The local planning
authority and the developer often have a community of interest in carrying
out a particular development: the developer gets its proposal granted and the
local authority obtains the revitalisation of the economy of an area, or the
creation of jobs, or some other economic benefit. (Indeed, developments by
local authorities and developers in partnership with each other are now quite
common.) In addition, arrangements between developers and local authorities in which 'planning gain' is bargained for are increasingly used to
supplement the regulatory controls (see p. 243).

It should also be borne in mind that the impact of planning control is in
many ways incomplete or inadequate. Planning permission is not required for
all environmentally harmful activities, for example for mobile pollutants such
as cars, or in relation to most agricultural activities. There are difficulties
where some form of continuing control is required, because of the limitations
on planning conditions, or where positive management is required, since it is
mainly a preventative system. The system also tends to get circumvented in
various ways where nationally important development is desired by Central
Government.

A further point is that the planning decision is a political one, and thus
environmental issues may be subordinated to other needs. As the Royal
Commission on Environmental Pollution commented in its Fifth Report in
relation to pollution prevention, 'Our concern is not that pollution is not
always given top priority; it is that it is often dealt with inadequately, and
sometimes forgotten altogether in the planning process' (Cmnd. 6371, 1976).

Nevertheless, the planning system is of central importance in many areas
of environmental law, especially when used in conjunction with other regulatory controls. This is seen clearly in relation to waste disposal, where
planning permission for a waste disposal site is required before a waste

management licence can be granted. In other areas, planning control is arguably of greatest importance where the enforcement of pollution control is inadequate, since non-enforcement at the operational end puts increased pressure on initial siting and design issues.

Town and country planning and some themes of this book

This brief summary of the town and country planning system shows how it illustrates a number of the major themes of this book. For instance, it is a good example of a sophisticated anticipatory regulatory mechanism and it emphasises prevention of harm. That also means that the predominant method of control is through negative, restrictive measures, rather than through positive mechanisms. Local decision-making dominates, although there has been an all too obvious shift of power towards Central Government in recent years (see p. 210). It is a highly discretionary system, in which decisions are made on a case-by-case basis and it is a democratic system in which ultimate political control rests with elected members rather than with officers (on appeal responsibility rests with an elected Secretary of State), although in practice most decisions are actually taken by officers. It is a fairly open and public system. Of course, this last point sets up one of the great conflicts of the system: the more open it is, the slower decisions tend to be.

Enforcement is under-emphasised, being almost exclusively the responsibility of the local planning authority and dependent on political and tactical factors.

But the most important point is that this is a highly political system of decision-making. Local planning authorities and the Secretary of State make discretionary decisions by balancing economic, political, environmental and social factors. It is therefore just as important to understand the prevailing policy in relation to a particular issue as it is to understand the relevant law.

The role of the law and the courts requires some explanation here. The planning system is one where the law exercises a supervisory, or review, function. It is there to define the various concepts used in the planning system (such as what development is, or what types of conditions are legitimate), to ensure that the correct procedures are used and to ensure that discretionary decisions are taken in the proper manner. The law is therefore ultimately about procedures, i.e. about ensuring that decisions are made correctly rather than that the correct decisions are made.

The planning legislation

As Lord Scarman stated in *Pioneer Aggregates (UK)* v *Secretary of State* [1984] 3 WLR 32, 'Planning control is the creature of Statute . . . Parliament has provided a comprehensive code of planning control'. This comprehensive code was originally created in the Town and Country Planning Act 1947, when a uniform and mandatory country-wide system of development control was introduced. One of the most remarkable things about planning is that, whilst there have been numerous detailed additions and amendments to the law, the basic structure of much of this system (apart from that relating to development plans) has remained unchanged since then, although the way in which it is operated has in practice changed quite radically.

The legislation is now consolidated in the Town and Country Planning Act 1990. Unless otherwise stated, wherever a section number is given in this chapter without reference to a particular Act, it refers to that Act.

The Planning and Compensation Act 1991 made substantial changes to the 1990 Act, especially in relation to development plans, enforcement and planning obligations. Perhaps the greatest impact of the 1991 Act, however, has been on the relationship between development plans and other material considerations, particularly Central Government policy guidance. This is because of a new statutory presumption, laid down in a new s. 54A to the 1990 Act, in favour of following the provisions of the development plan. The precise implications of this new presumption are still not entirely clear, but it obviously reflects a shift in emphasis away from 'developer-led' planning towards 'plan-led' planning (see p. 237). The 1991 Act was brought into force in a piecemeal manner and involved the passage of a large amount of subordinate legislation, but it was effectively fully implemented by the beginning of 1993.

It should be noted that much of the detail of the law on town and country planning is in subordinate legislation. Of particular importance are the Town and Country Planning (General Permitted Development) Order 1995 (SI 1995 No. 418) and the Town and Country Planning (General Development Procedure) Order 1995 (SI 1995 No. 419) which have consolidated the old GDO (SI 1988 No. 813). These regulations fulfil different functions: the former grants automatic planning permission for a large number of activities and the latter provides many of the procedures relating to an application for permission.

What is town and country planning?

One respected town planner has described town planning simply as 'How much of what is put where'. This reflects the fact that planning is a *process* through which decisions are made, rather than anything with an absolutely definitive subject matter. As befits a political system, the question of what planning covers has over the years largely been left to those who make planning decisions. The result has been an expansion of the idea, beyond straightforward amenity, public health and land use issues towards taking into account the economic and social impact of decisions.

This widening of the scope of planning has received the support of the courts. In exercising their supervisory jurisdiction they have often had to ask the question 'What is planning?' in order to decide whether a power has been used legitimately. In so doing they have proved willing to decide that most things are within the scope of planning. The most commonly used legal test is given by Lord Scarman in *Great Portland Estates Ltd* v *Westminster CC* [1984] 3 All ER 744, who suggested that town planning covers anything that 'relates to the character of the use of land'.

However, this accommodating legal attitude is not shared by all and in recent years there have been fundamental divisions over the legitimate role and scope of planning. Until the 1970s, town and country planning was a relatively uncontroversial topic in party political terms, with the exception of the questions of compensation for refusal of permission and taxation of profits resulting from a grant of permission. There was a degree of consensus over what planning should consist of and over the preferred policies. This has now broken down, with the result that there is open conflict over both the proper role of planning and over the content of the policies that should be adopted.

There is universal agreement that planning includes land use and amenity issues, such as the location and design of new developments. The key question is how far socio-economic issues are a legitimate part of it. Some see planning as one means by which a particular form of social development may be produced. Others wish to see planning restricted as much as possible on the grounds that it interferes unduly with the free market. The second view is effectively the one that has been espoused by the current Government, with its firm beliefs in deregulation, a minimalist approach to restrictions on commercial activity, the power of the market as a distributor of resources, and the consequent need for speed and certainty in any system of control.

Planning policy

Notwithstanding the retention of the basic structure of the system outlined above, town planning has changed radically since the 1970s. Only some of these changes have been to the law. Most have been brought about by administrative means, particularly by the concerted application of strong Central Government policy. This was summarised by Grant in the first updating supplement to *Urban Planning Law* (1986) as follows:

One of the most distinctive trends of the past five years has been the emergence of Government policy as a dominant force in development control. It has been brought about by a series of hard-hitting Circulars based on the Government's deregulatory and pro-development ideology, coupled to a new willingness to use the appeals process as a means of reinforcing the policies.

The pro-development ideology was arguably the most important aspect of the 1980s, as the Government sought to increase the role of the free market in generating development. Landmarks in this regard were the publication of Circular 22/80, with an overt encouragement of small businesses and private housing, and Circular 14/85 with its presumption in favour of development which stated 'There is always a presumption in favour of allowing applications for development, having regard to all material considerations, unless that development would cause demonstrable harm to interests of acknowledged importance'. Circular 1/85 also played an important role, emphasising that conditions should not be attached unless they could be justified on clear grounds. Their role was described as 'anodyne expedients by which objections to offensive developments can be assuaged' (Miller & Wood, *Planning and Pollution*, 1983).

Not only were these Circulars pro-development in terms of policy, they afforded such great weight to this that local planning authorities ignored them at their peril. The result was that in the 1980s these explicitly directory Circulars grew to have far greater importance than local policies such as development plans. As shown below, these were downgraded in importance in the 1980s, though they are enjoying a resurgence at present. The reason for this is straightforward; in a developer-led system, developers value the certainty that is provided by a framework of clear policies, rather than the uncertainty provided by a wholly market-based approach.

The appeals process was used to support this shift in power from local government to Central Government. Pearce ('The Changing Role of Planning Appeals', *Development and Planning*, ed. Cross and Whitehead, 1989) showed some dramatic changes here. In the early to mid–1970s the success rate of appeals against refusal of permission was in the region of 20%. This had grown to 32% by 1984 and 40% in 1986/7, at which level it stayed for the rest of the decade. Not surprisingly, the number of appeals also rose sharply, from around 8,000 in the mid–1970s to almost 30,000 each year in the late 1980's. This meant that a quarter of all refusals were appealed. A similar story was apparent in relation to appeals against enforcement notices.

In keeping with the policy of doctrinal neutrality on the content of planning policies, the courts did not interfere with these changes, except to preserve the rationality of the decision-making process by insisting that adequate reasons were given for decisions. In this respect it should be recognised that the planning system has always been pro-development to some extent. This stems from the prominence of property-based ideas within it and is evident in its very structure. For example, third parties and objectors are not given particularly wide rights within the system. Specifically, there is a right to appeal against the refusal of permission, but no right to appeal against a grant of permission (as there is in many other countries, such as Eire). The result is that permission will be granted if *either* the local planning authority or the Secretary of State is in favour of it.

There has also always been some sort of presumption in favour of granting permission; the difference is that this has changed in substance from the basic public law requirement that reasons be given for a decision affecting someone's right to develop to a *policy* in favour of development that may have a great weight attached to it by the decision-maker (see p. 236 for a discussion of the court's attitude to the presumption in favour of development). Similarly there have always been restrictions on the scope of conditions, with the courts adopting the attitude that conditions that take away private property rights without compensation are *ultra vires* (see p. 240). Lastly, the statistics on planning permission show that, of the current 450,000 applications made each year, 86% are granted (first quarter of 1993).

Deregulation

A separate, though related, strand of the changes in the 1980s was the theme of deregulation. This was illustrated by the titles of three White Papers setting out Government policy—*Lifting the Burden* (Cmnd. 9571, 1985), *Building Businesses, Not Barriers* (Cmnd. 9794, 1986) and *Releasing Enterprise* (Cm. 512). A major emphasis was the reduction of red tape and delays. Significant relaxations were made in the General Development Order in 1981, 1985 and 1988 and in the Use Classes Order in 1987 so as to cut out the need for planning permission in many situations, with the objective of encouraging the development of small businesses. Along with the other changes to development plans referred to at p. 214, the procedures for development plans were streamlined, so that they might be adopted more quickly, leading to a consequent reduction in public opportunities for participation in the process. Regular encouragement was given by Circulars to speed up the process of dealing with planning applications. The politically suspect metropolitan county councils were abolished in the Local Government Act 1985, and this led to the introduction of a new system of unitary development plans in those areas.

The uniformity of the system was also lost. Enterprise zones were introduced in the Local Government, Planning and Land Act 1980 and simplified planning zones in the Housing and Planning Act 1986. Both mechanisms operate so as to remove most or all planning controls in designated areas, though designation and the controls that are retained remain with the local authority. In contrast, urban development areas, also introduced in the Local Government, Planning and Land Act 1980, are designated (or imposed) solely by the Secretary of State and are put under the management of centrally appointed urban development corporations, with local planning authorities losing all their powers (see p. 232). A final point worth mentioning is that an increasing number of environmentally significant developments avoid the planning system entirely by using the more limited Private Bill procedures.

A change of direction?
In summary it can be said that in the 1980s the planning system became far more centralised. This was true in two senses: more decisions were taken at a central level and central policy pervaded every decision even at a local level. One effect was to shift power from local government to Central Government; another to increase the areas of conflict between the two levels. But, interestingly, at the same time the system became in a way less centralised. This was because the changes in policy were designed to increase the role of the market at the expense of the State, and to make the system more developer-led.

However, it is clear that in the 1990s these trends are slowly being reversed as the Government steers a slightly different course to that charted in the 1980s. There are signs that greater regard is being paid to local decisions (as represented by development plans) and this impression of a shift in the balance between Central Government and local government is reinforced by the new presumption in favour of following the development plan mentioned above.

The pace of change in planning policy has slowed significantly from the heady days of the mid to late 1980s. This reflects a number of factors, not the least of which is the deep recession in the development industry in the early to mid 1990s. When this is coupled with the strategic shift from central to local control via the development plan system, it is difficult to identify any significant policy emphasis from Central Government. Perhaps the most notable policy guidance in the mid-1990s has seen the use of the mechanism of planning to contribute to the goal of sustainable development. PPGs on planning and transport and retail development (and more specifically out-of-town retailing) have indicated that the Government is willing to use planning as a means of governing the location of development which would generate significant amounts of traffic. These policy initiatives have been reinforced by a spate of appeal decisions where the Secretary of State has upheld the turned down appeals for a number of out-of-town superstores. Ironically, the use of central policy to *promote* 'environmentally friendly' developments is a cumbersome mechanism, and can be overridden by both local decisions through the development plan process and the courts (see the House of Lords' decision in *Bolton MBC* v *Secretary of State for the Environment* [1995] JPL 581).

Local planning authorities

Initial responsibility for most planning decisions rests with local authorities, which in this context are generically called local planning authorities. In metropolitan areas all planning functions are carried out by the metropolitan district council. In non-metropolitan areas planning functions are split between county and district councils by schedule 1.

County councils (called county planning authorities) are responsible for:

(a) structure plans;
(b) local plans relating to certain county subjects, such as minerals planning and waste disposal;
(c) county matters in development control (including minerals developments and any related works or buildings, waste disposal applications, and applications relating to land in national parks);
(d) certain development control decisions where they are able to grant themselves planning permission;
(e) county councils are also consulted by the district planning authority over certain large-scale developments, principally those which affect the structure plan or county matters, and over highway matters in their capacity as highways authorities.

District councils (called district planning authorities) are responsible for all other local plans and for all development control decisions, *except* those relating to county matters.

There are a number of special areas where different rules apply:

(a)   In national parks, all planning decisions are taken by the national park authority, which will be either a joint board established for that purpose (this is the case in the Peak District and Lake District), or a committee of the county council. In each case the board or committee consists of representatives of the county and district councils within the national park, with one-third of the members appointed directly by the Secretary of State. Section 63 of the Environment Act 1995 will, however, convert the existing authorities into autonomous local authorities (see p. 504).

(b)   In the Broads, the similarly constituted Broads Authority takes all decisions (Norfolk and Suffolk Broads Act 1988).

(c)   In urban development areas the urban development corporation normally becomes the local planning authority. This was also the case with new town development corporations, but these have now virtually been phased out. (In enterprise zones and simplified planning zones the local planning authority stays the same).

Forward planning: development plans

Local planning authorities are responsible for producing development plans on a continuing basis, which then guide or influence development in the areas covered. In this country, all development plans are permissive, i.e. they lay down policies, aims, objectives and goals rather than state what is definitely going to happen in an area. They have no immediate effect other than as a statement of what the local planning authority considers is desirable. But they do have a great and growing importance in the decision whether or not to grant planning permission (see p. 234).

There is *no* national plan. The nearest equivalent is the Central Government policy set out in Planning Policy Guidance Notes and Government Circulars. There are also no formal regional plans, although groupings of local planning authorities do produce general regional strategies, and there is formal regional planning guidance issued by Central Government, often based on advice from these regional groupings.

For most areas the existing system is to have two tiers of plan—structure plans and local plans, collectively referred to as the development plan. However, in metropolitan areas, unitary development plans are taking over this function. They were first required by the Local Government Act 1985 (a consequence of the abolition of the metropolitan county councils), and although they are still in the course of being made, will replace structure plans and local plans in those areas in the next few years.

The history and future of development plans

The system of development plans has been one area within planning law where there seems to have been a constant state of change. The original development plans established under the 1947 Act were basically detailed, spatial, land use maps, drawn up by local authorities for all areas, but requiring Central Government approval. Delay was endemic both in making the plans and keeping them up-to-date, and public involvement was not properly catered for, with the result that the two-tier system of structure and local plans was introduced in the Town and Country Planning Act 1968. Increased public participation rights were added by the Town and Country Planning Act 1971.

Before these plans had much of a chance to prove themselves, they became unpopular with a Government unconvinced by the need for strong forward planning and antipathetic to the power of local authorities. Structure plans in particular were downgraded by comparison with local plans by the Local Government, Planning and Land Act 1980 and plans of all types were accorded ever-decreasing weight in decisions compared to Central Government policies. Numerous proposals for reform were produced, the major themes of which were the need for plans to be restricted to land use matters, for less detail to be included in them, and for procedures to be speeded up.

Ultimately, some important changes were enacted by the Planning and Compensation Act 1991, sch. 4, which remodelled the part of the Town and Country Planning Act 1990 dealing with development plans (Part II). The main changes, which came into force in February 1992, were as follows:

(a)   Despite some consideration having been given to their abolition, structure plans were retained. But they should now cover a more restricted range of topics than before.

(b)   The requirement that structure plans and modifications to them must be approved by the Secretary of State was removed.

(c)   It became mandatory for a local planning authority to make a *district-wide* local plan, something which few had done in the past, preferring to concentrate their plan-making activities on specific parts of their district.

(d)   Development plans for the area of a national park became mandatory for the first time, as did a local minerals plan and a waste local plan, the last being intended to complement the waste disposal plan required by the Environmental Protection Act 1990, s. 50, which has limited public involvement.

(e)   In relation to all these types of plan (and also to unitary development plans) the procedures were streamlined so as to reduce the delay between initial deposit and final adoption, though the main elements of public participation and consultation were retained.

These changes make it clear that the next few years will see a great deal of activity on plan-making, a fact that gains in significance when considered alongside the movement towards a plan-led system of development control and the consequent increase in practical importance of the plans. The following sections refer to the law as it now is after the changes made by the 1991 Act.

Structure plans

A structure plan is a statement of general strategic policies set out in the form of a written statement supplemented by representative diagrams and a written memorandum (which is not a formal part of the plan). It will contain major strategic policies for the area of a county. Planning Policy Guidance Note 12 sets out current Government policy, which is to restrict the scope of structure plans to topics undeniably connected with land use. These are listed as housing, green belts, conservation, the rural economy, the urban economy, major employment-generating development, strategic transport and highways issues, minerals matters, waste treatment and disposal, land reclamation, tourism, leisure and recreation, and energy generation, including renewable energy. The impact of the proposals on the environment should also be covered, including the question of the contribution that planning can play in combating global warming. There is a specific duty to include policies for 'the improvement of the physical environment' (s. 31(3)), and many structure plans now include policies on such things as air pollution. These will set out general objectives for the area and act as a framework for land use decisions (see Wood, *Planning Pollution Prevention*, 1989, Ch. 5). On the other hand, the Royal Society for the Protection of Birds has published a report critical of the generally inadequate treatment of nature conservation in structure plans (*RSPB Planscan*, 1990). The structure plan will be relevant to the process of filling out these policies in the local plan and to major development control decisions.

All areas now have a structure plan, but there is a continuing duty for a county planning authority to keep under review matters affecting the development and planning of their area (s. 30), and Planning Policy Guidance Note 12 envisages there should be a formal review every 15 years. In addition, some counties have different structure plans for different parts of the county and are now required to prepare revised plans on a county-wide basis. The procedures for modifying the plan are set out in ss. 31–35C and the Town and Country Planning (Development Plan) Regulations 1991 (SI 1991 No. 2794), which allow for limited public involvement. In essence, the county planning authority produces and publicises reasoned proposals. It must consult with a wide range of interested bodies (including the various regulatory agencies with environmental responsibilities), send a copy to the Secretary of State and allow at least six weeks for members of the public to make representations. Unless the Secretary of State directs otherwise, an examination in public (a limited form of public inquiry at which there is no right to present a case unless invited to do so) must be held. This appears to be dispensed with in over half the cases.

In the past, a structure plan required the approval of the Secretary of State. This requirement meant that the Secretary of State had the final say on the scope and content of the plan and its policies, and the power was often used to ensure that policies acceptable to Central Government were adopted rather than those originally proposed by the local planning authority. This requirement has now been dropped, but the Secretary of State has a power to call a plan in (s. 35A), and thus is able to exercise ultimate control over policy. The plan should be in conformity with the Regional Planning Guidance produced by the Secretary of State.

A challenge to a structure plan modification can be made within six weeks of the decision under s. 287 but, given the wide and subjective powers given to the local authority and the Secretary of State, unless the decision is perverse, totally unreasoned or internally contradictory, a successful challenge is most unlikely (see *E. Bradley & Sons* v *Secretary of State for the Environment* [1983] 47 P&CR 375).

Local plans

Local plans are more detailed, consisting of written policies and specific land use allocations by reference to a map, so their relevance to individual development control decisions is much greater. There are three types of local plan:

(a) district plans, including proposals for regulatory controls within a defined area: the district planning authority makes these;

(b) subject plans, covering proposals for particularly sensitive subjects in an area (e.g. green belt, minerals development, tourism): either county or district planning authorities may make these;

(c) action area plans, dealing with proposals for the comprehensive redevelopment of small areas.

In addition, urban development areas and the few remaining new towns may have their own plans. Automatic planning permission is granted by Special Development Order for the matters in such a plan.

Prior to the passage of the 1991 Act, the local planning authority was given a discretion to include environmental measures in a local plan, but policies varied from the detailed to the non-existent. There is now a duty to include such policies. It seems that no subject plan directly concerned with pollution control or nature conservation has yet been made, though Humberside CC has an Intensive Livestock Units Subject Plan.

Despite their importance for development control, until the passage of the 1991 Act there was no requirement for everywhere to have a local plan. According to the White Paper, *This Common Inheritance* (Cm. 1200, 1990), 55 of the 333 district planning authorities at that time had no local plan at all, and most others had only patchy coverage. One reason for this was undoubtedly that the making of local plans was actively discouraged by the Government throughout the 1980s, both in Circular guidance (e.g. Circular 22/84) and through the appeals system. However, there has been a distinct U-turn in policy on this point and the making of local plans became mandatory under the 1991 Act. Each district planning authority is now under a duty to make a district-wide local plan. Figures issued at the beginning of 1993 showed that 82 districts had district-wide plans in place, and it was expected that the system would be virtually complete by the end of 1996.

The procedures for making or modifying a local plan are set out in ss. 36–52 and the Town and Country Planning (Development Plan) Regulations 1991 (SI 1991 No. 2794). In the past these procedures allowed for greater individual involvement than structure plans, but the initial procedures are now effectively the same for each type of plan. One important difference is that, if an objection to a draft local plan is made and not withdrawn, the local planning authority *must* hold a public local inquiry before an inspector. Objectors must be given at least six weeks' notice and have a right to appear at the inquiry (s. 42). The procedure is governed by a *Code of Practice on Development Plans,* published as an Annex to Planning Policy Guidance Note 12. The local planning authority must consider the inspector's recommendations and can adopt the local plan formally by resolution, unless the Secretary of State exercises the right to call in the plan for approval—a very rare occurrence (ss. 44 and 45). The local plan should be reviewed every 10 years at least.

The local plan is required to be in 'general conformity' with the structure plan (s. 46). However, if there is a conflict between the two, it is the local plan which prevails, unless the structure plan specifically lists the local plan as not conforming with it (s. 48). Local plans may be challenged within six weeks of their adoption (s. 287). Owing to the procedural duties relating to the public local inquiry, a successful action is more likely than for a challenge to a structure plan.

Unitary development plans

The Local Government Act 1985 introduced unitary development plans to replace structure and local plans in metropolitan areas. This is being done gradually; only one unitary development plan has yet been made, but all metropolitan authorities have been directed to make one. Existing plans remain in force until the Secretary of State brings the new plan into force and existing local plans may be incorporated into it. It is expected that all unitary development plans will be in place by the end of 1995.

The unitary development plan will consist of two parts: Part I will in general correspond to the structure plan and Part II to the local plan. The procedures for them are set out in ss. 12–28. Essentially they allow for a mixture of the current procedures used for structure plans and local plans, combining central supervision over strategic and regional matters with a commitment to some public involvement in more detailed matters. There is a provision for all or part of the plan to be called in for central approval, although it is not expected that this will be usual, even for Part I. The Planning and Compensation Act 1991 imposed a duty to include environmental matters in both Parts I and II.

Development plans and development control

Statutory plans *must* be taken into account in any development control decision. Section 70(2) states that, when making a decision whether to grant planning permission, the local planning authority 'shall have regard to the provisions of the development plan, so far as material to the application, and to any other material considerations'.

This important issue will be covered at p. 234, but it should be noted that, after a period in the 1980s in which plans were downgraded in importance compared to Central Government policy, the Government has now placed increased emphasis on development plans as the framework within which individual planning decisions should be considered. A particular consideration is the need to provide certain guidance for developers on future policy, since, in a developer-led system, developers value clear policies, as opposed to the uncertainty provided by a wholly market-based approach. Section 54A added by the Planning and Compensation Act 1991, s. 26, states:

> where, in making any determination under the planning Acts, regard is to be had to the development plan, the determination shall be made in accordance with the development plan unless material considerations indicate otherwise.

Non-statutory plans and guidance

Local planning authorities frequently have other policies and drafts that have not gone through the statutory procedures. In practice, a large range of such 'non-statutory' material, ranging from draft local plans to design briefs and technical specifications, is used by local planning authorities in making decisions. But there are obvious problems in this practice, because it may be seen as subverting the statutory public participation requirements, and thus the democratic legitimacy of the planning process.

In *Great Portland Estates Ltd* v *Westminster CC* [1984] 3 All ER 744, a distinction was drawn between different types of non-statutory guidance. The House of Lords required that all matters of *policy* should be included in the statutory plan and that only supplementary matters of detail, or those which relate to the implementation of these policies, should be put in non-statutory guidance. However, as long as this non-statutory material is not illegal (i.e. it must relate to the character of the use of land) it is a material consideration under s. 70(2) and must be considered alongside the statutory development plan, although perhaps not always accorded the same weight. The weight attached to it will depend on the circumstances in which it was produced.

Development control: definition of development

It is in relation to the system of development control that the town and country planning system has its greatest impact on environmental law. Planning permission is required for the carrying out of any development (s. 57(1)). The general approach has been to define development very widely so that virtually everything is included initially, and then to exempt by reference to well-defined categories. This has the effect of shifting the focus in most practical situations from what is included to what is excluded (see the Use Classes Order and the General Permitted Development Order in particular).

Development is defined in s. 55(1), which provides:

> Development . . . . means the carrying out of building, engineering, mining or other operations in, on, over or under land, or the making of any material change in the use of any buildings or other land.

This definition has effectively remained unchanged since 1947, so past decisions of the courts, which are the ultimate interpreters of the meaning of the Act, are relevant. Decisions of the Secretary of State on appeal are also of importance in understanding the definition, although these are not binding as legal authority.

The courts have decided that the existence of development is a question of 'fact and degree' in each particular case. It is for the local planning authority (or the Secretary of State on appeal) to apply the relevant law to the facts of each case to decide whether there has been development. The courts limit themselves to supervising and reviewing these decisions, i.e. a decision by a local planning authority that a particular state of affairs amounts to development will only be overturned by the courts if the authority has used an incorrect test, or the correct test incorrectly, or has reached a perverse decision.

There are two limbs to the definition—operational development and change of use development. It is important to make this distinction because:

(a) enforcement action can only be taken against development that has taken place;
(b) an enforcement notice should specify which limb of development has taken place;
(c) the limitation period for serving an enforcement notice is different for the two categories (four years and 10 years respectively).

There are four types of operational development:

(a) building operations;
(b) engineering operations;
(c) mining operations; and
(d) other operations.

Building operations
These are defined very widely in s. 336. 'Building' 'includes any structure or erection, and any part of a building as so defined, but does not include plant or machinery comprised in a building'. 'Building operations' include rebuilding operations, structural alterations of or additions to buildings, and other operations normally undertaken by a person carrying on business as a builder.

Any significant works are included, such as rebuilding works, works of alteration, the buiding of an extension, and the erection of such things as shop canopies, window grilles, shutters, walls, flagpoles, fences, advertising hoardings, large sculptures, street furniture and many other things. In one celebrated example, the erection of a model shark emerging from the roof of a house was held to amount to a building operation (though it ultimately received planning permission [1993] JPL 194). It is normally considered that very minor alterations such as the installation of ordinary TV aerials, are not significant enough to amount to development.

Exceptions include the following:

(a) Maintenance, improvement or alterations to a building affecting only its interior, or not materially affecting the external appearance, are not development (s. 55(2)(a)).

(b) Large numbers of minor and public operations are exempted from the need for planning permission by the General Development Order (see p. 225)

(c) Moveable structures (e.g. caravans) are not normally buildings, unless attached to the land or made permanent in some way (see *Barvis v SSE* [1971] 22 P&CR 710).

Demolition raises some interesting points. Until recently the predominant view was that simple demolition of a building was not development, unless it involved such a large amount of removal of materials that it constituted an engineering operation (*Coleshill Investments v MHLG* [1969] 2 All ER 525). However, in *Cambridge CC v Secretary of State* [1991] JPL 428, David Widdicombe QC decided in the High Court that demolition of part of a building by the removal of roofing materials prior to total demolition was operational development. As a result (and despite the overruling of this decision by the Court of Appeal), in the Planning and Compensation Act 1991 the Government took the opportunity to amend s. 55 to include demolition within the definition of building operation. But, in order to avoid unnecessary regulatory control, the effect of this step was mitigated by a new s. 55(2)(g), which allows any description of building specified by the Secretary of State to be excluded from the need for planning permission. This power was used to exclude all buildings except dwellinghouses. Even then, the General Development Order (now adopted in the new Order) was amended to grant automatic planning permission in all cases apart from where a building was deliberately allowed to become unsafe or uninhabitable. Before these permitted development rights may be used, however, the developer must notify the local planning authority and the authority may impose restrictions on the method of demolition and the restoration of the site, thus retaining some control over the impact of the demolition on the area. Apart from this limited prior notification requirement, the position is thus that demolition requires planning permission only where an Article 4 direction has been served withdrawing the permitted development right (see p. 226), or the activity falls within the scope of the *Coleshill* decision, which remains good law.

Whatever the situation for ordinary buildings or structures, demolition of a listed building or of any building in a conservation area is subject to control (see Planning (Listed Buildings and Conservation Areas) Act 1990).

Engineering operations
These include road building, laying out of access to roads, drainage works, land reclamation, and earthmoving works. There are many exceptions for public works in s. 55 and the General Permitted Development Order.

Mining operations
These include all forms of extractive operation, such as mining, quarrying and the removal of materials from mineral deposits and waste tips. There are

additional powers over minerals development. County planning authorities are designated mineral planning authorities and given wide powers to review operations and to impose conditions relating to aftercare, restoration of sites and discontinuance of activities.

Other operations

This is a little discussed catch-all category. It appears designed to ensure that matters such as waste disposal and drilling are covered.

An operation has commenced as soon as it has an impact on the land. This includes digging trenches and laying out the lines of roads (s. 56 and *Malvern Hills DC* v *Secretary of State* [1983] 81 LGR 13). The time of commencement is important because every planning permission contains a condition requiring commencement of the work within a stated time, otherwise the permission lapses. If no time is stipulated by the local planning authority, the period is five years from the grant of permission (s. 91). It should also be noted that enforcement action must wait until commencement of the operation, but that the four-year limitation period for serving enforcement notices commences at the substantial completion of the operation.

Material change of use

The power to control changes in the use of land is virtually unique to British town and country planning, and makes it peculiarly able to exercise detailed control over land use. In the debates on the 1947 Act, Lord Reid, then a Conservative MP but later a Law Lord, is reported to have said of material change of use, 'Nobody knows what that means'. Very little guidance is given in the Act on the meaning of this rather vague phrase, but over the years the judges have filled in any gaps by the creation of a number of important explanatory concepts. Nevertheless, this remains a somewhat flexible phrase, and flexibility is aided by the fact that the decision whether development has taken place in any particular case is a matter for the local planning authority, applying the law to the facts.

It is the *change* that is development, not the use itself Accordingly, a use which has been carried on since before 1948 cannot be the subject of control. The change must be *material* in the sense that it has:

(a)   a physical impact on the land;
(b)   a substantial impact; and
(c)   an impact that is relevant to town and country planning.

For example, in *Snook* v *Secretary of State* [1977] 33 P&CR 1, a change from builder's storeyard to demolition person's storeyard was held not to be a material change because the change in nature did not have planning effects.

Some uses are *ancillary* or *incidental* to the main use of a property, such as keeping pets in a house. They are ignored for planning puposes. However, if the ancillary use extends beyond a normal degree, as it may do if, for example, extensive breeding of dogs takes place, it cannot be ignored and a change has occurred. There are then two *concurrent* uses (residential and dog breeding). In *Wallington* v *Secretary of State* [1991] JPL 942, a material change of use was found where 44 dogs were kept in a dwellinghouse and an enforcement notice limiting the number to six on noise grounds was upheld. Similarly, a factory will be treated as one use of a site, even though a number of different activities, such as manufacturing, storage, offices and distribution, are carried on.

The unit of land to be considered when ascertaining whether there has been a change of use is called the *planning unit*. This is normally the unit of occupation prior to the change and it is unusual to aggregate together more than one unit of occupation, or to subdivide one, unless 'two or more physically distinct areas are occupied for substantially different and unrelated purposes' (see *Burdle* v *Secretary of State* [1972] 3 All ER 240). Thus a factory is normally treated as one unit, allowing some internal shifting of activities between manufacturing, storage, office space and car parking. Two factories on separate sites in the same ownership would be treated as two units.

Intensification of an existing use of a site often causes problems. It is not development unless it results in the use becoming different in character or concept. For example, the *Wallington* case illustrates a change in character, whilst a factory which doubles its output, or begins 24-hour working, would not require planning permission.

Certain matters are stated in the Act to be material changes. These are: splitting a single dwellinghouse into separate dwellings (s. 55(3)(a)); the deposit of waste (s. 55(3)(b)); and the display of adverts (s. 55(5)). Conversely, certain matters are stated *not* to be material changes, though in some cases the application of the judicially invented tests would have reached the same conclusions. These include (s. 55(2)(d) and (e)):

   (d)   the use of any buildings or other land within the curtilage of a dwelling-house for any purpose incidental to the enjoyment of the dwellinghouse as such;
   (e)   the use of any land for the purpose of agriculture or forestry (including afforestation) and the use for any of those purposes of any building occupied together with land so used.

Use Classes Order

Any change within one of the Use Classes set out in the Schedule to the Town and Country Planning (Use Classes) Order 1987 (SI 1987 No. 764) is not development, thus removing planning barriers that might obstruct a change from one use to another with a similar environmental impact. It is significantly more liberal than previous Orders, part of the deregulatory strategy pursued by the Government in the 1980s aimed at encouraging changes in business structure. It should also be noted that the General Development Order grants automatic permission for certain innocuous changes from one use class to another.

It is not possible in a book of this kind to explain all of the Classes, but some of them are very wide. For example, Class A1 includes most shops, Class A2 all shop-front financial and professional services where the services are provided principally to visiting members of the public, and Class A3 most food and drink premises. Class B1—the general business class—is very important, since it includes both use as offices and use for any industrial process which can be carried out in a residential area without significant detriment to its environmental amenity. Class B2 is a general industrial class, including all industrial uses not in other Classes and permits a large range of industrial changes. This Class was extended considerably with an amendment of the 1987 Order which abolished the old Special Industrial Classes B4–7 and brought them under the general B2 Class (see the Town and Country Planning (Use Classes) Amendment Order 1995 (SI 1995 No. 297)). Class B3 was abolished in 1992.

The extension of Class B2 was justified on the basis that there are pollution control powers in place to control the activities of special industrial uses although the extent to which that control is efficient must be questionable. The changes are significant as Classes B4–7 included some of the more polluting developments, and now no permission is required to change between these uses. In addition, the nature of B2 uses has, traditionally, been somewhat more benign than the special uses. The change in the Classes could, for instance, see an engineering use replaced by a blood-boiling factory without any development taking place which would require planning permission. Although both could have an impact upon the amenity of the locality, the nature of the impact could differ widely.

In line with general principle, ancillary and incidental uses are ignored for the purposes of the Order. In addition, a subdivision of a unit (other than a dwelling-house) into two or more units all within the same Class (such as subdivision of a factory unit) is not development. However, it is possible for a planning permission to contain a condition restricting the future operation of the Use Classes Order in relation to that site (*City of London Corpn* v *Secretary of State* [1971] 23 P&CR 169), although this type of condition is not favoured by the Government as a matter of policy.

Many unusual uses will not be in any Class, and neither are concurrent uses where the components are in different Classes. The following uses are specifically stated *not* to be in any Class—theatres, amusement arcades, funfairs, launderettes, petrol stations, taxi businesses, car-hire businesses, scrapyards, mineral storeyards and car-breaking yards—so a change to these uses always requires planning permission.

In addition to the exemptions provided by the Use Classes Order, certain changes of use in breach of the law are immune from enforcement action. Prior to the passage of the Planning and Compensation Act 1991 these were changes that took place before 1 January 1964; under the 1991 Act immunity is conferred 10 years after any breach occurred. It should also be noted that s. 57 states that the resumption of a previous, lawful use after a temporary planning permission has expired, or after the service of an enforcement notice, does not require planning permission. The 1991 Act makes it clear, by adding a new s. 191(2), that a use which is immune from enforcement is a lawful use, thus reversing the House of Lords' decision in *Young* v *Secretary of State* [1983] 47 P&CR 165.

Existing uses

Normally there is a right to carry on the existing use of a site, unless it is in breach of planning control. This is roughly equivalent to a property right attaching to the land and has a distinct value. Of course, when the occupier of land voluntarily changes the use, the existing use right switches from the old to the new use.

Existing use rights have been described as 'hardy beasts with a great capacity for survival' (Lord Scarman in *Pioneer Aggregates* v *Secretary of State* [1984] 3 WLR 32), but they may be abandoned by a lengthy period of disuse (*Hartley* v *MHLG* [1970] 1 QB 413). It is also possible to lose the benefit of the existing use of a site by carrying out works or changes which effect a *radical change* to the site (*Jennings Motors* v *Secretary of State* [1982] 1 All ER 471). This applies whether planning permission is obtained or not. If there is a planning permission, any limitations in it will be operative; if there is no permission, then *any* use of the site will be in breach of planning control. Otherwise, an existing use right can only be removed by a discontinuance order (s. 102), or an order revoking planning permission (ss. 97–100). In both cases compensation is payable.

It is not possible to abandon a planning permission, since it is a public right attaching to the land not the occupier. This is illustrated by *Pioneer Aggregates* v *Secretary of State* [1984] 3 WLR 32, where a perpetual permission for quarrying was granted in 1950. Quarrying ceased in 1966 and, when it was recommenced in 1980, the local planning authority argued that the use had been abandoned. The House of Lords decided that the planning permission still applied to permit quarrying and any removal of that right would entail payment of compensation.

This position distinguishes planning control from most other areas of environmental control. There is no ability to vary a planning permission once it has been granted, even where circumstances have changed radically in a way that was not foreseen at the time the permission was granted. This emphasises that a grant of planning permission is an irrevocable event, effectively creating rights for the landowner in a way that a consent from a pollution control agency does not.

The General Development Orders

The Town and Country Planning (General Permitted Development) Order 1995 (SI 1995 No. 418) (known as the GDO) grants automatic planning permission for 34 classes of development, listed and defined in sch. 1. These are called 'permitted development rights'. There has been some relaxation of the GDO in order to remove what were seen as unnecessary restrictions on development. In addition, the Town and Country Planning (General Development Procedure) Order 1995 (SI 1995 No. 419) (GDPO) sets out various procedural requirements connected with both permitted development and normal planning applications.

Three general types of activity are exempted in this way:

(a) minor developments;
(b) developments carried out by a whole range of public services; and
(c) favoured activities, especially agriculture and forestry.

There are some general restrictions in the Order. An application must always be made for developments involving the formation or widening of an access to a trunk or classified road. Automatic rights may also be restricted by a condition imposed on an earlier grant of planning permission (*City of London Corpn* v *Secretary of State* [1971] 23 P&CR 169). In addition, permitted development rights are withdrawn for a number of developments including those which require environmental assessment (see the Town and Country Planning (Environmental Assessment and Permitted Development) Regulations 1995 at p. 269) or which are likely to have a significant impact upon a certain areas of nature conservation value. Certain automatic rights are more restricted in national parks, AONBs and conservation areas.

Under Article 4 of the GDPO, a local planning authority may restrict automatic rights by serving a direction withdrawing the automatic planning permission, in which case permission must be sought in the ordinary way. The direction may be general to a type of development or specific to a site. Directions under Article 4 normally require the approval of the Secretary of State, must be made before the development is started and involve the payment of compensation to owners and occupiers, because they amount effectively to the taking away of a right to develop.

Certain automatic rights are more restricted in national parks, areas of outstanding natural beauty and conservation areas (e.g. on extensions to buildings).

It is not possible in a book of this kind to explain all of the Parts to Schedule 1, but the following explanation gives a flavour of the wide range of matters that are covered. For example, Part 1 covers 'the enlargement, improvement or other alteration of a dwellinghouse', subject to very technical limitations on the size, height, forwardmost projection, proximity to a boundary and total coverage of the curtilage. These rights only apply to dwellings, not to offices, and there are further provisions relating to ancillary buildings and developments, such as porches, sheds, garages, animal shelters, stables, swimming pools, oil tanks, hardstanding for cars, and satellite antennae. The limitations have been altered many times, most recently in the 1980s in an attempt to reduce the number of trivial applications. Part 8 covers 'the extension or alteration of an industrial building or a warehouse', again with size, height and other limitations relating to loss of parking and external appearance of the site. Part 4 permits temporary buildings and works, and temporary uses of any type (apart from caravan sites) for up to 28 days in one year (except markets and motor racing, where 14 days only are allowed). Part 6 permits many agricultural operations on agricultural land and Part 7 most forestry operations, both with generous size and height limits, although local planning authorities are given extra powers over the siting and design of otherwise exempted agricultural and forestry buildings. For a more detailed review of agricultural and forestry operations see Chapter 17.

The remaining Parts include a wide range of works carried out by public bodies, many of which will have potentially large environmental effects. They include repairs to services, developments by drainage authorities, many developments on operational land by statutory undertakers (e.g. in connection with railways, waterways, harbours, water, gas, electricity, lighthouses and the Post Office), and ancillary mining activities at existing mines.

Is planning permission required?

There is a fairly simple mechanism for ascertaining whether planning permission is required. It is now set out in s. 192, which was introduced by the Planning and Compensation Act 1991 and replaced the old mechanism under s. 64, which has been repealed. Section 192 provides that anyone may apply to the district planning authority for a certificate of lawfulness of proposed use or development, specifying the proposed use or operation. A certificate must be granted if the authority is satisfied that the use or operation would be lawful if subsisting or carried out at the time of the application. This is then conclusive of the legality of the development, as long as circumstances do not change before the development takes place. In other words, a certificate is the equivalent of a planning permission for what it covers.

The exact procedures for an application are contained in the GDPO. Since the application has to be specific, it is not possible to make one that relates to a hypothetical situation. Neither is it possible to apply after the development has taken place. In such a situation, the only way of discovering the position would be to seek a declaration in the High Court (a very expensive step), or to await the service of an enforcement notice and then appeal against it. The applicant may appeal under s. 78 to the Secretary of State against a determination under s. 192, or against a failure to make one within eight weeks.

Applying for planning permission

Anyone can apply for planning permission. It is not necessary to be the owner or occupier of the property, or even a prospective occupier. An application may even be used as a form of publicity stunt. For example, Friends of the Earth once submitted an application for an oversize replica of the Leaning Tower of Pisa in order to draw attention to the inadequacy of the UK Atomic Energy Authority's application for a nuclear reprocessing plant at Dounreay.

There are several types of permission the applicant may seek:

(a) Full permission.

(b)   Retrospective permission (allowed under s. 63(2)).

(c)   An application for the renewal of a planning permission.

(d)   Outline permission (see s. 92 and GDO, Art. 3). This can be sought for building operations only. Matters of 'siting, design, external appearance, means of access, landscaping of the site' (reserved matters) need not be submitted. Subsequent approval of these is needed within three years of the permission, or any other period stipulated by the local planning authority (s. 92(2)) otherwise the outline permission will lapse. An outline planning permission is legally a full permission in that any conditions, apart from those relating to reserved matters, must be imposed at this stage, the normal publicity arrangements apply, and revocation entails the payment of compensation.

(e)   Approval of reserved matters (GDO, Art. 4). Any number of such applications can be made within the three-year period. As this is not a full planning application, no further publicity is required and no new conditions can be added. (It may also be necessary to apply to the local planning authority for other approvals, e.g. where a condition in the planning permission requires future approval of a landscaping plan.)

(f)   Under s. 73, an applicant can ask for a condition to be discharged without putting the rest of the planning permission at risk. The local planning authority (and the Secretary of State on appeal) is limited to considering the condition in question. This procedure is very important in providing a measure of continuing control over planning permissions. It enables a landowner to get an outdated or unwanted condition removed, but in so doing it jeopardises the local planning authority's original discretionary decision. This is because it enables applications for removal of conditions even where the application might never have been granted in the first place had the condition not been attached.

Steps for the applicant to take

The applicant must apply on a form provided by the local planning authority. It must also notify owners and tenants of the land and submit a certificate to the authority stating that it has done so. This enables these people to be aware of the application and to make representations that the authority must take into account. It is an offence knowingly to issue a false certificate.

In *Main* v *Swansea CC* [1985] 49 P&CR 26, the Court of Appeal decided that failure to carry out such procedures does not necessarily render a subsequent grant of planning permission void: it all depends on whether anyone with *locus standi* has been prejudiced as a result. This applies to most procedures under the Act. In any case, *R* v *Rotherham MBC ex parte Rankin* [1990] JEL 503 shows that an action to quash a permission must be brought without delay.

Fees are payable for all applications for planning permission and deemed applications in connection with an appeal against an enforcement notice. There are fixed charges for different types of application. The categories are set out in the Town and Country Planning (Fees for Applications and Deemed Applications) Regulations 1989 (SI 1989 No. 193). The local planning authority need not consider an application until the requisite fee has been paid.

The current rates (they are periodically increased) are set out in the Town and Country Planning (Fees for Applications and Deemed Applications) (Amendment) (No.2) Regulations 1992 (SI 1992 No. 3052). For example, the rate is £120 for each house and for a material change of use, and £60 for extensions. At present the fees do not cover the full administrative cost to the local planning authoriy of processing applications but, in line with Government policy, the level can be expected to rise so as to do so in the next few years.

Steps for the local planning authority to take

On receipt of an application, the local planning authority will consult with a wide range of public bodies as required for specified situations by the Town and Country Planning (General Development) Order, Art. 18. These include highways authorities, other local authorities, parish and community councils, the National Rivers Authority, British Coal, the Ministry of Agriculture, Fisheries and Food, and the relevant Nature Conservancy Councils. Interestingly there is no duty to consult Her Majesty's Inspectorate of Pollution. There is a Code of Conduct governing this consultation procedure and those consulted have procedural rights in the event of an appeal. Any representations that are made are material considerations which must be taken into account by the local planning authority before it decides the application. However, it must not slavishly follow the advice of another public body, otherwise the decision will be challengeable for fettering of discretion.

The local planning authority must also publicise *all* applications (GDO, Arts. 6–8). It reflects a major change from the position prior to 1992, when there were no statutory publicity requirements other than for applications which did not conform with the development plan, applications relating to a listed building or in a conservation area (the duties in this respect still exist in addition to those explained below), applications subject to environmental assessment (see Chapter 10), and applications for a number of somewhat randomly selected anti-social activities that were termed 'bad-neighbour' developments.

The rigours of the earlier position were mitigated by the fact that most local planning authorities included provision for publicity in a wider range of cases in their standing orders, and indeed were encouraged to do so by Circular advice. For example, neighbours and others likely to be affected would often be informed of an application. The Local Government Ombudsman formalised some of these practices by deciding that, where a local authority had a policy of publicising applications, it would amount to maladministration not to follow that policy in any given case (see the case at [1983] JPL 613). However, this approach is of limited use since, while it may result in an aggrieved neighbour receiving an apology or some compensation for not being notified, an Ombudsman cannot quash the planning permission. Nevertheless, it remains an alternative course of action should the statutory requirements be ignored.

The new publicity requirements set out in the General Development Order split applications into three categories:

(a)   major developments, such as developments on sites of more than one hectare, the building of 10 or more houses, developments involving 1,000 square metres or more of floor space, and mineral and waste applications—in these cases an advertisement must be placed in a local newspaper and either a site notice posted or neighbours notified;

(b)   applications covered by the need for an environmental assessment, or which do not accord with the provisions of the development plan, or which affect a public right of way—in these cases a newspaper advertisement and a site notice are required;

(c)   in all other cases either a site notice or neighbour notification can be used.

These requirements involve some discretion being given to the local planning authority. For example, in categories (a) and (c) it has a choice of publicity measures, whilst it has a general power to decide that any development is major enough to fall within category (a).

In addition, the Town and Country Planning (Development Plans and Consultation) Directions 1992 require that certain applications which do not accord with the provisions of the development plan should be referred to the Secretary of State so that a decision can be made whether to call them in.

It must be asked what the legal position is should these procedures not be complied with. On the basis of court decisions such as *Main* v *Swansea CC* [1985] 49 P&CR 26 and *R* v *St Edmundsbury BC ex parte Investors in Industry Commercial Properties Ltd* [1985] 1 WLR 1168, it must be assumed that a failure may invalidate a decision, but would not necessarily do so because of the hurdles thrown up by judicial review. Reference should also be made to a number of cases in which the courts developed some safeguards for neighbours through the concepts of legitimate expectations and fairness (for a discussion of these cases, see Hinds [1988] JPL 742). However, these cases stopped some way short of recognising any general principle that applications should be publicised and they are rendered of reduced significance by the introduction of statutory publicity in all cases.

Decisions by the local planning authority

The local planning authority may (a) grant planning permission, (b) grant permission subject to conditions, (c) refuse permission, or (d) grant permission for part of the application only, as long as what is granted is not different in substance from the original, or an effective denial of rights to would-be objectors (see *Bernard Wheatcroft Ltd* v *Secretary of State* [1981] 257 EG 934). The decision must be in writing and must include reasons for the decision and for the imposition of any conditions. These are normally brief and it seems that a failure to provide reasons does not make the decision void. In the event of a grievance, the correct (and cheaper) course would be to appeal to the Secretary of State. The decision should be made within eight weeks of receipt by the local planning authority and payment of the fee, otherwise the applicant can appeal to the Secretary of State as if the application had been refused (GDO, Art. 20). The applicant can agree to a longer time scale.

Section 69 requires the local planning authority to keep public registers of all planning applications and decisions. (There is a further public register of details of enforcement notices and stop notices kept under s. 188.) The GDO, Arts. 25 and 26 set out the form these registers must take. They are an invaluable source of information on the planning history of a site.

Planning permission attaches to the land, not to the applicant (s. 75(1)). Exceptionally, a condition may limit the persons who can take advantage of the planning permission, though such conditions are discouraged by the Secretary of State (see Circular 1/85). A permission cannot be abandoned, since it is a public document (*Pioneer Aggregates* v *Secretary of State* [1984] 3 WLR 32). However, it is possible for a permission to become spent, either through lapse of time, occurrence of a condition subsequent, or occurrence of a situation which renders carrying it out impossible (*Pilkington* v *Secretary of State* [1973] 1 WLR 1527). In any other case where a planning permission is taken away, compensation is payable (ss. 97–100).

Alternative and special procedures

The following are ways that ordinary planning procedures may be circumvented, mainly for public developments:

(a)   Local authorities are effectively allowed to grant themselves planning permission (s. 316 and the Town and Country Planning General Regulations 1992 (SI 1992 No. 1492)). They can do this for any land within their area which they own or intend to develop, although if they intend to carry out the work themselves the permission is a personal, non-transferable one. The procedures are simple: the local planning authority passes a resolution to seek planning permission, after which it must publicise the application. Having taken any representations into account as material considerations, it may then pass a second resolution granting permission. The resultant planning permission is deemed to have been granted by the Secretary of State, so there is no right of appeal: it can be challenged only by judicial review. In view of the possibility of a conflict of interest, the courts have interpreted the procedural requirements of the General Regulations very strictly (*Steeples* v *Derbyshire CC* [1984] 3 All ER 468). It is not, however, impermissible for a local planning authority to follow a well-defined policy, provided it considers other possibilities and does not fetter its discretion. Such a course is not contrary to natural justice (*R* v *Amber Valley DC ex parte Jackson* [1985] 1 WLR 298).

(b)   Developments authorised by a Government Department under other authorisation procedures do not require planning permission (s. 90). This prevents a duplication of effort, but it does result in the decision being taken centrally rather than locally. For example, this option is available in relation to applications for the construction of nuclear power stations, since permission for power stations is also required from the Department of Trade and Industry under the Electricity Act 1989.

(c) Permission may be granted by a Special Development Order made under s. 59. This process has been used for granting blanket permissions in new towns, urban development areas and enterprise zones. The Windscale Thermal Oxide Reprocessing Plant was also permitted by the Town and Country Planning (Windscale and Calder Works) Special Development Order 1978 (see SI 1978 No. 523). In that case the Order followed a public inquiry and a Parliamentary debate, but neither is strictly required.

(d) Increasing use is being made of Private or Hybrid Acts of Parliament which avoid any of the planning procedures and effectively give the decision to a small Parliamentary joint Committee, with limited public scrutiny. The Channel Tunnel Act 1987 is an example of such an Act with very important environmental effects.

(e) Under s. 294, Crown land (i.e. all land owned by the Crown, the Duchies of Lancaster and Cornwall, Government Departments, but not nationalised industries) is effectively excluded from the Act by the provision of immunity against service of an enforcement notice. Planning permission can be obtained prior to disposal to private hands and action can be taken against private individuals occupying Crown land. In Circular 18/84, it is stated that the Crown bodies have agreed to abide informally by the same procedures and requirements as apply to private developers, but this system is not legally enforceable. One exception is that Crown immunity has been removed from health authorities and NHS trusts by the National Health Service and Community Care Act 1990. In November 1992, the Government issued a consultation paper proposing the removal of Crown immunity in planning legislation, except for cases involving national security and where there was a need for a particular development to be completed urgently. However, the paper also proposed that the normal enforcement procedures would not apply to Crown land. Instead, a local planning authority would seek a declaration in the High Court and the body in breach would remedy matters of its own accord.

Special areas

One of the features of the 1947 Act was that it applied a uniform system of control nationwide. Exceptions were made for developments in the areas of the new towns, but it was not until the 1980s that further exceptions were made as part of the Government's strategy of deregulation, with the proclaimed aim of effecting regeneration of the inner cities.

Urban development areas

Urban development areas were introduced in the Local Government, Planning and Land Act 1980. Not only are ordinary planning rules virtually scrapped in these areas, but the local planning authority is replaced by an unelected body. Under s. 134 of the 1980 Act, the Secretary of State may designate an area an urban development area and appoint an urban development corporation, which has general powers to redevelop land, together with wide powers of acquisition, management and resale. It may submit to the Secretary of State proposals for the development of land in its area (s. 148), which establishes a form of master plan. The Secretary of State may then make a Special Development Order, which grants automatic permission for development in accordance with the approved master plan and normally designates the corporation the local planning authority for all planning purposes (1990 Act, s. 7). The local planning authority accordingly loses all planning powers, although there is provision for consultation between it and the corporation. Twelve urban development areas have been designated.

Enterprise zones
Enterprise zones were also introduced by the Local Government, Planning and Land Act 1980. The order establishing an enterprise zone, which is made by the Secretary of State after some limited publicity, grants automatic planning permission for categories of development specified in the enterprise zone scheme (1990 Act, s. 88). However, the local authority draws up the scheme to cover those matters it wishes to permit. Thus, while enterprise zones are formally designated by the Secretary of State, local authorities decide what is to be permitted. They also remain the local planning authority for other development not covered by the scheme.

An enterprise zone normally lasts for 10 years and involves fiscal and administrative advantages for those in it, as well as the planning exemptions. Few new zones are now expected to be made (there are currently 25), but development commenced before the expiry of the scheme retains the benefit of the automatic permission.

Simplified planning zones
These were introduced in the Housing and Planning Act 1986. As with an enterprise zone scheme, a simplified planning zone scheme grants automatic planning permission for the matters specified in it, but there are no non-planning effects (1990 Act, s. 82).

Every district planning authority has a duty to consider whether to impose a simplified planning zone in part of its area. It must prepare a scheme if satisfied it is expedient to do so. Anybody may request the making of a scheme and the Secretary of State may direct the making of one. The procedures for making one are set out in the 1990 Act, sch. 7, as amended by the Planning and Compensation Act 1991. There is no requirement that the scheme be approved by the Secretary of State, though it may be called in for approval. A simplified planning zone lasts for 10 years, but development commenced before the expiry of the scheme retains the benefit of the automatic permission. Only a handful have been made.

National parks, areas of outstanding natural beauty, conservation areas, sites of special scientific interest, and designated green belt cannot be the subject of a scheme. County matters are also excluded, as are matters covered by the need for an environmental assessment.

The Secretary of State's powers

Under s. 77, the Secretary of State has an unfettered power to call in any planning application for determination. This immediately transfers jurisdiction from the local planning authority to the Secretary of State. This power is used sparingly, usually only for matters of national or regional importance or of local controversy. There is a right to a public inquiry unless waived by the parties and the Secretary of State and one is normally held. The procedures are virtually the same as for appeals, suitably amended to provide for the fact that this is a first determination. There is no formal power to request the Secretary of State to call in an application: objectors should write to the Secretary of State putting their case for this to happen.

The Secretary of State also has power to make directions relating to an application; this is normally used only for certain classes of case (e.g. applications for large shopping centres must be referred to the Secretary of State), but may also be used to prevent a precipitate decision by a local authority in an individual case.

Summary of rights of third parties

Third parties or objectors have limited specific rights under the legislation, although statutory publicity is now required for all applications and the Local Government (Access to Information) Act 1985 ensures the right to attend council meetings (see p. 53). Any representations made to the local planning authority must be considered as a material consideration.

Since third parties have no right to appeal against a planning decision, they must apply for judicial review of any adverse decision. This entails having *locus standi*, acting without delay, and being able to afford the large costs involved, and has very little chance of success. Only local planning authority decisions can be subject to judicial review: decisions of the Secretary of State are immune from challenge except under s. 288 (see p. 249). If an appeal is brought by the applicant, third parties have wider procedural rights at that stage.

The local planning authority's discretion

Under s. 70(2), in deciding whether or not to grant permission, the local planning authority 'shall have regard to the provisions of the development plan, so far as material to the application, and to any other material considerations'. The Secretary of State is subject to the same requirements in relation to decisions on a s. 78 appeal, or which are called in under s. 77.

It is central to an understanding of planning law to appreciate the scope of s. 70(2):

(a)   It gives the local planning authority a very wide *discretion* whether or not to grant permission.

(b)   This discretion will be exercised on grounds of *policy*.

It should be noted that policy means 'planning policy'. Despite the fact that ultimate responsibility for local authority decisions rests with elected members, decisions may not be 'political' in the sense of being based on party political or personal factors. For example, a decision by elected members that an industrial development should be refused simply because the residents were opposed to it would be *ultra vires,* unless there were valid planning objections.

The discretion is controlled in two ways:

(a)   through judicial review of the legality of decisions; and
(b)   for decisions of the local planning authority, through the appeal system.

There is no doubt that the second way is more important, firstly because of the limited scope of the courts' supervisory jurisdiction, and secondly because of the willingness of the Secretary of State to use the appeals process to impose Central Government policy. In practice, the Secretary of State exercises a stranglehold over the content of the policies that are applied, and has the final say on policy in any case because of the applicant's unlimited right of appeal.

If a local planning authority refuses planning permission, its decision may thus be challenged either on legal grounds (for example, that the objections are not planning objections), or on policy grounds (for example, that too much weight was attached to the objections).

Judicial control of the discretion
The courts control and restrict the discretion through the application of ordinary principles of public law (see in general *E.C. Gransden* v *Secretary of State* [1986] JPL 519 and *Wycombe DC* v *Secretary of State* [1988] JPL 111). Failure to take something that is relevant into account (or, alternatively, taking into account something that is not relevant) means that the resultant decision is *ultra vires* and may be quashed, although the courts retain a discretion whether to do so. Whether something is relevant is a legal matter for the courts to decide.

As long as the policies that are applied are lawful (i.e. relevant to town planning), the courts do not interfere with their content. This is effectively a principle of non-intervention in policy matters. Accordingly, the *weight* given to any policy is a matter for the decision-maker, unless the decision is perverse. However, it is impermissible to have an absolute policy, or to apply it rigidly, since this would constitute an unlawful fettering of discretion (*Stringer* v *MHLG* [1970] 1 WLR 1281). The courts thus see their role as ensuring that decisions are made rationally in the light of all the town planning considerations. This is ensured by the requirement that *reasons* must be given for decisions: something that has attracted a great deal of attention in recent cases.

The application of policy

The decision whether to grant permission will be made by reference to:

(a) the facts of the case;

(b) development plans;

(c) other local policies;

(d) Central Government policies, especially as set out in Circulars and Planning Policy Guidance Notes (policy used to be published in Circulars, but Planning Policy Guidance Notes are now taking over this role, although the process of replacement is not complete, so reference still needs to be made to both types of document);

(e) representations received; and

(f) any other material considerations (see below).

As stated above, the weight given to each of these factors is ultimately a matter for the decision-maker, but, in practice, development plans and Central Government policies are the most important. In the past, this had little to do with the law, because the courts always refused to lay down a rigid hierarchy of the relative importance of the different considerations. Instead it followed from the way that policies were actually applied on appeal. However, things have changed greatly as a result of the enactment of s. 54A (see below).

Nevertheless, the prior legal position must be considered, since it helps to explain how s. 54A is being interpreted. Cases such as *Enfield LBC* v *Secretary of State* [1975] JPL 155, established that the policies laid down in a development plan must always be taken into account, but it was made clear that the plan is only one consideration, albeit an important one, in deciding whether to grant planning permission. Thus, unlike the situation in many other countries, a plan did not have to be followed; it was a statement of aims or objectives only. Circulars and Planning Policy Guidance Notes were also material considerations and must therefore be considered where relevant (*J.A. Pye Ltd* v *West Oxfordshire DC* [1982] 47 P&CR 125). However, it is now normally assumed that a Circular has been considered unless the reasoning is inconsistent with it, or it has obviously been ignored or misunderstood. The correct interpretation of a policy in a development plan or Circular is ultimately a legal matter for the courts to decide. Misunderstanding a policy is accordingly as bad as ignoring it. It is left to the decision-maker in each case to weigh up the competing issues. This shifts the emphasis of legal control on to the reasons given for the decision. As long as adequate reasons are given the courts will not interfere. In practice this means that Central Government policies will normally be applied on appeal.

This judicial reluctance to get involved in policy matters was crucial in the light of the development of Central Government policy in the 1980s. There was a complete overhaul of existing guidance, and the whole political shape of the planning system was altered by the publication of explicitly directory Circulars (such as 22/80 and 14/85) laying down very strong pro-development policies. For example, a policy presumption that development should be permitted 'unless the development would cause demonstrable harm to interests of acknowledged importance' was introduced in Circular 14/85 and repeated in the original Planning Policy Guidance Note 1. This presumption was not restricted in terms of the subject matter of the application, with the result that it applied as much to industrial development as it did to housing development. However, it did not apply where certain restraint policies were applied, such as where inappropriate development was proposed in the Green Belt (see Planning Policy Guidance Note 2), and it would be rebutted by a strong local policy, such as a policy against industrial development in a defined area.

The relevance of the presumption was addressed by the House of Lords in *London Residuary Body* v *Lambeth BC* [1990] 2 All ER 309, which decided that the policy presumption must be taken into account and had the weight attached to it by the decision-maker. As a matter of interpretation, it was not limited to resolving a deadlock where the factors in favour of permission equalled those against, as suggested by the Court of Appeal. This decision, by confirming the principle of non-intervention in the contents of policies, allowed the Government freedom to accord the presumption a very high value.

The presumption in favour of the development plan

This state of affairs has now changed. The first signs of any change were seen in a number of appeal decisions around the turn of the decade which decided that where there was an up-to-date plan with clear policies that were in conformity with regional and national policies, then it was likely to be followed. Legislative recognition of this point was provided by s. 54A, which was inserted by the Planning and Compensation Act 1991. This states:

Where, in making any determination under the planning Acts, regard is to be had to the development plan, the determination shall be made in accordance with the development plan unless material considerations indicate otherwise.

This section appears to introduce a presumption in favour of following the provisions of the development plan, because it replaces the existing duty to 'have regard to' the plan with a duty to act 'in accordance with' it. This is certainly the position that a number of Government Ministers have sought to promote in speeches that suggest that we have entered a period of 'plan-led' planning, rather than one which is 'market-' or 'developer-led'.

The legal position is still ambiguous to a degree. The courts have had occasion to consider s. 54A in a handful of cases, but without having to tackle the question directly. Unsurprisingly, they have suggested that s. 54A does set out a presumption in favour of the development plan, but that it can be rebutted fairly easily (at least as a matter of law, if not of policy) by other considerations, such as Central Government policy and the presumption in favour of development, as long as the reasoning is clear and rational (see, for example, *St Albans DC* v *Secretary of State* [1993] JPL 374). (This case also shows how the court's general discretion not to quash a decision if the failure identified does not make a difference to the result can be used to water down s. 54A, and that there is no need to mention the section specifically if it is obviously taken into account.)

More important than the legal position is the policy context, in particular the question of how the legal presumption laid down in s. 54A fits in with the *policy* presumption in favour of granting planning permission. This was partly answered by the publication of a revised Planning Policy Guidance Note 1 in March 1992. This reiterates that the planning system 'should operate on the basis that applications for development should be allowed, having regard to the development plan and all material considerations, unless the proposed development would cause demonstrable harm to interests of acknowledged importance'. In a way this suggests that little has changed from the earlier advice, but it is significant that the above statement has been moved from the section of the Guidance Note dealing specifically with planning applications to the introduction. The remainder of the Guidance Note shows clearly that the importance of the presumption in favour of development has been downgraded. The plan is said to be the starting point. If the proposal is in accordance with the plan, it would normally be granted permission. If the proposal is in conflict with it, the developer would normally have to produce 'convincing reasons' to show why the plan should not apply. If the plan is neutral, then the presumption in favour of development has a role to play as one of the material considerations. It is clear that importance will be attached to such things as the age of the plan, the strength of the relevant policies, how far they are consistent with other national and regional policies, and whether the Secretary of State had intervened during the making of the plan. On this last point, the Guidance Note states that if there was no formal intervention at the plan-making stage it may be assumed that the Secretary of State 'will attach commensurate weight' to the plan on any appeal.

In summary, it appears that the planning system has moved into an age which can be characterised by the description 'plan-led', but that this is no guarantee that the plan will always be followed. One point that has therefore acquired increased significance is the interpretation of development plans. In the past it has often been assumed that this is a matter of law for the courts to decide. This is undoubtedly correct, but it does not solve the question of whether the courts will impose their own interpretation or will be content to adopt the less interventionist method of reviewing whether the decision-maker's interpretation was a reasonable one. This is crucial to the extent to which the courts will interfere with decisions via s. 54A. Past experience suggests that they will continue with their normal non-interventionist approach and adopt the second method, thus reinforcing the view that the real change in planning that is envisaged in the 1990s will result from actual changes in policy rather than from anything the courts require.

Other material considerations

Various matters are always material considerations and thus always have to be taken into account—e.g. plans, Circulars, Planning Policy Guidance

Notes, the results of consultations, and any representations made by third parties or objectors. In addition, certain issues are clearly nearly always material on the facts—e.g. the effect on the amenity of an area, safety considerations, potential pollution problems, the effect on the local economy, transport and highways considerations, the balance of land use in an area, and the need for the proposed development. To be material they have to be material to planning and material to the application. 'Planning' has been given a wide meaning here and covers anything that relates to 'the character of the use of the land' (*Great Portland Estates* v *Westminster CC* [1984] 3 All ER 744).

This may be illustrated by the range of matters that have been held to be material in certain circumstances: the effect on private rights (*Stringer* v *MHLG* [1970] 1 WLR 1281); the existing use of the site (*Clyde & Co.* v *Secretary of State* [1977] JPL 521); the personal circumstances of the occupier (*Tameside MBC* v *Secretary of State* [1984] JPL 180); the precedent effect of a decision (*Collis Radio Ltd* v *Secretary of State* [1975] 29 P&CR 390); whether the application is premature in the light of an emerging development plan (*Arlington Securities Ltd* v *Secretary of State* [1989] JPL 166); the achievement of a separate planning objective of the local planning authority—in this case the protection of the Royal Opera House by allowing it to raise funds by carrying out the development permitted (*R* v *Westminster CC ex parte Monahan* [1988] JPL 557); the availability of alternative sites, which has great implications for objectors seeking to put forward the argument that another site elsewhere is more suitable for the development (see *Greater London Council* v *Secretary of State* [1986] JPL 193).

In relation to environmental matters, it is clear that planning permission may be refused on a number of grounds. An industrial development may be refused because of possible pollution or safety problems (e.g. it is possible to prevent a plant handling dangerous substances, or a waste disposal site, from being sited near to a sensitive watercourse). A housing estate may be refused because of the inadequacy of the existing sewerage provision. A new workplace may be refused because of the effect of noise on neighbouring properties. It is not just the potential harm the proposed development may cause that is relevant. Development may be refused because it would be within *a cordon sanitaire* around an existing installation. For example, *Stringer* v *MHLG* [1970] 1 WLR 1281 concerned an area around Jodrell Bank that was subject to a policy of restraint on development to prevent interference with the radio telescope.

However, it must be remembered that these are only some of the matters that must be taken into account. The final decision involves a balancing of all the factors. A clear example of the discretion given to the local planning authority to decide that other factors outweigh environmental ones is *R* v *Exeter CC ex parte J L Thomas & Co Ltd* [1990] 1 All ER 413. Permission was granted for a housing estate close to an existing animal waste processing plant, despite arguments put forward by the owners of the plant that this might mean that it could be closed down by the future occupants of the houses, exercising their rights in private nuisance. The court held that such a decision was unchallengeable, as long as the local planning authority had considered this factor: it had no *duty* to refuse permission on these grounds.

Conditions

Section 70(1) permits the local planning authority (and the Secretary of State on appeal) to impose such conditions 'as it thinks fit'. This wide discretionary power is limited by statutory guidance in ss. 72 and 75, judicial control over what is permissible, and Central Government policy.

Statutory guidance is limited and relatively unimportant. Section 72 states that conditions attached to other land under the control of the applicant, conditions requiring commencement of the development within a specified time, and temporary permissions are permissible. Section 75(3) enables new buildings to be used for the purpose for which they were designed, unless the permission expressly limits the use.

Legal tests for the validity of conditions

Over the years the courts have developed four tests of validity for conditions. In contrast with the decisions on material considerations, these have produced some rather restrictive results, possibly because the cases were mainly decided earlier, when a more overt policy of protection of private property rights was applied. A condition is *ultra vires* if it is:

  (a)   not related to planning purposes;
  (b)   not related to the development permitted;
  (c)   perverse ('so unreasonable that no reasonable authority could impose it'); or
  (d)   hopelessly uncertain.

(a)   Conditions not related to planning purposes
In applying this test, the courts have had to define the limits of 'planning'. They have done this by concluding that certain matters of a social planning nature do not relate to town and country planning. For example, in *R* v *Hillingdon BC ex parte Royco Homes* [1974] 2 QB 720, a condition requiring that houses be occupied by people on the local authority housing list, who should then be granted 10 years security of tenure, was held to be *ultra vires*. However, the dividing line is unclear. An occupancy condition restricting occupation of a rural dwelling to agricultural workers and dependants will be valid (*Fawcett Properties Ltd* v *Bucks CC* [1961] AC 636), as will a personal permission, although in each case the Secretary of State disapproves of the use of such conditions (see Circular 1/85).

(b)   Conditions not related to the development permitted
A condition must be geographically and functionally linked to the site to which the application relates. Thus conditions relating to other land controlled by the applicant are valid only if the other land is close by (*Pyx Granite*

Ltd v *MHLG* [1958] 1 QB 554). Equally, a condition requiring works to be carried out on land which is neither included in the application nor under the control of the applicant is *ultra vires* (*Ladbrokes Ltd* v *Secretary of State* [1981] JPL 427). Thus, a requirement to screen a site by planting trees on neighbouring land would be *ultra vires*, unless that land was under the control of the applicant.

(c) Conditions that are perverse

This test has normally been used as a means of preventing the use of conditions which undermine private property rights by requiring the dedication of land to the public without compensation. In *Hall* v *Shoreham UDC* [1964] 1 WLR 240, a condition was attached to a permission for industrial development which required an access road to be built at the developer's expense and dedicated to the public. This was held to be *ultra vires*, even though the Court of Appeal was clear that the condition was beneficial in planning terms since it created a usable access to otherwise inaccessible land. In *Bradford MBC* v *Secretary of State* [1986] JPL 598 this position was supported. The Court of Appeal stated that a condition requiring donation of land to the public for a road-widening scheme would be *ultra vires* even if the developer suggested it or agreed to it, since *vires* cannot be conferred by consent.

This restriction is bizarre, since it is surely the whole *raison d'être of* development control to take away existing rights without compensation. It ignores the community of interest between the developer and the local planning authority; in the *Bradford* case, the developer included the donation of the land in the application since it was clear that permission would not be granted unless the road was widened. It also prevents any great use of planning conditions to secure 'planning gain' for the local community. In *M J Shanley Ltd* v *Secretary of State* [1982] JPL 380, a condition requiring 40 acres of the developer's land to be landscaped and dedicated as public open space, in return for permission to carry out housing development on adjoining land, was stated to be *ultra vires*.

It is interesting, however, that the courts have accepted the validity of conditions restricting existing use rights, or the right to take future advantage of the Use Classes Order or General Permitted Development Order (*City of London Corpn* v *Secretary of State* [1971] 23 P&CR 169). They have also accepted negative conditions subjecting development to a condition precedent, even though the condition would be invalid if put in terms of a positive obligation (*Grampian RC* v *Aberdeen DC* [1984] 47 P&CR 633), and even though the condition precedent may be unlikely to occur (*British Railways Board* v *Secretary of State* (1990) *The Times*, 29 October).

(d) Conditions which are hopelessly uncertain

In this category it is clear that a mere ambiguity will not render the condition invalid. In *Alderson* v *Secretary of State* [1984] 49 P&CR 307, a condition requiring occupation by people who worked locally was valid because it was sufficiently certain to be understandable to the applicant.

If a condition is *ultra vires,* it may be challenged in the courts. This may result in the whole planning permission being declared void, unless the condition can be severed. Alternatives are to appeal against the condition to the Secretary of State, or to apply for a discharge of the condition under s. 73.

Conditions and policy

On appeal the Secretary of State can add, omit or amend any conditions as part of the total rehearing of the issues. This can be done on legal, factual or policy grounds, so an understanding of the Secretary of State's policy on conditions is essential.

Circular 1/85 requires conditions to be (a) necessary, (b) relevant to planning, (c) relevant to the development permitted, (d) enforceable, (e) precise, and (f) reasonable. In addition, it lays down some very important general policy tests: 'As a matter of policy, a condition ought not to be imposed unless there is a definite need for it'; 'a condition should not be retained unless there are sound and clear cut reasons for doing so'; a condition 'requires special and precise justification' if planning permission would not be refused if the condition were omitted. The local planning authority should also consider whether the imposition of any conditions may render an otherwise objectionable development acceptable, so as to save the application from being refused.

These are not legal requirements, but a local planning authority ignores these tests at its peril because of the applicant's right of appeal. It also appears from *Times Investments Ltd* v *Secretary of State* [1990] JPL 433 that a failure to have regard to these policies (e.g. not to demonstrate the harm that would be caused by omitting a particular condition) may render the decision *ultra vires* for failure to have regard to a material consideration. Once again, therefore, the Secretary of State's guidance imposes significant restrictions on the decisions that may be reached. Circular 1/85 notes types of condition that would normally be *ultra vires* and those that require exceptional justification. Appendix A includes a list of model conditions and Appendix B a list of unacceptable ones.

Planning conditions and pollution control

One particular issue relates to the use of planning conditions to achieve continuing pollution control objectives. Government policy (supported by the pollution control authorities and the Royal Commission on Environmental Pollution in its Fifth Report) has consistently been that planning conditions should not be used to deal with problems which are the subject of controls under separate environmental legislation. This prevents an unnecessary duplication of controls, or conflict over the correct conditions to impose. For example, conditions should not be used to impose acceptable levels on emissions or discharges to air or water, since those matters are best dealt with by the relevant pollution control authority. However, the widespread practice of imposing conditions on noise levels from premises illustrates that it is not the imposition of conditions relating to pollution as such which is discouraged, but the use of such conditions where there is an alternative system of preventative control.

This restriction may create a problem for the local planning authority, since it is clear that pollution conditions may not be enforced as rigorously as it may wish (see Chapter 6). Its main alternative, if it felt a risk was too great to take, would be to refuse permission altogether (after liaising with the relevant pollution control authority). However it is not *illegal* to impose conditions which duplicate controls. In allowing an appeal against an enforcement notice served on the Ferro-Alloys and Metals Smelter in Glossop, the Secretary of State attached conditions incorporating the requirements of an improvement notice served by HMIP into the permission (see [1990] 2 LMELR 176). The effect was that the requirements of the improvement notice would continue to apply even if it was later withdrawn by HMIP. Given the potential advantages to the local authority in having direct enforcement remedies available through planning law, this may well presage a greater use of such conditions in the future.

Planning obligations

The town and country planning legislation has always included powers under which a local planning authority could enter into an agreement relating to the development or use of land. Similar powers are provided in other legislation (e.g. the Local Government (Miscellaneous Provisions) Act 1982 and various Local Acts). Whilst for many years little use was made of these powers, in the 1970s and 1980s they came to be seen as a mechanism for the provision of some form of 'planning gain' (i.e. some gain to the community that would not necessarily have been obtained without the agreement). The increased importance of agreements illustrated the negotiative nature of modern town planning and showed that the concept of planning as a strict system of regulation in which the regulator imposes restrictions on a developer had become rather outdated. But it also gave rise to some concern. There was no need for approval of agreements by the Secretary of State, no provision for publicity or appeal, limited scrutiny of the content of agreements and limited potential for a successful challenge by a third party. As a result, there was a great danger that an agreement could be seen either in terms of the local planning authority 'selling' planning permission or the developer offering a bribe in return for favourable treatment.

When the Town and Country Planning Act was consolidated in 1990, the provisions on agreements were included as s. 106. However, they were soon completely rewritten by the Planning and Compensation Act 1991. The main change was that developers were enabled to give binding unilateral undertakings as well as to enter into agreements. The phrase 'planning obligations' is now used to cover both agreements and undertakings. The idea of unilateral undertakings was attacked by the opposition parties in Parliament as a 'developer's charter', but it appears that they have not been used on any major scale. They are of greatest importance for developers wishing to make proposals in relation to infrastructure costs and requirements and in situations where a local planning authority is unwilling to agree terms. But they can also be used to great effect during an appeal—a developer can lay its proposal on the table and thus enable the Secretary of State to take that into account in deciding whether to allow the appeal. Other changes made by the 1991 Act were that the various powers were set out far more clearly than under the existing legislation and that a new procedure was introduced in which an application can be made for the discharge or modification of an obligation. The Crown was also enabled to create planning obligations.

As a result, the redrafted s. 106 represents the current law, though the old provisions continue to apply to agreements made before 25 October 1991. Planning obligations can only be created by deed and by a person who has an interest in the relevant land. They may include positive as well as negative obligations (s. 106(1)). For example, a developer could offer to build and maintain some facility of benefit to the community on the site, or could agree that traffic flows on to the site would be regulated in a particular way. They are enforceable against successors in title (s. 106(3)) and are local land charges (s. 106(11)). Where there is a breach, they are enforceable by injunction (s. 106(5)), which is often a more attractive method of enforcement for a local planning authority than reliance on the enforcement notice procedures. The local planning authority has an alternative power to enter the land, carry out the appropriate operations and recover its costs, as long as it gives at least 21 days' notice of its intention to do so (s. 106(6)).

It is important to note that the creation of a s. 106 obligation does not replace the need to seek planning permission in the normal way. But the existence of a valid obligation is definitely a material consideration which should be taken into account under s. 70(2). The local planning authority will normally link the permission and the obligation by imposing a condition on the permission that implementation depends on the acceptance of a planning obligation. It thus appears that a planning obligation may enable the local planning authority and the developer to supplement a permission by achieving objectives which could not be achieved by planning conditions.

However, the exact legal extent of this has never been entirely clear, and was not clarified by the 1991 Act. In *R v Gillingham BC ex parte Parham Ltd* [1988] JPL 336, it was decided that an agreement made under the section as it was then drafted must relate to planning purposes and must not be perverse, although it need not be related to the development permitted. This clearly accepted that the test for agreements was more relaxed than that for conditions, which requires all three tests to be satisfied (see p. 240). The decision, which was supported in *R v Wealden DC ex parte Charles Church (South East) Ltd* [1989] JPL 837, in effect represented a judicial approval of the practice of obtaining planning gain, at least where it was reasonable to do so.

The Court of Appeal took a different view in *R v Plymouth CC ex parte Plymouth and South Devon Co-operative Society Ltd* [1993] JPL B81. In this case, the court had to examine the legality of the offer by two superstore developers of planning gain—including such things as construction of a tourist information centre, provision of a bird-watching hide, a contribution towards a 'Park and Ride' scheme, and up to £1m for infrastructure works at another site. The Court of Appeal decided that community benefits could be material considerations even where they were not necessary to overcome or alleviate planning objections. The court stated that a planning obligation had to satisfy the three tests which applied to conditions, i.e. (a) it must have a planning purpose; (b) it must fairly and reasonably relate to the permitted development; and (c) it must not be perverse or grossly unreasonable. The court decided that the proposed benefits satisfied these tests.

The House of Lords have subsequently refined this decision in *Tesco Stores Limited* v *Secretary of State for the Environment and others* [1995] JPL 581. Once again, the case involved competing superstore developers, one of whom had entered into a planning obligation offering planning gain in the form of private funding for a £6.6m new road, which was intended to relieve traffic congestion in the town of Witney in Oxfordshire, in return for the grant of planning permission for their site. On appeal, the Secretary of State decided that the offer of funding (or the lack of it) was not a good ground for either granting or refusing permission.

In the House of Lords it was argued that the offer of funding was a material consideration and that as the Secretary of State failed to have regard to it his decision was flawed. The House took a different approach to the Court of Appeal in *Plymouth* and distinguished the tests for the legality of conditions and planning obligations. In particular, Lord Hoffman, in an erudite judgment, held that a planning obligation could be valid even where it would not satisfy the second test set out in *Plymouth* (above). Thus, a planning obligation only has to satisfy tests (a) and (c) above. Whilst accepting that it would be unlawful to take into account an obligation which had no connection *whatsoever* with the development, the weight to be attached to the obligation was entirely a matter for the decision-maker (and different decision-makers could take opposing views on the weight to attach to the same obligation). The court did not, however, give any guidance on the sufficiency of the connection between the development and the obligation. It is difficult to envisage many obligations which could not be linked to the development in some manner (albeit that specific examples could be tortuous). Moreover, Lord Hoffman commented that it was not necessary for the obligation to be proportional to the development, nor did it have to be necessary to allow the development to go ahead.

The decision in the House of Lords in *Tesco* re-emphasises the fact that the earlier reported cases confused the *legal* question of the legitimacy of obligations with the *policy* test laid down in Circular 16/91 and its predecessors. In particular, the requirement that the development relates to a planning purpose merely reflects the legal requirement to take into account material considerations under s. 70(2) of the Town and Country Planning Act 1990.

Moreover, the third test of general reasonableness equates with normal principles of administrative law. On the other hand, the second test set out in *Plymouth* was a test of policy which was specified in Circular 16/91.

The legal tests are amplified by policy guidance on what is permissible by way of planning gain set out in Circular 16/91. Given that policy and practice have arguably been more important than law in this area in the past, the terms of the Circular are of special significance. They suggest that s. 106 should not be used so as to require a developer to provide more than that which is linked to the development in issue in terms of scale and kind. This appears to mean, for example, that a developer may be asked to provide extra sewerage which is needed for the works applied for, but not sewerage for the whole general area. But this limitation seems unenforceable in many cases, since neither the developer nor the local planning authority will wish to challenge an arrange- ment they have themselves reached (and which may indeed be encouraged by the local plan, which was the situation in the *Plymouth* case), and other objectors may well lack either knowledge of the agreement or *locus standi* to challenge it. It is significant that the reported cases on planning obligations nearly all concern claims by one developer that a rival is being given preferential treatment as a result of an offer of planning gain that is questionable in terms of law or policy. Lord Hoffman in *Tesco* examined the interface between the law and policy of planning obligations and suggested that there was nothing in the 1990 Act which required the Secretary of State to adopt the second test (i.e. necessity) notwithstanding that it was a policy which was consistent with the policy of a presumption in favour of develop- ment. He went on to say, however, that the Secretary of State was entitled to change that policy at any time. Indeed, he went on to suggest that it would be legitimate for the Secretary of State to pursue a policy of granting permissions for 'good reason' and that one of those 'good reasons' could be the willingness of the developer to provide related external benefits.

Section 106A includes provisions on the modification or discharge of obligations. This may be done by agreement, but there is also a right to apply to the local planning authority for modification or discharge after five years, with an appeal against refusal to the Secretary of State provided by s. 106B. The Town and Country Planning (Modification and Discharge of Planning Obligations) Regulations 1992 (SI 1992 No. 2832) provide the procedures for these sections, but it is clear that the right is narrower than that for discharge of conditions set out in s. 73, thus providing another good reason why local authorities may choose an obligation in preference to conditions. Agreements existing on 25 October 1991 are still covered by the old law on variation and extinguishment, which allows restrictive covenants to be looked at under the Law of Property Act 1925, s. 84.

Planning appeals

Section 78 provides a statutory right of appeal to the Secretary of State against refusals of permission or the imposition of any conditions, and where the local planning authority has failed to determine an application within eight weeks. Only the applicant can appeal.

An appeal amounts to a total rehearing of the application. The Secretary of State can make any decision originally open to the local planning authority, i.e. allow or refuse permission or attach any conditions. This is true even where the appeal is against a conditional grant of permission (but not where it is against an application for discharge of conditions under s. 73, since there the local planning authority itself would have been limited to a consideration of the relevant condition). An appeal is thus not primarily a contest, but a forum in which all relevant information may be produced and tested so that the Inspector may make a rational decision. However, it is clear that, over the years, appeals have come to resemble the confrontational model of court proceedings far more than was originally intended although research has indicated that many users of the system are unhappy, and changes to reduce inquiry times have been proposed.

There is also a right to seek judicial review of local planning authority decisions, although an applicant would normally be advised to appeal to the Secretary of State, because the appeal will encompass policy matters and is cheaper. A decision to grant planning permission can only be challenged through judicial review. Such action requires the person initiating the challenge to have *locus standi*, which is fairly easily satisfied for those with some interest in the case (see *R* v *Sheffield CC ex parte Mansfield* [1978] 37 P&CR 1). Alternatively, the Attorney-General can be requested to bring a relator action on behalf of the applicant.

The number of appeals increased rapidly in the 1980s, with a figure of 32,281 being reached in 1989/90. This fell to 22,121 in 1991/92. The success rate currently is around 33%, a significant increase on the 1970s, but not as high as the peak of 40% reached in the late 1980s. There is clear evidence that the appeals process has been politicised, with the opportunity being taken to impose Central Government policy unless there are strong and clear local policies applicable (e.g. in a local plan), or a clear restraint policy, such as the Green Belt, applies.

Procedure on appeals

Either party (or the Secretary of State) has a right to opt for a public hearing. Normally this will be a public inquiry under ss. 320 and 321, but increasing use is now being made of informal hearings. Otherwise the appeal will be decided by written representations, and currently over 80% of all appeals are decided in this way. The Town and Country Planning (Written Representations Procedure) Regulations 1987 (SI 1987 No. 701) introduced statutory rules for such procedures for the first time and laid down time limits for the various stages involved. Third parties have some limited rights to make representations on written appeals. However, it is clear that it will be very rare for a decision to be quashed because of inadequacies in the procedures actually adopted.

Apart from a very small number of matters of national importance, the decision is normally taken by an Inspector. In the remaining cases, the Inspector's report goes to the Secretary of State, who then makes the final decision in the light of the recommendations.

If a public inquiry is to be held, there are two similar sets of rules: the Town and Country Planning (Inquiries Procedure) Rules 1992 (SI 1992 No. 2038) and the Town and Country Planning (Determination by Inspectors)

(Inquiries Procedure) Rules 1992 (SI 1992 No. 2039). They are an attempt to solve previous criticisms about the delays and costs involved in a public inquiry by setting out formal rules on pre-inquiry exchanges of information and laying down timetables for the various stages. However, there is no remedy to ensure these time scales are kept, except an award of costs.

The inquiry must be public and anyone is entitled to attend. In general, the procedure to be followed is at the discretion of the Inspector, but the rules give the appellant and the local planning authority full participation rights, including access to evidence, calling of witnesses, and the right to cross-examine. A right to appear and present a case is also conferred on other people who have served a statement of case. However, since the rules are supplemented by the rules of natural justice, as indeed are the written representation procedures, an Inspector normally permits anyone with anything new and relevant to say to put their case properly. The Inspector is entitled to make a site inspection at any time, but this is not the place for hearing submissions.

Reasons must be given for the decision. Again, this duty has been supplemented by the courts, which require the reasons to be adequate, intelligible and not self-contradictory. The conclusions should follow from the evidence and all the main points raised at the inquiry should be dealt with (*Givaudan* v *MHLG* [1966] 3 All ER 696).

Unlike normal civil litigation where the loser will usually pay all the costs of an action, parties to a planning appeal are expected to pay their own costs unless there has been 'unreasonable behaviour' (as defined in Circular 8/93) by one of the parties which justifies an award of costs against them. On the whole, costs can only be awarded where there has been a public inquiry. Costs can also be awarded in the case of a written representations appeal where a public inquiry is cancelled as a result of the withdrawal of one or more grounds of refusal, but the appeal proceeds by way of written representation. However, there has been an increase in the number of successful claims in the last few years. The majority of awards are against the local planning authority, rather than the appellant, and very limited use has been made of the power to make awards against third parties. 'Unreasonable behaviour' for the appellant includes making an appeal that has no reasonable chance of success (e.g. an appeal against a refusal prompted by a clear planning policy such as the Green Belt—see the award in the *Bricket Wood* case [1989] JPL 629), and uncooperative behaviour. For the local planning authority, unreasonable refusal of the application is the main ground for an award, which puts great emphasis on the reasons for refusal and the statement of case submitted before the inquiry (see Walker [1988] JPL 598).

A number of cases are now heard by a less formal procedure, 'a hearing', but only if the appellant and the local planning authority both agree. Hearings are not normally offered by the Secretary of State where third-party evidence is expected, or there are disputed matters of fact, or complex matters of law or policy. The details are laid out in a Code of Conduct published as part of Circular 10/88, which stresses prehearing exchange of information.

Challenging the decision of the Secretary of State

The Secretary of State's decision can only be challenged under s. 288, owing to s. 284 which ousts all other challenges. Section 288 thus provides a statutory appeal: this must be distinguished from judicial review under RSC Ord. 53 (see Chapter 2). About 150 cases under s. 288 are brought each year. These are the main source of decisions on planning law.

The s. 288 grounds approximate to judicial review grounds. A decision can be challenged either if it is not within the powers of the Act , or if substantial prejudice has been caused by a failure to comply with the relevant procedures (e.g. the Inquiries Rules). These will cover bad faith, perverse decisions, failure to take account of relevant factors, taking into account irrelevant factors, mistakes of law, acting on no evidence, giving inadequate reasons, or a want of natural justice.

Under s. 288, the High Court is limited to quashing the decision of the Secretary of State and remitting the case. It cannot make the decision for the Secretary of State, but can make some fairly explicit directions as to the relevant law. Thus, even if an appeal under s. 288 is successful, there is no guarantee that the redetermination will be any more beneficial. The High Court also has a discretion whether to quash a decision and will refuse to do so if it considers that the defect made no difference to the eventual decision.

Any 'person aggrieved' by the decision can use s. 288. This includes all parties who appeared at the inquiry or made representations, as well as the appellant, the local planning authority, and owners and occupiers of the site (see *Turner* v *Secretary of State* [1973] 28 P&CR 123). The time limit for a s. 288 appeal is six weeks from the Secretary of State's decision, after which the decision is unchallengeable, no matter what the grounds of complaint (*Smith* v *East Elloe RDC* [1956] AC 736).

Enforcement of planning law

Planning law has a well-developed system of enforcement, which has just undergone some quite radical changes in the Planning and Compensation Act 1991. Most of these changes stem from the recommendations of the Carnwath Report (*Enforcing Planning Law,* 1989), but it is clear that the system of enforcement has in reality been a weak point of the planning system for many years. It has a number of features which differentiate it from most other enforcement mechanisms in environmental law. In particular, it is a two-stage procedure, in which an enforcement notice is first issued and then may be followed up with a prosecution if it is ignored.

Enforcement notices

The major tool for enforcement against breaches of planning control is the enforcement notice. This is an entirely discretionary procedure under which a local planning authority may serve an enforcement notice in respect of unauthorised development, requiring the owner or occupier to take specified steps to remedy a breach. Unlike most pollution control legislation, a breach of planning law is not in itself a criminal offence; the offence consists of failing to comply with an enforcement notice. There are additional powers relating to stop notices and to injunctions, though these have not been greatly used. There are also new powers on contravention notices and breach of condition notices.

A number of limitations of the enforcement notice procedure should be noted:

(a)   The legislation empowers no one other than the local planning authority to serve an enforcement notice (except the Secretary of State, who has a reserve power in s. 182 that appears never to have been used).

(b)   The local planning authority is given a wide and virtually unchallengeable discretion whether to serve an enforcement notice and over its content. One may be issued where the authority consider it 'expedient' to do so, having regard to the development plan and to any other material considerations (s. 172).

(c)   This makes the exercise of the discretion dependent on policy factors. Government policy advice in Planning Policy Guidance Note 18 is that enforcement action should be taken only where it is essential and commensurate with the breach to which it relates, and that the service of an enforcement notice should be treated as a last resort. The local planning authority will take into account effectively the same things as it would when deciding whether to grant planning permissions (after all, failing to enforce against a breach is almost tantamount to granting unconditional permission).

(d)   The whole process of serving an enforcement notice is very lengthy and excessively technical.

(e)   There is an appeal to the Secretary of State: not only does this delay matters, since the appeal suspends the operation of the notice, there is a very high success rate on appeal (averaging around 40% in recent years), mainly owing to the deregulatory policies of the Government.

In a survey carried out in 1983, Jowell and Millichap found that enforcement of the law was given a very low profile in many local planning authorities (see [1986] JPL 482), though matters may well have improved since then as a result of the wider range of effective powers now available. A significant number of authorities did not have anyone responsible for enforcement. Monitoring of compliance with conditions and agreements was *ad hoc* and not guaranteed. The most common method of discovery of a breach was from a complaint from a member of the public rather than from investigation. When it came to taking action, informal methods of solving the problem were favoured, such as warning letters and requests for details of ownership of the land (an easily recognised threat of more formal enforcement action). Even if an enforcement notice was served, there was no guarantee that it would itself be enforced if ignored. 40% of metropolitan authorities and 32% of non-metropolitan authorities had not prosecuted once in the two years preceding the survey, low fines being given as a significant reason for failing to do so. Even more starkly, 65% of authorities had not used a stop notice in the previous two years, with fear of compensation being cited as the main reason for reluctance here.

Further surveys have illustrated that enforcement action is more likely to be taken where economic circumstances permit it. For example, enforcement is more common in South East England than in depressed urban areas.

Immunity from enforcement
The following situations provide immunity from the service of an enforcement notice:

(a) Where four years have elapsed from the substantial completion of an operational development (s. 171B(1)).

(b) Where four years have elapsed from a change of use *to* a dwelling-house (s. 171B(2)).

(c) Where 10 years have elapsed from any other breach of planning control (s. 171B(3)). This is a change introduced by the Planning and Compensation Act 1991; prior to that Act there was immunity for changes of use only if the breach took place before 1 January 1964. All cases where there is a breach of a condition attached to a planning permission are now covered by the 10-year period of immunity, thus mitigating the effect of *Harvey* v *Secretary of State for Wales* [1990] JPL 420, which decided, on the original wording of the 1990 Act, that conditions attaching to an operational permission were subject to the four-year rule. This created some potential difficulties for the enforcement of continuing conditions, such as occupancy conditions or those relating to the operation of a site. However, *Harvey* still applies to any breach which took place before the 1991 Act came into force, which was 2 January 1992.

(d) Where there is a certificate of lawfulness of existing use or development, a certificate of lawfulness of proposed use or development, or an established use certificate granted under earlier legislation relating to the alleged breach (see ss. 191–194). These certificates are conclusive as to the lawfulness of the matters to which they relate.

(e) Development by, or on behalf of, the Crown on Crown land (s. 294), although it is possible for a special enforcement notice to be served on a private individual who is occupying Crown land (s. 294(3)), a power that is primarily available for the control of trespassers.

Procedure for issuing an enforcement notice
An enforcement notice is first issued by the local planning authority (normally the district planning authority, though the county planning authority has some powers over county matters). It must then be served on all owners and occupiers of the relevant premises, including licensees. The enforcement notice must specify the alleged breach, the steps required to remedy it (these may include any steps to alleviate an injury to amenity), the reasons for issuing the enforcement notice, and the relevant land. It also has to specify the date on which it takes effect, which must be at least 28 days from the date

of service, and a further period after that which is for compliance with its requirements.

At the end of the period for compliance, the owner of the land (or in some cases a person with control of or an interest in the land) commits a criminal offence if its requirements have not been met (s. 179). It should be noted that compliance with an enforcement notice does not discharge it: it attaches permanently to the land (s. 181). However, an enforcement notice is a local land charge, so future purchasers of the land should find out about its existence. Each district planning authority must keep a public register of enforcement notices and stop notices (s. 188).

The maximum penalty for these offences is £20,000 on summary conviction, or an unlimited fine for conviction on indictment. In determining the amount of any fine, the court must have regard to any financial benefit accruing to the convicted person. There is no provision for imprisonment. The local planning authority also has a power to enter the land and remedy a breach at the owner's expense (s. 178).

Appeals

Any person with an interest in the relevant land (or an occupier with a written licence) may appeal against the enforcement notice to the Secretary of State. The appeal must be in writing and must be received by the Secretary of State before the enforcement notice takes effect. Thus the period in which an appeal must be lodged could be as short as 28 days.

An appeal will suspend the operation of the enforcement notice until the appeal is finally determined. In *R* v *Kuxhaus* [1988] 2 All ER 705, it was held that this could mean until a subsequent court action had been heard; in that case the number of successive appeals meant that the enforcement notice was suspended for over six years. The effect of that decision has now been reversed by the Planning and Compensation Act 1991. Nevertheless, the enforcement notice is still suspended until after the Secretary of State's decision, and it is quite clear that a determined and experienced operator may delay the final operation of an enforcement notice for a considerable period.

There are seven grounds of appeal set out in s. 174(2):

(a) planning permission ought to be granted for the development, or the relevant condition ought to be discharged;

(b) the alleged breach has not in fact taken place;

(c) the matters alleged in the enforcement notice do not in law constitute a breach of planning control;

(d) the matters alleged in the enforcement notice are immune from enforcement action;

(e) failures to carry out the correct procedures in serving the enforcement notice;

(f) the steps required to remedy the breach are excessive;

(g) the time allowed for compliance with the enforcement notice is unreasonably short.

These grounds are very wide, and cover both policy and legal grounds. Ground (a) is effectively an application for planning permission from the Secretary of State, hence a fee is payable for making an enforcement notice appeal (this is refundable if the appeal is allowed on grounds (b)–(e) or the enforcement notice is withdrawn).

Ground (f) is also important. A local planning authority may not 'over-enforce', i.e. put the recipient of an enforcement notice in a worse position than before the breach took place. This relates mainly to ancillary uses; the local planning authority may not require a developer to cease a use which would always have been ancillary (see *Mansi v Elstree RDC* [1964] 16 P&CR 153).

The procedure for enforcement appeals is very similar to that for planning appeals. They are governed by the Town and Country Planning (Enforcement Notices and Appeals) Regulations 1991 (SI 1991 No. 2804) and the Town and Country Planning (Enforcement) (Inquiries Procedure) Rules 1992 (SI 1992 No. 1903). A choice of procedure is provided between a public inquiry, an informal hearing and a written representation procedure, and most cases are decided by Inspectors. Intelligible reasons must be given for the decision.

The Secretary of State may (a) uphold an enforcement notice and refuse the appeal; (b) quash it (often this involves granting retrospective planning permission); (c) vary its terms; or (d) amend it. In the last two cases any error in the enforcement notice may be corrected if it would not cause injustice to the appellant or the local planning authority.

Challenging the validity of an enforcement notice

The service of an enforcement notice is the first step towards the creation of a possible criminal offence, so the procedures set out in the legislation must be strictly observed. However, there is the possibility that the Secretary of State can amend an enforcement notice on appeal. In the past, the courts have tended to adopt very technical reasoning in this area, and have suggested that many procedural shortcomings render an enforcement notice invalid and not capable of correction, but recent decisions suggest that this attitude is changing. In *R v Tower Hamlets LBC ex parte Ahern (London) Ltd* [1989] JPL 757, it is made clear that, as long as the enforcement notice tells the recipient what must be done and why, most technicalities may be corrected by the Secretary of State on appeal, if that can be done without prejudice to either party. This point was reinforced by the redrafting of s. 173, on the contents of an enforcement notice, in the Planning and Compensation Act 1991.

Appeal is made the exclusive remedy for the matters laid out in grounds (a) to (g): it is not possible to seek judicial review of an enforcement notice on these grounds (s. 285). However, some may be challenged in the High Court through judicial review as nullities (and therefore void). This may be the case if the notice is hopelessly ambiguous as to what is required, or if essential procedural requirements are not met (see *Miller-Mead v MHLG* [1963] 2 QB 196). The validity of an enforcement notice may not be challenged in a prosecution for breach (*R v Smith* [1985] JPL 183).

There is a further right of appeal on a point of law to the High Court against the decision of the Secretary of State (s. 289). It has no jurisdiction to quash an enforcement notice; if the judge thinks the Secretary of State was wrong in law the matter will be remitted to the Secretary of State.

Stop notices

One of the problems with enforcement notices is that immediate action to remedy the breach cannot be ensured. Accordingly, under s. 183, the local planning authority is given power to serve a stop notice on anyone carrying on an unlawful activity. This makes it an offence to continue any activity which is specified in the notice once it has come into force, which may be between 3 and 28 days from service. The penalties are the same as for breach of an enforcement notice.

There are limits on the application of stop notices. A stop notice is parasitic on an enforcement notice; that is it must be served together with one or after one has been served, and will automatically cease to have effect if the enforcement notice is withdrawn or successfully appealed. It may not be served to stop use as a dwellinghouse, or where an activity has been carried on for more than four years. Most importantly, compensation is payable by the local planning authority if the enforcement notice or the stop notice is withdrawn, or if an enforcement notice appeal is allowed on any other ground than ground (a)—the policy ground. This threat of compensation has meant that service of a stop notice has been quite a rare occurrence, but the availability of compensation has now been limited by the Planning and Compensation Act 1991 so that it is not payable if the activity stopped is in breach of planning control.

There is no appeal against service of a stop notice. Accordingly, it is permissible to challenge the validity of a stop notice when prosecuted for ignoring it (*R* v *Jenner* [1983] 2 All ER 46).

Injunctions

Under s. 222 of the Local Government Act 1972, a local planning authority has always had a power to seek an injunction against any breach of the law where it is considered 'expedient for the promotion or protection of the interests of the inhabitants of their area'. This power has been interpreted fairly widely in the House of Lords in *Stoke on Trent CC* v *B & Q Retail Ltd* [1984] AC 754, with the result that an injunction may be sought not only where there has been a deliberate and flagrant flouting of the law but where the normal enforcement procedures prove inadequate to deal with the problem. For example, in *Westminster CC* v *Jones* [1981] JPL 750, a chemist's shop in a residential area was converted to an amusement arcade. The owner ignored an enforcement notice and appealed against it, thus delaying the enforcement process, but the court granted an injunction in the light of the damage to amenity in the area and the deliberate nature of Jones's actions. A new s. 187B provides a specific power for the local planning authority to seek an injunction if it considers it necessary or expedient to restrain an actual or potential breach of planning control, thus removing the need to rely on the Local Government Act 1972. In *Kirklees MBC* v *Wickes Building Supplies Ltd* [1992] 3 All ER 717, the House of Lords established that any public authority exercising the functions of law enforcement does not always have to give a cross-undertaking in damages when seeking injunctions, thus removing a serious practical obstacle that had previously restricted their use.

An injunction is a discretionary remedy and will not be granted by a court unless the circumstances warrant such a strong solution. The penalty for breach of an injunction is potentially far higher than for breach of an enforcement notice, since the developer is in contempt of court and imprisonment is a possibility. It seems, however, that there is no requirement that other enforcement methods have been exhausted first.

Other enforcement powers

The Planning and Compensation Act 1991 introduced an additional three enforcement powers as follows:

(a) The local planning authority may serve a planning contravention notice on any owner, occupier, or other person who is using or carrying out operations on land, seeking information from them relating to its use or occupation (s. 171C). It is a summary offence to ignore such a notice, or knowingly to provide incorrect information (s. 171D). The idea behind the procedure is to obtain information relating to suspected breaches and to enable the breach to be remedied without recourse to more formal enforcement procedures. Clearly, the issuing of such a notice will warn the recipient that the local planning authority will take further action if necessary.

(b) A breach of condition notice provides for a simple summary procedure whereby a local planning authority may serve written notice on a person responsible for non-compliance with a condition, or having control over the relevant land, requiring compliance in a period of not less than 28 days (s. 187A). It is an offence not to comply with such a notice, the maximum fine being £1,000. As with enforcement notices, it is made clear that a continuation of the non-compliance constitutes a further offence.

(c) Local planning authorities are provided with wide powers to enter land at any reasonable time to ascertain whether there has been a breach of planning control and what remedial steps may be required (ss. 196A, 196B and 196C).

Enforcement where there is no breach of planning law

There are some courses of action available to the local planning authority where there is no breach of the planning legislation. Normally these require the payment of compensation for the loss of any rights which have been taken away, so they are little used. But they are of importance as reserve powers where there is something creating an environmental problem that may not be removed or controlled in any other way.

Under s. 102 a local planning authority may serve a discontinuance order, which may require that any use be discontinued or that any buildings or works be removed or altered. Under s. 97 a local planning authority may revoke or modify a planning permission that has already been granted. In both these cases there are provisions for a public local inquiry to be held and compensation to be paid. The Secretary of State must also confirm these orders before they have effect and has reserve powers to make either type. Indeed, in March 1991, the Secretary of State took the exceptional step of making an order revoking a planning permission which Poole DC had granted to itself for housing on land designated a site of special scientific interest (SSSI) on Canford Heath in Dorset (thus belatedly rendering unnecessary the litigation in *R* v *Poole BC ex parte Beebee* [1991] JPL 643).

The local planning authority may also conclude a planning agreement under s. 106 in order to remove an existing building or use, although obviously the owner will require something of benefit in return.

Planning and hazardous substances

The storage of hazardous substances was traditionally dealt with under normal planning procedures. There were, however, many occasions when the storage of large amounts of hazardous materials fell outside the scope of existing controls as it was either permitted automatically under the GDO/UCO or it did not amount to development at all. Thus, it became necessary to control the siting of hazardous materials under a separate but complementary set of controls.

The Planning (Hazardous Substances) Act 1990 was brought into force on 1 June 1992. It requires hazardous substances consent (HSC) to be obtained if hazardous substances are present on, over or under land in an amount at or above a controlled quantity. The Act gives hazardous substances authorities (HSAs) the opportunity to consider whether the proposed storage or use of a hazardous substance is appropriate in a particular location, having regard to the risks arising to persons in the surrounding area, the wider implications for the community and other material considerations.

The controls under the Act are not intended to duplicate the effect of other statutory controls. Thus the Act does not apply to controlled or radioactive wastes. Also, the controls do not apply to explosives, the location of which is controlled by licences specifically issued by the HSE. The Planning (Hazardous Substances) Regulations 1992 (SI 1992 No. 656) outline the categories of substances which are controlled by the Act and the level at which they become subject to the provisions of the Act.

The Act operates by requiring any person wishing to store any listed substances at or above prescribed controlled quantities to obtain prior consent from the relevant HSA.

The role of the hazardous substances authorities
HSAs are defined in ss. 1 and 3 of the 1990 Act. The provisions in the Act are designed to ensure that the HSA will usually be the same council or other

body that would act as local planning authority in dealing with an associated application for planning permission.

The relevant responsible bodies are:
— in non-metropolitan areas, the district council;
— in metropolitan areas, the metropolitan authority;
— in Greater London, the borough councils;
— county councils for county matters and nationals parks;
— miscellaneous bodies where they are responsible for the planning functions of the area (e.g. planning boards, UDCs, the Broads Authority, and housing action trusts).

The extent of control

The 1992 Regulations list 71 substances which are subject to control (sch. 1). Section 4(3) and reg. 4 exempt the temporary storage of a controlled amount of a hazardous substance whilst it is being transported or transferred from one mode of transport to another. The exemptions under the Regulations also include aerosol dispensers, substances in pipelines, ammonium nitrates and substances stored on land as a result of a maritime emergency.

Applications for consent

Applications for HSC must be made on a prescribed form and be accompanied by:

(a) a site plan;
(b) a plan indicating the intended location of the controlled substances, the plant which the substance will be present in and access points to the site.

Notice of the application must be given in a local newspaper and on a site notice at least 21 days prior to making the application (reg. 6). In addition, an ownership certificate must be submitted with the application on a similar basis to that in a planning application.

The basis for giving consent

Section 9 of the Planning (Hazardous Substances) Act 1990 sets out the powers and duty of HSAs in relation to their decisions on an application for consent. Section 9(1) gives the HSA the power to grant consent either with or without conditions, or to refuse consent. Section 9(5) requires the HSA to have regard to any material considerations and specifies certain considerations to which the HSA shall have regard.

Section 9(2)(d) makes the provisions of a development plan relevant when determining whether to grant consent. It is important to note that the Act is a 'planning Act' within the definition of s. 336 of the Town and Country Planning Act 1990. Thus, s. 54A of the Town and Country Planning Act 1990 applies to the determination of any consent. Consequently, the determination should be in accordance with the development plan unless material considerations indicate otherwise. It is therefore clearly important for a HSA to consider any policies contained in the relevant development plan.

Regulation 10 of the 1992 Regulations sets out a list of bodies that the HSA must consult before granting hazardous substances consent. The list includes, amongst others, the HSE and the NRA.

The role of the Health and Safety Executive

Although the Planning (Hazardous Substances) Act gives the HSE a purely consultative role in the decision-making process that the HSA must undertake, it is clear from Central Government guidance that a great deal of importance is placed upon the expertise that the HSE have in assessing risks to persons from the presence of hazardous substances.

Section 10(2) of the 1990 Act makes particular provision for the conditions that may have been imposed by the HSA. It states that any condition relating to how a hazardous substance is to be kept or used should be imposed only if the HSE have advised the HSA that any consent should be subject to such conditions. Thus, the HSA does not have a free hand when imposing conditions on any consent that it wishes to give. Central guidance in Circular 11/92 states that any advice from the HSE along the lines that hazardous substance consent should be refused should not be overridden without careful consideration. Where an HSA wishes to grant consent against the HSE's advice, it should give advance notice of that intention and allow 21 days for the HSE to give further consideration to the matter. During this period the HSE can request the Secretary of State for the Environment to call in the application for his own determination.

Furthermore, the controls under the Act are designed to complement and not override or duplicate the requirements of the Health and Safety at Work etc. Act 1974 and its relevant statutory provisions. If an HSA, in exercising its powers under the Act, omits or requires something to be done which is (or which becomes) contrary to any of the above statutory provisions, s. 29 of the 1990 Act is designed to ensure that those safety provisions will prevail, as safety must be the overriding concern. Thus, the statutory provisions relating to health and safety clearly take precedence over any consent given by a HSA, and since it is the HSE who enforce safety provisions, it is also clear that they would have the final word if such a conflict arose.

Relationship with other planning controls

The provisions of the 1990 Act and the relevant regulations were designed to fill the gaps in existing planning controls by enabling specific control to be exercised over the presence of hazardous substances, whether or not associated development was involved. Thus, it is now possible for a local body to have control over the siting of hazardous substances even if development has not occurred.

The new requirement for hazardous substances consent, however, does not override the need for planning permission to be obtained where development is involved. This may arise, for example, where it is proposed to erect a building for the storage or processing of hazardous substances. Where both planning permission and hazardous substances consent are required, two separate applications will be necessary and the respective statutory requirements will need to be followed.

Enforcement
Any person in control of land, or any person who knowingly causes or allows:

(a) more than the controlled quantity of a hazardous substance to be present in, over, or under land without consent or in excess of the quantity allowed by the consent;

(b) a breach of any condition of a hazardous substances consent;

will be guilty of an offence (s. 23).

The maximum penalty on summary conviction is £20,000 and on indictment an unlimited fine, and regard must be had of any financial benefit which has accrued or is likely to accrue to the defendant as a result of the offence (s. 23(4A)).

It is a defence to prove that the defendant took all reasonable precautions and exercised all diligence to avoid the commission of an offence, or that the defendant did not know and had no reason to believe that an offence had been committed.

Hazardous substances contravention notice
Where it appears to the HSA that there has been a contravention of HSC, s. 24 of the 1990 Act provides for the service of a hazardous substances contravention notice. The notice must be served on the owner and/or person in control of the land and/or anyone with an interest in the land who is materially affected by the notice. The notice must:

(a) specify the alleged breach;

(b) outline the steps which are to be taken to remedy the breach;

(c) identify the land to which notice relates;

(d) state the date on which the notice takes effect and the time limit for remedying the breach.

There is a right of appeal against the notice prior to the date on which the notice takes effect. Section 26 enables the HSA to apply for an injunction where it considers it necessary or expedient to do so, whether or not it has exercised any other enforcement powers. Under s. 36, a duly authorised person has the power to enter land at any reasonable time for the purpose of surveying in connection with any application for HSC, or for considering the issue of a hazardous substances contravention notice. Furthermore, s. 178 of the Town and Country Planning Act 1990 gives the HSA power to enter land where a notice has not been complied with, to take the steps specified in the notice and to recover the costs of doing so from the landowner.

Modification of consents
There is a variety of mechanisms available to modify existing consents. Under s. 13, applicants can apply to remove or modify conditions on existing consents. In considering the application the HSA must consider only the condition(s) which is (are) to be removed or modified and not the decision about whether or not to grant consent.

The HSA can revoke or modify a consent by order under s. 14 if it considers it expedient to do so having regard to material considerations. Any order made is subject to confirmation by the Secretary of State. Compensation is payable to any person in circumstances where that person has suffered loss as a result of:

(a)   disturbance in the enjoyment of their land;
(b)   depreciation of the value of their land.

Compensation will not be paid where a consent is revoked and:

(a)   planning permission for a change of use is implemented;
(b)   there has been a material change of use to the land in any event;
(c)   controlled substances have not been present on, over or under land for the preceding five years.

Deemed consent

Section 11 of the 1990 Act enabled a deemed consent to be claimed where hazardous substances had been present during the period of 12 months immediately preceding the commencement of the Act (i.e. 1 June 1992). The purpose of this provision was to avoid undue disruption by enabling the continuation of previous operations involving hazardous substances in a similar way to that which was then in existence, but with some facility for controlled expansion, without a specific grant of consent being required from the HSA.

Provided a valid claim was made prior to 30 November 1992 (i.e. the submitted information was complete and accurate and the statutory requirements of s. 11 and reg. 14 were met), HSC was automatically deemed to be granted, subject to the standard conditions set out in s. 11(7)(a) of the Act and in sch. 3 to the Regulations. The jurisdiction of the HSA to consider the application was limited to the validity of the application submitted and not the criteria in s. 9.

It is clear from s. 11(8) that the quantity of hazardous substances permitted in the case of deemed consent may be up to twice that which was last notified to the HSE under the Notification of Installations Handling Hazardous Substances Regulations 1982 (SI 1982 No. 1357). Therefore, the introduction of the full, established quantity of a hazardous substance as authorised under a deemed consent may well result in the contravention of health and safety provisions.

Hazardous substances register

Section 28 of the 1990 Act requires every HSA to keep a register containing information about a variety of matters. Regulation 23 sets out the detailed requirements for the manner in which the register should be kept. The register contains details of:

(a)   applications for HSC;

    (b)   information about deemed consents;
    (c)   enforcement action;
    (d)   decisions of the HSA and directions of the Secretary of State.

Fees

All applications for full HSC must be accompanied by a fee. Regulations 24 and 25 of the 1992 Regulations set out the detailed provisions relating to fees, the level of which is between £200 and £400, depending on the quantity of substances involved. The aim of the fee is to enable the local authority to cover normal administration costs.

TEN
Environmental assessment

The assessment of the environmental effects of a development has always been an implicit part of the decision-making process in the system of town and country planning operating in Britain. Indeed, there have also been explicit examples where detailed assessments of the environmental effects of developments have been carried out, for instance in relation to power stations and motorways. Environmental harm has always been a material consideration when deciding whether or not to grant planning permission and there are many developments which have had planning permission refused because of their detrimental environmental effects.

This implicit mechanism was raised to a more formal level with the adoption of EC Directive 85/337 on the Assessment of the Effects of Certain Private and Public Projects on the Environment. This Directive established the need for the preparation of a statement outlining the effects of a development on the environment as a mandatory component of the decision-making process in relation to certain specified projects.

The Directive was the subject of fierce debate between the Member States (and has remained controversial ever since). After much discussion, and some alterations, the Directive was implemented in England and Wales by the Town and Country Planning (Assessment of Environmental Effects) Regulations 1988 (SI 1988 No. 1199) (there are similar regulations which apply in Scotland). These regulations were enacted in Britain under the European Communities Act 1972 and are specifically limited, therefore, to the categories of development listed in the Directive. Section 15 of the Planning and Compensation Act 1991 inserted s. 71A of the Town and Country Planning Act 1990, which provides the Secretary of State with the power to make regulations extending the categories of projects which are to be the subject of environmental assessment, and consequently environmental assessment now has a place in primary legislation. This power was used for the first time when the Secretary of State extended the classes of project which are subject to environmental assessment within the Town and Country Planning (Assessment of Environmental Effects) (Amendment) Regulations 1994 (SI 1994

No. 677). This extended the requirement for environmental assessment to wind turbines, motorway service areas, coast protection works and financed toll roads (although it is only in the latter case that a environmental assessment is mandatory).

The Town and Country (Assessment of Environmental Effects) Regulations 1988 ('the Regulations') cover projects which require planning permission and are listed in the Directive. Additionally, certain projects which either do not constitute development, or are permitted under a development order or are dealt with under separate consent procedures, have separate specific regulations. These include such proposals as afforestation, highways, harbour works, salmon farms, power stations and overhead transmission lines. The separate regulations all follow the framework of the general regulations, but specifically apply to projects which do not require planning permission.

What is environmental assessment?

On a simple level, environmental assessment is merely an information-gathering exercise carried out by the developer and other bodies which enables a local planning authority to understand the environmental effects of a development before deciding whether or not to grant planning permission for that proposal. On this level, however, there is little to distinguish this concept from the normal planning process under which environmental effects are a material consideration. The innovation behind the formal environmental assessment process is the systematic use of the best objective sources of information and the emphasis on the use of the best techniques to gather that information. The ideal environmental assessment would involve a totally bias-free collation of information produced in a form which would be coherent, sound and complete. It should then allow the local planning authority and members of the public to scrutinise the proposal, assess the weight of predicted effects and suggest modifications or mitigation where appropriate.

Thus, environmental assessment is a technique and a process. It is inanimate rather than tangible. The end product of the assessment is known as the 'environmental statement' and is submitted on behalf of the developer. This 'environmental statement' is the ultimate submission which is made to the determining authority. It forms part of the overall assessment which is brought together from a number of sources. Clearly, most of the information will be supplied by the developer. There are, however, a number of other sources from which information can, and should, be drawn. There are a number of other participants in the process, and these would normally include statutory consultees (NRA, MAFF, HSE, etc.), independent third parties (conservation groups and the like), members of the public, and even the local planning authority itself. The large range of bodies involved in the assessment re-emphasises the underlying concept behind environmental assessment as being based on the systematic analysis of all the relevant facts—these relevant facts being drawn from the widest possible sources.

The theory of the stated objectives of environmental assessment is seemingly simple enough. Unfortunately, the difficulties involved in the coordination of a proper assessment have led to a number of criticisms of the process (as to which see p. 279).

Environmental Assessment Directive

Directive 85/337 on the assessment of the effects of certain public and private projects on the environment requires Member States to ensure that projects Likely to have significant effects on the environment by virtue of their nature, size or location are assessed with regard to their environmental impact before development consent is given. Projects are categorised into Annex I (where environmental assessment is compulsory) and Annex II (where it is discretionary).

Whereas the term 'project' is defined as the execution of construction works or of other installations or schemes (which would equate roughly with the concept of 'development' in English planning law), 'development consent' is defined as the decision of the competent authority which entitles the developer to proceed with the project. There is some difficulty with the definition of 'proceeding with the project'. This does not necessarily equate with planning permission, as other statutory consents could be required. Whilst certain developments could be built they could not be operated without other licenses.

On one interpretation therefore, it could be argued that, under the terms of the directive, a WRA or, subsequently, the Environment Agency (for example) could request an environmental assessment when considering an application for a waste management licence where the local planning authority had failed to require an assessment. Although this is not the case in UK legislation it arguably could be if the Directive was to have direct effect (as to which see below).

The Directive goes on to set out the detailed requirements for an assessment, which should include direct and indirect effects of a project on a variety of factors, including human beings, fauna, flora, the environment and material assets and the cultural heritage.

The developer must then submit certain specified information to the authority dealing with the application (see below for the contents of an environmental statement). There are also provisions for consultation with both the authorities likely to be concerned with the project and members of the general public, although the detailed arrangements for consultation are left to individual Member States.

A number of proposed amendments have been put forward by the EC Commission. The changes were considered to be necessary because of the wide discrepancies between both the quantity and the quality of assessments carried out in all Member States. There are three main changes. First, there will be a requirement to undertake a formal screening process whereby the decision on whether to require an environmental assessment for an Annex II project would have to be made after considering certain criteria with the publication of the results of the formal process. Secondly, there would be an official scoping exercise with consultation with the various statutory consultees and others to determine the nature of the subjects which would be assessed. Finally, there would be changes to the general consultation procedures requiring consultation with statutory consultees and the public. All three of these initiatives have some existing role in UK practice, although only the latter of these are already a formal feature of environmental assessment in the UK.

Environmental Assessment Directive and direct effect

Unlike more recent directives (e.g. on Access to information (92/313), Habitats (92/43), and Waste (91/271)), the Environmental Assessment Directive was not translated 'literally' when transposed into UK legislation. Moreover, most Member States (including the UK) failed to implement the Directive within the time frame laid down. This has led to a number of challenges to decisions made on projects which purportedly fall within the terms of the Directive. A central issue in all cases was whether the Directive had direct effect within UK legislation (for a general discussion of the direct effect doctrine in relation to environmental Directives see p. 87).

The answer to the question of whether the Directive has direct effect in the UK is, unfortunately, unclear. Most of the cases involved 'pipe-line projects', i.e. projects which fell within one of the Annexes of the Directive and were applied for or published before the date of the implementation of the directive (3 July 1988) (without the benefit of an environmental assessment) but received consent afterwards or which were applied for after 3 July but before the implementation date for the relevant domestic legislation (15 July 1988).

In *Twyford Parish Council* v *The Secretary of State For the Environment and the Secretary of State for Transport* [1992] 1 Env LR 37, McCullough J appeared to accept that the Directive passed the test of being 'unconditional and sufficiently precise' in its terms and was therefore capable of having direct effect in relation to all projects under the Directive (and on the facts to the extension of the M3 motorway across Twyford Down—an Annex I project).

Subsequently, in the Scottish Court of Session in *Kincardine and Deeside DC* v *The Forestry Commissioners* [1992] 1 Env LR 151, Lord Coulsfield (without referring to the *Twyford* decision) held that Art. 4.2 of the Directive (which lays down the framework for Annex II projects) was not 'plain and unconditional' as it allowed the authorities a discretion not as to the means of implementation of the Directive but as to whether an assessment should be required. Therefore, the Directive would not appear to have direct effect in respect of Annex II projects.

Thus, the decision in *Kincardine* could be distinguished from the *Twyford* decision and it would have appeared to have been a sensible position for the directive to have direct effect in respect of Annex I projects where Member States have no discretion.

Unfortunately, the decision of Tucker J in *Wychavon DC* v *Secretary of State for the Environment and Velcourt Ltd* [1994] Env LR 239 has thrown the issue into some confusion. In that case an application for poultry houses and dwellings was submitted on 11 July 1988 (i.e. after the implementation date for the Directive but before the implementation of the domestic regulations). The High Court held that the Directive had no direct effect in relation to any Annex I or Annex II projects.

Tucker J held that it was unnecessary to analyse each Article of the Directive in order to identify whether every one was sufficiently precise; it was enough to make out one Article which was imprecise and the direct effect of the whole Directive would fall. He proceeded to identify some Articles within the terms of the Directive which were, in his view, insufficiently precise and, therefore, offended the principles which lay behind the direct effect doctrine. Whilst this argument could be supported on the ground that the Directive should be seen as a unified set of rules (i.e. all the provisions are interdependent) it is clearly wrong when compared to other Directives which have had partial direct effect. Thus, we are left with the position that three separate courts (which did not refer to any of the other decisions) have arrived at different views as to the direct effect of the Directive. Indeed, the decision in *Wychavon* directly contradicts the previous two decisions without seeking to distinguish them.

The UK courts' attitude to the direct effect doctrine and the Environmental Assessment directive is also demonstrated by the fact that in both the *Twyford* and *Wychavon* decisions the court went on to discuss its findings on the basis that the Directive had direct effect. In both cases the court expressed the view that the challenges would have been dismissed as the applicant had not suffered substantial prejudice (*Twyford*) and there was a general reluctance to exercise any discretion and grant relief. The European Court of Justice has yet to rule directly on the issue of whether the Directive has direct effect (although see Case C-396/92 *ENDS Report* 237 at p. 43). It will be interesting to see whether the ECJ adopts any of the judicial thinking put forward in the High Court. It is tentatively suggested that the ECJ would probably come to a different conclusion from most, if not all, of the decisions in the UK courts.

The use of the direct effect doctrine in the UK courts has normally been on the basis that the Directive has not been fully or properly implemented in UK legislation. Notwithstanding the courts' views of these challenges, the Government has accepted that the original regulations were ineffective in implementing the Directive (see environmental assessment and permitted development below).

Is the project subject to environmental assessment?

The process of environmental assessment can be broken down into a number of discrete stages. The first stage is to determine whether or not the project falls within the criteria for the requirement of environmental assessment. The projects which should be subject to environmental assessment are listed in a variety of regulations, the main ones being the Town and Country Planning (Assessment of Environmental Effects) Regulations 1988. As mentioned above, there are developments which fall outside the control of the Town and Country Planning Acts which are dealt with in specific regulations. For the purposes of this chapter, reference will be made only to the main regulations.

The Regulations apply to the main groups of projects under what are known as schedule one projects and schedule two projects. Projects falling within schedule one of the Regulations *must* be the subject of environmental assessment, whereas projects falling within schedule two of the Regulations only require environmental assessment where there are *likely to be significant environmental effects.*

Schedule one projects—mandatory environmental assessment
As might be expected, the projects falling within schedule one of the Regulations include major infrastructure projects. For example:

— crude-oil refineries;
— thermal power stations;
— installations for the disposal of radioactive waste;
— chemical installations;
— motorways and major roads;
— trading ports;
— special waste incineration, treatment or landfill.

This list of examples for which environmental assessment is mandatory is not particularly surprising. Indeed, most of these types of projects will have been the subject of some form of environmental assessment before the introduction of the Regulations. Projects of this type have always been subject to thorough scrutiny and are usually considered at major public inquiries which involve many months of preparation and a vast range of documentation. It is fair to say that until recently the public was largely excluded from the technical debate unless they had the financial resources to instruct experts to act on their behalf. If the environmental assessment process operates satisfactorily in disseminating information in intelligible terms, then the public may be able to play a more effective role in these inquiries.

For most projects falling within schedule one, the definition of the project is self-explanatory. There are, however, in certain instances, thresholds which seek to define further the types of project to which mandatory environmental assessment applies. For instance, a thermal power station other than a nuclear power station is subject to mandatory environmental assessment only where it has a heat output of 300 megawatts or more. Where there is any degree of uncertainty over whether or not a project falls within schedule one, a ruling on the need for an assessment can be obtained from either the Secretary of State or the local planning authority (see p. 273).

Schedule two projects—discretionary environmental assessment
The projects within schedule two of the Regulations are, by and large, the types of development which are less sensitive in nature. For example:

— pig/poultry units;
— mineral extraction;
— metal processing;
— glass-making;
— food manufacture;
— holiday villages;
— knackers' yards;
— wool scouring units;
— tanneries;
— paper manufacturers.

The fact that a project falls within schedule two does not mean that environmental assessment is necessarily required. There is a requirement for environmental assessment only where such projects 'are likely to have significant effects on the environment by virtue of factors such as their nature, size or location'.

There is no statutory definition or guidance on what is meant by the phrase 'significant effects on the environment'. There is, however, guidance in the DoE Circular 15/88, which lays down three general criteria as to whether the environmental effects are likely to be 'significant':

(a)   whether the project is of more than local significance in terms of its size and physical scale;

(b)   the sensitivity of the location of the development (where it is proposed to be located in areas such as national parks, areas of outstanding natural beauty or a site of special scientific interest, the effects of the development will undoubtedly increase);

(c)   the polluting effect of the development and whether or not it is likely to give rise to complex or adverse effects.

Aside from these general criteria the Circular sets out specific indicative criteria and thresholds relative to each schedule two project. These thresholds are merely advisory and illustrative and each project is to be taken on a case-by-case basis. Experience has shown that some local planning authorities view the threshold levels as being obligatory, but there is little uniformity in the approach. Most thresholds are size related. For instance, intensive pig-rearing units will normally not require environmental assessment unless they exceed 400 sows or 5,000 fattening pigs. Other thresholds concentrate on the amount of land-take. Manufacturing plants, for example, may require environmental assessments when they exceed 30 hectares in area. There is no apparent allowance made for the cumulative effect of a number of smaller, separate proposals. Thus, the construction of two 15 hectare manufacturing plants would arguably not fall within the criteria for environmental assessment. However, for a judicial view see *R* v *Swale BC ex parte RSPB* (p. 271).

Environmental assessment and permitted development

Although many developments which do not require planning permission are dealt with under Regulations which are separate from the main Town and Country Planning Regulations (e.g. afforestation and fish farms), there were still, however, some anomalies which enabled developments which gained automatic planning permission by virtue of the General Development Order to escape from the need to have an environmental assessment whereas in other circumstances an assessment, would be required.

Therefore, the Town and Country Planning (General Permitted Development) Order 1995 (SI 1995 No. 418) withdraws permitted development rights from developments which fall within sch. 1 of the 1988 Regulations (mandatory assessment) and for schedule 2 projects where the development is likely to have significant effects. The effect of the Regulations is to require developments with automatic permitted development rights to apply for planning permission where an environmental assessment is required.

In addition, new Regulations set down procedures to be followed where the otherwise permitted development falls within the environmental assessment regime (see the Town and Country Planning (Environmental Assessment and Permitted Development) Regulations 1995 (SI 1995 No. 417)). Where the development is normally permitted and falls within sch. 2 the developer can apply to the local planning authority for a determination as to whether an environmental assessment is required, with a right of appeal to the Secretary of State in cases of dips. Circular 3/95 sets out indicative criteria for nine classes of development which would normally be permitted but which fall within the classes of projects subject to the Regulations. These include field drainage works, reclamation of land from the sea, surface storage of fossil fuels, petroleum, natural gas and chemical products, local authority roads, the construction of harbours and marinas, long-distance aqueducts and water pipelines, waste-water treatment plants and sewage sludge lagoons.

The amendments have been made necessary as a result of pressure from the EC, which has insisted that the Environmental Assessment Directive requires the assessment of all developments listed in the Annexes regardless of the national position in relation to automatic development consent. Although it is not expected to make a dramatic impact upon UK practice there will be a few circumstances where the ability of a planning authority to investigate the impact of a development which would otherwise have automatic permission could prove to be decisive.

In particular, it is interesting to note that the introduction of the new Regulations specifically goes against other deregulatory initiatives brought forward by the Government and, in effect, places hurdles in the way of developers which were absent previously (albeit at the urging of the EC). There is one cautionary note, however; the advice to local authorities contained in the Circular suggests that 'full, clear and precise reasons' are required before the authority can demand an environmental assessment of a development which is viewed in the Government's eyes as being suitable for automatic planning permission. Indeed, it could be argued that there would have to be a particularly serious environmental consequence for the Secretary of State to uphold a planning refusal in circumstances where it would normally receive automatic planning permission.

Pre-application procedures for establishing the need for environmental assessment

With the vagueness of the indicative criteria for schedule two projects and the uncertainty of interpreting the definition for schedule one projects, there is a number of pre-planning application procedures which establish whether or not environmental assessment is required. Many developers of major projects will need to know at an early stage of the development process whether or not an environmental assessment is required, as the potential for delay and expense is great once a planning application has been submitted.

Under reg. 5(1) of the Regulations, it is open to an applicant at any time prior to making a planning application to seek an opinion from the local planning authority as to whether or not a proposed development falls within schedule one or schedule two, and whether it exceeds thresholds or is in any other way suitable for environmental assessment. This request is made to the appropriate planning authority dealing with the application, whether it be the county authority, district authority or metropolitan authority.

When making an application for an adjudication the applicant must provide some basic minimum information about the proposal, including:

(a)   a site plan;
(b)   a description of the development and its nature and purpose;
(c)   its possible effects on the environment.

Local planning authorities can request further information if they consider it to be necessary (reg. 5(3)). They must determine the request within three weeks or any longer period as the developer may agree. If the authority determines that environmental information is required it must give clear and precise reasons for its opinion (reg. 5(4)). All documents relating to the request, including the opinion of the local planning authority and the accompanying statement of reasons, are placed on the public register (reg. 5(5)).

If the local planning authority either fails to give an opinion within the determination period or requires the provision of environmental information before granting planning permission the developer may refer the matter to the Secretary of State for a direction (reg. 5(6)).

Pre-application directions from the Secretary of State

Where developers wish to challenge the local planning authority's determination they are required to send a copy of all the relevant documentation, including any representations made in the light of the local planning authority's opinion and statement of reasons, to the Department of the Environment. The Secretary of State will then give a direction concerning the requirement for environmental assessment within three weeks of the date of the application (reg. 6). Where the direction states that an environmental assessment is required, it must be accompanied by a statement of reasons, giving a full explanation of the Secretary of State's view (reg. 6(5)). The Secretary of State also has a residual power under reg. 3 to direct that a particular form of development is exempt from environmental assessment.

Challenges to the decisions of the Secretary of State or local planning authority

There is clearly a considerable amount of discretion over whether or not an environmental assessment is required. The courts have been given guidance on the exercise of that discretion in two cases, both of which suggest that they will seldom intervene in the decision of a determining authority. In *R v Swale Borough Council and Medway Ports Authority ex parte The Royal Society for the Protection of Birds* [1991] JPL 39, Swale Borough Council granted planning permission for 'land reclamation' on an area of mud-flats near the mouth of the River Medway. This application for planning permission was to be the first stage in a proposed development of the area for further dock uses and a business park. Notwithstanding these proposals, the application for land reclamation was necessary because of dredging which was taking place in the area. No environmental assessment of the project took place. The RSPB challenged the decision to grant planning permission. One of the grounds of challenge related to the failure to carry out an environmental assessment as required by the Regulations. The RSPB argued that the application could not be viewed in isolation and was part of an integrated development strategy. As such it was either a schedule one project (i.e. a trading port), or a schedule two project with significant environmental effects. The court held that the question of whether or not the project fell within a particular schedule or class was essentially a matter of fact and degree for the determining authority. The issue as to the cumulative effect of other applications was to be dealt with strictly by looking at the nature of the project requiring permission and not any further proposals. However, in assessing the environmental effects of a schedule two project, it was possible, in Simon Brown J's view, to consider the environmental effects of a development in total even though this would mean considering more than what was being applied for. This would seem to go further than the advice laid down in Circular 15/88, which states: 'The individual developer can be asked to provide an environmental statement only in respect of the particular development he proposes'.

The point may well be academic when considering that the main thrust of the decision concerned the discretionary nature of the decision to request an environmental assessment. It does not come as any great surprise that the court was willing to intervene only when the decision was unreasonable in the *Wednesbury* sense. To that extent, it would be open to a local planning authority to request an environmental assessment where the project fell within the class in schedule one or schedule two, but was under the threshold levels, when the environmental effects of the development could not be viewed in isolation. This would not be the case, however, where a number of separate developments which fell outside the Regulations amounted cumulatively to a single development which was above the threshold criteria and would have significant environmental effects. The position may alter, however, if current EC proposals to amend the Directive in respect of requirements to 'screen' and 'scope' any assessment (see pp. 264-5).

In *R v Poole Borough Council ex parte Beebee and others* [1991] JPL 643, Poole Borough Council granted itself planning permission without consiering whether or not an environmental assessment was required. Schiemann J took the view that the purpose of an environmental assessment was to draw to the attention of the decision-maker any relevant information which would assist in reaching a decision. On the facts, he thought that the local planning authority had all the relevant information before it and that an environmental statement would have been superfluous. All the information which might have been gleaned from a formal environmental statement had already emerged and ensured that the council had not arrived at an irrational decision.

As the purpose of environmental assessment is to produce a *systematic* approach to the consideration of environmental effects using best practicable techniques and best available sources of information, it is bold to assert that the local planning authority had all the information that would have been contained in an environmental assessment before the assessment itself has been carried out. Indeed, the transcript of the case suggests that the officers' reports to the decision-making committee had a number of omissions, which would imply that there were deficiencies in the local authority's decision.

Other procedures for determining the need for environmental assessment

Although the pre-application procedure will be utilised in most cases, where there is uncertainty over the requirement for an environmental assessment there is a number of alternative methods which can be used.

First, it is open to a developer to volunteer an environmental statement and to state expressly that the document is to be viewed as being an environmental statement for the purposes of the Regulations. This in turn means that the local planning authority has to carry out the other information-gathering exercises for the environmental assessment process. This has led to the growth in the submission of quasi-environmental statements. These documents contain the information which would normally be contained within an environmental statement, but are not submitted as formal statements for the purposes of the Regulations. In such circumstances, if there is any doubt as to the need for environmental assessment the local planning authority can gather the information from one source (i.e. the developer), but is not obliged to go through the whole environmental assessment exercise. One of the consequences of this approach has been that there is a tendency to concentrate on the subjectivity of the developer's assessment of the environmental effects. Thus, the whole purpose and concept of the environmental assessment can be undermined unless this quasi-assessment is carried out thoroughly.

If an environmental statement is submitted and it is not referred to as a statement for the purposes of the Regulations, the local planning authority should consider whether a formal environmental assessment should be undertaken. If it decides that it should be carried out, the statement can be considered as the environmental statement for the purposes of the Regulations. If the authority takes the view that environmental assessment is not required, it is still required to take the information into account when deciding the planning application.

Post-planning application determinations on the need for environmental assessment

Where a planning application has been submitted without an environmental statement the local planning authority should consider whether the application falls within one of the schedules to the Regulations. Additionally, it should check to see if the Secretary of State has made any directions, or if the authority itself has made any prior determinations on the relevant project.

Where the local planning authority considers that the project falls within one of the schedules, it must inform the applicant within three weeks of the need for an environmental statement to accompany the planning application, giving its full reasons for doing so. Thereafter, the applicant can either ask the Secretary of State for a direction within three weeks, or supply the environmental statement. Failure to do so would mean that the application could not be decided until a statement had been submitted, unless the local planning authority was minded to refuse the application.

Appeals and called-in applications

There is even scope for the Secretary of State to request an environmental statement after he has called in an application or it has gone to appeal. Where there is a direction that an environmental assessment is required, the Secretary of State or an inspector cannot grant planning permission on appeal or after a call-in unless the environmental statement is submitted.

The environmental statement

The main component of any environmental assessment is the environmental statement. The prohibition governing the undertaking of environmental assessment is that planning permission cannot be granted for a project falling within the schedules without the developer submitting an environmental statement. There may, of course, be any number of reasons why a local planning authority might refuse an application on grounds other than the environmental effects of the project, but it would be necessary before granting planning permission to consider information contained within the environmental statement.

There is no statutory provision as to the form of an environmental statement, but it must contain the information contained in schedule three of the Regulations, which reflects Arts. 3 and 5 of Annex III of the Directive. This 'specified information' includes:

(a)   a description of the proposed development, including:

    (i)   the site,
    (ii)   the design,
    (iii) the size and scale of the development;

(b)   the data necessary to identify and assess the main effects which that development is likely to have on the environment;
(c)   a description and assessment of the likely significant effects, direct or indirect, by reference to:

    (i)   human beings, fauna and flora,
    (ii)   soil, water, air, climate and landscape,
    (iii) the interaction between these factors,
    (iv)   material assets and the cultural heritage;

(d)   where significant adverse effects are identified, a description of the measures envisaged to avoid, reduce or remedy those effects.

Furthermore, an environmental statement *may* be supported by further information which can amplify or explain any of the specified information. This includes:

(a)   the physical characteristics of the proposed development, and the land use requirements;
(b)   the main characteristics of the production processes proposed;
(c)   the estimated type and quantity of expected emissions resulting from the operation of the proposed development;
(d)   the main alternatives studied by the applicant;
(e)   the likely significant direct and indirect effects on the environment resulting from:

    (i)   use of natural resources,
    (ii)   the emission of pollutants, the creation of nuiances, and the elimination of waste.

The environmental statement should also have a non-technical summary of the information to enable non-experts to understand its findings.

When considering the types of information to be included in the environmental statement it is important that the project is viewed as having two distinct phases—the construction (and commissioning) phase and the operational phase. Clearly the effects of construction may be different from the long-term operational effects.

The Department of the Environment's *Guide to Environmental Assessment* has a checklist of items for inclusion in an environmental statement, which comprises:

(a) information describing the process;
(b) information describing the site and its environment;
(c) assessment of the effects;
(d) mitigating measures and their likely effectiveness;
(e) risk of accidents.

Not all environmental statements should cover every conceivable aspect of a project's potential effects. An environmental statement should deal primarily with the main or significant effects to which a project may give rise. In many cases, the environmental statement should deal only with a few aspects in depth. It is important that there is agreement between the developer and the local planning authority as to the pertinent issues to be dealt with in an environmental statement. This requires a 'screening' and 'scoping' exercise.

Undertaking the process of environmental assessment

Alternative site selection
Although there is no absolute requirement to undertake an alternative site assessment as part of an environmental assessment, it is nevertheless important to consider the rationale behind the choice of the site in question and why alternatives were not thought to be suitable. The decision to carry out a site selection process must be based upon the applicant's assessment of the need to minimise and the possibility of mitigating the environmental impact when selecting the site for the proposed development.

Clearly, the type of development has a marked effect on the depth of search carried out. Where the proposal is for a nuclear power station there would be a significant obligation to undertake a thorough search for the best available site. This may well mean undertaking a national, or at least regional, investigation. Alternatively, if the proposal is to establish an intensive pig-rearing unit there would not be the same degree of obligation. Notwithstanding this, where a farmer managed a 10,000 acre farm there would be an expectation that the site identified for the unit would be the site giving rise to minimal environmental effects.

The site selection process should identify the basis upon which a balance has been struck between the following factors:

(a) operational requirements;
(b) economic constraints;
(c) environmental effects.

Any analysis of these issues, and particularly the weight being attached to the operational economic considerations, is capable of being challenged. It is incumbent upon the developer to establish the criteria and indicate how the particular site chosen strikes an acceptable balance.

The process of identifying the site by reference to other sites is known as the macro-siting process. Once the site has been identified there is then usually a range of alternatives for micro-siting within the site itself. Environmental impacts can be mitigated by adopting the best configuration of the development within the site.

Screening the effects
The key to the need for an environmental assessment is to identify the likely significance of the impacts. In order to deal with this the developer needs to apply a two-stage test:

(a) Which impacts resulting from the project are likely to be significant (known as the screening process)?

(b) What is the magnitude and significance of these impacts, identifying which issues should be addressed for each impact?

There are EC proposals to lift this somewhat informal process to a more formal level with a requirement that the local authority publish its findings in relation to the 'screening' process.

Scoping
Once a developer has completed a full analysis of the likely environmental implications of a project it is necessary to proceed to undertake a scoping exercise. This involves preliminary meetings with the local planning authority and other relevant consultees in order to ascertain the scope of the environmental issues to be examined and the degree of investigation that has to be undertaken. The object of the Directive was to ensure that parties other than the developer and the local planning authority have a role to play in development process. The scoping exercise should enable the environmental assessment to acquire the objectivity which provides an accurate assessment of the environmental effects.

Although the scoping exercise will provide a common ground as to the issues raised by a development, it does not necessarily mean that all parties will agree on the acceptability of those effects. Once again, the EC has recommended the formalisation of the scoping exercise with a statutory requirement to consult various bodies before deciding on the scope of the assessment.

Consultation
In gathering information developers are not only expected to consult local planning authorities; they must also seek views from the statutory consultees and possibly non-statutory consultees.

Ordinarily, the developer will go to the local planning authority first to discuss the project. At that stage the local planning authority may wish to identify the bodies with whom consultations should be undertaken. Such consultees will often extend beyond the range of those specified in the Regulations as statutory consultees. Regulation 8 provides that the statutory consultees should include those bodies which the local planning authority is required by Art. 18 of the Town and Country Planning (General Development) Order 1988 to consult on the determination of a planning application. These include, where appropriate, the HSE, British Coal, the NRA, the highway authority, English Heritage, the Ministry of Agriculture, Food and Fisheries and the Waste Regulation Authority. The width of consultation depends precisely upon the type of development proposed. In addition reg. 8 provides that English Nature, the Countryside Commission and HMIP should be consulted.

It is the developer's responsibility to approach the statutory consultees. Regulation 22 imposes a duty on the statutory consultees to make available, on request, any information in their possession which is relevant to the preparation of the environmental statement. This does not, however, require the public bodies to obtain information they do not have or to disclose confidential information. The consultees Can levy a reasonable charge for making such information available (reg. 20).

The information which it is envisaged would be made available would include specialised information, such as the results of ecological monitoring, which would help the identification and assessment of the envoronmental effects.

Furthermore, there may be non-statutory consultees who could assist with this information. Developers can consult with these bodies where they offer some particular expertise or local insight. This type of non-statutory consultee could include such bodies as the RSPB, CPRE, local nature groups and members of the general public.

The consultation exercise (often extensive) forms the backbone of the whole environmental assessment process and produces a number of advantages. First, quite often in development projects some environmental issues are obvious. The benefit of the consultation exercise, however, is that it identifies those issues which are perhaps not so clear. Secondly, a methodical, even approach to the objective analysis of environmental impacts enables alterations to be made to a project at an early stage without great expense or inconvenience. These alterations can mitigate or eliminate adverse effects. Thirdly, where a full and adequate consultation is carried out before a planning application is submitted, the amount of time taken by the local planning authority and other consultees to consider the application when submitted will be greatly reduced. Finally, the consultation process affords the developer the opportunity of communicating with all parties who are likely to have an interest in the project. Misunderstandings can be cleared up on both sides. This then enables the developer and the local planning authority to concentrate on the relevant issues.

Determination of the planning application

The developer is responsible for the content of the environmental statement which is finally submitted. Where the local planning authority considers that the information given is insufficient to allow for proper consideration of the environmental effects of the development, further information can be requested (reg. 21). Where the process of consultation has been carried out properly this should not arise.

Once an environmental statement has been prepared and submitted together with the planning application, there are further procedural steps which closely follow the standard procedure for planning applications. The two main differences are that the determination period for the application is extended to 16 weeks (regs. 14 and 16) and there are increased publicity requirements to ensure that the planning application including the environmental statement is advertised in the local newspaper and in a site notice (reg. 12(3) GDO 1988 (SI 1988 No. 1813, as amended)).

Additionally, each statutory consultee is entitled to a copy of the environmental statement free of charge, and a reasonable number of copies should be made available for sale to the public at a charge which reflects their printing and distribution costs (regs. 18 and 20).

The local planning authority then notifies the statutory consultees of the application (if this is necessary) and they have a minimum of 14 days to comment on the environmental statement.

As a result of the Town and Country Planning (Assessment of Environmental Effects) (Amendment) Regulations 1992 (SI 1992 No. 1494), these procedural requirements now apply in situations where the local planning authority is itself the applicant for planning permission.

It is not open to the local planning authority to invalidate an environmental statement because of its view of the inadequacies of the information supplied. Should it take the view that the environmental statement is inadequate, it should use its powers to seek further information under reg. 21. Where the developer fails to provide further information and the local planning authority decides to refuse planning permission, or fails to determine the application within the 16-week period, the developer has the usual right of appeal to the Secretary of State.

Environmental assessment in simplified planning zones and enterprise zones

A separate system for environmental assessment is operated in simplified planning zones. Because of their deregulated nature there is a danger that projects which would normally require environmental assessment would not be subject to the Regulations or the Directive. By way of clarification, the DoE Circular 24/88 states that, generally, permission ought not to be given in simplified planning zones created since July 1988 for any project which should be the subject of an environmental assessment.

Schedule one projects are excluded from all simplified planning zone permissions. Where a simplified planning zone scheme purportedly grants permission for a schedule one project, authorities should include a provision expressly excluding development that falls within the definition of a project requiring mandatory environmental assessment.

There are two different approaches for schedule two projects:

(a)   Where a simplified planning zone prescribes the particular types of development permitted, the permission can be divided in such a way that it excludes projects requiring environmental assessment.

(b)   For other simplified planning zones, it will be necessary to include provisions requiring developers to establish with the planning authority that an environmental assessment is not necessary. If an environmental assessment is necessary a separate planning application will be required.

Enterprise zones designated before July 1988 are not affected by the provisions of the Directive. The vast majority of enterprise zones fall into this category. The Government has recognised, however, that there might be exceptional circumstances for the creation of a new enterprise zone (e.g. in Lanarkshire to compensate for the loss of Ravenscraig). This situation is to be dealt with in a similar way to simplified planning zones.

Environmental assessment in practice

Research by the Institute of Environmental Assessment (IEA) showed that 1,131 projects were the subject of environmental assessment between July 1988 and July 1992. The research suggested that the experience of environmental assessments in general had been mixed. Over 50% of local planning authorities had not received an environmental statement in that time, and over 40% had received only one. Kent County Council, on the other hand, had received 15. In the first few years since the introduction of the system both the environmental assessment process and the environmental statement in particular have been the subject of a number of criticisms.

The low quality of environmental statements
As with any new system, there has been a relatively short period to accumulate the amount of knowledge required to deal with an issue as complex as the environmental effects of a large-scale project. Although many developers have taken a framework for environmental assessment from experience gained in the United States with environmental impact assessment, the IEA found that when they reviewed a sample of environmental statements 30% of their content was graded as unsatisfactory to poor. Most of these deficiencies were to be found in the assessment of the environmental impacts of the project. There are no agreed 'standards' covering the assessment of these impacts and this has led to a wide diversity in the quality of environmental statements.

Lack of objectivity
Many environmental statements have received criticism for being statements of the developer's case in favour of their planning application. Often this is the result of the inadequacy of the scoping exercise. There is no requirement to carry out any form of scoping exercise. One survey showed that as many as 50% of local planning authorities were not consulted at the scoping stage. Thus the assessment may fail to consider material issues which should have

been addressed. Where scoping does take place there is a good chance that the environmental assessment will throw up negative effects which can be mitigated. Furthermore, the scoping exercise can sometimes take the form of a general consultation where the developer tells the local planning authority of the issues which need to be addressed. Unfortunately, a combination of factors, including lack of resources, lack of central guidance and a lack of technical support, often dictates that a scoping exercise of such a 'subjective' nature cannot be widened without a contribution from the local authority.

Lack of central guidance
There is an amount of general guidance on the procedural and legal aspects of environmental assessment, but there is very little guidance on the methodology of assessing impact, or on the types of impact which any particular project might produce. The depth to which an assessment is carried out can also be critical, particularly in relation to archaeological or ecological interests. Thus, there is a danger that there will be a period where mistakes will be made and effects unassessed or not dealt with sufficiently. There is now an amount of material available from previous assessments which can demonstrate the 'do's and don'ts' of the process. These environmental statements are not freely available, although the IEA does have a library.

Lack of a consistent approach
A major criticism of the environmental assessment system to date has focused on the failure of the local planning authorities to have a consistent approach when determining the need for environmental assessment. Research carried out on behalf of the DoE showed that 50% of local planning authorities who had not received any environmental statements had planning applications on their planning registers which were above the relevant thresholds for schedule two projects and which could have been suitable for environmental assessment. A large number of these projects were of the same type or similar in size to projects in other areas which had been the subject of environmental assessment. When questioned further the local planning authorities admitted that a principal cause for these discrepancies was their unfamiliarity with the Regulations.

Complexity of the task
One of the main concerns of the Government when introducing the Regulations was to ensure that environmental assessment did not become another bureaucratic hurdle for developers. Thus the determination period for environmental assessment projects was extended to 16 weeks. In practice, however, only about half of the planning applications were determined within the statutory period. The average period for determination has been around the 36-week mark, with almost a quarter taking over a year to decide. The delay would seem to stem from disagreement between the main parties over the scope of an environmental assessment and the alleged impacts of the development.

The case for reform?

Although the system has been the subject of criticism from both sides of the development industry, very few changes to either the law or practice of environmental assessment have taken place. One suggestion which has been put forward by a number of bodies is that there should be a formal, independent 'Council for Environmental Assessment' who would help with scoping and quality review. This suggestion was formally proposed as an unsuccessful amendment to the Planning and Compensation Bill in 1991 by Lord Nathan.

The EC has, however, proposed a number of formal changes to the Environmental Assessment Directive which would address some of these criticisms (see above). On a national level, in 1994, after a long wait (it was promised in 1990), the Government finally published some guidance on the quality of environmental statements. The guide sets out a set of procedures which should be followed when preparing an environmental statement. The main emphasis of the guidance is on the need to use approved methodologies for calculating impacts and to differentiate between scientific calculation of impacts and the evaluation of the significance of the impact, which is at best an informed judgment. The statement should, it is suggested, contain a method statement which should set out an explanation of the approach to carrying out the assessment, including an outline of the scoping exercise, the techniques and methods used to assess impacts and the approach taken in appraising the significance and scale of the impacts. Although concrete guidance is to be welcomed, the improvement in the quality of environmental statements is dependent upon local planning authorities and third parties evaluating draft statements and rejecting them if they are below an acceptable standard.

ELEVEN
Integrated pollution control

The development of the regulatory system of pollution control has tradition-ally been pragmatic, reacting to environmental problems in a piecemeal fashion. Consequently, the approach has been fragmented; specific media have been controlled by diverse administrative and enforcement agencies. Many examples of the reactive nature of environmental law can be seen throughout this book. The Clean Air Act, the Alkali Act, and the Deposit of Poisonous Wastes Act all related to specific problems at a particular time which had given rise to public concern. The *ad hoc* nature of these controls resulted in a haphazard approach characterised by legislation with loopholes enabling offenders to avoid liability.

The end result was that by the 1970s, the British system of pollution control was characterised by a division in the means of control; there were separate controls for emissions into the atmosphere, environmental problems on land, and emissions into the aqueous environment.

Pollution of the atmosphere

Traditionally, the role of environmental law was targeted towards the protec-tion of public health. Although the secondary purpose of such controls was that the environment was protected from harm, this was not the main purpose of the legislation. In the 1830s standards of sanitation in the major cities created a great deal of concern amongst those enlightened individuals who took an interest in the poorer classes. Consequently, between the years 1840 to 1875, attempts were made to deal with the problem by the setting up of special local boards of commissioners which were the predecessors of today's local authorities. These boards were made responsible for the enforce-ment of minimal sanitation standards.

At approximately the same time, industry started to utilise new materials and new industrial sectors were formed, such as alkali works, which produced highly noxious and polluting chemicals as a by-product of their processes. Even in this respect, the problem was not viewed in purely environmental terms and the main thrust of the controls was based on technological answers to what were perceived as scientific problems. Thus the Alkali Inspectorate was created in 1863 to fulfil a technical and advisory role in the combating of pollution. However, the legislation was neither properly enforced nor did it address all the difficulties emissions into the atmosphere could cause. Consequently, although noxious fumes were controlled, there was no prohibition on the emission of smoke into the atmosphere, which brought about problems of lower-level pollution with the production of smog. Thus, although the law sought to deal with one problem another problem arose elsewhere.

As new environmental issues emerged, legislation was introduced which often resulted in separate bodies being responsible for enforcement in respect of overlapping emissions. For example, in relation to air pollution the Alkali Inspectorate dealt with noxious fumes under the Alkali Act, but local authorities were responsible for the control of smoke under the Clean Air Acts. Other bodies were created to deal with a variety of subject matters such as the control of health and safety within factories, the control of nuclear installations and the control of mines and quarries. The control of emissions to the atmosphere was pieced together by a haphazard jigsaw of administrative controls enforced by a number of different bodies. As will be seen, air pollution was not the only area of confusion. Although the aims of these statutory bodies were different, the reactive approach often meant that the mechanisms used to control individual areas of concern overlapped. This resulted in over-complicated and ineffective enforcement.

The Robens Committee was set up in the early–1970s to report on health and safety at work and to answer specifically some of the criticisms that had been levelled at the many different authorities administering different sectors. In 1972, the Committee recommended that a new unified body should be set up to deal with all aspects of health, safety and welfare at work. Traditionally, there had been some confusion as to the role of the Alkali Inspectorate and whether or not its aim was to protect the environment or to safeguard the health of workers. The Robens Committee recommended that a new Health and Safety Executive (HSE) should be established to include the Alkali Inspectorate. This was duly formed in 1974, in the first real attempt to unify a number of different inspectorates under one organisational umbrella.

Environmentalists viewed this as a retrogressive step. The HSE was a factory-based control agency and sought specifically to protect the interests of workers rather than dealing with environmental protection on a broader basis. Secondly, focusing protection on the factory environment did not necessarily take into account the many environmental difficulties suffered as a result of emissions, although other sectors were subject to statutory control through alternative mechanisms.

Pollution on land

The Control of Pollution Act 1974 created new bodies which were known as waste disposal authorities and had responsibility for the disposal of waste to land. These functions were primarily the responsibility of county authorities. Clearly, this protection was not part of the factory-based approach but, unfortunately, in practice there was little or no coordination between the HSE and those controlling waste disposal, notwithstanding that there is a connection between the production of waste in factories regulated by the HSE and the disposal of waste on sites controlled by waste disposal authorities.

Control of water pollution

Notwithstanding the separation of responsibilities for the control of pollution within factories and on land, there was a further complication with the separation of the control over emissions into water. The River Boards Act 1948 created a number of river boards to control land drainage, fisheries and the prevention of river pollution. Then, under the Water Resources Act 1963, 27 river authorities were created to take over responsibility from the river boards; they themselves were then superseded with the creation of the regional water authorities under the Water Act 1973. (See Chapter 14.)

The regional water authorities were given sole responsibility for regulating all matters concerned with water. Thus, they had control over prevention of river pollution, the supply of water, the control of sewage, water conservation, fisheries and water recreation. The Water Act 1989 attempted to overcome the inherent difficulties by separating the operational side of the authorities from the regulatory side. In dividing the poacher from the gamekeeper, a further two bodies entered the administrative jungle of environmental protection.

The administrative jungle and the mechanisms of protection

Although attempts were made by the Department of the Environment to rationalise environmental control, the plethora of enforcement agencies, including such bodies as the HSE, local authorities, the water authorities, and later the successor to the Alkali Inspectorate (the Industrial Air Pollution Inspectorate) and the waste disposal authorities, created a complicated web of fragmented control. There was no unified concept of environmental protection; a theoretical and unrealistic sectoral approach had fundamental flaws which constantly served to undermine the authority of the law.

In addition to the jungle of administrative bodies, environmental control was also hampered by the vast number of powers and procedures available to each individual enforcement agency. Where powers to control pollution were available to a number of bodies, overlapping controls often meant that a particular incident or process could be regulated by as many as four different authorities. For example, a factory which was subject to control under the Alkali Etc. Works Regulation Act 1906, which produced dark smoke and discharged trade effluent into the nearby river could be controlled by the Alkali Inspectorate, the local environmental health department, and the water authority. This often created difficulties, particularly as a particular problem could be approached by each different enforcement body using different enforcement powers. In many cases there were elements of 'too many cooks spoiling the broth'.

The controls available to each enforcement agency also varied tremendously. The traditional basis for environmental pollution control has always been seen as discretionary and technical in a scientific sense. Historically, the main basis of this control has been by the operation of the principle of 'best practicable means' (BPM). This principle was first applied in 1842 in an attempt to control smoke nuisances in Leeds, and was further utilised in the Alkali Acts to control *all* noxious emissions from alkali works by 1874. The concept of BPM has since formed the basis of emission control for all media. Although explicit in the Alkali Acts and other statutes (e.g. the Public Health Act 1936 in relation to statutory nuisances) the *principle* of BPM governed other areas of control implicitly. Even where no statutory reference to the phrase could be found, consideration was given to BPM to guide standard-setting and enforcement.

The phrase 'best practicable means' incorporates both a scientific approach ('means') and a discretionary approach ('best' and 'practicable'). There were three main aims of the BPM legislation. First, there was a prohibition on any emission which could constitute a recognised health hazard. Secondly, emissions had to be reduced to the lowest level, always balancing that requirement with local conditions and circumstances, the current state of pollution control technology, the effects of the substances emitted, the financial effect upon a company using such equipment and the means that were to be used to control the emissions. Thirdly, where there were harmful emissions, the aim was that such emissions should be, so far as possible, diluted and dispersed.

The statutory guidance as to what constituted BPM was sparse so as not to fetter the discretion of the regulatory bodies. Certain guidelines were contained within the various statutory controls (e.g. the Control of Pollution Act 1974, s. 72), but effectively, the concept utilised a presumptive control mechanism. Thus, where the individualised emission levels were complied with, it was presumed that there were no better practicable means in controlling emissions. In practice, the Alkali Inspectorate used the concept of BPM to balance any cost implications with the statutory objective of controlling noxious or offensive gases. The 1981 report of the Alkali Inspectorate put it thus:

The expression 'BPM' takes into account economics and all of its financial implications and we interpret this not just in the narrow sense of a works dipping into its own pocket, but including the wider effect on the community. In the long run it is not the owners of the works who pay for clean air but the public, and it is our duty to see that money is wisely spent on the public's behalf. The country's industries and world's current financial situation have to be weighed against the benefits for which we strive and careful thought has to be given to decisions which could seriously impair competitiveness in the national and international markets. Never do we lose sight of our ultimate goal—that all scheduled works should operate harmlessly and inoffensively and that this state shall be attained at the earliest possible moment.

Notwithstanding this 'ultimate goal' there was no clearly defined environmental quality standard. The use of presumptive standards contained in guidance notes issued on a year to year basis attempted to impose some limits on emissions to the atmosphere. It was clear, however, that these limits were to be applied flexibly and on an individualised basis to ensure that in each particular case the emission controls were 'practicable'.

The flexibility that BPM gave to the Inspectorate meant that there could be a co-operative rather than a confrontational approach to industry. It was only when all the possible avenues of co-operation had been exhausted that breaches of the presumptive standards would result in enforcement action (for some possible explanations of this, see Chapter 6).

Although not explicit within the water industry, similar considerations applied to the control of emissions into water. However, there was one distinguishing feature. EC environmental policy sought to introduce into the legislation of Member States the concept of water quality standards or objectives. These directives covered such areas as the quality of drinking water, bathing waters, and the quality of groundwater. Previously there had been no legally binding limits, although both the National Water Council and the Secretary of State had fulfilled secondary roles in setting administrative standards of quality. In order to implement Directives (e.g. 80/778 and 75/440 on Drinking Water and Surface Water for Drinking), the water authorities utilised their powers in setting limits for emission levels on discharge consents. There was still a certain amount of balancing required between the financial implications of the cost of pollution abatement equipment and the requirement to bring water quality up to certain standards.

Overall, as Britain entered the 1980s, there was a fragmented, individualised, sectoral approach which did not reflect the growing trend within Europe for an integrated approach to the environment with specific quality objectives. As the move to make a fundamental change from the 'British approach' gathered pace, the consequences of the traditional basis of pollution control became clear.

Consequences of the fragmented approach

(a) Failure to view the environment as a whole
One of the main concerns of those who criticised the sectoral approach to pollution control in Britain was that there was a failure to deal with the environment as a whole. Each individual medium was seen as a separate area of control and no consideration was given to the possible consequences of imposing control on one sector in relation to others. For instance, where strict controls were placed upon the levels of effluent discharge into water, a simple alteration to the production process may shift the effluent to another sector, such as by incineration (air) or landfill.

The environment as a concept is a series of interdependent sectors. When individual bodies controlled separate sectors there was often a reluctance to deal with a problem on a unified basis. Administratively, the idea of two separate bodies with overlapping responsibilities created tremendous logistical difficulties, misunderstandings arose, inter-departmental communication had its own problems, which led to inefficient control.

(b) The discretionary decision-making process
The different regulatory bodies possessed wide discretionary powers with which to enforce their statutory duties. Too much discretion led to uncertainty. Certain bodies took a more rigorous view of enforcement whereas others were content to pursue a conciliatory approach. When a number of statutory bodies controlled the same process, the use of these different criteria led to an imbalance in the protection of the environment as a whole. Where an enforcement body showed a tendency to pursue rigorous levels of enforcement, emissions in that sector were kept at an artificially low level. However, this was often counterbalanced by an increase of emission levels to another medium in relation to which the alternative enforcement bodies exercised their discretion leniently.

(c) The development of a co-operational approach to enforcement
The lack of definitive standards in many areas saw the development of the co-operative approach by many enforcement agencies. It has been argued in favour of such an approach that compliance with standards has resulted rather than producing a wholesale enforcement holiday. However, other consequences have also been identified (see Chapter 6).

(d) Overlapping controls
One of the consequences of failing to deal with the environment as a whole was that each individual enforcement agency had a prescribed area of responsibility. Where, however, there were overlaps in that responsibility, an uncoordinated approach brought about ineffective enforcement of the regulations in question.

For example, where there was a spillage of a hazardous substance within a factory site there could have been as many as five different agencies who could have taken individual action against the company involved. If the substance found its way into a water-course the water authority could take action. Where there was a statutory nuisance arising from smells and fumes, the local environmental health officer could take action. If the substance came within the COSHH Regulations, the Factory Inspectorate could have taken action. The water services company could have also prosecuted for the breach of a discharge consent into sewers, the National Rivers Authority could have prosecuted for pollution of controlled waters and the Fire Service could have taken action for the breach of any storage licence conditions. Where such complex administrative mechanisms are required to cope with a simple single incident there is a chance that the proper mechanism is not utilised. The nature of the bureaucratic system of control was such that where administra-

tive controls overlap, any failure of communication between the enforcement
agencies rendered proper enforcement more difficult.

(e)   Lack of public accountability

Lastly, where there were so many enforcement agencies, there was often a
problem with a lack of public accountability. The trained professional could
have difficulty in ascertaining which body is responsible for a particular
activity. The person in the street had very little chance of knowing who to
turn to. Normally, the local environmental health officer was the first person
to receive complaints, not necessarily because the local authority was the
proper controlling body for a particular process, but because the public
identified the environmental health department of a local authority as being
the 'right place' to which to complain. Other more obscure agencies were not
fully recognised by members of the public. Where there was such uncertainty
then the accountability of these bodies was also obscured. For an administrative and bureaucratic system to work effectively, the public needed to
recognise who controls what and how they did so.

Time for a change

The consequences of this fragmented approach were recognised when, in an
attempt to address them, the Secretary of State for the Environment asked
the Royal Commission on Environmental Pollution in their Fifth Report in
1976 to 'review the efficacy of the methods of the control of air pollution from
domestic and industrial sources and to consider the relation between relevant
authorities'. After receiving many representations, the Royal Commission
identified many of the problems which have already been outlined above.
They pointed out specifically that, by treating the disposal of waste to air,
land and water as three separate issues, there was a danger that the 'allocation
of available resources to each of the media will not reflect an overall view of
where the problems are most severe' and also that such an approach would
result in the 'haphazard disposal' of emissions to one particular sector without
taking into account which of the media a particular pollutant would be best
disposed into. As a background to the considerations of the Commission, the
proposals of the Robens Committee were being implemented and thus,
instead of taking a unified approach to the environment, there was a move
away from environmental protection to a more factory-based approach with
the creation of the HSE.

Before attempting to deal with the procedural aspects of a unified environmental protection system, there had to be an administrative body in place which
could effectively use the powers given to it. Thus, the Commission proposed two
changes. First, the Commission recommended that there should be a single
unified body to ensure that any regulatory system imposed could be enforced
effectively and the full environmental consequences of an operation could be
assessed. Secondly, in order to assess the full environmental effect of a process
rather than just assessing its impact in terms of different media, it recommended
that the new concept of the 'best practicable environmental option' be utilised.

Best practicable environmental option

The concept of 'best practicable environmental option' (BPEO) was intended to adopt some of the more positive benefits of the previous BPM tests whilst maintaining some environmental utility. First, the test allowed the enforcement agency to set emission standards relating to specific prescribed substances and specific prescribed processes. Secondly, they acknowledged that the scientific and technical background that a properly trained Inspectorate could bring to the system of control would provide a technological advantage and would imply that any enforcement agency was seen as more than merely an environmental police force, but also as an adviser/consultant. The concept of BPEO sought to keep the more legalistic standard-setting idea, whilst maintaining the scientific and technological approach to pollution abatement.

The basis of BPEO was in part an extension of the BPM concept but it introduced consideration of the environment as a whole when setting emission standards for industrial processes. In 1988, in their Twelfth Report, the Commission suggested a definition for BPEO as being:

> . . . the outcome of a systematic consultative and decision-making procedure which emphasises the protection of the environment across land, air and water. The BPEO procedure establishes, for a given set of objectives, the option that provides the most benefit or least damage to the environment as a whole, at acceptable cost, in the long as well as the short term.

Thus, although the BPEO concept was considered to be an extension of the BPM test it was much more than that. It was to form the *philosophical basis* for a more practical test.

These recommendations were ignored by Central Government for some time, mainly for political reasons. In 1982, the Department of the Environment's Pollution Paper No. 18 investigated the role of a unified administrative body without taking specific action. However in 1983, William Waldegrave, a new Minister in the Department of the Environment, pressed for a unified agency to implement the Royal Commission's recommendation. Tim O'Riordan and Albert Weale ([1989] PA 277) point out a number of motivating factors for this sudden re-emergence. Amongst the factors identified was the need to implement the idea of BPEO. In the period since their Fifth Report the Royal Commission had not kept quiet about the concept. In particular, the Tenth Report, *Tackling Pollution—Experiences and Prospects*, was particularly scathing in its criticism of Government inaction. However, with the administrative set-up in the 1980s there was no one regulatory body to oversee the new system. The weaknesses of the fragmented, reactive approach finally received official recognition. Mr Waldegrave told the House of Lords Select Committee on the European Communities:

> I have been struck by how often we appear to be dealing with subjects not really on the basis of an objective assessment of environmental priorities but as a result of the changing fashions in pressure from outside.

The difficulties of quasi-governmental organisations being influenced by party political pressures tended to detract from the main priority of environmental protection. Thus, a feeling grew in the Conservative Government and elsewhere that a free-standing body was necessary.

The EC's role in change

At about the same time as the Fifth Report of the Royal Commission on Environmental Pollution, the EC was formally adopting its First Action Programme for the environment. The approach for this Action Programme was fundamentally different to that of Britain as it adopted a continental approach which contained few elements of British tradition. The continental approach was to take a proactive rather than a reactive stance. Thus, its driving principle was one of anticipation of environmental pollution problems rather than trying to deal with problems as they arose on a piecemeal basis.

From the date of implementation of the First Action Programme, a number of Directives were introduced which emphasised these differences in approach. Directive 76/464 on Pollution caused by Dangerous Substances Discharged into the Aquatic Environment was introduced to eliminate or reduce the pollution of water by dangerous substances. This was to be implemented by means of emission standards on authorisations to sewers and controlled waters. Similar Directives were later introduced for Air Pollution (84/360) and Emissions from Large Combustion Plants (86/609).

Increasingly, the flexibility of standard-setting in Britain did not reflect this move towards European-style emission standards defined with reference to 'permissible maximum concentrations of substances' and 'quality objectives'. Other countries within the EC were already developing new and different ideas.

Vorsorgeprinzip: anticipation through foresight

In the 1970s, as environmental issues started to percolate through the political systems of the Member States of the EC, the methodology of pollution control in other Member States was starting to develop significantly. In West Germany, for instance, environmental control evolved around the somewhat different mechanism of the *vorsorgeprinzip*. This was a stated principle which was to be adhered to when considering the environmental impact of a process and which operated on two bases: first, that the environment should be able to restore itself notwithstanding the effect of industrial activity, and secondly, that environmental controls on emission standards should be set as high as they could, taking into account available technology. These two bases work in tandem to create an overall scheme which takes into account available technology but does not sacrifice environmental quality by putting standards at the margins of environmental deterioration. However, even with the principle of *vorsorgeprinzip* there was also some need to take into account an economic factor. Thus, the principle of proportionality, which takes into account the balance between the environmental improvement achieved and the cost needed to attain that improvement, was also a factor.

The natural consequence of this three-pronged approach was translated into EC policy in the Directive on Atmospheric Emissions from Industrial Plants (84/360). This required that 'all appropriate preventive measures against air pollution be taken, including the application of best available technology, provided that the application of such measures does not entail excessive cost'. The introduction of this new system—'the best available technology not entailing excessive cost' or BATNEEC—was to play an important part in the development of an integrated pollution control system in Britain.

Some saw this new principle as being not very far removed from the old principle of BPM, but the method of its utilisation within the British legislation, when coupled with environmental quality objectives, ensured that there was to be a fundamental restructuring of pollution control within Britain.

HMIP—a unified body

Although the Royal Commission on Environmental Pollution made strong recommendations that a unified body be created to deal with environmental problems, this was specifically rejected by the Government of the day and ignored for approximately 10 years until its Tenth Report raised the issue again when considering the concept of BPEO. Whilst considering the *vorsorgeprinzip* from Germany and the concept of BPEO, the Commission accepted the benefits of such a system, but pointed out that for BPEO to operate effectively it would require a single agency to deal with the day-to-day regulation of environmental matters.

Finally, after an investigation of the efficiency of the Health and Safety Executive, a recommendation was made to create a unified Inspectorate which could not only overcome some of the historical problems surrounding environmental protection but also implement the new system of integrated pollution control.

The Environment Agency and IPC

Although the EPA 1990 attempted to deal with the problems of a diverse range of agencies, some difficulties were still experienced at the boundaries of each agency's controls. In order to deal with some of the obvious areas of overlap a memorandum of understanding was agreed between HMIP and the NRA to cover situations where there were overlapping responsibilities. In the field of waste management, HMIP acted in a technical and advisory capacity, with the regulation of the final disposal of waste on land remaining with local authorities.

The introduction of the Environment Agency is, in one sense therefore, the logical conclusion of the move towards an integrated system of control over pollution. Initially, administrative integration is perhaps the most significant challenge, but there are still a number of legal anomalies which need to be dealt with. For example there is a wider range of enforcement powers available to deal with IPC processes than discharge consents. In time, however, the assimilation of all the powers which were available to the old enforcement agencies should see more consistency in both decision-making and enforcement.

The introduction of integrated pollution control

Any new system of control needed to take into account the requirements of assessing the environment as a whole. With a new administrative agency, Her Majesty's Inspectorate of Pollution, ready to deal with an integrated approach, all that was required was the setting up of the legislation to break down the boundaries between the different sectors. Many of the elements of the new system of integrated pollution control contained some similarity to previous environmental legislation (e.g. the Health and Safety at Work etc. Act 1974 and the Alkali Etc. Works Regulation Act 1906). However, there were a number of new concepts which were introduced to enable Britain to fulfil its obligations under the EEC Treaty and also to take a proactive approach to environmental protection.

Thus, the EPA 1990 introduced a system of integrated pollution control (IPC) to improve the regulation of pollution control arising from industrial processes. Part I of the Act establishes two separate systems: first, IPC controlled by HMIP; and secondly, air pollution control (APC) controlled by the local authority environmental health department (see Chapter 12). Both systems contain the same principal mechanisms, but differ in two aspects. IPC controls the more polluting processes and is intended to prevent or minimise pollution of any environmental medium, whereas APC solely controls atmospheric releases from the less polluting processes.

The system of integrated pollution control works on the principle that to carry out a scheduled process without an authorisation from HMIP is a criminal offence. Secondly, when granting an authorisation, various statutory objectives are required to be met before such an authorisation can be granted. Lastly, the scope of control is wide. When assessing an application for an authorisation in relation to the more polluting (and potentially more damaging) processes, account has to be taken of emission to all three media when calculating the effect of a process upon the environment as a whole.

Organisation and administration of the system of integrated pollution control

The legislation controlling integrated pollution control is contained in Part I of the EPA 1990. The EPA 1990 is something of a lawyers' paradise in that it is only a framework which requires regulations to be passed to fill out various areas of the primary legislation. The reasons for this have more to do with the need for flexibility in controlling environmental matters than any desire to avoid responsibility within the main Act. It is possible to pass new regulations quickly and this allows for new research into environmental problems to be taken into account when assessing what particular matters ought to fall under the control of the framework legislation. The power to make regulations has been used to amend the scope of control significantly at least three times since the implementation of the EPA 1990.

Thus, the EPA 1990 itself forms only a small part of the controlling legislation. There are further statutory controls under the Environmental Protection (Prescribed Processes and Substances) Regulations 1991 (SI 1991 No. 472 as amended), the Environmental Protection (Applications, Appeals and Registers) Regulations 1991 (SI 1991 No. 507) and the Environmental Protection (Authorisation of Processes) (Determination Periods) Order 1991 (SI 1991 No. 513). Furthermore, there is a system of guidance notes issued by HMIP, providing detailed guidance processes which are covered under the regime.

The system of integrated pollution control is administered centrally by HMIP (EPA 1990, s. 4(2)). It is referred to in the Act as 'the enforcing authority'. A similar system, which relates solely to the control of emissions into the atmosphere from less polluting processes, is controlled by local authorities under the air pollution control regime (see Chapter 13).

The Department of the Environment has stated that the main objectives of integrated pollution control (IPC) are two-fold:

(a) to prevent or minimise the release of prescribed substances and to render harmless any such substances which are released;

(b) to develop an approach to pollution control that considers discharges from industrial processes to all media in the context of the effect on the environment as a whole.

Additionally, the system aims to improve the administrative structure of pollution control by clarifying the functions and responsibilities of HMIP and other statutory bodies and by providing 'one-stop shopping' for those carrying out the most environmentally damaging processes. It is also hoped that the system will improve public accountability by making the relevant enforcement body easily indentifiable, removing doubts as to who is doing what, and by making it possible to obtain information quickly and simply. Finally, it is hoped that the system will allow a certain degree of flexibility in allowing alterations to be made to the scientific methods of abatement where new information is received, both in respect of abatement technology and in respect of the effect of pollutants. Account can also be taken of new emission standards, whether imposed by the EC or on a more international scale (EPA 1990, s. 7).

The requirement for authorisation

The IPC system applies to any process carried out in England and Wales which has been prescribed as being subject to such control by the Secretary of State (EPA 1990, s. 2(1)). The Secretary of State has exercised this power under the Environmental Protection (Prescribed Processes and Substances) Regulations 1991 (SI 1991 No. 472). These Regulations include a list of processes and substances which are controlled either under the IPC system or the air pollution control system. Accordingly the regulations split processes and substances into two parts, Part A and Part B. Part A processes are prescribed for IPC. Part B processes are prescribed for local authority air pollution control (APC) which, although governed by similar principles, has different detailed guidance (see Chapter 12).

Approximately 5,000 installations are regulated in respect of solid, liquid and gaseous wastes under IPC, whereas roughly 27,000 are subject to control purely in respect of the emissions to the atmosphere by local authority environmental health departments. Whether a process is controlled under the system depends on whether it is a process contained in the schedule of prescribed processes in addition to whether or not it is likely to release certain prescribed substances into specified media.

Determination of the need for an authorisation

Unlike the Town and Country Planning Act, there is no formal mechanism for determining whether or not a process falls within the terms of the Regulations. Furthermore, there is no discretion as to whether or not HMIP can extend the categories in the Regulations to include extraordinary processes. Therefore, where there is uncertainty, the only mechanism for clarifying the position is to apply for a declaration in the High Court. In certain instances the Regulations which define prescribed processes and substances have been extended (see the Environmental Protection (Prescribed Processes and Substances) (Amendment) Regulations 1992 (SI 1992 No. 614)). Other difficulties of interpretation are dealt with in specific IPC Notes and General Guidance Notes issued by HMIP.

Clearly, one of the main difficulties with seeking to avoid making an application for a prescribed process which does not fall within any definition as specified in the Regulations is that there is a risk of prosecution. For most operators that risk will be too great and it will be more appropriate to agree with HMIP the scope of the description of the process.

Prescribed processes

Schedule 1 to the Regulations contains a list of the prescribed processes. This list is split into six main chapters outlining various areas of industry. These areas are:

(a)   the fuel and power industry;
(b)   the chemical industry;
(c)   the minerals industry;
(d)   the metal industry;
(e)   the waste disposal industry; and
(f)   miscellaneous industry.

Within these six different headings the processes are further split into those processes likely to cause greater pollution, contained in Part A, and those more suitable for Part B control. Each individual industry grouping also has subsections.

Fuel and power industry
Gasification processes, carbonisation processes, combustion processes and petroleum processes.

Chemical industry
Petrochemical processes, organic processes, chemical pesticide processes, pharmaceutical processes, acid manufacturing processes, halogen processes, chemical fertilizer processes, bulk chemical storage processes and inorganic chemical processes.

Minerals industry
Cement processes, asbestos processes, fibre processes and ceramic processes.

Metal industry
Iron and steel processes, smelting processes and non-ferrous processes.

Waste disposal industry
Incineration processes, chemical recovery processes and waste-derived fuel processes.

Miscellaneous industry
Paper manufacturing processes, di-isocyanate processes, tar and bitumen processes, uranium processes, coating processes, coating manufacturing processes, timber processes, animal and plant treatment processes.

All in all, approximately 105 processes covering some 5,000 different installations are covered under Part A of the Regulations. Essentially, the list of processes extends the previous list regulated under the Health and Safety at Work etc. Act 1974 by including processes which give rise to significant quantities of special waste and processes which give rise to the emission into sewers or controlled waters of Red List substances, which have a particularly damaging effect on the environment.

Meaning of process

Industrial processes are often made up of many individual component parts but, in terms of the integrated pollution control system, a process is defined in relation to the operator and the location. So, where there are a number of processes falling within the same class in sch. 1, only one authorisation will be required if there is only one person operating the process. Where there is an overlap between the control of Part A processes and Part B processes, then the Part A processes will take precedence. Thus, where a small element of the process is subject to APC and one element is subject to IPC, HMIP will govern the whole of the process and only one authorisation will be required. Where the processes fall into different categories under sch. 1, different authorisations will be required. Thus, a process involving bulk chemical storage and chemical recovery requires two authorisations. However, it could be possible for one process to fall within Part A whilst another process is within Part B of a different class. In that particular situation, responsibility for each process would fall to different controlling authorities.

The authorisations themselves cover all operations relating to the main process itself. Therefore, where the production of waste from the main operation is incidental to the overall operation of a plant, that would not necessarily fall within the waste disposal class under sch. 1.

The Government has amended the detailed provisions on the scope of Part A and B processes as part of the deregulatory thrust. In the first set of amendments set down in 1994, eight processes were brought within control for the first time, whilst a number were 'demoted' from IPC to LAAPC. Perhaps the most significant change, however, was the alteration of some of the thresholds which took certain processes outside control (see p. 341). Further amendments to the regulations were proposed in June 1995, with deregulation being the aim yet again. In particular the definition of the 'triviality' exemption (see p. 298) in relation to specific levels of releases will exclude many processes in the pulp and paper and leather industries.

Release of prescribed substances

Alongside the regulations controlling individual processes there are also controls over the release of prescribed substances. Often, the release of prescribed substances will be an integral part of the process controlled. However, specific obligations fall upon operators to deal with the listed substances in a particular way. Schedules 4, 5 and 6 of the Regulations lay down those substances which are controlled in this way.

Schedule 4—Releases into the air
The substances listed under sch. 4 are subject to control not only under IPC but also under APC. They are:

Oxides of sulphur and other sulphur compounds.
Oxides of nitrogen and other nitrogen compounds.
Oxides of carbon.
Organic compounds and partial oxidation products.
Metals, metalloids and their compounds.
Asbestos (suspended particulate matter and fibres), glass fibres and mineral fibres.
Halogens and their compounds.
Phosphorus and its compounds.
Particulate matter.

Schedule 5—Releases into water
This list reflects the Red List, which governs the input of substances which are a danger. The following are listed:

Mercury and its compounds.
Cadmium and its compounds.
All isomers of hexachlorocyclohexane.
All isomers of DDT.
Pentachlorophenol and its compounds.
Hexachlorobenzene.
Hexachlorobutadiene.
Aldrin.
Dieldrin.
Endrin.
Polychlorinated biphenyls (PCBs).
Dichlorvos.
1, 2-Dichloroethane.
All isomers of trichlorobenzene.
Atrazine.
Simazine.
Tributyltin.
Triphenyltin.
Trifluralin.
Fenitrothion.
Azinphos-methyl.
Malathion.
Endosulfan.

Schedule 6—Releases to land
The following substances are listed in sch. 6:

Organic solvents.
Azides.
Halogens and their covalent compounds.
Metal carbonyls.
Organo metallic compounds.
Oxidising agents.
Polychlorinated dibenzofuran and any congener thereof.
Polychlorinated dibenzo-p-dioxin and any other congener thereof.
Polyhalogenated biphenyls, terphenyls and naphthalenes.
Phosphorus.
Pesticides.
Alkali metals and their oxides and alkaline earth materials and their oxides.

Exceptions

As in many similar environmental control regulations there are exceptions to the general rule that processes in Part A are to be controlled under the IPC system. Regulation 4 and sch. 2 give a list of creiteria for exemptions. A process is exempted if:

(a)   it cannot result in emissions to air of a substance contained in sch. 4 or, if there are such emissions, the release of those substances to cause any harm as it is in such trivial amounts;

(b)   it cannot result in any discharges to water of any substance listed in sch. 5 beyond background concentration;

(c)   it cannot result in any substance listed in sch. 6 being released into land, or if such substances are released they are released in such trivial amounts that the release cannot do any harm.

There is no statutory definition of the term 'trivial', although the thresholds set down in the process regulations can specify concentrations which are to be regarded as 'trivial'. The burden of proving that the release is trivial lies, in effect, with the applicant as the burden of demonstrating that an exception applies in any subsequent prosecution lies with the operator (see *Tandridge DC* v *P&S Civil Engineering Ltd* [1995] Env LR 67).

Other processes excluded include those carried out in:

(a)   working museums demonstrating an industrial process of historic interest, or a school (reg. 4(3));

(b)   certain engines powering aircraft, ships, trains and cars (reg. 4(4));

(c)   those processes carried out as domestic activities in connection with private dwelling.

Notwithstanding these exceptions, if the process gives rise to an offensive smell noticeable outside the premises where the process is carried on then it will be subject to control under Part I.

Overlapping controls

The deposit of controlled waste

Section 28(1) of the EPA 1990 provides that no condition may be attached to an authorisation which regulates the final disposal by deposit in or on land of controlled waste. There is a greater degree of uncertainty, however, over the overlapping responsibilities where waste is treated or kept. The Secretary of State has the power to draw up regulations excluding the deposit, treatment or keeping of waste from the need for a waste management licence under Part II of the Act (s. 33(3)). Under the Waste Management Licensing Regulations 1994 (SI 1994 No. 1056), two main categories of processes are excluded from the waste management regime. Regulation 16(1)(a) excludes any recovery or disposal of waste where it forms part of an IPC process (although s. 28(1) still applies to the final deposit of waste). In addition, reg. 16(1)(b) excludes waste incineration which falls within LAAPC. This exclusion applies only to the parts of the process which are controlled under LAAPC (i.e. the release of prescribed substances to the atmosphere) and does not cover other aspects of the process (including storage and handling of waste).

The pollution of controlled waters

Where an authorisation covers the discharge of substances to water, the control of such a process remains with HMIP. Section 88 of the Water Resources Act 1991, provides that any discharges made in compliance with that authorisation would not amount to an offence under s. 85. In other words, there is no need to obtain a discharge consent from the NRA. There are a number of caveats to this recentralisation of control to HMIP. First, the NRA has the power to certify that in its opinion the release of substances into controlled waters from any process will result in, or contribute to, a failure to achieve any water quality objective set under the Water Resources Act 1991 (s. 28(3)(a)). In such circumstances, HMIP is not allowed to grant an authorisation. Secondly, the NRA is entitled to notify HMIP in writing as to appropriate conditions to appear in the authorisation (s. 28(3)(b)), and finally, the NRA can write to HMIP requiring it to issue a variation notice (s. 28(4)) (see further p. 445).

The discharge of effluent into sewers

Part I of EPA 1990 applies to the discharge of trade effluent. Thus, where effluent is produced as part of a prescribed process an IPC authorisation will specify conditions relating to discharges to sewers. There is an overlap in the controls in that consent is also required from the sewerage undertaker for a discharge consent under s. 118 of the Water Industry Act 1991. Such a consent would cover the volume, composition, temperature of the discharge in addition to setting out the consent fee (see p. 465).

Statutory nuisance

Where a local authority wishes to initiate its statutory nuisance powers in relation to a prescribed process it must first obtain the Secretary of State's consent (s. 10). This power applies only in relation to smoke emitted from premises, dust, steam, smell or other effluvia arising on industrial, trade or business premises, or any accumulation or deposit.

Planning permission

There is no reference to the overlap between the planning system and IPC. There is no obligation on an operator to obtain a planning permission for any development associated with a new or altered process prior to authorisation under Part I of the EPA 1990 (the reverse is also true). PPG 23 on Planning and Pollution Control recommends that both applications are submitted together. There are, of course, inherent dangers of applying for any one before the other as different considerations are taken into account when determining each application. An illustration of the problems was seen in the case of the Point of Ayr gas terminal in North Wales. Planning permission was granted for the project after a public inquiry in 1992. When the IPC application was lodged (on the basis of the location of plant which had received planning permission) in 1994 the application was refused by HMIP as the process did not represent BATNEEC. This led to a fresh application with changes to plant design at a reported cost of several million pounds (see *ENDS Report* 245 at p. 13 and 246 at p. 7).

It is quite normal for a planning application to be submitted along with a staged application for an IPC application (see p. 302). When dealing with the planning application, local authorities are advised to consider only the land-use implications of the development. This leads to the question of the nature of 'land-use' implications. The courts have examined the nature of the overlap between planning and pollution control in *Gateshead MBC v Secretary of State for the Environment and Northumbrian Water Group* [1995] Env LR 37. In that case the Secretary of State granted planning permission for a clinical waste incinerator in the north-east. The inspector appointed to hear the appeal recommended that permission be refused. One of the issues which was taken into account by the inspector was the public fear that pollution from the site would be unacceptable. The Secretary of State concluded that the issue could be satisfactorily addressed as part of the IPC application and granted planning permission. That decision was challenged by the local planning authority on the basis that the two systems were so closely inter-linked that it was unreasonable to grant planning permission without knowing if emissions could be adequately controlled under the IPC system. In the High Court, Sullivan J decided that although the two statutory regimes overlapped, the extent of the overlap would vary on every occasion. It was envisaged that there would be a whole range of cases, from those where environmental considerations could be dealt with adequately under the IPC system to those where environmental considerations could not be overcome by the mere grant of an authorisation. The correct legal test was whether or not it was reasonable in the *Wednesbury* sense to arrive at the decision reached by the decision-maker. On appeal, the Court of Appeal affirmed this decision with only a slight variation of judgment. The issue of whether there was an unacceptable risk was, in the court's view, a matter for HMIP and the fact that the public had expressed concern about the issue was not conclusive. The court went on to say, however, that the fact that planning permission had been granted should not be viewed as a restriction upon HMIP's discretion to refuse the application for IPC authorisation if it thought fit to do so. Thus, the courts have affirmed the Government's implicit view as contained in PPG 23 that there is no definite dividing line between planning and IPC applications, and that each decision-maker is entitled to arrive at different conclusions if it exercises its discretion reasonably.

Transitional controls

As the IPC system is being phased in over a five-year period, some intricate Parliamentary drafting covers the transitional arrangements. In appropriate cases, the Clean Air Act, Health & Safety at Work etc. Act 1974 and the Alkali Etc. Works Regulation Act 1906 are being progressively repealed. As an authorisation is granted, refused or determined on appeal, controls under the appropriate Act will cease (EPA 1990, sch. 15).

Applications for authorisation

When IPC governs a prescribed process an authorisation has to be obtained from HMIP before that process can be carried out (EPA 1990, s. 6(1)). To carry out a process without authorisation is a criminal offence (s. 23(1)). Thus, the first step in the IPC procedure is to apply for an authorisation.

The Environmental Protection (Applications, Appeals and Registers) Regulations 1991 (SI 1991 No. 507) lay down the procedure for an application. Regulation 2 prescribes the information required by HMIP. Clearly, certain authorisations can be very complicated and a great deal of information is required. This information includes:

(a) The name, address and telephone number of the applicant.

(b) A map of the area within which the process is to be located, with indications of the exact location of the process, the name of the local authority, and the address of the location of the prescribed process.

(c) A proper description of the process, including such information as relates to the concept of BATNEEC (as to which, see below). This is wider than the information required under the BPM tests and the techniques employed must be described fully.

(d) Where there is a prescribed substance involved in the process, information regarding the quantity and nature of the releases and also whether or not raw materials are used in the process itself.

(e) Where techniques are used to prevent or minimise the release of prescribed substances, or such substances are rendered harmless, a full description of the methods used. There should be information as to how waste will be discharged.

(f) A detailed assessment of the environmental implications of the process. This has to be carried out specifically in relation to the BPEO. It does not have to be a definitive description of the environmental effects but rather an assessment of the environmental impact on a local, regional or global basis and, alongside this, there has to be a justification of the process used in an attempt to balance the harm caused by a process with the techniques used.

(g) Information regarding the monitoring of the released substances.

Where HMIP wishes to impose additional conditions but does not have sufficient information to enable itself to do so, it may ask the applicant to furnish such information as is necessary. If that information is not forthcoming, EPA 1990, sch. 1, para. 1(3) allows HMIP to give notice in writing to the operator of the requirement to give any further information within a specified period so that the application can be determined properly.

A number of changes have been proposed to the application procedure. A consultation paper was issued in August 1994 which set out a number of minor amendments to the existing regulations. The most significant change which it proposed is that where an application is submitted for a variation to an existing process which results in 'environmental gains or a reduction in the environmental impact of the process' there would be no requirement to advertise or consult with the public. This, of course, begs a number of questions about the judgment of 'environmental gains', as it could be either a marginal gain or a gain made at the expense of some other environmental 'loss'. Other changes would include the ability to withdraw information from the register when an application was withdrawn, the disclosure of information on parent companies and an increase in the requirement to advertise applications.

The application form

The only requirement for a valid application in relation to its form is that it be made in writing. There is, however, an application form available from HMIP, which is a short document dealing with the relevant names and addresses of the applicant and the prescribed processes, the application fee, and details of the bodies who may be statutory consultees. Lastly, there is a section which deals with applications for confidentiality.

Additional information

The official application form provided by HMIP deals with only a small proportion of the information which is necessary for an application to be determined properly. The vast majority of the information prescribed under the Regulations relates to technical information and is usually provided in separate documentation. Although there is no formal requirement to present the information in a particular way, HMIP has suggested that applications can be dealt with swiftly and properly where the technical detail is structured by focusing on the detailed description of the process, the abatement techniques utilised and the environmental effects of the prescribed releases.

Special cases

Although generally the procedure for making an application is the same for every process, there is a number of exceptions to the rule which were either introduced at the outset of the system or have evolved since its inception as a result of unforeseen difficulties.

Staged applications

The development of industrial sites for new and particularly complicated processes inevitably takes many years. Often proposals develop over time and a variety of changes can be made to the plans. In these cases, HMIP can agree to a staged application procedure whereby the applicant submits the application for authorisation over an agreed period of time so that there is a degree of flexibility.

Where such a phasing has been agreed it is normal for the applicant to submit an outline of the process design as an initial step. Once this step is complete the application will not be determined within the usual period. Instead, an agreed timetable will be adhered to in which the operator submits details of the process during the design, construction and commissioning stages.

Clearly, the advantage of such an approach from the operator's point of view is that it enables HMIP's suggestions for improvements to be made at the design stage so that they can be incorporated in the final proposal.

Aside from the timing of the application all normal procedures will be followed, including publication, consultation and the payment of a fee. There will, however, be a final determination only when it is agreed that such a determination will be appropriate—usually at the commissioning stage.

Envelope applications

The particular operational requirements of the chemicals industry have led to a change in accepted procedures where the process involves either a pilot plant or a facility for manufacturing products under contract. Normally, there is a four-month time limit for issuing an authorisation for a process, although this may be increased by agreement between the parties. This suggests that there would be tremendous difficulties for chemical operators in particular, where they were producing chemicals in response to a particular demand at a particular time. Furthermore, many manufacturers produce small scale runs of products when trying to assess the commercial viability of a particular product. Where operators were obliged to apply for new authorisations every time they received a new contract or carried out a trial, there would not be sufficient time under the normal procedure for the application to be processed. Thus, HMIP introduced the concept of the envelope authorisation procedure.

For contract operations the envelope application will define the areas of processes which can be carried out before a further authorisation would be required. Essentially, the opportunity is given to applicants to demonstrate that they are competent to deal with a wide range of activities within a single authorisation.

Once the boundary of the envelope has been determined it is still possible to manufacture products outside the envelope by submitting an application for a 'non-substantial variation'. This non-substantial variation is not a full application but would normally be processed relatively quickly so long as it fell within a band of the same or similar processes as those contained within the envelope.

For pilot plants, however, there is a much wider regime. As the processes involved are relatively small-scale the environmental impact is also likely to be small. Therefore, an envelope authorisation for a pilot plant can be much broader. Normally, once an envelope authorisation has been granted it will be necessary only to give HMIP seven days' notice of a new project. This procedure will be followed unless the trial is likely to result in the previously agreed envelope limits being exceeded or new processes being utilised.

Complex sites

Although many sites will feature the use of specific waste treatment facilities, there are complex industrial sites where a number of processes may feed into common effluent and/or other abatement facilities. These processes raise difficulties where the processes are of a different nature, some of which may fall within the IPC regime, some of which may not; and even where all the processes are covered by IPC they may come within IPC at different times. HMIP has responded to such complicated situations by introducing the concept of 'ring fencing'. The idea of ring fencing is to separate each individual process into artificial 'ring fenced' areas. An application for the processes within each ring fence will be determined separately and on the basis of the release of prescribed processes from the particular process to the common treatment plant. As new processes come within IPC they will all be controlled separately and the limits on the effluent from each process will be dealt with by means of individual authorisations.

When all the processes which feed into the effluent treatment plant have been dealt with by HMIP, a unified authorisation can then be considered.

Fees

A valid application has to be accompanied by the appropriate fee (s. 6(2)). Section 8 of the EPA 1990 makes provision for a statutory charging scheme to be introduced to recover the administrative costs of operating IPC. The scheme is a statutory scheme although it is not made under regulations.

The charges scheme operates on three levels:

(a)   An application fee—this is specifically linked to the costs of processing particular applications.

(b)   An annual subsistence charge, which covers the annual maintenance of an authorisation, including monitoring, inspection charges and enforcement.

(c)   A substantial variation fee—this is levied at a different level to the annual fee and covers the costs of considering an application for a substantial variation of an existing authorisation.

The charges are levied on a component basis. Therefore, there is a flat rate which is multiplied by the number of components in each process. The definition of 'component' is different for each individual process and is contained in an appendix to the charging scheme.

Fee levels
Fee levels are set annually and take effect from 1 April in each year.

The level of fees has risen by almost 100% in the last three years as a direct result of underestimating the costs of administering the system. Therefore, applications submitted in the early years have an additional charge which is intended to recoup the shortfall of income in that period.

Where there has been a mis-calculation as to the amount of fees required, there is provision to enable HMIP to send a further invoice to the applicant. If there has been an over-payment this will be refunded.

Where an application is not accompanied by the appropriate fee, or a fee has not been paid within 28 days of being invoiced, HMIP has a discretion to decline to consider the application and cannot issue the authorisation.

Where the subsistence charge is not paid it is open to HMIP to revoke the authorisation or take other enforcement action (s. 8(8)).

Although the charging mechanism has always been seen as a method of raising revenue which contributed to the running costs of HMIP (indeed HMIP is under a statutory duty to recover costs), it has traditionally been spread equally between all operators. HMIP has investigated the use of different charging mechanisms (for the annual subsistence fee) in seeking to make the operators of more polluting processes pay proportionately more by way of charges. HMIP announced a major review of the charging system in the light of the introduction of the Environment Agency with the aim of introducing any new system in 1997.

HMIP has put forward five basic models of charging with alternative suggestions (to the present system of charging per component) based upon risk assessment (see OPRA below), level of emissions (taken from the Chemical Release inventory) and charging only for time spent and materials used in policing the process.

The Operator and Pollution Risk Appraisal (OPRA) scheme has been through a pilot scheme and will probably be introduced in 1996/7 (although it is only one of the options to be considered for the new charging scheme). The scheme is intended to provide an objective method of assessing the pollution risk posed by a process. Those processes with lower OPRA ratings could receive less inspection visits from HMIP and could consequently be expected to pay lower subsistence fees. More importantly, there would be an incentive for operators to reduce the OPRA rating which applied to their process and receive the benefit of lower fees.

Public participation and other consultation procedures

The right of the public to be notified of environmentally harmful processes has been virtually non-existent in the past. This has been altered under the Environmental Protection (Applications, Appeals and Registers) Regulations 1991 (SI 1991 No. 507). Regulation 5 obliges the operator of a process to advertise all applications for authorisation and all variations of an authorisation involving a substantial change. This advert has to be published in a local newspaper circulating in the area in which the process is to be operated, and must contain details including:

(a)   the name and address of the applicant and the premises where the process is carried on;

(b)   a description of the process;

(c)   the availability of information on the registers and where those registers can be inspected;

(d)   an invitation for representations to be made within 28 days to HMIP.

This advertisement has to appear between 14 and 42 days after the application was made or the day on which the variation notice was served upon the applicant.

Other consultees are given the right to make representations under reg. 4. The list of consultees reflects the many impacts that a process may have upon different areas not only of the environment but also the workplace. The bodies entitled to be consulted include:

(a) the Health and Safety Executive, specifically in relation to the health and safety at work of people involved in the process;
(b) the National Rivers Authority in relation to any process which may result in the release of any substance into controlled waters;
(c) water services companies or any other sewerage undertaker, in relation to the release of any substance into a sewer;
(d) the Minister of Agriculture, Fisheries and Food;
(e) the relevant Nature Conservancy Council, in relation to the release of a substance which may affect a site of special scientific interest;
(f) a harbour authority, in relation to the release of any substance into a harbour;
(g) Local authorities, particlarly in relation to conditions to be imposed which have an impact on air quality management plans under the Environment Act 1995 (see p. 328).

These statutory consultees are entitled to notification within 14 days of receipt of an application for authorisation or variation (EPA 1990, sch. 1). They are then allowed to make representations within 28 days, and any representations made have to be taken into account as a consideration when deciding an application.

Where an application does not contain commercially confidential information, the Environmental Protection (Authorisation of Processes) (Determination Periods) Order 1991 (SI 1991 No. 513) provides that there is a four-month period for determining applications, beginning with the date of receipt (see also EPA 1990, sch. 1, paras. 5(1) and (3)). This time limit can be extended by agreement between the applicant and the enforcing authority.

Call-in procedure

As with an application for planning permission, the Secretary of State has the ability to 'call in' an application for an authorisation, thus ousting the jurisdiction of the enforcing authority (EPA 1990, sch. 3, para. 3(1)). This power can be exercised at the discretion of the Secretary of State. However, it is probable that this power will only be used for particularly sensitive applications, applications of local or national importance, or applications which arouse a great deal of public interest.

When an application is called in, the Secretary of State has no power to grant the authorisation, but instead must direct the enforcing authority as to whether to grant the application and, if so, as to the conditions which are to be attached (sch. 1, para. 3(5)). The manner by which the Secretary of State decides such an issue may be by public local inquiry or by means of informal hearings.

Commercial confidentiality and national security

In normal circumstances, the EPA 1990 seeks to allow free public access to information regarding an application for an authorisation. However, there are exceptions to this on the ground of commercial confidentiality and in relation to issues affecting national security. Where an applicant believes that any information contained within an application should be restricted, then an application may be made under ss. 21 and 22 to exclude such information from the public registers. This application is included along with the information relating to the authorisation, and HMIP (in relation to IPC) has to determine whether or not such information is commercially confidential (s. 22(2)(a)).

In the case of information relating to national security, the only criterion is that the Secretary of State has to be of the opinion that the inclusion in the register of that information would be contrary to the interests of national security. On commercial confidentiality grounds, the enforcing authority have 14 days in which to determine whether the information is commercially confidential and, if they fail to make a determination, it is deemed to be treated as such (s. 22(3)). Where the enforcing authority determine that the information is not commercially confidential, they must not enter such information on the register for 21 days so as to allow an applicant to appeal against the decision to the Secretary of State (s. 22(5)). Pending any appeal, the information is also excluded from the register.

The determination of an application

Once HMIP has received all representations, it is entitled to grant the authorisation, subject to any conditions required, or to refuse it (s. 6(3)). It is under a duty to refuse an authorisation if it is of the view that an applicant would be unable to carry on the process in compliance with any conditions which would be included in an authorisation (EPA 1990, s. 6(4)). Other grounds for refusal are if information required under the Environmental Protection (Applications, Appeals and Registers) Regulations 1991 (SI 1991 No. 507) was not supplied, or the proper fee had not accompanied the application. There is a residual power available to the Secretary of State under s. 6(5) to direct the enforcing authority either to grant or to refuse the authorisation.

In considering whether or not to grant an authorisation, there are a number of statutory objectives which have to be taken into account (s. 7). This section has introduced a new concept into environmental control within Britain of taking a proactive environmental quality approach to emissions to the environment as a whole. The statutory objectives have to be achieved in every authorisation and most of the conditions in an authorisation will relate to them. These objectives are contained in s. 7(2) and are:

(a)   ensuring that, in carrying on a prescribed process, the best available techniques not entailing excessive cost (BATNEEC) will be used:

(i)   for preventing the release of substances prescribed for any environmental medium into that medium or, where that is not practicable by such means, for reducing the release of such substances to a minimum and for rendering harmless any such substances which are so released; and

(ii)   for rendering harmless any other substances which might cause harm if released into any environmental medium;

(b)   compliance with any directions by the Secretary of State given for the implementation of any obligations of the United Kingdom under EC Treaties or international law relating to environmental protection;

(c)   compliance with any limits or requirements and achievement of any quality standards or quality objectives prescribed by the Secretary of State under any of the relevant enactments;

(d)   compliance with any requirements applicable to the grant of authorisations specified by or under a statutory plan made by the Secretary of State under s. 3(5) of the EPA 1990.

Section 7(1) provides for three different types of conditions which may be included in an authorisation:

(a)   Conditions to meet the statutory objectives as laid down in s. 7(2).
(b)   Conditions imposed by the Secretary of State under s. 7(3).
(c)   Any other appropriate conditions.

There is also a general implied condition that a process will be carried on using BATNEEC. Additionally, s. 7(7) specifically provides, in relation to IPC processes involving the release of substances into more than one environmental medium, that BATNEEC will be used for minimising the pollution which may be caused to the environment taken as a whole by the releases, having regard to the best practicable environmental option (BPEO) available in respect of the substances which may be released. Thus, the dual concepts of BATNEEC and BPEO are incorporated into the statutory objectives of Part I as far as IPC is concerned.

BATNEEC

All of the processes controlled by HMIP under IPC are subject to the requirement of BATNEEC. BATNEEC is to be applied specifically to each individual process taking into account various individual problems on a case by case basis. The concept of BATNEEC is somewhat wider than the traditional BPM model in that it includes not only the technical means and technology of pollution abatement, but also the number, qualifications, training and supervision of persons employed in the process, in addition to the design, construction, lay-out and maintenance of the buildings in which it is carried on (s. 7(10)). Thus, the umbrella of the control mechanisms covers a whole range of subjects which need to be taken into account on a strategic level.

'Best available techniques'

By way of further guidance as to the meaning of the phrase, the Department of the Environment's guide to IPC states that 'available' should be taken to mean procurable by the operator of the process in question; this does not imply that the technique is in general use, but it does require general accessibility. It includes a technique which has been developed (or proven) at a scale which allows its implementation in the relevant industrial context with the necessary business confidence. It does not imply that sources outside Britain are 'unavailable'. Nor does it imply a competitive supply market; if there is a monopoly supplier, the technique counts as being available provided that the operator can procure it.

This would suggest that the use of easily available abatement equipment would not necessarily satisfy the criteria. Efforts may need to be made to investigate other avenues of technology. 'Best' is defined in relation to the effectiveness of the techniques in minimising, preventing or rendering harmless noxious emissions. 'Best' is not an absolute term and it has been indicated that there may well be a number of different techniques which qualify under this particular word.

The statutory terms are deliberately vague in an attempt to import some flexibility into the decision-making process. There is, however, supplementary guidance contained in the IPC notes. Unfortunately, there has been very little indication of HMIP's (or perhaps more importantly, the Secretary of State's views) on the meaning of 'BAT' other than the guidance set out in the IPC notes that there have been very few refusals of authorisations or enforcement notices and therefore few consequent appeals in which policy could be clarified. The first batch of contentious appeals related mainly to the postponement of upgrading requirements to allow ageing equipment to last until the process was abandoned. The first widely reported decision on the issue, however, does clarify certain aspects of the 'BAT' principle (although it concerned a process which was controlled under the LAAPC system, little turns on the point).

Operators of a foundry in Yorkshire were served with an enforcement notice as emission levels for particulates from the process were unacceptably high. The notice required the installation of modern abatement equipment before the time limit for other operators of similar plant. The operators appealed on the basis that the equipment was not 'available' as it was being used only on a trial basis in the UK notwithstanding the fact that it was being used extensively throughout the world.

On appeal the inspector decided that the installation of the equipment would not entail excessive cost and that it would satisfy all the elements of the 'BAT' test, bar one. As there was a residual risk that the equipment would cause a fire when used under UK conditions the inspector decided that it was not truly 'available'. The Secretary of State accepted his Inspector's recommendations and upheld the appeal. Although the decision has no binding effect, it would seem as if the term 'available' could take on a more parochial meaning in circumstances where local conditions might differ from the world market.

The DoE is keenly aware that people within industry are particularly concerned that the meaning of BATNEEC should have a clearer definition than that contained in the Act. Overall, the onus is on an applicant to supply a system which properly and effectively deals with emissions so that they minimise the harm caused to the environment as a whole. It need not be the most up-to-date equipment, but it certainly requires an attempt to demonstrate that the particular system used is effective and that there are no more effective methods of dealing with the waste products of an industrial process.

'Not entailing excessive cost'

However, as pointed out earlier, there is always the need to balance one part of the BATNEEC requirement against the other. Thus, if the cost of a particular technique is excessive then, even though it might be the 'best available technique', it need not necessarily become a condition of any authorisation that that technique be used. There are, however, different considerations to take into account, depending on whether a process is an existing process or a new process.

Clearly, where there is an existing process to update, account needs to be taken of the financial consequences of introducing new equipment. Therefore, it is anticipated that the introduction of new plant and equipment will be phased-in over a number of years. Thus, the cost of upgrading environmental plant will be spread over a number of years so that the two balancing factors of 'best available techniques' and 'not entailing excessive cost' can be taken into account.

Although it is clear that some account has to be taken of economic factors, what is yet to be determined is the extent to which the costs will be allowed to tip the balance. There has been comment made that those who cannot afford to equip their factories with up-to-date plant and machinery should not be allowed to carry out operations which could contaminate the environment. It is this unknown factor which could mean that the concept of BATNEEC will be much harsher than that of the traditional best practicable means. Certainly, with new processes, applicants will be required to show that there has been a cost/benefit analysis to show that whatever they are claiming to be excessive in a financial and economic sense is excessive by objective criteria in relation to the pollution caused.

HMIP has made available its internal guidance notes which form part of the Inspectorate's Manual on IPC. These have made it clear that when issuing authorisations they will be viewing an application in terms of a process standard rather than purely looking at the emission levels. Operators will have to demonstrate the options that they have considered when selecting the best available techniques. However, they have pointed out that in a situation where the best technique is not put forward, the applicant must be able to justify the technique on the grounds that the selection of another option would involve entailing excessive cost. The note stresses the onus is on the operator to:

describe excessive cost in absolute terms without reference to the cost of the product. The applicant must be able to demonstrate that the increased cost of the product produced by the best available technique is grossly disproportionate to any environmental benefit likely to accrue from that method of production. The extra cost must represent a significant fraction of the cost of the finished product.

Additionally, HMIP may be able to relax the BATNEEC requirements where substances are released and are to be rendered harmless. The note goes on to say that the process standard for new processes will be different to that for existing plant. Geographical effects, such as the volume of water carrying away effluent, could affect whether something is BATNEEC in one place but not in another.

However, the guidance is different for the prevention or minimisation of releases of prescribed substances. In those circumstances no account is to be taken of the absolute value of any local environmental effects of the releases.

There are, however, to be different considerations when dealing with existing plant. It is stressed that existing processes will have to be upgraded to the BATNEEC standards applicable to new plant within four years of the original date of authorisation. There may be allowable derogations from this period, but HMIP has stated that these may not be allowed for more than four years. The tone of the new guidance is that HMIP will certainly be looking towards the upgrading of existing plant with as much severity as the implementation of new plant.

Best practicable environmental option
In addition to demonstrating that the process constitutes the BATNEEC, operators must demonstrate that it represents the 'best practicable environmental option' (BPEO). Section 7(7) of the EPA 1990 provides that where the process is subject to control by HMIP and results in the release of substances to more than one environmental medium the operator has to demonstrate that the BATNEEC is being used to minimise the release of substances to the environment *having regard* to the BPEO.

Although the Royal Commission on Environmental Pollution (RCEP) put forward a definition in its Report (see p. 289) there is no statutory definition and it has proved to be a particularly difficult concept to pin down in practice. Whilst a BPEO assessment has a number of similarities with a formal environmental assessment, it is the distinguishing features which make the concept of BPEO both wider and narrower than the assessment of a construction project. It is narrower in the sense that with a BPEO assessment there is only a requirement to assess the effects of releases of substances upon air, water and land. It is, however, wider in that there is a requirement to assess the availability and relative cost-benefit ratios of other process options which could be used to deal with the releases.

In a study carried out by the *ENDS Report* the vast majority of operators were found to have ignored other alternative process options and failed to have provided any data on the costs of other options when demonstrating that they were excessive. HMIP has issued draft guidance on carrying out a BPEO assessment in which there is an attempt to set down a framework for operators to assess the impact of a variety of process options. It includes advice on the selection of options, the assessment of environmental effects and a system for ranking the process options. The underlying concept for the assessment is based upon the assessment of each process option as a proportion of the environmental quality standard for particular substances. In the absence of an environmental quality standard for any particular substance HMIP would determine an environmental assessment level (EAL) which would act as the guideline. Many critics complained that the EALs were both arbitrary and imprecise. Although the basis of the methodology has been criticised, it is clear that the introduction of some formal guidance on the issue of carrying out a BPEO assessment is necessary in order for the concept to have any meaning. One of the critics of HMIP's approach, the RCEP has promised to look at the issue of BPEO in its next report (after dealing with soil protection). In particular, it will examine the underlying concept behind BPEO and the setting down of environmental quality standards, in an attempt to lay down some ground rules to underpin the comparison of different environmental options.

Integrated pollution control notes

In addition to the limited definition contained within the Act, an inspector determining an application for an authorisation must take into account the particular guidance note applicable to the class of process which is subject to the authorisation. The notes are supposed to provide a coherent context in which decisions can be made in relation to conditions to be imposed upon authorisations. Thus, all parties to an authorisation will know of the ground rules. The introduction of an element of certainty into the system increases both public accountability and also procedural fairness. As general guidance, the guidance note serves as a framework within which the details can be supplemented by scientific and technological advice from HMIP. The notes:

(a)   give the rationale behind the designation of the process for IPC;

(b)   state the environmental quality standards which are relevant to the process;

(c)   state HMIP's views as to the achievable standards;

(d)   describe a number of ways by which those standards can be reached;

(e)   give guidance as to what would amount to a substantial change and therefore require authorisation under the variation procedures.

The details contained within the guidance notes act as standards which new processes will have to meet. On the other hand, existing processes are given an appropriate timescale within which to achieve these standards. To ensure that each note represents the 'state of the art' they are to be reviewed at least every four years.

There are over 200 integrated pollution control notes and these obviously require a significant review of the existing guidance. Thus, in respect of applications made before any guidance is issued, there must be consultation with HMIP as to the standards required.

Implementation of the IPC system

IPC was introduced for new processes, substantial variations of existing processes, and large combustion plants on 1 April 1991. Other existing processes are to be introduced over a five-year period ending on 31 January 1996.

The introduction of a timetable for the implementation of IPC was a direct result of concern expressed over the ineffective implementation of the Control of Pollution Act 1974. Various amendments were proposed to the Environmental Protection Bill requiring implementation within a certain time period. In order to counter such suggestions an official timetable for the implementation of the system was introduced. (See sch. 3 Environmental Protection (Prescribed Processes and Substances) Regulations 1991 (SI 1991 No. 472.)

Transfer of authorisations

An authorisation is personal to an applicant/operator. However, it is possible to transfer an authorisation from one operator to another. Therefore, if a business has been sold, it is possible to transfer an existing authorisation to the new owner.

Section 9 of the EPA 1990 provides that the person to whom the authorisation is transferred must notify HMIP of the transfer within 21 days. This will allow HMIP to take into account any new considerations arising out of the transfer and provides an opportunity for variation notices to be served. Failure to notify HMIP of the transfer of an authorisation is an offence (EPA 1990, s. 23).

Enforcement powers

HMIP has probably the widest range of enforcement powers available to any of the environmental agencies. This includes a series of administrative sanctions such as enforcement, revocation and prohibition notices. This flexibility gives HMIP the scope to take action against a variety of breaches of legislation. This is evidenced by the fact that although the rate of prosecutions is low, with approximately 13–14 cases a year brought on average, there has been a widespread use of enforcement notices and other administrative mechanisms. The use of enforcement action is publicised heavily by HMIP, but the effect of its general enforcement policy is hard to discern, with public complaints about prescribed processes increasing (see further pp. 136–7). In particular, there are some doubts about the use of administrative sanctions as there are few indicators to demonstrate whether the enforcement notices served are complied with or to what extent they result in improvements.

Variation notices

The ability to vary an authorisation is not strictly an enforcement power when compared with, for example, enforcement and prohibition notices. However, the effect of a variation may be such that an operator would view it as having no practical distinction from an enforcement notice. The distinctive character of a variation notice relates more to the proactive approach rather than the punitive approach. Where new pollution abatement systems are introduced, or there is an understanding of new environmental dangers, then a variation notice can be served to bring operators 'uptodate' (s. 11). Indeed, the Chief Inspector of HMIP is under a statutory duty to follow developments in pollution abatement technology and techniques (EPA 1990, s. 4(9)).

Where HMIP considers that the conditions to which the authorisation originally applied have changed, it is under a duty under s. 10 of the Act to vary that authorisation. The variation notice specifies what type of variation is required and the date on which the variations have to take effect (s. 10(3)).

It is also open to the applicant to apply for a variation where plant is upgraded or replaced (EPA 1990, s. 11). Thus, s. 11 provides that an operator wishing to make a 'relevant change' can notify HMIP and ask for a determination:

(a)   whether the proposed change would involve a breach of any condition of the authorisation;

(b)   if it would not involve such a breach, whether the authority would be likely to vary the conditions of the authorisation as a result of the change;

(c)   if it would involve such a breach, whether the authority would consider varying the conditions of the authorisation so that the change may be made; and

(d)   whether the change would involve a substantial change in the manner in which the process is being carried on.

A relevant change in a prescribed process is defined as a 'change in the manner of carrying on the process which is capable of altering the substances released from the process or of affecting the amount or any other characteristic of any substance so released' (s. 11(11)). Where the change would amount to a substantial change in the manner in which the process is being carried on, this is to be treated as a fresh application and various consultation procedures must be undertaken.

These powers allow a degree of flexibility into the system so that changes which do not affect the authorisation can be made without a great deal of administrative intervention. On the other hand, where there is a change in the circumstances surrounding the authorisation, clearly HMIP ought to be able to intervene directly and request certain amendments.

The procedure mentioned above is only a preliminary procedure. Where HMIP decides that a formal variation is required, such an application has to be made. The only other alternative for an operator is to request a variation of the conditions of an authorisation.

There are further powers of variation contained in s. 11(5) and (6). The DoE envisages that these particular sections will be used during the construction of a plant where a variation in the authorisation is required but no 'relevant change' as defined in s. 11(11) of the Act is to take place. On the other hand, s. 11(6) allows for a variation of the conditions of an authorisation to take account of a relevant change.

The procedure governing a variation under s. 11 is contained in the Environmental Protection (Applications, Appeals and Registers) Regulations 1991 (SI 1991 No. 507). Regulation 3 states that when an application is made by an operator it must be in writing and include the name, address and telephone number of the operator and the address of the premises where the prescribed process is carried on. The request also has to include a description of the change, any change to the overall techniques used in the process, and any further information which the operator wishes the inspector to take into account.

Revocation notices

Section 12 of the EPA 1990 gives HMIP the power to revoke an authorisation at any time by giving notice in writing (s. 12(1)). This power is subject to the right of appeal or subsequently from challenge by way of judicial review. An appeal against a revocation notice suspends the action of the notice. Notwithstanding the nature of this power, HMIP is able to revoke an authorisation where it has reason to believe that a prescribed process in respect of which there is an authorisation has not been carried on for a period of 12 months (s. 12(2)). Thus, where authorisations are seen to be redundant, the power to revoke will be exercised to ensure that there is no question of restarting the process. When a revocation notice is served, there is a minimum period of 28 days before it can take effect (s. 12(3)). There is also a residual power open to the Secretary of State to direct HMIP as to whether or not it should revoke the authorisation.

The seriousness of this power is illustrated by the fact that it has only been used on one occasion in the first five years of operation of the IPC system (see [1995] *ENDS Report* 240 at p. 8).

Enforcement notices

Where HMIP is of the opinion that an operator is contravening any condition of an authorisation, or is likely to contravene a condition, it is under a duty to serve an enforcement notice (s. 13). The power to serve such a notice is discretionary as HMIP is entitled to arrive at a judgment about the likelihood of contravention. A decision not to take action would be challengeable by way of judicial review.

An enforcement notice must contain the following details:

(a) that the enforcing authority is of the opinion that there has been a contravention or that it is likely that there will be;
(b) the matters which constitute the contravention or give rise to the likelihood that there will be a contravention;
(c) the steps required to remedy the situation;
(d) the period within which those steps should be taken (s. 13(2)).

There is a residual power for the Secretary of State to direct HMIP to take enforcement action (s. 13(3)).

Prohibition notices

If HMIP is of the opinion that the carrying on of an authorised process in a particular manner involves an imminent risk of serious pollution, it is under a mandatory duty to serve a prohibition notice, whether or not the operator is contravening the authorisation (s. 14(1)). The prohibition notice has to include details of the authority's assessment of the risk involved in the process, as well as specifying the steps that must be taken to remove it and the period within which they must be taken. The meaning of imminent risk to the environment is open to all manner of interpretation. Section 1(2) defines the environment as 'all, or any, of the following media, namely, the air, water and land', whereas pollution of the environment means 'pollution of the environment due to the release (into any environmental medium) from any process of substances which are capable of causing harm to man or any other living organisms supported by the environment'. It will be a matter for the subjective judgment of the inspectors as to what amounts to an 'imminent risk' and what amounts to 'serious pollution'.

The prohibition notice empowers HMIP to prohibit an authorisation either as a whole or, if it is felt that the risk could be avoided by withdrawing part, then by prohibiting that part only. Additionally, there is power under s. 14 to impose new conditions on the original authorisation and thus avoid imminent risk of serious pollution of the environment.

In attempting to clarify the difference between prohibition notices and enforcement notices, when the Environmental Protection Bill passed through the House of Lords, Lord Reay explained that a prohibition notice would cover:

> circumstances in which a process is being operated in a perfectly reasonable manner and within the conditions of the authorisation, but where some event external to the process requires quick and decisive action. For example, an accident at one process could release substances which could react with those normally allowed to be released at a nearby process, so causing serious pollution. In those circumstances, it would be right to close down temporarily the second process even though it was operating within its authorisation.

Therefore, when considering the nature of the prohibition notice, it has to be borne in mind that such a Draconian power cannot be used too widely. The width of this power can be seen in s. 14(3), where it is stated that until the notice is withdrawn, an authorisation will cease to have any effect.

Powers of inspectors

These particular methods of enforcement will be used only as a final resort. Attempts also have to be made to ascertain whether or not such enforcement is appropriate. Therefore, the Act provides inspectors with a very wide range of powers to enable them to carry out their functions. Under s. 17, an inspector may:

(a) enter premises—normally this must be at any reasonable time, but where there is an imminent risk of serious pollution, entry can be made at any time;

(b) examine and investigate any process contained in any premises;

(c) direct that any premises and items contained on those premises remain undisturbed;

(d) take measurements, photographs and make recordings;

(e) take samples of air, water, articles or substances on or in the vicinity of the premises;

(f) require any articles or substances to be dismantled or subjected to any process or test;

(g) take possession of and detain any article or substance;

(h) require persons to answer questions if the inspector reasonably believes them to be able to give relevant information and, once they have supplied answers, to sign a declaration as to the truth of those answers;

(i) require the production of any records;

(j) require any assistance or facilities necessary to carry out any of the duties mentioned above;

(k) seize and render harmless any article or substance which is believed to be the cause of imminent danger.

These powers will be revoked when the EA comes into being and the unified powers come into force (see p. 45).

Offences and remedies

Section 23 of the EPA 1990 gives a long list of offences under Part I. It is a criminal offence to:

(a) operate a prescribed process without an authorisation;

(b) contravene the conditions of an authorisation;

(c) fail to give notice of transfer of an authorisation;

(d) fail to comply with an enforcement or prohibition notice;

(e) without reasonable excuse, fail to comply with a requirement imposed by an inspector under the powers in s. 17; or

(f) intentionally make a false entry in any record required to be kept as a condition of an authorisation.

All offences are triable either way, with the more serious offences having a maximum fine level in the magistrates' court of £20,000. In the Crown Court all offences are subject to a maximum term of imprisonment of two years and/or an unlimited fine (s. 23(2)). The Act also gives rights of audience to inspectors to present prosecutions even though they are not legally qualified (s. 23(5)). In any trial relating to the breach of the implied condition relating to the use of BATNEEC, the onus of proof falls upon the operator of the process to show that there was no better available technique not entailing excessive cost which could be employed for that particular process (s. 25(1)).

It is open to any court in sentencing an offender for failure to comply with an enforcement or prohibition notice to order that the effects of the offence be remedied (s. 26). This allows for clean-up and compensation costs to come directly out of the offender's pocket. In many instances, these costs will far outstrip any reasonable fine that could be imposed. Perhaps even more importantly, where a process has been operated without any authorisation or has not been in compliance with a condition of an authorisation, the Chief Inspector can arrange for reasonable steps to be taken towards remedying any harm caused as a consequence and recover the costs of taking such steps from any person committing the offence (s. 27(1)). Before doing so, however, the Chief Inspector must obtain the Secretary of State's approval in writing. Thus, even where a court is not willing to impose the high financial burden of clean-up costs on an offender, it will be open to the Inspectorate to remedy such harm. There are further remedies available to HMIP in the High Court, under s. 24, where there has been a failure to comply with an enforcement or a prohibition notice. This allows HMIP to seek injunctions where the enforcement of the criminal law is not securing adequate compliance.

Corporate liability

In an age where the concept of individual responsibility for corporate actions is being accepted by both the courts and the general public, s. 157 of the EPA 1990 provides that where an offence is committed by a company and it can be shown that a director, manager, or similar person in the company either consented, connived or was negligent, then criminal liability can attach individually as well as on a corporate basis. Furthermore, where an offence is committed owing to the act of default of an independent third party, proceedings can be brought against either or both under s. 158. These provisions would cover coprorate officers who acknowledged that there was a risk of environmental contanimation from certain activities and took that risk in the full knowledge of the consequences. Furthermore, acitivites where an act of environmental damage is caused by a breach of Part I owing to the activities of an independent contractor and notwithstanding the absence of fault on behalf of the operator of the process, both parties can be prosecuted.

Crown immunity

As in other legislation the Crown will be immune from criminal proceedings by virtue of s. 159. However, where the Crown operates processes subject to IPC it will not be exempt from the general control mechanisms under Part I. Thus there is a need to apply for authorisations and the same statutory objectives will apply as in the case of non-Crown bodies.

There is, under s. 159(2), a subsidiary power which allows for the Crown to be taken to the High Court and any breach of any authorisation to be declared unlawful. It is difficult to envisage a situation where this would be useful except in a case where the proof of civil liability depended to a certain extent upon the ability to show unlawful action on behalf of the Crown.

Appeals

Section 15 of the EPA 1990 governs appeals. It provides that there is a right of appeal against:

(a) revocation, variation, enforcement and prohibition notices;
(b) the refusal to grant or vary an authorisation;
(c) the imposition of unreasonable conditions.

Furthermore, s. 22 gives an applicant a right of appeal where HMIP has notified the operator that information contained within an authorisation or an application for an authorisation is not commercially confidential.

The detailed appeals procedure is contained in the Environmental Protection (Applications, Appeals and Registers) Regulations 1991 (SI 1991 No. 507). Generally, the time limit for appeals is similar to that in the planning system, being six months from a refusal or a deemed refusal to grant an authorisation. Where there is an appeal against an enforcement, prohibition or variation notice, the time limit is two months from the date of the notice. Where HMIP is seeking notice to revoke an authorisation, the appeal must be submitted before the notice takes effect. Lastly, where there is an appeal concerning commercial confidentiality, it must be submitted within 21 days from the refusal.

Pending the hearing of the appeal, a revocation notice will not have effect. However, in all other cases involving appeals against statutory notices, although there is an appeal made, there is no suspension of the notice. Thus, an operator cannot gain an economic advantage where there is a rush order by appealing against a notice so as to stop the enforcement process, continuing to pollute until the order is completed, and then stopping the process before the appeal is heard.

An appeal must be made in writing to the Secretary of State (reg. 9). The appeal has to be accompanied by any relevant information, including any application, authorisation, correspondence or decision and a statement as to how the appellant wishes the appeal to be determined.

Modes of appeal

An appeal can be heard in one of two ways: either by way of written representations or by a hearing. If either party to the appeal requests that it be heard by way of hearing the Secretary of State has no discretion in the matter, he must hold the hearing (s. 15(5)(a)) although there is a discretion as to whether the hearing is in public. The Secretary of State also has the power to direct that a public inquiry be held (s. 15(5)(b)). There has been an attempt by the DoE to ensure that hearings do not take on a quasi-legal nature, as has happened in the planning system. Thus, the system has very few rules. The DoE Guidance states:

the procedure at a hearing will be left to the Appeals Inspector. He may hear the parties in whatever order he thinks most suitable for the clarification of issues. He may, for instance, review the case based on the papers already provided and then outline what he considers to be the main issues and indicate those matters which require further explanation or clarification. This will not preclude the appellant or the enforcing authority from referring to other aspects which they consider to be relevant. The approach that will be encouraged will be one of informality, for example, hearings may often take the form of a round table discussion, rather than a formal presentation of evidence.

This air of informality is supposedly to alter the hearing system from being adversarial, as is often the case in planning appeals, to inquisitorial. There is to a certain extent a degree of public participation in that reg. 13 states that notice has to be given at least 28 days before the date of the hearing of the date, time and place for the holding of the hearing. The Department does however concede that in more controversial proposals it may be necessary to adopt a formal procedure. Presumably, where issues are likely to be of great consequence to members of the public, there needs to be some element of the adversarial approach to ensure that there is adequate accountability. Otherwise, public confidence in an appeals system, which to the untrained eye and ear would appear to be a meeting of highly trained, highly specialised people discussing hypothetical problems around a table, would be seriously undermined.

The written representations appeal procedure will contain an exchange of views on paper as to the suitability of any proposals. The procedure will vary little from the planning system.

The Secretary of State cannot delegate the above decision-making powers. The inspector who heard the appeal is required to report to the Secretary of State as to any conclusions and recommendations. The Secretary of State in making the decision has to take into account these recommendations but does not have to follow them. The Secretary of State then issues the decision to all interested parties.

The European approach to integrated pollution prevention and control

An integrated approach to pollution control is reflected in a proposed Directive on Integrated Pollution Prevention and Control (IPPC). It is envisaged that a system along similar lines to IPC will be introduced in all Member States under a framework Directive setting out the principles of the legislation which is to be implemented in each Member State.

The draft Directive contains a list of industrial activities which would be the subject of detailed legislation in each country. All of these industries would then fall under the control of a system of IPPC permits during a 10-year period.

To ensure that there is harmonisation of environmental standards, triennial reports are to be submitted by each Member State, setting out emission/release limits and related process standards designed to achieve these limits for each individual industrial sector. The intention is eventually to implement daughter Directives for each industry sector to ensure uniform quality standards throughout the Community.

Much of the proposed Directive broadly follows the IPC system in Britain. There are, however, a few points of distinction. The range of industrial processes and substances subject to control is considerably wider than under the Prescribed Processes and Substances Regulations in force in Britain. This would require amendment of the existing legislation with at least 5,000 processes not currently under control found in the draft Directive.

Under the Directive, any permit granted must contain a condition requiring the restoration of any process which has permanently ceased operation so as to ensure that there is no harm to the environment. It is expected that the use of conditions in planning permissions would be able to perform this role.

Lastly, there is to be no deadline for upgrading processes to the required process standards for achieving emission/release limits. Thus, the regulatory pressure on operators to improve quality standards would be left to each Member State. Britain has already gone somewhat further in imposing an open-ended process standard when requiring emission limits ultimately to be reduced to a minimum.

TWELVE
Atmospheric pollution

The range of problems affecting the atmosphere stretches across the full range of human activities, from highly toxic fumes emitted from a complicated industrial process to such seemingly mundane activities as lighting a fire, driving a car or using spray-on deodorant. The history of atmospheric pollution dates back to early times. The prohibitions on certain activities producing smoke are probably the first instances of environment pollution legislation in Great Britain.

Because such a wide range of activities affects the atmosphere, the range of environmental issues is also wide. On the one hand, there have always been difficulties with polluting activities affecting the locality in which they were situated. International difficulties have arisen with the creation of acid rain. In recent years we have seen a realisation amongst the international community that individual nations' actions can combine to create truly global difficulties. The destruction of the ozone layer and the issue of global warning have brought home the truly awesome consequences of the combined effect of certain industrial activities.

Local atmospheric pollution

The pollution of the local atmosphere from emissions has traditionally been easy to identify. Such problems date back to the early uses of coal in domestic fires. The production of fumes and particulates from fires caused pulmonary infections and related lung diseases. Notwithstanding this effect, coal continued to be used. In 1661, John Evelyn published his famous work on air pollution in city areas, *Fumi Fugium*, which not only outlined the problems that atmospheric pollution from smoke caused, but also, more importantly, tried to suggest methods by which the problems could be resolved.

With the advent of more complicated processes in the late-eighteenth century, the problems of atmospheric pollution grew more severe. The industrial revolution increased the use of coal to drive new machinery and, more importantly, produced very acidic emissions as a consequence of the 'alkali works'. These works used the leblanc process to produce soda, but the by-product of the chemical process used meant that hydrochloric gas was emitted into the atmosphere which, when mixed with water, created a new phenomenon—acid rain.

The consequences of these new processes were that areas of the country were rendered desolate by this very highly acidic moist air, burning trees, shrubs and hedges. One of the centres for the alkali industry, St Helens in Lancashire, was reported as not having a single tree with any foliage on it. Even amongst the people working in such factories, concern was expressed. This concern led to the setting-up of a Royal Commission to look into the problem of alkali pollution, which subsequently made the recommendations which led to the first Alkali Act, passed in 1863. Under this Act, a new Alkali Inspector was appointed who regulated such alkali processes. Although the Act did not attempt to deal with smoke, it did introduce new stricter controls over the production of acidic emissions. It made the first attempts at restricting the composition of emissions with the introduction of primitive emission standard requirements. Under the Act, there was a requirement that 95% of all noxious emissions should be arrested within the plant, so that only 5% of the previously emitted fumes were allowed into the atmosphere.

Even though there were strict emission standards on the volume of noxious gases produced, there were also the first signs of a proactive approach from the newly created Alkali Inspectorate in that they would encourage manufacturers to reduce the emissions to less than 5% in order to protect the environment.

The initial effect of the legislation was a dramatic reduction in the production of acidic emissions from almost 14,000 tonnes to about 45 tonnes. This improvement, however, was only temporary. Within a short time the inadequacy of the legislation was brought home. The imposition of individualised emission standards could not take into account the cumulative effect of a large concentration of such operations. As the Act had only set a reduction for acidic emissions in terms of a percentage for each plant, the overall concentration of such emissions rose as the number of factories increased.

The introduction of the Alkali Act of 1874 attempted to redress the balance by introducing the concept of best practicable means (BPM). The application of BPM was used to widen the scope of the previous emission limits to include all noxious or offensive gases. In essence, the application of BPM relied upon these presumptive limits. The limits saw the introduction of the first proper emission standards in British legislation by specifying actual amounts of certain substances per cubic metre of emitted gas. If these emission limits were being met, then it was presumed that any legislation was being complied with and that the best practicable means were being used. Interestingly, the emission limits set for hydrogen chloride in the 1874 Act, 0.2 grains per cubic foot, still stands today. The use of the concept of best practicable means ensured that there was to be a conciliatory and co-operational approach as the Alkali Inspectorate sought a method of enforcement which would not place 'an undue burden on manufacturing industry'.

Neither of these Acts, nor the consolidation Act of 1906, dealt specifically with the control of smoke from either industrial or commercial premises. Attempts were made to control the emission of smoke through such Acts as the Public Health Act 1875, the Public Health (Smoke Abatement) Act 1926 and the Public Health Act 1936, but these dealt generally with smoke nuisances. These powers could not rid industrial cities of the problems of smoke pollution. The physical evidence of this pollution could be seen on blackened buildings, and by the frequency of smog, which was prevalent from Victorian times. Such smog was caused by fog forming in winter months and combining with smoke particles to produce a compound of gases which could cut visibility to very low levels. Of more concern, however, was the effect that these smogs had upon the dispersion of pollution. With a heavy concentration of smog hanging over a city the air was very still and convection was low. With the onset of these calm conditions, the dispersal of emissions was much more difficult. Such a lethal cocktail was bound to produce tragic effects, but these were fairly minimal until December 1952 when a smog descended upon London which did not clear for five days. Nothing unusual was noticed until prize cattle at the Smithfield Show started to suffer from respiratory problems. The smog got everywhere, even inside the Sadlers Wells Theatre, which resulted in the stoppage of a performance because of the difficulty of seeing the stage. When the smog had lifted it was estimated that nearly 4,000 people had lost their lives as a consequence of the smoke and other emissions.

The Government immediately responded by setting up the Beaver Committee to report on the difficulties surrounding smoke pollution. The recommendation of the Committee was to introduce legislation to eliminate particulate emissions such as smoke, dust and grit so that such conditions would not arise again. With the introduction of the Clean Air Act 1956, later supplemented by the Clean Air Act 1968, controls were introduced for the first time to restrict the production of smoke, grit and dust from all commercial and industrial activities not covered by the Alkali Acts but also, more importantly, domestic fires as well. The Acts introduced such concepts as smoke control areas and the complete prohibition on 'dark smoke' from chimneys.

During the 1970s, the problems of the emission of smoke, dirt, dust and grit lessened and coupled with the new approach to industrial processes a gradual improvement took place in the quality of the atmosphere in the UK. There was a move away from the use of coal as fuel to smokeless substances such as coke and gas. Additionally, the gap left behind with the introduction of clean air zones was met by an increase in the use of electricity for power and heat. The main generator of electricity in Britain, the Central Electricity Generating Board, changed its practices in a direct reaction to the difficulties encountered with local pollution by replacing the short chimneys traditionally used in power stations with larger and taller stacks. The basis of this change was to disperse pollution at a higher level in the hope that any substances would be diluted over greater distances. The consequence would be a reduction in the concentrations of pollutants in the nearby locality. Unfortunately, this reduction in the levels of local pollution only shifted the problems to a different location. Whilst the pollution of the atmosphere declined nationally, the concern internationally rose. The change of policy from short to tall stacks for chimneys saw the creation of the first environmental problem which could properly be identified across national boundaries—the problem of acid rain.

International difficulties: acid rain

The production of electricity from power stations burning fossil fuels produces, amongst other things, sulphur dioxide, nitrous oxide and nitrogen dioxide. The sulphur dioxide created from power stations amounts to some 80% of all such emissions into the atmosphere. In 1953 the Beaver Report had recommended that such plants should be fitted with desulphurisation equipment, but that was rejected specifically at the time as being impracticable for the particular process. Instead, the change from using short chimneys to a dilution and dispersal method from tall chimneys was introduced. It was thought that the dispersal of such emissions into the upper levels of the atmosphere would render such substances harmless before they could contaminate an area. This applied to the areas around the emission plants but, further afield, the evidence suggested that it had little effect.

In smoothly flowing medium speed winds, plumes from power stations travel in a concentrated stream for hundreds of miles. Tall stacks (Drax Power Station is 259 metres tall) can take emissions above a layer of air trapped near the ground into smooth air streams. On a steady south westerly, a plume from Eggborough Power Station, labelled with sodium hexafluoride was tracked all the way across the North Sea to Denmark . . . in clear skies sulphur was being slowly oxidised and deposited. Once it entered low mountain cloud, production of acid increased 14 fold and fall out increased over 200%. The total removal rate shot up to 27% an hour, depositing the sulphur in a concentrated drizzle (Rose, *The Dirty Man of Europe*).

The combination of sulphur dioxide and other acids from power stations and traffic combined with the atmosphere to produce not only acid rain, but also acid deposits in the atmosphere made of ammonium sulphate particles.

The effects of the production of such substances into the atmosphere has increased the acidity of rainfall in some areas to over 40 times the natural level. This has had a terrible effect upon areas of not only England, Scotland and Wales but also other countries within Europe where the prevailing winds have carried such emissions. The Scandinavian countries in particular have received a large percentage of the 'export' of Britain's production of sulphur dioxide and acid rain. Vegetation suffers from the increased acidity, trees and shrubs die and, in Southern Norway, it has been shown that there has been a steady increase in the acidity of lakes so that some lakes and rivers no longer support any life. The specific effects of certain pollutants can range from speckled areas on leaves brought about by acidic deposits through to complete death. These problems require a co-operative approach to be taken between nations. There has been a long running dispute between Britain and the Scandinavian countries as to the cause of the acidic deposits on their countries. The EC has made some steps towards introducing a desulphurisation programme, but it remains to be seen whether or not this is to be successful.

Global issues: ozone depletion and global warming

The Department of the Environment's White Paper *This Common Inheritance,* published in September 1990, brought the international problem of global warming to the top of the environmental agenda.

Global warming is one of the biggest environmental challenges now facing the world. It calls for action by all the world's nations, as no single nation can solve the problem on its own.

The greenhouse effect, as it has come to be known, has arisen because the production of various 'greenhouse' gases have increased in the past century with progressive industrialisation. In the lower atmosphere the production of emissions from power stations, car exhausts and industrial plants have increased by almost 100%. These emissions absorb radiated heat and create a higher ambient temperature level which has led to speculation that there could be shrinking global icecaps and rising water levels.

Additionally, the amount of ozone in the upper atmosphere screens the earth from harmful UV-B radiation. This screen has deteriorated and there have been studies showing a 'hole' above Antarctica. This depletion of ozone has been linked to the use of chlorofluorocarbons (CFCs). The creation of greenhouse gases and the depletion of the ozone layer are worldwide problems which require international co-operation to solve. The use of international law as a mechanism for environmental protection is relatively unusual and there are some limitations to its usefulness. However, the nature of the problems facing the world in terms of these two issues have led to significant steps being taken to prevent any further harm.

Global issues

The Earth Summit in Brazil, attended by over 160 countries, was seen as a watershed in the fight against climate change. At the conference the Climate Treaty was signed in an attempt to reduce the emission of greenhouse gases to 1990 levels by 2000. The Treaty was ratified by 50 countries (including the EU and the UK) and came into force in March 1994. The relative weakness of the use of international obligations to enforce environmental improvements can be seen in the fact that the UK's commitment to the Treaty (as set out in Climate Change—the UK Programme) consists of a set of voluntary measures with the aim of reducing energy consumption, with regulatory or economic instruments only being used where necessary.

Air pollution policy

The control of air pollution has, as noted above, been the classic example of the use of reactive legal controls to regulate specific problems as they arise. Policy approaches have, until very recently, been sparse and incoherent. Although the legal controls have been modernised and broadened, it is only in the 1990s that a coherent strategy has been developed to deal with the problems of atmospheric pollution. When the Government published its policy on sustainable development in January 1994, urban air quality was identified as a priority area for improvement. In March 1994 the DoE issued a consultation paper on air quality which bluntly described previous policy initiatives on air pollution as 'the fortuitous sum of a large number of unrelated regulatory decisions and individual choices'. It was not until the beginning of 1995 that the first steps were taken towards a coherent air quality management system and the Environment Act 1995 has a variety of framework provisions which are described below.

A variety of factors has led to this acceleration of policy-making. First, there has been increasing evidence linking health problems with poor air quality, with the increase of the incidence of asthma and other diseases connected with a variety of atmospheric pollutants. There has also been a number of occasions (particularly in the summer months) when pollution levels have risen to dangerous levels in cities.

Secondly, the quality of provision of information on air quality has been improved with the number of background monitoring stations increased. Although air quality standards (AQS) have been introduced for a number of pollutants any assessment of measuring improvement depends to a large extent upon the availability of long-term data. Most of England's major cities now have stations to monitor base data in order to assess compliance with standards for the main polluting emissions. It is anticipated that this will increase as the move towards established AQS grows over the next few years (for more on monitoring see p. 329).

Thirdly, the link between air pollution and transport, in particular motor transport, has become much more pronounced. The RCEP's Eighteenth Report concentrated on the environmental effects of vehicle emissions. In addition there has been a range of measures designed to tackle pollution from motor vehicle (see p. 344).

Finally, as in other areas of environmental policy, the EC has made moves towards streamlining policy on atmospheric pollution. This culminated in a proposal for a new framework Directive on air quality assessment and management with further proposals to set AQS for 12 significant pollutants by 1999 (see p. 331).

Air quality strategy

The cornerstone of policy on air pollution is a new National Strategy for Air Quality. The broad outline of the new strategy was identified in a Consultation Paper 'Air Quality: Meeting the Challenge', published in January 1995.

The strategy as outlined in the Consultation Paper consists of three broad areas for action. Overall, the aim of the strategy was to establish, for the first time, clear identifiable goals within a framework of air quality management.

A framework of air quality standards and targets
The implementation of the strategy is largely dependent upon the introduction of AQS for nine pollutants. The standards are generally set in relation to the effect of each pollutant on human health, although the effect upon the environment might also be considered. There are two main levels:

(a)   *The alert threshold:* This level is reached when air quality is so poor that an immediate response would be justified to prevent serious damage to health or the environment.

(b)   *The guideline level:* This level is to be seen as a long-term goal and represents an equilibrium point at which the pollutant in question is considered to be harmless to health and the environment and which can be achieved through cost effective measures such as the introduction of new plant and technology.

These levels are to be set alongside a timetable for achieving the new objectives, although some doubts have been expressed in relation to the Government's desire to enforce these time limits. The Expert Panel on Air Quality Standards is to have the role of advising in relation to the setting down the numerical standards. As mentioned above, work has already been carried out (and in most cases completed) in respect of the guideline levels, although the more difficult alert threshold is as yet undetermined.

Local air quality management areas
The national framework of new two-level AQS will be implemented on a practical level with the introduction of air quality management areas (AQMAs) laid down and regulated by local authorities (EA 1995, ss. 83–4).

Local authorities have a duty to carry out regular assessments of air quality in their areas with a view to the identification of targeted areas for action. It is expected that all major urban areas will be surveyed before the end of 1997.

Where the local authority has identified an area for action it must consider whether to declare an AQMA where it has been shown that the AQS set out in the National Strategy are not likely to be met solely as a result of national policies. The criteria for doing so is to be the subject of Central Government advice. The procedure for declaring an AQMA and the proposed action to comply with the AQS laid down is to be similar to that of the designation of a smoke control area (see p. 339) involving consultation with a variety of bodies (DoE, EA, public and neighbouring councils).

The Environment Act 1995 also contains wide regulation-making powers to enable local authorities to control levels of pollution in AQMAs (s. 84).

Advisory bodies with responsibility for air pollution
There are a number of bodies carrying out an advisory function within the area of air pollution. Three of particular importance are:

(a) The Expert Panel on Air Quality Standards (EPAQS), set up by the DoE which makes recommendations in respect of AQS. Although the Government seeks advice from a variety of bodies, this group, made up of both medical and air pollution experts, is seen to have the greatest influence when setting new AQS. It has made recommendations for AQS for ozone, benzene, 1,3-butadiene and carbon monoxide with other pollutants to follow over a period of time.

(b) The Quality of Urban Air Review Group (QUARG) reviews the state on urban air quality and makes recommendations in relation to monitoring stations/networks, types of pollutants monitored, information made available to the public and areas for further research.

(c) The National Environmental Technology Centre (NETCEN) is responsible for a variety of functions relating to the measurement of air pollution. It coordinates the UK Smoke and Sulphur Dioxide Monitoring Network, prepares an annual National Atmospheric Emissions Inventory giving estimates of atmospheric pollution from all sources and provides training for local authorities in relation to the Enhanced Urban Network (EUN) (see below).

Monitoring of air pollution

The introduction of AQS for a variety of pollutants will rely heavily on the systematic measurement of those pollutants in the atmosphere. Monitoring of smoke, sulphur dioxide, grit and dust has, in fact, taken place since the early part of this century. This is unsurprising given the major impact that these pollutants had upon health and the environment and the relatively unsophisticated methods of measurement. In 1961, the establishment of the National Survey of Air Pollution led to a coordinated network of monitoring sites situated throughout the country. These sites concentrated on the accumulation of data on smoke and sulphur dioxide. The network was, however, unwieldy (nearly 1,200 sites) and unreliable. The National Survey was, in turn, replaced with a more workable Smoke and Sulphur Dioxide Monitoring Network with 240 sites. Of these, 156 monitor compliance with EU Directives on sulphur dioxide and suspended particulates, with the rest forming the Basic Urban Network, providing basic information for urban areas. There are other monitoring sites which gather information on nitrogen dioxide (7), lead in the atmosphere (16) and acid deposition (32).

The most significant recent development in monitoring air pollution has been the introduction of the Enhanced Urban Network (EUN) in 1992 (with an expansion in 1995). A range of pollutants (ozone, nitrogen oxide, sulphur dioxide, carbon monoxide and particulates) are measured continuously at 23 sites throughout the country (Belfast, Birmingham, Bradford, Bristol, Cardiff, Edinburgh, Glasgow, Hull, Leeds, Leicester, Liverpool, London (× 3), Manchester, Newcastle, Norwich, Nottingham, Plymouth, Sheffield, Southampton, Stoke-on-Trent and Wolverhampton).

Information on pollutants which are likely to affect health is gathered from the EUN and disseminated to the public via the Met Office weather bulletins, the media, a telephone service and the Internet.

There are specific and separate requirements for the monitoring and dissemination of information on ozone levels. The Ozone Monitoring and Information Regulations 1994 (SI 1994 No. 440) implemented the EC Directive on Air Pollution by Ozone (92/72). The Regulations require the establishment of a monitoring network, the dissemination of information, and a system whereby the public are warned when excessive levels of ozone are in the atmosphere. These warnings should be communicated as soon as possible and on a sufficiently wide scale to enable the public to take precautionary measures. The warnings should contain details of the area affected, the length of time that levels are likely to be excessive and precautionary measures which should be taken. The regulations are implemented by means of the EUN and the public information systems outlined above.

The introduction and expansion of the EUN has been widely welcomed but the quality and accuracy of past monitoring of air pollution has been criticised strongly. The main criticisms have centred around the selection and quantity of sites. The effectiveness of any monitoring network is primarily dependent upon the location of the monitoring equipment. It has been argued that the monitoring sites are not generally located in areas of high exposure and therefore give a false impression of levels of pollution. Secondly, although coverage of monitoring sites is spreading there are still large gaps, particularly in some areas of heavy industry and traffic. More specifically, the EC has criticised the UK for failing to provide an adequate number of sites to monitor nitrogen dioxide levels. The introduction of a National Air Quality Strategy based around specific targets and AQS means that the base data provided by the EUN has to be credible and sufficiently broad to indicate true levels of improvement.

The EC and air pollution

The protection of the atmosphere was not seen as a priority by the EC until the mid 1980s. Indeed, relatively few proposals based purely on environmental protection (as opposed to market harmonisation) were published before 1984. The reasons for this were twofold. First, a lack of political will and, secondly, a genuine desire to move forward in other areas. As a result of the effects of acid rain, however, the German Government pressed for swift action in 1983 and the main framework Directive on emissions from industrial plant (84/360) was introduced nearly 10 years after the framework Directives for waste and water pollution. Since that time, though, the concern about trans-boundary pollution and wider issues such as global warming and ozone depletion has led to a wide range of Directives being introduced.

The Commission's approach to the protection of the atmosphere has been wide-ranging in its scope. Various mechanisms have been used.

Environmental quality standards
Directive 80/779 on Smoke and Sulphur Dioxide sets limit values for the ground level concentration of smoke and sulphur dioxide which must be

adhered to for specified periods. Furthermore, there are more stringent guide levels which can be set in areas of special need. Other approaches of this sort are to be found in Directives on Lead (82/884) and Nitrogen Oxide (85/203). In Britain, these Directives have been implemented by means of the Air Quality Standards Regulations 1989 (SI 1989 No. 317).

In June 1995 a common position was agreed on a Directive on Air Quality Assessment and Management. The Directive is intended to provide a framework for 12 pollutants (in the process replacing Directives 80/779, 85/203 and 82/884).

The first daughter Directives—for sulphur dioxide, particulates, lead and nitrogen dioxide—are to be produced by the end of 1996. The remaining daughter Directives are expected to be approved by 1999 at the latest.

It is intended that the Framework Directive will apply three types of quality objective—a limit value, a guide value and an alert threshold (which mirrors, to some extent the new framework found in the draft of the air quality strategy to be produced under the Environment Act 1995).

Emission limits
Certain Directives impose limits upon the emission levels of pollutants. In the framework Directive 84/360 this is used in conjunction with the process standard 'best available technology not entailing excessive cost'.

Directive 88/609 dealing with emissions from large combustion plants utilises a variation on the normal emission standard. Under that Directive, each Member State is allocated a total national limit for emissions from power stations and other large combustion plants. These so-called 'bubble' limits are then reduced over a period of time. This enables each Member State to have a degree of flexibility when imposing individual emission limits whilst still maintaining an overall ceiling. In Britain, these Directives based upon specific emission levels have been implemented through Part I of the EPA 1990.

The introduction of a national 'plan' for the 'bubble' limits for sulphur dioxide and nitrogen oxide from combustion plants has been implemented under s. 3(5) of the EPA 1990. This plan has imposed particular limits upon individual power stations which cumulatively fall within the overall limits under the Directive. The national plan is not binding, however, and the limits which have been placed upon the Part I authorisations for these power stations are, on the whole, more stringent. This allows an operator with a number of plants to exceed its allocation under the national plan for one plant if that can be offset by low levels of emissions at another, provided that it falls within the limit set by the Part I authorisation.

Product standards
The protection of the atmosphere is one of the few areas where product standards have been used extensively. One of the main reasons for this is that, previously, the introduction of such standards was seen to be justifiable in terms of market harmonisation where environmental justifications were not accepted by every Member State. Relevant Directives include: lead in petrol

(85/210); emissions from vehicles (88/76, 89/458 and 91/441); and the sulphur content of gas oil (87/219).

Prohibitions
The phasing out and prohibition of CFCs under Regulations 3322/88 and 594/91 is one of the few examples of that mechanism.

Market mechanisms
Proposals for an EC carbon/energy tax have been progressing through various stages for some time. Compulsory taxation on carbon-based fuel has been accepted by the majority of Member States, with Britain being the main dissenter. The future of the proposal is somewhat uncertain but it is envisaged that some form of taxation will be introduced by the late–1990s.

EC action on a worldwide basis
The EC has encouraged a number of worldwide initiatives by negotiating in its own right on issues which require global action. Thus, the EC is a signatory to the Vienna Convention on Ozone Layer protection. This in turn led to the implementation of Regulations 3322/88 and 594/91 on CFCs.

Future proposals
A new framework Directive on Air Quality Standards has recently been agreed (see above). This proposal will replace Directives 80/779, 85/203 and 82/884 in respect of air quality and introduce limit values for a range of over 20 substances. The objective of the new proposal will be to harmonise the present Directives by putting forward three types of quality objectives which will apply to all substances under the Directive: first, a limit value, secondly, a guide value and, thirdly, an alert threshold. Not all of the substances would be subject to the three parameters immediately and further daughter Directives will be introduced to phase in those substances which are not limited in every category.

The Air Quality Standards Regulations 1989

As Britain was under a duty to implement EC Directives on air quality, steps were taken (prior to the introduction of the provisons under Part I of EPA 1990) to move away from the informal, flexible standards under previous legislation. Therefore, in 1989, mandatory air quality standards were introduced under the Air Quality Standards Regulations 1989 (SI 1989 No. 317). These regulations impose an obligation upon the Secretary of State to ensure that levels of sulphur dioxide, nitrogen dioxide, lead and smoke do not rise above EC limits, and to set up a system of sampling stations to measure air quality.

The control of smoke under the Clean Air Act 1993

As we have seen, the control of smoke, dust and dirt from industrial and domestic fires was largely ineffective in dealing with the problems associated with such emissions in the early part of the twentieth century. Although the Public Health (Smoke Abatement) Act 1926 attempted to control certain categories of industrial smoke, domestic smoke was prohibited only if it amounted to a 'nuisance'. The Clean Air Act 1956, later amended and supplemented by the Clean Air Act 1968, provided a comprehensive control mechanism for the protection of the environment from smoke, dust and fumes. These Acts were consolidated in the Clean Air Act 1993.

This Act constitutes a separate and distinct area of control. Essentially, it controls smoke, dust and grit from all fires and furnaces.

Overlap with Part I of EPA 1990
Section 41 of the 1993 Act specifically excludes prescribed processes from controls regulating the production of smoke and dust. Under that section, Parts I–III of the 1993 Act do not apply to any prescribed process as from the date on which an application for authorisation is granted or refused (whether or not on appeal).

The enforcement agency responsible for the Clean Air Act 1993 is the district authority, metropolitan authority or London borough council (s. 55).

Control of smoke from chimneys
Section 1 of the 1993 Act prohibits the emission of 'dark smoke' from the chimney of any building. Any occupier who breaches s. 1 will be guilty of a criminal offence. The section applies to all types of buildings, from domestic houses to industrial premises and crematoria. The mechanism of control specifically applies to chimneys from buildings. Although the definition of the word 'building' covers such structures as a greenhouse, it would have to be a part of a recognised structure (*Clifford* v *Holt* [1899] 1 Ch 698).

The prohibition applies only to 'dark smoke'; other types of emissions are covered either elsewhere in the Act or under different statutes. In attempting to determine whether smoke is 'dark', enforcement officers are forced to make a visual assessment of the shade of the smoke emission by comparing the darkness of the smoke with a uniform chart known as a Ringelmann chart. The chart contains five shades of grey by cross hatching black lines on a white background from clear (number 0) to black (number 4). The chart is rectangular in shape, measuring some 581 mm × 127 mm. The chart is used in accordance with certain guidelines laid down in British Standard 2742. It is held up by the operator and compared to the smoke from a distance of at least 15 metres and then comparisons are made between the colour of the smoke and the colour on the chart. If the colour of the smoke is as dark as, or darker than, shade 2 on the Ringelmann Scale it then qualifies as dark smoke (s. 3(1)). Where, however, an operator is experienced, s. 3(2) allows for an assessment to be made independent of the Ringelmann chart, often by the use of a smaller, more portable smoke chart (129 mm × 69 mm). Some officers rely purely on their experience to assess whether or not the smoke is darker than shade 2.

The prohibition also only covers smoke emitted from chimneys. The definition of a chimney can be found in s. 64 and is wide enough to cover all structures or openings through which smoke is emitted. Thus, smoke from outdoor fires or, for instance, burning straw or stubble is not covered by s. 1.

Strict liability

As in other environmental legislation, liability is strict, therefore prima facie *any* dark smoke emitted from a chimney would give rise to liability under s. 1. The Act imposes liabililty on an occupier of a building from which smoke is emitted, irrespective of responsibility.

Exemptions and defences

Section 1(3) provides for certain exemptions to be made by the Secretary of State. These exemptions are restricted by the duration of emissions. The Dark Smoke (Permitted Periods) Regulations 1958 (SI 1958 No. 498) allows three main exemptions for smoke from chimneys. There are time-limits imposed of anything between 10 and 40 minutes during any period of eight hours for emission of dark smoke depending on both the number of furnaces used and whether or not soot is blowing. Secondly, there is a limit of four minutes of continuous emissions of dark smoke where the cause is not owed to burning soot. Lastly, there is a limit of two minutes in each period of 30 minutes where smoke is black (that is, smoke as dark as, or darker than, shade 4 on the Ringelmann chart).

Furthermore, s. 1(4) lays down three statutory defences. These defences are not absolute and require certain qualifying steps to be taken to ensure that the defences apply. The section provides that it is a defence to a charge under s. 1(1) that the emission was:

(a)   solely due to the lighting of a furnace, and that all practicable steps were taken to minimise or prevent emissions;

(b)   solely due to the failure of a furnace, and that the contravention of s. 1(1) could not reasonably have been foreseen or provided against and prevented by action taken after the failure;

(c)   solely due to the unavoidable use of the least unsuitable fuel available when suitable fuel was unavailable, and that practicable steps were taken to minimise or prevent emissions;

(d)   any combination of (a), (b) and (c).

Enforcement and offences

Local authorities can take action against dark smoke emitted from outside the area which they control if it affects their area (s. 55(2)). An important prerequisite of bringing a prosecution is that the enforcement authority are under a duty to notify occupiers of the existence of the offence 'as soon as may be'. This notification will normally be given orally by the relevant enforcement officer. If such oral notification is given, it must be confirmed in writing within four days of the date on which the officer became aware of the offence. In any event, written notice of the offence must be given within that time. If notification is not given, it is a defence to charges under ss. 1, 2 or 20 of the Act (s. 51(3)). The offence is only triable in the magistrates' court.

There are different maximum levels of fine for emissions from private dwellings (level 3 on the standard scale) and for any other case (level 5 on the standard scale) (s. 1(5)).

Emissions of dark smoke from industrial plants
Section 2 of the Act prohibits the emissions of dark smoke from industrial trade premises other than from a chimney of a building (which is covered under s. 1). 'Premises' include the grounds of factories and open areas such as demolition sites (*Sheffield CC v ADH Demolition* (1984) 82 LGR 177). Section 2(2)(b) gives the Secretary of State power to pass regulations giving an exemption to the burning of prescribed matter which emits dark smoke in the open. The Clean Air (Emission of Dark Smoke) (Exemption) Regulations 1969 (SI 1969 No. 1263) exempt certain material such as timber, explosives, tar, and waste from animal or poultry carcases. Section 2(6) provides that industrial or trade premises include premises not used for industrial or trade purposes but on which substances or matter are burnt in connection with such processes. Thus, open areas without any connection to industrial activities would fall within control under this section.

Section 2(3) refers to the burden of proof required when attempting to show the causation of dark smoke. On trade or business premises, where circumstances are such that the burning of material would be likely to give rise to an emission of dark smoke, such an emission can be taken as proved unless the occupier or person accused of the offence can show that no dark smoke actually was emitted. When fires have been extinguished but dark smoke has already been emitted there has often been difficulty in proving the source of the dark smoke. This section allows environmental health officers to act against smoke pollution even though there is no smoke emanating from the premises. The prohibition under s. 2 applies not only to occupiers but also to any person who causes or permits the emission of dark smoke from industrial or trade premises.

There is a statutory defence under s. 2(4) that the emission of dark smoke was 'inadvertent'. This would suggest that although the offence has an absolute liability, some degree of blameworthiness is necessary for an action to be successful. If the emission was inadvertent, it is also necessary to show that all practicable steps have been taken to prevent or minimise the emission of dark smoke. Practicability is defined in s. 64 as meaning reasonably practicable having regard to local conditions and circumstances, to the financial implications and to the current state of technical knowledge. An offence under s. 2 is triable only in a magistrates' court, the maximum fine being set at level 5 on the standard scale (s. 2(5)).

The control of grit, dust and fumes

The Act does not only cover smoke. Emissions from furnaces can also contain particulate matter and the Act extends to cover such particulate matter, ranging from the largest (being grit as defined in the Clean Air (Emission of Grit and Dust from Furnaces) Regulations 1971 (SI 1971 No. 162)), through dust and small solid particles between 1 and 75 μm in diameter (as defined in BS3405), to fumes (which are defined as any airborne solid matter smaller than dust) (s. 64). There are proactive measures for preventing smoke, dust, grit and fumes being emitted from furnaces. Section 4 provides that furnaces over a certain energy value (excluding domestic boilers) should, as far as practicable, be smokeless when using a fuel for which it was designed. This control is implemented by s. 4(1), under which anyone wishing to install a furnace has to notify the local authority before doing so. Where the local authority is notified and authorisation has been given, then the furnace is deemed to comply with the provision. This, however, does not exempt the furnace from being subject to the prohibition on dark smoke under s. 1. Where a furnace is operated without such an approval then the person who installed the furnace will be guilty of an offence (s. 4(4)).

This proactive approach is further strengthened by the requirement for grit and dust arrestment plant to be fitted to furnaces. This power is extended by ss. 6 and 7, which control all furnaces partly installed or for which there is an agreement to install after 1 October 1969. Again, details of the type of arrestment plant must be given to the local authority. Prior to 1 October 1969, the only furnaces covered were those in buildings burning pulverised fuel or solid waste or fuel at a rate of 1 tonne or more an hour. After that date, the Clean Air Act 1968 extended the powers to include furnaces in which solid, liquid or gaseous matter is burnt as well as reducing the rate of the use of solid matter to a minimum 100 pounds per hour. The statutory requirements are fleshed out by the Clean Air (Emission of Grit and Dust from Furnaces) Regulations 1971 (SI 1971 No. 162), which contain information as to the quantities of grit and dust which may be emitted by reference to either the heat put out by the furnace or the heat taken in by the furnace.

Exemptions

There are exemptions to the requirement to supply details of plant to the local authority under s. 6; s. 7 gives two main areas of exemption. First, the Secretary of State can exempt certain furnaces by way of the Clean Air (Arrestment Plant) (Exemption) Regulations 1969 (SI 1969 No. 1262), which exclude mobile or transportable furnaces, and certain other furnaces. Secondly, the local authority has a power to exempt a specific furnace if it is satisfied that the emissions from the furnace will not be prejudicial to health or a nuisance. Application for this exemption has to be made by the person installing the furnace. The local authority has eight weeks in which to give a written decision and if no decision is forthcoming in that period then exemption is deemed to have been granted. Where there is a refusal of an application, there is a right of appeal within 28 days from the date of the decision.

Monitoring provisions

To enable the local authority to enforce its responsibilities effectively, s. 10 allows the Secretary of State to make regulations which allow the local authority to monitor the emission of grit and dust from furnaces. This provision does not apply to fumes unless they are controlled specifically under other legislation.

The provisions regulating the measurement of grit and dust are contained in the Clean Air (Measurement of Grit and Dust) Regulations 1971 (SI 1971 No. 616) and the Clean Air (Units of Measurement) Regulations 1992 (SI 1992 No. 35). Under these regulations, the local authority has to give occupiers of premises not less than six weeks' notice in writing requiring them to make adaptations to any chimney serving a furnace to allow for plant and machinery to be installed to monitor the dust and grit from the furnace. Thereafter the local authority must give at least 28 days' notice in writing requiring a test to be carried out in accordance with the procedure specified in an otherwise obscure book, *The Measurement of Solids in Flue Gases* by P G W Hawksley, S Badzioch and J H Blackett. Then, after giving at least 48 hours' notice in writing of the date and time of the tests, the occupier must send to the local authority within 14 days the report of the results of the test, including the date, the number of furnaces and the results in terms of pounds of grit and dust emitted per hour.

These provisions apply only to a number of specific types of furnace including those that burn pulverised fuel or any other solid matter at a rate of 45 kilograms or more per hour.

The control of height of chimneys

As one of the main mechanisms for the control of environmental pollution into the atmosphere was to increase the height of chimneys to disperse the pollutant over a wider area, there is specific legislation to control the height of chimneys. The argument used by many scientists has been that the higher the chimney the higher the emission point, and thus the more diluted any emissions will be when they eventually come back down to the ground.

Under ss. 14 and 15, an application for chimney height approval is required to enable the local authority to assess the height required, taking into account the geographical features and the constitution of the emissions, so as to avoid localised pollution. If approval is not obtained, it will only be an offence if the chimney is used once it has been constructed. The application form is prescribed by the Clean Air (Height of Chimneys) (Prescribed Form) Regulations 1969 (SI 1969 No. 412). An application must be made in the following circumstances:

(a)   where a new chimney is erected;

(b)   where the combustion space of a furnace serving an existing chimney is enlarged by adding a new furnace to an existing number of furnaces all serving the same chimney;

(c)   where a furnace is removed, or replaced, but only where a furnace burns pulverised fuel, or burns solid matter at a rate of 100 pounds or more per hour, or burns more than 1.25 million BTU per hour of any liquid or gas.

In addition to these controls, planning permission must also be applied for.

When deciding whether or not to grant chimney height approval, the local authority must be satisfied that the chimney height will be sufficient to prevent, so far as is practicable, the smoke, grit, dust, gases or fumes emitted from the chimney from being prejudicial to health or a nuisance when taking into account (s. 15(2)):

(a)   the purpose of the chimney;
(b)   the position and descriptions of buildings near it;
(c)   the levels of the neighbouring ground;
(d)   any other matters requiring consideration in the circumstances.

If the local authority decides to grant approval, it can grant it with or without conditions, but these must relate only to the rate and quality of emissions from the chimney (s. 15(3)). If the local authority turns down an application, it has to notify the applicant of its decision in writing with its reasons and an indication as to what it thinks the lowest acceptable height would be. The applicant may appeal to the Secretary of State within 28 days of notification of the decision (s. 15(6)).

As in other areas of control in the Clean Air Act, the Secretary of State has the power to exempt certain boilers or plants from this control for chimney height approval. These exemptions can be found in the Clean Air (Heights of Chimneys) (Exemption) Regulations 1969 (SI 1969 No. 411). The Regulations specifically relate to the need for approval to construct a chimney under s. 10 and include mostly temporary or mobile boilers or plant.

The guidelines on assessing chimney heights are contained in the *Third Memorandum on Chimney Heights,* published by HMSO. This provides specific mathematical calculations which take into account background levels of pollution. Where pollution levels are higher there is a requirement that a chimney should be higher as well. The memorandum indicates that the chimney height required should vary according to the type of area concerned among other factors. It identifies the following types of area:

(a)   an undeveloped area where development is unlikely;
(b)   a partially developed area with scattered houses;
(c)   a built-up residential area;
(d)   an urban area of mixed industrial and residential development;
(e)   a large city or an urban area of mixed heavy industrial and dense residential development.

By assessing the level of pollution in the atmosphere in these generalised ways, it is hoped to achieve an idea of the required height for a particular chimney. In a large city or urban area it will be a requirement that chimneys should be at their highest.

Miscellaneous controls

Aside from chimneys serving a furnace, s. 16 applies similar restrictions on chimneys serving a non-combustion process. There is a much simpler procedure for obtaining approval by submitting building regulation plans. The local authority is entitled to reject the plans if the chimney is not adequate to prevent emissions from becoming prejudicial to health or a nuisance. There is a right of appeal against refusal.

The Building Regulations 1991 (SI 1991 No. 2768) apply not only to non-combustible furnace chimneys but also to those controlled by s. 15. Building regulation approval is therefore required for all chimneys.

Smoke control areas

In order to improve conditions over wide areas and to control non-dark smoke, s. 18 allows local authorities to designate areas which will be smoke control areas. As there are difficulties in defining areas in relation to land, two or more authorities are entitled to join together and declare that a larger area than their own area is to be a smoke control area (s. 61(3)). Most smoke control areas were designated soon after the introduction of the Clean Air Act 1956. Although the process has slowed down since that time, the number of smoke control orders continues to rise. By 1990, nearly 10 million premises were subject to control, and the success of the orders was a major factor in the achievement of compliance with EC Directive 80/779.

The effect of designating a smoke control area is to make it an offence for occupiers of premises to allow any smoke emissions from a chimney.

The Act exempts both authorised fuel and certain fireplaces from control. The Smoke Control Areas (Authorised Fuels) Regulations 1991 (SI 1991 No. 1282), consolidate 17 different regulations made since 1956. These Regulations include all the types of material which can be burnt without emitting smoke. Fireplaces are exempted under various Smoke Control (Exempted Fireplaces) Orders. Therefore, either authorised fuel can be used *per se* or unauthorised fuel can be used on exempted fireplaces, and the use of either could amount to a defence to a prosecution under s. 20. The burden of proof for showing that such exemptions apply falls upon the occupier.

The local authority is entitled under s. 18(2) to exempt specified buildings, classes of building or fireplaces from the smoke control area. It may make different provision for different parts of the area or limit their operation to specified classes of buildings in the area, such as factories rather than houses.

The process for making an order designating a smoke control area is contained in sch. 1. There is a requirement for general publicity, which enables the public to make objections. This publicity is effected by placing advertisements in the *London Gazette* in addition to notices being posted around the area. If there are any objections to the order they must be taken into account as material considerations in deciding whether or not to ratify the order. Where an order is made, its operation is delayed for a minimum of six months whilst the authority brings the effect of the order to the notice of the people within the area.

Department of the Environment Circular 11/81 suggests that there should be sufficient supplies of authorised fuel in the area and the operation of the order should be implemented at some time between 1 July and 1 November to ensure that there are adequate provisions of fuel stocks.

The future of the smoke control area programme is in some doubt. Circular 9/93 states that the system of clean air grants from Central Government to help with the financing of the programme is to be scrapped in 1995. The main justification for this step is that full compliance with EC Directive 880/779 on particulates and sulphur dioxide has been achieved now that the areas of the country which were the subject of a derogation from the standards have been improved.

Central finance will be unavailable to fund smoke control programmes unless there is a continued breach of EC standards and the programme cannot be paid for out of the local funds or central credit approvals. Outside these criteria, all schemes will be at the discretion of the relevant authority. This move has been criticised in the light of moves to re-draft the framework Directive on air quality standards.

The control of noxious emissions to the atmosphere other than smoke, dust, grit, and fumes

Although the control of smoke has remained relatively unaffected by the EPA 1990, the control of more noxious pollutants is controlled under the air pollution control (APC) system contained in Part I of that Act.

The general framework of control under the APC regime is similar to that under IPC. Such things as application procedures, appeals, conditions and enforcement powers broadly reflect the IPC system, as to which see Chapter 11. It is not, therefore, intended to reproduce all the statutory provisions but to concentrate on the distinguishing features of APC where they depart significantly from the IPC system.

Under APC, local authorities regulate atmospheric emissions from a variety of industrial processes and mobile plant. New processes or existing processes which were substantially modified were required to apply for authorisation from 1 April 1991. Unlike IPC all existing processes covered under APC were required to apply for authorisation before the end of 1993.

The scope of air pollution control

The Environmental Protection (Prescribed Processes and Substances) Regulations 1991 (SI 1991 No. 472) (as amended) lists those processes which are to be controlled by the local authority, known as Part B processes. Since the introduction of the Regulations in 1991 there have been two major changes to the content of the Part B list. In a strong deregulatory move in 1994 there was a streamlining of the process list with some Part A processes (under IPC) being transferred to Part B and many threshold levels being raised to take processes outside regulatory control. Further draft deregulatory proposals were published in mid-1995 and the moves towards streamlining the system are expected to continue. These amendments should be viewed in the same context as the continuing review of APC guidance notes (see below). As in the planning field, the Government has used both regulatory amendments and policy guidance to refine the scope of the system in an attempt to eliminate what is considered to unnecessary bureaucracy. Critics have, however, argued that the raising of thresholds and other amendments have had a significant impact upon the number of process which are not subject to any regulation. In particular, the choice of defined threshold limits has lead to claims that some limits are almost arbitrary. For example, the threshold for prescribing processes involving the sale of coal and coal products was lifted from a throughput of 3,000 tonnes to 10,000 tonnes. Whilst it might be argued that the impact of operations with a throughput at the former level was insignificant, it is much more difficult to argue that the latter level is a precise indication of a significant impact. If this is the case, is the impact insignificant at a throughput of 9,995 tonnes per year? It is for this reason that some operators have chosen to alter processes to fall beneath the threshold limits and escape direct control.

The substances controlled under APC are set out in sch. 4 to the Regulations and are controlled only in relation to their impact on the atmosphere rather than land or water (see p. 296).

Applications

All Part B process applications must be made to the local authority for the area in which the process will be carried on (in the case of mobile plant it is the local authority in which the applicant's principal place of business is situated). The form and content of the application is set out in the Environmental Protection (Applications, Appeals and Registers) Regulations 1991 (SI 1991 No. 507). A application fee is payable under the APC charging scheme (see p. 304). An annual fee is payable thereafter.

An application must contain general information about the location of the process, a description of the process and the name and address of the operator. It should also contain details of any prescribed substances released from the process, with an assessment of the environmental consequences of the emissions and methods of abatement and monitoring all with reference to the BATNEEC for that particular process. It should be borne in mind that this information relates only to atmospheric emissions (s. 7(5)), it is not necessary to include any information on discharges to water and production of solid wastes. It is also not necessary to undertake an exercise to identify the BPEO in relation to the process as this only applies to IPC (s. 7(7)).

The local authority has the power to request further information in writing (sch. 1 para. 1(3)). The procedure in relation to consultation and publicity is similar to that for IPC, with HSE and nature conservation bodies being statutory consultees and publication of details of the application in a newspaper within 42 days of the application being made. Representations can be made within 28 days of the publication of the details of the application. Under the Environmental Protection (Authorisation of Processes) (Determination Periods) Order 1991 (SI 1991 No. 513) the determination period for applications involving new processes is four months whereas this can be extended to nine months for an existing process (see SI 1994 No. 2847). In every case the deadline can be extended with the agreement of the parties.

Various amendments to the application procedure were proposed in 1994, including increasing the requirements for advertising an application, details of any parent company to be included in all applications (to enable the public to identify where the ultimate responsibility for a process lay) and amendments to the details contained on the public register.

The determination of the application

The local authority has two choices when determining an application. It can grant the application subject to conditions (including conditions imposed by s. 7) or refuse the application (s. 6(3)). It must refuse an application where it considers that the applicant will not be able to comply with the conditions which would be imposed under the authorisation. Although not explicit, it would appear that this refers to the ability of the applicant to achieve the standards set down by the conditions rather than the selection of the process components and their capabilities. Where there are doubts about the adequacy of the components there should be a refusal on the ground that the process does not fulfil the BATNEEC requirement.

Each APC authorisation has an implied condition (where not explicit) that the BATNEEC will be used for preventing the release of prescribed substances into the air or, where that is not practicable, for reducing the release of that substance to a minimum or rendering it harmless. There is a residual duty to render harmless the release of any substance which might cause harm to the air.

Explicit conditions can be imposed to achieve the BATNEEC standards and to ensure compliance with any standards or limits set down by the Secretary of State. It is particularly important to consider the lawfulness of conditions imposed in relation to APC authorisations. GG2 sets out a list of model conditions with tests of clarity, relevance and workability proposed for determining lawfulness. As in a number of other areas where conditions overlap (most notably planning and waste disposal) it is not necessarily easy to identify clear subject boundaries. It should be possible, however, to limit the conditions purely to the operation of the process itself and the consequences for atmospheric emissions. Most guidance notes contain a list of the matters which should be made the subject of conditions.

Air pollution guidance notes

Unlike the IPC guidance note system, central guidance notes for APC are issued centrally by the DoE. There is a large number of guidance notes which cover all Part B processes. Each note contains information relating to recommended emission limits, requirements for monitoring, reporting and record-keeping, as well as miscellaneous matters including the use of equipment to abate pollution, the handling of certain materials and the construction of chimneys and other emission points.

Significantly, the guidance notes cover situations where existing operations must be upgraded to meet new quality objectives. The notes are reviewed on a four-yearly cycle, with the first reviews being completed by the end of 1995.

In a similar fashion to the Prescribed Processes and Substances Regulations, the review has been seen as an attempt to deregulate the system and to simplify, in particular, ongoing requirements for monitoring. It has been suggested that where monitoring information has been initially validated by an external independent party, the gap between a further regular monitoring period may be extended. It is presumed that this is justified by the demonstrated reliability of the information. This move has also been criticised as it increases the chance that breaches of conditions in relation to emissions limits will be much more difficult to detect.

Although the system has been operating for some time, it is difficult to discern the true weight of the guidance contained in the APC notes because of the lack of information relating to decisions on appeal. More specifically, there has been no reported examples of successful appeals against local authorities imposing more stringent requirements than those set down in the APC notes. Whilst the notes are not viewed as determinative and local circumstances can prevail, it is thought that there would have to be clear justification from a departure from the standards contained in central guidance.

Enforcement provisions

Sections 11 to 14 of the EPA 1990 enable local authorities to enforce the APC system. The provisions are the same as for IPC and include:

(a) variation notices to take into account changes in circumstances (s. 11);

(b) enforcement notices requiring certain steps to be taken (s. 13);

(c) revocation notices to be issued in situations where a process has not been carried out for twelve months (s. 12);

(d) prohibition notices in situations where there is a imminent risk of serious pollution (s. 14).

There is a right of appeal under s. 15. Environmental health officers have the same powers as HMIP inspectors when dealing with the obtaining of information.

Public registers

Under ss. 20 to 22 of the EPA 1990, there is a duty on local authorities to keep registers and information relating to applications and authorisations, convictions, and monitoring data. They must also hold registers in relation to the IPC system.

Overlap with other controls

Where an authorisation is required under both parts of the regulations, i.e. there are components of a process subject to IPC control and related components subject to Part B of the regulations, HMIP will have full control.

The Secretary of State also has power to transfer processes under APC control to HMIP (this is intended to smooth the administrative functions of the system in that, where a process is substantially controlled by HMIP, but there are a number of processes which are controlled under APC, it would make administrative sense to amalgamate the two controls under HMIP). It is also thought that such a power could be used where the Secretary of State is of the opinion that the local authority is not conducting its duties properly.

Where matters which could amount to a statutory nuisance are more properly controlled under APC, the Secretary of State's consent is required before a local authority can institute summary proceedings (s. 79(10)). It is important to note that this is not a complete prohibition on the bringing of an action in statutory nuisance. Indeed, where an operator of a process is guilty of an offence under s. 22, it is undoubtedly for a local authority to fulfil its statutory duty under s. 79 to ensure that statutory nuisances within its area are abated.

The control of emissions from motor vehicles

The effect of transport on the environment is varied. Noise, land-take for roads and other projects and the use of raw materials (petrol, diesel, in addition to manufacturing materials). Emissions from vehicles are, however, probably the most significant issue which needs to be regulated and controlled.

The problems of pollution from motor vehicles was acknowledged as significant in the RCEP's first report where the Royal Commission warned of the dangers of ignoring the environmental implications of traffic growth. With growth forecasts for road traffic of over 140% between 1988 and 2025 the original warnings have taken on a repetitive nature. In particular, the RCEP's Eighteenth Report on Transport and the Environment set out eight key objectives which were intended to make transport policy more sustainable. In relation to atmospheric pollution this included targets for air quality and the reduction of CO_2 emissions.

The law in relation to the control of emissions from motor vehicles is under constant review and too detailed to be covered, other than in principle, in a book of this type. Most controls target product standards in relation to vehicle-type approval, specified emission limits from vehicles, the content of fuel and maintenance tests. Most limits have their origin within EC legislation (see below).

When a new motor vehicle is produced it must comply with all relevant standards, including EC emission limits. The Motor Vehicles (Type Approval) (Great Britain) Regulations (SI 1994 No. 981) sets out type-approval procedures which are applied to specimen examples of vehicles prior to general sale.

The Road Vehicle (Construction and Use) Regulations, are a series of Regulations which set out requirements in reaction to a variety of construction details, including catalytic convertors, the use of unleaded petrol, and emission levels for vehicles in use. In particular, the annual MOT tests (and, more recently, roadside checks) have standards for smoke and carbon monoxide which must not be exceeded.

European policy on motor vehicles

The EC has combined policy with legislative initiatives on transport generally, and motor vehicles specifically, for some time (the earliest Directive on emissions from engines dates back to 1970). European transport policy is to be found in a Green Paper on the Impact of Transport on the Environment, adopted in 1992. UK policy mirrors the approach contained in this document with its integrated approach to transport policy ('sustainable mobility') with an increasing overlap between transport policy and other areas, such as planning and economic policy.

Vehicle emissions have been controlled under a number of increasingly complex amendments to the original controlling Directive 70/220. Generally, Directives have set product standards by fixing emission limits for carbon monoxide, HC and NO_2 and particulates. Various amendments have culminated in Directive 94/12 which sets out limits for cars and light vans which will come into force in 1997 for all new registrations and 1996 for new models. Emissions from larger vans and heavy duty vehicles are controlled under separate Directives (93/59 and 91/542 respectively).

In addition to the fixed emission limits, there have been a number of Directives controlling the roadworthiness of vehicles to ensure that the original product standards are being maintained. Directives 91/238 and 92/55 set out procedures for checking the roadworthiness of private cars and light vehicles and catalytic converters respectively.

These Directives are implemented in UK legislation through the Construction and Use Regulations and the Type Approval Regulations (see above).

THIRTEEN
Waste management

The production of waste is a natural consequence of life in an industrialised society. In the past, both the volume and the types of waste produced were easily dealt with in small, country rubbish dumps. This, of course, was in the days before plastic packaging, aluminium cans and other composite materials which make up a large amount of domestic waste in Britain. Furthermore, the amount of domestic waste disposed of in Britain represents only a small fraction of the total amount of waste produced. In the Second Report of the House of Commons Environment Committee on toxic waste, it was shown that in 1989 Britain produced approximately 2,500m tonnes of waste, of which only 1.5m tonnes was domestic and trade waste. Other types of waste included liquid industrial effluent, agricultural waste, waste from mines and quarries, sewage sludge, waste from power stations, solid industrial waste and hazardous waste.

These vast amounts of waste have increased in recent years. The consumer boom of the post-war Britain has led to the production of more and more products with less and less durability. As consumption increases so does the volume of waste, and a strong impression builds up that we live in a society with a throwaway mentality. The culprits are, however, not just the end users of products, but also the producers and designers of them.

Most of the waste disposed of in Britain is deposited in large holes in the ground, such as old quarries. The difficulties of burying waste are numerous. Substances may break down after a number of years to produce contaminating liquids or hazardous gases, which may then escape from the site. In 1989 and 1990, the House of Commons Environment Committee reported on the issues of toxic waste and contaminated land. The evidence submitted to the Committee painted a horrifying picture of the extent to which there are problems with the state of contaminated land in Britain. Estimates of the area of land contaminated range from a very conservative 10,000 hectares to a possible 100,000 hectares. Britain has already experienced the dangers of waste disposal sites. In 1986, methane produced from a landfill site at Loscoe in Derbyshire exploded, causing injury. Other examples could be given from around the world of housing estates that have been abandoned because of contamination of the land on which they were built, severely polluted water supplies, deaths caused by indiscriminate dumping of waste, and areas that are wholly unusable owing to long-term pollution problems caused by dumping.

Landfill is not the only option for the disposal of waste. Large quantities of waste are discharged to sewers or to natural waters, both matters which are dealt with elsewhere in this book. A small percentage of waste is incinerated or dumped at sea.

Each of these methods of disposal creates its own pollution problems and controversies. As suggested above, landfill sites may give rise to problems of methane emissions and of water pollution as a result of leachate. They also give rise to effects that will be only too obvious to those who live nearby, such as smells, noise, air-borne dust and rubbish, and increased traffic generation. As a result, landfill sites are amongst the uses of land that are most vigorously opposed by local communities. A further factor is that there is a marked tendency for landfill sites to be proposed on 'waste land', which is often precisely that land which is of greatest importance in nature conservation and amenity terms. However, in the 1990s the most important point is simply that many existing sites are reaching their full capacity and that the supply of suitable new locations for landfill sites is very limited indeed. In some areas the problem is acute, leading to the need to transport waste long distances. A particular problem for Britain is that, unlike many other European countries, it has traditionally followed a policy of co-disposal on landfill sites, meaning that different sorts of waste are mixed together.

In relation to incineration, there are obvious problems of air pollution, especially concerning the release of such things as dioxins as a result of incomplete combustion. More recently, the publication of a draft US EPA Report on the effects of dioxins has led some people to take the view that any level of dioxin production, however small, could cause significant harm to both humans and the environment. It is becoming clear that the application of EC standards on air pollution to British incinerators will lead to a reduction in their number and that replacement facilities are being opposed and delayed through the town and country planning system and latterly the authorisation process under EPA 1990, Part I. However, in May 1993, the Royal Commission on Environmental Pollution in its Seventeenth Report, *Incineration of Waste* (Cmd. 2181), recommended that waste incineration should play a key role in the future development of waste disposal, though critics have pointed to the weakness of the Royal Commission's arguments on waste minimisation.

Dumping at sea is now heavily restricted through international conventions and must be seen as an option which has virtually disappeared. For example, dumping of industrial waste at sea has now effectively ceased and Britain, the only EC country still dumping sewage sludge at sea, has agreed to discontinue this practice by 1998.

These problems illustrate the need to establish a clear framework of policy to provide for the proper disposal of waste, particularly toxic and hazardous waste. However, more importantly, they establish the need to develop policies relating to the reduction of waste and its recycling or re-use.

Waste policy

The response has been to seek to develop policies that tackle the problem of waste at source if possible. The Government's White Paper, *This Common Inheritance,* states that 'the Government's first priority is to reduce waste at source to a minimum'. It further states that the Government is committed to the promotion of recycling of as much waste as possible and to the tightening of controls over waste disposal standards. This official policy can be summarised as being that waste minimisation is to be preferred to recycling, and recycling preferred to disposal. These policies reflect those of the EC (see below).

Although there has been a tremendous upsurge in policy initiatives in the field of waste management there has been a feeling that the growth has been unstructured and the overall objectives have been difficult to discern. It has also become important to establish central policy themes in order to set down the manner in which the policy objectives can, in practice, be achieved. There has therefore been a need to bring together the various initiatives in a coherent structure and to iron out any minor inconsistencies between individual strategies. The status of official policy on waste management has thus taken a further step forward with the introduction of a formal National Waste Strategy for England and Wales. Section 44A of the Environmental Protection Act 1990 (inserted by s. 92 of the Environment Act 1995) provides for the Secretary of State to prepare a statement containing policies in relation to the recovery and disposal of waste. It is intended that the Strategy will replace waste disposal plans which have been drawn up by waste regulation authorities under s. 50 of EPA 1990 in addition to meeting the requirements of the EC Framework Directive's provisions in relation to waste management plans.

A pre-cursor to the plan was published in consultation form in January 1995. Although it does not have any statutory status, this consultation paper is likely to form the basis for the statutory plan under the EPA 1990. Underpinning the Strategy are the three key objectives for waste management: to reduce the amount of waste that society produces; to make best use of the waste that is produced; and to choose waste management practices which minimise the risks of immediate and future environmental pollution and harm to human health. The mechanism for achieving these three objectives is the previously outlined waste hierarchy of waste reduction, reuse, recovery, and disposal.

The plan then goes on to set a variety of general and specific targets for a selection of waste streams with a five-point plan to achieve the aims of the Strategy. This plan comprises strategies based upon regulation, economic instruments, the Town and Country Planning system, promoting waste minimisation techniques to industry; and the provision of sound information about the sources, amounts and types of waste which are managed.

Although Britain has now firmly established the concept of a hierarchy of waste management it must be recognised that Britain is still some way behind other EC countries in the amount of waste that is recycled and in developing recycling policies. For example, a recent report suggested that less than 6% of British household waste is recycled, against a Government target of 50%, which it believes can mainly be achieved through the use of economic instruments and charging mechanisms. In this respect, the Government's Advisory Committee on Business and the Environment recommended in its first report in November 1991 that the most effective method of encouraging recycling would be to raise landfill prices significantly—they are currently far lower than in many other countries. This is a simple example of the use of an economic instrument.

The introduction of a tax on waste disposed to landfill has been considered for some time. The idea received support from the Royal Commission on Environmental Pollution. The tax looks likely to be implemented within the fiscal year 1996–97 although a lot of issues have yet to be sorted out (see below). After the tax is introduced landfill costs are expected to rise by up to 50%.

The impact of the recent legislation on firms producing waste is clear, particularly when coupled with developments in relation to discharges to sewers and controls over incineration. Waste minimisation is to be encouraged because the costs of disposal, by whatever route, are likely to increase significantly throughout the 1990s.

As has frequently been the case in environmental matters, the British approach to the clean-up of contaminated land has tended to be a fairly pragmatic one. Unlike the position in some other countries, where land is cleaned up to uniformly high standards, the British approach is in general to consider the proposed use of land and to question whether there is any immediate threat of pollution or harm to human health. The British clean-up powers tend, therefore, not to be activated until there is some problem, and then are used only to the extent that is necessary to remove the problem, rather than to provide an absolutely pristine site (even if that were technically achievable).

This chapter will concentrate on the management of waste throughout the disposal chain and the clean-up of contaminated land. This should not, however, obscure the point that increasingly developments in waste minimisation techniques and recycling technologies are likely to dominate over the coming years.

The use of economic instruments and waste management

The waste management system has seen the largest number of active initiatives in relation to the use of economic instruments in the field of environmental protection. In particular, provisions to encourage the recycling and the proposed tax on disposal of waste to landfill are intended to reflect the environmental costs of disposing of waste to land.

The landfill tax

A tax on the disposal of waste to landfill has been promised for some time. A consultation paper was finally published in March 1995 by a number of Government Departments (including DoE, HM Customs and Excise, DTI and the Treasury) which set out the details of the propose levy. The tax is intended to come into effect on 1 October 1996 and it is anticipated that the legislation might be introduced with the Finance Act 1995 after the November Budget. The tax is likely to have a large impact upon those companies which dispose of significant volumes of waste to landfill, although this will be offset by some of the changes in other taxation. Furthermore, it is anticipated that there will be an incentive to produce less waste or recycle where appropriate. Other technologies for waste disposal (e.g. *in-situ* sewage treatment of liquid waste) are also expected to become more prominent as existing price differentials narrow. There have, however, been a number of criticisms of the proposed tax and allegations that it will only lead to more waste being dumped in poorly engineered and unsuitable sites.

The tax is intended to reflect the full environmental costs of disposing of waste to landfill and to apply the 'polluter pays' principle. It is also hoped that the amount of waste going to final disposal will be reduced by 20% over a 20-year period as waste producers seek to reduce costs. It is estimated that approximately 100 million tonnes of waste is dumped in landfill sites every year, with an average cost of £10 per tonne. The consultation paper asserts that 'the tax will seek to reflect the environmental costs of landfill which are not already reflected in the price paid'. It was initially proposed that the tax would be collected on an *ad valorem* basis on the disposal price paid (i.e. the tax was to be levied as a percentage addition to the charge of landfilling waste). The tax mirrors the existing arrangements for VAT. All operators of landfill sites would be required to register with HM Customs and Excise and would have to account for the tax. Unlike VAT, however, the tax would not be deductible by the producers of the waste as an input tax.

There were over 700 responses to the consultation paper, mostly critical of the proposed method of calculating the tax. The main criticism was that the *ad valorem* basis for collecting the tax would lead to adverse environmental consequences. The consultation paper suggested that, by relating the tax to price, the revenue raised would accurately reflect the environmental costs of waste disposal in two ways. First, waste which was relatively less harmful to the environment (e.g. demolition and construction wastes) commands a lower disposal price and therefore would attract a lower tax penalty. Secondly, waste which was disposed of in areas where landfill sites are scarce (and, consequently, it is argued, often environmentally more damaging) would also command higher disposal costs and thus a higher tax penalty.

These views were criticised as they did not reflect an accurate picture of the waste management industry. Moreover, by relating the tax to price it was argued that waste producers would simply opt to dispose of waste in sites which were cheaper and not necessarily better equipped to cope with the wastes which were disposed. Many of the consultees argued that an *ad valorem* tax would increase the tax differentials between sites with higher and lower environmental standards, produce a disincentive to produce higher standards and increase the likelihood that waste would be transported over longer distances to cheaper sites. Responding to this criticism the Chancellor (with the Treasury having primary responsibility for the tax) announced that the tax would be weight-based, charged per tonne of waste and that inert waste would be subject to a reduced rate of tax.

No specific rate of tax was given in the consultation paper although it is intended to raise receipts of between £300–500m, implying a rate of between 30% and 50% The intention is to offset the money raised by making compensatory reductions in the level of employer National Insurance contributions. A landfill rate of 50%, for instance, could, according to the Chancellor, lead to a 0.2% reduction in the main rate of employers' contributions or more than 1% in the lower rates of employers' contributions.

Generally, the use of the tax income to reduce National Insurance contributions has been welcomed, but some commentators have criticised the failure to allow the income to be set-aside solely for environmental purposes. The Government has attempted to address these criticisms by raising the possibility of introducing environmental trusts. These trusts would be private sector, non-profit-making bodies, under a duty to distribute funds for approved environmental purposes—reflecting the bodies set up to administrate the proceeds of the National Lottery. In particular, it is intended that most of the funds will be set aside for paying for the clean-up of contaminated sites or closed landfills where primary responsibility cannot be clearly identified. This would be one of the few examples of a hypothecated tax and certainly an unusual innovation in the environmental field, which could gain favour with a large number of environmental groups. It is envisaged that landfill tax bills would be abated by 90% of any payments made by waste producers to the environmental trusts in the previous quarter. They will be financed primarily from these rebates but the waste industry will still have to contribute 10% of their funds. They will disburse their funds on broad purposes to be approved by the Government. These are likely to include research and the remediation costs involved in cleaning up sites where liability is unclear. A working party is to be established with representatives from the waste industry and others to discuss the issue further.

Recycling

There is now a number of powers in the legislation which aim to encourage recycling. for example in accordance with Directive 91/156, many types of waste recycling facility are likely to be exempt from the waste management licensings, system and require only to be registered with the WRA. However, it is clear that government belief is that recycling ought to be encouraged by voluntary and economic mechanisms rather than be required through compulsory controls. As a result, British legislation does not formally include many specific duties to recycle. This attitude partly explains, for example, the

Government's opposition to the introduction of strict recycling targets in the proposed EC Directive on packaging waste.

The authority with the most important role in relation to recycling is the waste collection authority, since it collects most domestic and commercial waste and is able to separate recyclable wastes at an early stage. The authority may require separate receptacles to be used for household wastes that are to be recycled and those which are not (s. 46(2)). It may buy or acquire waste with a view to recycling it (s. 55) and, if it makes arrangements for recycling waste, it does not have to deliver the waste to the waste disposal authority, as it would otherwise have to do under s. 48. It is also under a duty to draw up a waste recycling plan for its area, which involves publicising the arrangements it intends to make to facilitate recycling (s. 49). By the middle of 1993 all authorities had submitted their draft plan to the Secretary of State.

Perhaps most significant in the light of the Government's policy on economic instruments is that the waste collection authority is entitled to a recycling credit from the waste disposal authority under s. 52 where it recycles waste. The idea behind this provision is that it acts as an incentive to recycle waste by getting the waste disposal authority to pay the waste collection authority the amount of money it saves by not having to dispose of the waste. The amount payable is based on the net saving the waste disposal authority makes as a result of the recycling activities. At present the rate is fixed at half the average cost saving to the waste disposal authority, but the Government has announced that this is to rise to the full amount. The waste disposal authority *may* also make such a payment to anyone else who recycles waste and thus removes it from the waste stream (s. 52(3)).

Legislative history

The disposal of waste was not seen as an important issue until a public outcry concerning the deposit of hazardous waste in the West Midlands in the early-1970s led to the passage of the Deposit of Poisonous Wastes Act 1972. This Act is a classic example of the reactive nature of environmental legislation in Britain, since it approached the deposit of waste from a narrow viewpoint and sought mainly to combat the type of incident that had occurred. However, it remains the case that the 1972 Act was one of the first ever controls over the deposit of hazardous waste in the world.

The 1972 Act was soon replaced by Part I of the Control of Pollution Act 1974 (COPA 1974). COPA 1974 introduced a more comprehensive system in which a waste disposal licence was required from the waste disposal authority before 'controlled waste' could be disposed of either to landfill or for incineration. This system provided a model for other countries, and in particular for the EC framework Directive on Waste (75/442). At that stage, Britain led the way in legislating against the dumping of waste.

However, over the years COPA 1974 gave rise to a number of problems and itself proved to be too narrow. Accordingly, in Part II of the Environmental Protection Act 1990 (EPA 1990) the framework for a new system of waste management was established. The change in concept from 'waste

disposal' (as used in COPA 1974) to that of 'waste management' is significant, since it illustrates that increased control is to be exercised over the whole
of the waste cycle 'from cradle to grave'. In particular, the EPA 1990 involves
greater controls over waste producers and waste carriers than was the case
under COPA 1974. As a result, the full implementation of the EPA 1990
changed the way in which waste is dealt with fundamentally.

After many stops and starts the main provisions of Part II of the EPA 1990
were finally implemented on 1 May 1994. Anyone who would like to think
that the statutory regime is now settled and sensibly structured is unfortunately faced with labyrinth of regulations and guidance notes. It is also likely
that the detail of the legislation will change within a short period.

The main reason for the delay—and subsequent deluge of statutory and
non-statutory material—has been the need to implement the framework
Directive on Waste (91/156). In common with many other areas of environmental law the Act itself now provides only a framework which is fleshed out
by numerous other documents. In addition to the Waste Management
Licensing Regulations (SI 1994 No. 1056) which forms the main body of
supplementary legislation, there is the Waste Management Licensing (Fees
and Charges) Scheme, Waste Management Papers on the Licensing of Waste
Management Facilities (No. 4) and Landfill Completion (No. 26A), and
Government guidance in the form of the Department of the Environment
Circular 11/94 on Waste Management Licencing and the Framework Directive on Waste. The effect of all this and future material is that the law has
now become even more complex and difficult to interpret. In this chapter an
attempt will be made to explain some of the principles of the new legislation;
unfortunately, the detail of the law falls outside the scope of such a work as
this. Although COPA 1974 has now been largely superseded appropriate
reference will be made to its provisions where the courts have interpreted
concepts which are relevant to Part II of EPA 1990.

Transitional provisions

Most waste disposal licences granted under COPA 1974 and in force on 1
May 1994 are automatically treated as if they were a waste management
license under Part II of EPA 1990. There are, however, four situations where
the old Act continues to apply (although the significance of each diminishes
with passing time):

(a) old (i.e. made prior to 1 May 1994) applications for a waste disposal
licence which are undetermined;
(b) undetermined appeals against the revocation of a waste disposal
licence;
(c) activities which fall under Part I of the EPA 1990 but which are not
yet covered and are exempt from the need for a licence under Part II;
(d) scrap metal activities which are exempt from the need for a licence
under Part II but are controlled under a waste management licence.

All of these transitional arrangements continue to be regulated under COPA 1974. Where applications or appeals are determined there will be an automatic transfer to a waste management licence as if it were 1 May 1994.

Waste disposal and town planning

The disposal of waste on land presents some difficult questions of a land use nature. It has always been necessary to acquire planning permission for landfill operations. Indeed, the Town and Country Planning Acts were the primary control over waste before COPA 1974 was enacted. They still provide an additional, and complementary, layer of controls, one that will remain largely unchanged by the introduction of the EPA 1990.

Waste local plans

On the whole, county authorities have traditionally incorporated policies on waste disposal into county structure plans. Some counties prepared subject local plans, but coverage has been sparse. There is now, however, a duty imposed under s. 38 of the Town and Country Planning Act 1990 (as amended by the Planning and Compensation Act 1991), upon non-metropolitan authorities alone, to prepare a waste local plan.

The plan should cover a variety of issues and should include references to the full range of waste management considerations, including such issues as:

scrap yards, incineration, landfill and landraise, recycling and waste transfer, waste processing, composting, storage and treatment centres.

The plan should be in general conformity with the structure plan and take into account any minerals local plan. It should aim to identify sites already in use, future sites and broad areas of search within which sites may be located. It should also identify policies setting out criteria against which applications for waste management facilities will be determined.

In metropolitan areas, waste policies should be included in unitary development plans in respect of development which involves the depositing of refuse or waste materials other than mineral waste.

When drawing up plans, local planning authorities should take into account factors such as the principle of self-sufficiency, whereby the authority should aim to allocate sufficient land and/or facilities to deal with the waste arising within that area. Other factors which need to be taken into account include targets of waste minimisation and recycling, incineration to reduce land take, the variety of treatment methods which may be required prior to disposal and waste disposal plans made under s. 50 of the EPA 1990.

Waste local plans and waste disposal plans

Waste disposal plans have to be drawn up by the WRA (see p. 382). Waste disposal plans are primarily concerned with strategic aspects of treating and disposing of waste as opposed to the issues surrounding land use aspects. Thus, waste disposal plans include reference to the types and amounts of waste arisings, the import and export of waste from an area, site operating standards and licensing criteria and a hierarchy of disposal methods. The overlap between waste local plans and waste disposal plans should be minimised.

Development control
Section 55(3)(b) of the Town and Country Planning Act 1990 provides that the deposit of refuse or waste materials on land involves the material change in the use of that land if the area of the deposit is extended or the height of the deposit is extended above the original ground level. In addition, depending upon the facts of the case, tipping can amount to an engineering operation (if it involves technical supervision for instance), or even fall within the catch-all definition of an 'other operation'.

A planning application for the use of land, or the carrying out of operations in or on land, for the deposit of refuse or waste materials and/or the erection of any building, plant or machinery designed to be used wholly or mainly for the purposes of treating, storing, processing or disposing of refuse or waste materials is a county matter (see Town and Country Planning Act 1990, sch. 1). The application is made direct to the county planning authority, which is then under a duty to notify the district authority within 14 days as part of the consultation procedure (art. 19 of the GDO).

Areas of doubt
Not every application will clearly fall within the above definitions. The ancillary use of waste disposal or management facilities as part of a larger operation would not amount to a county matter. Often the district authority will view an application as being a district matter even though it involves an element of waste disposal. It is the primary intention behind a particular planning application which is important. Where applications *primarily* relate to a process resulting in the final *deposit* of waste it is the DoE's view that this would be a county matter. On the other hand, planning applications involving the storage, treatment or processing of waste, but which do not end with the depositing of waste, are to be viewed as district matters.

Planning conditions and obligations
The difficulties with using planning conditions to control environmentally sensitive developments have been covered elsewhere (see p. 242). Planning permissions for waste disposal operations require special consideration. The main criterion for conditions on a planning permission for waste disposal is that they be for a planning purpose. Examples of matters which would normally be dealt with by way of conditions on the planning permission include:

(a)   phasing of operations;
(b)   the extent of tipping;
(c)   access to and from the site;
(d)   the *general* nature of the waste;

(e)   restoration plans, including site contours, minimum depth of top soil etc.;

(f)   aftercare for a short-term period.

To avoid duplicating environmental controls there are certain areas which should not normally be covered as they are more properly dealt with under the waste management regime. These include:

(a)   the duration of activity;

(b)   supervision of activities (including site offices and other administrative responsibilities);

(c)   the specific types of waste to be covered;

(d)   keeping of records;

(e)   associated works.

As stated above (p. 242), although it is advisable to separate the two areas of control, it is not unlawful to impose conditions which overlap.

EC Directives on waste

In keeping with the general aims of EC environmental policy set out in Art. 130R(2), the EC has adopted as a specific aim the prevention of waste at source through proper design of products and processes. This is linked with such initiatives as the development of clean technology, eco-labelling and the discipline of life cycle analysis. A second aim is to recycle or to re-use waste that is produced, with particular emphasis to be placed on the use of waste as a source of energy, for example through combined heat and power schemes linked to waste incinerators. An obvious example of the EC's role in this area is its development of a Directive on the recycling of packaging waste (although this is in fact based on existing legislation in other EC countries). A third aim is that waste should be disposed of in its country of origin, thus leading to restrictions on the transfrontier shipment of waste.

These aims have been translated into a number of Directives on waste management, each of which has had, and will continue to have, a great impact on the shape of British law in this area. The framework Directive on Waste 75/442 established a general framework of controls for waste management. In accordance with the EC's general policies, it aimed to encourage the recovery of waste and its management at the point of production. It has been significantly amended by Directive 91/156 which should have been complied with by April 1993. The Directive has been fully implemented with the introduction of the Waste Management Licensing Regulations (SI 1994 No. 1056). Together, the two Directives require that a public agency plans waste disposal properly, that waste disposal facilities are licensed by a competent public agency and that any exemptions from the licensing system fall within certain categories and are properly justified. They also lay down a definition of waste. In Case C155/91, *Commission v Council* [1993] *Water Law* 109, the European Court of Justice decided that the principal objective of the amending Directive 91/156 was the protection of the environment rather than the removal of trade barriers.

There is a separate framework Directive on Hazardous Waste (78/319, as amended by 91/689). These Directives lay down similar requirements to those applicable to all waste. Their main significance is that the amendments set out in 91/689 seek to lay down a common definition of hazardous waste across the EC based on the generic features and constituents of the waste. Implementation of the Directive depended upon the preparation of a list of hazardous wastes by the EC, which were determinative of its scope. The list was finally agreed (after much discussion) in December 1994 and at the time of writing new special waste regulations were being prepared to implement the new definition (see further p. 407).

There is also a Directive on Sewage Sludge (86/278), which lays down restrictions on the content of sewage sludge used on agricultural land. It has a knock-on effect on what sewerage undertakers will allow to be discharged into their sewers.

The EC is preparing Directives on landfills and on civil liability for damage caused by waste. The landfill proposals seek to harmonise landfill standards across the EC by laying down requirements on most matters concerned with the design and operation of a site, including permits, location, operating practices, leachate controls, financial guarantees, site closure, aftercare and liability for harm caused. The civil liability proposals seek to establish a wide-ranging strict liability regime for any harm caused by waste (see p. 408). However, in each case the detail of the proposals has given rise to a great amount of controversy and there is no guarantee of the final form any Directive will take. A Directive on Packaging and Packaging Waste was adopted in December 1994. The objective of the Directive is to harmonise national measures on packaging waste. Member States must take action to achieve certain recycling targets. By June 2001, between 50% and 65% by weight of packaging waste is to be recovered, with 25–45% of this to be recycled. Implementation must take place before the beginning of 1998. In the UK a 'Producer Responsibility Initiative' was launched in July 1993 to prompt industry to take the lead on packaging waste. The Environment Act 1995, ss. 93–95 provide for the drawing up of regulations to impose producer responsibility for packaging waste, although there has been no decision as to who will bear the cost of implementation.

As far as transfrontier shipment of waste is concerned, Regulation 259/93 introduces a system of control of shipments of waste within, into and out of the EC. It implements the provisions of the Basle Convention on the Control of Transboundary Movement of Hazardous Wastes and their Disposal 1989 (Cm. 984). The central feature of these instruments is a requirement that all shipments of waste must be subject to prior notification to the competent authorities. Transfrontier shipment of wastes, although a topic of great importance, is outside the scope of this book.

Lastly, there are Directives on the incineration of waste. Directives 89/369 and 89/429 respectively cover new and old municipal incinerators. Both are 'daughter Directives' of the Directive on Air Pollution from Industrial Plants

84/360. They lay down EC standards based on best available technology and are expected to lead to the shutdown of a number of British incinerators that cannot meet those standards. A Directive on hazardous waste incineration was adopted in December 1994: amongst other things, this lays down strict emission limits based on the most up-to-date technology. The provisions of all these Directives are implemented in British law through the integrated pollution control and air pollution control systems in Part I of the EPA 1990.

Waste disposal under the Control of Pollution Act 1974

Part I of COPA 1990 introduced a fairly comprehensive system of licensing under which a waste disposal licence was required from the waste disposal authority (WDA) for the deposit of household, industrial or commercial waste, referred to generically as 'controlled waste'. Mineral and agricultural wastes were, in general, exempt. So too was a range of activities listed in sch. 6 of the Control of Pollution (Collection and Disposal) Regulations 1988 (SI 1988 No. 819).

In non-metropolitan areas, the WDA was the county council in England and the district council in Wales. In metropolitan areas, it was normally the district council, although in some areas a joint body was established. The WDA had a range of administrative and regulatory functions, including a duty to arrange for the disposal of controlled waste (s. 13), a duty to make a waste disposal plan (s. 2), and responsibility for the operation of the licensing system (s. 5).

An application for a waste disposal licence had to be made in writing to the WDA (s. 51(1)). There were no publicity requirements, although there was a duty for the WDA to consult with the waste collection authority (normally the district council) and the NRA (s. 5(4)). The only mechanism for refusal on environmental grounds was that the disposal would pose a threat of water pollution or to public health (s. 5(3)). The WDA could attach conditions relating to waste disposal (s. 6), but the legislation was narrowly drafted in this respect and a number of desirable conditions were held to be outside its scope. There was a right of appeal to the Secretary of State against refusal or against any conditions (s. 10).

There were, however, parallel controls operated through the town planning system. Before a waste disposal licence could be granted, a valid planning permission (or equivalent exemption under the planning legislation) had to be in existence for the use of the site for waste disposal (s. 5(2)). This requirement placed the emphasis on whether and where to have a waste disposal site at the planning permission stage. Since it was clear that conditions attached to a waste disposal licence should not overlap with the types of condition that could be imposed on a planning permission, it also meant that the conditions attached to the planning permission were crucial to the operation of the site. For example, conditions relating to such important matters as aftercare and traffic movements to and from the site would be included in the planning permission rather than the waste disposal licence, with all the implications for enforcement that were entailed should breach of conditions occur.

Once a licence had been granted, the WDA had a number of supervisory duties (s. 9). However, its powers to take action were limited. Variation or revocation of the licence was possible only in restricted circumstances (s. 7). There were few limitations on the transfer of a licence (s. 8). Most significantly, there were no limitations whatsoever on the surrender of a licence, with the result that a licence holder could abandon its responsibilities under a licence at any time (s. 8(4)). There was a public register of current disposal licences (s. 6(4)).

It was a strict liability offence to deposit, or to cause or knowingly permit the deposit of, controlled waste without a licence (s. 3). Supplementary powers enabled the WDA to carry out a clean-up of illegal deposits of waste (s. 16), and there were provisions establishing strict civil liability for certain illegal deposits (s. 88).

The failings of COPA 1974

Although COPA 1974 provided the first system of comprehensive control over waste disposal in Britain, the practical effect of the Act turned out to be disappointing. Some of the defects were inherent in the system, whilst others became apparent as time passed. In referring to the state of waste management in Britain, the Second Report of the House of Commons Environment Committee on Toxic Waste contained some of the strongest words ever published by a Parliamentary Committee:

> Never, in any of our enquiries into environmental problems, have we experienced such consistent and universal criticism of existing legislation and of central and local government as we have done during the course of this inquiry.

After what appeared to be a bright future in 1974, what went wrong?

(a) Organisational problems
COPA 1974 created a system in which WDAs operated disposal sites themselves at the same time as regulating private sites by means of the licensing system. The inherent conflict between these two activities proved to be the cause of many difficulties. The perception that the WDAs were acting as both 'poacher and gamekeeper' undermined public confidence in the whole waste disposal industry.

(b) A lack of central guidance on acceptable standards
There was a great disparity between standards of control in different parts of the country. Evidence submitted to the House of Commons Environment Committee had shown that different WDAs used different standards when setting and enforcing conditions in disposal licences. As the Committee put it:

> Against this *laissez faire* background, it is not surprising to find that there is no consistency of standards between one waste disposal authority and

another. In many, the standards are extremely low, encouraging the operation of contractors who have no regard for the potential dangers to the environment.

A major reason for this *'laissez faire'* approach was the lack of Central Government guidance. The DoE had the task of supplying WDAs with scientific guidance as to the manner in which the system ought to be operated, which could then introduce uniformity into the controls. It committed itself to producing some 13 waste management papers in the 1980s, but this target was missed and many of the papers were not produced on time. As Lawrence put it ([1989] 3 Env Law 4):

These examples of Central Government complacency and neglect send clear signals out to the local authorities that waste regulation is not taken seriously in this country. This does nothing to engender the professionalism, technical competence and status that is required for efficient waste regulation.

(c) A lack of strategic plans

The introduction of waste disposal plans under s. 2 was a mandatory requirement of EC Directive 75/442. But, for example, by 1 October 1989, only 23 WDAs out of 79 had completed their plans. Obviously, little long-term planning could take place where there was no plan, since it should have provided the strategic background to the disposal of waste in an area.

(d) The need to prove deposit related offences

COPA 1974 emphasised the control of the deposit of waste. But problems also arise in relation to the storage, treatment and transportation of waste. These problems could not be tackled effectively by COPA 1974. The need to prove a deposit in order to activate many of the enforcement provisions also had the effect of concentrating on the element that was the most difficult to prove. For example, if waste was fly-tipped, under COPA 1974 only the person who made the deposit, or who caused or knowingly permitted it, could be prosecuted, leaving others further up the disposal chain free from control, even though they may have had a significant degree of responsibility for what happened. Even when a prosecution was brought, the maximum penalties were low.

One particular case that illustrated some of the problems in this area was *Leigh Land Reclamation Ltd* v *Walsall MBC* [1991] 191 *ENDS Report* 37. Charges were brought against the holder of a waste disposal licence alleging that it was depositing waste at a time when a number of conditions relating to the overall operation of the site were not being complied with. For example, waste was not being compacted and progressively covered during the day as required. The Divisional Court held that, as long as the *deposit* was in accordance with the conditions, it was irrelevant that other conditions relating to the site were not being complied with. Since COPA 1974 included no separate offence of failure to comply with a condition, this rather literal decision meant that there was effectively no way of enforcing many administrative and operational conditions attached to a disposal licence.

(e) Inability to control 'cowboys'

There were some severe defects in the licensing system which meant that proper control over standards was difficult. For example, there were only very limited opportunities to refuse a grant of a waste disposal licence, or to refuse a transfer, or to vary or revoke a licence. In consequence, great weight was placed on the planning permission stage, though in many cases the planning permission had been granted many years previously and did not fully take environmental considerations into account. (Of course, one of the features of the town planning system is that it is not possible to alter or revoke a planning permission once it has been granted, without the payment of compensation.)

A further problem was that, because of the way the legislation was drafted, WDAs were unable to attach some types of condition. For example, aftercare and restoration conditions were not permitted in a waste disposal licence, although they could be attached to a planning permission. A condition that a site should be operated 'so as to avoid creating a nuisance to the inhabitants of the neighbourhood' was held not to be appropriate in a waste disposal licence (*Attorney General's Reference (No. 2 of 1988)* [1990] JEL 80). The reasoning was that it did not fall within the limited purposes of COPA 1974, Part I, which were assumed (by reference to s. 5) to be the prevention of harm to public health, water pollution and serious detriment to the locality. In addition, the court considered that such matters should be controlled through the statutory nuisance procedures.

(f) The ability to surrender a licence

Site operators had a right to surrender a disposal licence at any time, in which case any conditions attached to it would automatically cease to have any effect. In practice, this meant that an operator could abandon a site and relinquish any future responsibility for supervision of it. For example, an operator who was financially or technically incompetent to deal with problems that had arisen on the land could avoid them simply by giving notice to the WDA. Of course, the operator would not thereby avoid any responsibilities imposed by the planning permission, or, if it owned the land, which arose out of ownership, but this right effectively undermined any attempt to impose a proper system of monitoring of waste sites once operations had ceased.

The Environmental Protection Act 1990, Part II

The EPA 1990, Part II enacted a wide range of new powers designed to strengthen control over waste 'from cradle to grave'. It also attempted to grapple with most of the difficulties thrown up by COPA 1974. Unfortunately, implementation of the EPA 1990, Part II has been beset with problems. No timetable for its introduction was originally written into the Act or promised in the debates on the Bill. To some extent this was understandable, since the Act itself largely set out a framework into which details would be inserted by regulations, and it was always accepted that the drafting of the appropriate regulations would involve the solution of some difficult and complex problems. Extensive consultation has taken place on various aspects of the new provisions. Some of these gave rise to great controversy, particularly as far as the waste disposal industry is concerned. As a result, there were persistent delays, a situation that has not been helped by the uncertainty caused by the announcement in 1992 of the Government's intention to create a national Environment Agency, which would take over the waste regulation functions currently exercised by local authorities. In the end, implementation has been piecemeal. The provisions on duty of care were brought into force on 1 April 1992. But, despite several promises of commencement dates, the new waste management licensing system was not brought into operation until 1 May 1994.

The main features of the EPA 1990, Part II are the following:

(a)   The operational and regulatory functions of local authorities have been separated, thus avoiding the implication that the regulatory system is biased. The operational body must be at arm's length from the regulatory authority and is subject to competitive tendering from the private sector. These provisions have been in force since 1991.

(b)   A criminal duty of care, which applies to all those who deal with controlled waste, was introduced on 1 April 1992. This important duty is an attempt to ensure that waste is dealt with properly from its production to its ultimate disposal. It imposes greater duties on the producers and intermediate handlers of waste than ever before and effectively necessitates the introduction of effective systems of waste management within firms.

(c)   A new, all-embracing criminal offence of treating, keeping or disposing of controlled waste in a manner likely to cause pollution of the environment or harm to human health was introduced on 1 April 1992. It operates independently of the licensing system and effectively imposes minimum standards on the way waste is handled.

(d)   A number of sections designed to encourage the recycling of waste have been introduced.

(e)   Provisions were enacted establishing a new system of waste management licensing. These seek to remedy many of the defects and close many of the loopholes in the licensing system established under COPA 1974. In particular, there are expanded powers to refuse licences on environmental grounds, new powers to refuse licences on the ground that the applicant is not a 'fit and proper person', more sophisticated powers to modify, suspend and revoke licences, greater powers to impose appropriate conditions, enhanced powers of enforcement, and increased maximum penalties in the event of a breach. A particular feature of the system is that an operator will no longer be able to surrender a licence, but will be subject to the licence conditions until released from these obligations by the Environment Agency issuing a certificate of completion. A complementary change is that the EPA 1990 enables conditions to be attached to site licences which will continue to apply after the site has ceased to be used for depositing waste.

The EPA 1990, Part II is supplemented by the provisions of the Control of Pollution (Amendment) Act 1989, which was brought into force on 1 April 1992. This Act introduced a system of registration of carriers of controlled waste, with strong penalties for operating an unregistered vehicle. Further supplementation is provided by the EPA 1990, Part IV, which creates a fairly comprehensive regime relating to the control of litter.

It is clear that the combined impact of the above changes will be that the whole of the waste cycle is regulated more rigorously than at any stage in the past. Producers of waste will be subject to a number of controls on the production and transfer of waste that did not affect them before. Tighter standards than before will operate in relation to where and how waste can be disposed of. There is little doubt that the cost of disposing of solid waste is set to rise significantly, and that producers should turn their attention to waste minimisation.

Waste authorities under the EPA 1990

The Environment Agency will take over the powers of the WRAs and WDAs when the relevant part of the Environment Act 1995 comes into force. Until that time the EPA 1990 sets out the powers and responsibilities of the waste management agencies.

For the purposes of the EPA 1990, s. 30 defines three types of authority:

(a) *The waste collection authority* is the district council or London borough council. It has a duty to arrange for the collection of household waste, and a further duty to arrange for the collection of commercial waste if requested by the occupier to do so (s. 45(1)). It may collect industrial waste if it gets the consent of the waste disposal authority (s. 45(2)). It has a duty to draw up plans for recycling household and commercial waste (s. 49). The detail of the law on the collection of waste is outside the scope of this book.

(b) *The waste regulation authority (WRA)* is the county council in English non-metropolitan areas and the district council in Wales. In metropolitan areas it is the metropolitan district council or London borough council, except that in Greater London, Greater Manchester and Merseyside a joint body for each has been established. The Secretary of State may alter these arrangements by establishing a regional authority under s. 31. This has been done in South Yorkshire, for example.

The WRA is effectively a pollution control body with regulatory responsibilities in relation to the whole of the waste stream. In particular, it is responsible for the operation of the waste management licensing system, the system of licensing of waste carriers, the special waste provisions, the operation of the duty of care, and the enforcement of the law. Each WRA must compile and publish an annual report on the discharge of its functions under the EPA 1990 (s. 67).

(c) *The waste disposal authority* is the same authority as the WRA, except that Wigan is allowed to control its own waste disposal despite being in Greater Manchester.

Section 30 and sch. 2 of the Act require the separation of the regulatory and organisational functions of the WRA and the waste disposal authority. In a move echoing the division of the regional water authorities into the National Rivers Authority and the water services companies, WRAs which wish to carry on waste disposal functions have to establish an arm's length local authority waste disposal company (LAWDC).

Under s. 51, the waste disposal authority has a duty to arrange for the disposal of controlled waste collected by the waste collection authority and to provide household waste sites ('dump-it' sites) for the public. As part of the Government's privatisation programme, in each case the disposal is to be by a contractor, which may either be a private firm or the LAWDC. Authorities were required to put waste disposal operations out to competitive tender from 31 May 1991.

What is waste?

The concept of waste has proved to be particularly difficult to define with any certainty. The main reason for this is the subjective nature of the view which one can take when considering whether material is waste. In particular, one person's waste can be another person's raw material, or, as Purdue put it ('Defining Waste' [1990] JEL 259):

the old newspapers blowing down the street may be gathered by boy scouts to be recycled or even used by a vagrant to keep warm. Even at the same moment in time one person may regard an object as waste, while another has a use for it. This makes legal definition difficult.

Of course, the adoption of the waste management hierarchy as outlined above simply adds to the complexity of the tests. Where an emphasis is placed upon the reuse and recycling of material it would not make a great deal of sense to overregulate unnecessarily and thereby discourage those seeking to minimise the final production of waste. On the other hand, many recycling and reclamation processes have the capability of causing harm to the environment if left unregulated. The legislation seeks to balance these two competing considerations.

For many years the definition of waste included substances or articles which were scrap or which required to be disposed of because it was broken, worn out, contaminated or otherwise spoilt (s. 30 COPA 1974 and s. 75 EPA 1990). Under the amendments to the framework Directive, however, a common definition of waste was agreed to apply to all Member States. This differs from the previous definition and thus required amendments to UK legislation. Other amendments have been necessary to ensure full implementation of the Directive. All of the amendments have been incorporated within the Waste Management Licensing Regulations 1994 with subsequent amendments to the EPA 1990.

The Regulations are very complicated and the guidance in Circular 11/94 runs to almost 200 pages. In an attempt to distill the detail into broad principles it is possible to put forward two propositions:

(a) the only waste which is regulated by the WRAs is now known as *Directive waste* to reflect the description of waste as contained in the Directive;

(b) generally, the activities which are controlled under Part II of the EPA 1990 are now known as *Directive disposal* and *Directive recovery*. These two phrases replace the old single phrase of 'treating keeping or disposing of waste' as contained in s. 33 of EPA 1990.

Directive waste

Article 1 of the framework Directive amends the definition of waste within the UK. Schedule 22 of the Environment Act 1995 formally repeals s. 75(2) of EPA 1990 and the practical effect upon English law is that the previous statutory definition of waste contained in that section has been replaced by the definition of 'Directive waste' which is, itself, contained in regs. 1(3), 24(8) of and para. 9 of sch 4 to the Waste Management Licensing Regulations 1994. These provisions amend the definition of controlled waste in the Controlled Waste Regulations to provide that waste which is not Directive waste shall not be treated as controlled waste (and therefore shall fall outside the scheme of control of Part II of the Act).

The general definition of Directive waste is:

. . . any substance or object which the holder discards or intends or is required to discard . . .

The crucial concept in determining whether material is waste would appear to be 'discarding'. Further guidance on this concept is contained in Circular 11/94 which poses the question:

has the substance or object been discarded so that it is no longer part of the normal commercial cycle or chain of utility?

If the answer to this question is 'no', it should be a reasonable indication that the substance or object is not waste. The Circular goes on to provide the example of glass bottles which are subject to a refundable deposit on safe return. The DoE contends that the bottles are not waste in the hands of the buyer, the shop to which they are returned or the supplier who takes it from the shop. In these circumstances the bottle never leaves the 'chain of utility'. On the other hand bottles, which are placed in a 'bottle bank' for recycling are discarded and should be treated as waste. 'Discard' can also mean 'dispose of' and/or 'get rid of' but attempting to come up with an all-encompassing definition would be impossible.

Further clarification of the concept is given in four broad categories of potential waste:

(1) worn, but functioning, substances or objects which are still usable (albeit after repair) for the purpose for which they were made—generally not waste;

(2) substances or objects which can be put to immediate use otherwise than by a specialised waste recovery establishment or undertaking—generally not waste;

(3)   degenerated substances or objects which can be put to use only by establishments or undertakings specialising in waste recovery—generally waste even if transferred for value;

(4)   Substances or objects which the holder does not want and which he has to pay to have taken away—depends upon the facts of the particular disposal. Where there is an intention that the material/substance will be used by the recipient and no special recovery process is required, that material/ substance will not be waste, notwithstanding that a price is paid.

Many difficult cases will depend largely upon their facts and the intentions of the parties and it is not possible to give anything other than a general picture.

In addition to the general definition there are more specific categories of Directive waste contained in Part II of sch. 4 of the Waste Management Licensing Regulations 1994. The long list of categories includes residual products from industrial processes, products for which the holder has no further use (e.g. household, agricultural, office, commercial and agricultural discards) and production or consumption residues not otherwise mentioned in the Schedule.

There is also a general all inclusive category which includes *any* materials, substances or products which are not contained in any of the other categories. The effect of this category is that there is a two-stage test which applies to the question of whether a substance, material or product is Directive waste:

(a)   is it a substance, material or product and does it therefore come within any of the categories set out in the specific definitions in sch. 4?; *and*

(b)   has the substance, material or product been discarded by its holder or is there an intention or requirement to discard it?.

It is the second of these two questions, however, which gives the key to the definition of Directive waste. For example, material is not waste merely because it falls within sch. 4, nor even because it has been sent to a waste recovery process. The overriding issue is whether it has been discarded.

Waste recovery operations and specialised recovery operations
One of the notable features of the detailed guidance on the definition of Directive waste is the manner in which recycling and recovery operations are dealt with. In an attempt to balance the need for control with the need to encourage reuse the Circular seeks to distinguish waste recovery operations from specialised recovery operations. Waste recovery operations are listed in sch. 4, Pt. IV to the Waste Management Licensing Regulations 1994. These processes cover the reclamation or recycling of a variety of substances, including solvents, acids and oils. A substance is not considered to be waste solely on the ground that it has been consigned to a recovery process. The main reason for this is that some of the processes listed in the Regulations cannot be distinguished easily from the normal commercial chain of utility (i.e. the recovery process is part and parcel of the overall process). Therefore, the substance might not have been discarded within the meaning of the

definition of Directive waste. One example might be the reuse/recovery of waste oil from a process as a source of fuel for another process.

On the other hand, waste consigned to special recovery operations will always be considered to be waste. There is no specific definition of the phrase 'special recovery operations' within the Regulations or the guidance. The phrase is, however, intended to cover operations which either reuse substances or objects which are waste because they have fallen out of the chain of utility or recycles them in a way which eliminates or diminishes sufficiently the threat posed by their original production as waste and produces a raw material which can be used in the same way as raw material of a non-waste compound. Thus, where contaminated waste oil is disposed of to a third party and that third party utilises the waste for its own purposes (after cleaning the oil) the oil will be waste as it will have to the subject of a special recovery operation.

Can the identity of waste change over time?

In the examples above it can be seen that a substance which has been waste can be purified and utilised. Where waste is 'recovered' under the Directive the substance ceases to be waste—this follows the accepted position after the decision in *Kent CC v Queenborough Rolling Mill Co. Ltd* (see below). The waste is 'recovered' when it is a substance of sufficient beneficial use to eliminate or sufficiently diminish the threat posed by the original production of the waste. In addition, the waste can be altered by a change of intention on behalf of the recipient of the waste. For example, someone who receives a broken, discarded product can mend it so that it ceases to be waste.

Case law

The courts have examined the definition of waste on a number of occasions. Although these decisions are based upon the definition under previous legislation they assist in helping with the interpretation of Directive waste as the principles can, in some cases, be extended to cover the new definition. In *Long v Brook* [1980] Crim LR 109 the Crown Court decided upon its true construction; COPA 1974 defined 'waste' from the point of view of the person discarding the material. This was followed in *Kent CC v Queenborough Rolling Mill Co. Ltd* [1990] JEL 257 where the defendant company was charged with depositing waste on land without a disposal licence contrary to COPA 1974 (s. 3). The material concerned consisted of ballast, china, china clay and broken pottery from a disused site which was being cleared by a demolition company. It was used to fill an area subject to subsidence. The magistrates decided that such material was not waste as it was inert and was being used for the purposes of infill. On appeal to the Divisional Court the council argued that the material was waste by its very nature. The defendant company argued that the material was not waste because it was put to a useful purpose and therefore was not unwanted. The Divisional Court held that, although the material was put to a useful purpose, that was not a relevant factor in deciding whether the material was waste. The important factor was the nature of the material when it was discarded. If it was waste it would always remain waste until it was adequately reconstituted or recycled. This would still be the case with the redefintion of waste under the Waste Management Licensing Regulations 1994.

In *Cheshire CC* v *Armstrong's Transport (Wigan) Ltd* [1995] Env LR 62 the defendant company was responsible for processing building site rubble before returning the crushed material to its original site to assist in rebuilding works. The Defendant was prosecuted as it did not seek a waste disposal licence under COPA 1974. The magistrates found that the material was not waste as it was a product. The defendant was able to demonstrate that there was no intention to discard on behalf of the last holder of the material as they were under a contractual obligation to return the material to the site once it had been processed. The Divisional Court held that this obligation meant that the rubble was not waste as the original holder had not wished to dispose of it. Such evidence would, of course, also be required to demonstrate that material had not left the 'chain of utility'.

In *Meston Technical Services Ltd and Wright* v *Warwickshire County Council* [1995] Env LR D36 the defendants operated a waste recycling business from a site in an industrial park. They traded in the receipt of liquid controlled waste which was received from various companies and was reprocessed into substances which would either be sold on for industrial or commercial use or otherwise disposed of by way of landfill or incineration. The defendant was prosecuted for breach of licence conditions under COPA 1974. On appeal the defendants argued that the drums of material were not 'waste' within the meaning of COPA 1974 and that the licence did not apply to the storage of the drums. It was argued, that the drums (and the material within it) were not waste because it was wanted by the appellants and was valuable to them. Secondly, it was argued that the defendants could only be guilty of an offence where they themselves regarded the relevant material as waste. If they did not regard it as waste but intended to sell it on if they could, it was not waste and no offence was committed. The Divisional Court held that the value of the material or the views of the defendant were irrelevant when considering the definition of the material as waste, and it was not appropriate to examine the aims and purposes of the holder of the waste when considering what was waste under the Environmental Protection Act 1990. The new, wider definition of Directive waste would support this interpretation of 'waste'.

These national decisions are in line with a decision of the European Court of Justice in linked Cases 206 and 207/88 *Vessoso* and *Zanetti* [1990] LMELR 133. In these cases, two Italians had been charged with collecting, transporting and storing waste without authorisation, contrary to Italian Presidential Decree. It was argued on their behalf that the material was recyclable raw material and not waste. In its judgment, the Court stated that the definition of waste contained in the original framework Directive on Waste (75/442) was concerned with the potential health and pollution hazard that the materials could bring, and concluded by finding that although recycling was to be encouraged, material could be waste notwithstanding its potential for future use. This has now been clarified with the expansion of the definition of waste in the updated framework Directive (91/156) and the amendments to British legislation.

What is controlled waste?

Most of the provisions of the EPA 1990 apply to controlled waste. The primary definition of controlled waste is defined in EPA 1990, s. 75(4) as meaning household, industrial or commercial waste or any such waste. In *Thanet DC* v *Kent CC* [1993] Env LR 391 the Divisional Court held that the phrase 'any such waste' is limited to waste coming within any of the categories and would not cover seaweed deposited on agricultural land. The definition of controlled waste has been amended by the Waste Management Licensing Regulations 1994. Regulation 24(8) amends the Controlled Waste Regulations 1992 (SI 1992 No. 588) by providing that waste which is not Directive waste shall not be treated as household, industrial or commercial waste. Thus, the practical effect is that the previous categories of household, industrial or commercial waste have been amended to the single class of Directive waste.

Exemptions

Regulation 1(3) of the 1994 Regulations excludes anything excluded from the scope of the Directive from the definition of Directive waste (and thus controlled waste). The justification for these exemptions is that they are already covered under existing legislation. There are, however, a few anomalies. Six main categories of waste are exempted.

(a)   Gaseous effluent emitted into the atmosphere: controlled under Part I of the EPA 1990 and the Clean Air Act 1993. Emissions from waste management are, however, covered under the Directive (e.g. from incineration).

(b)   Radioactive waste: controlled under the Radioactive Substances Act 1993.

(c)   Waste resulting from prospecting, extraction, treatment, and storage of mineral resources and the working of quarries: controlled under the Mines and Quarries (Tips) Act 1969. This also accords with s. 75(7) of EPA 1990 which excludes all waste from mines and quarries from the definition of controlled waste. The issue of non-mineral waste from mines and quarries is, however, far from clear-cut. Although the EPA 1990 would exclude this waste from the definition of controlled waste the DoE has said that this would fall within the definition of Directive waste.

(d)   Animal carcasses and the following agricultural waste; faecal matter and other natural, non-dangerous substances used in farming: controlled under the Animal By-Products Order 1992 (SI 1992 No. 3303); there is, however, a similar problem to the position in respect of minerals wastes. Agricultural waste is excluded form the definition of controlled waste under s. 75(7) of EPA 1990, yet the DoE takes the view that it should fall within the definition of Directive waste where it falls outside the above exemption.

(e)   Waste waters, with the exception of waste in liquid form: broadly controlled under the Water Resources Act 1991 and Water Industry Act 1991. Where, however, waste water or liquid is subjected to Directive recovery or disposal (e.g. effluent treatment plants) the DoE has advised that it is its view that this will amount to the treatment of Directive waste and a licence will be required.

(f) Decommissioned explosives: controlled under the Explosives Act 1875, the Control of Explosives Regulations 1991 (SI 1991 No. 1531), various regulations under the Health and Safety at Work Act 1974 and the Road Traffic (Carriage of Explosives) Regulations 1989 (SI 1989 No. 615).

There is a residual degree of control over non-Directive waste. Any person who deposits or who knowingly causes or knowingly permits the deposit of any non-controlled waste commits an offence if the waste has the characteristics of special waste and is not deposited in accordance with a licence or permission of some description (EPA 1990, s. 63(2)). This rather convoluted subsection appears designed to cover such things as the irresponsible disposal of toxic materials. The maximum penalty is the same as under s. 33. In addition, the Secretary of State may make regulations under s. 63(1) applying specified parts of the EPA 1990 to exempt wastes (specifically agricultural and mine wastes), although no such regulations have ever been made.

The meaning of 'deposit'

One final definition that must be explained is of the word 'deposit' since it is central to the operation of the EPA 1990 (and indeed also central to COPA 1974). It is now clear from the decision of the Divisional Court in *R v Metropolitan Stipendiary Magistrate ex parte London Waste Regulation Authority* [1993] 3 All ER 113, that this word applies to temporary deposits as well as to permanent ones, which seems to reflect both common sense and the intent of the legislation. The court departed from the earlier case of *Leigh Land Reclamation Ltd v Walsall MBC* [1991] 191 *ENDS Report* 37, where it was held that waste was deposited at a landfill site only when there was no realistic prospect of further examination or inspection and it had reached its final resting place. The *Leigh* decision had caused enormous problems for the operation of COPA 1974 and had effectively led to many WRA imposing a moratorium on prosecutions and use of their clean-up powers because of the possibility of the defendant arguing that the waste was going to be moved in the future.

Waste plans

The WRA should have started drawing up a waste disposal plan under s. 50, since that section was brought into force on 31 May 1991. This plan should identify the current provision for waste disposal in the area and should set out the WRA's policies for waste disposal and recycling in its area. It should cover toxic and hazardous waste as well as other controlled waste. It is the duty of the WRA to have regard to the desirability, where reasonably practicable, of giving priority to recycling waste (s. 50(4)). In drawing up the plan, the WRA must consult with the NRA , waste collection authorities, the county council (in Wales only) and representatives of the waste management industry locally.

It must also publicise the draft plan and allow members of the public to make representations, and send a copy of the draft plan to the Secretary of State. It can then be adopted. The WRA must also carry out further investigations from time to time and has powers to modify the plan. The waste disposal plan is required in addition to the waste local plan to be drawn up by the local planning authority (see p. 354).

The waste collection authority is under a duty to draw up a waste recycling plan for its area in relation to household and commercial waste. This will involve a survey of the type and quantity of controlled waste it expects to collect, before setting out the arrangements it intends to make to facilitate recycling. There is no formal requirement to publicise the plan before it is made, except to send it in draft form to the Secretary of State. However, the plan must be publicised once it is made and must be available for inspection free of charge. There is a duty to carry out further investigations from time to time and the authority has powers to modify the plan. The exact status of a waste recycling plan is unclear, since the waste collection authority has few powers except over the waste it collects. It could be used to set recycling targets, although it appears these would not have the force of law. All waste collection authorities had submitted a draft plan to the DoE by the middle of 1993. The national waste strategy proposed under s. 44A is intended to replace these waste plans over time (see p. 348).

Waste management licensing

As with the definition of waste, the requirement for a waste management license has been affected by the need to implement the framework Directive. A waste management licence is required for the disposal, keeping or treatment of controlled waste on land or by means of a mobile plant. The effect of the Waste Management Licencing Regulations 1994, however, when taken with the prohibition on the unlawful management of waste in s. 33 is to limit the phrase 'treatment, keeping or disposal of waste' to Directive disposal and recovery operations (sch. 4, para. 9).

Directive disposal operations

The list of Directive disposal operations is found in Part III of sch. 4 to the 1994 Regulations. It includes landfill, incineration on land and at sea, permanent storage of waste, e.g. in a mine, the treatment of waste prior to final disposal and the injection of waste into the earth.

Directive recovery operations

The list of Directive recovery operations is found in Part IV of sch. 4. It includes the reclamation or recycling of a variety of substances (e.g. solvents, organic substances, acids and metals) and the use of wastes obtained from recycling or reclamation.

Exemptions

A lengthy list of exemptions from the need for a waste management licence is set out in reg. 17 and sch. 3. It is not possible in a book of this nature to go through the whole list, or to provide exact details of those things that are mentioned, but the main types of activity that are covered are as follows:

(a)   activities that are carried on in accordance with the provisions of consents or authorisations granted under other legislation (e.g. a discharge consent granted under the Water Resources Act 1991, or a licence to dump at sea granted under the Food and Environment Protection Act 1985);

(b)   the storage of Directive waste at the place at which it is produced pending its treatment or disposal elsewhere (this will cover such things as storing waste in a skip—there is no time limit as long as the producer can show that it is genuinely going to be collected);

(c)   the storage of special waste at the place at which it is produced pending its treatment or disposal elsewhere, as long as certain conditions on quantity and security are met;

(d)   various activities relating to the recovery or reuse of waste, such as sorting waste at the place at which it is produced, baling it, shredding it and compacting it;

(e)   storage or deposit of demolition or construction wastes for the purposes of construction work being undertaken on the land;

(f)   deposit of certain organic matter for the purposes of fertilising or conditioning land;

(g)   in order to encourage recycling, a great variety of recycling activities are exempted, although often subject to detailed restrictions on quantity (for example, the collection of paper and cardboard, aluminium and steel cans, plastics, glass and textiles for recycling, or the cleaning and washing of packaging or containers so that they can be reused).

In most of these categories the exemption will not apply if the waste is special waste (see p. 406).

The requirement for a waste management licence (and the exemptions from the need for a licence) must read in conjunction with the offence of unlawful waste management set out in s. 33 (see p. 384). The general offence in s. 33(1)(c) of keeping, treating or disposing of Directive waste in a manner likely to cause pollution of the environment or harm to human health (see p. 387) will remain applicable in all the above exemptions apart from those in category (a). By contrast household waste from a private dwelling which is treated, kept or disposed of within the curtilage of the dwelling by, or with the permission of, the occupier, is entirely exempt from s. 33 (s. 33(2)).

Registration
A new requirement of the 1994 Regulations, made necessary by the provisions of Article 11 of the framework Directive, is that certain activities must be registered with the WRA even though exempted from the waste management licensing system. The new registration system is based around a new offence in support of the requirement to register. Under reg. 18(1) it is an offence to carry on an exempt activity involving the recovery or disposal of waste without being registered with the appropriate registration authority.

The requirement to register covers 'establishments or undertakings' it does not include private individuals. Registration is effected simply by notifying the WRA of the relevant activities, where they are carried on, and the exemption which is being relied on (reg. 18(3)). The WRA is required to keep a register of exemptions containing the particulars of the registration (reg. 18(4)). The tone of Government advice in Circular 11/94 is that the requirement to register is more administrative in nature than any great step forward in environmental protection. Indeed, the advice in the Circular would suggest that prosecution for the failure to register an exempt activity would only be a last resort. Where serious environmental harm had arisen from exempt activities it would be preferable to rely upon prosecution powers under s. 33(1)(c), if possible (see p. 387).

Applications for a licence

If a waste management licence is required, an application must be made in writing to the WRA. There is a standard application form available from all WRA's.. It is an offence to make a statement in an application for a licence (or in an application for modification, transfer or surrender) knowing it to be false in a material particular, or reckless as to such an event (s. 44). The maximum penalty on conviction in the magistrates' court is a £5,000 fine, but in the Crown Court the maximum penalty is an unlimited fine and/or two years in prison.

Where the licence relates to the keeping, treating, or disposal of waste in or on land the licence is called a 'site licence', and the application is made to the WRA where the site is situated. An application for a licence for mobile plant is made to the WRA where the applicant has its principal place of business, thus allowing for a number of pieces of plant to be covered by one licence. Section 35(2) states that only the occupier of the land or the operator of a mobile plant can apply for a licence. There is no definition of an occupier in the Act, but it must be assumed that it relates to the ability to control the waste operation and the use of the land.

The WRA must consult with a number of other public bodies if it proposes to issue a licence, and must consider any representations that those bodies make within 21 days. The NRA and the Health and Safety Executive are statutory consultees in all cases. In any case where the site is notified as a site of special scientific interest (SSSI), the relevant NCC is also a statutory consultee, reflecting the fact that a number of SSSIs have been lost to waste disposal over the years—though current planning guidance makes it less likely that planning permission will be granted for waste disposal on a SSSI in the future.

The NRA is a very important consultee because of the strong risk of water pollution should leachate escape from the site. It has published a set of strong and clear policies for the protection of groundwater, to which it will refer when formulating its response to the WRA (see NRA, *Policy and Practice for the Protection of Groundwater*, 1992). In addition, if the NRA disagrees with the WRA over whether the site is suitable for the issue of a licence, or over the conditions that should be attached, the dispute can be referred to the Secretary of State for a decision (s. 36(5)). It would normally be appropriate for an applicant to consult the NRA informally before making an application, since opposition from the NRA will make a successful application unlikely.

The WRA must also take into account any Central Government guidance (s. 35(8)). This will be provided in the form of waste management papers and it is intended that they should produce a situation where a more uniform approach is adopted across the country than has been the case in the past. The most significant paper is Waste Management Paper No. 4, *Licensing of Waste Facilities*, which seeks to provide comprehensive guidance on the criteria for granting a licence, such as the definition of a 'fit and proper person' and on conditions. WMP4 contains a policy that licences should be reviewed annually and fully reconsidered at least every five years. It will also be appropriate to consider the Central Guidance to be found in 11/94.

One feature that is missing is any element of public participation, since the application does not have to be advertised. This situation arises because it is perceived that the grant of a waste management licence is a technical question: the wider question of the appropriateness of the site will have been considered when planning permission was sought.

The powers of the WRA

The WRA has a discretion to grant or refuse a licence. But this is subject to a number of restrictions. (Similar restrictions apply to the WRA's discretion on questions relating to the transfer, modification, suspension or revocation of a licence, though the wording of the relevant sections is usually more restrictive—see below.)

First, an application *must* be refused if planning permission is required for the use of the land and there is no such permission (s. 36(2)). For these purposes, a lawful development certificate granted under the Town and Country Planning Act 1990, s. 191, is treated as a planning permission. An established use certificate granted under earlier legislation will also normally suffice.

Secondly, the WRA *may* refuse a licence if it is satisfied that such a step is necessary to prevent pollution of the environment or harm to human health. This gives a fairly wide discretion to the WRA, since s. 29 defines pollution of the environment to mean pollution due to the release or escape of substances capable of causing harm to any living organism from the land in or on which waste is kept, treated or deposited. Where there is no planning permission in force (i.e. because it was not required—this would cover a site open since before 1948), the WRA may refuse a licence if that is necessary to prevent serious detriment to the amenities of the locality (s. 36(3)).

Further guidance on this point is provided by the Waste Management Licensing Regulations. In order to ensure compliance with Directive 80/68 on Groundwater, WRAs are required only to grant applications if technical precautions, enforceable through conditions, can be taken to prevent the discharge of List I substances and to prevent groundwater pollution by List II substances. WRAs are also required to review existing licences that may lead to discharges of List I or List II substances and to use their modification and revocation powers accordingly.

Thirdly, a licence *may* be refused if the applicant is not a fit and proper person. The meaning of this phrase is set out in general terms in s. 74 and in more specific terms in the Waste Management Licensing Regulations. The final form of the Regulations and the guidance on their use was the subject of great controversy and debate between the Government and the waste disposal industry in 1992 and 1993, leading to a position where the standards are not as strict as was once envisaged.

Section 74(3) states that an applicant is not a fit and proper person if:

(a)   the applicant or any other relevant person has committed a relevant offence; or

(b)   the mangement of the site will not be in the hands of a technically competent person; or

(c)   the applicant cannot make financial provision adequate to discharge the obligations arising under the licence.

Section 74(7) explains that a relevant person has committed a relevant offence in this context if:

(i)   any employee of the applicant has been convicted of a relevant offence;

(ii)   a company of which the applicant was a director, manager, secretary or similar officer has been convicted of a relevant offence; or

(iii)   where the applicant is a company, any current director, manager, secretary or similar officer of the company has been convicted of a relevant offence, or was an officer of another company when that company was convicted of a relevant offence. The question of who constitutes a manager will be construed narrowly to mean someone who is part of the 'controlling mind' of the company (see *R* v *Boal* [1992] 3 All ER 177 and *Woodhouse* v *Walsall MBC* [1994] Env LR 30).

For the purpose of these provisions, a list of relevant offences is contained in the Waste Management Licensing Regulations 1994, reg. 3). Since the list is wide (but by no means exhaustive of environmental offences), the WRA can choose to ignore a conviction if it wishes to do so (s. 74(4)). Waste Management Paper No. 4, Chapter 3 contains guidance on these provisions. It suggests that four factors should be taken into account in exercising the discretion to ignore a conviction. These are: the type of applicant (i.e. individual, partnership or corporate body); whether it is the applicant or another relevant person who has been convicted of the relevant offence; the nature and gravity of the relevant offence(s); and the number of relevant offences which have been committed.

As far as technical competence is concerned reg. 4 applies to the person responsible for the proper management of the site. The regulation provides that a person is technically competent in relation to the prescribed facilities set out in reg. 4 only if they are the holder of the relevant certificate of technical competence awarded by the Waste Management Industry Training Board (WAMITAB).

There are various transitional arrangements for those managers who have experience within the waste industry prior to the implementation of Part II of the EPA 1990 (known as 'existing managers'). A person will qualify as an existing manager if they registered with WAMITAB before 10 August 1994 and in the 12 months prior to that date were a manager of a relevant type of facility. An operator of a site previously controlled under COPA 1974 is also assumed to be a 'fit and proper' person. Both exemptions last until 1999 to enable those who are exempt to gain WAMITAB certification.

The position with regard to financial provision is much less clear cut. WMP 4 suggests that the main ways of providing such financial provision is through insurance via a third party or, if that is not possible, through self-insurance. The paper also identifies four stages in relation to landfill where financial provision may be relevant: site acquisition and preparation; site operation; site restoration and landscaping, or aftercare for a new use; and post-closure control and monitoring. Specific financial provision may be included in a licence in order to meet specified obligations under the licence. The assessment of the financial provision of an applicant is not to be specifically detailed. It is only to be considered in general terms in relation to the obligations under the licence. WMP4 suggests that the main thing that the WRA will want to see when assessing financial capability will be a business plan showing the various stages of the life of the landfill. Unfortunately, as history has shown, the provision of a sound business plan does not necessarily guarantee the long-term success of the operation. It is this long-term position which remains to be assessed.

If the WRA decides that the applicant is a fit and proper person, it is under a duty to grant a licence (s. 36(3)). This suggests that if the impediment can be avoided by the imposition of appropriate conditions, the licence should be granted with those conditions attached.

Conditions

The WRA is given a wide discretion to attach 'appropriate' conditions to a licence (s. 35(3)). Applying ordinary public law principles, conditions must relate to the purposes of Part II of the EPA 1990. In *Attorney-General's Reference (No. 2 of 1988)* [1990] JEL 80, the Court of Appeal decided that a condition requiring the site to be operated so as to avoid creating a nuisance was not permissible under COPA 1974, since it did not relate to the purposes of that Act. Even though the purposes of the EPA 1990 are wider than those of COPA 1974 (in that they relate to the protection of the environment as a whole, rather than the protection of water resources), it is still unclear whether such a condition would be acceptable under s. 35(3), since it is still arguable that such matters are more appropriately dealt with under the statutory nuisance provisions in Part III of the EPA 1990.

Unlike many pieces of environmental legislation, the EPA 1990 does not provide a list of the types of conditions that are appropriate. This function however, is carried out by Waste Management Paper 4. This provides a checklist of matters that should be covered, and stresses that they should relate to the operation and management of the site, so as not to duplicate the conditions attached to the planning permission. The Paper also states that conditions should be enforceable, unambiguous, necessary and comprehensive, and that operators should know exactly what they have to do to comply with them. It appears from decisions of the Secretary of State on appeal that conditions should not impose an unreasonable burden on the operator of a site (see Bates, *UK Waste Law* (1992), p. 203). This seems to water down somewhat the environmental protection aim of the legislation, though it is clearly in line with Government policies on restricting unnecessary regulation and on balancing environmental factors with economic ones.

The range of conditions imposed under the EPA 1990 can be wider than under COPA 1974 in a number of ways. Section 35(3) states that conditions may be imposed which must be complied with before activities begin or after they have ceased. For example, conditions requiring insurance cover to be effected before the site is opened, or the monitoring of a site for methane emissions or for leachate after disposal has finished, are legitimate. Under COPA 1974, such aftercare conditions can be imposed only at the planning permission stage. Section 35(4) provides that conditions may require the applicant to carry out works that need the consent of another person. If they do so, the person whose consent is required must grant any rights in relation to the land that will enable the licence holder to comply with the conditions. For example, this subsection could be used to override landlord and tenant law by allowing a tenant to carry out works that would normally require the landlord's consent.

Regulations may be made prescribing conditions which are or are not to be included (s. 35(6)). In addition, the Secretary of State is given wide powers to direct that specified conditions are, or are not, included in a licence (s. 35). For example, the Waste Management Licensing Regulations stipulate that no conditions designed solely to secure health and safety at work can be imposed (reg. 12), and that, in order to comply with Directive 75/439 on Waste Oils, certain conditions relating to waste oils must be included (reg. 14).

Transfer of a licence
A waste management licence may be transferred by the WRA under s. 40 if the holder and the proposed transferee make a joint application to the WRA. Unless the WRA considers that the proposed transferee is not a fit and proper person, it must make the transfer. An application for a transfer has to be made in writing. It must be determined within two months (or any longer period if agreed between the parties). In the absence of any agreement the application is claimed to have been refused.

Surrender of a licence
Under s. 39, a site licence cannot be surrendered at will, though a mobile plant licence can. A surrender of a site licence can take place only if the licence holder applies to the WRA and it accepts the surrender. Before that happens, the WRA must inspect the land and determine whether it is likely or unlikely that the condition of the land will cause pollution of the environment or harm to human health. In making that determination, it must take into account only matters that relate to the keeping, treatment or disposal of waste on the site, and not extraneous factors.

If the WRA considers that the condition of the land is likely to cause such pollution or harm, it *must* refuse the application (s. 39(6)). But if it is satisfied that the condition of the land is unlikely to cause pollution or harm, it *must* accept the surrender, though not before consulting with the NRA and considering any representations it makes. If the NRA requests that surrender be refused, the matter can be referred to the Secretary of State for a decision (s. 39(7)). Where a surrender is accepted, the WRA will issue a certificate of completion, and any obligations under the licence (such as to monitor for methane emissions) then come to an end. Since s. 39 requires the WRA to issue a certificate where pollution or harm is unlikely, it is possible that an operator will be able to surrender a licence even though it has not fully complied with the licence conditions. However, any conditions attached to the planning permission for the site will still apply after surrender: these could cover such things as a requirement to restore the land to its previous use or to landscape it appropriately.

This procedure is of great importance, since until the implementation of the EPA 1990 holders of waste disposal licences can surrender them at will, and thus relinquish any continuing responsibilities for the site. This will no longer be possible under the EPA 1990. One side effect of this change was that, in anticipation of the introduction of stricter standards and more rigorous enforcement powers under the EPA 1990, many holders of waste disposal licences under COPA 1974 surrendered them prior to the implementation of the new system, resulting in a significant shake-out of the waste disposal industry.

Detailed guidance for applying for a surrender have been set out in WMP 4 and WMP 26A which must, as a result of s. 35(8), be taken into account by the WRA). Applications for the surrender of a licence must include: information on the licence holder; site location; number of the site licence; and a description of all the different activities (whether licensed or not) which were carried out on the site, the location of those activities, the period over which they were carried out and an estimate of the quantity of waste dealt with at the site. Where the site has involved the disposal of waste to landfill, further detailed information is required relating to such matters as hydrogeology, production of gas and leachate and the quality of groundwater.

Once all the formalities have been complied with, the certificate can be issued and the licence ceases to have effect. There is little experience of WRAs accepting the surrender of licences and there has been considerable disagreement between those who consider that, as a matter of commercial fairness, a certificate of completion should be granted as of right where certain specified standards are met, and those who wish to see the WRA have greater discretion. It remains to be seen how willing WRAs will be to issue a certificate, since not only do they lose any income derived from the annual licence charges, but they may also become liable for future clean-up costs.

The provisions on surrender have given rise to a degree of disagreement between those who consider that, as a matter of commercial fairness, a certificate of completion should be granted virtually as of right where certain specified standards, agreed in advance, are met, and those who wish to see the WRA have greater discretion. It remains to be seen how willing WRAs will be to issue a certificate, since not only do they lose any income derived from the annual licence charges, but they may also become liable for any future clean-up costs.

Enforcement powers

It is one of the features of most modern systems of pollution control that the regulatory agencies have strong enforcement powers. These are not limited to bringing prosecutions for breaches of the law, but extend to powers to vary and to revoke licences without compensation. These administrative remedies often represent a greater threat to operators than prosecution because of the potential financial consequences. The WRA has some of the widest and most varied sets of powers in this respect, including powers to modify a licence, to revoke it in whole or in part, to suspend the operation of licensed activities, and to order the carrying out of specified works. In order to ensure that these powers are used, s. 42 imposes supervisory duties on the WRA. In a number of cases the legislation places the WRA under a duty to take enforcement action.

The enforcement powers in the EPA 1990 are significantly wider than under COPA 1974. In addition, many of the restrictions that applied to waste disposal licences granted under COPA 1974, for example on the permissible scope of conditions, are removed by the EPA 1990. Many licences granted under COPA 1974 do not protect the environment as much as they might have done. But when (or if) they automatically become waste management licences subject to the EPA 1990 (as a result of s. 77), the modification, suspension and revocation powers can be used to impose new standards more in keeping with modern expectations.

Supervision of a licence
Section 42 puts the WRA under a duty to supervise waste management licences. It must take the steps that are needed to ensure that pollution of the environment, harm to human health or serious detriment to the amenities of the locality do not occur. it must also take steps to ensure that licence conditions are complied with. If at any time it appears that water pollution is likely to be caused by the activities to which the licence relates, the WRA must consult with the NRA over how it should exercise this supervisory duty (s. 42(2)).

Where there is an emergency, specific powers are given by s. 42(3). The WRA may carry out necessary works on land or in relation to plant or equipment, and may recover any expenditure from the licence holder.

Modification of a licence
Powers to modify a licence are of particular importance where circumstances have changed since the initial grant of the licence. The WRA may, at its discretion, modify the conditions of a licence where it considers this is

desirable and is unlikely to require unreasonable expense on the part of the licence holder (s. 37(1)(a)). But if it considers that in order to ensure that the authorised activities do not cause pollution of the environment or harm to human health, or become seriously detrimental to the amenities of the locality, it is necessary to modify the conditions, it *must* do so to the extent necessary (s. 37(2)). Alternatively, in such circumstances it may decide to revoke the licence under s. 38(1). The consultation requirements apply to a WRA proposal to modify a licence in virtually the same way that they apply to an application under s. 36, except that, in an emergency, a reference to a consultee may be postponed. There is a separate right for the licence holder to apply for a modification (s. 37(1)(b)). In each situation any modification made under s. 37 must be by notice and must specify when it takes effect (s. 37(4)).

Suspension of a licence
The powers to suspend and to revoke a licence are of great use where licensed activities are giving rise to problems, for example where the site is being inadequately managed or is causing pollution. The grounds for their use are, in general terms, similar to those relating to the refusal of an initial licence application, though they are in fact slightly less wide. They provide an opportunity to police the licence on a continuing basis and may be used in addition to other enforcement mechanisms, such as prosecution or ordering a clean-up.

The WRA may suspend a licence by serving a notice on the licence holder. Such a notice must specify when the suspension is to take effect and when it is to cease. This may be on the occurrence either of a specified date or a specified event. A suspension cannot be of the whole of a licence, but can only relate to those parts of the licence that authorise the carrying on of activities. For example, the WRA may suspend a licence in so far as it allows certain types of waste to be deposited, whilst retaining in force any conditions that relate to measures the licence holder must take to protect against pollution. Whilst a part of a licence is suspended it does not authorise the licence holder to carry on the activities specified.

The power to suspend is new in the EPA 1990. It is provided for in two separate sections: one where there has been a failure to comply with the licence (s. 42(6)), and another which applies more generally (s. 38(6)).

(a) Under s. 38(6), if the WRA considers that the site is no longer in the hands of a technically competent person, it may suspend those parts of the licence that authorise the carrying on of activities. The same power applies if the WRA considers that serious pollution of the environment or serious harm to human health has been caused, or is about to be caused, or that the continuation of the activities will cause serious pollution of the environment or serious harm to human health.

(b) The alternative power is that if, in exercising its supervisory powers under s. 42, it appears to the WRA that a condition is not being complied with, it may by notice require the licence holder to comply within a specified time. If the licence holder does not do so, the WRA may suspend the licence

(s. 42(6)). In this situation, the availability of the suspension power acts as an incentive to the proper implementation of conditions.

One limitation on these powers is that, if the Secretary of State determines on appeal that the WRA acted unreasonably in suspending a licence, the licence holder can claim compensation for consequential loss from the WRA (s. 43(7)). This potential financial liability may act as a brake on the use of suspension notices by the WRA.

Whilst a licence is suspended, the WRA may require the licence holder to take such measures to deal with or avert pollution or harm as it thinks fit (s. 38(9)). Significantly, this may include matters which fall outside the scope of the original licence conditions. It is an offence to fail to comply with such a requirement (s. 38(10)). The maximum penalty is, on conviction in the magistrates' court, a fine of £5,000 or, on conviction in the Crown Court, two years' imprisonment and/or an unlimited fine. If the waste is special waste, a magistrates' court may imprison for up to six months, and the maximum term of imprisonment on conviction in the Crown Court is five years.

Revocation of a licence

The WRA may revoke a licence by serving a notice on the licence holder, specifying when the revocation is to take effect. A revocation may be of the whole of a licence or of part of it—this includes revocation of those parts of the licence that authorise the carrying on of activities, whilst retaining other parts. For example, the WRA may revoke a licence in so far as it allows special waste to be deposited, leaving the rest of the licence in force. Revocation of the whole of the licence is likely to be inappropriate in many cases, since it means that any conditions attached to the licence cease to have effect (s. 35(11)). As these may include conditions requiring the licence holder to carry out works of pollution control, or conditions relating to the restoration and aftercare of a site, revocation would effectively remove most of the licence holder's responsibilities. It was once possible that the WRA could avoid this difficulty by exercising its powers under s. 61 (a section which has now been repealed), but that section only allowed costs to be recovered from the owner of the site, who may not be the same person as the former licence holder, particularly if the pollution occurs some years later.

(a) Under s. 38(1), if the WRA considers that the holder of a licence has ceased to be a fit and proper person by reason of being convicted of a relevant offence, it may revoke the licence, wholly or in part. The same power applies if the WRA considers that the continuation of the activities authorised by the licence would cause pollution of the environment or harm to human health, or would be seriously detrimental to the amenities of the locality, except that, in such a case, it must also consider that the pollution, harm or detriment cannot be avoided by modifying the conditions of the licence.

(b) Under s. 38(2), if the WRA considers that the site is no longer in the hands of a technically competent person, it may revoke those parts of the licence that authorise the carrying out of activities, but not the rest of it.

(c)   The same power of partial revocation applies if the licence holder fails
to pay an annual subsistence charge (s. 41(7)).

(d)   As with the power to suspend a licence, if the licence holder fails to
comply with a notice served under s. 42 requiring compliance with a
condition, the WRA may revoke the licence, either wholly or in part
(s. 42(6)).

Fees and charges

As part of the Government's objective of transferring funding of the regulation of pollution from the public to polluters, the EPA 1990, s. 41 introduces
fees and charges for licences for the first time (see the Waste Management
Licensing (Fees and Charges) Scheme 1994). The scheme is a cost-recovery
scheme, meaning that the levels are supposed to be fixed by the Secretary of
State so as to cover, in general terms, the cost to the WRA of processing an
application and supervising a licence.

In order to achieve this objective and to ensure that different operations pay
a reasonably fair charge relative to each other, a fairly complex scheme has
been implemented. The types of licensable activity are divided into four main
classes, although these are then subdivided to take account of such things as
whether the waste is being reused, reclaimed or recycled. These classes are:
the treatment of controlled waste; the keeping of controlled waste; the
disposal of controlled waste; and situations where a site has closed and a
certificate of completion is being sought. Having established these general
classes, the type of waste which is concerned (for example, whether it is inert
waste, household waste, industrial waste or special waste), and the amount
of waste that the site is licensed to receive annually, are taken into account
so that the precise category into which the activity falls can be ascertained.
The various fees and charges are then worked out by reference to that
category.

There are separate fees for initial applications for a licence, and for
applications for transfer, modification and surrender respectively. An annual
subsistence charge is also payable, which will normally run into thousands of
pounds, depending on the type of facility. To reflect the importance of the
NRA's role in waste management licensing, an amount is payable to the NRA
out of the appropriate fee or charge where it is consulted by the WRA in
relation to a licence (s. 41(5)). The WRA has a power to revoke a licence in
part if the annual charge is not paid (s. 41(7)).

Public registers

The WRA is under a duty to maintain a public register of a wide range of
information relating to the waste management licensing system (s. 64,
supplemented by the Waste Management Licensing Regulations 1994 (SI
No. 1056). Further details of the requirements are given in Chapter 7.

In outline, the registers must contain details of the following: all current or
recently current licences and applications, together with any relevant support-

ing documentation, representations and directions; modification, suspension and revocation notices; matters relating to an application to surrender a licence; reports and monitoring information produced or obtained by the WRA in discharging its functions; remedial action taken by the WRA; consignment notes and records made for the purposes of the special waste provisions; convictions of licence holders under Part II of the Act; and appeals. A licence is no longer recent 12 months after it ceases to be in force, and an application no longer recent 12 months after its rejection, meaning that the registers are of limited use for historical purposes.

There are powers for the Secretary of State to exclude information from the registers on the ground that its inclusion would be contrary to the interests of national security (s. 65), and for the WRA to exclude information on commercial confidentiality grounds (s. 66), though there is an appeal to the Secretary of State if the WRA refuses to do so. In relation to exclusions dealt with under s. 66, the register will contain an entry indicating the existence of the information.

These fairly comprehensive registers will provide much useful information to environmental groups. But they will also be of great help to those who need to comply with the duty of care, since a search of the register may answer many relevant questions about waste carriers and waste disposal sites.

The powers of the Secretary of State

Apart from the wide-ranging powers to make regulations under the Act and to issue policy guidance, the Secretary of State is provided with very wide powers to give directions to the WRA. For example, where an application is made, the Secretary of State may give a binding direction to the WRA in relation to the terms and conditions that must, or must not, be included in the licence (s. 35(7)). This power is the equivalent of the call-in powers that exist in other areas of the law. There are similar powers to give binding directions relating to modification (s. 37(3)) and to suspension and revocation (ss. 38(7) and 42(8))—in these cases the Secretary of State can effectively force the WRA to take action. There is a more general power contained in s. 72, under which the Secretary of State can declare a WRA in default if satisfied that it has failed to carry out any particular function. If the WRA fails to remedy the default, the Secretary of State may take over the relevant function.

Appeals

There are wide-ranging rights of appeal to the Secretary of State contained in s. 43. An appeal can be made where:

(a) an application for a licence is rejected (or is not determined within four months);
(b) a licence is subject to conditions;
(c) the conditions are modified;

(d) an application for a modification of conditions is rejected (or is not determined within two months);

(e)   a licence is suspended;

(f)   a licence is revoked;

(g) an application to surrender a licence is rejected (or is not determined within three months);

(h) an application for a transfer of a licence is rejected (or is not determined within two months).

One exception is where the Secretary of State made the original decision under the various powers of direction. In such a case, an action for judicial review would be the only available option.

There are no specified grounds of appeal. The procedures relating to appeals will be set out in regulations. The Waste Management Licensing Regulations 1994 state that an appeal must be brought within six months of the relevant decision (or deemed decision in cases where the appeal is against a non-determination within the required timescale). As is normal in environmental matters the appellant and the WRA have a choice as to whether the appeal is in the form of a hearing or by written representations. Unusually, if a hearing is held, s. 43(2)(c) states that it is open to the person who hears the appeal to hold it in private, in whole or in part. The appeal will commonly be referred to an inspector or other person, who will normally make the decision on behalf of the Secretary of State.

Modifications and revocations normally have no effect while an appeal is pending or being heard (s. 43(4)). However, the WRA may reverse this rule by stating in its notice that this is necessary for the purpose of preventing or minimising pollution of the environment or harm to human health (s. 43(6)). Suspension notices are not affected by an appeal (s. 43(5)). One limitation on the exercise of the power under s. 43(6) is that a licence holder may ask the Secretary of State to determine whether the WRA acted unreasonably in activating s. 43(6), or in suspending a licence. If the decision goes in favour of the licence holder, it can claim compensation for consequential loss from the WRA (s. 43(7)). This may limit the use of suspension notices and of s. 43(6).

Offences

With the introduction of the concepts of Directive waste and Directive disposal and recovery operations the original offences under s. 33 of EPA 1990 have now been reinterpreted. Unless one of the exemptions applies, a combination of s. 33(1) of EPA 1990, reg. 1(3) and sch. 4 of the Waste Management Licensing Regulations 1994 makes it a criminal offence to do the following:

(a) deposit Directive waste in or on land unless it is in accordance with a waste management licence. This applies to any deposit, whether temporary or permanent, and is not restricted to Directive disposal and recovery operations;

(b) treat, keep or dispose of Directive waste unless it is under and in accordance with a waste management licence—this offence can be committed either in or on land, or by means of mobile plant. As pointed out above this offence now extends only to Directive disposal and recovery operations;

(c) knowingly cause or knowingly permit either of the above.

These offences are considerably wider than those under COPA 1974 because they are not limited to deposits but extend to keeping, treating or disposing of controlled waste. However, many acts of storage and treatment will in fact be exempted, as the Waste Management Licensing Regulations 1994 show. It is clear that offences in categories (a) and (b) above are ones of strict liability, but it should be noted that (c) interposes 'knowingly' in front of both 'cause' and 'permit'.

The meaning of 'knowingly permit' was discussed in *Ashcroft* v *Cambro Waste Products Ltd* [1981] 3 All ER 699. The defendant was charged with knowingly permitting the deposit of controlled waste in contravention of a condition in a waste disposal licence. He argued that although he knew of the deposit of the waste, he did not know it was in breach of the condition. The court held that it was sufficient for the prosecution to show that he knowingly permitted the deposit: it did not need to show that he knew he was in breach of the licence. The more recent case of *Kent CC* v *Beaney* [1991] 5 Env Law 89, suggests that knowing permission may be inferred from the facts of a case where it must have been obvious to the landowner what was going on. This appears to widen the concept considerably to include cases of acquiescence.

As far as the concept of causation is concerned, this has been discussed on a number of occasions in relation to the similar offences under the Water Resources Act 1991. However, analogies with these cases should be made with care, since they do not consider the situation where 'knowingly' is inserted in front of 'cause'. This appears to suggest that someone who orders another to deposit waste will be guilty under this section only if it is shown that they knew the deposit was to take place unlawfully. One subsection that may help here is s. 33(5), which states that where controlled waste is deposited from a motor vehicle, the person who controls the vehicle, or who is in a position to control its use, will be treated as knowingly causing the deposit. See p. 430 for discussion of the meaning of 'cause or knowingly permit' in the context of the Water Resources Act 1991. There is a separate strict liability offence of contravening any condition of a waste management licence (s. 33(6)). This removes the loophole revealed by *Leigh Land Reclamation Ltd* v *Walsall MBC* (see p. 360).

The maximum penalty for these offences is, on conviction in the magistrates' court, six months' imprisonment and/or a fine of £20,000 or, on conviction in the Crown Court, two years' imprisonment and/or an unlimited fine. If the waste is special waste, the maximum term of imprisonment on conviction in the Crown Court is five years. An injunction may also be sought in appropriate cases.

Any director, manager, secretary or other similar officer of a corporate body can be prosecuted personally if the offence is committed with their consent or connivance, or is attributable to their neglect (s. 157). As stated earlier, a 'manager' only covers someone who is part of the 'controlling mind' of the company (see *R v Boal* [1992] 3 All ER 177, a case on very similar wording in the Fire Precautions Act 1971). This liability is additional to the individual liability of the person who carried out, or knowingly caused or knowingly permitted the deposit. Waste management is one area of environmental law where sentences of imprisonment have actually been imposed, though they have been reserved for serious offences and where an offender offends repeatedly.

The decision in *Boal* has been applied recently in relation to waste management offences under COPA 1974. In *Woodhouse v Walsall MBC* [1994] Env LR 30, the general manager of a waste disposal site (along with his employers) was convicted of a waste offence under the Act. Following the decision in *Boal* the crucial issue in determining personal (as opposed to corporate liability) was whether the defendant was 'in a position of real authority' having both 'the power and responsibility to decide corporate policy and strategy'. This is something more than mere authority itself (such as the power to 'hire and fire'). The important test was whether a defendant was in a position to control and guide the corporate body in terms of policy and strategy. This is, of course, a question of fact and degree in every case. For a possible view of the other side of the coin (i.e. corporate liability for the actions of its employees in relation to the Water Resources Act 1991) see *NRA v Alfred McAlpine Homes South Ltd* [1994] Env LR 198 and p. 433.

Defences

There is a defence under s. 33(7)(a) where the defendant took all reasonable precautions and exercised all due diligence to avoid the commission of the offence. This is a familiar defence that is included in many pieces of regulatory legislation. Essentially, it involves the defendant showing either that it took the appropriate steps on the facts of the case, or that it set up an adequate system. In many ways, the requirements are similar to those laid down by the duty of care. For example, the defence is of great use for receivers of waste (i.e. carriers and waste disposal site operators), who may inadvertently deal with it in an illegal fashion if they are misled by the consignor. However, it does impose quite a high standard on them to take steps to ensure that the consignment contains what it is meant to contain. It is arguable that this defence introduces an element of self-policing into the waste disposal chain. For example, in *Durham CC v Peter Connors Industrial Services Ltd* [1993] Env LR 197, a system of operation which relied upon the person disposing of waste regularly collecting a skip which had been filled with waste by another without checking on the contents of the skip every time, was not sufficient to come within an analogous defence under s. 3(4) of COPA 1974. In that case, the court said that the collector of waste had to take care to inform itself on each occasion that it collected the waste as to the nature of the contents of the skip. The defence required a specific enquiry to be made of any person who knew what the waste was and whether or not the future deposit of that waste would involve a breach of the Act.

There are further defences in s. 33(7)(b) and (c) relating respectively to employees who act under instructions from their employer and in ingnorance of the offence, and to acts carried out in an emergency in order to avoid danger to the public (although not danger to the environment) . The onus of proof establishing whether or not an emergency exists rests with the defendant upon the balance of probabilities. In *Waste Incineration Services Ltd* v *Dudley MBC* [1992] Env LR 29 the court viewed the phrase 'emergency' (as used in a condition of a waste disposal licence) objectively and without reference to how the licence holder perceived a given set of facts.

Dangerous disposal of waste

There is a very important further offence created by s. 33(1)(c). It is an offence to treat, keep or dispose of controlled waste in a manner likely to cause pollution of the environment or harm to human health. The importance of this paragraph is that it applies irrespective of the need for a waste management licence. In other words, activities which are exempted from the need for a licence are still governed by what is in effect a general requirement to act safely. The paragraph could also be said to supplement the licensing system by acting as a form of residual condition attached to a licence, since in theory it applies even where a licence is being complied with. The offence is drafted remarkably widely, as pollution of the environment is defined in s. 29 by reference to harm to *any* living organism. Harm in this context means any harm to the health of living organisms or interference with the ecological systems of which they form a part.

The paragraph is mainly targeted at providing a straightforward offence that can be used in relation to fly-tipping and other forms of irresponsible waste disposal. However, it also covers such things as storage of wastes on the production site—the harm to human health could be a harm to employees. The maximum penalty for breach of s. 33(1)(c) is the same as for offences relating to a waste management licence. The section does not, however, apply to activities which are under regulations made under s. 33(3). This has only been done in the cases of activities which are adequately controlled under regimes other than waste management.

Overlap with EPA 1990, Part I

Regulation 16 of the Waste Management Licensing Regulations 1994 covers the overlap between control under Parts I and II of the EPA 1990. In relation to integrated pollution control, reg. 16(1)(a) provides that the recovery or disposal of waste under an IPC authorisation, where the activity is or forms part of a process is exempt from the licensing. What is not clear is the extent to which an activity is 'part of the process'. The problem is particularly acute in respect of incineration and other combustion processes which use waste fuels. In particular, where waste is stored or treated on the site of an incinerator it is unclear as to whether a waste management licence is required.

In addition, despite the fact that it is meant to provide an integrated system of control, no condition can be attached to an authorisation which regulates the final disposal of Directive waste in or on land (s. 28(1)). This is a matter left entirely to the WRA. HMIP and local authorities are, however, required to notify the relevant WRA of the fact that a process involves the final disposal of waste in or on land. When the Environment Agency is introduced some of these artificial boundaries will, of course, cease.

In relation to other processes, most incinerators (except for very small ones), a number of waste recovery operations, and some other processes in which waste is burned as a fuel are subject to control under the local authority air pollution control provisions of Part I of the EPA 1990 (see Part B of section 5.1 (incineration) of the Prescribed Processes etc Regulations 1991 (SI 1991 No. 472). In these restricted circumstances, where an authorisation is required under Part I of the EPA 1990, this will exempt the premises from the need for a waste management licence. In practice, however, many operators will have operations ancillary to the main process (e.g. waste storage or delivery) and will seek a waste management licence to cover these aspects.

Clean-up powers

Section 59 gives WRAs and waste collection authorities powers to require the removal of controlled waste. They apply whenever controlled waste has been deposited on land in contravention of s. 33(1), i.e. the deposit was not in accordance with a waste management licence or it breached s. 33(1)(c).

The initial responsibility falls on the occupier of the land. The WRA may serve a notice on the occupier requiring the waste to be removed, or steps to be taken to mitigate the consequences of the deposit. The notice must specify a period within which this action should be taken, though it cannot be less than 21 days. There is a right to appeal to the magistrates' court during the 21-day period. Such an appeal must be allowed if the court is satisfied that the appellant neither deposited nor knowingly caused or knowingly permitted the deposit, or if there is a material defect in the notice (s. 59(3)). An appeal suspends the operation of the notice until it is determined (s. 59(4)). It is a summary offence, with a maximum fine of £5,000 to fail to comply with a notice served under s. 59 (s. 59(5)). This offence is a continuing one and a further fine of up to £1,000 can be imposed for every day on which the failure to comply continues after conviction. Ultimately, the WRA has default powers to carry out the steps specified in the notice itself and to recover any expenses reasonably incurred from the person on whom it was served (s. 59(6)).

Where the occupier did not make or knowingly permit the unlawful deposit, or there is no occupier, the WRA may remove the waste or take mitigating steps immediately. This course of action is also available if these steps were immediately necessary to remove or prevent pollution or harm to human health (s. 59(7)). The WRA may then recover its costs from any person who deposited the waste, or knowingly caused or knowingly permitted its deposit, unless that person can show that the cost was incurred unnecessarily (s. 59(8)). Ultimate responsibility for unlawfully deposited waste therefore falls on the person who deposited it rather than on the occupier.

However, it may not be possible to trace the person responsible, or they may have no money to pay the WRA's costs, in which case the position is in practice that the WRA has a choice whether to leave the waste where it is or pick up the bill itself. Nevertheless, this is an important power which can be used in addition to a prosecution under s. 33, since it tackles directly the problem that faces the WRA.

The NRA's powers under the Water Resources Act 1991, s. 161, should also be considered in this context, since they may be used to deal with deposits of waste that threaten controlled waters (see p. 450).

Contaminated land

Britain has an industrial legacy which has led to the contamination of some areas of the country. Traditionally, active emissions from industrial processes have been controlled, whereas the long-term harm caused from ground contamination has been ignored. It has been estimated that approximately 27,000 hectares of land in the UK are regarded as potentially contaminated. The law in relation to the harm caused by contaminated land has, however, been pragmatic and piecemeal. Various mechanisms are available to deal with the specific problems associated with contaminated land (see p. 397). Until relatively recently, however, the need to legislate specifically in order to control the problem has not been acknowledged. There is now a recognition of the need to reuse old industrial land and the understanding of the consequences of land contamination has increased. Subsequently, the law and policy in relation to the clean-up of contaminated land is in the process of change.

The Environment Act 1995 has introduced a new system of control specifically targeted at the clean-up of contaminated land. The principles of the system work in a similar way to the statutory nuisance provisions in the EPA 1990, although there is a hierarchy of sites which involve slightly different actions. Indeed, the new provisions have been inserted into Part II of the EPA 1990 and now sit alongside the nuisance provisions.

Like many other areas of environmental law the framework of the legislation gives only a small part of the legislative picture. Most of the detail is likely to be fleshed out in the guise of Government guidance. At the time of writing only a portion of this guidance has been issued (albeit only in draft and for consultation purposes). It is likely, therefore, that a unified body of law and policy on the clean-up of contaminated land will only be available some (considerable?) time after the Royal Assent of the Environment Act 1995.

The introduction of the Environment Act 1995 was a direct result of the failure of the first initiative intended to deal with the problem, the contaminative uses register. The origin of the register was to be found in the Parliamentary Select Commitee's report on contaminated land in 1989, which recommended the abolition of the *caveat emptor* rule in relation to the sale and purchase of land so that the seller was under an obligation to inform the buyer of any of the defects with the land (including contamination). The Government responded with a consultation paper, *Let the Buyer be Better*

Informed. The primary thrust of the proposals was the introduction of a set of registers which would form an objective list of potentially contaminated sites by reference to a selection of potentially contaminative uses. It was intended that regulations prescribing the form of the register were to be introduced in late 1991.

The response to the consultation exercise was overwhelming and generally negative. In the light of many of the observations which were made, the DoE issued a second consultation paper on 31 July 1992. On this occasion, a set of draft regulations was included which were intended to indicate the framework for the registers. It was envisaged that the regulations would be implemented in late 1992 and subsequently local authorities would be given 15 months in which to compile the data which was to form the registers before they would be available for the public.

The second consultation exercise differed from the first in that fewer categories of potentially contaminative uses which would be included on the register were proposed than on the original list. It was intended that the register would cover land on which there had been such uses as oil refineries, chemical works, scrap metal stores, waste tips, lead works and steel works.

Many objections were raised at both stages of the consultation process. It was pointed out that there were no provisions for the removal of the sites from the register even if the land had subsequently been cleaned up. It was suggested therefore that there was little incentive to clean up a site as it would still be included on the register.

The second major area of concern was the problem of blight on land which was included on the register. It was argued that it would be unlikely that developers would wish to buy an identified 'problem' site, as any subsequent resale or leasing would involve an investigation from potential purchasers into the contamination on site.

This in turn, it was argued, would lead to a disincentive to regenerate vacant and derelict land, which would be contrary to existing Government policy. As developers refused to develop on inner-city areas this would subsequently lead to pressures on edge-of-town sites.

Banks and building societies predicted that there would be a large scale reduction in the value of land included on the register. This would lead to lending institutions being reluctant to fund property development on sites included on the register. Thus, it was argued that sites included on the register would be effectively sterilised.

More fundamental criticisms were aimed at the registers and there were many suggestions that the concept behind them was seriously flawed. Most of the criticisms related to the fact that the registers would not record actual contamination but instead would rely upon the previous or existing uses of land. It was suggested that such a blanket approach would not provide sufficient certainty of the presence of contamination. Indeed, there would be a significant number of sites which were heavily contaminated which would not appear on the register at all.

The fundamental problem, however, was that the registers did not seek to do anything positive to assist remediation where land had been identified as being contaminated. It was argued that it was not the main priority to identify which areas had a chance of being contaminated, as such information was generally acknowledged to be available. Once contamination has been identified, the crucial issue to be addressed is the liability for the costs of remediation and the recovery of those costs. The registers, of course did not attempt to deal with these complicated issues.

In the light of these criticisms it was announced in March 1993 that the Government was withdrawing its proposals to set up the register of contaminative uses. At the same time it was announced that there would be a wide-ranging review of the clean-up of contaminated land including such issues as treatment, allocation of liabilities and cost recovery. The Consultation Paper, *Paying for Our Past* was issued in March 1994. The aim of the paper was to set out a number of 'preliminary conclusions' on a series of seven issues dealing with Government policy objectives, the statutory framework, the relationship with the common law, the extension of strict liability, the identity of the person liable for clean-up, providing the markets with information and the role of public sector bodies.

In November 1994 the Government announced the outcome of the consultation exercise. The result was a policy document, *The Framework for Contaminated Land*. The document sets out the broad future strategy for dealing with contaminated land. The principal elements of this strategy are:

(a)   the adoption of the 'suitable for use' approach when dealing with the issue of clean-up. Thus, remedial action will only be required where the contamination poses unacceptable actual or potential risks to health or the environment. This is to be balanced against the appropriateness and cost effectiveness of the measures, taking into account the actual or intended use of the site. Therefore, the measure required to clean up a site which was to be used for housing would be more stringent than if it were to be used for car-parking;

(b)   to prioritise action to deal with the most urgent and real problems whilst balancing the economic constraints within the economy as a whole and on private businesses and landowners;

(c)   to clarify the law on the clean-up of contaminated sites, thus enabling a proper market to be created for those who own sites which are or have been contaminated;

(d)   to supplement the existing statutory nuisance provisions with a new, modern, specific power to deal with contaminated land.

In addition it was announced that ss. 143 and 61 of the EPA 1990 dealing with the contaminative uses register and closed landfills were to be repealed.

What is contaminated land?
For a number of years there has been some discussion about the precise definition of the phrase 'contaminated land'. The main difficulty in seeking to define the phrase is that 'contamination' (with no necessary link to any harm/damage) refers merely to the presence of a foreign substance. This is

not the same as 'pollution' which is linked to harm. Thus, arguably, land could be contaminated and pose no threat to either the environment or human health. In such a case it would be unnecessary to carry out any clean-up operations. The DoE, in evidence to the House of Commons Select Committee select, took the view that contaminated land should be defined as land 'which represents an actual hazard to public health or the environment as a result of current or previous use'.

In any event the discussion has now been superseded by the statutory definition contained in s. 78A(2) of the EPA 1990 (as inserted by the Environment Act 1995). In that section 'contaminated land' is defined as being:

land which appears to the local authority in whose area it is situated to be in such a condition, by reason of substances in, on or under land, that

(a)   significant harm is being caused or there is a significant possibility of such harm being caused; or
(b)   pollution of controlled waters is being or is likely to be, caused.

Local authorities are under a duty to have regard to any guidance issued by the Secretary of State when assessing whether land is contaminated (s. 78B(2)). In addition, the assessment of 'significant' harm is also to be the subject of further guidance. There is, however, express provision within the Act for such guidance to make provision for different weight to be attached to different descriptions of harm to health or property and other factors.

Draft guidance was issued by the Secretary of State when the Environment Bill was passing through Parliament. The draft guidance 'shadows' the Act and proposes limitations on the statutory definitions of 'contaminated land' and 'significant harm'. In essence, the guidance sets out the details of a risk assessment by attempting to differentiate between different levels of risk for different categories of human health.

Environment Agency
The primary responsibility for the role of identifying and cleaning up contaminated land will fall to the district and metropolitan authorities. The local authorities are guided by the Environment Agency (EA), which provides technical expertise and advice. The EA is also responsible for continuing the Government's research programme into contaminated land, with particular reference to publishing guidelines for priority contaminants (s. 78A(6)). Finally, the EA will play an active role in the clean-up of the most contaminated sites (known as 'special sites') after notification from the local authorities (see below). The EA has inspection and entry powers in relation to special sites (s. 78Q). In particular, the EA can terminate the designation of a special site where it appears to the EA that it is no longer suitable for designation (s. 78Q(4)). The EA is under a duty to prepare a report on the state of contaminated land in England, Wales and Scotland with assistance from local authorities (s. 78U).

The identification of contaminated land

Under s. 78B of the EPA 1990 each local authority is under a duty to inspect its area from time to time for the purposes of identifying:

(a)   contaminated land;
(b)   special sites.

Special sites are designated by the EA after notification by the local authority after carrying out their general inspection duty. Special sites are regulated directly by the EA and will be defined in separate regulations which have yet to be published. The general criteria for special sites are the seriousness of the harm or water pollution which would be (or is being) caused and whether the EA is more likely to have the expertise to act on those particular sites (s. 78C(10)).

When identifying sites, the enforcing authority is entitled to take into account the cumulative impact of two or more sites when assessing the 'significant harm' or 'pollution'. This will be important where the 'cocktail' effect of a number of contaminated sites causes significant harm, whereas any individual site will not give rise to any notable pollution (s. 78X).

The issue of the nature of the inspection duty is at the time of writing unclear. On the one hand it could be little more than a paper exercise, on the other a full site investigation of every potentially contaminated site might be necessary. The practical conclusion is that local authorities will probably be under a duty to investigate sites which are acknowledged to be problem sites by reference to some objective evidence. It would be unreasonable to expect the duty to cover inspection of all potential sites within the locality. Therefore in a similar way to the analogous provisions in relation to statutory nuisances it is likely that the provisions will be used in a reactive rather than proactive manner.

Once land has been identified as being contaminated the local authority is under a duty to notify the Agency, the owner/occupier of the land, and anyone who is considered to be the 'appropriate person' (see below).

Remediation notices

Once a site has been identified as contaminated land or a special site the relevant authority is under a duty to prepare, and serve on the 'appropriate person', a remediation notice specifying what must be done by way of remediation (s. 78E). This reflects the existing responsibilities in relation to statutory nuisances. There are, however, a number of circumstances where the duty to serve a remediation notice does not apply. Where the enforcing authority is satisfied that a site is contaminated but remediation works cannot be specified the duty to serve a remediation notice does not apply. Instead, it must publish a remediation document setting out the grounds for taking the view that remediation works cannot be specified (s. 78H(5)–(16)).

If a remediation notice is to be served the relevant authority is then under a duty to carry out a formal consultation exercise before service (s. 78H(1)). This duty does not apply in cases where it appears to the authority that there is an imminent danger of serious harm or pollution of controlled waters (s. 78(H)(4)). The authority is required to notify the appropriate person(s) on whom a notice would be served, the owner of the land, and any person who appears to be in occupation of the whole or part of the land, at least three months before the date of service of the notice (s. 78H(3)).

It is intended that this time would be used by the potential recipient of the notice to come up with alternative proposals for remediation or to locate any alternative person responsible for the contamination.

In an attempt to encourage more voluntary remediation work, the relevant authority is precluded from serving a remediation notice where it is satisfied that appropriate steps are being, or will be taken, without the service of a notice (s. 78H(5)). The appropriate person is required to prepare, within a reasonable period, a remediation statement setting out the works which will be carried out within a specified period.

The remediation notice is to be served on the appropriate persons and is required to set out what must be done and the time period for carrying out the specified steps (s. 78E(1)). In specifying the steps required under a remediation notice the authority is under a duty to take into account guidance produced by the EA and to balance the costs of carrying out the work with the seriousness of the harm/pollution caused (s. 78E(4)). This cost-benefit analysis which is to be carried out by the relevant authority will be crucial in determining the effectiveness of the new provisions. A further restriction is placed upon the authority in that cannot issue a notice where powers are available to the EA under s. 27 of the EPA 1990 in relation to remediation of pollution caused by prescribed processes.

The 'appropriate person'
Although the practicalities of the new system are fairly straightforward, the issue of the identity of the 'appropriate person' on whom the remediation notice is served is perhaps the central element of the new system. In accordance with the 'polluter pays' principle the aropriate person is defined as the person, or any of the persons, who caused or knowingly permitted the substances, or any of the substances, which have been the cause of the contamination to be in or under the land (s. 78E).

Where there are two or more parties responsible for the presence of contaminative substances in or under land the Act makes provision for joint and several liability in restricted circumstances. Different remediation notices can require different things to be done by way of remediation (s. 78E(2)) although each 'appropriate person' may only be served with a notice in connection with any remediation which is 'to any extent referable' to substances caused or knowingly permitted by that party (s. 78F(9)). On the other hand, it is no defence for the recipient of a remediation notice to argue that any remediation would not be required in consequence only of the presence of the substance introduced by the recipient of the notice. Where the same remediation activity is required from different parties a remediation notice cannot be served requiring remediation measures in respect of other contaminating substances whose presence was not caused or knowingly permitted by them. In such circumstances, where the 'appropriate person' who *is* responsible for the remediation activity cannot be found, after reasonable inquiry, the owner or occupier become 'appropriate persons' (see below). Where there are two or more 'appropriate persons' in relation to any remediation works they will only be responsible for a relative portion of the costs and/or the works and the remediation notice must specify the proportion of the costs which they are liable to bear (s. 78F(7)).

Although primary responsibility for remediation rests with the person who caused or knowingly permitted the substance to be present in land a residual responsibility falls upon owners and occupiers. Where, after reasonable inquiry, the original polluter cannot be 'found' the owner or the occupier for the time being are deemed to be persons (s. 78F(4)). The liability of owners and occupiers is restricted in relation to remediation works in relation to the pollution of controlled waters (s. 78J). Where a party finds themselves responsible for remediation works solely as a result of their ownership or occupation of land (as opposed to being the original polluter) they will not be liable for any works relating to the pollution of controlled waters (s. 78J(2)). There are other restrictions in relation to liability for contamination which escapes to other land (see below).

'Owner' is defined in s. 78A as being the person entitled to receive the rent for the property. It specifically excludes mortgagees not in possession, which means that lenders can receive remediation notices where they are mortgagees in possession. Insolvency practitioners are also protected from personal liability unless the contamination is attributable to their own negligence (s. 78X). 'Occupier' is not defined.

Escapes of substances to other land
As contamination does not necessarily confine itself to boundaries of ownership or occupation there is provision for the service of remediation notices where substances have escaped from their original resting place onto other land. The basic principle is that the original polluter can be responsible for contamination which has escaped from the original land onto other land (s. 78K(1)). Owners and occupiers are not liable to carry out remediation works in respect of substances which have migrated onto their land other than remediation to land within their ownership or occupation (s. 78K(3)). In addition, owners of land adjoining contaminated land are not liable for remediation in respect of other, further land to which substances have migrated, unless they are the owner of that land (s. 78K(4)).

Although these provisions in respect of responsibility for contamination provide a complicated hierarchy of liability, the practical difficulties of establishing responsibility must not be overlooked. Unfortunately, contamination does not necessarily carry clear identification of responsibility. In particular, in areas where there has been a long history of industrial activity, distinguishing between different polluters will present evidential hurdles which will have to be overcome before a remediation notice can be served. In these circumstances it is clear that the service of a remediation notice will not be a quick-fire remedy.

Non-compliance with a remediation notice

It is an offence to fail to comply with a remediation notice without reasonable excuse (s. 78M). There are, however, relatively minor penalties which undermines the deterrence factor. The offence can only be tried in the magistrates' court. Where the contaminated land is currently industrial, trade or business premises, the maximum penalty is a fine of £20,000, with a further daily fine of up to £2,000 for every day before the enforcing authority has carried out any remediation (s. 00). In cases of other contaminated land the maximum fine is £5,000, with a maximum daily fine of £500 (10% of Level 5).

The relevant authority has the power to carry out remediation works where the recipient of the remediation has failed to comply either with or without the appropriate person's agreement (s. 78N). The agency has the power to recover all or part of its reasonable costs. In recovering costs, regard must be had to any hardship which the cost-recovery might impose. In England and Wales the relevant authority also has the power to serve a charging notice on the owner which will constitute a charge on the premises which consist of or include the contaminated land in question. The costs of any charge may be paid by instalments over a maximum 30-year period. A person served with the charging notice has a right of appeal which must be made to the county court within 21 days of the receipt of the notice (s. 78P(8)).

Appeals

Any person who is the recipient of a remediation notice has the right of appeal within 21 days of the service of the notice. Where the notice was served by a local authority the appeal is made to the magistrates' court; in relation to special sites, the right of appeal is to the Secretary of State (s. 78L). The details of the appeals process are to be the subject of regulations which have yet to be published, but it is expected that they will broadly follow the pattern of appeals against statutory nuisances (see p. 78R).

Registers

There is a public register which contains details of remediation statements, notices, appeals and information about remediation work notified to the authority, although there is no official guarantee of compliance with remediation notices.

Other statutory provisions for the clean-up of contaminated land

The new provisions in the Environment Act are designed to replace (and not supplement) the existing statutory nuisance provisions in Part III of the EPA. Once the new provisions in the Environment Act are brought into force, s. 79 of the EPA will be amended to exclude contaminated land from the definition of statutory nuisances (see sch. 22, para. 89, Environment Act 1995). There may, however be occasions where the land in question does not fall within the specific statutory definition of contaminated land under s. 79A and the statutory nuisance provisions could be used to enforce a clean-up.

Although the introduction of the new contaminated land provisions in the Environment Act 1995 is an attempt to update the law there are still a number of other statutory provisions which can be utilised in dealing with land which is causing or likely to cause harm to the environment.

Most statutory powers rely upon the need to prevent actual harm and do not seek to remediate contamination which is in existence but causing no harm. Thus, there is no statutory obligation to clean up contamination unless certain pre-conditions are met. The only occasions where remediation is required as a matter of law is where contamination is likely to lead to:

(a) pollution of the environment;
(b) adverse effects on human health or safety;
(c) an escape of pollutants.

Where remediation is required as a matter of statute the steps which would be taken would only normally be limited to the minimisation of one of these three risks rather than making the site 'clean'. As a matter of practice, however, when sites are remediated it is normally to an accepted standard.

Statutory powers to clean up contaminated land

Statutory nuisances
Sections 79 and 80 of the EPA 1990 require local authorities to inspect their areas in order to detect the presence of statutory nuisances. This includes any accumulation or deposit which is prejudicial to health or a nuisance. Once they have detected a statutory nuisance they are under a duty to serve notices requiring abatement of the nuisance. The notice is to be served on the person responsible for the nuisance or, if that person is unable to be found, the owner or occupier of the site. The local authority has a residual right to carry out the works if the owner/occupier does not do so (see s. 81(3)).

Pollution of controlled waters
Section 161 of the Water Resources Act 1991 enables the National Rivers Authority to take preventative action and/or remediation action to deal with actual or threatened pollution of controlled waters. Again, the notice is to be served on the person responsible for the pollution and the NRA can carry out the works and recover the costs from that person (see p. 450).

Section 215 of the Town and Country Planning Act 1990
Local planning authorities have the power to require steps to be taken for remedying the condition of land which adversely affects the amenity of their area. They may serve an appropriate notice upon the owner and occupier of that land. This notice can be the subject of an appeal which can effectively negate the power.

Section 61 of the Environmental Protection Act 1990

Under s. 61 of the EPA 1990, a section never implemented and now repealed, certain pieces of land were to be inspected by the WRA to check whether or not there was anything affecting the land so that it caused pollution or harm to human health (s. 61(1)). This duty to carry out inspections from time to time arose in respect of any land on which controlled waste had been deposited (whether under a licence or at any other time), or where the authority had reason to believe that there were concentrations or accumulations of landfill gases or noxious liquids (s. 61(3)). Where such sites were, in the opinion of the authority, likely to cause pollution or harm to human health, they were under a duty to carry out work or take other steps on the land or adjacent land to avoid such harm or pollution (s. 61(7)). In such circumstances, the costs or any part of such cost could be recovered from the owner of the land, unless the costs were incurred unreasonably. There may, of course, have been instances when the owner of the land was not responsible for the build-up of pollution. Thus, where costs were sought from the owner, account had to be taken of any hardship suffered by the owner in paying costs (s. 61(10)).

As in the case of the Contaminative Uses Register this section was the subject of much criticism for the potentially damaging effects upon innocent owners. Consequently it has been repealed by the Environment Act 1995. It is nevertheless an important section in that it demonstrates the historical background to the new provisions.

Civil liabilities

In addition to the statutory powers which can be used to remediate con-taminated land, there are also potential civil liabilities for damage caused from contamination. These liabilities also depend upon actual loss rather than anticipated loss, although it may be possible to bring a mandatory injunction to prevent any damage arising (see Chapter 8).

Section 73 of the Environmental Protection Act

As outlined below (see p. 408) this section applies where any damage is caused by a deposit of controlled waste in contravention of ss. 33(1) or 63(2) (i.e. the deposit was not in accordance with a waste management licence, or it breached s. 33(1)(c), or it breached the provision on disposal of non-controlled waste).

Rylands v Fletcher

Strict liability under the rule in *Rylands* v *Fletcher* can be utilised to pay for the clean-up of contaminated sites (see p. 187). There are a number of limitations on this rule in relation to contaminated land:

(a)   it is only the person who brought the substance which escapes on to the land who can be the defendant;

(b)   the thing on the land must truly escape rather than be the conse-quence of an 'action' (compare spillages of material over a period of time (an action) with the leaking of a faulty underground storage tank (an escape));

(c)   the escape must cause the damage to the plaintiff;

(d)   the use of land must be non-natural.

Many of these issues have been considered in relation to the pollution of ground water in *Cambridge Water Company* v *Eastern Counties Leather* (see p. 182). It is not clear as to the extent to which the principles in that decision will apply to contaminated land, but there would be good grounds to suggest that it would be followed in such cases.

Nuisance

It may be possible to bring an action in private nuisance on the grounds that contamination has caused a substantial and unreasonable interference with the use of adjoining property. Again, the person liable would be the person responsible or, if that person was not found, the owner/occupier of the site (see p. 172).

Other liabilities might arise in negligence and/or breach of statutory duty. Clearly each of these causes of action would depend to a large extent upon the specific circumstances of the contamination.

Duty of care

The most significant new control introduced by the EPA 1990 is the criminal duty of care imposed by s. 34, which came into force on 1 April 1992. All those who deal with controlled waste are required to take reasonable and appropriate steps in relation to it, otherwise they commit a criminal offence. This entails such things as storing and packaging waste properly, describing clearly what it consists of, dealing only with an authorised carrier, providing the carrier with an accurate transfer note relating to the waste, and taking steps to ensure that it is ultimately disposed of correctly. What is reasonable will depend on the exact circumstances and on the identity and resources of the person concerned. Additional, more specific, requirements apply to special waste (see p. 405).

The introduction of the duty of care was prompted primarily by the publication of the Eleventh Report of the Royal Commission on Environmental Pollution, *Managing Waste: The Duty of Care*, in 1985 (Cmd 9675). This concluded:

The first task is for society to identify where the responsibility lies for ensuring that wastes are properly handled and disposed of. In our judgment, this must rest with the individual or organisation who produces the wastes. The producer incurs a duty of care which is owed to society, and we would like to see this duty reflected in public attitudes and enshrined in legislation and codes of practice.

The Royal Commission went on to stress the need to pass the responsibility for waste from person to person down the disposal chain, thereby suggesting that, rather than the producer retaining total responsibility for the waste, the duty of care would operate by ensuring that everyone in the chain checks the competence of those with whom they deal with regard to handling the waste safely and without harm to the environment. The main purpose behind the duty of care is thus clear. It is to encourage anyone who holds waste to deal with it in a responsible fashion, so that a 'cradle to grave' approach is applied to its management and disposal. It is no longer the case that producers and others necessarily lose responsibility for waste when they cease to have possession of it.

What does the duty entail?

Section 34 provides that the duty of care applies to any person who produces, imports, carries, keeps, treats or disposes of controlled waste, or who, as a broker, has control of it. The only exception is that occupiers of domestic premises are not subject to the duty with regard to household waste produced on the property (s. 34(2)). The duty applies only to controlled waste.

The section itself states that any person to whom the duty applies should take reasonable steps to:

(a)   prevent any other person contravening s. 33 (i.e. the law relating to the unauthorised deposit, keeping, treatment or disposal of controlled waste);

(b)   prevent the escape of waste;

(c)   ensure that the waste is transferred only to an authorised person;

(d)   ensure that an adequate written description of the waste is given to anyone to whom the waste is transferred.

Each of these four limbs is discussed below.

The bare duty in s. 34 is supplemented by the Environmental Protection (Duty of Care) Regulations 1991 (SI 1991 No. 2839), which lay down some additional documentation requirements. Contravention of these regulations automatically results in the commission of a criminal offence. There is also a *Code of Practice on the Duty of Care,* made by the Secretary of State. This is a statutory code, made under s. 34(7). Contravention of its provisions is not of itself a criminal offence, but it could be said that contravention gives rise to a presumption that the duty has been breached, since s. 34(10) states that it should be taken into account in deciding whether the duty has been complied with and in fixing any penalty. (The Code may also be used as evidence in civil cases and in prosecutions under s. 33.) The combined effect of s. 34, the regulations and the Code of Practice is to lay down a mixture of general and specific requirements.

It is a criminal offence to breach the duty of care. The maximum penalty is, on conviction in the magistrates' court, a £5,000 fine or, on conviction in the Crown Court, an unlimited fine.

The steps required to be taken under s. 34 (see above) comprise the following:

(a)   *The prevention of breaches of s. 33*—This part of the duty of care is concerned with ensuring that a holder of waste (i.e. the person who has control of it at any time) takes responsibility for checking that the waste is dealt with properly by others further down the waste disposal chain. For example, it entails that the transferor of waste should know where the waste is going before parting with it, which in turn involves checking that the site where the waste is to be taken is licensed to take it and that the carrier is actually taking it there. The Code of Practice requires that a transferor of waste must be prepared to stop a transfer of waste if not satisfied that it is being dealt with properly. The standard is objective in the sense that holders of waste ought to act on signs that something is amiss. For example, a transferor of waste who suspects that a carrier is not tipping the waste where it says it is (for instance, because of the short periods of time between journeys), or who is quoted an unrealistically low price for the disposal of waste, ought to check what is actually happening. However, the standard is also related to the resources and knowledge of the individual, with the result that large firms may be expected to carry out more rigorous investigations than small ones.

(b) *Prevention of the escape of waste*—This requirement is mainly related to the correct packaging and labelling of waste. For instance, if waste spills from inadequate drums whilst they are on the back of a lorry, the transferor of the drums may well be in breach as well as the lorry driver. Other examples relate to the nature of the packaging; for example, fire resistant packaging should be used for inflammable wastes. This limb also imposes a duty to ensure that waste is properly stored—using an open skip which allows waste to be blown off by the wind may amount to a breach.

(c) *Transfer to an authorised person*—There are various stages to the disposal of waste and who constitutes an authorised person will vary from stage to stage. If waste is entrusted to a carrier, the duty of care clearly establishes that it should only be given to a carrier who is registered under the Control of Pollution (Amendment) Act 1989 (see below), or who is exempted from registration under that Act. Accordingly, the Code of Practice states that a transferor should check the carrier's certificate of registration, or its grounds for exemption. It even states that a photocopy of the registration certificate is not adequate for this purpose, only an original copy issued by the WRA.

If waste is being delivered to a waste disposal site or an incinerator, an authorised person is one who holds a waste management or waste disposal licence or is exempt from the need for one.

(d) *Description of the waste*—The purpose behind this requirement is fairly clear. It is to enable everyone who deals with the waste to know what it consists of. In that way, it should not be treated incorrectly through ignorance. The detail required in a description will depend on the nature of the waste. For example, if it is hazardous the exact nature of the hazard should be identified, whereas in many other cases a general description will suffice. Consideration of the purpose of the requirement should enable decisions to be taken on what is an adequate description. For example, omitting to mention that a skip includes a small amount of dangerous chemicals may lead to the contents being deposited at a site that is not equipped to take it, or to an undesirable mixing of incompatible wastes. Alternatively, a false description could have catastrophic results in the event of a road accident if it meant that the emergency services dealt with it inappropriately.

The requirement of an adequate description is supplemented by the 1991 Regulations (SI 1991 No. 2839). These require that when controlled waste is transferred there must be a transfer note, though this does not actually have to travel with the waste. The transfer note must identify the waste and state its quantity, the kind of container it is in, the time and place of transfer, and the name, address and other relevant details of the transferor and transferee. The Regulations also require that the transferor and transferee sign the transfer note and that the transfer note and the written description are kept for at least two years from the date of transfer. WRAs have powers to demand production of the transfer note or written description within this period. The written description and the transfer note may be combined in one document as long as each requirement is fully met. A standard form of transfer note is set out in the Code of Practice. Because of the width of the concept of a transfer, these requirements cover a range of circumstances where the recipient may not at first glance seem like a typical 'waste disposal firm'—for example, a landlord of an industrial estate, office block or large shopping centre could require a transfer note if the waste was collected centrally, unless the transfer was construed as being 'within the same premises'.

It is permissible for multiple consignments of waste up to one year to be covered by one transfer note, as long as the description of the waste, the identity of the parties and all other details remain the same for each consignment.

Enforcement of the duty of care
It should be noted that the duty of care is broken irrespective of whether harm is caused. It is the failure to take reasonable steps that is the criminal offence, not any damage that results from it. This creates a position where offences will be committed frequently. The control mechanism is whether any breach comes to the attention of the WRA and whether it considers any enforcement action is justified. In this context, the Government has made it quite clear in its Circular advice that WRAs are meant to be reactive in their approach to policing the duty of care and are not expected to go out of their way to look for breaches. Instead, they should treat enforcement work as part of their existing duty to supervise the waste management licensing system. Certainly no extra resources have been given to WRAs in order to enable them to monitor the duty of care provisions.

It should also be remembered that everyone in the waste chain is subject to the duty of care. The system should therefore have an element of self-policing. For example, a producer of waste would be well advised not to transfer it to someone they suspect of being a 'cowboy', because if the waste is fly-tipped that could lead the WRA to prosecute the producer for breach of the duty of care (and also give rise to possible criminal actions for knowingly permitting the deposit, and to potential liability in civil law, or under the clean-up powers). Equally, a waste carrier should not accept improperly labelled or packaged waste, and should make periodic checks on the waste it receives, since it will have responsibility under the duty of care if there is something wrong.

In summary, the preceding discussion suggests that the main function of the duty of care is to encourage responsible behaviour and the development of appropriate management systems for the storage, transfer and monitoring of waste, rather than to punish wrongdoing. Because of the documentation procedures, it also makes waste consignments easier to trace. The first reported prosecutions illustrate these points. For example, in one case a demolition contractor was fined £800 for failing to ensure that a skip contained only materials described in the transfer note—the infringement came about because employees had not been given sufficient instruction that only certain materials could be put in the skip. However, one of the lessons from the early prosecutions appears to be that the courts are treating many of the breaches, such as failing to make out a transfer note, as technical in nature, and thus are imposing only small fines. This seems to underplay the importance of this type of management-based control.

Carriage of waste

Intimately connected with the duty of care is the requirement that all carriers of waste are registered with the WRA. The requirements in this respect arise out of the Control of Pollution (Amendment) Act 1989. This was a private member's bill (although it did ultimately have Government support) which sought to deal with the growing problem of fly-tipping by providing some powers over carriers. The Act is supplemented by the Controlled Waste (Registration of Carriers and Seizure of Vehicles) Regulations 1991 (SI 1991 No. 1624). It came into force on 1 April 1992.

It is an offence under the 1989 Act, s. 1(1), to carry controlled waste without being registered with the WRA. The offence is a summary one only, with a maximum fine of £5,000. The defences are very similar to those available for offences under the EPA 1990, s. 33 (see p. 336). It should be remembered that it is normally a separate offence under the duty of care to deal with an unregistered carrier.

Local authorities, British Rail, and charities and voluntary groups are specifically exempt from the requirement to register by virtue of reg. 2, which also states that a producer may carry its own wastes without having to seek registration, as long as the waste is not demolition or construction waste. In addition, s. 1(1) refers only to carrying waste in the course of a business or with a view to profit, meaning that such things as carrying waste to a local authority waste site on behalf of a neighbour are not covered.

An application for registration must be made to the WRA where the carrier has its principal place of business (reg. 4). There is only one substantive ground for refusal of registration, which is that the applicant is not a desirable carrier. This fulfils a similar function to the 'fit and proper person' requirement in the waste management licensing system. It has two elements: (i) that the carrier, or someone closely connected with the carrier's business, has been convicted of one of the relevant offences listed in sch. 1 to the Regulations; and (ii) that the WRA considers it undesirable for the carrier to be authorised to carry controlled waste (reg. 5). There is a power to revoke a registration on these grounds (reg. 10). However, the impact of these provisions is limited somewhat by the Rehabilitation of Offenders Act 1974, which effectively will allow most convictions to become spent after five years. In addition, there is a right to appeal to the Secretary of State against refusal or revocation and, in a recent example, in accordance with the advice in Circular 11/91, a refusal to register was overturned even though the applicant had been convicted of seven waste offences in the past (see [1993] 217 *ENDS Report* 13). Unless revoked, a registration lasts for three years, when it must be renewed, though the carrier may surrender a registration at any time. A fee is payable for an application or a renewal (reg. 4(9)). WRAs must keep a public register, to be open for inspection free of charge, of firms that are registered in their area (reg. 3).

Enforcement of the Act is mainly in the hands of the WRA. WRA officers (and also police officers) are given powers to stop and search vehicles, as long as they have reasonable grounds for believing that controlled waste is being carried by an unregistered carrier (s. 5(1)). They may also require the carrier to produce its certificate of registration. It is a summary offence intentionally to obstruct an officer exercising these powers, with a maximum penalty of £5,000. WRA officers also have the powers provided under the EPA 1990, ss. 69–71 (see below).

In addition, there are separate powers relating to the seizure of vehicles used for unlawful activities (s. 6). If the WRA is unable to obtain through its general powers information about the ownership of a vehicle it has reason to believe has been involved in unlawful disposal operations, it may apply for a warrant from a magistrate to seize the vehicle. Once the vehicle has been seized, the WRA may take specified publicity measures and, if no one claims it, dispose of it (reg. 23). If the WRA does discover who owns the vehicle it can bring a prosecution under the 1989 Act and/or under the EPA 1990, ss. 33 and 34, though in those circumstances it has no power to seize the vehicle.

Waste brokers

There is a growing business in arranging for the disposal or movement of other people's wastes. These people may not require a waste management licence because they never actually handle the waste themselves. The Waste Management Licensing Regulations 1994 now control such brokers/dealers in waste. Regulation 20 makes it an offence for any establishment or undertaking to arrange, as a dealer or broker, for the disposal or recovery of Directive waste on behalf of another person unless they are registered with the WRA. Exemptions apply to those with a waste management licence, or other statutory consents (e.g. a discharge consent), charitable or voluntary registered waste carriers, and bodies with statutory responsibilities for waste management (e.g. waste collection and disposal authorities).

Schedule 5 to the Regulations sets out the procedure for registration. Perhaps the most important consideration in determining whether an establishment/undertaking shall be registered is the number of 'relevant offences' committed by the applicant or connected persons. Generally the considerations are the same as the test for 'fit and proper persons' in relation to applications for a waste management licence. A fee is payable on application for registration and the entry in the register is available to the general public. The entry in the register lasts for a maximum of three years unless it is renewed.

General powers of WRAs

Sections 69–71 provide WRAs with powers that can be exercised in relation to any of their functions, not just in relation to waste management licensing. There are wide powers to require information by notice (s. 71). It is a criminal offence to fail to provide, without reasonable excuse, the information required, or knowingly to provide false information. The maximum penalty is a fine of £5,000 on summary conviction, or an unlimited fine and/or two years in prison on conviction on indictment. When serving such a notice, the WRA must have admissible evidence upon which they can base an argument as to their reasons for needing the information in order to fulfil their statutory functions. It is not possible to use these powers as a 'fishing expedition' where no other evidence is available, as there must be cogent evidence available which can form the foundation of any further requests (*JB and M Motor Haulage Ltd* v *LWRA* [1993] Env LR 243).

WRA inspectors have wide powers which are set out in s. 69. These include rights of entry, rights to carry out investigations on premises, and rights to take and remove samples, including the power to take samples which will be used as evidence and taken into account by the Secretary of State on appeal (*Polymeric Treatments* v *Walsall MBC* [1993] Env LR 427). The inspector may also require any person to answer questions and provide information relevant to the investigation.

A further power in s. 71 allows inspectors who are carrying out investigations to seize and render harmless any article or substance (not just waste) which appears to be a cause of imminent danger of serious pollution or serious harm to human health.

Special waste

As stated earlier, there are additional controls over hazardous waste, which is referred to in the British context as 'special waste'. In general terms this is waste that is dangerous or difficult to dispose of. The Directive on Hazardous Waste (91/689) was adopted in December 1991 and replaced an earlier Directive on Toxic and Dangerous Waste (78/319). Implementation of the new Directive depended upon the preparation of a list of hazardous waste which was finally established in December 1994 and is intended to be incorporated into the new Special Waste Regulations (see below p. 407). The

EPA 1990, s. 62, enables new regulations to be made concerning special waste and it is anticipated that the power will be used before the end of 1995 (see 'Proposals for change', below). As a result of the anticipated changes, only an outline of the provisions in existence at the time of writing will be given. The Regulations will be supplemented by a revised edition of Waste Management Paper 23. This guidance will classify waste by hazard criteria and will set out recommended procedures for deciding the hazardous properties of a particular consignment of waste. Until such time as the revised version of WMP 23 is produced the Government has issued interim guidance to assist in the process of identification of special waste.

Definition of special waste
In the 1980 Regulations 'special waste' is defined as follows:

(a)   All medicinal products (as defined in the Medicines Act 1968, s. 130) which are available only in accordance with a prescription are special waste (reg. 2(1)(b)).

(b)   Any controlled waste which consists of or contains any of the substances listed in sch. 1, Part I, is special waste if it is also either—

(i)   dangerous to life, or
(ii)   has a flash point of 21 degrees Celsius or less.

The list in sch. 1, Part I is a lengthy one that includes all acids and alkalis, asbestos, many metals, biocides, and such things as organic halogen compounds. 'Dangerous to life' is defined very precisely in sch. 1, Part II by reference to toxicological tests. Mixed waste is covered if *any* five cubic centimetres of the waste would be covered by the description, which suggests that producers should separate out special wastes if possible. In practice, the flexibility of the definition, particularly when dealing with residual quantities of special waste, such as used tins of paint or solvent, means that the WRA has a fair degree of discretion in individual borderline cases.

Consignment notes
If waste is special waste, a system of consignment notes is established, so that the progress of the waste may be traced from its place of origin to the place of disposal. The consignment note must travel with the waste, and at every relevant stage a copy must be sent to the WRA. The central element of the system is that advance notice must be given of special waste movements. The producer of special waste must prepare six copies of a note, which should consist of five Parts, lettered A to E. Parts A and B are to be filled in and signed by the producer and must describe the waste precisely, including the size, type and number of containers in which it is packed, and record its collection point and destination. A copy must be sent to the WRA for the area where the waste is to be disposed of so as to arrive not more than one month and not less than three days before the waste is removed from the site. Part C is a certificate that must be filled in by the carrier of the waste before

it is removed. At that stage the producer must also complete and sign Part D, which contains a statement that the carrier was told of any appropriate precautionary measures. Part E is to be completed by the disposer of the waste to certify receipt. The disposer sends the completed note to the WRA immediately. The disposer must also keep a record of the location of any special waste that is deposited (reg. 14).

This is a complex system, so where there is a regular consignment to one disposal site a WRA may give written notice that the requirement of separate notification of every consignment is waived and instead require the notes to be forwarded at least every 12 months (reg. 9). There is an appeal to the Secretary of State if such an arrangement is refused (reg. 11).

Producers of special waste have to keep a register of all consignment notes at the production site for at least two years. Carriers and disposers have obligations to keep similar registers. The WRA will keep consignment notes as part of the public register kept under s. 64.

It is a criminal offence to fail to comply with any of the regulations. The maximum penalty for a conviction in the magistrates' court is £2,500. The maximum penalty for conviction on indictment is an unlimited fine and/or two years' imprisonment. There are defences relating to emergencies and where the offender took all reasonable precautions to avoid the commission of an offence.

These regulations pre-date the duty of care introduced by the EPA 1990. The requirements are cumulative, with the result that the duty of care requirements must also be complied with (see p. 399).

Carriage of special waste

There are numerous provisions on the carriage of special waste. In general terms, special waste will fall within the requirements of the Chemical Hazard Information and Packaging Regulations 1993 (SI 1993 No. 1746). The name of these Regulations accurately summarises their scope. They are supplemented by further regulations and orders relating specifically to carriage by road, carriage in tankers, carriage by rail, carriage by air and carriage by sea, which include detailed provisions on such things as the design of containers and the training of those responsible for the waste.

Proposals for change

At the time of writing, the Special Waste Regulations were scheduled to be repealed and replaced by the Special Waste Regulations 1995 in order to implement the Hazardous Waste Directive. A consultation paper was issued by the DoE in March 1995 setting out proposals for changes in the definition of special waste and the procedures for dealing with it. In general terms the following proposals were put forward:

(a) An extension of the definition of 'special waste', which embraces both the EC list of hazardous waste and any other waste which is viewed as special under existing legislation. The EC list contains nearly 250 classes of waste which are defined by reference to their origin or chemical character. They will be treated as special waste in domestic legislation if they posses any of 14 hazardous properties including flammability, toxicity or carcinogenicity. Where wastes are presently controlled under the domestic legislation but are excluded from the EC list, the new Regulations will contain a set of qualifying criteria (probably based on the 14 classes set out above with additional qualifying thresholds).

(b)   The pre-notification procedure for waste movements will be simplified in the case of repeat consignments and cross-boundary transfers. Under the new Regulations waste producers and others in the system will be able to use the standard notification procedure as outlined above for *all* transfers of the same waste to the same destination without the level of administrative intervention in the old system. Moreover where waste is transferred across authority boundaries there will be no need to notify both authorities. Finally, where a single carrier collects special waste with the same broad characteristics from a series of different premises it will be possible for pre-notification to take place only once, as opposed to the situation at present which requires separate notification for each pick-up.

(c)   A new cost-recovery charging system will be introduced. A fee will be payable both for single and repetitive consignments or the collection of waste from different sites. The charges will be paid with the copy of the consignment notice and any transfer of waste without paying the fee would be a criminal offence.

(d)   A number of restrictions will be imposed as a result of the Hazardous Waste Directive. In particular, there will be a prohibition on the mixing of special wastes from different categories and of special waste with non-special waste unless it is specifically authorised under a waste management licence or is exempted from control.

These proposals supersede a previous consultation paper issued in 1993 which effectively proposed the abolition of the special waste rules including the advance notification requirement. The fact that the new proposals have returned to a relatively regulated system reflected the strong opposition that the waste management industry put forward to the previous proposals. Inevitably, the new system has been deregulated, but it is quite clear from the waste industry's earlier reaction that it plays an important part in dealing with the difficult issue of transfers of waste.

Civil liability for unlawful disposal of waste

Civil liability is provided for in s. 73(6), which is significantly wider than the equivalent provision in COPA 1974 (COPA 1974, s. 88). This subsection applies where any damage is caused by a deposit of controlled waste in contravention of ss. 33(1) or 63(2) (i.e. the deposit was not in accordance with a waste management licence, or it breached s. 33(1)(c), or it breached the provision on unlawful disposal of non-controlled waste). Any person who deposited the waste is liable to pay damages for any personal injury or property damage that was caused, except where it was due wholly to the fault of the person who suffered it, or they voluntarily accepted the risk of the damage. Liability also attaches to any person who knowingly caused or knowingly permitted such waste to be deposited, with the result that anyone who orders an unlawful deposit, or who stands by in the knowledge that it is happening, will also be liable. Since liability is linked to the commission of an offence under ss. 33 or 63(2), it is strict and fault need not be shown, though the defences available under those sections will also apply.

Section 73(6) provides an alternative to the common law causes of action which are explained in Chapter 8. The leading case on waste sites is the Canadian case of *Gertsen* v *Municipality of Toronto* [1973] 41 DLR (3d) 646, where an occupier of land successfully claimed damages for personal injury. His injuries were the result of an explosion caused by the spark from his car engine when he started it up in his garage, which had filled with high levels of methane escaping from the disused landfill site on which it was built. The action was successful under *Rylands* v *Fletcher*, nuisance and negligence, although it must be doubted whether, on the current state of the law, all these causes of action would have succeeded in an English court. Section 73(6) will avoid some of the difficulties associated with the common law actions where there has been an unlawful deposit.

Future development of civil law
It is probable that the width of civil liability will be extended in the future, since the EC has a draft Directive on civil liability for damage caused by waste and the Council of Europe has a Convention on Civil Liability for Damage Resulting From Activities Dangerous to the Environment. Both these documents, if adopted, would involve strict liability on a wider scale than in current British law. In March 1993, the EC also issued a green paper on civil liability for environmental damage, which proposed the establishment of a strict liability regime in combination with the provision of central funds to pay for a clean-up where no liable party could be found. These developments are in line with the EC's commitment in its Fifth Action Programme to the development of civil law as an instrument of environmental protection. It is possible that the EC will adopt the Council of Europe Convention, which covers activities such as production and handling of dangerous substances and waste treatment and disposal, though the British Government has refused to ratify it.

The draft Directive has gone through a number of drafts, the most recent of which dates from June 1991 (see [1991] OJ C192). However, it may not survive in its current draft form (it has given rise to a great amount of controversy and debate), so its provisions will not be considered in great detail. It applies to all kinds of waste, with only minor exceptions where there is some other form of liability (e.g. as there is for radioactive waste). It seeks to employ the 'polluter pays' principle to minimise the generation of waste by imposing strict civil liability for damage caused by waste on the producer, who will remain liable until the waste is transferred to a licensed disposal facility. The most significant feature of the draft Directive is that the definition of 'damage' is very wide indeed. It covers not only personal injury and damage to property but also purely environmental harm, referred to as 'impairment of the environment'. Liability is envisaged to include the costs incurred by a public agency or the occupier in restoring the environment to the state it was in before the damage occurred. The potential remedies are also seen as very wide and include: the prohibition of activities; damages to compensate for damage caused; restoration of the environment; reimbursement of expenditure incurred in preventing damage; and reimbursement of expenses incurred in correcting any damage. It appears to be intended that amenity and action groups should have a right to bring an action for the costs they have incurred in preventing or remedying environmental harm. Many of these things would involve some extension of British law, especially in relation to standing to bring an action, the availability of remedies, and the extent of damages that are recoverable. As a result, if the Directive is ever adopted, it would entail a number of far-reaching changes in British laws on tort and procedure. However, despite the fears expressed by some commentators, the current draft still does not approximate to the notorious US 'Superfund' system established in the Comprehensive Environmental Response Compensation and Liability Act 1981, where public bodies may force clean-up irrespective of actual harm and may then recover costs on the basis of strict, joint and several and retroactive liability.

In this respect, the main restriction in the draft Directive is that it is not intended to be retroactive. It is specifically provided that the Directive is only to apply to damage arising from an incident giving rise to injury or damage taking place after the Directive comes into effect. But this does not fully clarify the situation, since it is unclear when an incident takes place. If, for example, cylinders containing hazardous material are dumped and then, after some months of decay, begin to leak into a nearby watercourse and continue to leak for a long period, it is arguable whether the incident causing the damage took place when the cylinders were dumped, or when the leakage occurred, or is a continuing incident as long as the leakage continues. In other words, it is not clear how far the draft Directive will apply to latent damage.

FOURTEEN
Water pollution

This chapter is about the protection of the water environment. It will concentrate on the control of pollution of inland and coastal waters and will not seek to cover in any detail the very wide range of environmental and other issues that arise from the activities of the water industry. Some of these issues, such as the provision of a clean water supply, will be covered briefly, since, although they do not directly concern the protection of inland and coastal waters, they have a significant impact on water pollution policy and controls. Others, such as the effects of land drainage on the landscape and on nature conservation, will be relevant to other chapters. Marine pollution, where different controls apply, will not be covered as it is outside the scope of this book. Discharges to sewers, which have as much in common with waste disposal as with water pollution and which have their own, more basic, regulatory system operated by sewerage undertakers, are dealt with in Chapter 15.

Over the years, the law on water pollution has tended to be the most developed of the systems of pollution control. It has also had the greatest degree of coherence, both in terms of the institutional arrangements and in terms of substantive law. Since 1974, control has been exercised through a relatively sophisticated and public regulatory system, which has thereafter been updated on a number of occasions.

The current position is that the National Rivers Authority (NRA) has general responsibility for water pollution under the Water Resources Act 1991. The regulatory system involves the setting of water quality objectives for inland, coastal, estuarial and ground waters and a requirement that a discharge consent is obtained from the NRA for discharges of trade or sewage effluent to these waters. This system is backed up by criminal offences, including one of discharging trade or sewage effluent without a consent and a general offence which applies when pollution is caused by other matter. It is also supported by further regulatory and administrative controls, notably in relation to the prevention of harm, and by some well-developed and frequently used common law principles. Discharges from certain environmentally hazardous processes are at present controlled by Her Majesty's Inspectorate of Pollution (HMIP) under the integrated pollution control provisions of the EPA 1990, but this split of responsibilities (although not the separate legislative powers) will disappear when the Environment Act 1995 brings together the NRA and HMIP and their functions in the Environment Agency from 1 April 1996.

Water pollution

Pollutants of water come in many forms, including:

(a) deoxygenating materials, for example, sewage and other organic wastes, such as silage, farm wastes and wastes from a number of heavily polluting industrial processes (e.g. food processing and the production of smokeless fuel, textiles, paper and dairy products);

(b) nutrient enrichment by such things as fertilisers, which may give rise to eutrophication, causing an accelerated growth of plants and algae and leading to a decline in water quality;

(c) solids, which may impede flows, or block out light for growth;

(d) toxic materials: some materials, such as heavy metals, pesticides or nitrate, are toxic to humans, animals, plants, or all three, often depending on the level of the dose received;

(e) materials which cause an impact on amenity, such as car tyres or shopping trolleys, or old boots in canals;

(f) disease-carrying agents, such as bacteria;

(g) heat, which may affect biological conditions and also deoxygenates water.

The effect of any potential pollutant will vary according to the size, temperature, rate of flow and oxygen content of the receiving waters, as well as the local geology and the presence of other pollutants and any resulting synergistic effects. The use made of a stream is also of enormous importance in deciding whether it can be said to be polluted, and this factor has a large impact on the attitude of the regulatory bodies towards the setting of standards and their enforcement. It is not sufficient to look at pollution of surface waters, since 35% of the public water supply is taken from ground waters. As a result the control of water pollution encompasses the control of liquid discharges to land.

The sources of pollution are also varied. For example:

(a) There are over 100,000 discharges where there is consent for discharge to waters. Many of these will involve toxic materials or organic pollutants.

(b) There are over 4,300 sewage works with discharge consents. The organic content of these discharges makes them highly polluting, and they have had a particularly important role in the history of water pollution.

(c) Agricultural pollution is significant: discharges and escapes of farm wastes are of great importance and accounted for 2,883 pollution incidents in

1993, most incidents being related to slurry stores and escapes of silage (see *Water Pollution Incidents in England and Wales—1993*, NRA, 1994). A new phenomenon of recent years has been discharges of wastes from fish farms. Run-off from pesticides and fertilisers also create major problems.

(d) Discharges of waste waters from mines are often highly contaminated (and *abandoned* mines are still largely exempt from the regulatory system, although the exemption will be removed from 31 December 1999 by the Environment Act 1995, s. 60).

(e) Accidents are frequent causes of pollution, particularly from the storage and transport of hazardous chemicals.

(f) Leachate from waste sites, including disused ones, is also significant.

The River Quality Survey takes place every five years to give an accurate national picture of water pollution. The 1990 Survey (covering the period 1985–1990) showed a slight deterioration in overall river quality, although this may to some extent have been due to changes in survey methods. However, closer analysis reveals that there was a significant deterioration in some areas, matched by an improvement in others. Given that the period in question coincided with a deep industrial recession and the increased utilisation of alternative disposal routes for wastes, this position reflects a serious problem. The main causes of deterioration were discharges from sewage works and agricultural pollution. The latter is reducing the quality of many once clean rural rivers. Other significant polluters were identified as discharges from mines, run-off from waste tips and fish farms. This illustrates that one issue for the future is how to control non-point discharges and that more inventive legal mechanisms than those used in the past are needed.

The NRA is introducing a new classification system known as the 'general quality assessment' which will replace the existing methods used for the River Quality Survey and will provide a uniform mechanism for measuring water quality. Applying the new system, the NRA found that water quality improved by 10% between 1990 and 1992 (see *The Quality of Rivers and Canals in England and Wales (1990 to 1992)*, NRA, 1994). However, the NRA only looked at the chemical quality of waters, whilst the general quality assessment will ultimately have four separate elements, covering chemical, biological, nutrient and aesthetic matters, and will thus give a more rounded view of overall water quality.

The water industry

The water industry has traditionally been thought of as including a wide range of rather different matters: water collection, treatment and supply; the provision of sewers, sewage works and sewage disposal; water pollution control; the regulation of bodies providing water services; fisheries; navigation; flood defence and land drainage; recreational activities; and conservation responsibilities. From this list it is clear that in reality this is a set of industries, connected in the sense that they all relate to the water cycle, but separate in their objectives. Not all of these matters are relevant to the themes of this book; pollution control is only one function of the water industry, but its place in relation to these other activities needs to be understood.

The industry has historically been dominated by water supply and sewage disposal. Up to the Second World War these tasks largely were carried out by municipal authorities. However, activities such as fishing and pollution control increasingly came to be organised on a river basin basis through a number of specialist, river-related institutions, such as catchment boards (for land drainage), fisheries boards and internal drainage boards, although a significant responsibility for pollution control still rested with the local authorities through their public health functions.

These trends led to an attempt to create a more logical system. The River Boards Act 1948 established 32 river boards, organised on a catchment area basis, which took over a number of regulatory functions. In 1963 the Water Resources Act converted these boards into 27 river authorities, which had a range of regulatory functions, including pollution control and responsibility for the new system of licensing abstractions of water. Water supply and sewage disposal remained in general a local authority function, although the number of water supply undertakings was steadily reduced over the years.

The Water Act 1973 established a fully integrated system of river and water management. Ten regional water authorities became responsible for all water related functions within river basin areas. These included the management of water provision, water treatment and water supply, sewerage, sewage works and sewage disposal, land drainage and flood defence, pollution control, inland fisheries, recreational uses of water and ecological and amenity matters. The idea was to set up a completely planned and integrated service as opposed to the fragmented system then in existence (prior to 1973, there were 27 river authorities, 157 water supply undertakings and no less than 1,393 sewage authorities). The only real exception was the retention of 29 private water companies responsible for water supply in defined areas.

However, this system came to be seen as ineffective. For a start, the industry was clearly massively underfunded, with the result that capital and other works were postponed and the quality of service declined. In consequence, the problem of water quality was never really addressed and this contributed to a general decline in standards. A particular cause of these declining standards was the inadequacy of many sewage works operated by the regional water authorities themselves, which came to be seen as acting the part of both poacher and gamekeeper in relation to water pollution. This conflict of interest led to specific changes in the Water Act 1989.

The Water Act 1989 and the Water Resources Act 1991

The Water Act 1989 carried out a fundamental restructuring of the water industry. The main impetus was undoubtedly the Government's policy of privatisation. One stated aim of this was to increase accountability, though exactly whether this means the industry should be accountable to the public, the Government, or to shareholders is unclear. A further aim was to remove the previous cash limits on public spending that had restricted the regional water authorities, thus opening the way for improvements in the quality of water services, but at a cost to the consumer of those services, who will pay for them.

Originally it was intended to privatise the whole industry en bloc, but the inadequacy of the proposed regulatory mechanisms, particularly those for pollution control, led to the privatisation of the operational end of the industry only (i.e. water supply, sewerage services and certain recreational services) in the form of 10 water services companies. These double as water undertakers and sewerage undertakers in areas corresponding with the old regional water authority ones. The 29 water companies were retained as statutory water companies, having responsibility for water supply only.

The position of Director General of Water Services, who is in charge of the Office of Water Services (OFWAT), was created to exercise regulatory functions in relation to water supply and sewerage provision. The NRA was created as a wide-ranging and independent regulatory agency with responsibility for tackling water pollution amongst other things. Unlike the old regional water authorities, it had no operational responsibilities in relation to sewage works to conflict with its environmental protection role. For a more detailed explanation of the NRA, see p. 48. These arrangements were consolidated in the Water Resources Act 1991 and the Water Industry Act 1991. However, from 1 April 1996 the NRA will be subsumed within the Environment Agency (see p. 40).

Water pollution controls

The modern system of control really begins with the Rivers (Prevention of Pollution) Act 1951, a rather rudimentary control system in which consent from the river board was required for industrial or sewage discharges into most inland waters. Prior to that, there had been the Rivers Pollution Prevention Act 1876, which imposed an absolute prohibition on pollution but proved almost totally unworkable. The Clean Rivers (Estuaries and Tidal Waters) Act 1960 extended the controls to tidal and estuarial waters and the Rivers (Prevention of Pollution) Act 1961 ensured that a large number of discharges that had hitherto been exempted were controlled, including those commenced prior to 1951. The Water Resources Act 1963 extended the system to discharges to certain underground waters. However, the system remained essentially secret and with little public accountability. Control over sewage effluents was also compromised because of the local authorities' control of the river authorities.

The next major step forward was in the Control of Pollution Act 1974, which again extended the geographical coverage of the controls so that most discharges to inland, underground, tidal or coastal waters out to the 'three-mile limit' were covered. More importantly, COPA 1974 introduced some advanced provisions on public participation in decisions, established public registers of information and allowed for private prosecutions, which had previously been excluded. In addition a more sophisticated set of preventative and remedial measures was introduced.

However COPA 1974 did not come into force immediately. Like much environmental legislation its implementation relied on commencement orders, and the main measures were not brought into force until the mid-1980s: a delay mainly due to the Government's worries over the economic cost of the new controls, particularly in relation to underperforming sewage works operated by the regional water authorities. Even when COPA 1974 was brought into force, the transitional provisions meant that the full impact was not felt immediately, and indeed certain of the provisions never were implemented.

As explained above, the Water Act 1989 created the NRA. It also continued the process of refining and improving the law. The system of consents set out in COPA 1974 remained roughly the same, though with a few amendments. Important changes included the introduction of sections providing for statutory water quality objectives for the first time, the introduction of a system of charging for trade and sewage discharges, and the improvement of the available preventative and remedial powers. Water pollution law was then consolidated in the Water Resources Act 1991.

The EPA 1990 did not alter the main structure of water pollution law, but, under the Act, Her Majesty's Inspectorate of Pollution took the lead role in relation to processes subject to integrated pollution control, thus robbing the NRA of total control over discharges to inland and coastal waters. The bringing together of the NRA and HMIP in the Environment Agency means that the institutional control of water pollution is once more unified.

Throughout this history the emphasis has been on flexible standards, with most consents being set on an individualised basis by reference to the effect of a discharge on the receiving waters. Particular emphasis has been placed on biochemical oxygen demand (BOD) and the level of suspended solids, rather than on such things as metals and toxic substances, especially in relation to sewage discharges. In a sense, the method of setting consents could almost be described as a 'rule of thumb' method. This approach is, however, changing in response to EC Directives and as a result of the NRA's commitment to creating a more uniform system of control nationwide.

Scotland

It should be noted that in Scotland a different system applies, since the water industry has not been privatised there. At present, regional councils are responsible for the provision of the water supply and for sewerage and sewage disposal. Apart from the three island councils, which are all-purpose authorities, water pollution is the responsibility of the seven river purification boards. These are independent catchment area bodies with their own budgets financed out of precepts on the regional councils, and with one third of their members appointed by each of the following, namely, regional councils, district councils and the Secretary of State. The Water Act 1989 did not make any institutional changes, but in sch. 23 it did amend the Control of Pollution Act 1974, which still remains in force in Scotland. Unfortunately, this has meant that there are slightly different wordings for some sections on each side of the border. Whilst water pollution law is thus very similar in Scotland, it cannot always be guaranteed that it is exactly the same.

This position is in the process of being altered. The Local Government etc (Scotland) Act 1995 will restructure local government in Scotland by introducing unitary authorities for the mainland, although the three existing island councils will be retained. It also establishes three publicly owned combined water and sewerage authorities, respectively called the East of Scotland, West of Scotland and North of Scotland Water Authorities, to take over from the regional councils. The Environment Act 1995 establishes the Scottish Environment Protection Agency (SEPA), which will replace the river purification boards and Her Majesty's Industrial Pollution Inspectorate (HMIPI) and thus brings together all water pollution functions in one body.

Pollution policy

Until 1989, it was difficult to identify a coherent national water pollution policy. The Department of the Environment had overall responsibility for all water matters, but most policy decisions were left to the regional water authorities, with the DoE appearing more preoccupied with financial matters than with water quality. The one national body in this area, the National Water Council, was abolished in 1983 as superfluous. Of course, there were often unspoken aims, such as that of getting treatable wastes into the sewerage system if possible, and cleaning up waters for economic reasons, since the public water supply was increasingly taken from them. In addition, EC standards effectively laid down a set of priorities, leading to such things as a policy to minimise the discharge of dangerous substances and if possible to cut them out entirely—effectively a 'precautionary' policy.

The establishment of the NRA meant that the opportunity could be taken to establish a truly national policy on water pollution—or at least one applicable to England and Wales. At a general level, this has been achieved through the NRA's Corporate Plans, which set out a number of aims on water pollution, such as the assessment of the present quality of waters, the establishment of classification systems so that comparisons can be made, the review of existing policy in relation to the granting of consents and compliance with them, increased attention to prevention of harm in such areas as farm pollution and pollution from abandoned mines, and a more rigorous enforcement policy involving greater use of prosecution. The NRA also has a range of policies and strategy documents on other aspects of the water cycle, including aquifer protection, conservation issues, recreational opportunities and water resources. The general approach adopted by the NRA is that river catchments should be managed on a integrated basis. This process is a good example of aspects of environmental policy being set by a body other than Central Government. However, the Government also has an important role to play here. In *River Quality: The Government's Proposals* (DoE, 1992), it sets out its general strategy for water quality. This makes it quite clear that the cost-effectiveness of environmental improvements—and the question of who should pay for them—is a major factor in Government policy, hence the slow progress that is being made on such things as statutory water quality objectives.

More specifically, the NRA has been involved in trying to establish uniformity and consistency on such things as sampling, setting of consents and public participation, where in the past there have tended to be different attitudes in different regions. In the Kinnersley Report (*Discharge Consent and Compliance Policy: A Blueprint for the Future*, NRA, July 1990), the NRA suggested some mechanisms for unifying the totally different procedures and levels of consents that it inherited from the 10 regional water authorities. It established a national strategy for reviewing all existing consents on a catchment area basis, and this included bringing sewage works consents into line with industrial consents. However, it remains the case that consents are mainly set on an individualised basis, with the main determinant being the effect on the receiving waters.

The EC and water pollution

The EC has had an enormous impact on water pollution law and policy over the years. The First Action Programme on the Environment in 1973 picked out water pollution as a priority matter, and there has been a steady stream of Directives since. These have tackled such diverse topics as the reduction of pollution from dangerous substances, the improvement of the quality of bathing waters, nitrates in water and the progressive introduction of adequate sewage treatment systems. However, it remains the case that EC law only covers water pollution in a selective manner—not all pollutants in all waters are yet covered, although the Commission has proposed a Directive on ecological quality that will apply to all water bodies in the EC (see below).

EC water Directives tend to follow two basic models (see Somsen, 'EC Water Directives' [1990] *Water Law* 93):

(a) those which adopt emission standards, which are mainly used for reducing dangerous substances; and

(b) those which impose quality objectives on waters that are mainly set according to the use that is to be made of those waters.

For a full discussion of all the EC Directives relating to water and their implementation, see Haigh, *Manual of Environmental Policy: the EC and Britain*, Longman.

Emission standard approaches
One of the first water Directives, and arguably the most important, is 76/464 on Dangerous Substances in Water. This is a framework Directive passed with the aim of reducing or eliminating certain dangerous substances from water. It covers essentially the same waters as those controlled by the NRA and has led to very tight controls over dangerous substances in discharge consents.

The Directive lays down two lists of substances:

(a)   List I (the 'black list'); and
(b)   List II (the 'grey list').

In relation to black list substances, the Directive seeks the elimination of pollution. Any discharge of a black list substance must be subject to some form of authorisation granted by a competent national authority. Such an authorisation must conform to very strict requirements. It must *either* set an emission standard which does not exceed the appropriate EC limit value, or the emission standard must be set so that the EC environmental quality standard for the receiving waters is kept to at all times. Only Britain has adopted the second approach (see below), the competent authority being either the NRA or HMIP, which operate the discharge consent systems so as to ensure that the EC environmental quality standards are met at all times.

However, implementation of this part of the Directive is proceeding slowly. The Directive itself identifies potential black list substances in general terms only—they are those which are highly toxic, persistent, carcinogenic or liable to bio-accumulate. Although in 1982 the EC Commission published a specific list of 129 potential black list substances (made up mainly of pesticides, organic solvents, and a small number of heavy metals), implementation of the Directive ultimately depends on the agreement of subsidiary 'daughter Directives' which set the EC standards for individual substances. Only a few such daughter Directives have been agreed, covering the following substances: cadmium (Directive 83/513); mercury (82/176 and 84/156); hexachlorocyclohexane (84/491); carbon tetrachloride, pentachlorophenol and DDT (86/280); chloroform, hexachlorobenzene, hexachlorobutadiene and the pesticides aldrin, dieldrin, endrin and isodrin (88/347); and 1, 2-dichloroethane, trichloroethylene, tetrachloroethylene and trichlorobenzene (90/415). Where a daughter Directive has not been agreed for a potential black list substance, the substance is treated as on the grey list (see below). The list of 129 (amended slightly in the intervening years) therefore acts as a priority list for future daughter Directives.

For grey list substances, the Directive again lays down a fairly general list. This includes a range of metals (such as zinc, copper, tin, nickel and chromium), biocides, cyanides, fluorides, ammonia and nitrites. The objective is that pollution by these substances should be reduced. Accordingly, if any such substance has a deleterious effect on the aquatic environment, the Directive requires Member States to develop a national environmental quality standard and to ensure that it is met in the receiving waters. These standards are set at a national, rather than at an EC, level. The Member State must also introduce a reduction programme for grey list substances and must control discharges by setting standards in discharge consents which enable the environmental quality standards to be achieved. Britain has either set or has proposed environmental quality standards for all substances on the 'red list' (see p. 297) and for a number of other substances on the grey list (see *Dangerous Substances in Water: A Practical Guide*, Environmental Data Services Ltd, 1992).

It was Directive 76/464 which first demonstrated the differences between Britain and the rest of the EC over standard setting. Britain's system of a decentralised setting of non-uniform consents by reference to the quality of the receiving waters was seen to be directly contradictory to the EC desire for uniform, centrally set emission standards for dangerous substances. After much argument, this led to the agreement of the alternative approaches for 'black list' substances in the Directive explained above. The same conflict has also led to delays in the process of agreeing daughter Directives, since unanimity is required on the setting of the limit values and environmental quality objectives.

Directive 76/464 has had an enormous impact on British pollution control. Having claimed that it set its consents by reference to quality objectives for the receiving waters, the British Government was forced to introduce such a system on a formal basis, and water quality objectives were introduced for the first time in the late–1970s, at first by administrative action. This was insufficient for compliance with EC law and sections relating to *statutory* water quality objectives were first introduced in the Water Act 1989.

The Directive also led to specific changes in relation to controls over dangerous substances. For example, whilst many existing discharges were given deemed consent when COPA 1974 was finally brought into force, those involving dangerous substances were subject to specified emission standards. In general, significant discharges of 'black list' and 'grey list' substances are subject to integrated pollution control. The rules providing for control by HMIP of prescribed substances discharged to sewers are also a result of this Directive.

A similar story attaches to Directive 80/68 on Groundwater, except in this case List I substances are to be prevented from entering ground waters, whilst discharges of List II substances should be limited, in both cases by a consent system. The EC Council has issued a Resolution calling upon the Commission to prepare an action programme for groundwater protection and to draft proposals for a revision of Directive 80/68 (see OJ 1995 C49/1).

One problem with the emission standards approach is that it does not work well for pollution from non-point (i.e. diffuse) sources, nor where there are multiple polluters in one catchment area. Directive 86/280 attempts to tackle this issue by requiring all *sources* of 'black list' substances to be monitored.

Quality objective approaches

For the quality approach there are a number of stages:

(a) water with particular uses must first be identified (this is usually left to the discretion of the Member States);

(b) the EC must establish a number of parameters: these are normally expressed either as Imperative (I) Values, which must be kept to, or Guide (G) Values, which Member States must try to achieve;

(c) environmental quality objectives must be set for the waters, having regard to the parameters;

(d) a competent national authority must be established for monitoring purposes and uniform sampling techniques are set by EC Directives (e.g. 79/869 on Sampling Surface Water for Drinking);

(e) procedures are established for updating the I and G Values in the light of new knowledge.

Directives which have adopted this approach include those on Surface Water for Drinking 75/440, Shellfish Waters 79/923, Water Standards for Freshwater Fish 78/659, Bathing Waters 76/160 and Drinking Water 80/778.

The Directive on Surface Water for Drinking lays down three classes of waters (A1, A2 and A3), and 46 relevant parameters that waters must comply with to fall within any class (see **Water supply** below).

The two Directives on Freshwater Fish and Shellfish lay down standards for waters designated by Member States. The power to designate these waters was delegated to the regional water authorities (now the NRA)—another example of a decentralised implementation of policy. But, there is no duty to designate and the main effect of these Directives has been to increase sampling and monitoring of relevant waters.

The Directive on Bathing Waters lays down 19 parameters (mainly bacteriological) with which all 'traditional' bathing waters must comply, within specified percentile compliance rates. It covers fresh and marine waters. The Directive is very vague as to precisely which waters are covered, but unlike the previous two Directives there appears to be no need for any designation for the Directive to apply. The British response was unenthusiastic: identification of the relevant waters was left to the regional water authorities and only 27 were initially identified—fewer than, for example, land-locked Luxembourg. No doubt the reason was the fear of the cost of cleaning up discharges of sewage effluent to the sea. In consequence of a reasoned opinion on non-implementation from the EC Commission, and intense EC and public pressure, the number of designated beaches is now over 400. Nevertheless, Britain was taken to the European Court of Justice over non-implementation of the Directive and in July 1993 was found to be in breach in relation to standards on Blackpool and Southport beaches (see *Commission* v *United Kingdom* [1993] *Water Law* 168). 82.5% of designated beaches complied with the standards in 1994.

The Directive on Drinking Water is probably the best known of the water quality Directives. It lays down 62 parameters relating to the quality of all water provided for human consumption or for the purposes of food manufacturing, except for natural mineral waters (as to which, see Directive 80/777). It led directly to the setting in Britain of the first statutory standards of wholesomeness for drinking water, in the Water Supply (Water Quality) Regulations 1989 (SI 1989 No. 1147).

Apart from the delay in complying with the Directive until well after the formal date set for compliance, argument has centred over the provisions for derogating from the Directive, because of problems in some areas in complying with the standards on lead, nitrate and certain pesticides. For example, the Government sought to grant derogations for nitrate levels by reference to Article 9 of the Directive, which refers to geological conditions. This was argued by the Commission to be an inaccurate interpretation of Article 9, since nitrate levels result from self-induced effects on the soil. The British

Government has now been held by the European Court of Justice to be in breach of the Directive in relation to nitrate levels in a number of supply areas (see *Commission* v *United Kingdom* [1993] *Water Law* 59). This case also decided that the duty to comply with the standards laid down in the Directive is absolute, rather than simply to take all practicable steps to comply. However, in *R* v *Secretary of State ex parte Friends of the Earth* [1995] 245 *ENDS Report* 44, the question arose whether the Secretary of State was in breach of EC law by accepting undertakings from a number of water companies in relation to admitted breaches of the pesticide standards set out in the Directive. The Court of Appeal decided that there was no breach, because the Secretary of State had taken sufficiently speedy action to remedy the breach.

The Directive on Nitrates 91/676 also adopts a form of quality approach. It requires Member States to designate 'nitrate vulnerable zones' by December 1993. These are defined in the Directive as being where inland waters intended for drinking or groundwaters are likely to contain more than 50mg/1 nitrate if protective action is not taken; or where any inland or coastal waters are liable to suffer from eutrophication if protective action is not taken. Within these designated 'nitrate vulnerable zones', detailed regulatory requirements are laid down in the Directive. For more detail on the Directive and its implementation in Britain, see p. 453.

Other Directives on water pollution

The Directive on Urban Waste Water Treatment 91/271 is potentially the most significant Directive for the future direction of water pollution policy. It lays down minimum standards for the treatment of urban waste waters (i.e. domestic sewage and industrial waste waters). These treatment standards, and the time-scales within which they must be met, vary according to the population of the urban area concerned, but the basic idea is that secondary treatment should be usual for domestic wastes. For example, a secondary or equivalent system of sewage treatment is required by the end of 2000 for a town with a population equivalent of more than 15,000. Stricter standards are required in sensitive areas and lower standards are permitted in certain less-sensitive areas.

Accordingly, the Directive will have an impact on treatment standards (and therefore costs) for most wastes discharged to sewers. It will have a special impact on those areas of Europe where sewage treatment systems are in their infancy and on those countries, such as Britain, which have followed a 'dilute and disperse' policy of discharging virtually untreated sewage into the sea. For example, it has been estimated that only about 2% of British sewage outfalls into the sea receive secondary treatment. The Directive also requires all Member States to cease dumping sewage sludge in the sea by the end of 1998, as agreed at the Conference for the Protection of the North Sea in March 1990, with an obligation progressively to reduce toxic, persistent or bioaccumulable materials in sludge before then. Britain is the only country currently carrying out this practice.

Directive 91/271 has given rise to the Urban Waste Water Treatment (England and Wales) Regulations 1994 (SI 1994 No. 2841). Although belated in terms of formal implementation of the Directive, these Regulations largely adopt the wording of the Directive, except that instead of 'less-sensitive areas' the Regulations refer to 'high natural dispersion areas'. In addition, there is currently controversy over the classification of a number of estuarial waters as coastal for the purposes of the Regulations, thus allowing lower levels of treatment to be applied. In 1994, the Government announced the identification of 33 sensitive areas and 58 high natural dispersion areas, although more may be classified in the future.

Finally, there are two other Directives worth a mention in the light of their different approaches to control. Directive 73/404 on Detergents sets a product standard by prohibiting the marketing of detergents with average biodegradability of less than 90%. Directive 78/176 on Titanium Dioxide sets standards in relation to a specific industry.

Summary of the impact of EC law

The EC has thus had a great impact on British water pollution practice. Whilst there have been many arguments about technical matters, such as the levels laid down for nitrate in drinking water and the need for a Bathing Waters Directive at all, most of the standards required have been introduced in one way or another, although normally belatedly. A formal system of water quality classifications and objectives, statutory regulations on drinking water quality, the introduction of specific standards for dangerous substances, and a dramatic shift in relation to the discharge of sewage effluent to the sea can all be attributed to EC initiatives. The general approach to pollution control has also been altered significantly.

Perhaps the greatest impact, however, has been the great publicity that has been engendered by having specific standards set at EC level against which Government action can be measured. This has certainly contributed to the intensity of the debate over nitrate. EC requirements also had an impact on the proposals for the privatisation of the water industry. It became clear that the EC would not accept a private pollution regulator as a 'competent authority' for the purposes of Directives, and this was one reason for the creation of the NRA (and also a separate Drinking Water Inspectorate).

Future of EC water pollution policy

EC water pollution policy is currently in a state of flux. Although the EC institutions appear to have fought off arguments that some of the water Directives should be repealed, that various timescales for compliance should be relaxed and that Member States should recover jurisdiction under the doctrine of subsidiarity, alterations to existing Directives are likely. It is especially likely that amendments will be made to the earlier Directives in the light of more recent scientific and environmental attitudes. For example, there are proposals to revise Directive 80/778 on Drinking Water with a smaller number of parameters, although it appears that the controversial parameters for pesticides and nitrates will remain. A proposal for amendment of Directive 76/160 on Bathing Waters has also been published (OJ 1994

C112/3). This involves a reduction in the number of parameters with which traditional bathing waters must comply to 12, the relaxation of some of these values, and the extension of powers for Member States to derogate from the Directive. The definition of traditional bathing waters is not, however, changed. As noted above, Directive 80/68 on Groundwater is also likely to be revised.

In addition, a draft Directive on the ecological quality of water has been published (OJ 1994 C222/1). In terms of the legislative mechanism adopted, the proposal reveals a distinct change of policy. Instead of laying down clear and precise standards, as most water Directives have done in the past, the Directive will simply set out a procedural framework within which Member States should act. It will thus provide Member States with a large amount of discretion and, in theory, will enable them to adapt the provisions to fit with local conditions. According to the draft, they will be required to do the following: define operational targets for good ecological water quality for all surface waters and for the territorial sea; draw up an inventory of pollution sources; establish a system for controlling water quality; monitor, assess and inform the public of water quality in accordance with specified criteria; and draw up and implement integrated programmes for improving water quality, the measures contained in which should be based largely on best available technology and best environmental practice. This change of legislative policy will clearly affect not only the uniformity of standards across Europe, but also the potential use of the doctrine of direct effects by individuals and amenity groups in the event of non-compliance by Member States. According to the draft, the Directive will also consolidate the law, since it will result in the repeal of Directives 79/923 on Shellfish Waters and 78/659 on Water Standards for Freshwater Fish.

Water supply

Strictly speaking, the provision of a clean water supply is a consumer protection rather than an environmental protection measure. However, there is an intimate relationship between water supply and pollution control. The public water supply is abstracted from inland and ground waters, so pollution of those waters will lead to a reduction in the available source and to an increase in the cost of treatment of the water that is abstracted. To this end, it is an offence to pollute any 'waterworks' likely to be used for human consumption, which covers pollution of springs, wells, boreholes and service reservoirs (Water Industry Act 1991, s. 72). In addition, Directive 75/440 on Surface Water for Drinking has imposed controls on the quality of inland waters. This Directive seeks to ensure that surface waters which are abstracted for drinking are fit for that purpose and divides waters into three categories—A1, A2 and A3. Classification in these categories depends on the waters meeting the limits set out in the Directive. Any water of below A3 quality should not be abstracted for drinking except in exceptional circumstances. These requirements are implemented in British law by the Surface Waters (Classification) Regulations 1989 (SI 1989 No. 1148), which set out categories DW1, DW2 and DW3 corresponding to those in the Directive, and by the Water Supply (Water Quality) Regulations 1989 (SI 1989 No. 1147).

There is also a more indirect link which is tied up with the highly charged political question of who should pay for the cost of environmental protection, and which requires some understanding of how the water industry as a whole is regulated and paid for. As pointed out earlier in the chapter, the water industry was massively underfunded when it was in public control prior to 1989, with the result that sewage works were major sources of pollution, and the quality of the public water supply was questionable. Since 1989, the public water supply and sewerage services have been provided by the privatised water undertakers under the regulatory oversight of the Director General of Water Services (OFWAT) and the Secretary of State. Water bills have risen considerably above inflation and, compared with the position prior to 1989, the way in which consumers pay for water and sewerage services is more explicit, since the full amount is paid in charges rather than a proportion being hidden in general taxation. However, the water companies' overall charges for water and sewerage services are regulated by the Director General under the Water Industry Act 1991. This is achieved by reference to a formula, known as RPI + K, under which the weighted average charge is allowed to increase by the retail price index plus a company-specific factor set by the Director General (known as the K factor). The Director General has to take water companies' costs, including the cost of 'environmental' improvements such as upgrading of sewage works and improvements in drinking water quality, into account when setting the K factor. Once the K factor is set, the water companies have to operate within it. This means that the trade-offs between environmental improvements by the water companies (for example, improved performance from sewage works, improved water quality from the public water supply and reduced losses from leakage), improvements in levels of service, efficiency savings and increased company profits and directors' pay, are very clear.

The K factors, which were originally set by the Secretary of State in 1989, were redetermined by the Director General in July 1994. In the run-up to that redetermination, there was a very public debate about the cost of environmental improvements. This debate focussed in particular on the cost of complying with EC Directives such as Directive 91/271 on Urban Waste Water Treatment, which requires the upgrading of a large number of sewage works, although the whole issue was complicated by wildly differing views on the actual costs involved. Some, including the Director General to some extent, argued that the economic cost of the environmental standards set out in the Directives was too high a price for consumers to pay, whilst others argued that basic environmental standards must be paid for, and that water companies rather than consumers should pay by making efficiency savings and reducing excessive profits and directors' pay (for a more detailed analysis, see Wilkinson, 'The Re-determination of the K Factors' [1994] *Water Law* 153).

There is a separate issue concerning overall usage of water, which is rising rapidly, and the question whether current patterns of water use are sustainable in the long term. At present, domestic consumers pay mainly for water under a formula that relates to the rateable value of their houses. This method is likely to remain despite the fact that rateable values are redundant for all other purposes, since the Government is opposed to the use of council tax bands for fixing water bills. However, many (including the Director General) argue that such a method provides no incentive to consumers to reduce or control their water usage and that water metering would have the twin benefits of reducing overall usage and of producing a fair system of payment linked to actual usage. Other commentators, however, argue that metering would unfairly penalise those on low incomes in relation to usage of a basic human resource and would lead to social problems. The Environment Act 1995 places a new duty on water companies to promote the efficient use of water by their customers.

As far as the quality of the public water supply is concerned, under the Water Industry Act 1991, s. 67, domestic water must be 'wholesome', a term which was defined in legislation for the first time in the Water Supply (Water Quality) Regulations 1989 (SI 1989 No. 1147). These Regulations lay down a large number of specific criteria with which water must comply if it is supplied for domestic purposes or for the purposes of food production. In each case the limits have been set so as to conform with Directive 80/778 on Drinking Water. The Regulations require that information on water quality must be made available to the public. In addition, it is an offence under the Water Industry Act 1991, s. 70 to supply water that is unfit for human consumption, although prosecutions for this offence may only be brought by the Secretary of State or the Director of Public Prosecutions. A Drinking Water Inspectorate has been established within the Department of the Environment with responsibility for monitoring the provisions relating to water quality. There have now been successful prosecutions of Severn Trent Water (in this case for the s. 70 offence, see [1995] 243 *ENDS Report* 45) and of Dwr Cymru (Welsh Water) (in this case for contravention of the Regulations, see [1995] *Water Law* 61). There is also the possibility of an action at common law for breach of statutory duty or negligence (see *Read* v *Croydon Corporation* [1938] 4 All ER 631, where a ratepayer successfully sued in negligence for water supplied to his household which caused his daughter to contract typhoid).

Consents for the discharge of trade or sewage effluents

A consent is required from the NRA for:

(a)   any discharge of trade or sewage effluent into 'controlled waters';
(b)   any discharge of trade or sewage effluent through a pipe from land into the sea outside the limits of 'controlled waters';
(c)   any discharge where a prohibition is in force.

It is an offence under the Water Resources Act 1991, s. 85 to 'cause or knowingly permit' such a discharge, although there is a defence if it is carried out in accordance with a consent. This means it is also an offence to breach any conditions attached to a consent, a point made explicit by s. 85(6). There is no need to show that the discharge has polluted the receiving waters because the offence consists of discharging otherwise than in accordance with the consent.

'Trade effluent' is defined in s. 221 and includes any effluent from trade premises (these include agricultural, fish farming and research establishments), other than domestic sewage or surface water. 'Sewage effluent', also defined in s. 221, includes any effluent, other than surface water, from a sewerage works. The discharge must be of effluent, so it seems that if trade materials, such as fuel oil, escape they are covered by the general pollution offence (see below). But there is some doubt here since effluent is defined in s. 221 to mean 'any liquid' and is not specifically limited to wastes.

A further problem relates to the interpretation of the word 'discharge'. This word is not defined in the Act. It is capable of carrying either an active meaning (i.e. that the release of materials has to be part of a deliberate trade or sewage process) or a passive meaning (as in the discharge of blood from a wound). It is suggested that it carries an active meaning, because otherwise potential dischargers would be in the impossible position of having to apply for a consent for something that was not meant to happen. The effect of this reasoning is that accidental and non-routine emissions of trade or sewage effluent do not require a consent and are covered by the general water pollution offence (see below).

The prohibition is a new device first introduced by the Water Act 1989. It is designed to cover those cases where the type of discharge is not necessarily harmful and thus the blanket requirement of a consent is not justified. By prohibiting discharges on a selective basis, control can be exercised over just those situations where it is required.

There are three situations where a prohibition may apply:

(a) Where the NRA by notice prohibits a discharge of trade or sewage effluent from a building or fixed plant to any land or land-locked waters outside the definition of controlled waters. This includes such situations as soakaways from trade premises and some agricultural activities.

(b) Where it prohibits a discharge of matter other than trade or sewage effluent from a drain or sewer. Trade and sewage effluent are automatically covered by the need for a consent, so the intention here is to restrict such things as discharges of dangerous substances from a storm drain.

(c) In addition, any such discharges involving substances prescribed by regulations *automatically* invoke the prohibition.

In relation to the first two categories, the prohibition can only come into force three months after notice to the discharger, unless the NRA is satisfied that there is an emergency.

Controlled waters
The meaning of 'controlled waters' is given in s. 104. There has been a change in the meaning of this phrase since its usage in COPA 1974 and it

now includes virtually all inland and coastal waters. Controlled waters are made up of four sub-categories:

(a)   relevant territorial waters (i.e. the sea within a line three miles out from the baselines from which the territorial sea is measured, despite the extension of the territorial limit to 12 miles in the Territorial Sea Act 1987);

(b)   coastal waters (i.e. the sea within those baselines up to the line of the highest tide, and tidal waters up to the fresh water limit as defined by the Secretary of State on maps produced for that purpose);

(c)   inland waters (i.e. rivers, streams, underground streams, canals, lakes and reservoirs, including those that are temporarily dry); and

(d)   groundwaters (i.e. any waters contained in underground strata or in wells or boreholes).

The only waters that are excluded are land-locked waters that do not drain into other controlled waters. However, the Secretary of State has power to include or exclude specific waters by order. This has been done in the Controlled Waters (Lakes and Ponds) Order 1989 (SI 1989 No. 1149), which includes any reservoirs, apart from those intended for public water supply, which would otherwise be excluded. Water supply mains and pipes, and sewers and drains (where separate controls on discharges apply), are also excluded from the definition of controlled waters.

General pollution offence

There is a general offence under s. 85(1)(a) of causing or knowingly permitting any poisonous, noxious or polluting matter or any solid waste to enter controlled waters. As is common within the flexible definitions of British pollution control, the words 'poisonous, noxious or polluting' are not defined. However, the wording is very wide and in R v Dovermoss Ltd [1995] ELM 106, the Court of Appeal decided that 'polluting' requires simply that a likelihood or *capability* of causing harm to animals, plants or those who use the water could be demonstrated. Actual harm is not necessary.

This general offence complements the more specific offence of discharging trade or sewage effluent without consent. Obviously it covers any entry of polluting matter which is not trade or sewage effluent. But, unlike COPA 1974, where the general and the specific offences were made exclusive of each other by s. 31(2)(e), under later Acts this exclusivity has been removed, so an illegal discharge of trade or sewage effluent also amounts to an offence under the general offence if it causes pollution. Indeed, because of the evidential problems of providing a legal sample to prove a breach of a discharge consent, it has been normal for the general offence to be charged even for discharges of trade or sewage effluent.

The general offence also covers accidental and non-routine escapes of trade or sewage effluent because, whilst the specific offence requires a 'discharge', the general offence only requires an entry. In addition, non-point discharges, such as agricultural run-off, are potentially covered by the general offence.

There is a further offence in s. 85(5) of substantially aggravating pollution by impeding the proper flow of inland, non-tidal waters.

Penalties

For all s. 85 offences the potential penalties are the same. On summary conviction there is a maximum fine of £20,000 (this was raised by the EPA 1990, s. 145(1) from the previous maximum of £2,000), and/or three months in prison. On conviction on indictment, there can be an unlimited fine and/ or a two-year jail sentence. The normal six-month period for a summary prosecution to be brought is extended to 12 months by the Water Resources Act 1991, s. 101, as it is for all offences in Part III of the Act.

Defences

A number of defences to these water pollution offences is set out in s. 88. A discharge or entry made in accordance with the following is a defence:

(a) a consent from the NRA, or the equivalent consent granted or deemed to have been granted under COPA 1974 or earlier legislation;
(b) an authorisation in relation to integrated pollution control granted under Part I of the EPA 1990;
(c) a waste management licence or a waste disposal licence from the waste regulation authority (except where the offence is of discharging trade or sewage effluent or where a prohibition is in force);
(d) a licence permitting dumping at sea granted by the Ministry of Agriculture, Fisheries and Food under the Food and Environment Protection Act 1985;
(e) an Act of Parliament;
(f) any statutory order (such as a drought order).

Section 89 provides a further defence if the entry or discharge was made in an emergency in order to avoid danger to life or health: in such a case the discharger must inform the NRA as soon as reasonably practicable and take reasonable steps to minimise any pollution. It must be assumed that only a danger to human life or health would suffice. In addition, s. 89 excludes from the operation of s. 85 sewage effluent from vessels (which is covered under by-laws) and solid refuse from mines where the NRA has given consent for its deposit. There is also a block exemption order relating to certain discharges which had never required a consent until COPA 1974 came into force. This granted transitional exemption for these discharges, but it is being progressively withdrawn and few discharges are now covered.

There is also a defence in s. 89(3) for water from abandoned mines. However, the defence applies only to the situation where the defendant 'permits' the entry of polluted waters. It is strongly arguable that it does not provide a defence to a charge of 'causing' pollution, which may well be justified where a mine owner abandons a mine knowing that to cease pumping water from it will inevitably lead to an overflow and to pollution (see below and *Lockhart* v *National Coal Board* [1981] SLT 161). In any case, the exemption for abandoned mines is to be withdrawn from 31 December 1999 (see the Environment Act 1995, s. 60). The Environment Act 1995 also defines the concept of abandonment for the first time and imposes a duty on mine operators to give the Environment Agency at least six months' notice of a proposed abandonment.

There are some complex provisions in s. 87 relating to responsibility for discharges from sewage works. In addition to the impact of the wide interpretation given to the concept of 'causing' on sewerage undertakers (see below), s. 87(1) deems sewerage undertakers to have caused a discharge of sewage effluent if they were bound to receive into the sewer or works matter included in the discharge. In other words, they are responsible for all discharges from sewers or works unless the pollution is caused by an illegal (i.e. unconsented) discharge into the sewer. However, s. 87(2) provides a defence where a contravention of s. 85 is attributable to an unconsented discharge into the sewerage system by a third party which the sewerage undertaker could not reasonably have been expected to prevent. In *National Rivers Authority* v *Yorkshire Water Services Ltd* [1995] 1 All ER 225, the House of Lords decided that, notwithstanding the precise wording of s. 87(2), the defence applies to all the offences in s. 85. It should be noted that the defence covers the situation where the sewerage undertaker could not reasonably have prevented the discharge *into* the sewer, rather than *from* the sewer, but that the original discharger into the sewer can be prosecuted under s. 85 for causing pollution of controlled waters as well as under the Water Industry Act 1991, s. 118, for the illegal discharge to the sewer (see Chapter 15).

Under COPA 1974, there was a defence to the general offence if it was committed by a farmer who was acting in accordance with good agricultural practice. This was defined in a Code of Guidance issued by the Minister of Agriculture, Fisheries and Food. The defence has been repealed. In its place is a non-binding *Code of Good Agricultural Practice for the Protection of Water*, issued jointly in 1991 by MAFF and the Secretary of State after consultation with the NRA. This code has no legal effect. Contravention does not amount to a criminal offence and compliance does not afford a legal defence, but obviously conformity with the Code will affect any decision whether to prosecute and the level of any fine imposed.

Meaning of 'cause or knowingly permit'

The offences under s. 85 require that the defendant 'cause or knowingly permit' the relevant discharge or entry. This phrase has been interpreted in many cases and it is clear that there are two separate offences, 'causing' and 'knowingly permitting', and that the former lays down an offence of strict liability because it is not conditioned by any requirement of knowledge. Indeed, *Alphacell Ltd* v *Woodward* [1972] AC 824, a case on this wording in the Rivers (Prevention of Pollution) Act 1951, is one of the leading cases in criminal law on the meaning of strict liability.

In *Alphacell* v *Woodward*, settling tanks at a paper factory overflowed into the River Irwell. The biochemical oxygen demand (BOD) of the discharge was well above the level permitted in the consent. Although the magistrates did not find that the firm had been negligent (a strange decision since pumps which should have stopped the overflow were blocked), the House of Lords held that there was no need to prove negligence or fault. Alphacell were guilty of the general offence of causing pollution simply by carrying on the activity which caused the pollution. As long as their activity was itself intentional all that needed to be shown was a causal link between it and the discharge. The directness of the entry was also irrelevant: in this case the entry was via a channel into the river.

This test has been reiterated in many cases. In *Southern Water Authority* v *Pegrum* [1989] *Local Government Review* 672 effluent from the defendants' pig farm ran into tanks and from there into specially built lagoons. Owing to a fissure in one of the lagoons, when it reached a certain level it leaked, polluting a nearby stream. The Divisional Court held that, as long as the farmers carried on an active operation such as this and there was no effective intervening cause of the pollution, such as a trespasser or an Act of God, the general offence of causing pollution under COPA 1974, s. 31 (which involved identical wording) had been committed. The defence that the lagoon was filled by heavy rain was rejected on the grounds that it required something quite out of the ordinary to break the causal link. Similarly, in *Wrothwell Ltd* v *Yorkshire Water Authority* [1984] Crim LR 43, it was held that a director of a company who had poured herbicide into what he thought was a drain leading to the public sewer, but which in fact led to a nearby stream, was guilty of causing pollution of the stream, despite the unintended result of his action.

More recently, in *National Rivers Authority* v *Yorkshire Water Services Ltd* [1995] 1 All ER 225, the House of Lords has reaffirmed the *Alphacell* test, emphasising that the issue of causation is a question of fact in each case. In *Yorkshire Water Services* an industrial solvent had been discharged illegally into the sewers by an unidentified industrial firm. The solvent had travelled through the sewers and, as a result of the design of the sewage works, into controlled waters, in a virtually undiluted condition. The House of Lords stated that there was ample evidence on which a tribunal of fact could find that the sewerage undertaker had caused the discharge from the sewage works (although in fact the conviction was quashed because the sewerage under-taker could take advantage of the special defence in s. 87(2)). In *Attorney General's Reference (No. 1 of 1994)* [1995] 2 All ER 1007, this case was applied by the Court of Appeal, which decided that where a sewerage undertaker had run a sewerage system in an unmaintained state it could be guilty of causing polluting matter to enter controlled waters. It had been argued that this amounted to an omission rather than an active operation, but the court reformulated the issue by pointing out that the active operation was running a sewage disposal system in an unmaintained state. The court also added that it was possible for more than one person to be liable for causing one pollution incident—the offence simply required that the defendant caused the discharge or entry, not that it was the sole, or even the principal, cause. (For example, on the facts of the *Yorkshire Water Services* case, it was entirely possible for both the original discharger into the sewer and the sewerage undertaker to have caused the entry into the river.)

A final case worth mentioning in this context is *CPC (UK) Ltd v National Rivers Authority* [1995] Env LR 131, where the operator of a factory was held to have caused polluting matter to have entered controlled waters when a pipe carrying cleaning fluid had fractured, allowing the fluid to flow into a river via a storm drain. The conviction was upheld even though the cause of the fracture was defective work carried out by subcontractors of the previous owner some time before the current owners had bought the premises. The reasoning was quite straightforward: the current owners had caused the pollution because they were operating the site when the polluting incident took place. Care must be taken, however, in referring to causation as a question of fact in each case. It does not mean that the tribunal of fact has total discretion, since its decision could be overturned if it failed the *Wednesbury* reasonableness requirement.

There have been two lines of cases which have suggested some limits to this wide interpretation of the concept of causing pollution. One line concerns the situation where a third party has acted in such a way as to interrupt the chain of causation. In *Impress (Worcester) Ltd v Rees* [1971] 2 All ER 357, fuel oil from a tank was released into the River Severn. The defendant successfully pleaded that this was the act of a trespasser. Similarly, in *Welsh Water Authority v Williams Motors (Cwmdu) Ltd, The Times,* 5 December 1988, the owner of a petrol station was held not guilty of causing oil pollution where an independent lorry driver had spilt a delivery of diesel oil. In *National Rivers Authority v Wright Engineering Co. Ltd* [1994] Env LR 186, vandals had interfered with an oil storage tank, which had then leaked into controlled waters. Once again, the company was held not to have caused the polluting entry, although it was accepted that the foreseeability of vandalism would be one relevant factor in deciding who caused the pollution incident. It should also be recognised that the decision in *Attorney General's Reference (No. 1 of 1994)* that more than one person can cause one pollution incident (see above) must mean that the availability of a defence cannot be taken for granted whenever a third party is involved.

The second line of cases relates to situations where the defendant can be said to be passive rather than active. It is illustrated most clearly by *Price v Cromack* [1975] 1 WLR 988, where a farmer had a contract permitting an animal products firm to discharge waste into lagoons on his land. One lagoon wall failed and the resulting escape severely polluted a river. The farmer was charged with causing pollution, but was acquitted on the ground that he had only permitted the accumulation and had not caused the pollution. *Price v Cromack* was followed in *Wychavon DC v NRA* [1993] JEL 121 and *NRA v Welsh Development Agency* [1993] Env LR 407. In the *Wychavon* case, raw sewage escaped from a sewer that was under the control of Wychavon DC, which was at the time acting as agent of the water company in maintaining and repairing the sewerage system. The immediate cause was a blockage in the sewer. The Divisional Court decided that the Council was not guilty of the causing offence since it had not done anything positive but had merely remained inactive. In the *Welsh Development Agency* case, the court decided that the landlord of an industrial estate did not cause a discharge of trade effluent from the estate's surface water drains when the effluent originated from one of the units on the estate. These two cases both purport to follow Lord Wilberforce's statement in *Alphacell* v *Woodward* that causing 'must involve some active operation or chain of operations involving as the result the pollution of the stream'. But both appear to ignore the fact that in *Alphacell* it is made clear that it is not the immediate cause of the pollution that must be active, but the operation that underlies it. (For example, the active operation in *Alphacell* was identified as a complex one that involved the carrying on of a paper factory with an effluent treatment plant situated next to a river and which had an overflow channel that led directly to a river: it was inevitable that if something went wrong, polluting matter would enter the river.) None of these cases has been overruled, but they must be treated as limited to their own facts as a result of the reaffirmation of *Alphacell* in *National Rivers Authority* v *Yorkshire Water Services Ltd* and *Attorney General's Reference (No. 1 of 1994)*

The offence of 'knowingly permitting' has given rise to fewer cases and is clearly more limited than the 'causing' offence because of the knowledge requirement. However, it may be of use in situations where a person is passive even after knowing of the polluting incident. For example, in *Price* v *Cromack* the judge suggested the farmer could well have been charged with knowingly permitting the pollution; and in the *Wychavon* case it is fairly clear that the local authority could have been charged with knowingly permitting the pollution once it had been drawn to its attention (on the facts it had delayed for some time before taking steps to remedy the situation). One issue of great importance to the 'knowingly permitting' offence is the level of knowledge required. In *Schulmans Incorporated Ltd* v *National Rivers Authority* [1993] Env LR D1 the judge held that constructive knowledge was sufficient, although he did not go on to elaborate the point (see Wilkinson, 'Causing and knowingly permitting pollution offences: a review' [1993] *Water Law* 25, for a discussion of the possible implications of this case).

Two final cases are of importance for the s. 85 offences. In *Taylor Woodrow Property Management Ltd* v *National Rivers Authority* [1995] JEL 55, a property company held a discharge consent relating to an outfall from an industrial estate. Even though it did not itself actually make any discharge, it was held liable under s. 85(6) for contravening the conditions of the consent. It thus appears that the holder of a consent is always capable of being prosecuted for breach of positive conditions attached to the consent. It can also be noted that this is a very neat way of avoiding any argument concerning whether the defendant has carried out an active operation, but only where there is a consent.

In *National Rivers Authority* v *Alfred McAlpine Homes (East) Ltd* [1995] JEL 60, the company was held to be vicariously liable for acts of its employees, irrespective of whether those employees exercised 'the controlling mind' of the company. This appears to be a straightforward application of the principle of vicarious liability, but it does illustrate the need for companies to establish proper environmental management systems. The *McAlpine* case is also noteworthy for the approach of Morland J, who commented that any other answer 'would render important environmental legislation almost entirely nugatory', before stating:

> In my judgment to make the offence an effective weapon in the defence of environmental protection a company must by necessary implication be criminally liable for the acts or omissions of its servants or agents during activities being done for the company. I do not find that this offends our concept of a just and fair criminal legal system having regard to the magnitude of environmental pollution, even though no due diligence defence was provided for.

It is quite clear from this quotation, and from other comments in the cases referred to above, that the judges have been prepared to adopt a fairly purposive view of the legislation in order to further the aim of environmental protection. One result has been that the s. 85 offences have been given a very wide interpretation. This has had a number of implications. First, a wide range of accidental occurrences are offences. Secondly, any excess over the requirements of a numerical consent amounts to a criminal offence, no matter how small it is. Thirdly, firms are given a clear incentive to adopt an appropriate environmental management system so that accidents and breaches of consent do not occur. (This is, of course, accentuated by the possible personal liability of directors and senior managers under s. 217.) Fourthly, when a prosecution is brought there is a very high success rate (it is currently over 95%). However, the NRA has a discretion whether to prosecute and has traditionally adopted a policy which means that a prosecution will not be brought in every possible case (see p. 449).

The consent system

The system for acquiring a consent is set out in the Water Resources Act 1991, sch. 10, which involves a higher degree of public involvement than many other licensing-type systems. However, the Environment Act 1995 substitutes a new sch. 10, which will come into force when the Environment Agency comes into existence. As part of the Government's deregulation strategy the new sch. 10 waters down some of the publicity and other procedural requirements. The original sch. 10 is referred to below.

Consents which have already been granted under COPA 1974 or earlier legislation are simply translated into valid consents for the purposes of the Act. However, they may be varied or revoked in the future under the terms of sch. 10 (see below).

A consent is required for each discharge, so if a factory has three discharge pipes it needs a consent for each one. The applicant applies to the NRA, which has a discretion as to the details required. Normally the applicant will have to state the place, nature, quantity, rate of flow, composition and temperature of the proposed discharge. It is an offence under s. 206 to give incorrect information.

The NRA must publicise the application in a local newspaper and in the *London Gazette* and notify any relevant local authorities and water undertakers, at the applicant's expense. However, this publicity may be dispensed with if the NRA considers that the discharge will have 'no appreciable effect' on the receiving waters. Great use was made of this dispensation by the regional water authorities in the past, so that an estimated 90% of all applications were exempted from publicity in this way. Guidance on this vague and subjective discretion is given in DoE Circular 17/84, which suggests a complex set of tests to be considered, the main one being that a change is not to be considered appreciable if there is less than a 10% increase on all relevant parameters, unless some significant environmental amenity is affected. This is a good example of the use of administrative methods to define a legal requirement. It is objectionable that the operation of such an important publicity procedure rests on a rather restrictive interpretation given in a Departmental Circular.

Under sch. 10, para. 1(7), an applicant may apply to the Secretary of State for a certificate of exemption from these publicity requirements. Such a certificate will be granted if the Secretary of State is satisfied that publicity would be contrary to the public interest or would prejudice information about a trade secret to an unreasonable degree. A certificate will also exempt the discharge and discharger from the provisions of the public register under s. 190. It seems that this exemption is rarely used.

The NRA must take into account written representations made within six weeks of the notice appearing in the *London Gazette*. It has the power to grant consent, either unconditionally or subject to conditions, or to refuse consent. If it proposes to grant a consent it must inform anyone who made representations and wait a further 21 days. This is to enable an objector to request the Secretary of State to call the matter in.

A fee for making an application for a new or revised consent was introduced from 1 October 1990. The intention is that the NRA should recover the overall costs incurred in processing applications. A standard charge is payable for each new or revised consent. There is a reduced charge for certain minor discharges of sewage effluent or cooling waters and for those surface water discharges which require consent (see *NRA Scheme of Charges in Respect of Applications and Consents for Discharges to Controlled Waters*).

Conditions

The NRA may attach 'such conditions as it may think fit' and sch. 10, para. 2(5) includes a non-exhaustive list. This includes such things as the quality, quantity, nature, composition and temperature of the discharge, the siting and design of the outlet, the provision of meters for measuring these matters, the taking and recording of samples by the discharger, and the provision of information to the NRA. Frequently the most significant conditions will relate to biochemical oxygen demand, levels of toxic or dangerous materials, and suspended solids, although the NRA has suggested, amongst other recommendations relating to consents, the introduction of a more sophisticated test based on the toxicity of the discharge (*Discharge Consent and Compliance Policy: A Blueprint for the Future*, NRA, 1990). For industrial discharges it is normal to attach absolute numerical limits for the various parameters covered in the consent, with the result that any excess amounts to a breach of the consent. For sewage discharges a test based on 95% compliance has in the past been more normal, though sewage works consents are now being brought into line with industrial consents (see p. 446).

Conditions requiring a specified treatment process are legal, but it remains to be seen whether such conditions will be imposed, since in the past it has been Government policy to require compliance with environmental standards whilst giving a discharger a choice of methods to achieve the standard. It is permissible for conditions to be staggered so that they get progressively stricter. This was accepted in *Trent River Authority* v *F. H. Drabble & Sons Ltd* [1970] 1 WLR 98 and is now specifically covered in sch. 10.

A consent attaches to the discharge and is not personal to the applicant, so the benefit can be passed on to a new owner (sch. 10, para. 2(6)).

There is a procedure for granting a retrospective consent in para. 5. This involves the payment of the relevant fee and the same publicity requirements as for any other application. However, the paragraph is not fully retrospective since it affords no immunity for offences committed before the consent was granted. It enables the NRA to formalise the legal position in relation to a discharge and also to attach conditions to an existing discharge.

A significant problem under COPA 1974 was the position of new pollutants. This phrase covers substances which the discharger introduces into the discharge after the consent has been obtained, or new substances unknown at the time the consent was set, or substances which were only later traceable or later considered to be polluting. Such substances would not be mentioned in the consent, and it appeared that discharging them may not have been in breach of the consent, since there was a breach only if the conditions were not met. It seems that this possible loophole has been avoided by the Water Resources Act 1991, which requires that the discharge must be 'under and in accordance with' the consent in order for the defence in s. 88 to apply. However, to make matters clear, the NRA has recommended that all consents should include a general condition excluding the discharge of any substance not specified in the consent.

Revocation and variation

Under sch. 10, para. 6 it is the duty of the NRA to review consents from time to time, although this will be changed to a dicretionary power under the Environment Act 1995. A variation or a revocation can be made simply by notifying the discharger. Alternatively the Secretary of State may direct that a variation take place. No compensation is payable except in one case considered below. There is no provision for public participation in relation to a variation or revocation. This power to make variations or revocations is a wide one which reflects the need to cater for new circumstances, such as a new polluter in the catchment area, or a newly perceived pollution threat, or a change in EC or international obligations. It also reasserts the position that no one has a right to pollute.

However, there are limits on when a variation or revocation can be made. A period will be stipulated in the original consent (in the past this could not be less than two years, but the Environment Act 1995 extends it to four years) and a variation or revocation cannot take place within that period (measured from the setting of the original consent or the last variation), except with the permission of the discharger. Exceptionally, the Secretary of State may direct a modification within the period in order to give effect to an EC or international obligation, or to protect public health, or flora and fauna dependent on an aquatic environment. There is no right to vary early solely because the discharger has been in breach of the consent, or in order to cater for a new pollutant: both are situations where such a right would be desirable. The NRA will have to pay compensation to the discharger if a direction is made on the public health or protection of flora and fauna ground within the period.

Transitional provisions

In any regulatory system, when a new Act comes into force the transitional provisions are of importance. For the Water Act 1989, because most discharges were already covered by the provisions of COPA 1974, the transition was fairly straightforward. Existing consents were simply translated into Water Act consents and later into consents under the Water Resources Act 1991. This hides a continuation of a transitional provision from COPA 1974. Some discharges which did not require a consent before that Act were deemed to have been granted consent for the current level of discharge under COPA 1974, s. 40(4), as long as an application was made. These applications are slowly being decided by the NRA but the process is not yet complete. Such discharges include many pre–1974 discharges to estuaries, which are effectively permitted to continue with their previous discharge uncontrolled.

Annual charges for discharge consents

The NRA is empowered to make annual charges for discharge consents under the Water Resources Act 1991, s. 131, although any such scheme requires the approval of the Secretary of State and the consent of the Treasury. Accordingly, the *NRA Scheme of Charges in Respect of Applications and Consents for Discharges to Controlled Waters* has been made. It came into force on 1 July 1991.

The basic philosophy underpinning the Scheme is that of cost-recovery charging, i.e. that the NRA should recover from dischargers the actual cost of its activities connected with discharges. This includes the sampling of discharges, inspection of discharges, discharge-related impact monitoring, work on the review of consents, laboratory services and direct administration connected to these matters. Expenditure on general water quality monitoring, general administration and pollution incidents is not recovered by these charges, but will come from the general budget of the NRA. It is estimated that over £40m will be recovered through charges annually, thus increasing the Authority's independence from Government.

Further principles are that the charges are uniform throughout the country and are not to vary locally; that they relate to what is consented to rather than to the actual discharge; and that they are set according to a formula which has three separate elements—the volume of the discharge, its content, and the nature of the receiving waters. For each of these three elements broad bands have been devised, each being accorded a weighted value (i.e. a number of units). For volume, there are eight broad bands, with larger volume discharges having a higher value than lower ones. There are exceptions for emergency discharges, intermittent discharges and rainwater drains. For content, there are seven bands, reflecting the relative complexity and cost of monitoring the discharge. For receiving waters, there are four bands, with estuarine waters having a higher weighting than inland watercourses, which in turn are weighted more highly than discharges to coastal waters or to groundwaters.

Each discharge thus has three separate values, which are multiplied together to give a final figure in terms of a number of units. This final figure is then multiplied by a national financial factor, so that all dischargers know in advance what their charge is going to be. This financial factor will be varied annually. It can be expected that most dischargers will face a significant annual bill for their discharges.

At present there is no proposal for additional charges for 'Red List' or other hazardous substances on the grounds that the presence of these in a discharge will tend to take it into the more highly weighted categories as far as content is concerned. In a way, therefore, the polluter pays principle is being partially operated in relation to these charges. However, the White Paper (*This Common Inheritance,* 1990, Cmd 1200, para. 12.25 and Annex A) suggests that the Government is looking at charging methods related to the pollution load, or environmental effect, of a discharge, and is commissioning studies to look at such a system. This would be far more in keeping with the true meaning of the polluter pays principle.

The role of the Secretary of State

The Secretary of State has a general, and very wide, power under the Water Resources Act 1991, s. 5 to issue directions of a general or specific nature to the NRA in relation to pollution control, amongst other matters (this will be replaced by the Environment Act 1995, s. 40 when the Environment Agency comes into existence). The supplementary powers of the Secretary of State to require information from the NRA in ss. 196 and 202 should also be noted. The reason for the width of the s. 5 power is the fact that large policy-making powers have effectively been delegated to the NRA, making some mechanism for central control desirable. The use of directions to achieve this should be compared with the use of Circular guidance in other areas of environmental law, since they fulfil similar purposes.

The s. 5 power is exercisable, except in an emergency, only after consultation with the NRA, but it could be used if the NRA failed to act on a certain matter. It is envisaged that it will be used to give effect to EC or international obligations if there is no other way of achieving this. Directions made under s. 5 must be listed in the NRA's Annual Report: otherwise there is no requirement for them to be published.

At any stage the Secretary of State may call in an application for decision (sch. 10, para. 4). This is an unfettered discretion and ousts the jurisdiction of the NRA to consider the consent. It is rarely exercised.

Appeals

The applicant or discharger has a right to appeal to the Secretary of State against a refusal of consent, the attachment of unreasonable conditions, any adverse variation or revocation of a consent, or the setting of the period in which a consent cannot be varied (s. 91). An application is deemed to have been refused if no decision is given within four months.

An appeal is a general rehearing of the matter in issue and the Secretary of State has the same powers as the NRA originally had. Compared to the system of planning appeals, which accords enormous opportunities for argument on policy, it seems that this appeal right will be less commonly used, since there is little perceived difference in policy between the Secretary of State and the NRA. However, one criticism that has been made of the appeals system is the length of time it takes for appeals to be decided, with the result that an understanding of the principles to be applied on appeal is only building up slowly.

The procedures for called in applications and for appeals are set out in the Control of Pollution (Consents for Discharges etc.) (Secretary of State's Functions) Regulations 1989 (SI 1989 No. 1151). These regulations retain the procedures for other applications with modified wording, and also provide for the rights of objectors. One significant change is that the discretion not to publicise where there is no appreciable effect on the receiving waters does not apply.

A final power of the Secretary of State is that the NRA must apply to the Secretary of State if it wishes to make any discharges. Similar procedures apply as for ordinary consent applications (Control of Pollution (Discharges by the NRA) Regulations 1989 (SI 1989 No. 1157)). Given the limited operational activities of the NRA, few such applications will be necessary.

How are consents set?

The NRA, or the Secretary of State on appeal, has a wide discretion in setting the consent and it will be set by reference to a variety of factors. Although sch. 10 is silent as to the factors which must be taken into account, applying ordinary public law principles the NRA must have regard to all material considerations. In addition, certain requirements appear from other sections of the Act, especially s. 84, and from EC law.

As stated before, it is important to grasp the individualised and flexible nature of these consents, although uniformity and consistency is now being sought by the NRA. Relevant matters include:

(a) The water quality objectives and standards set for the receiving waters under s. 83 (see below). This emphasises that one of the crucial elements in fixing a consent is the effect on the receiving waters. This in turn depends on the use that is intended for those receiving waters.

(b) Any other effects on the receiving waters, such as on a fishery or downstream user. In particular, regard will be had to whether the waters are used for abstraction for water supply or irrigation.

(c) Any relevant EC standards for the discharge concerned or for the quality of the receiving waters.

(d) Any 'cocktail' effect of the discharge. The NRA will consider not only the immediate effect of the discharge but also any impact the discharge will have in combination with the current contents of the waters and any potential future discharges.

(e) The desirability of minimising discharges of hazardous substances as far as possible in accordance with Directive 76/464 (see p. 418).

(f) The NRA's environmental duties laid out in s. 16 (see p. 49).

(g) The specific duty in relation to sites of special scientific interest set out in s. 17 (see p. 482).

(h) Any relevant objections and representations made and the results of any consultation carried out.

(i) Certain informal standard tests for particular types of discharge. For example, 'normal' standards for sewage works were suggested by the Eighth Report of the Royal Commission on Sewage Disposal in 1912 and these were applied for many years. The NRA is now seeking to establish some uniformity of standards across the country for all types of discharge.

(j) Any other material considerations.

Water quality objectives

Although the British approach to the control of water pollution has tended over the years to concentrate on the environmental impact of pollutants, the development of *statutory* water quality objectives owes a great deal to the EC. In the 1970s, in debates on EC Directives such as 76/464 on Dangerous Substances in Water, the British Government argued that its system of water pollution control was different to the systems operated by other EC Member States in that it was based on individualised consent standards set by reference to local environmental quality objectives, rather than on uniform emission standards or limit values which did not take the environmental effects fully into account. At the time, however, there were no formally set quality objectives, so in order to show that this was indeed how the system worked, the Government was forced to introduce more explicit objectives.

In 1978, the National Water Council developed a water quality classification (see *River Water Quality: The Next Stage*, National Water Council, 1978). This had five basic classes of river waters (there was a similar but separate classification for estuaries):

1A   High quality waters suitable for all abstraction purposes with only modest treatment. Capable of supporting game or other high class fisheries. High amenity value.

1B   Good quality waters usable for substantially the same purposes as 1A though not as high quality.

2   Fair quality waters viable as coarse fisheries and capable of use for drinking water provided advanced treatment is given. Moderate amenity value.

3   Poor waters polluted to the extent that fish are absent or only sporadically present. Suitable only for low grade industrial abstractions.

4   Bad quality waters which are grossly polluted and likely to cause a nuisance.

This classification was adopted by the regional water authorities in setting informal river quality objectives over the next few years. It was also used for the five-yearly national survey of water quality. However, as an administrative method of implementing EC Directives, it was clearly insufficient to satisfy EC law (see *Commission* v *Belgium* [1982] CMLR 627, which requires implementation of EC Directives to be done by legislative means), so it became inevitable that a statutory system would be adopted.

The Water Act 1989 introduced statutory water quality classifications and objectives for the first time. The provisions are now reproduced in the Water Resources Act 1991, ss. 82–84. When fully operational (which will not be for many years), statutory water quality objectives will make the system more open and will be an important element in the general process of establishing a rationally planned, transparent and properly accountable system of water resources management.

The essential features are that, over the next few years, classification regulations will be made which set the standards that waters must reach in order to come within a certain classification. This will be done under s. 82. The Secretary of State will then establish (under s. 83) a water quality *objective* for each stretch of controlled waters. This will set specified classifications as an objective, and will accordingly incorporate the relevant water quality *standards*. These will then act as explicit policy goals for the NRA, which will be under a legal duty under s. 84 to exercise its functions, including the granting of discharge consents, so as to achieve and maintain the statutory water quality objective at all times, at least as far as it is practicable to do so. There are thus three different processes involved, although these are intertwined.

The first process is the setting of classification systems for waters under s. 82. In order to comply with certain EC Directives, this process was started with the publication of three sets of regulations:

(a)   The Surface Waters (Classification) Regulations 1989 (SI 1989 No. 1148), which classify inland waters (i.e. fresh waters) into three categories according to their suitability as drinking waters. The classification is based on the mandatory values in Directive 75/440 on Surface Water for Drinking. To qualify as within any category, the specified limits must not be exceeded.

(b)   The Bathing Waters (Classification) Regulations 1991 (SI 1991 No. 1597), which establish a classification that reflects the mandatory standards laid down in Directive 76/160 on Bathing Waters.

(c)   The Surface Waters (Dangerous Substances) (Classification) Regulations 1989 and 1992 (SIs 1989 No. 2286 and 1992 No. 337), which set classifications in accordance with Directive 76/464 on Dangerous Substances in Water and its daughter Directives. These Regulations specify annual mean concentrations of a limited range of substances (mainly 'Red List' substances) which should not be exceeded. In order to comply with EC law, these classifications have also been issued as initial water quality objectives under s. 83, this action having been taken by the Secretary of State under the power to make directions now contained in s. 5 of the Act. In so doing the publicity requirements set out in s. 83(4) were dispensed with.

The process has now been taken further with the Surface Waters (River Ecosystem) (Classification) Regulations 1994 (SI 1994 No. 1057), which were introduced following extensive consultation. These Regulations lay down five classifications, RE1–RE5, which are defined according to conformity with seven parameters: dissolved oxygen, biochemical oxygen demand (BOD), total ammonia, un-ionised ammonia, pH, dissolved copper and total zinc. Standard sampling and analysis methods are laid down, as are methods for determining compliance with the classifications. The absence of biological parameters, which were originally proposed by the NRA, has been criticised, but the view has been taken that they would be inappropriate for the statutory classification scheme. They will, however, be used in future as part of a uniform system of analysis for the five-yearly national survey of water quality (see p. 413). Classification systems are still awaited for controlled waters apart from rivers.

The second process is that water quality objectives for individual stretches of controlled waters may be set by the Secretary of State (s. 83). The choice of an objective by the Secretary of State would mean that the appropriate standards laid down for that objective in the classification regulations would apply to the stretch of water. In addition, appropriate EC standards laid down in Directives would be incorporated where relevant (for example, if the waters were bathing waters designated under Directive 76/160).

The procedures for setting a statutory water quality objective involve at least three months' publicity of the proposed objective 'in such manner as the Secretary of State considers appropriate for bringing it to the attention of persons likely to be affected by it' (i.e. these provisions are less specific than many other publicity provisions in relation to pollution control). The NRA must also be notified. All representations and objections must be considered, and the Secretary of State may modify the proposals in the light of these representations. A public local inquiry may be held under s. 213. Obviously it is in the interests of anyone discharging into a catchment to get involved in the setting of these objectives. Similar advice applies to those who discharge into sewers, because discharges from sewage works will also be affected by the statutory water quality objective. The Secretary of State may review and, in the light of the review, vary water quality objectives by going through the same procedures, but this may only take place five years after the objective was last set or varied, or alternatively if the NRA requests a review, which it may do only after consulting relevant water undertakers.

The third process is that, as stated above, under s. 84 the NRA and Secretary of State are placed under a duty to exercise their powers under the Act so as to achieve statutory water quality objectives at all times, so far as it is practicable to do so. This duty already applies to the objectives set in the Surface Waters (Dangerous Substances) (Classification) Regulations, but will only apply to other objectives when they are formally established. It does not follow that the NRA is in breach of s. 84 simply by failing to achieve the appropriate standards. But it does mean that its powers in relation to the setting and variation of consents, remedial and enforcement action, and preventative controls should be exercised to achieve the standards if practicable, since a judicial review action could conceivably be brought to ensure the enforcement of the duty. Under the EPA 1990, s. 7(2)(c), a similar duty is placed on HMIP to try to achieve statutory water quality objectives when considering authorisations for integrated pollution control. These duties will transfer to the Environment Agency when it comes into existence.

One of the criticisms of the sections on statutory water quality objectives when they were first passed was that no timetable was set for the introduction of the system. It is now clear that full implementation will take many years. There is still some work to be done on the development of precise classification criteria. After that, the process of setting individual objectives will, in the Government's words, extend 'over a number of years', starting with a very limited number of selected river catchments. Even then, the current proposals relate only to rivers—statutory water quality objectives for estuaries, coastal waters, groundwaters, canals and lakes are clearly many years off. The existing informal river quality objectives will remain in force until superseded by the statutory objectives. There is little doubt that the Government has little enthusiasm for the costs involved in setting statutory water quality objectives, despite the great benefits they would produce in terms of a rational and transparent system of pollution control.

Public registers

For the first time, the Control of Pollution Act 1974 provided for public registers of a range of environmental information relating to water pollution, although these provisions were not implemented until 1985. Prior to that the system tended to be operated with a fair degree of secrecy about consents and samples taken. The relevant provisions are repeated in the Water Resources Act 1991 with some amendments.

Under s. 190, a public register must be kept by the NRA of all applications for consent, consents actually granted, any conditions attached to a consent, notices of water quality objectives made under s. 83 and (at present) certificates issued under sch. 10, para. 1(7) exempting applicants from the publicity requirements of the Act. Prescribed details of authorisations granted for the purposes of integrated pollution control must also be recorded on the water registers. In addition, the results of any samples of the receiving waters or of effluent, and any information produced by analysis of them, must be registered. This requirement is worded more widely than under COPA 1974, and samples taken by *any* person must be registered; this includes samples taken by a discharger as a condition of consent.

Section 190 requires that the register is open for inspection by any member of the public free of charge at all reasonable times and that reasonable facilities for taking copies are afforded on payment of a reasonable fee. The Control of Pollution (Registers) Regulations 1989 (SI 1989 No. 1160) specify the detailed shape of the registers, including a requirement that details of any sample must be entered on the register within two months of the date of the sample.

The public register provides an invaluable database for groups and individuals wishing to monitor water quality. It can be used to mount a private prosecution (as in *Wales* v *Thames Water Authority* [1987] 1/3 *Environmental Law* 3, where the Water Authority was successfully prosecuted for pollution from a sewage works in reliance on the information which it had itself recorded on the register), or to provide evidence for a civil claim, or to provide general information on the state of the water environment. The admissibility of the registers as evidence seems quite clear now that they are kept by the NRA (see p. 448).

It is currently possible to obtain a certificate of exemption from the Secretary of State exempting an applicant from the requirements of the register in relation to an application, a consent, any conditions attached or any sample of effluent from the discharge (sch. 10, para. 1(7)). This involves satisfying the Secretary of State that registration would either prejudice a trade secret to an unreasonable degree or would be contrary to the public interest. Circular 13/85 suggests that such a situation will be rare, and the existence of the certificate itself must be registered, but the exemption does illustrate a particularly property-based view of the control of pollution. These povisions will be replaced by similar ones, allowing exclusion from the register on the grounds of commercial confidentiality and that inclusion would be contrary to the interests of national security, when the Environment Agency comes into existence.

In addition, s. 204 prohibits the NRA or any officer from disclosing information obtained under the Act. Any person who does disclose such information without the permission of the person or company which provided it is guilty of an offence and liable, on summary conviction, to a fine not exceeding £5,000, and on conviction on indictment, to imprisonment for up to two years or an unlimited fine, or both. Of course, this restriction does not apply to matters required to be entered on the register. Nor does it apply to such things as the disclosure of information for criminal proceedings, or in pursuance of an EC obligation, and a range of other matters listed in s. 204. It also does not apply where a company has ceased trading.

Integrated pollution control

For those processes prescribed for Part I of the EPA 1990 (i.e. those processes subject to integrated pollution control), the NRA loses its powers in relation to consents for discharges to controlled waters. Instead, HMIP has responsibility for operating and enforcing the system of authorisations for processes set up under the 1990 Act. Acting in accordance with an integrated pollution control authorisation will be a defence to the water pollution offences under s. 85 of the Water Resources Act 1991.

However, the NRA does not lose all its control over water pollution. In deciding whether to grant an authorisation, HMIP must consult with the NRA and, in setting the authorisation, HMIP must take into account such things as any relevant water quality objectives set under the Water Resources Act 1991. Most importantly, under s. 28 of the EPA 1990, the NRA may effectively dictate certain matters. to HMIP where a release into controlled waters is concerned:

(a)   Under s. 28(3)(a), the NRA may certify its opinion that a release will result in, or contribute to, a failure to achieve a statutory water quality objective. If it does so, HMIP cannot grant an authorisation at all.

(b)   Under s. 28(3)(b), the NRA may dictate whatever conditions it thinks are appropriate. If it does so, HMIP must include these conditions, though it may make them more onerous and it may add others.

(c)   Under s. 28(4), the NRA may require HMIP to vary any conditions of an authorisation if it considers such a variation appropriate. If it does so, HMIP must vary the conditions as required, using its powers under s. 10 of EPA 1990. This can be done at any time by serving a notice on the holder of an authorisation. (The exercise of all these powers is governed by a Memorandum of Understanding between HMIP and the NRA—see [1991] Water Law 86.)

Since the NRA has responsibility for controlled waters, and HMIP has responsibility for all prescribed processes, there was always going to be a conflict where the two controls overlapped. The NRA's position was that it should be the decision-making body in relation to controlled waters, with HMIP having powers to make directions to it. However, this was not accepted in the legislation, and HMIP was given the lead role. In particular, the NRA has no effective policing powers in relation to prescribed processes (with the exception of the right to bring a prosecution for breach of the 1990 Act), even though it is ultimately responsible for water quality. The EPA 1990 provides some extensive administrative provisions on the enforcement of the system, such as prohibition notices, yet the NRA will be unable to use these and will have to rely for enforcement on HMIP.

The significant powers given to the NRA under EPA 1990, s. 28, provide one resolution of this conflict. But it must be said that they do take away some of the internal logic of the integrated pollution control system by allowing the NRA effectively to interfere with the terms of an authorisation, thus potentially upsetting any balance HMIP was trying to reach. Of course, in one sense all these conflicts disappear with the joining together of the NRA and HMIP in the Environment Agency, but there is still scope for internal disagreements between different parts of the Agency.

Sewage discharges

Sewage discharges have always caused problems, firstly because of their potent polluting power and secondly because of the conflict of interest between regulator and regulated. These points were seen at their clearest in the 1970s and 1980s when capital expenditure cuts led to a number of badly underperforming sewage works at a time when the regulator and regulated was the same body, the regional water authority. However, the same conflict also existed prior to that: the local authorities which ran the sewage works also provided members for the rivers authorities, for example, and thus exercised an influence on their decisions.

Under the Water Resources Act 1991, there is no conflict of interest. Sewerage undertakers are treated similarly to other dischargers in requiring a consent from the NRA. One slight difference relates to the offences under s. 85. Because sewerage undertakers treat wastes discharged by other people, and thus have limited control over what is actually put into the sewers, they have a special defence under s. 87(2). This operates if the contravention of their discharge consent was due to an unconsented discharge made into the sewer by another person which they could not reasonably have prevented (see *National Rivers Authority* v *Yorkshire Water Services Ltd* [1995] 1 All ER 225, which is discussed at p. 430).

A more significant difference is that sewage works have traditionally had their consents set on different terms from other dischargers. The standard practice for other dischargers has been to set absolute numerical limits, with the result that any breach of the limit amounts to a criminal offence. For sewage discharges, in the past the conditions of consents have normally been set by reference to 'look-up tables' intended to ensure a 95% compliance rate over a rolling 12-month period. This leeway was allowed for in recognition of the variable quality of sewage effluents and the comparative lack of control that sewage works operators could exercise over them. The result is that it has been difficult to prove the offence under s. 85, since a single sample which exceeds the consent will not amount to a breach, and a number of legal samples over a 12-month period are needed.

The NRA is currently reviewing its treatment of sewage works. It is introducing consents that set absolute limits, although it is also retaining some percentile compliance tests in order to provide greater control over discharges (see *Discharge Consent and Compliance Policy: A Blueprint for the Future*, NRA, 1990). It is also reviewing and tightening the levels of many consents. These steps have led to a steady rise in the number of prosecutions for illegal sewage discharges and have also had a marked knock-on effect on trade effluent consents granted by the sewerage undertakers under the Water Industry Act 1991.

An understanding of the present position requires some explanation of the position prior to 1989. Between 1951 and 1985 (when the relevant provisions of the Control of Pollution Act 1974 came into force), consents had been set and monitored in virtual secrecy, though they tended to follow the biochemical oxygen demand (BOD) and suspended solids standards recommended by the Eighth Report of the Royal Commission on Sewage Disposal in 1912. Under the 1974 Act, because of the conflict of interest within regional water authorities, a special procedure was established whereby consents were formally set by the Secretary of State (through HMIP after 1987). Similar procedures for applying for consent to those set up for industrial discharges were provided for in regulations. However, most sewage works consents were already in existence, which meant that under COPA 1974, s. 40 there was no need for a new application and hence the publicity requirements were rarely used.

In the 1970s and 1980s many consents were relaxed. For example, the National Water Council had commenced a review of consents in the late-1970s which led to the relaxation of some sewage works consents. This review was never completed and the results never published. Consents were also relaxed in the 1980s in anticipation of the implementation of COPA and the consequent availability of a right to bring private prosecutions, and again in the run-up to water privatisation in order to protect the sewerage undertakers. Notwithstanding these events, there was evidence that up to a quarter of sewage works were still regularly exceeding their consents in 1989. The NRA's recent actions are clearly an attempt to control sewage discharges more rigorously and it is also significant that the privatised water companies figure prominently in lists of those who have been prosecuted most frequently.

Radioactive discharges

Under the Control of Pollution (Radioactive Waste) Regulations, 1989 (SI 1989 No. 1158), the radioactivity of a discharge is to be ignored for the purposes of the Water Resources Act 1991. In other words, the non-radioactive elements of a discharge or entry are dealt with under the Water Resources Act 1991 and the radioactive elements under the Radioactive Substances Act 1993 by HMIP or the Minister of Agriculture, Fisheries and Food.

Sampling and enforcement powers

NRA officers have wide rights of entry to property under the Water Resources Act 1991, ss. 169–174, to ascertain if any powers or duties require implementation, or to inspect for breaches of controls. Reserve powers of entry under a warrant from a magistrate are granted in sch. 20 for cases of difficulty.

The powers include a right to take samples of water or effluent or to install monitoring equipment. However, until its prospective repeal by the Environment Act 1995, s. 111, s. 209 posed some problems in this respect. Under s. 209, the result of the analysis of a sample taken on behalf of the NRA was not admissible in legal proceedings unless it was a 'legal', or tripartite, sample (i.e. one that was taken in accordance with s. 209(1), which required that the occupier of the land concerned was notified of the intention to have the sample analysed and it was divided into three parts, one of which was sent for analysis, one given to the occupier and one retained for future comparison). Despite the fact that there is no requirement that a sample be produced in evidence at all (some cases, for example, can easily be proved by visual evidence or the presence of dead fish), this section provided some practical difficulties for the NRA, especially since it costs approximately five times as much to take a tripartite sample as it does to take a routine one.

The section was discussed in a number of cases. In *National Rivers Authority v Harcros Timber and Building Supplies Ltd* [1992] Env LR 172, the Divisional Court decided that the requirement of a legal sample applied to both samples of effluent and samples of the receiving waters. In *CPC (UK) Ltd v National Rivers Authority* [1995] Env LR 131, a more restrictive interpretation was adopted by the Court of Appeal and it was decided that, where readings were obtained by the NRA from a continuous water monitor, this was not a 'sample' for the purposes of s. 209. In *Attorney General's Reference (No. 2 of 1994)* [1995] Env LR 143, the Court of Appeal adopted a purposive view of the section and decided that the notification to the occupier did not necessarily have to precede the taking of the sample or its division, and that the requirement that the sample be divided 'there and then' simply meant at *or proximate to* the site and on the occasion of taking the sample, which is effectively a continuous event rather than a single moment in time. It would also appear from the wording of the section that it applied only to samples taken by or on behalf of the NRA; therefore, a privately taken sample would be admissible, although its scientific accuracy might be challenged. It is worth noting that a private sample taken by trespassing on the discharger's land, although admissible, may be excluded as improperly obtained evidence at the discretion of the court, although such a course of action is unlikely (see the Police and Criminal Evidence Act 1984, s. 78).

The Environment Act 1995 circumvents this rather confusing position by repealing s. 209, although not without significant opposition in Parliament from industrial interests. Section 111 states simply that information provided or obtained as a result of a licence condition is admissible, including where it is provided by means of an apparatus (i.e. some form of measuring device). There is a rebuttable presumption that such an apparatus is accurate. This should reduce the number of offenders who escape prosecution on evidential technicalities.

There is also a potential problem relating to the admissibility of the public registers, since it is fairly clearly hearsay evidence. It appears that samples taken by the NRA are admissible under the Criminal Justice Act 1988, s. 24. This section also seems to avoid any problem relating to self-incrimination where the discharger's own data are used, as that data will count as a confession (see the Police and Criminal Evidence Act 1984, ss. 76 and 82).

Enforcement policy

A central issue relating to water pollution, and indeed of this whole book, is whether the rules are actually enforced by the regulators (see Chapter 6 for a general survey of attitudes towards enforcement by regulatory bodies). The NRA has established a national prosecution policy and it is clear that the traditional recipe of a conciliatory approach to enforcement with low prosecution rates has been rapidly reformulated.

For example, from 1980 to 1987 the regional water authorities collectively prosecuted between 91 and 254 cases of water pollution each year (Birch, *Poison in the System*, Greenpeace, 1988). By comparison, in its first year of operation (1989/90), the NRA successfully prosecuted 370 cases. Fuller details of more recent prosecutions are given in *Water Pollution Incidents in England and Wales*—1993, NRA, 1994. This report records 25,299 substantiated pollution incidents in 1993 and states that by 31 March 1994, 286 prosecutions had been brought, with a further 133 cases still to come to court. (This actually compares with a figure of 592 prosecutions for incidents occurring in 1990, which can be explained by the higher number of major incidents that year, which was a time of drought in many areas.) In addition, in a further 206 cases a formal caution was issued, this course of action being used where the polluter admits the offence yet a prosecution is considered unnecessary.

This increase in prosecution activity is linked to the NRA's internal practices. It divides pollution incidents into three categories according to their severity—major, significant and minor. For example, a major incident involves one or more of the following:

(a)   a potential or actual persistent effect on water quality or aquatic life;
(b)   the closure of a potable water, industrial or agricultural abstraction point;
(c)   an extensive fish kill;
(d)   excessive breaches of consent conditions;
(e)   a major effect on amenity values; or
(f)   extensive remedial measures are necessary.

It then applies its internal prosecution policy. Although this remains unpublished, essentially it involves prosecuting for major incidents where there is sufficient evidence to do so, and leaving it to the discretion of individual officers where a significant incident has occurred (see Jewell, *Agricultural Water Pollution Issues and NRA Enforcement Policy* [1991] LMELR 110). The proportion of major incidents for which a prosecution is brought is over 30%.

However, it remains the case that most prosecutions are for accidental or other unusual incidents, rather than for consistent breaches of consent, a characteristic that was noted by Greenpeace in *Poison in the System*, and which has given rise to continued complaints from environmental groups that the NRA is not taking action against persistent polluters with sufficient rigour. In this regard, it is appropriate to note that private prosecution remains a possibility under the Water Resources Act 1991. Whilst little used, its availability remains a threat to dischargers, particularly in the light of the information on the public registers, and it may also be used by environmental groups as a means of registering their disquiet over the NRA's perceived failure to take action over certain discharges. This was the case, for example, when Greenpeace successfully prosecuted Albright & Wilson in 1991.

Owing to the strict liability nature of the offences most prosecutions are successful. Of the 286 prosecutions referred to above, 277 resulted in conviction, a success rate of 97%. The level of fines imposed by magistrates is also rising. Before the EPA 1990 raised the maximum fine on summary conviction to £20,000, it was £2,000. However, even this was rarely imposed and the average fine in the late–1980s was estimated to be around £250. This has clearly increased since then, most probably as a result of greater publicity of the costs of environmental pollution, so that the maximum fine has been imposed on a number of occasions and a fine of over £1,000 would now be expected in most cases. Another emerging trend is an increased willingness by the NRA to bring a prosecution in the Crown Court, where fines may be higher. This has resulted in several very large fines, most notably the £1m fine imposed on Shell (*National Rivers Authority* v *Shell (UK)* [1990] *Water Law* 40). There has, as yet, been no reported case of a sentence of imprisonment being imposed for a water pollution offence.

Preventative and remedial powers

One of the special features of the regulatory system on water pollution is the extent of powers in relation to the prevention of harm. The exercise of these powers is undoubtedly aided by the presence of water quality objectives against which action may be justified.

Under s. 161, the NRA has widely drafted powers to prevent pollution incidents where there is a threat of water pollution, to clean up after them and to carry out remedial or restorative works. For example, s. 161 covers such things as diverting a potential pollutant spilt in an accident in order to prevent it from entering a watercourse, cleaning up the effects of a spillage, and restocking a river with fish. As a result of an amendment made by the Environment Act 1995, s. 60, it will also cover investigations into pollution incidents. The 1995 Act does, however, introduce a new procedure, which will come into force when the Environment Agency takes over the s. 161 power from the NRA. This procedure is that the power to carry out works and operations will be exercisable only where a works notice is served on the appropriate responsible person in accordance with s. 161B, unless it is necessary to carry out the works 'forthwith'. There is a right to appeal against such a notice. Far from restricting the use of s. 161, this procedure arguably extends the usefulness of the section where a notice is served to prevent pollution occurring, because it will be an offence to fail to comply with a works notice.

The NRA can recover the costs incurred in these works, operations or investigations from anyone who has caused or knowingly permitted the pollutant to be present in controlled waters, or who has caused or knowingly permitted the pollutant to be a threat to controlled waters. It is arguable that this wide formulation may cover requiring current owners to clean up contaminated sites. There are two exceptions: expenses cannot normally be recovered in relation to waters from an abandoned mine (these are also exempted from some of the criminal provisions in the Act), although this exemption will lapse after 31 December 1999 as a result of an amendment made by the Environment Act 1995, s. 60; and these powers cannot be exercised so as to impede or prevent the making of a discharge in pursuance of a consent. In this second case the NRA is limited to a consideration of whether the consent should be varied, though it should be noted that there is no power to override the period of immunity against variation merely on the grounds that a discharger has committed a breach or an act of pollution.

Section 161 is mainly used for accidental acts of pollution, although it can be used where there has been a breach of the conditions of a consent. It is particularly useful because the potential cost may act as a greater deterrent than the threat of prosecution. The costs of a clean-up operation are likely in many cases to be higher than the potential fine. For example, in *National Rivers Authority* v *Shell (UK)* [1990] *Water Law* 40, Shell was fined £1m for a major leak of oil into the River Mersey, but it has been reported as having paid over £6m in clean-up costs. In *Bruton and National Rivers Authority* v *Clarke* [1994] *Water Law* 145, a county court case concerning damage to a fishery, the approach to valuing a claim under s. 161 is shown, with the judge limiting the NRA to costs necessarily incurred as a result of the pollution incident and not allowing costs incurred in *improving* the fishery. The case also illustrated that there does not have to be a successful prosecution for s. 161 to be successful. However, in *National Rivers Authority: River Pollution from Farms in England* (National Audit Office, 1995), the National Audit Office reports that the NRA only obtains recovery of costs in a minority of cases (42% of the sample taken), which is a low figure considering the NRA's stated policy that polluters should pay for the consequences of their actions.

Precautions against pollution

Under s. 92, the Secretary of State is empowered to make regulations concerning precautions to be taken in relation to any poisonous, noxious or polluting matter to prevent it from entering controlled waters. Such regulations may prevent anyone having custody or control of poisonous, noxious or polluting matter unless the steps required in the regulations or specified by the NRA are carried out. These regulations may create additional criminal offences and administrative remedies in relation to breaches, although these may not have penalties higher than for the pollution offences under s. 85.

The Control of Pollution (Silage, Slurry and Agricultural Fuel Oil) Regulations 1991 (SI 1991 No. 324) are, as yet, the only regulations made under s. 92. They introduce precautionary controls over the design and operation of some potentially very polluting activities by imposing specific controls over silage making operations, slurry stores and agricultural fuel oil stores. All new or substantially altered facilities are covered by the new standards (many of which are performance standards rather than strict design requirements), though it is possible for the NRA to bring existing activities under control if it is satisfied there is a significant risk of pollution to controlled waters. These Regulations have the potential to complement the planning system in preventing pollution problems arising. However, control is exercisable over operational details in a more specific way than is possible through the planning system, oversight and monitoring will be carried out by a more specialist body, and the controls relate to agricultural matters not normally covered by planning powers. Further regulations relating to industrial fuel oil stores have been promised by the Government on a number of occasions but, as yet, no such regulations have been made.

Water protection zones

Under s. 93, the Secretary of State may designate water protection zones by order. Such an order may effectively establish a system of local law within the zone with regard to water pollution. It is envisaged that an order under this section may either prohibit or restrict specified activities within the designated zone with a view to preventing or controlling the entry of poisonous, noxious or polluting matter into controlled waters, or provide for a system whereby the NRA determine prohibited or restricted activities. It is not possible to require the carrying out of positive works. An order may also include provisions relating to procedures for obtaining consent for such restricted activities from the NRA, with criminal sanctions being available for breaches.

The procedure for the making of an order is set out in sch. 11. This requires that the NRA must apply for an order by submitting a draft to the Secretary of State. Fairly precise publicity requirements are laid down, including a duty to notify any local authority and water undertaker within the designated area. The Secretary of State may modify the order and has a power (not a duty) to hold a public inquiry before making it. In England, the Secretary of State must consult with the Minister of Agriculture, Fisheries and Food.

Similar provisions were included in COPA 1974 but were never used, and no water protection zones have yet been designated under the Water Resources Act either, though one has been proposed for the River Dee catchment. They would be excellent tools for protecting certain sensitive areas and for combating non-point discharges, such as pesticide or fertiliser run-off, and would enable steps to be taken to protect against groundwater pollution. However, the use of these powers has always been strongly opposed by agricultural interests. Significantly, there is no specific provision in the Act for an order to include compensation payments, but it may include such supplemental and consequential provision as the Secretary of State 'considers appropriate'.

One limitation, in s. 93(3), is that a water protection zone should not concern itself with nitrate from agricultural sources. This is because protection against nitrate is provided for in s. 94: a section which was hurriedly written into the legislation during its passage in response to public worries about nitrate in groundwaters used for water supply and the action against the British Government in the European Court of Justice for non-compliance with EC Directive 80/778 on Drinking Water. From a legal point of view it is difficult to see why the nitrate problem could not have been tackled through the designation of water protection zones, and it is hard to avoid the conclusion that specific nitrate sensitive area provisions are something of a political gesture.

Nitrate sensitive areas

The powers in relation to nitrate are set out in s. 94, which provides that an area may be designated a nitrate sensitive area by order with a view to preventing or controlling the entry of nitrate into controlled waters as a result of agriculture. In this case the designation is made by the Secretary of State and the Minister of Agriculture, Fisheries and Food acting jointly if the area is in England, and by the Secretary of State for Wales alone if it is in Wales. An order can only be made if requested by the NRA, which must identify controlled waters likely to be affected and the agricultural land likely to result in the entry of nitrate into waters. It must also appear to the NRA that its other powers are inadequate to control nitrate pollution before applying for an order. The consent of the Treasury is required before an order is made.

There are two types of order that may be made, respectively imposing voluntary and mandatory controls. Voluntary controls are available where *any* nitrate sensitive area has been designated: the Minister of Agriculture, Fisheries and Food may enter into a management agreement with any owner of an interest in agricultural land, with compensation payable. Such an agreement will bind those deriving title from the original party.

A mandatory order is similar to an order designating a water protection zone. However, there are significant differences. In nitrate sensitive areas the order may require positive obligations, such as the construction of containment walls around agricultural stores, as well as prohibitions and restrictions on activities. If consent is required, it is obtained from the Minister responsible for the designation, not the NRA. In addition, the order may provide for compensation to be paid to anyone affected by the obligations. No guidelines on the criteria for awarding compensation are set out in the Act.

The procedure for making a mandatory order is set out in sch. 12. This requires that the NRA must apply for an order by submitting a draft to the relevant Minister. Once again, precise publicity requirements are laid down, including a duty to notify any local authority and water undertaker within the designated area, and to notify any owner or occupier appearing to the relevant Minister to be likely to be affected by the compensation provisions. The relevant Minister may modify an order and has a power (not a duty) to hold a public inquiry before making an order.

The Government has made public its intention to use only the voluntary methods initially, in keeping with its stated preference for such methods. It designated 10 pilot areas in the Nitrate Sensitive Areas (Designation) Order 1990 (SI 1990 No. 1013), which provided for two types of scheme, a 'basic scheme' and a 'premium scheme', with more significant restrictions on agricultural operations (and higher payments) available in the latter than in the former. The take-up rate was, in general, good (about 87% of the agricultural land in the 10 areas), but the premium scheme was little used, so the payment rates were increased in an amendment order (SI 1993 No. 3198).

Since then, the perceived success of the pilot scheme has led the Government to expand the number of nitrate sensitive areas to 22 and to introduce a new scheme in the Nitrate Sensitive Areas Regulations 1994 (SI 1994 No. 1729). These Regulations are formally made under the European Communities Act 1972, s. 2(2), in order to comply with the EC Agri-Environment Regulation 2078/92, and thus technically concern the de-intensification of agriculture rather than pollution control. They provide for three separate schemes: a 'premium arable scheme', a 'premium grass scheme' and a 'basic scheme', with farmers being required to give undertakings as to their farming operations for a period of five years in return for payments of specified amounts per hectare per year. It is significant that the payment rates may be revised during the five years.

In relation to Directive 91/676 on Nitrates, the position is less clear. The Government failed to meet the December 1993 deadline for designating nitrate vulnerable zones and only set out the proposed zones in a consultation paper in May 1994, although admittedly it did propose that an area of about 650,000 hectares be designated. The next deadline under the Directive is that action programmes for the nitrate vulnerable zones have to be established by December 1995. Whilst there is no doubt that the 1994 Regulations represent a fairly sophisticated response to nitrate pollution in the designated nitrate sensitive areas, it is clear that the Regulations, and accompanying voluntary mechanisms such as the *Code of Good Agricultural Practice for the Protection of Water*, issued by the Ministry of Agriculture, Fisheries and Food, are insufficient to comply with the Directive. It appears that mandatory measures may have to be adopted within the next few years. It is also probable that these will not involve the levels of compensation that are currently paid to farmers, since that would appear to conflict with the polluter pays principle, although it may be possible to justify the continuation of such payments as part of the EC's agriculture policy as represented by the Agri-Environment Regulation 2078/92.

Planning controls

Local planning authorities have the ability to make important decisions relating to water pollution through the town and country planning system. However. it is clearly recommended in Central Government guidance, such as Circular 1/85 on planning conditions and Planning Policy Guidance Note

23, *Planning and Pollution Control* (PPG 23, 1994), that planning powers should be used mainly for locational and siting decisions and that matters about the regulation of pollution should be left to the specialist regulators to control through the specialist consent systems.

It is clear that potential water pollution arising from a proposed development is a material consideration in any planning decision, and the NRA is a statutory consultee under the General Development Procedure Order in relation to many applications for planning permission. This is of great importance in relation to groundwaters, since the NRA has published a set of very strong policy statements on the protection of groundwater (*Policy and Practice for the Protection of Groundwater*, NRA, 1992). In addition, planning permission may be refused because of inadequate sewerage in the area. Of course, the NRA will also have an important role to play in the making of development plans. The generous exemptions for agricultural activities and buildings may be of significance in the context of increasing evidence of water pollution by agriculture.

Other water pollution offences

There are a number of other offences which may be committed in relation to water pollution. A few of the main ones are considered here: to these should be added offences concerning the dumping of waste, which often involve the pollution of water, and many by-laws of a local or specific nature.

Under the Water Resources Act 1991, s. 90(1), it is an offence to remove any part of the bed of inland waters so as to cause it to be carried away in suspension. Section 90(2) provides for an offence of causing or permitting vegetation to be cut or uprooted so as to fall into inland waters, and then failing to take reasonable steps to remove it. In both cases the NRA may grant its consent subject to any conditions it considers appropriate. The offences are summary only, with a maximum fine of £2,500.

Under the Water Resources Act 1991, sch. 25, the NRA has powers to make by-laws in relation to the washing or cleaning of anything in controlled waters, or in relation to sanitary appliances on vessels. The maximum fine for an offence under these by-laws is £2,500.

Under the Salmon and Freshwater Fisheries Act 1975, s. 4(1), it is an offence to cause or knowingly permit any liquid or solid matter to flow or be put into waters containing fish so as to cause those waters to be poisonous or injurious to fish, their food or their spawning grounds. This offence is more limited than the Water Resoures Act 1991, s. 85; it requires proof of the presence of fish and injury to them. A prosecution cannot be brought except by the NRA or anyone who has obtained a certificate from the Minister of Agriculture, Fisheries and Food (or, in Wales, the Secretary of State) that they have a material interest in the waters affected. The maximum fine on summary conviction is also less than for s. 85 (£5,000 rather than £20,000) although the penalties for conviction on indictment are the same. The Water Consolidation (Consequential Provisions) Act 1991, sch. 1 provides that a consent under the 1991 Act is a defence to the offence under the 1975 Act.

Under EPA 1990, s. 140, the Secretary of State is given powers to make regulations to prohibit the importation, use, supply or storage of any substance or article for the purpose of preventing it causing pollution of the environment, or harm to the health of humans, animals or plants. This very wide power includes the power to order the disposal or treatment of restricted articles. It replaces the similar power under COPA 1974, s. 100. That section was used to make regulations banning the supply of lead weights for use by anglers (see Control of Pollution (Anglers' Lead Weights) Regulations 1986 (SI 1986 No. 1992)), prohibiting the supply and use of PCBs (see Control of Pollution (Supply and Use of Injurious Substances) Regulations 1986 (SI 1986 No. 902)), and prohibiting the supply of tri-organotin compound paints (see Control of Pollution (Anti-Fouling Paints and Treatments) Regulations 1987 (SI 1987 No. 783)). Interestingly, the regulations on anglers' lead weights have been amended as a result of the EC single internal market. The original regulations had banned the import of lead weights as well as their supply. The Control of Pollution (Anglers' Lead Weights) (Amendment) Regulations 1993 (SI 1993 No. 49) amended this so that only their supply is banned, since the Government considered, despite the clear implications of the *Danish Bottles* case (see p. 76), that the import ban could no longer be justified.

Statutory nuisances

In addition to the statutory nuisances listed in Part III of the EPA 1990 (see p. 192), two further statutory nuisances are provided for in the Public Health Act 1936, s. 259. Section 259(1)(a) provides that any pool, pond, ditch, gutter or watercourse which is in a state that is prejudicial to health or a nuisance is a statutory nuisance. This will cover small ponds and ditches which are not within the consent system, as well as controlled waters. Section 259(1)(b) covers any watercourse which is silted up or choked so as to obstruct the proper flow of water and thus causing a nuisance or which is prejudicial to health. This is limited to watercourses which are not normally navigated. The normal procedures for statutory nuisance apply to these situations, thus creating an alternative course of action for a local authority or individual wishing to clean up a grossly polluted watercourse.

Water pollution and the common law

The common law still plays a significant role in the control of water pollution. Indeed, for various technical reasons it is probably of greater use for water pollution than for other forms of pollution and may be used to produce, directly or indirectly, environmental improvements.

One right which has already been mentioned is the right of private prosecution for breaches of the criminal law. This has been available for many water pollution offences since 1985 as a result of the removal by COPA 1974 of the restrictions on it. More significant, however, are the various civil law claims that may be brought. For example, the Anglers' Cooperative Association is estimated to have been involved in over 1,000 cases involving water pollution since the Second World War. The two main remedies available are damages to compensate an owner of the river bed, the river banks, or a fishery for any losses caused, and an injunction to restrain future breaches of the law.

There are a number of reasons why water pollution cases have proved easier to bring than air pollution cases:

(a) Causation is easier to show because of the defined channels in which water normally flows.

(b) Many rural landowners have the money to bring an action: indeed, pollution to fisheries will often justify an action in commercial terms, as the claim by pop star Roger Daltrey for the loss of an estimated 500,000 fish from his fish farm, caused by the bursting of an upstream fertiliser storage tank, illustrates (*Beju Bop Ltd* v *Home Farm (Iwerne Minister) Ltd* [1990] *Water Law* 90). Damages of £500,000 were claimed, although the case was settled out of court for £150,000.

(c) There are a number of campaigning and amenity bodies concerned with water problems, far more than are concerned with air or noise pollution.

(d) The acquisition of evidence is more straightforward, particularly since the advent of the public registers, which may provide evidence relating to the quality of the receiving waters before and after an incident and also relating to discharges. Nevertheless, there will still be problems with an individual acquiring scientifically valid evidence (see Macrory, *Water Law,* Ch. 5:2).

Riparian rights
The usefulness of the civil law in this area stems mainly from the nature of riparian rights. Owners of land adjoining a watercourse (including estuaries), termed riparian owners, normally own the river bed, but not the water itself. However, as a natural incident of the soil itself, they have the right to receive the water in its natural state, subject only to reasonable usage by an upstream owner for ordinary purposes (*Chasemore* v *Richards* [1859] 7 HLC 349). Owners of other property rights such as fisheries have the same right.

The most authoritative statement of this principle was given by Lord Macnaghten in *Young & Co.* v *Bankier Distillery Co.* [1893] AC 698. He stated:

A riparian proprietor is entitled to have the water of the stream, on the bank of which his property lies, flow down as it has been accustomed to flow down to his property, subject to the ordinary use of the flowing water by upper proprietors, and to such further use, if any, on their part in connection with their property as may be reasonable in the circumstances. Every riparian owner is thus entitled to the water of his stream, in its natural flow, without sensible diminution or increase, and without sensible alteration in its character or quality.

This means that any interference with the natural quantity or quality of the water is an actionable nuisance. The strictness of this test was shown in *Young*

& Co. v *Bankier Distillery Co.* An upstream mineowner discharged water into a stream from a mine. This altered the chemistry of the water from soft to hard and thus altered the quality of the downstream distillery's whisky. The water had not been made impure, but the distillery obtained an injunction because the nature of the water had been changed. The case illustrates the relative nature of the definition of water pollution and indeed emphasises that the common law does not lay down any absolute standards in relation to water quality. It is worth noting, however, that this test only applies where the upstream usage is not ordinary; a good example of the balancing process the law of nuisance tries to carry out.

Some of the technical difficulties relating to the law of nuisance, such as the causation question and the locality doctrine, have been neatly answered in the water pollution cases. It appears from the reasoning in *Young & Co.* v *Bankier Distillery Co.* (above) that an invasion of the natural right to water is treated as equivalent to damage to land, thus circumventing the locality doctrine. It is also clear that actual harm need not be shown, merely a 'sensible alteration', a position that is supported by *Nicholls* v *Ely Sugar Factory Ltd* [1936] Ch 343, where the claim of interference with riparian rights was held to be analogous to trespass. It follows that an action can be brought against any upstream polluter, even if only one of many and responsible for only a part of the whole pollution. All that needs to be shown is that the polluter is contributing to the pollution (*Crossley* v *Lightowler* [1866] 11 Ch App Cas 478).

Pollution of groundwater

Liability will also arise in nuisance for polluting percolating groundwaters, as long as causation can be shown. This was first established in *Ballard* v *Tomlinson* [1885] 29 ChD 115, where a brewery sued successfully for the contamination of its well caused by a neighbour who used his own well for the disposal of sewage. However, the exact extent of this liability has recently been clarified by the House of Lords in *Cambridge Water Company Ltd* v *Eastern Counties Leather plc* [1994] 1 All ER 53. In this case, a water company claimed £1m damages for the pollution of one of its boreholes by spillages of organic solvents from a nearby leather tannery. These solvents had seeped into the aquifer over a number of years, resulting in water abstracted from the borehole failing the standards laid down in EC Directive 80/778 on Drinking Water by large margins. The Court of Appeal had followed *Ballard* v *Tomlinson* and decided that the tannery had interfered with a natural right incidental to the water company's ownership, that liability was strict, and that all the water company needed to do was to show causation, which it had done. This was hailed by some commentators as an acceptance of the central role of strict liability in water pollution law and a reflection of the 'polluter pays' principle. However, other observers, including those representing most potential polluters, argued that the Court of Appeal's decision raised the question of retrospective strict liability, since the spillages in issue had taken place many years previously. In this regard, the judge at first instance had decided that it was not foreseeable at the time the spillages took place that they might lead to the contamination of the public water supply.

The House of Lords allowed the appeal on the ground that, following Lord Reid's comments in *The Wagon Mound (No. 2)* [1967] 1 AC 617, the recovery of damages in private nuisance depends on foreseeability by the defendant of the type of damage that occurred. It also considered that the same foreseeability requirement applied to liability under the rule in *Rylands* v *Fletcher*. *Ballard* v *Tomlinson*, where this point did not arise, was distinguished.

This decision places significant restrictions on liability for *past* activities. However, it does not necessarily restrict the recovery of damages, or the imposition of an injunction, in cases where polluting activities *currently* cause damage to groundwaters or, indeed, where the cause of the pollution was recent. It must also be pointed out that liability in nuisance is personal in the sense that, even if the original polluter is liable for pollution damage, it does not follow that a subsequent purchaser of the site would also be liable. But, purchasers of potentially contaminated land must bear in mind the possible implications of cases such as *Goldman* v *Hargrave* [1967] 1 AC 645, which establish that there is liability for 'adopting' a nuisance in certain circumstances.

Other claims

Other common law claims may also be available. In *Jones* v *Llanrwst UDC* [1908] All ER 922, the owner of a river bed claimed successfully in trespass for deposits of solid wastes. In *Scott-Whitehead* v *National Coal Board* [1987] 53 P&CR 263, Southern Water Authority was held liable in negligence for the loss of a farmer's potato crop. The loss was caused by saline water abstracted in accordance with an abstraction licence granted by the Authority: the salinity in turn was caused by an upstream colliery discharge permitted by the Authority, which was not being diluted properly in the circumstances of the 1976 drought. The judge held the Authority liable for not warning the farmer of the potential damage to his crop if he used excessively saline water, although the exact reasoning behind this decision must now be reassessed in the light of the restriction on the liability of public authorities for negligence in the exercise of their duties in *Murphy* v *Brentwood DC* [1990] 2 All ER 908.

Lastly, it is often stated that a prescriptive right to acquire an easement to pollute can be acquired. Whilst this remains true as a matter of principle, such an occurrence will be rare owing to the fact that it is not possible to acquire a prescriptive right where the act relied upon to gain the right is illegal. In most water pollution cases the polluting activity will be illegal.

Remedies

Damages will be recoverable for any loss to the person whose rights have been infringed. This will include such things as any clean-up costs, the cost of restocking the water with fish, any loss of profits from subscriptions for such things as fishing rights and, in some circumstances, loss of amenity (see *Bruton and National Rivers Authority* v *Clarke* [1994] *Water Law* 145).

Injunctions are also available for water pollution, though they will normally be suspended to allow the defendants time to correct matters. For example, in *Pride of Derby Angling Assoc.* v *British Celanese Ltd* [1952] Ch 149, injunctions and damages were obtained against British Celanese Ltd (for industrial effluent), Derby Corporation (for untreated sewage), and the British Electricity Authority (for thermal pollution from a power station).

It is important to note that acting within the terms of a discharge consent does not act as a defence to a civil action, since the private law system operates separately from the public regulatory mechanisms. This is made explicit in the Water Resources Act 1991, s. 100(b), but it can also be implied from the important decision in *Wheeler* v *JJ Saunders Ltd* [1995] 2 All ER 697, which decided that a planning permission cannot license what is otherwise a nuisance.

FIFTEEN
Disposal of waste to sewers

In this book disposals of waste to the sewerage system are dealt with in a self-contained chapter because they are a separate form of waste disposal with their own particular and unique regulatory regime. The treatment of wastes at sewage works is an integral part of general policies on waste disposal and protection of the natural environment. The alternative to such disposal (waste minimisation apart) is often some form of direct discharge to the environment, so sewage treatment offers an important weapon in the search for the best practicable environmental option (BPEO).

There are other links with environmental protection that justify detailed consideration of sewage disposal. Sewage treatment is only an intermediate step in the ultimate disposal of waste and the operators of sewers and sewage works must dispose of their own wastes. This will often (though not always) be after a treatment process and will involve a combination of liquid discharges into watercourses or the sea, the dumping of sludge on land or at sea, and incineration. Indeed, sewage works have been responsible for the low quality of many of our inland and coastal waters (see *The Quality of Rivers, Canals and Estuaries in England and Wales*, NRA, 1991). The Government announced a commitment to phase out the dumping of sewage sludge at sea by 1998 at the Third International Conference for the Protection of the North Sea in March 1990.

Sewerage and sewage treatment have always been closely related with the water industry and most books have tended to treat discharges to sewers as a part of the law on water pollution. This can be explained on the grounds that discharges to sewers are liquid and that most sewage works themselves discharge into watercourses, but it also relates to the historical institutional connections. Sewerage, public water supply and the prevention of water pollution have often been carried out by the same bodies, most notably between 1974 and 1989 when the 10 regional water authorities in England and Wales carried out all functions in relation to water and sewage on an integrated basis. This included regulating discharges both to the sewers and to surface waters.

Since 1 September 1989 there has been a reversion to a system of split responsibilities. Private water and sewerage undertakers provide the public water supply and own and operate the sewerage network and the sewage works, as well as regulating discharges to sewers, whilst the National Rivers Authority regulates abstractions from and discharges to the natural environment and has responsibility for combating surface water pollution. Under the Environment Act 1995, all the NRA's responsibilities will be taken over by the Environment Agency.

Trade effluent discharges

The sewerage undertaker plays its most important environmental protection role in the regulation of trade effluent discharges, although since 1989 certain dangerous discharges have been regulated by HMIP (see below). Measured in terms of pollutant load, a far greater quantity of industrial effluent is discharged into the sewers than directly into surface waters or by any other disposal route.

The regulatory regime relating to discharges to sewers is an old and somewhat rudimentary one, though there have been periodic developments designed to bring it more up-to-date. It involves a rather basic system of individualised consents set by the operators of the sewers, involving little input from other bodies or from the public at any of the various stages of policy-making, standard-setting, consent-setting or enforcement. The legislation is contained in the Water Industry Act 1991, to which all section numbers refer.

It is a criminal offence to discharge any trade effluent from trade premises into sewers unless a trade effluent consent is obtained from the sewerage undertaker (s. 118). 'Trade effluent' and 'trade premises' are defined widely in s. 141 to include all liquid discharges from industry, shops, research establishments, launderettes and agriculture, except for domestic sewage. It is also an offence to breach the terms of a consent. This is a unique system of control in that it is the only example in this country of a private body exercising regulatory functions with regard to environmental protection.

Applying for a trade effluent consent

The discharger applies for a trade effluent consent by serving a trade effluent notice on the sewerage undertaker at least two months prior to the commencement of the discharge. This notice is effectively an application and must state the nature and composition of the proposed effluent, the maximum daily volume and the maximum rate of discharge in order to enable the sewerage undertaker to establish its likely effect.

The sewerage undertaker then has a discretion whether to grant or refuse consent, though if the sewerage system can cope with the discharge, it is normal for consent to be granted subject to conditions. The scope of these conditions is laid down in s. 121. They may include such matters as the place of discharge, the nature, temperature and composition of the discharge (including requirements as to the elimination or maximum concentration of any specified constituent), the rate and timing of discharges, and ancillary matters such as the fixing of meters to register the volume of the discharge, the monitoring of the nature and volume of the discharge and the keeping of records. Most importantly, conditions on the payment of effluent charges will also be included.

It is not permissible to attach conditions which require the fitting of specified treatment plant. The normal practice is to specify the effluent standards that must be met and to leave it to the discharger to determine how to meet those standards, albeit often with advice from the sewerage undertaker. One reason for this is the widespread belief that most effluent is better and more efficiently treated at the sewage works than at each factory, but it also reflects the policy of preserving some element of choice for producers.

How are consents set?

Since discharges to sewers are distinct from other discharges in being to an artificial environment, the matters that are taken into account in setting a consent differ from other consents and licences. In particular, environmental protection is only one factor.

The objectives of trade effluent control are set out clearly in a booklet produced by the Water Authorities Association in September 1986 entitled *Trade Effluent Discharged to the Sewer*. They are that the system of control seeks:

(a)   to protect the sewerage system and the personnel who work in it;

(b)   to protect the sewage works and their efficient operation (for example, most sewage works operate by a biological process and care has to be taken not to neutralise that process);

(c)   to protect the environment generally from the residues of the sewage treatment process or from direct discharges from parts of the system such as storm drains; and

(d)   to ensure that dischargers pay a reasonable charge for the cost of the treatment.

In addition, the booklet stresses that it is important for correct information on discharges to be kept, so that dischargers can know how to improve their trade effluent control and sewerage undertakers can plan for future sewerage provision and operate the treatment process efficiently.

With these factors in mind, the consent will in general be set by reference to the receiving capabilities of the sewer and sewage works. If the works are already overburdened, the consent may be refused or subject to tight limits, whereas if there is spare capacity at the works, the limits will be much more generous. Certain pollutants, such as heavy metals or persistent chemicals, may be unsuitable for sewage treatment and may be banned from the discharge. The discharger may then have to pre-treat the effluent to remove these constituents, or find an alternative method of disposal. Other relevant matters are taken into account, such as the sewerage undertaker's own potential liability for discharges from the works under the Water Resources Act 1991 and the requirements of EC law.

The sewerage undertaker has a power to vary a consent unilaterally by giving two months' notice to the discharger (s. 124). This enables it to take steps to meet the terms of the consent for the sewage works set by the NRA. Since 1989, variation has been a common occurrence, as sewerage undertakers have renegotiated consents inherited from the regional water authorities and established a more uniform system for their areas and also as the NRA has tightened consents relating to discharges from sewage works. It should be noted, however, that there is no power for the sewerage undertaker to revoke a consent.

Variation of a consent is, however, possible only after two years have elapsed from the grant of the consent or the last variation. Exceptionally, a variation may be made within this period if it is necessary to provide proper protection for people likely to be affected by the discharge. In this situation, compensation will be payable to the discharger unless the variation was necessary as a result of a change of circumstances unforeseeable at the time of the grant of the consent or its last variation (s. 125).

The discharger has a right of appeal to the Director General of Water Services (i.e. to OFWAT) against a refusal or variation of consent or the imposition of conditions, except that there is no appeal against trade effluent charges (ss. 122, 126). An appeal against a deemed refusal may also be brought if no decision is given on the trade effluent notice within two months. (It used to be the case that such a failure to determine an application led to an automatic consent, but that rule was removed by the Water Act 1989.) As with planning appeals, an appeal is effectively a rehearing and the Director General may make any decision that the sewerage undertaker could have made. There is a further right of appeal to the High Court on a matter of law.

An alternative to seeking a consent is for the discharger and the sewerage undertaker to reach an agreement for the reception or disposal of trade effluent under s. 129. Such an agreement may provide for the discharger to pay for works necessary to treat the wastes, such as an extension to a sewage works.

Trade effluent charges

Trade effluent charges are levied for discharges to sewers and a charges scheme may be made under the Water Industry Act 1991, s. 143. All the sewerage undertakers currently use a similar formula based on the so-called 'Mogden Formula', in which charges are calculated according to the volume and strength of the effluent, as measured by the chemical oxygen demand (COD) and the solids content. Dischargers are therefore advised to consider whether their processes can be changed so as to minimise wastes, and thus costs. No extra charges are currently levied by the sewerage undertakers in relation to metals or other hazardous items: undesirable levels of these are controlled by the consent limits rather than by charging mechanisms. However, levels of charges are rising as a consequence of the fact that sewerage undertakers are themselves liable for charges for their own discharges from sewage works. The charging system thus operates in tandem with the consent system to reduce discharges. To a limited extent it encourages the reduction of pollution, although it does not make dischargers fully responsible for the environmental costs of their discharges. It remains to be seen whether a system of incentive charging will be introduced in this area: that would require legislation.

Public participation

Public rights in relation to the trade effluent system are very limited. There is no right for a member of the public to be informed of an application for a trade effluent consent and no right to participate in the decision whether to grant one, or in any appeal. Under the Water Industry Act 1991, s. 196, all consents, variations, agreements and directions by the sewerage undertaker or the Director General, and all decisions by the Secretary of State (effectively HMIP in this context) must be placed on a public register.

However, this is a limited right, since there is no public right to information on any samples taken. Indeed, it is a criminal offence under s. 206 for an employee of the sewerage undertaker to disclose information furnished under the Act. There is also no right of private prosecution for breach of a consent, except by a 'person aggrieved' or with the consent of the Attorney-General. It remains to be seen whether the Environmental Information Regulations 1992 (SI 1992 No. 3240) will confer wider rights (see p. 161).

'Red List' substances

In order to ensure compliance with EC Directives, such as 76/464 on Dangerous Substances in Water, an additional control has been introduced for specified dangerous substances. The Secretary of State is empowered to prescribe certain substances or processes for which HMIP is effectively made the consenting body (the Environment Agency will take over the function when it comes into existence). Currently 24 such substances are listed in sch. 1 to the Trade Effluents (Prescribed Processes and Substances) Regulations 1989 (SI 1989 No. 1156, as amended by SI 1990 No. 1629), and five processes involving asbestos or chloroform are listed in sch. 2. The 24 prescribed substances consist of the 'Red List' (see p. 297), plus carbon tetrachloride.

All discharges where any of these substances is present in more than background concentration, or where a prescribed process is carried on, must be referred to HMIP, which may then issue a direction (against which there is no appeal) to the sewerage undertaker on whether to grant a consent and on any conditions it might impose. Before deciding an application, HMIP must provide the sewerage undertaker and the applicant with an opportunity to make representations. The same procedures apply where more than 30 kg per year of trichloroethylene or perchloroethylene is discharged (Trade

Effluent (Prescribed Processes and Substances) Regulations (SI 1992 No. 339)).

Existing discharges covered by the regulations are also reviewable by HMIP. As with ordinary trade effluent discharges, a review may not normally be made within two years of the previous review. However, review is possible within two years if there has been a contravention of a consent or agreement, to give effect to an international or EC obligation, or to protect public health or aquatic flora and fauna. Compensation is payable in some of these circumstances, unless the review resulted from a change of circumstances unforeseeable at the time of the setting of the consent or the previous review.

This system is affected by the introduction of integrated pollution control in the EPA 1990. Any process discharging significant amounts of 'Red List' substances will normally be a prescribed process for the purposes of integrated pollution control and therefore will require an authorisation from HMIP (when the relevant process is brought under control). In these circumstances a trade effluent consent will be required as well as an authorisation.

Enforcement

The penalty for the offence of discharging without consent, or in breach of a condition, is, on summary conviction, a fine not exceeding £5,000, and on conviction on indictment, an unlimited fine (ss. 118, 121).

Enforcement of the legislation is by the sewerage undertaker. In the past this has led to a conciliatory approach to enforcement, since officials have seen themselves as problem-solvers rather than as police officers. Indeed, one of the main surveys of enforcement attitudes (Richardson, Ogus and Burrows, *Policing Pollution,* 1983) was a survey of trade effluent control officers. This approach has, in the past, been reinforced by the requirement for a 'legal sample' to be taken in order for it to be admissible as evidence in court (s. 171), but this limitation is being removed by the Environment Act 1995, s. 111. (For the meaning of 'legal sample', see p. 447.)

Discharges from sewage works

Under the Water Resources Act 1991, sewerage undertakers have consents set for their own discharges into controlled waters and may be prosecuted by the NRA or any individual if they breach them. They are responsible for all discharges from their sewers or works, subject only to a defence that the breach was caused by an illegal discharge to the sewer that they could not reasonably have been expected to prevent (Water Resources Act 1991, s. 87(2) and *National Rivers Authority* v *Yorkshire Water Services Ltd* [1995] 1 All ER 225). This means that sewerage undertakers are ultimately responsible if they are unable to treat adequately discharges they have permitted. They thus have an incentive to restrict discharges to those which are treatable.

Domestic sewage discharges

Some discharges are prohibited entirely by the Water Industry Act 1991, s. 111 (although a trade effluent consent is a defence). These are discharges of anything liable to damage the sewer, or to stop its flow, or to prejudice the sewage works treatment; any chemicals, or any liquids over 110°F, which will be dangerous or a nuisance; and any petroleum spirit, including motor oils. For example, drainage of used car oils is an offence under this section. The maximum penalties are, on summary conviction, a fine of up to £5,000, and, on conviction on indictment, an unlimited fine and/or up to two years imprisonment.

Otherwise, there is no restriction on discharges of domestic sewage. There is a right of connection to the public sewer conferred on owners and occupiers by the Water Industry Act 1991, s. 106, with very limited powers of refusal. These do not include the potential overloading of the system: as Upjohn J stated in *Smeaton* v *Ilford Corporation* [1954] 1 Ch 450, 'they [i.e. the sewerage undertakers] are bound to permit occupiers of premises to make connections to the sewer and to discharge their sewage therein'. Powers to requisition new sewers for domestic purposes are set out in the Water Industry Act 1991, s. 98.

However, it is permissible for the local planning authority to refuse planning permission on the ground that the local sewage works are overburdened or inadequate, since that is a material consideration. Alternatively, it could seek some planning gain in relation to the provision of sewers by the use of conditions or planning obligations under the Town and Country Planning Act 1990 (see Chapter 9 for the limitations on this course of action).

SIXTEEN
The conservation of nature

This chapter looks at the laws which set out specifically to protect plants, animals and habitat. This has become a popular subject in recent years, partly as a result of the dramatic growth of interest in all things connected with nature and conservation, but also as a consequence of the appalling rate of decline in and loss of the natural environment. The Wildlife and Countryside Act 1981, the major piece of legislation in this area, reflects this popularity: it still holds the record for the number of amendments tabled to a Parliamentary Bill and its controversial passage brought nature conservation firmly into the arena of political debate, where it has stayed.

At the outset, a distinction must be made between nature conservation and matters of amenity and landscape, which are dealt with in Chapter 17. Even though these topics are often closely related, it is possible to distinguish between those laws which are justified as a matter of straight wildlife protection and those which relate more to human uses of the environment. It must also be borne in mind that the preservation of a balanced ecosystem and the survival of many species depends as much on the responses to the other environmental threats covered in this book, such as pollution and development, as on the specific methods of protection mentioned in this chapter, which would probably be useless if applied in isolation.

History

A brief history of nature conservation will help to explain the current structure of the law. Up to less than 200 years ago, the need to protect wildlife was normally perceived solely in human terms, such as the desirability of preserving game and quarry species and protected areas in which to hunt them. There is little doubt that an incidental benefit of this human-centred approach was the protection of other animals and plants and the preservation of whole areas (for example the New Forest) in a fairly natural state, but there were few laws designed specifically to protect wildlife.

From Victorian times, the tendency was to enact legislation outlawing unwelcome activities in response to particular problems as they were identified. The rationale for this intervention was as much based on concern about cruelty as on any positive desire to conserve nature for its own sake. Some good examples are the Sea Birds Protection Acts of 1869, 1872 and 1880, passed to combat the slaughter of birds at places such as Flamborough Head, and various pieces of legislation intended to restrict the international trade in feathers for clothing and hats. However, there was no grand design underlying these restrictions. The weight of conservation fell on voluntary organisations—indeed Britain had the world's first developed conservation movement—and no official bodies were established to monitor or enforce the legislation that did exist. This unplanned approach persisted; the Protection of Birds Act 1954, which established protection for birds that was far stronger than that for other animals and plants, was a Private Member's Bill brought forward on behalf of the Royal Society for the Protection of Birds.

These voluntary organisations gradually developed a strategy which became, and remains, the typical approach to nature conservation. This is the designation of selected areas or sites that are specially protected. The first modern uses of this technique related to the protection of common lands for recreational purposes, but it was soon used for the development of nature reserves, even though at this time they were seen as a somewhat peripheral interest of the nature conservation movement. For example, the National Trust acquired parts of Wicken Fen in 1899, the Norfolk Naturalists Trust was founded to buy Cley Marshes in 1926 and the Royal Society for the Protection of Birds bought its first nature reserve (on Romney Marsh) in 1929. However, in the absence of any legislative protection for such sites, their safety lay in the exercise of ordinary property rights. After all, the property owner's freedom to exclude others and to use the land for any purposes is one mechanism for controlling land use in limited areas. The limitations of this approach are well illustrated by the RSPB's first reserve, which had to be abandoned when drainage activities on neighbouring land destroyed its natural interest.

The post-war period

In the immediate post-war period, the site designation approach was adopted as a matter of national policy. The beginning of the modern age of nature conservation can be traced to that time in the publication of two influential reports, *Conservation of Nature in England and Wales* from the Wildlife Conservation Special Committee (the Huxley Committee, Cmd 7122) and *Nature Reserves in Scotland* from the Scottish Wild Life Conservation Committee (the Ritchie Committee, Cmd 7184), many (though not all) of whose recommendations were accepted and acted upon.

A specialist national nature conservation body—the Nature Conservancy—was established and one of its main roles was to create a series of protected sites across the nation, rather than the somewhat random series produced by private acquisition. The two main habitat protection measures, the national nature reserve (NNR) and the site of special scientific interest (SSSI), both date from this period. The scientific basis of nature conservation was emphasised and it was linked firmly to education and research on the natural environment. Nature conservation was also split from amenity, recreation and landscape matters, which were given their own separate institutions and laws, and it is worth reflecting that the powers for nature conservation at that time were both stronger and met with far less opposition than those for recreation in the countryside.

Current policy

Many of the features of this post-war structure remain, but the climate in which they operate has changed radically, with the result that many of the similarities the current system has with that structure are illusory. There have been devastating changes in both the urban and rural environments and these have altered the role of site designation dramatically from an educational to a safeguarding one. One result has been the expansion of the NNR and SSSI system way beyond that envisaged, or indeed considered necessary, by the Huxley and Ritchie Committees, in order to ensure that at least a basic pool of key sites is protected.

Another result is that general environmental awareness has now shifted the focus of policy away from the designation and protection of certain key sites towards the protection of the wider countryside. It is now accepted that there is little future in having isolated and ever-decreasing areas of protected wildlife in an otherwise barren countryside, and so nature conservation is increasingly seen as a factor to weigh in the balance when considering all rural policies. This adds to the political dimension which nature conservation has rapidly acquired. It also leads nature conservation law into a potential head-on collision with traditional views of property and personal rights.

In addition, the enjoyment of nature has emerged as a major leisure pursuit, blurring the distinction in the public mind and in policy between nature conservation as a scientifically justified discipline and as a recreation. There has been an undreamt-of increase in voluntary activity in relation to the countryside, resulting in large numbers of reserves and sites protected by voluntary bodies and non-statutory designations. There has also been an increase in international activity on the natural environment, mainly through conventions such as the Washington Convention on International Trade in Endangered Species (usually known as CITES), and the pressure on the Government to carry out internationally agreed policies is immense. Nowhere is it greater than in relation to the EC, which has important Directives on Wild Birds and on Habitats. The Wild Birds Directive (79/409) required changes in British law and led to the Wildlife and Countryside Act 1981, effectively the first major Government sponsored measure on nature conservation and one that revealed some severe differences in philosophy between the political parties, whilst the Habitats Directive (92/43) has led to a significant increase in protection for certain internationally important sites.

Types of legal protection

From this brief historical survey it can be seen that the protections offered by the law can be divided into four rough categories:

(a) protecting individual animals and plants;
(b) habitat protection through the designation of key sites;
(c) the use of grants and incentives; and
(d) incidental protection.

(a) Protecting individual animals and plants

This is still done on a somewhat ad hoc basis, though a degree of coherence is provided by the Wildlife and Countryside Act 1981. Nature conservation is not the only aim being pursued: there is still a large element of protection against cruelty, and there are important exceptions relating to game and quarry species.

(b) Habitat protection through the designation of key sites

This has been a favoured technique, and a bewildering array of legislative designations has built up, the special rules and protections differing for each one. There is quite a degree of overlap here and many designations are cumulative. In *Nature Conservation in Great Britain* (1984), the Nature Conservancy Council set out its policy that 10% of the country be covered by one designation or another, so that a bedrock of essential sites may be protected.

(c) The use of grants and incentives in the wider countryside

The realisation that the protection of isolated sites is insufficient, both in scientific terms and in terms of the expectations of people who are interested in nature, has led to the search for general policies conducive to nature conservation, especially as part of agriculture and forestry policy. This is all part of the general trend towards integrating environmental considerations into all aspects of policy.

(d) Incidental protection

It remains clear that nature conservation interests are often served by taking advantage of legal powers which were not designed with nature conservation in mind. The best example is the purchase of private nature reserves by voluntary bodies, thus taking advantage of ordinary property rights, but another good example is the nature conservation value of the large tracts of land used for Ministry of Defence training grounds.

The nature conservation agencies

In 1949, on the basis of recommendations contained in the Huxley and Ritchie Reports, the Nature Conservancy was established by Royal Charter. This was a scientifically-orientated national body with responsibility through-out Great Britain for nature conservation matters ranging from education and research to the designation and management of national nature reserves. Under the Nature Conservancy Council Act 1973, this body became the Nature Conservancy Council (NCC), an autonomous body independent of government departments, but whose Council members were appointed by the Secretaries of State. However, the new NCC was split from its active research ecology arm (this is now the Institute of Terrestrial Ecology), a separation which resulted in a greater concentration on its remaining roles of advice and site protection. When coupled with the increasingly political flavour of nature conservation in the 1970s and 1980s, this turned the NCC into what could almost be described as a pressure group within Government.

Under the EPA 1990, from 1 April 1991 the NCC (and hence responsibilty for nature conservation) was split into three national bodies; an NCC for England (called English Nature); a Countryside Council for Wales, combining the functions of the NCC and the Countryside Commission in the principality (i.e. combining nature conservation with amenity and recreational matters); and an NCC for Scotland. In the case of Scotland, the position was further changed by the Natural Heritage (Scotland) Act 1991. This Act established a new body called Scottish Natural Heritage, effectively through a merger of the NCC for Scotland with the Countryside Commission for Scotland. In the EPA, the three national bodies—English Nature, the Countryside Council for Wales and Scottish Natural Heritage—inherited most of the responsibilities of the NCC within the appropriate geographical area and thus have very similar powers and duties relating to nature conservation to each other. For ease of explanation, the name 'NCC' is retained throughout this book to refer to the relevant national body in its own area.

Each of the three national bodies is established on a similar basis to the old NCC (see EPA 1990, sch. 6). They receive annual grant in aid from the Treasury and have to submit annual reports and accounts to Parliament. Council members are appointed by the appropriate Secretary of State. They are the Government's statutory advisers on nature conservation issues, with specific responsibilities for advising on species and habitat protection, the dissemination of knowledge about nature conservation, the support and conduct of research into nature conservation, and the safeguarding of protected sites (see EPA 1990, s. 132). In particular, they are responsible for the selection and management of NNRs and for the designation and oversight of SSSIs. They are also statutory consultees in relation to a large number of decisions made by other public bodies, including decisions on applications for planning permission and for pollution consents. In one sense, therefore, the three bodies are classic quangos and could be said to be largely unaccountable for many of their decisions: but they could also be said to be accountable to the interests of wildlife and ecology.

The dismantling of the NCC was undoubtedly the most controversial part of the EPA 1990. The Conservative Government sought to justify it on the ground of administrative efficiency, but the result has been to add to the adminstrative complexity (and thus to the administrative cost) of nature conservation activities. A further justification was that power was devolved to Scotland and Wales and away from a GB body based in Peterborough. Whilst there was a significant degree of support for such devolution, particularly in Scotland, this explanation scarcely fits in with the Government's general record on devolution of powers. The clear impression that is left is that the main motivation behind the splitting up of the NCC was the political desirability of reducing the NCC's power in Scotland, where it had been active in opposing such things as afforestation of the unique flow country of Caithness and Sutherland.

Critics of the dismantling of the NCC point to the irrationality of dividing responsibility for nature conservation along national borders, when ecological criteria demand that a wider approach is adopted. They also stress the fact that three smaller bodies are inevitably weaker than one large one. In addition, there is a significant possibility that uniformity in the implementation of the law will be lost. This follows inexorably from the wide discretions in the legislation and the fact that in Scotland and Wales in particular there is a greater willingness to accept that economic factors outweigh nature conservation considerations. As the last Chairman of the NCC, Sir William Wilkinson, put it when presenting the NCC's 16th Annual Report, 'As a result of the Government's attitude, nature conservation has been set back three, or possibly up to five, years'.

The controversy over the splitting up of the NCC led to the establishment in the EPA 1990 of a further GB-wide body. There was initial opposition to such an idea from the Government, but during the debates on the Bill a separate Joint Nature Conservation Committee emerged. The final form of this body is provided for in sch. 7. It has few executive functions, but carries out important roles in relation to the international responsibilities of the old NCC (e.g. under the Ramsar Convention and other international agreements), matters affecting Great Britain as a whole, and the retention of common standards throughout Great Britain (for example, common criteria for the designation of SSSIs). Since it is really a committee of the three national bodies, the Joint Nature Conservation Committee relies on them for its funding, staffing and other resources. It consists of an independent chair and three other independent people appointed by the Secretary of State, together with two representatives from each of the three national bodies and the chair of the English Countryside Commission. Two non-voting members are appointed by the Department of the Environment for Northern Ireland.

The protection of individual animals and plants

The common law is generally unsympathetic to wild creatures, according them no rights of their own. However, property rights may usefully be exercised in order to protect them. Wild animals are subject to the qualified ownership of the landowner whose land they are on, whilst wild plants are part of the land itself. As a result, wild animals and plants have no common law protection against the landowner. But anyone else who kills or injures a wild animal or picks a wild plant commits the torts of trespass and interference with property. Whilst the normal remedy would be damages for the value of the item taken (and thus is of little practical use), it would be possible to seek an injunction to restrain continued breaches. An owner of a nature reserve could in theory use these property rights to protect against threats to the wildlife on it. In addition, a person who uproots plants may commit the crimes of theft and criminal damage, though there is an exception in the Theft Act 1968, s. 4(3) for picking flowers, fruit, foliage and fungi.

As a consequence of the limitations of the common law, the main protection for wild creatures is statutory. The Wildlife and Countryside Act 1981, Part I, contains the bulk of the law in this area, although the Conservation (Natural Habitats etc.) Regulations 1994 (SI 1994 No. 2716) have made some changes to ensure compliance with the Habitats Directive 92/43. Two more specific conservation Acts are the Conservation of Seals Act 1970 and the Protection of Badgers Act 1992. There are numerous pieces of legislation relating to hunted species, such as deer, game birds, wildfowl, rabbits and of course fish, though in all these Acts protection of individual animals is incidental. Reference to specialist books is recommended.

The chosen method of control is to establish blanket criminal offences of interfering with specified wildlife, together with a long list of exceptions and defences for acceptable activities, many of which require permission or a licence from an official body. The strongest provisions relate to wild birds (a legacy of the historical influence of the voluntary bodies here, but also a result of the EC Directive on Wild Birds 79/409, which requires certain legislative protections) in the sense that they are reverse listed—i.e. the Act applies unless they are exempted in the Schedules covering pest and quarry species. Animals and plants are covered only if specifically listed in other Schedules. As with all Schedules under the Act, the Secretary of State has powers to vary them by order to include or exclude species (s. 22), and this power has been exercised fairly frequently to take account of changes in the conservation status of the species concerned. The Joint Nature Conservation Committee has a specific duty to carry out a quinquennial review of schs. 5 and 8, which deal with protected animals and plants respectively, although its advice is not binding on the Secretary of State.

Wild birds

It is an offence intentionally to kill, injure or take any wild bird and this is backed up by offences of intentionally taking, damaging or destroying a nest whilst it is in use or being built and intentionally taking or destroying eggs (s. 1(1)). It is also an offence to be in possession of a wild bird or egg, live or dead (s. 1(2)). There are further offences relating to illegal methods of killing or taking wild birds (s. 5) and the sale or advertising for sale of wild birds (s. 6). For these purposes a bird is presumed to be wild unless proved otherwise.

Birds are divided into two categories. Rarer birds are listed in sch. 1 and are specially protected. This means that the maximum penalty for committing any of these offences is increased from the normal £1,000 to £5,000 (s. 1(4)). In addition, intentionally disturbing a Schedule 1 bird on or near its nest, or disturbing its dependent young, is an offence (s. 1(5)).

Areas may be designated as bird sanctuaries by the Secretary of State, but only with the consent or acquiescence of the owners and occupiers. By-laws may be made for bird sanctuaries which create extra offences, including unauthorised access to the site (s. 3).

There are a number of exceptions and defences to these various offences. Game birds (i.e. pheasant, partridge, grouse and ptarmigan) are excluded from the protection provided by the Act, apart from that relating to illegal methods of killing or taking them (s. 27). Wildfowl listed in sch. 2, Part I may be killed or taken outside the close season (s. 2(1)). (The close season can be varied by the Secretary of State and there is also a power to provide for special protection periods in the event of bad weather in the open season.) Pest species listed in sch. 2, Part II may be killed or taken and their nests or eggs destroyed, but only by the owner or occupier of the land or any other authorised person (s. 2(2)).

Under s. 4, there are defences relating to the killing of injured birds and where the action is an 'incidental result of a lawful operation and could not reasonably have been avoided', or where it is necessary for crop protection, disease prevention or the protection of public health and safety. None of these defences requires permission, though the last three are only available to owners and occupiers and other authorised persons.

Section 16 also includes a long list of further exceptions which apply if a licence has been obtained from the appropriate official authority. It includes such things as the carrying out of research, educational activities, ringing of birds, falconry and keeping bird or egg collections.

Animals

Only the animals listed in sch. 5 are protected by the legislation. This includes all bats, reptiles and amphibians, but only the rarest mammals, fish, butterflies and other forms of life.

For those animals which are protected, there is a range of offences similar to those for wild birds. It is an offence intentionally to kill, injure or take any scheduled wild animal (s. 9(1)), or to have in one's possession any such animal, live or dead, or any part of one (s. 9(2)). Additional offences relate to the sale or advertisement for sale of wild animals (s. 9(5)), illegal methods of killing or taking any wild animal (s. 11(1)), and illegal methods of killing or taking those animals listed in sch. 6 (s. 11(2)). There is also an offence of intentionally damaging, destroying or obstructing any structure or place used for shelter or protection by a sch. 5 animal, or disturbing such an animal whilst it is occupying such a structure (s. 9(4)). This provision is of greatest significance for the protection of bats roosting in such typical places as attics, outbuildings, caves and belfries, since they cannot be disturbed by, for example, rebuilding or timber treatment unless the NCC is notified in advance. For all these offences the maximum penalty is £5,000. In ss. 10 and 16 there are similar provisions relating to defences and licences to those available for wild birds.

In addition, the Conservation (Natural Habitats etc.) Regulations 1994 (SI 1994 No. 2716) create some further offences in relation to the animals defined as 'European protected species', which are listed in sch. 2 to the Regulations (this is a short list which includes all native bats, the dormouse, the great crested newt, the otter, the large blue butterfly and a few other species). In order to ensure compliance with the Habitats Directive 92/43, the

Government has chosen to set out the requirements of the Directive in full, rather than seek to amend the existing legislation. The result is that the Regulations cover similar ground to the 1981 Act, but with some occasional subtle changes in wording to make the offences wider: for example, it is an offence under reg. 39 deliberately to disturb an animal of a European protected species or deliberately to take or destroy the eggs of such an animal.

Badgers

Badgers are given special protection under their own legislation. This has been developed over many years and is now consolidated in the Protection of Badgers Act 1992. The general scheme is similar to that for animals protected under the Wildlife and Countryside Act 1981, sch. 5, but there are some unique features to the provisions. It is an offence to do any of the following: wilfully kill, injure or take a badger, or attempt any of those things (s. 1(1)); possess a dead badger (s. 1(3)); cruelly ill-treat a badger, use badger tongs, or dig for a badger (s. 2); sell or have possession of a live badger (s. 4); mark or attach a marking device to a badger, except under licence (s. 5). In recognition of the evidential problems thrown up in prosecutions for the barbaric activity of badger baiting, in relation to the attempt offences under s. 1(1) and the offence of digging for a badger, the burden of proof is effectively reversed. Once there is reasonable evidence of the offence it is up to the defendant to prove that no offence has been committed. For all these offences there is a defence if a licence is obtained from the appropriate authority (s. 10).

There is a further, very important, offence of interference with a badger sett that shows signs of current use (s. 3). This covers such things as damaging the sett, destroying it, obstructing access to it, causing a dog to enter it, or disturbing a badger that is in occupation. The provisions are unusually strong in that, even where there is a valid planning permission, a separate licence will be required under s. 10 if the carrying out of the permission would involve damage or disturbance to a sett. This has led to a situation where the existence of a badger sett is a very significant factor if development is envisaged. There is a general defence if the action was the incidental result of a lawful operation and could not reasonably have been avoided, and a more specific defence in relation to temporary interference in the course of fox-hunting (s. 8).

The maximum fine for all the offences under the 1992 Act is £5,000 per badger affected, and in relation to most of the offences a prison term of up to six months may also be imposed. If a dog is used in connection with the offence, the court may order its destruction or disposal.

Plants

Section 13 makes it an offence for anyone other than the owner, occupier or other authorised person intentionally to uproot any wild plant. In addition, it is an offence for anyone intentionally to pick, uproot or destroy any of the numerous species of rare wild plants listed in sch. 8. The sale or advertisement for sale of sch. 8 plants is also an offence. Once again, there are similar provisions relating to defences and licences to those available for wild birds.

In addition, the Conservation (Natural Habitats etc.) Regulations 1994 (SI 1994 No. 2716) create some further offences in relation to the small number of European protected species of plants which are listed in sch. 4. As with the offences concerning European protected species of animals, in order to ensure compliance with the Habitats Directive 92/43, the offences are similar to, but slightly wider than, those in the 1981 Act: for example, it is an offence deliberately to collect or cut a wild plant of a European protected species.

Introducing foreign animals or plants to Great Britain

A final section of the 1981 Act worth mentioning is s. 14, which makes it an offence to introduce into the wild any animal not normally resident in Great Britain or any wild animal or plant listed in sch. 9. This section aims to protect against further repetitions of the ecological havoc wrought by alien introductions such as grey squirrel, coypu and giant hogweed.

Habitat protection

Although there is a rapidly growing number of protective designations for areas of habitat, the main domestic ones remain the interrelated categories of NNR and SSSI. The increasingly important international designations are discussed later in this chapter. Both NNRs and SSSIs were originally introduced in the National Parks and Access to the Countryside Act 1949 on the recommendation of the Huxley and Ritchie Committees. The NNR powers remain essentially those enacted in 1949, but the SSSI provisions have been significantly altered and strengthened by the Wildlife and Countryside Act 1981, Part II. This reflects the changing role of SSSIs in the light of the enormous environmental changes since 1949.

Two preliminary points need to be made about the 1981 Act, the passage of which would justify a book by itself. First, the whole structure of Part II rests on the policy of voluntariness favoured by the Conservative Government. This is the view that compulsory controls should only be used as a last resort, because they will only serve to antagonise landowners, who are seen as having the main responsibility for site protection. Pursuant to this policy, the favoured mechanism of control is the management agreement: the NCC is to seek to enter into agreements with landowners to protect the site, with compensation being paid for losses incurred by owners (see p. 486). In order to achieve this, many of the legal requirements focus on a duty to notify the NCC of threats to sites.

Secondly, Part II was significantly altered during its passage through Parliament. Originally the Government intended to confer statutory protection only on the limited number of sites to be accorded nature conservation order status, leaving the majority of SSSIs protected by the narrow existing limitations on development in the planning system. Many saw this as wholly inadequate, particularly when the NCC released statistics showing that between 10 and 15% of SSSIs had suffered significant damage or loss in 1980 alone, the majority of the damage being caused by agriculture rather than urban-type developments. Statutory powers relating to *all* SSSIs were hurriedly introduced. One effect is that the provisions on SSSIs (and the confusingly similar nature conservation orders) are not well drafted and many detailed matters remain particularly unclear, although there have subsequently been drafting amendments in the Wildlife and Countryside (Amendment) Act 1985, the Wildlife and Countryside (Service of Notices) Act 1985 and the EPA 1990.

The difference between NNRs and SSSIs can best be explained by saying that NNRs are actively controlled and managed by the NCC, whereas in SSSIs the occupier of the land retains control subject to a number of restrictions on use decided by the NCC. In one sense, therefore, the NNRs are the top tier of sites which merit extra controls and the expenditure of money on positive management. However, since they are all notified as SSSIs and benefit from the restrictions on them, it is clearer if the protections available to SSSIs are explained first.

Sites of special scientific interest (SSSIs)

It is important to understand the function of SSSIs. In an explanatory paper, *The Selection of Sites of Special Scientific Interest,* it is explained that they are a representative sample of British habitats, with each site seen as 'an integral part of a national series' established with the aim of 'maintaining the present diversity of wild animals and plants in Great Britain'. It is emphasised that selection is on scientific grounds rather than to enhance amenity or provide recreation. For biological sites, the best examples of various habitat types (including natural, semi-natural and man-made landscapes) are chosen, determined on the basis of 'naturalness, diversity, typicalness and size', along with sites catering for rare habitats and species. A geographical spread is ensured by selecting typical sites within sub-regional areas (see, in general, *Guidelines for Selection of Biological SSSIs.* NCC, 1989). Geological SSSIs are treated differently, the intention being to 'conserve those localities essential to the continued conduct of research and education in the earth sciences'. again in the context of a national representative series (see *Geological Conservation Review,* NCC).

By the end of March 1992, throughout Great Britain there were 5,801 SSSIs notified under the 1981 Act (3,621 in England, 841 in Wales, and 1,339 in Scotland). Together they covered 1,777,619 hectares, which is over 7% of the land area, though the proportion is far higher in some regions. The size of individual SSSIs ranges from over 10,000 hectares for some upland moorland sites, to less than one hectare. Also included are a number of linear sites, such as rivers.

The NCC is given a wide discretion both to formulate reasonable criteria for notification and to carry out the task of individual selection. The 1981 Act, s. 28(1), states:

Where the Nature Conservancy Council are of the opinion that any area of land is of special interest by reason of any of its flora, fauna, or geological

or physiographical features, it shall be the duty of the Council to notify that
fact —

(a) to the local planning authority in whose area the land is situated;
(b) to every owner and occupier of any of that land; and
(c) to the Secretary of State.

One effect of this definition is that the list is not unchanging. New SSSIs will
be notified as new information about sites is acquired, and as the importance
of safeguarding certain habitats increases. It must also be understood that, in
an age when sites are being damaged and destroyed, one site may become of
greater importance simply because of the loss of another site. The NCC will,
in practice, denotify a site which loses its scientific interest, although it is
unclear whether there is any legislative sanction for such a step.

Section 28(1) states that it is the 'duty' of the NCC to notify the people
and bodies listed. This is a very rare example, as far as environmental
legislation is concerned, of a duty rather than a discretionary power being
referred to. It is especially remarkable given the largely unaccountable nature
of the notifying agencies. It has now been discussed in *R v Nature Conservancy
Council ex parte London Brick Property Ltd* [1995] ELM 95, which concerned
a challenge to the notification of a SSSI on a brickworks in Peterborough.
May J discussed the procedures for establishing a SSSI and decided that there
are, in fact, two steps involved.

(a) Under s. 28(1), a *duty* is imposed on the NCC to notify a site which
fulfils the appropriate scientific criteria. This notification has provisional
effect, but a period of three months is provided during which representations or objections can be made (s. 28(2), as inserted by the Wildlife and
Countryside (Amendment) Act 1985).
(b) The NCC must consider these representations or objections and
then has a *discretion* under s. 28(4A) whether to confirm the notification
(with or without modifications). If confirmation is not made within nine
months of the date when the notification was served, the notification lapses.

May J then went on to accept that English Nature's policy normally to
confirm a notification unless the site is unavoidably going to be destroyed is
a reasonable policy, and he upheld the confirmation.

The implications of this decision are significant, since it suggests that it
would be illegal for the NCC to refuse to notify on political or tactical
grounds (although it could arguably refuse to confirm a notification), and that
it may well be possible for an environmental group to succeed in an action to
compel the NCC to notify a site. Conversely, it appears that it will be difficult
to mount a successful challenge against an unwelcome notification where the
requisite special interest can be shown.

It is up to the NCC to define the boundaries of the SSSI and it appears
from *Sweet v Secretary of State and Nature Conservancy Council* [1989] JEL 245
(actually a case about s. 29, as to which, see below) that it is permissible for

land of lesser intrinsic scientific interest to be notified if it is part of the same environmental unit as land which is of interest. However the position of surrounding buffer lands is less clear and it must be doubted whether they could be notified. One geographical limitation is that SSSIs cannot be notified for waters below the low water mark (thus excluding many estuaries), although inland waters are included within the definition of land in the Act.

In carrying out the notification to owners and occupiers, the NCC must specify the features of the land which are of special interest and must also specify any operations which are likely to damage those features. These have traditionally been called 'potentially damaging operations' and it is clear from the decision in *Sweet* that a very wide interpretation will be given to this phrase. It can include virtually anything that has an impact on the site and 'operations' is not limited to its meaning under the Town and Country Planning Act 1990. In *Sweet*, it was held to include:

> cultivation, including ploughing, rotavation, harrowing and reseeding; grazing; mowing or other methods of cutting vegetation; application of manure, fertilisers and lime; burning; the release into the site of any wild feral or domestic animal, reptile, amphibian, bird, fish or invertebrate, or any plant or seed; the storage of materials; the use of materials; the use of vehicles or craft likely to damage or disturb features of interest.

Such things as drainage, building operations and the application of pesticides are clearly covered. One thing which is not covered, however, is doing nothing, and on many sites this is potentially bad for the nature conservation interest.

In the Scottish case of *North Uist Fisheries Ltd* v *Secretary of State for Scotland* [1991] SLT 333 (again a case on similar wording in s. 29), the judge suggested that the use of the word 'likely' required any potential damage to be probable rather than a bare possibility. If this interpretation (which was strictly *obiter*) is correct, it would undermine the whole of the legislation on SSSIs. It is submitted that the judge's reasoning should not be followed, since it seems to be based on an entirely incorrect understanding of the context of the legislation.

Duties on owners and occupiers

The process of notification is a lengthy one, since every owner and occupier, which includes approximately 30,000 people, must be notified in relation to the whole of each site. The NCC has only recently finished the process, started in 1981, of renotifying all the sites which existed at that time. This was important because, until it did so, the protection of the 1981 Act did not apply to those sites.

Once they have been notified, owners and occupiers are placed under a reciprocal duty. They must notify the NCC in writing before carrying out any potentially damaging operation. However, four months after this notification, or earlier if the written consent of the NCC is obtained, the operation can go ahead unimpeded—unless of course it requires and fails to get planning permission, which must still be sought for operations and material changes of use as defined in the Town and Country Planning Act 1990. It is an offence 'without reasonable excuse' to carry out a potentially damaging operation either without notifying the NCC, or within the four-month period, but the maximum penalty is only a £2,500 fine. The restrictive effect of designation as an SSSI is therefore to impose a four-month ban on potentially damaging operations.

Liability for the commission of the offence is strict, but it can only be committed by owners and occupiers of the SSSI. They should know about the designation, either because they have been notified, or because it is a local land charge (s. 28(11)). There are two specific defences available: that the operation was carried out in an emergency, and that planning permission had been granted by the local planning authority. This does not include a permission granted by the General Development Order (s. 28(8)), but it does mean that a planning permission overrides a SSSI designation.

These provisions illustrate the 'voluntary' mechanism which is favoured by the Conservative Government. The whole purpose of the reciprocal notification requirement and the four-month ban is to give the NCC an opportunity to arrange a management agreement with the owner or occupier.

One question which has often arisen relates to the meaning of the word 'occupier' in this context. This is important because there is no need for the NCC to notify anyone who is less than an occupier. It is also true that such a person cannot commit an offence under s. 28 and cannot be offered a management agreement. In *Southern Water Authority* v *Nature Conservancy Council* [1992] 3 All ER 481, the House of Lords decided that for the purposes of s. 28 someone is an occupier if they have some form of stable relationship with the land. As a result, a water authority which carried out drainage works whilst temporarily on an SSSI did not commit an offence under s. 28, even though it knew that these were potentially damaging operations and that they would cause significant harm (the House of Lords referred to its actions as 'ecological vandalism'). This decision did not specifically answer the important question whether commoners are covered by the definition of an occupier, but it is the practice of the NCC to treat them as such, relying on a clear statement to that effect given by a Government Minister during the debates on the Environmental Protection Bill (see Withrington & Jones, 'The Enforcement of Conservation Legislation' in *Agriculture, Conservation and Land Use*, ed. Howarth and Rodgers, University of Wales Press, 1992). Support for this stance can now be gained from the House of Lords decision in *Pepper* v *Hart* [1993] 1 All ER 42 that it is permissible to refer to Parliamentary debates in certain limited circumstances to establish the meaning of a statute, since the statement was given in the context of a refusal to bring forward an amendment to clarify the situation on the grounds that the position was already clear.

As pointed out earlier in this chapter, the drafting of the provisions of the 1981 Act leave a lot to be desired. But maybe the final words on the effectiveness of the provisions on SSSIs should be left to Lord Mustill in *Southern Water Authority* v *Nature Conservancy Council*, who stated (at p. 484):

It needs only a moment to see that this regime is toothless, for it demands no more from the owner or occupier of an SSSI than a little patience . . . In truth the Act does no more in the great majority of cases than give the Council a breathing space within which to apply moral pressure, with a view to persuading the owner or occupier to make a voluntary agreement.

Specific duties in the water industry

Specific duties in relation to SSSIs are imposed in a number of pieces of legislation, most notably in the Water Resources Act 1991, s. 17 and the Water Industry Act 1991, s. 4. The NCC must notify 'relevant bodies' (i.e. the NRA, water and sewerage undertakers and internal drainage boards) of SSSIs that may be affected by their activities. If a relevant body is notified, it must consult the NCC over any operation or activity it intends to carry out which it thinks is likely to damage or destroy the SSSI. In addition, the NRA is obliged to consult the NCC before authorising anything it thinks is likely to damage the SSSI. This includes granting abstraction licences, discharge consents and land drainage consents. A published Code of Practice suggests that *all* operations should be notified to the NCC, rather than just those the 'relevant body' *thinks* will damage the SSSI, otherwise detrimental ones may inadvertently be missed *(Code of Practice on Conservation, Access and Recreation,* July 1989).

These duties are wider than the normal ones imposed on owners and occupiers. They apply to all operations, not just to potentially damaging operations notified by the NCC, and they cover activities in the vicinity of an SSSI which may affect it, such as drainage works, or an upstream discharge. However, since there is no remedy if the relevant body fails to consult with the NCC, these duties are unenforceable unless the NCC brings a successful action for judicial review. This reflects the fact that the real purpose of these duties is to bring the matter to the attention of the NCC so that it may give advice (it does not normally offer a management agreement to public bodies, considering that their general environmental duties should suffice to make them act in a responsible fashion).

The Water Resources Act 1991, s. 17 is being replaced by the Environment Act 1995, s. 8, which is essentially worded in identical manner, except that the duty now applies to the Environment Agency. This has the effect of extending the duty to the Agency's functions under the Environmental Protection Act 1990, Part I and the Radioactive Substances Act 1993, where it did not previously apply. The more general environmental duties in the Water Resources Act 1991, ss. 16 and 18, the Land Drainage Act 1991, ss. 61A–61E, and the Environment Act 1995, ss. 6, 7, and 9, should also be noted (see Chapter 3).

Nature conservation orders

Section 29 provides stronger powers for areas subject to a nature conservation order. Even so, they have been sparingly used. About 40 have been made over the years, mainly to protect sites imminently threatened with destruction.

The powers in relation to nature conservation orders are superficially similar to those on SSSIs, but there are significant differences. The order will list potentially damaging operations which must be notified to the NCC before being carried out, and a three month ban is imposed. The NCC can extend this ban to 12 months by offering a management agreement, or by offering to purchase the interest of the person seeking to carry out the operation. At the end of the 12 months, the operation can go ahead. Once again, the purpose of this ban is to enable the NCC to conclude a management agreement, or terms for the purchase of the site.

It is an offence to carry out a potentially damaging operation without notifying the NCC, or within the period of the ban. The offence carries a maximum fine of £5,000 on summary conviction, or an unlimited fine for a conviction on indictment, and it can be committed by anyone, not just owners and occupiers. Thus, contractors, trespassers or visiting members of the public could be prosecuted under this section, a position justified by the publicity given to a nature conservation order (see below).

Certain ancillary arrangements differ from s. 28. The NCC is authorised to enter land to see if an order ought to be made, or to see if an offence against one has been committed (s. 51), powers which are not available for SSSIs (a significant gap in the legislation). Anyone can prosecute for a s. 29 offence (under s. 28 it is only the NCC and anyone who has the permission of the Director of Public Prosecutions). A convicting court has powers to make a restoration order (s. 31), ordering that the offender carry out specified works for the purpose of restoring the land to its former condition, although in many cases this power will be next to useless because the damage will be irreversible. Compensation is also payable to the owner or occupier for any reduction in the value of an agricultural holding as a result of an order, and for any loss directly attributable to the ban on operations (s. 30).

These wider powers are complemented by a much more complex system for making nature conservation orders. After consulting the NCC, the Secretary of State is empowered to designate areas by order. They must be of special interest and national importance, or required to ensure the survival in Great Britain of a plant or animal, or to comply with an international obligation. Although it is arguable that all SSSIs are of national importance, it is apparent that the Secretary of State has in practice refused to designate some SSSIs under s. 29 on the grounds that the land was not of national importance, even when the NCC has requested it. It is clear from *Sweet* v *Secretary of State and Nature Conservancy Council* [1989] JEL 245 that it is permissible to designate the whole of an environmental unit even though only part of it is of national importance.

Schedule 11 provides for the making of an order. It comes into effect immediately it is made. It must then be notified to owners, occupiers and the local planning authority and must be publicised generally for any objections to be made. Twenty-eight days are allowed for representations to the Secretary of State, who must appoint an inspector or hold a public inquiry if any objections are not withdrawn. The Secretary of State has a discretion to confirm the order, or to amend or revoke it.

Despite their complexity, nature conservation orders provide the NCC with few extra powers not available for all SSSIs. They are basically used to provide more time for the NCC to negotiate a management agreement where the owner or occupier is being awkward. They also serve notice of intent to use whatever powers are available to protect the site. This may include compulsory purchase (see below). For example, in *Sweet* the land was eventually obtained in 1989 as part of a new national nature reserve.

National nature reserves (NNRs)

NNRs owe their existence to the National Parks and Access to the Countryside Act 1949, s. 15, which defines them as areas managed for study or research into flora, fauna or geological or physiographical interest, or for preserving such features which are of special interest. Before declaring an area an NNR, the NCC must consider that it is expedient in the national interest to manage the area as an NNR.

Designation as an NNR is a simple process: the NCC merely declares that an area is one. In order to do this it has to have control of the site so that it can manage it. Control may be achieved either by buying the land, leasing it, or entering into a nature reserve agreement with the owner under the National Parks and Access to the Countryside Act, s. 16. Such an agreement is enforceable against successors in title. In addition, the Wildlife and Countryside Act 1981, s. 35 permits the NCC to declare an NNR on land which is of national importance and which is being managed by an approved body (meaning a voluntary conservation organisation).

The NCC also has powers to seek a compulsory purchase order if it is unable to conclude a satisfactory management agreement with the owner (1949 Act, s. 17), or if an unremedied breach of an agreement occurs. An order will require the approval of the Secretary of State. These compulsory powers are intended as reserve powers only and are very rarely used. However, they remain the only compulsory powers available to the NCC: if a maverick landowner were to refuse to enter into a management agreement on an SSSI and refused to sell the property, a compulsory purchase order would be the only remaining weapon.

There are no additional statutory restrictions on the use of a NNR other than those imposed on all SSSIs (as a matter of practice all NNRs are designated as SSSIs), since the nature reserve agreement will cover anything extra. However, the NCC is empowered to make by-laws for the protection of the reserve (1949 Act, s. 20). They require confirmation by the Secretary of State and the procedures for making them are set out in the 1949 Act, s. 106. These by-laws may include wide restrictions on such things as entry to the reserve, taking, killing or interference with animals, plants or the soil, dropping of litter and lighting fires. Shooting of birds can also be restricted in areas surrounding the reserve. By-laws may not restrict the rights of the owner or occupier, public rights of way (though this does not include rights of navigation—*Evans* v *Godber* [1974] 3 All ER 341), or statutory undertakers and some other public bodies carrying out their statutory functions.

There are over 250 NNRs in Great Britain, but it cannot be assumed that they are necessarily the very best sites. Designation of a site as an NNR imposes heavy costs on the NCC, which has accordingly to be selective, and it has tended to follow a policy of opportunism. Given a chronic shortage of money, it will buy or take control of sites that are threatened or available, rather than those which are in safe hands, such as those owned by a voluntary conservation body. Notwithstanding this, the NCC does have a list of proposed nature reserves, and has published *A Nature Conservation Review* (Ratcliffe, 1977 and updated), a description of around 900 key sites representing the range of British flora and fauna, which provides a list of possible future NNRs.

Local nature reserves

Under the National Parks and Access to the Countryside Act 1949, s. 21, local authorities are given the same powers to designate and manage local nature reserves as the NCC has in relation to NNRs. A local nature reserve must have local, as opposed to national, importance and the local authority must consult with the NCC before designation.

Marine nature reserves (MNRs)

MNRs are the counterparts to NNRs in tidal and coastal waters and may be designated for any area of land or water from the high tide mark to a line three miles from the baselines established for measuring the territorial sea (see the Territorial Sea Act 1987). They are provided for in the Wildlife and Countryside Act 1981, s. 36, and may be designated on the same grounds of conservation and study as NNRs. They are actively managed by the NCC.

There are a number of differences from NNRs. Some stem from the absence of property rights over most of the potential area of MNRS, others are a consequence of the limited vision of MNRs in the 1981 Act. Designation of an MNR is by the Secretary of State on the application of the NCC. There is a lengthy procedure, similar to that for nature conservation orders, in which the proposed designation and any by-laws are publicised, followed by a period for representations from interested parties, with the possibility of a public inquiry and of a judicial review both being catered for (see Wildlife and Countryside Act 1981, sch. 12). Only two MNRs have ever been designated (around the islands of Lundy and Skomer), although this may reflect the fact that the NCC's priorities lay elsewhere in the 1980s. It is also true that there are a few voluntary marine reserves.

In common with NNRs, the main additional control conferred by MNR status is the power of the NCC to make by-laws. These may be made as part of the original designation, or may be issued separately, but in either case require confirmation by the Secretary of State. The 1981 Act, s. 37, sets out the range of possible by-laws, which is much more limited than the range for NNRs. Restrictions may be introduced on the killing, taking and disturbance of plants and animals and on the deposit of litter. The by-laws may also prohibit or restrict access by people or vessels to the MNR, but this is limited by the provision in s. 37(3) that by-laws may not restrict any lawful right of passage by vessels, except for pleasure boats. This is an important limitation, since most boats will be able to take advantage of the right of passage in tidal waters, and there are no proprietary limitations on access in such waters. In addition, it must be noted that MNRs cannot take any real advantage from the protection relating to SSSIs, since SSSIs cannot be designated below the low water mark.

Limestone pavements

Limestone pavements are rare landscape features limited to a small number of areas in North-West Europe. In the light of the devastating damage that has been done to them, particularly in gathering stone for garden rockeries, specific powers to protect them were introduced in the Wildlife and Countryside Act 1981, s. 34.

There are two distinct controls. Under s. 34(1), the NCC or the Countryside Commission must notify limestone pavements of special interest to the local planning authority. Amongst other things this will then be taken into account in any planning application. Under s. 34(2), the Secretary of State, a county planning authority or a national park authority may by order prohibit the removal from, or disturbance of, any limestone on a site notified under s. 34(1), if they consider it is likely to be affected adversely by such acts. The making of a limestone pavement order is subject to the same procedures as a nature conservation order (1981 Act, sch. 11). It is an offence without reasonable excuse to remove or disturb any limestone on or in an area subject to an order, although it is a defence to have planning permission to do so. The penalty is a maximum fine of £5,000 on summary conviction and an unlimited fine on conviction on indictment. It was originally intended to protect most areas of substantial pavement, but the cumbersome nature of designation has meant that only a handful of orders have ever been made, mainly (as with nature conservation orders) to deal with threats of imminent damage.

This dual form of protection differs from all other conservation designations. But it must be noted that this is the form that the Government originally proposed in 1981 should apply to SSSIs, with only a few specially protected areas having extra restrictions and the ordinary SSSIs being protected only by notification to the local planning authority.

Management agreements

The NCC has a power to enter into management agreements with owners and occupiers of SSSIs (Countryside Act 1968, s. 15). This was extended by the EPA 1990, sch. 9 to enable agreements to be made with owners or occupiers of land adjoining an SSSI, which will be of use, for example, in wetland areas to control drainage. There is a similar power to make nature reserve agreements for NNRs (National Parks and Access to the Countryside

Act 1949, s. 16), although these normally provide for the NCC to manage the land itself.

Management agreements underpin the voluntary approach to nature conservation favoured by the current Government. They are effectively contracts in which owners or occupiers of land agree to manage it in the interests of nature conservation in return for payment from the NCC. They normally provide for positive management of the site as well as for restrictions, but it appears that only restrictive arrangements in the agreement will be binding on successors in title (s. 15(4)).

Prior to the Wildlife and Countryside Act 1981, little use was made of management agreements—only 70 were in force in 1980/81. But since the 1981 Act, numbers have grown, so that in 1990/91 the NCC paid out over £6.85m on 2,032 management agreements on SSSIs (see NCC 16th Annual Report).

Standard rates of compensation have been established in financial guidelines made by Ministers under the 1981 Act, s. 50 (these are set out in the Appendix to Circular 4/83). These are generous to landowners, because they are based on the principle of compensation for profits forgone, which will include such things as lost agricultural grants or lost revenues had the land been converted to a more profitable use. The owner or occupier also has a choice between a lump sum payment or an index-linked annual payment. However, one of the drawbacks of the legislation is that, unlike the position for agreements in environmentally sensitive areas (see p. 508) and under many other schemes, the terms of each SSSI management agreement have to be negotiated individually. This uses up valuable time and resources and has led to a much slower rate of agreement than under these other schemes. Land of outstanding scientific interest may also qualify for tax relief (see *Capital Taxation and Nature Conservation*, English Nature, 1992). Another drawback is that the legislation revolves around compensating people for *not* doing something, rather than paying them to do something, which is inappropriate in nature conservation terms.

There is little doubt that the cost of management agreements has proved more expensive than the Government originally anticipated. Only £600,000 was originally provided for them in 1981, although this figure has risen considerably since. It is also clear that lack of money has caused the NCC to be inhibited in negotiations. For example, in 1982 in Romney Marsh the NCC pulled out of negotiations when no extra Government money was provided for a potentially expensive agreement (see *Cash or Crisis*, Rose and Secrett, 1982). However, when the current figures for damage to SSSIs are considered (see below), it appears that the strategy of relying on management agreements has had some success in reducing damage caused by agricultural activities (although wider issues connected with the profitability of agriculture are also probably of great significance).

Planning permission

In addition to any controls specific to SSSIs and NNRs, planning permission will be required for operations and material changes of use which fall within the definition of development in the Town and Country Planning Act 1990, s. 55 (see p. 219). Where the application relates to an SSSI or is likely to affect an SSSI, the Town and Country Planning (General Development Procedure) Order 1995, Art. 10, requires the local planning authority to consult with the NCC before making a decision. The objective is the familiar one of informing the NCC in advance of a potential threat to the site, so it may give advice or offer a management agreement. Prior to the 1981 Act, this was the *only* legal protection for SSSIs.

These requirements are very limited in practice. Many activities likely to damage SSSIs, such as those relating to agriculture, forestry and works carried out by statutory undertakers, are not covered by the need for planning permission, either because they are not development or because they are granted exemption. In any case, the local planning authority is not bound by the NCC's advice—it is just one material consideration to be taken into account. The economic and other arguments in favour of the development may well outweigh the need to protect the SSSI. For example, in 1990 Havering DC granted outline planning permission for a large theme park on Rainham Marshes, the largest SSSI in Greater London. The Secretary of State refused to call the application in, even though this would have been the largest ever loss of SSSI land to a development with planning permission (it has not gone ahead). In another example, Poole BC granted itself planning permission for housing on Canford Heath, an SSSI within the town's boundaries. After an unsuccessful High Court challenge (see *R* v *Poole BC ex parte Beebee* [1991] JPL 643), the Secretary of State took the almost unprecedented step of revoking the planning permission under the Town and Country Planning Act 1990, s. 100.

Government policy on planning and nature conservation is now set out in Planning Policy Guidance Note 9, *Nature Conservation* (PPG 9, October 1994). As well as explaining the various statutory and international protections, PPG 9 emphasises that the nature conservation interest of a site, and the importance of the site in national and international terms, is clearly a material consideration when it comes to a decision whether to grant planning permission, although it does refer to the potential use of conditions or planning obligations to avoid damaging impacts. In particular, PPG 9 includes some especially strong policies in relation to international sites, including that environmental assessment will normally be required where such a site (including a proposed site) could be affected (see below for a discussion of internationally important sites).

However, there is a difficulty here concerning the relationship between safeguarding sites through the planning machinery and the formal designation of SSSIs. If a formal policy against granting planning permission on internationally important sites is adopted, which is likely, many people would then argue that the procedures for designation of those sites need to be upgraded so as to include rights of objection, the possibility of a public inquiry and so on, since such a restraint policy would effectively take away any real chance of realising the development value of the land.

If planning permission is granted for development, it acts as a defence to a prosecution for damaging an SSSI (1981 Act, s. 28(8)). This does not just apply to new permissions. It also exempts existing mineral and peat extraction permissions over SSSIs from the 1981 Act. These are on sites which tend not to have been identified as of importance when the permission was originally granted. The NCC's options are limited and all involve the payment of potentially large sums of money: revocation of the planning permission entails a liability to pay compensation, a management agreement would have to compensate for lost profits, and purchase would normally be at the market price.

Loss and damage to SSSIs

Despite the strengthening of the law relating to SSSIs in the 1981 Act, it remains clear that damage and loss to sites is still continuing, though probably at lower rates than before the passage of the Act. The three national conservation agencies currently divide incidents into four categories: complete loss, partial loss, long-term damage and short-term damage (although it must be recognised that the three agencies adopt slightly different criteria and that short-term damage can easily turn into long-term damage if appropriate management of a site is not undertaken). In 1991/92 they reported a total of one complete loss, six cases of partial loss, 46 cases of long-term damage and 196 cases of short-term damage. In 1994, the National Audit Office reported that 869 SSSIs in England suffered loss and damage between 1987 and 1993, which amounts to over one-fifth of the total number of SSSIs notified, although there was some element of double counting in these figures. These continuing losses illustrate that the traditional British approach to environmental issues identified in Chapter 5, of balancing the various factors and reaching a compromise, simply does not work when it comes to safeguarding key nature conservation sites.

The statistics on loss and damage show that the causes of damage have changed somewhat over the last 14 years, a point reinforced by a number of independent analyses (see Rowell, *SSSIs: A Health Check*, Wildlife Link, 1991). It is true that agricultural activities still account for the majority of incidents, but nowadays only a small proportion of these give rise to the loss of a site. The major problems in relation to agriculture appear to be those with which the Act is ill-equipped to deal, such as overgrazing (especially by commoners) and neglect, both of which create difficult issues of management and control. This point, that the main causes of damage are from those things that the Act cannot deal with properly, is reinforced when non-agricultural causes are looked at. Many cases of loss or long-term damage are caused by activities that are effectively exempt from the Act, such as: activities granted planning permission (for example, the perpetual permissions for peat extraction on lowland moors); major developments promoted by government departments (such as the Channel Tunnel, or the road-building programme); activities by statutory undertakers (the prosecution of Southern Water Authority mentioned earlier is a good example); recreational activities, which are often not controlled because those who are neither owners nor occupiers cannot commit an offence under s. 28; and activities taking place below the low water mark. These cases all point towards the existence of a number of defects in the scheme of the Act which urgently require to be addressed.

The international perspective

There are some international conventions relating to nature conservation whose significance in the context of domestic law should not be under-estimated. The Bern Convention on the Conservation of European Wildlife and Natural Habitats (Cmnd. 8738, 1979), could, arguably, be seen as the driving force behind the two EC Directives discussed in detail below, whilst the Ramsar Convention on Wetlands of International Importance (Cmnd. 6465, 1971, which is discussed below) has played a key role in relation to the protection of one particular habitat which the UK has in relative abundance. There is also the Bonn Convention on the Conservation of Migratory Species of Wild Animals, 1979 and the Washington Convention on International Trade in Endangered Species of Wild Fauna and Flora (Cmnd. 6647, 1973).

However, in terms of the impact on British law, two EC Directives, the Wild Birds Directive 79/409 and the Habitats Directive 92/43, have un-doubtedly had the greatest influence and will continue to be of importance in the future. The main reason relates to the very specific requirements that these Directives lay down concerning the designation of protected sites, but they also include some significant measures on the protection of individual animals and plants (which have been discussed above).

EC Wild Birds Directive 79/409

Under the Wild Birds Directive, Member States are required in general terms to take measures, including the creation of protected areas, to maintain a sufficient diversity of habitats for *all* European bird species (Arts. 1, 2 and 3). They are also required to take special conservation measures to conserve the habitats of the rare or vulnerable species listed in Annex I and of all regularly occurring migratory species (Art. 4). These special measures should include the designation of special protection areas for such birds. Once a special protection area has been designated, Member States must take appropriate steps to avoid significant pollution or deterioration of the habitat or disturb-ance of the birds within it (Art. 4(4)).

In Case C355/90, *Commission* v *Spain* [1993] *Water Law* 209, the European Court of Justice held that the Spanish Government was in breach of Art. 4 by failing to designate an important wetland area, the Marismas de Santoña, as a special protection area. The case established that a Member State is effectively under a duty to designate an area as a special protection area (and thus to protect it) if it fulfils the objective ornithological criteria laid down in the Directive.

In an earlier, though no less important, case, *Commission* v *Germany* [1991] ECR 883, the European Court of Justice addressed the meaning of Art. 4(4) in relation to an area known as the Leybucht Dykes. It established that reduction in the area of a special protection area was only justified on very limited grounds, such as where the works were necessary for reasons of public health or public safety (which was actually the situation in the case itself), and that works could not be permitted for economic or recreational reasons, thus creating a strong presumption against development in such an area. This point was reinforced by *Commission v Spain*, which applied the same test to the deterioration of a site as a result of pollution or other works and also suggested that Art. 4(4) is sufficiently clear to be directly effective. The effect of these rulings was very quickly mitigated by an amendment that was made to Art. 4 by the Habitats Directive, which brought the Wild Birds Directive into line with the less restrictive exceptions laid down in Art. 6(4) of that Directive (see below), but a more limited presumption against development in special protection areas remains. Special protection areas, whether actually classified or merely fulfilling the criteria, are thus to be given very strong protection.

Apart from the requirement to designate special protection areas, the Directive does not specify how its objectives are to be achieved, giving a degree of flexibility to Member States. In Britain, the approach that was adopted was initially to provide protection through the town planning and SSSI systems. All special protection areas are, in practice, notified as SSSIs before being designated, but it should be noted that, prior to the passage of the Conservation (Natural Habitats etc.) Regulations 1994 (which are discussed in detail below), designation as a special protection area (or as a Ramsar site, where a similar policy was adopted) did not impose any additional domestic requirements on owners or occupiers to those applicable to all SSSIs. There is also a crucial gap in the legislation on SSSIs in that there is no SSSI protection for parts of many special protection areas (and also many Ramsar sites) because they are below low-water mark. Estuarine sites in particular are under great pressure; an NCC report has shown that 56 out of 136 estuarine SSSIs suffered damage between 1986 and 1989, many through permanent developments (see *Nature Conservation and Estuaries in Great Britain* (NCC, 1991)). The two European Court of Justice cases suggested that the British approach was no longer adequate and the position has now been radically altered by the 1994 Regulations.

The NCC has produced some extensive criteria for qualification as a special protection area (see *Protecting Internationally Important Bird Sites* (NCC, 1990), in which it identified a total of 218 candidate sites and stated that it was considering the merits of a further 43). At present, 106 sites have been designated, covering 350,000 hectares, although new designations are still being made. It is also important to note that the Government has accepted, as a matter of planning policy, that all sites that meet the criteria for designation as a special protection area should be treated as if they had been formally designated. For example, in July 1992 the Secretary of State refused planning permission for a number of major developments in North Kent, giving the need to protect a candidate special protection area as one of the main reasons (see [1993] *Water Law* 89). This policy is now enshrined in Planning Policy Guidance Note 9, *Nature Conservation* (PPG 9, October 1994).

EC Habitats Directive 92/43

The full title of this Directive refers to the Conservation of Natural Habitats and of Wild Fauna and Flora. However, whilst it does require some measures of importance to the protection of individual animals and plants to be taken, its main importance relates to habitat protection. Accordingly, it is commonly referred to as the Habitats Directive. It was adopted in May 1992 after many years of argument within the EC and has led to some important changes to British law and policy on habitat protection, which are discussed below.

The central feature of the Directive is that it provides for the creation of a coherent ecological network of special areas of conservation, which will make up a system of European sites known as Natura 2000. The network will consist of sites containing the natural habitat types listed in Annex I of the Directive and sites containing the habitats of the species listed in Annex II. It will incorporate the special protection areas classified under the Wild Birds Directive. However, the Directive also includes some more general duties, including a requirement that Member States monitor the conservation status of *all* habitats and species (Art. 11) and a general duty relating to the management of certain important landscape features (Art. 10).

The procedures for producing the list of special areas of conservation are complex. By June 1995, Member States were required to send to the Commission a list of proposed sites, drawn up by reference to the criteria laid down in Annex III (Stage 1). The Commission is then under a duty to draw up, by June 1998, a draft list of 'sites of Community importance', taking account of the criteria set out in Annex III (Stage 2). The Commission adopts a final list thereafter in the light of scientific advice from a committee of independent experts. The Commission will produce a separate list of those sites which host one or more of the *priority* habitat types or species which are identified in Annexes I and II (these can be termed 'priority sites'). There are provisions for a bilateral consultation process between the Commission and a Member State where the Commission considers that a priority site has been left off a Member State's list, with ultimate recourse to the EC Council (Art. 5). In addition, the Commission is under a duty to review the list in the future, whilst Member States and the Commission are required to submit detailed implementation reports. Once the Commission has adopted the list of sites of Community importance, Member States are under a duty to designate any site on the list as a special area of conservation as soon as possible and within six years at the latest (Art. 4(4)).

The protection provided by the Habitats Directive is as follows:

(a) for special areas of conservation (once designated), Member States must adopt 'necessary conservation measures' and 'appropriate statutory, administrative or contractual measures' (Art 6(1));

(b)   for sites adopted by the Commission as sites of Community import-ance, special protection areas designated under the Wild Birds Directive and sites subject to the Art. 5 consultation procedure, Member States are required to take appropriate steps to avoid the deterioration of the sites and significant disturbance of the species for which the areas have been designated (Art. 6(2)); and

(c) for sites adopted by the Commission as sites of Community import-ance and special protection areas designated under the Wild Birds Directive, any plan or project not directly connected with the management of the site which is likely to have a significant effect on it must be subject to an appropriate assessment of the implications; the competent national authori-ties can then agree to the plan or project only if it will not 'adversely affect the integrity of the site concerned' (Art. 6(3)).

However, if there is no alternative solution, a plan or project may be carried out if there are 'imperative reasons of overriding public interest, including those of a social or economic nature'. In such a case, the Member State has to take compensatory measures in order to ensure the overall coherence of Natura 2000 and must inform the Commission of those measures. When compared with the position set out in *Commission* v *Germany* (the *Leybucht Dykes* case), this exception lessens the protection that is offered. However, for priority sites the exception is limited to considerations relating to human health or public safety, situations where the impact is beneficial to the environment, and cases where the Commission has accepted that there are reasons of overriding public interest (art 6(4)), in effect retaining the *Leybucht Dykes* position for priority sites. It is of relevance, therefore, that there are no priority bird species, and thus the stronger controls applicable to priority sites cannot apply to special protection areas designated under the Wild Birds Directive.

The 1994 Regulations

Initially, the British Government envisaged that the Habitats Directive could be implemented without new legislation. It intended to adopt the approach that had hitherto been used in relation to the Wild Birds Directive, i.e. judicious use of the SSSI and town planning systems. However, in the light of the two European Court of Justice cases it became clear that this would be inadequate in legal terms. As a result, in order to implement the provisions of the Directive, the European Communities Act 1972, s. 2(2) was used to pass the Conservation (Natural Habitats etc.) Regulations 1994 (SI 1994 No. 2716).

However, rather than remodel the law on nature conservation entirely, the Government adopted a minimalist approach. It simply engrafted onto the existing SSSI and town planning mechanisms the additional protections required by the Directive, and then only where absolutely necessary. In essence, the Regulations apply additional protections to 'European sites', which are defined as follows:

(a) a special area of conservation (once designated—the Regulations reproduce the procedures and timetable in the Directive relating to designa-tion, the Secretary of State being placed under a duty to propose a list of sites on or before 5 June 1995 (reg. 7) and required to designate sites adopted by the Commission as special areas of conservation 'as soon as possible and within six years at most' (reg. 8));

(b)   a site adopted by the Commission as a site of Community importance;

(c)   a special protection area designated under the Wild Birds Directive; and

(d)   a site subject to consultation under Art. 5 of the Directive (although in this case the protection is limited in the same way as under the Directive to the obligations under Art. 6(2)).

The Secretary of State will draw up a public register of European sites (Art. 11) and notify them to English Nature (Art. 12), which will then notify local planning authorities, owners and occupiers and anyone else the Secretary of State may direct (Art.13).

Under the Regulations, the basic protection given to terrestrial European sites is the same as under the Wildlife and Countryside Act 1981, s. 28 for all SSSIs, with the following exceptions:

(a)   English Nature may amend the original notification made under s. 28 of the special interest of the site and of the potentially damaging operations (reg. 18);

(b)   the process through which English Nature grants consent for potentially damaging operations is altered in the light of Art. 6 of the Directive so that:

(i)   if it appears to English Nature that a plan or project is likely to have a significant effect on the site, it must carry out an appropriate assessment and may only give consent if the plan or project will not affect the integrity of the site; and

(ii)   if it considers that there is a risk that the operation will be carried out without consent, it must notify the Secretary of State, who has the powers described below to make a special nature conservation order (reg. 20);

(c)   existing consents must be reviewed by English Nature and may be withdrawn or modified without compensation (reg. 21); and

(d)   by-laws may be made for terrestrial European sites (and over surrounding or adjoining sites) as if they were nature reserves (reg. 28).

In addition, the Secretary of State has a power to make a special nature conservation order over a European site (reg. 22). This is a new type of protection, which, although based on the Wildlife and Countryside Act 1981, s. 29, is potentially far stronger because it produces a situation where the ban on potentially damaging operations is permanent.

Where a special nature conservation order has been made, reg. 24 sets out the procedure to be followed where an owner or occupier applies for consent to carry out a plan or project. If it appears to English Nature that the plan or project is likely to have a significant effect on the site, it must carry out an appropriate assessment and *must* refuse consent, unless it is satisfied that the plan or project will not affect the integrity of the site. The owner or occupier may refer the refusal to the Secretary of State, who is given a power to direct English Nature to grant consent. But this power of direction can be used only if: (i) there is no alternative solution; and (ii) the plan or project must be carried out 'for imperative reasons of overriding public interest' (which is defined as in Art. 6(4) of the Directive and includes the more restrictive test for priority sites). If consent is granted, appropriate compensatory measures must be carried out.

This is the central feature of the whole Regulations, since it provides a form of absolute protection by introducing a mechanism through which a damaging activity may be prevented permanently. However, the success of the whole Regulations (at least in terms of whether the Directive is properly implemented in practice) depends on the willingness of the Secretary of State to make a special nature conservation order and then to refuse consent where appropriate. These are matters that may not become clear for some time since, until the Commission adopts the list of sites of Community importance, the only sites that are covered by the Habitats Directive are the special protection areas designated under the Wild Birds Directive. Nevertheless, it is clear from the whole scheme of protection that the Government envisages special nature conservation orders as instruments of last resort to be used only when absolutely necessary. Set against that, reg. 3(2) requires the Secretary of State and the nature conservation bodies to exercise their nature conservation functions 'so as to secure compliance' with the Directive. It must also be noted that the Regulations repeat many of the opaque words and phrases used in the Directive; in line with standard principles of EC law, these should be interpreted in accordance with the Directive.

European marine sites

As far as European sites which are marine or tidal are concerned, the Regulations are far more loosely worded. Every public body having functions relevant to marine conservation is required to exercise its functions so as to secure compliance with the requirements of the Directive (reg. 3(3)). In addition, more specific powers and duties are laid down in regs. 33–36. English Nature must advise other relevant authorities (a term which includes local authorities, the NRA, water and sewerage undertakers, internal drainage boards, navigation authorities, harbour authorities, lighthouse authorities and fisheries committees) as to the conservation objectives for the site and any potentially damaging operations. Any relevant authority *may* then establish a management scheme for the site and English Nature *may* make by-laws under the Wildlife and Countryside Act 1981, s. 37 as if the site were a marine nature reserve. The relevant Minister is given a wide power to make directions to the relevant authorities concerning management schemes. It must be doubted whether these vague arrangements, which in the absence of town planning and SSSI controls are the only real powers available below the low-water mark, are adequate to ensure the proper implementation of the Directive.

European sites and other regulatory systems

The Regulations also make important amendments to a number of regulatory systems. Where a plan or project is likely to have a significant effect on a European site, before granting such things as planning permission or a pollution authorisation, the relevant regulatory agency must consult with English Nature and carry out an appropriate assessment of the implications of the plan or project for the site (reg. 48). The agency must agree to the plan or project only if it will not adversely affect the integrity of the site, unless the provisions of regs. 49 and 53 are satisfied (these repeat the exceptions laid down in Art. 6(4) of the Directive). The Secretary of State is also given powers to prohibit the plan or project, either temporarily or permanently. In addition, existing permissions, consents and authorisations must be reviewed as soon as reasonably practicable. If the integrity of the site is adversely affected, the agency should use its normal powers of revocation or modification, paying compensation if that would be the usual position. There are also restrictions on a developer taking advantage of a development order in order to carry out development on a European site (regs. 60–64).

In relation to applications for planning permission, PPG 9, *Nature Conservation* (October 1994), creates some additional protections as a matter of policy, including that for development control purposes potential special protection areas and candidate special areas of conservation included in the list sent to the EC Commission should be treated in the same way as designated sites, and that environmental assessment will normally be required where a Ramsar site or a candidate or designated European site could be affected.

The Ramsar Convention

The Ramsar Convention on Wetlands of International Importance Especially as Waterfowl Habitat, 1971, was the first international convention dealing solely with habitat. It came into force in 1975 and currently there are over 50 Contracting Parties, of which the UK is one.

The Convention establishes a number of protections, though it can be criticised for being too general and unenforceable. First it imposes on the Contracting Parties a general duty to promote the conservation of wetlands and waterfowl, especially by establishing nature reserves. Secondly it adopts a site designation approach and provides for the compilation of a list of wetlands of international importance. Contracting Parties are under a duty to formulate their planning so as to promote the conservation of wetlands included in the list. Each Contracting Party must designate at least one site within its territory and deletion or reduction in size of a site is allowed only on the grounds of 'urgent national interests'. Guidelines on the definition of international importance have been drawn up, although ultimately it is up to each Contracting Party to decide whether and where it will designate. In addition to these powers, there are provisions under the Convention for the monitoring of wetlands, the establishment of a database, the funding of projects, educational work and publications. It also provides for a Ramsar Bureau, which is based in Switzerland.

'Wetland' is interpreted very widely to include 'areas of marsh, fen, peatland or water, whether natural or artificial, permanent or temporary, with water that is static or flowing, fresh, brackish or salt, including areas of marine water the depth of which does not exceed six metres'. Designation may also include adjacent areas of land, such as coasts, riverbanks and islands.

As with the Wild Birds Directive, the Ramsar Convention was initially implemented through the planning and SSSI systems. In practice, this still remains the case, since the sites are not European sites for the purposes of the 1994 Regulations. However, it must be pointed out that Ramsar sites are now given significant protection in practice through PPG 9 and that many of the 90 sites designated (which cover 385,000 hectares) are also special protection areas under the Wild Birds Directive or candidate special areas of conservation.

Summary of protection of internationally important sites

There is little doubt that the 1994 Regulations have increased the protection available to European sites and that PPG 9 reinforces that protection within the planning system. However, it is difficult to say whether they implement the Habitats Directive fully, since the crucial issues relate to whether the powers will be used in practice. As pointed out above, the willingness of the Secretary of State to designate European sites and then to protect them by making special nature conservation orders is central. In this respect it is relevant that on 20 June 1995 the Government sent to the EC Commission a list of 136 candidate special areas of conservation, although it was accepted that this was not a final list and that it did not include any marine areas. The Government's approach to the selection of appropriate sites was set out in *A List of Possible Special Areas of Conservation in the UK*, issued in March 1995, which confirmed that there will be few priority sites in the UK.

There are other potential defects with the Regulations. They impose a very heavy administrative burden on English Nature and the various regulatory agencies which are required to review consents. This burden may well prove to be too great. It must also be asked whether the extra attention paid to European sites means that, in practice, the resources and goodwill available to protect other sites has been significantly eroded. Many commentators have already queried why, in the light of the defects identified in the legislation relating to SSSIs, the opportunity was not taken to improve the protection given to *all* SSSIs.

As a postscript, there is one ongoing case that is of relevance to the selection of European sites. In this case the Royal Society for the Protection of Birds has challenged the failure of the Government to designate an area known as Lappel Bank within the Medway Estuary and Marshes as a special protection area for birds. The argument centres around whether it is permissible to take economic factors into account in the decision whether, and over what area, to designate a special protection area, with the Government arguing that it is and the RSPB relying on the European Court of Justice decision in *Commission* v *Spain* [1993] *Water Law* 209 (the *Marismas de Santoña* case) to argue that only ornithological criteria apply at this stage. In the Court of Appeal the judges were split, with the majority deciding in the Government's favour (unreported, 18 August 1994). However, the RSPB has appealed to the House of Lords, which refused interim relief but referred the matter to the European Court of Justice under Article 177 of the EC Treaty (unreported, 9 February 1995). The judgment of the European Court of Justice is awaited, but is certain to add to the law on the area. In the meantime it is worth reflecting that in *Commission* v *Spain* the Court held that the Spanish Government was in breach of the Wild Birds Directive by failing to designate an important wetland area. It also suggested that Art. 4(4) of the Wild Birds Directive is directly effective. Since Arts. 6(2), 6(3) and 6(4) of the Habitats Directive are in similar terms and also lay down clear requirements, it is arguable that they are also directly effective, with all the implications for enforcement of the law that that entails.

SEVENTEEN
The protection of the countryside

This chapter looks at the protection of the features which make the British countryside distinctive. There are a number of different things involved here: the restriction of urban expansion and urban developments in the country-side; the preservation of the particularly rural character of an area; and the protection of distinctive landscapes or landscape types. Since the shape of most of what is to be protected is the result of hundreds of years of human intervention, its protection poses some difficult problems, involving positive action as well as restrictive controls.

Three main methods of control may be discerned:

(a) One is to rely on the town and country planning legislation to control developments in the countryside in the same way that they are controlled in towns.

(b) A second is to impose special protections in designated areas, or in relation to designated features. In practice, these added protections often tend to stem from the town and country planning system as well, though there are some that do not.

(c) A third mechanism is to utilise grants and other incentives to ensure the proper care of the countryside, again with special schemes available in selected areas.

A particular feature of both the second and third mechanisms is the reliance on voluntary controls, rather than on compulsion.

Town and country planning

The starting point for the protection of the countryside has always been the development control system. But it has never proved particularly successful, because despite its name, it has always had an urban bias. There have been very few adaptations of the basic structure to cope with countryside matters. Indeed, it is commonly referred to as the 'town planning' system, the countryside aspect being forgotten.

There are a number of reasons for this. A major one is the history of the system, which had a consequent effect on the nature of the legal mechanisms that were adopted. The town and country planning system developed in 1947 was specifically designed to meet predominantly urban problems, such as community layout and design, industrial location, post-war reconstruction, public health and overcrowding, and transportation changes. As far as the rural environment was concerned, the main policy was the protection of the countryside against urban creep and expansion. The legal mechanisms that were adopted were thus mainly negative, such as the need for planning permission, and did not reflect the need for positive management in the countryside.

In addition, there was in 1947 perceived to be little need to control developments in the countryside, since it was generally considered that landowners and farmers had done a good job in shaping the landscape, and in any case agriculture itself required protection after the rural depression of the 1930s and the Atlantic Blockade of the Second World War. Agriculture and forestry, the two main activities likely to have an impact on the landscape, were granted generous exemptions in the legislation which, despite some minor changes, still remain today.

As a result there are distinct limitations on the use of development control in the countryside, and its most important role is in controlling new buildings and structures:

(a)   Many rural activities which have a significant impact on the landscape do not constitute development. For example, afforestation or deforestation, hedgerow or stone wall removal, ploughing, and the cultivation of new crops (such as oil seed rape) are all entirely excluded from the development control system.

(b)   The Town and Country Planning Act 1990, s. 55(2)(e), provides that a change of use to agriculture or forestry is not development. Whilst it is obvious that this covers a change from an urban to a rural use, in landscape terms it is more significant that this paragraph excludes from development control a change from unused land (often of high nature conservation or landscape value) to agriculture or forestry, or from agriculture to forestry, or from forestry to agriculture, or from one type of agriculture or forestry to another. 'Agriculture' is defined very widely in the Town and Country Planning Act 1990, s. 336, to include such diverse things as intensive livestock production, fish farming, horticulture and extensive grazing.

(c)   Further exemptions are set out in the Town and Country Planning (General Permitted Development) Order 1995 (SI 1995 No. 418) (the GDO) sch. 2, under which blanket automatic planning permissions (permitted development rights) are granted. For example, the GDO exempts the construction of fences and walls up to 2 metres in height, and temporary uses up to 28 days per year (although not war games, motor sports and clay pigeon shooting within SSSIs).

(d)   The GDO, sch. 2, parts 6 and 7 provide permitted development rights for a wide range of agricultural and forestry operations, such as new roads, buildings, drainage works and excavations, subject to some generous limitations on size and height (for example, each building may be up to 465 square metres in area and 12 metres in height). There are other, more technical limitations, such as that the erection or alteration of structures for the accommodation of livestock, or for storing slurry or sewage sludge, within 400 metres of non-agricultural dwellings or other buildings is not permitted under the GDO.

Prior to 1992, the exemption in part 6 applied to all farms over 0.4 hectares. An amendment that came into force in January 1992 raised that limit for most operations (termed 'Class A operations') to 5 hectares (even then, development is not permitted on a seperate parcel of land which is less than 1 hectare in area). A far more limited list of 'Class B operations' is granted permitted development rights on units between 0.4 and 5 hectares. There are thus different permitted development rights depending on the size of the farm concerned. In relation to both Class A and Class B operations, the development has to be reasonably necessary for the purposes of agriculture within the agricultural unit.

(e)   A final limitation on the usefulness of the development control system in the countryside is that this is a political system. Decisions are made by local planning authorities and are likely to reflect the economic needs and policy preferences of local residents, although reference must always be made to Plannings Policy Guidance Note 7, *The Countryside and the Rural Economy*, which sets out general Government planning policies towards the countryside. Local authorities may also underestimate the importance of a local area in national terms. (In passing it should be noted that these same limitations explain why the network of SSSIs is not protected properly by controls dependent on the town and country planning system (see p. 487).

Extra protections

In some circumstances, there are extra protections provided by the town and country planning system in the countryside:

(a)   The extent of development permitted under the GDO is limited in national parks, the Norfolk and Suffolk Broads, areas of outstanding natural beauty, conservation areas and any area specified by the Secretary of State and Minister of Agriculture under the Wildlife and Countryside Act 1981, s. 41(3) (collectively these areas are known as Article 1(5) land). Whilst the limitations are not great, this does mean that stricter controls apply to such things as extensions to houses and other buildings.

(b)   A system of prior notification applies to farm or forestry developments otherwise permitted by the GDO, sch. 2, parts 6 and 7. This means that 28 days' prior notification of the proposed development must be submitted to the local planning authority, which may then impose conditions relating to the siting, design and external appearance of the development in the light of the likely effects on the surroundings. In making this decision, the local planning authority is required to take into account not only the visual aspects of the development, but also the desirability of preserving ancient monuments and their settings, archaeological sites, the setting of listed buildings and sites of recognised nature conservation value. A fee is payable with the initial notification. Between 1950 and 1992 this requirement applied only in national parks and certain adjoining areas, but from the beginning of 1992 it was extended to all parts of England and Wales.

(c) As a matter of policy, the local planning authority may impose restrictive conditions on activities requiring permission. For example, specific design criteria are commonly imposed where there is a local style. It may also make non-statutory designations of such things as sites of high landscape value in its development plan.

(d) An Article 4 direction may be imposed under the GDO, requiring planning permission to be sought for something that would otherwise be granted automatic permission (see p. 226). For example, this mechanism was used on Halvergate Marsh in the Norfolk grazing marshes in 1984 to prevent agricultural drainage and ploughing damaging the landscape importance of the area, though in confirming the direction, the DoE stressed that the main purpose was to compel the farmer involved to accept a management agreement on the land. Since Article 4 directions entail the payment of compensation by the local planning authority if planning permission is then refused, their use is rare (even though the cost is sometimes grant-aided by central government agencies).

The Countryside Commission

The Countryside Commission was originally created in 1949 as the National Parks Commission. It is now established as an independent body, with its members appointed by the Secretary of State and with its finance provided by grant aid from central government (Wildlife and Countryside Act 1981, sch. 13). It has responsibilities in relation to the preservation and enhancement of natural beauty in England and the provision of recreational activities, including rights of way. These amenity functions distinguish its role from that of English Nature. It has few operational powers, apart from the designation of national parks and areas of outstanding natural beauty, but it has an important role in providing advice and finance in relation to its objectives. The equivalent responsibilities are carried out in Scotland by Scottish Natural Heritage and in Wales by the Countryside Council for Wales.

Landscape protection and management agreements

Apart from the limited protection accorded to landscapes by planning law, there are a number of designations of land that may be made. However, these depend ultimately either on the town planning system, or on voluntary powers. There are few, if any, compulsory powers to support landscape protection.

In line with this voluntary philosophy, there is a power for any local planning authority to enter into a management agreement with any owner of land for conserving or enhancing its natural beauty or amenity, or for promoting its enjoyment by the public (Wildlife and Countryside Act 1981, s. 39). Such an agreement is grant aided by the Countryside Commission. Unlike the position for agreements made in relation to SSSIs, the financial guidelines laid down in the Wildlife and Countryside Act 1981, s. 50 do not apply to agreements made under s. 39 (see p. 487 for those guidelines).

National parks

National parks in Britain do not equate to the concept of a national park used in most other countries. instead of being wilderness areas with few, if any, inhabitants, they contain land on which large numbers of people live. They are effectively working environments. The aim of national park designation is to plan and manage the area so as to create a balance between recreation, amenity, wildlife and economic development. Land ownership is unaffected by designation, although various public bodies are given powers to purchase land, and in practice much of some parks is in the ownership of a public body, or of the National Trust.

National parks were first provided for in the National Parks and Access to the Countryside Act 1949. This Act still provides the basic structure of the legislation on national parks, although it has been much amended, especially by the Countryside Act 1968 and the Environment Act 1995, Part III, which came into force on 20 September 1995. The purposes of national parks were originally stated in the Hobhouse Report (*National Parks in England and Wales*, 1947), and set out in the National Parks and Access to the Countryside Act 1949, s. 5, in terms of two general objectives: the preservation and enhancement of the natural beauty of the areas; and the promotion of their enjoyment by the public. In recognition of the way that attitudes towards the national parks have changed since 1949, the Environment Act 1995, s. 61 substitutes a new s. 5 which sets out somewhat wider purposes:

(a)   conserving and enhancing the natural beauty, wildlife and cultural heritage of the areas . . .; and
(b)   . . . promoting opportunities for the understanding and enjoyment of the special qualities of those areas by the public.

The impact of the changed purposes is reinforced by a new s. 11A(2) to the 1949 Act, which requires all public bodies and statutory undertakers to have regard to the new purposes when exercising or performing any functions affecting land in a national park. The new s. 11A(2) also gives statutory effect to the so-called 'Sandford principle', which is that where there is a conflict between purposes (a) and (b), then greater weight should be attached to purpose (a). The balance between environmental, amenity and economic factors is also made explicit in a new s. 11A(1), which requires national park authorities to seek to foster the economic and social well-being of local communities within the national park, albeit in the context of pursuing the purposes set out in s. 5.

Responsibility for proposing and designating a national park originally lay with the National Parks Commission, which designated the 10 existing parks in the 1950s. This responsibility has now devolved to the Countryside Commission and the Countryside Council for Wales, which are currently reviewing the boundaries of existing parks and the question of new designations. If a new park is proposed (and it has been suggested that the New Forest, which is currently managed by the Forestry Commission, with environmental purposes very much to the fore, should be formally recognised as a national park), it would require extensive publicity and consultation and would normally also require a public inquiry, after which the designation requires confirmation by the Secretary of State.

Currently there are 10 national parks, covering 9% of the area of England and Wales and with almost 250,000 permanent residents. There is no national park in Scotland, although there are designations with a roughly similar impact. The parks are the Peak District, the Lake District, the Yorkshire Dales, the North York Moors, Northumberland, Snowdonia, the Brecon Beacons, the Pembrokeshire Coast, Exmoor and Dartmoor. In addition, the Broads Authority was established by the Norfolk and Suffolk Broads Act 1988. This has a similar constitution and powers to the national parks, with the inclusion of powers over navigation and water space. For the purposes of most legal protections it is treated as a national park.

The national parks are the only areas where a new institutional structure has been created in an attempt to protect the countryside. However, control remains essentially local, since the Countryside Commission and the Countryside Council for Wales have no executive functions. At present, each park is run either by a committee of the relevant county council (a joint committee is possible in cases where the park spreads over a county boundary) or a separate, autonomous board. In each case one-third of the members are appointed by the appropriate Secretary of State and at least one-seventh of the members are appointed by the constituent district councils, with the remainder representing the county councils concerned. Two boards have been created, the Peak Park Joint Planning Board and the Lake District Special Planning Board, both of which are effectively semi-independent local authorities with their own staffing and budget.

The Environment Act 1995, Part III, will alter this position. Section 63 enables the Secretary of State to establish by order a national park authority in the form set out in sch. 7. It is clear that this section will be used to convert the existing authorities into what will effectively be autonomous local authorities (and also to establish national park authorities on this model for any new national parks that are designated). Schedule 7 provides that a national park authority shall be a body corporate and shall be subject to most legislative provisions affecting local authorities, including those on access to meetings, audit, competitive tendering and the jurisdiction of the Commissioner for Local Administration (the Ombudsman). Following a late amendment to the Act, for national parks in England the balance between the various appointees to the authorities has been altered, a change that has led to accusations from some quarters that national park authorities will be turned into centralised quangos. (In Wales, one-third of the members are still to be appointed by the Secretary of State, after consultation with the Countryside Council for Wales, and two-thirds appointed by the constituent local authorities.) One half plus two of the members will be appointed by the constituent county and district councils, with the remainder appointed by the Secretary of State, after consultation with the Countryside Commission. Of those Secretary of State appointees, one half minus one must be members of parish councils in the national park. The total number on the authority and the exact number of appointees each local authority will have will be set out in the specific order establishing each national park authority. The authority will then elect its own chair and deputy chair.

Each national park currently has a national park officer and a national park management plan. This position remains the same for the new authorities, which are empowered to adopt the existing management plan, subject to provisions concerning regular review (Environment Act 1995, s. 66). At present, 75% of the finance for the national parks is provided centrally through the national park supplementary grant. The new authorities will be in a similar position: the Environment Act 1995, s. 72 gives the relevant Secretary of State a wide discretion to make grants to a national park authority, whilst s. 71 empowers the authorities to issue levies to the constituent local authorities, and it has been announced that the principle of 75% central funding will remain. In addition, it should be noted that grants from the Countryside Commission and the Countryside Council for Wales for works and schemes are normally payable at a higher rate in a national park than they are outside.

Protection of the parks has always been strongly tied to the town and country planning system. The national park committee or board will be the local planning authority for the area and, as well as taking any decisions on the control of development in the area, will have drawn up any relevant local plans in the past. It will currently be drawing up the national park development plan that was first required by the Planning and Compensation Act 1991. (As with all plan-making in national parks, this requires consultation with the Countryside Commission or the Countryside Council for Wales.) The Environment Act 1995 enables the new national park authority to be designated the sole local planning authority for its area, and will take over all these planning functions. One exception concerns tree preservation orders, where the district council retains concurrent jurisdiction with the national park authority.

As far as the substantive details of planning law is concerned, apart from the limited restrictions referred to above, the main protection lies in the formulation and application of sensitive policies for the protection of the park through the planning process. But national parks are certainly not inviolable, as the siting of Fylingdales Early Warning Station, Milford Haven Oil Terminal, and numerous quarries in the Peak District illustrate. National park authorities also have positive powers in relation to such things as the purchase of land, the arrangement of public access, the provision of facilities and the appointment of rangers.

Every national park authority is under a duty to prepare a map of 'any area of mountain' moor, heath, woodland, down, cliff or foreshore' within the national park, whose natural beauty it is important to conserve (Wildlife and Countryside Act 1981, s. 43, as amended by the Wildlife and Countryside (Amendment) Act 1985). These maps will provide a reliable picture of the landscape of the parks and how it is changing. They will be used as the basis for policies relating to landscape protection within the parks, in line with guidance issued by the Countryside Commission.

Areas of outstanding natural beauty

Areas of outstanding natural beauty (AONBs) are designated under the National Parks and Access to the Countryside Act 1949, s. 87, for their natural beauty, with the objective of protecting and enhancing these features. Even though in landscape terms they are meant to be the equivalent of national parks, by comparison with the parks they are little known and understood, and many of the powers available within them are optional for the local planning authority. Indeed, Marion Shoard in *The Theft of the Countryside* (1981) described them as the 'Cinderellas of the planning system'.

AONBs have a number of similarities with national parks. They tend to be extensive areas: 41 have been designated, covering over 14% of England and Wales. They are designated in the same way as national parks, i.e. the Countryside Commission makes a proposal for designation which requires confirmation by the Secretary of State, normally after extensive consultation and a public inquiry. They rely on town planning procedures for their legal protection and the town planning powers are essentially the same as in national parks, including the duty to consult with the Countryside Commission over the making of development plans.

However, there are significant differences too. AONBs do not have a statutory role as far as recreation is concerned. No specific extra finance is provided for AONBs. But perhaps the major difference from national parks is that the local planning authority remains unchanged. In order to combat some of the weaknesses inherent in the powers relating to AONBs, the Countryside Commission issued a policy statement in which it suggested the preparation of a management plan for each one and the appointment of AONB officers, similar to national park officers. Current policy is also to encourage the coordinated planning of AONBs by the creation of joint advisory committees in those areas where more than one local planning authority has responsibility for the area.

Other landscape protections

A further type of designation is heritage coast. Areas are selected by the Countryside Commission and the local planning authority acting together and are subject to protective policies within the planning process. Forty-four areas covering 1,493 km of coast were designated by 1991. It should also be noted that there is a fairly strong Planning Policy Guidance Note No. 20, entitled *Coastal Planning,* which establishes a number of restraint policies on coastal development.

There is a power for the Secretary of State and the Minister of Agriculture to make moorland conservation orders by statutory instrument (Wildlife and

Countryside Act 1981, s. 42). These orders impose a notification requirement similar to that applied to SSSIs, with the intention that the national
park authority may offer a management agreement. It is accordingly a
criminal offence to plough or convert any moor or heath subject to an order
which has not been agricultural land within the preceding 20 years, unless the
national park authority has been notified in advance. This section is distinctly
limited. Orders can only be made in a national park and only provide for a
temporary ban on operations, and works can go ahead after 12 months even
if the national park authority refuses consent for them. It does not appear that
any such orders have ever been made.

Landscape protection orders were recommended by the House of Commons Select Committee on the Environment in 1985. Despite support from
the Countryside Commission, this proposal produced a very limited response
from the Government, which envisaged their use only as a stopgap power
pending the making of a management agreement, and the proposals have
never been acted upon.

Agriculture and landscape

There is insufficient space in this book to trace the history of agricultural
grants and their relationship with damage to the countryside, but in the past
their availability has often been held responsible for a great number of
damaging changes (see, for example, Shoard, *The Theft of The Countryside*,
1981). The nature of agricultural grants and, indeed, of the whole shape of
agriculture has changed dramatically in the last few years, and this is reflected
in such things as the so-called EC Agri-Environment Regulation 2078/92, the
EC scheme on agricultural set-aside, and the domestic Farm and Conservation Grant Scheme. There is also a number of schemes seeking to protect
landscapes, such as the Countryside Stewardship Scheme, introduced in
1991 by the Countryside Commission with the aim of encouraging farmers
to recreate traditional landscapes in return for incentive payments, although
the Ministry of Agriculture, Fisheries and Food will take this over in 1996.

There are three protective procedures which have an important impact on
the protection of the landscape and deserve greater attention:

(a) Prior notification

Since 1980 there has been a scheme in which farmers in national parks and
the Broads should give advance notification to the national park authority of
their intention to seek agricultural grants. (A similar scheme applies in
relation to SSSIs, requiring prior notification of the relevant NCC.) The
scheme is non-statutory and therefore is not backed up by any legal sanctions,
but it has had a high success rate in preventing objectionable proposals from
being carried out (see *Farm Grant Notifications in National Parks*, Countryside
Commission, 1987). The Countryside Commission has recommended that
the scheme be extended to cover AONBs.

The scheme works as follows. The farmer should notify the national park
authority of an intention to seek agricultural grant. If no objection is received,

the work may go ahead. If there is an objection, discussions follow between the two parties, and the Agricultural Development and Advisory Service of the Ministry of Agriculture, Fisheries and Food (ADAS) are able to mediate at this stage. If a satisfactory arrangement cannot be reached informally, one solution is for a management agreement to be concluded under the Wildlife and Countryside Act, s. 39.

If no agreement can be reached, the farmer may seek a decision on the grant from the Minister of Agriculture, who may approve or refuse it. The possibilities for damaging development are thus either:

(a)   that the Minister approves the grant against the opposition of the national park authority; or

(b)   that the farmer goes ahead with the works without grant.

It should be noted that, in making the decision, the Minister is under a duty to seek to achieve a reasonable balance between the interests of agriculture and of conservation of the natural beauty of the countryside (Agriculture Act 1986, s. 17), and this may be given as the reason for a refusal. However, the Minister may give as the reason for the refusal of grant the objection by the national park authority, in which case the authority is under a duty to offer a management agreement, to which the financial guidelines made under the Wildlife and Countryside Act 1981, s. 50 will apply (see the 1981 Act, s. 41(4)), although it does not appear that this procedure has ever been used.

(b)   Environmentally sensitive areas (ESAs)

These designations formally date from EC Regulation 797/85 on Improving the Efficiency of Agricultural Structures, which permitted Member States to give special aid to farmers in environmentally sensitive areas. However, the current powers are modelled on an experimental scheme established earlier in the Broads to solve the problems experienced in Halvergate Marsh as a result of proposals to plough part of the Marsh (see the Broads Grazing Marshes Conservation Scheme 1985–88). Effect was given to the EC Regulation in Britain by the Agriculture Act 1986, s. 18, which allows MAFF to designate an ESA after consultation with the Countryside Commission and the relevant NCC, with the aim of conserving landscape and wildlife. Over 20 ESAs have been designated in England and Wales.

Within these ESAs standard rates of annual payment are made by MAFF to farmers in return for their agreeing to farm in accordance with specified practices. The order establishing each ESA includes a list of practices (and of grant rates) specially tailored for that ESA, but the exact terms of each agreement are a matter for the management agreement between the farmer and MAFF. One important point about these protections, apart from the fact that they rely wholly on the voluntary agreement of the farmer, is that payment is made by MAFF rather than by the conservation bodies. Another is that, by providing for standard rates of payment for standard practices, the system is administratively far simpler than the one established for SSSIs, where each management agreement has to be negotiated individually. As a result, the take-up rate for the ESA scheme is far higher. The Countryside Commission has proposed that ESA-type arrangements should be available throughout the whole country (see *Protected Landscapes in the UK*, 1987).

(c)   Grant schemes under the Agri-Environment Regulation 2078/92

Four sets of regulations were made in 1994 in order to assist in the implementation of Regulation 2078/92. Each of them enables the Minister of Agriculture, Fisheries and Food to make payments for certain types of countryside management and each specifies rates of payment and precise management requirements. In keeping with the usual Government policy in this area, occupiers are given a choice whether to join the schemes or not. The Habitat (Water Fringe) Regulations 1994 (SI 1994 No. 1291) apply where an occupier within 20 metres of a designated watercourse or lake agrees not to use arable land or permanent grassland for agricultural purposes for 20 years and undertakes to manage the land to protect or improve a wildlife habitat. The Habitat (Salt-Marsh) Regulations 1994 (SI 1994 No. 1293) apply where the occupier undertakes to manage land with the objective of establishing an area of salt-marsh. The Habitat (Former Set-Aside Land) Regulations 1994 (SI 1994 No. 1292) apply a similar system in relation to land which has previously been the subject of agricultural set-aside. The fourth set of regulations, the Nitrate Sensitive Areas Regulations 1994 (SI 1994 No. 1729), are discussed in Chapter 14 in the context of nitrate sensitive areas, although their impact is somewhat wider than pollution control. Finally, under the Environment Act 1995, s. 98, the Minister of Agriculture, Fisheries and Food and the Secretary of State for Wales are empowered to make grants for any purposes which are conducive to the conservation or enhancement of the natural beauty or amenity of the countryside (including its flora and fauna) or any features of archaeological interest, or the promotion of the enjoyment of the countryside by the public.

EIGHTEEN

The protection of trees and woodlands

In seeking to protect trees and woodlands, the law has to grapple with two familiar and related difficulties—controlling destructive, rather than constructive, acts and establishing adequate control over natural things. There have been protections for selected trees in the town and country planning legislation since 1932, and the powers have been strengthened regularly since then. But planning law tends to concentrate on negative, restrictive controls while the proper management of natural resources such as trees requires positive measures. Ordinary town planning rules have a limited impact, but further protection for trees comes from specific legislation. This is now mainly provided by ss. 197–214 of the Town and Country Planning Act 1990, which deal with tree preservation orders (TPOs), and all references to section numbers in this chapter refer to this Act.

TPO protection is based on considerations of amenity rather than the nature conservation value of the trees. There are no nature conservation protections specific to trees, but most of the nature conservation and landscape designations may be used to protect trees. There are also protections which arise out of the forestry legislation, though this primarily tends to concern trees as commercial items, and will therefore be covered only briefly.

Trees and planning permission

Planning permission is not required for the planting or cutting down of trees or woodland, because trees, being natural, are not structures or buildings for the purposes of the development control system. Section 55(2)(e) also excludes from the definition of development any change of use of land to forestry or woodland.

However, s. 197 imposes a general duty on local planning authorities to make adequate provision for trees when planning permission is granted. This may involve attaching conditions relating to trees to the permission (e.g. that certain trees should be retained or replaced by others, or that new trees should be planted as part of the landscaping of the site). It also involves considering whether to impose a TPO on any existing trees. A further possibility is to refuse permission on the grounds that existing trees or woodland should be retained. Full advice on trees and the planning system is given in DoE Circular 36/78, which is how supplemented by *Tree Preservation Orders: A Guide to the Law and Good Practice* (DoE, 1994).

Tree preservation orders (TPOs)

A TPO is a means by which individual trees, groups of trees or woodlands may be protected against damage. A TPO may be imposed on specified trees 'if it appears to a local planning authority that it is expedient in the interests of amenity' (s. 198). Since the section refers explictly to amenity, it does not seem that a tree could be protected for nature conservation purposes. Most TPOs are made in urban areas, though rural woodland may also be protected.

TPO offences
Any person who, in contravention of a TPO, '(a) cuts down, uproots or wilfully destroys a tree, or (b) wilfully damages, tops or lops a tree in such a manner as to be likely to destroy it', commits an offence, unless consent has been obtained from the local planning authority (s. 210(1)). The maximum penalties for this offence were increased by the Planning and Compensation Act 1991. On summary conviction the maximum fine is £20,000. On conviction on indictment the level of the fine is unlimited. In determining the amount of any fine, the court must have regard to the financial benefit accruing, or likely to accrue, to the convicted person in consequence of the offence. This is a significant provision, since many offences against TPOs are committed by developers who stand to make a substantial gain on the development value of their land (see, for example, the £50,000 fine imposed on a property company for deliberately felling 25 trees after designation, which is reported at [1991] JPL 101). There is a further offence of contravening the provisions of a TPO (s. 210(4)), for which the maximum fine is £2,500. This will cover such things as ignoring conditions imposed on works permitted by a TPO. If no other enforcement action works, an injunction to stop contravention of a TPO is available (s. 214A), though courts will be reluctant to exercise their discretion to issue an injunction except in clear cases. One notorious persistent offender (a Kent farmer) has, however, been imprisoned for failing to comply with the terms of an injunction.

These offences may be committed by any person, not just the owner or occupier of the property. They are offences of strict liability. Thus, in *Maidstone BC v Mortimer* [1980] 3 All ER 552, a contractor was held to have committed an offence even though the owner of the site had assured him that consent for the works had been given. (It seems that the owner would also commit an offence in such a situation, because the contractor is acting as an agent.) This strict position is justified by the fact that a TPO is a public document (it is a local land charge), so anyone can check the position before carrying out works.

Part of the offence requires that it be committed 'wilfully'. This has been interpreted to mean that it is the act of damaging or destroying the tree that must be wilful (i.e. deliberate), not the contravention of the TPO. *Barnet LBC v Eastern Electricity Board* [1973] 2 All ER 319, illustrates that this may include a negligent act. In that case, contractors negligently damaged the roots of six trees subject to a TPO, shortening their life expectancy. The Divisional Court held that this amounted to a wilful destruction. The case also illustrates that the concept of destruction includes something less than immediate death to the tree.

Making a TPO
The local planning authority has responsibility for making TPOs. This normally means the district planning authority, or the national park authority in a national park, though a county planning authority does have jurisdiction over its own land and where it grants planning permission (e.g. on waste disposal or minerals applications). The authority which imposes the TPO is then the relevant local authority for all procedures for consent and for enforcement purposes. The Secretary of State has a reserve power to make a TPO under s. 202, although this is unlikely to be used much.

The procedures for making a TPO are set out in the Town and Country Planning (Tree Preservation Order) Regulations 1969 (SI 1969 No. 17, as amended by SI 1981 No. 14 and SI 1988 No. 963), which are made under the authority of s. 199. The local planning authority produces a draft TPO, which is placed on public deposit, and all owners, occupiers and those with felling rights are notified. At least 28 days are then allowed for objections, which must be considered before the local planning authority itself confirms the TPO (prior to 1980 a TPO required confirmation by the Secretary of State). There is no appeal against the making of a TPO, though there is right to challenge its validity in the High Court under s. 288. In practice, arguments about the desirability of protecting the tree are considered at the stage of seeking consent to fell.

Normally a TPO does not have effect until it is confirmed. But under s. 201 a provisional (or interim) TPO may be made by the local planning authority. This is done simply by stating that s. 201 applies and the TPO will then have immediate effect, though it will lapse if not confirmed within six months. Such a provisional TPO is of obvious use where there is an imminent threat of felling.

Each TPO is separately drafted and accompanied by a map. This position allows for flexibility (for example, conditions specific to that TPO may be attached, or permitted woodland management operations may be established for a coppiced woodland), but it does make the making of a TPO quite a cumbersome process—certainly more cumberstone than those protective designations where all that is required is that standard rules or restrictions apply to the designated land. However, there is a standard form, which is set out in the schedule to the 1969 Regulations, and accordingly most TPOs will be substantially in the form set out in the schedule. The normal position is therefore that TPOs include a list of permitted operations and of prohibited operations, some of which are especially tailored for that site.

One particular difficulty relates to the definition of a tree. In *Kent CC v Batchelor* [1976] 33 P&CR 185, Lord Denning MR somewhat arbitrarily suggested that a diameter of 7–8 inches at least was needed before something could be said to be a tree. However, this was expressly not accepted by Phillips J in *Bullock* v *Secretary of State* [1980] 40 P&CR 246, who thought that anything ordinarily called a tree could be covered by a TPO. In that case he accepted expressly that a coppiced woodland could be covered, a position which seems sensible, since from an ecological point of view a coppice is effectively a single entity and not a collection of unconnected trees. Phillips J's view is to be preferred and is supported by s. 206(4), which states that a TPO will attach to any tree planted as a replacement for one subject to a TPO—such a replacement will often be a sapling or smaller tree. However, although the dividing line is imprecise, it remains clear that some things cannot be the subject of a TPO, such as hedges, bushes and shrubs. It appears to be accepted that a stump of a tree is capable of remaining a tree if it is still alive—a proposition that enables a TPO to continue to apply to trees which have been felled, but not to those which have been uprooted.

A further issue relates to whether local authorities actually have the resources to make TPOs. It appears that a number of local authorities have adopted a policy of not making any further TPOs because of the time and expense involved. The legality of such a policy must be questioned, as it appears to amount to an effective fettering of discretion.

Defences to TPO offences

There is a number of exceptions to these offences:

(a) Some works are permitted in the TPO itself. For example, the standard form of TPO exempts many works by statutory undertakers on operational land, and also works on cultivated fruit trees. More importantly, it exempts from control 'cutting down, topping or lopping a tree . . . where immediately required for the purpose of carrying out development authorised by a planning permission' (this includes a permission granted by the GDO—as to which, see p. 225).

(b) It is possible to seek consent from the local planning authority (see below).

(c) It is an exception to cut down, uproot, to or lop trees which are dead, dying or dangerous, or 'so far as may be necessary for the prevention or abatement of a nuisance' (s. 198(6)). The nuisance exception relates to the position where a tree is a civil nuisance. It is potentially a very wide exception, because it is a civil nuisance for a tree to affect a neighbour's foundations or access. *Elliott* v *Islington LBC* [1990] 4/4 Env Law 9 illustrates the potential for conflict between public and private rights when dealing with private nuisance. Mr Elliott obtained a mandatory injunction against Islington LBC requiring that a horse chestnut tree, which was in an adjoininig park and was damaging his garden wall, be removed. (The tree was not actually subject to a TPO because it was the Council's practice not to designate trees on their own land, but this does not affect the point being made.) It is believed that the injunction was in fact never enforced following a later compromise agreed between the parties, but in the Court of Appeal Lord Donaldson MR showed the primacy accorded to private rights over the public interest when he stated, 'It is not generally appropriate to refuse to enforce specific private rights on the basis that that would cause hardship to the public: the court would be legislating to deprive people of their rights'.

(d) There are further exceptions where the Forestry Commission is already effectively controlling forestry activities on the land through a forestry dedication covenant, or a grant or loan made under the Forestry Acts (s. 200).

Consent

It is possible to apply to the local planning authority for consent to carry out any works which are prohibited by a TPO. Any consent which is granted may be subject to conditions, such as the planting of replacement trees. There are no publicity requirements for an application for consent, though Circular 36/78 encourages it and notification of neighbours and the placing of site notices are common. There is an appeal to the Secretary of State against a refusal of consent, and the procedures and powers on an appeal are exactly the same as for an appeal against refusal of planning permission. Technically, the Secretary of State cannot remove a TPO, but granting consent to fell with no obligation to replant achieves the same result.

Replacement trees

The replacement of trees covered by a TPO may be required by the terms of the TPO itself (e.g. in return for permitted works), by a condition attached to a planning permission, by the terms of a consent, or by s. 206.

Section 206 provides that, if a tree is removed or destroyed in contravention of a TPO, or because it was dead, dying or dangerous, a replacement tree of appropriate size and species must be planted at the same place as soon as reasonably possible. The owner may ask the local planning authority for this requirement to be lifted. The TPO attaches to the replacement tree.

Special provisions apply to woodlands. There is no need to replace a dead, dying or dangerous tree, and the obligation is to replace the same number of trees on or near those removed, or as agreed by the local planning authority. Flexibility has been provided in such a case because it will often be impossible to determine exactly how many trees were removed and from where.

Enforcement notices

Since contravening a TPO is itself a criminal offence, there is less need for an enforcement notice requirement than for ordinary breaches of development control. But there is a power for the local planning authority to serve an enforcement notice where a replanting obligation is not complied with. Such a notice must be served within four years of the failure and may require such replanting as is specified by the authority (s. 207). There is a right of appeal against an enforcement notice to the Secretary of State, who may uphold, modify, or quash it (s. 208).

Failure to comply with an enforcement notice is not a criminal offence but the local planning authority may enter the relevant land, carry out the replanting as required, and recover the cost from the owner (s. 209).

Conservation areas

All trees in a designated conservation area are subject to a statutory restriction (effectively a statutory TPO) which prohibits the cutting down, lopping, topping, uprooting, wilful damage or wilful destruction of the tree (s. 211). This is more limited than most individual TPOs. In addition, regulations may be made by the Secretary of State that exempt specified works (s. 212).

There is one crucial difference between these statutory TPOs and ordinary ones: prohibited acts may go ahead six weeks after notification of an intention to do them has been given to the local planning authority. The purpose of this section is to enable the local planning authority to have prior notification of potentially damaging works to trees in conservation areas. (A similar form of control is applied for the protection of SSSIs—see p. 480.) It then has six weeks in which to decide whether to impose a TPO: if it does not the works may go ahead. It is an offence to do any of the prohibited acts without notifying the local planning authority and waiting six weeks, unless consent is given earlier. The penalties for this offence, and the replanting and enforcement provisions, are the same as for ordinary TPOs.

Compensation

No compensation is payable for the imposition of a TPO, but it is payable where loss or damage is caused by a refusal of consent or by a conditional consent (s. 203).

Originally it was thought that this compensation was payable to compensate for the value of cut timber forgone, but this assumption was shown to be unwarranted by *Bell* v *Canterbury CC* [1989] 1 JEL 90. In this case the Court of Appeal confirmed that the level of compensation payable was for the loss in value of the land. Accordingly, it awarded compensation at £1,000 per acre to a farmer who was prevented from converting a coppiced woodland to beef or sheep farming. Such large amounts of compensation would obviously limit the use of TPOs by local authorities, especially on woodlands which may have potential for agricultural or urban development.

An immediate response was to alter the TPO Regulations. It had always been possible for the local planning authority to certify that refusal was in the interests of good forestry or that the trees were of outstanding or special amenity value: in such a case no compensation would be payable. This certificate was originally available for individual trees, but the Regulations were amended (in SI 1988 No. 963) to apply the procedure to woodlands. However, a more significant response was to alter the practice of the Forestry Commission in relation to woodland TPOs. In woodland, the volume of timber being cut will normally require a felling licence from the Forestry Commission (see below). Normally, the Commission would refer any application relating to trees subject to a TPO to the local planning authority. However, a change of practice consequent to *Bell* v *Canterbury CC* was that the Commission agreed to refuse a felling licence if TPO consent would be refused. The effect is that the Commission pays compensation, but at the level set out in the Forestry Act 1967, which relates to the value of the timber.

Felling licences

Under s. 9(2) of the Forestry Act 1967, a felling licence is required from the Forestry Commission for the felling of trees over 8 cm in diameter (15 cm in coppices) measured 1.3 m from the ground. It is an offence to fell without a licence, which again may be committed by anyone (see *Forestry Commission* v *Frost* [1990] JPL 929). This control is based on commercial factors, rather than on amenity factors. However, the Forestry Commission is under a duty to endeavour to achieve a balance between the management of forests and the conservation of landscape and nature (Forestry Act 1967 s. 1(3A), inserted by the Wildlife and Countryside (Amendment) Act 1985 s. 4). A felling licence is not required for fruit trees, trees in gardens, orchards, churchyards or public open space, topping or lopping of trees, operations under a forestry dedication scheme, or where less than 30 cm^3 of timber per quarter is harvested.

To avoid duplication of effort, if a felling licence is required and there is a TPO in force, the following procedure applies. The application goes to the Forestry Commission, which has three choices: it may refer the matter to the local planning authority, in which case the TPO legislation applies; it may refuse the licence, in which case it will pay compensation under the Forestry Act 1967; or it may grant a licence. A felling licence is the equivalent of a TPO consent, but before the Commission grants a licence it must consult with the local planning authority. If the authority objects to a proposed grant of a licence, the matter is referred to the Secretary of State for decision. If a licence is granted there is an obligation to restock the land, unless the Commission waives it (see the Forestry Act 1986).

Proposals for change

In December 1990, the Government issued a consultation paper entitled *Review of Tree Preservation Policies and Legislation,* which stated its intention to strengthen the TPO legislation. These proposals included the establishment of a standard form of TPO in legislation, that all TPOs should have immediate effect, more flexible arrangements on the siting of replacement trees, and legislation to limit compensation for refusal of consent in woodlands to the value of the lost timber. There are also proposals to give local authorities positive powers to demand works on protected trees.

In 1994 the Government announced its intention to implement many of these proposals and thus to make the TPO legislation more coherent. However, no Parliamentary time was found during the passage of the Environment Act 1995, which perhaps suggests that the Government's commitment to amendment of the law is somewhat qualified. In addition, it is extremely disappointing that neither Circular 36/78 nor the 1969 Regulations, both of which still refer to legislation which is now completely out-of-date, has ever been updated to reflect the significant changes in society and the law since then.

Hedgerows

There has been an enormous loss of hedgerows since 1945, mainly as a result of agricultural intensification. However, hedges have never had the same protection as trees, because the definition of a tree means that the TPO legislation does not apply to them, though it is capable of applying to trees in hedgerows. Numerous promises have been made in relation to hedgerow protection. In the White Paper, *This Common Inheritance* (1990), the Government proposed 'to enable local authorities to protect hedgerows of key importance by making preservation orders, with appropriate payments to farmers to look after them properly'. Similar promises were made in the Government's 1992 General Election manifesto and in Parliament in the context of opposing Private Member's Bills on the subject. The December 1990 consultation paper referred to above also proposed the introduction of hedgerow management orders.

The Environment Act 1995, s. 97, has finally taken the first steps on the road to protecting hedgerows. Surprisingly, it does not provide for hedgerow management orders backed up by compensation payments, but instead envisages a much simpler system in which regulations may be made prohibiting the removal, damage or destruction of 'important hedgerows', together with ancillary provisions about offences and appeals. The crucial question of the meaning of the phrase 'important hedgerow' is left to be defined in the regulations, but it is quite clear that any regulations that are made will create a system of compulsory controls that is similar in scope to the TPO system, rather than a voluntary system of the type usually preferred by the current Government.

Bibliography

This bibliography is intended as slightly more than just a list of books mentioned in the text. Because of our sparing use of references (which we think often serve to distract the reader), we have sought to identify, with brief comments, some of the more important pieces of writing on each area.

As the book tries to illustrate, there is a need to be familiar with the policy of environmental protection as well as with the law: indeed, the two are often indistinguishable. One way to achieve this is to read official publications and a clear picture of the whole range of policies and issues can be obtained from the Government's White Paper on the Environment, *This Common Inheritance: Britain's Environmental Strategy* (Cm. 1200, 1990). This has been supplemented by annual reports on the progress that is being made on the policies set out in it. More recently, the Government issued four, more reflective, documents in January 1994, *Sustainable Development: The UK Strategy* (Cm. 2426), *Climate Change: The UK Programme* (Cm. 2427), *Biodiversity: The UK Action Plan* (Cm. 2428); and *Sustainable Forestry: The UK Programme* (Cm. 2429). A further White Paper on sustainable development and the environment is expected early 1996.

Any Report by the Royal Commission on Environmental Pollution, the House of Commons Select Committee on the Environment, or the House of Lords Select Committee on the European Communities is worth reading. Each of these bodies has a firm grasp of the policy issues and is not afraid to challenge the adequacy of the existing situation.

However, often the best way to get an insight into what is happening is to read literature produced by environmentalists and environmental organisations. We recommend Rose, *The Dirty Man of Europe: The Great British Pollution Scandal* (Simon & Schuster, 1990) and Secrett & Porritt, *The Environment: The Government's Record* (Friends of the Earth, 1989), which is a good antidote to the claims in *This Common Inheritance*. In recent years, there have also been some interesting books attempting to counter what are seen by some as an excessive 'green pessimism': a good example of the genre is North, *Life on a Modern Planet: A Manifesto for Progress* (Manchester University Press, 1995).

For those seeking an overview of environmental law, the books can be divided into two main categories: those for environmental practitioners and those that are written for a more general audience.

In the first category, there is a range of texts covering the practice of environmental law. In particular, *The Encyclopaedia of Environmental Law* (Sweet & Maxwell), *Commercial Environmental Law and Liability* (FT Law & Tax), and *Garner's Environmental Law* (Butterworths) are all loose-leaf works which provide comprehensive and regularly updated coverage of the law and some important policy documents. Other titles of interest include *Tolley's Environmental Handbook* (Tolley, 1993), which has a very wide coverage of subject matter in the form of chapters written by different authors, and Salter, *Corporate Environmental Responsibility - Law and Practice* (Butterworths, 1992), though neither has much analysis at times.

As far as general textbooks are concerned, Hughes, *Environmental Law* (2nd ed. Butterworths, 1992) contains more detail and width of coverage than we provide in this book, whilst clear and accessible accounts of the law are given in Leeson, *Environmental Law* (Pitman, 1995), Mumma, *Environmental Law: Meeting UK and EC Requirements* (McGraw-Hill, 1995) and *NSCA Pollution Handbook* (National Society for Clean Air), which is updated annually. An introductory guide for the complete beginner is Murdie, *Environmental Law and Citizen Action* (Earthscan, 1993), although further detailed research would be necessary in conjunction with this book. It should also be noted that, since environmental law is heavily based on statutes, some good (if disjointed) discussions can be found in the various commentaries on the relevant Acts. There is also Duxbury and Morton, *Blackstone's Statutes on Environmental Law* (1994), which includes the text of the most useful Acts and pieces of delegated legislation.

Frontiers of Environmental Law, ed. Lomas (Chancery Law Publishing, 1991) is a stimulating set of essays on the subject: Chapter 2 by Macrory on the 'new formalism' is particularly valuable. A further set of essays entitled *Law, Policy and the Environment*, a special issue of the *Journal of Law and Society*, edited by Churchill, Gibson and Warren, 1991, includes background material on a number of areas. In particular, the article by Churchill, 'International Environmental Law and the UK', is an excellent survey of the role of international law. *Public Interest Perspectives in Environmental Law*, ed. Robinson & Dunkley (Wiley Chancery, 1995) is an excellent and valuable set of essays: it includes good chapters on public interest environmental litigation in the US and access to justice in the EC, as well as on the Australian experience of environmental courts, legal standing in the UK and the whole concept of public interest environmental law. Essays explaining the position in Scotland are collected in *Green's Guide to Environmental Law in Scotland*, ed. Reid (W.Green & Son, 1992).

Birnie and Boyle, *International Law and the Environment* (Oxford, 1992) is an excellent and comprehensive book that more than fills the gap on international law left in the text of this book. Sands, *Principles of International Environmental Law* (Manchester University Press, 1995) is also highly recommended.

Journals

Of course one of the most important things in environmental law is keeping up-to-date. There are a number of journals which attempt to do this, though one thing that any environmental law researcher quickly discovers is just how difficult it is to establish what has happened recently and what is going to happen next. This is perhaps a good illustration of the secrecy traditionally surrounding policy-making in this country (though the difficulties pale into insignificance when compared with those involved in finding material on EC proposals). There are many Consultation Papers currently being produced by Government on proposed changes in the law. These often summarise the current position and the reasons for change. The problem is finding out about their existence.

Since environmental law includes news and policy from a wide range of sources, the best way to keep up is to read *ENDS Report* (Environmental Data Services Ltd), a topical monthly digest of a wide range of news on environmental matters, with good coverage of legal and policy developments.

Environmental Law and Management (Wiley Chancery), formerly *Land Management and Environmental Law Report,* appears bi-monthly and attempts to cover all areas of environmental law through articles and current survey. *Water Law* (Wiley Chancery) is also bi-monthly, and as its name suggests, covers those things connected to the water industry, also through articles and current survey.

The Journal of Environmental Law (Oxford University Press), is published twice a year and includes more lengthy and reflective articles. It can be said to fill the need for a more academic journal, though a disadvantage is the slowness with which it is published. There is also *Environmental Law,* the journal of the UK Environmental Law Association (UKELA), published four times a year and including short articles and items of news.

All these journals — and the *Journal of Planning and Environment Law* (Sweet & Maxwell) — include summaries and reports of cases, usually with illuminating comments. The *Environmental Law Reports* (quarterly, Sweet & Maxwell) are the only source in which to find the full transcripts of environmental cases. There is scope for legitimate debate over the inclusion of certain cases, but as this book seeks to make clear, the boundaries of the subject are, by their very definition, blurred. For an international view, *Environmental Liability* (bi-monthly, Sweet & Maxwell) provides coverage of a variety of national approaches to environmental law.

Chapters 1, 2, 3 and 5

These chapters attempt to tackle in introductory form a number of more general issues. An excellent starting point for any deeper reading is Rehbinder and Stewart, *Environmental Protection Policy* (De Gruyter, 1985), though McLoughlin & Bellinger, *Environmental Pollution Control: An Introduction to Principles and Practice of Administration* (Graham & Trotman, 1993) is a very readable account which combines legal and administrative insights. On the specific issue of the various types of standard that are available, see Haigh, *EEC Environmental Policy and Britain* (2nd ed. Longmans, 1989), Chapter 3. There is also some useful material in Department of the Environment Pollution Paper No. 11, *Environmental Standards — The UK Practice* (1975) and Wood, *Planning Pollution Prevention* (Heinemann Newnes, 1989).

On the 'British approach' to pollution control, see Vogel, *National Styles of Regulation* (Cornell University Press, 1986), a comparison of British and American approaches, though it is somewhat out-of-date in the 1990s. Ridley, *Policies Against Pollution: The Conservative Record and Principles* (Centre for Policy Studies, 1989) includes an explanation of Government policy in the late 1980s, though it is easier to look at the policy documents mentioned earlier for an explanation of what may be happening in the 1990s. Also recommended are an, as yet, unpublished PhD thesis from the University of Sheffield, Hilson, *Pollution Control and the Rule of Law* (1995), which addresses whether current regulatory and market mechanisms fulfil the requirements of equity, efficiency, effectiveness and accountability, and Ogus, *Regulation: Legal Form and Economic Theory* (Oxford, 1994).

For a sound explanation of general legal principles in the UK, see Waite, 'Criminal and Administrative Sanctions in English Environmental Law' [1989–90] LMELR 38 and 74. For some thoughts on the civil liability system, see Ball, 'Liability for Environmental Harm' [1995] *Contemporary Issues in Law*, vol. 2. Some useful reflections on *locus standi* are Purdue, 'A Harpoon for Greenpeace?: Judicial Review of the Regulation of Radioactive Substances' [1994] JEL 297; Geddes, '*Locus Standi* and EEC Environmental Measures' [1992] JEL 29; and Macrory, 'Environmental Assessment and EC Law' [1992] JEL 273.

The relationship between economics and environmental law is covered in many books, but the starting point should be Pearce, Markandya and Barbier, *Blueprint for a Green Economy* (Earthscan, 1989), which now has a sequel, Pearce *et al*, *Blueprint 3: Measuring Sustainable Development* (Earthscan, 1993). Alternative views can be read in Bowers, *Economics of the Environment: The Conservationists' Response to the Pearce Report* (British Association of Nature Conservationists, 1990) and Jacobs, *The Green Economy* (Pluto Press, 1991).

Some other useful articles on issues that are relevant to the future of environmental law are Walton, Ross-Robertson and Rowan-Robinson, 'The Precautionary Principle and the UK Planning System' [1995] ELM 35; Winter, 'Planning and Sustainability: An Examination of the Role of the Planning System as an Instrument for the Delivery of Sustainable Development' [1994] JPL 883; and Fairley, 'Environmental Policy and Audit — What's In It For Us?' [1995] ELM 31. As suggested in the text, the creation of an environmental court has been discussed on a number of occasions. See, especially, Woolf, 'Are the Judiciary Environmentally Myopic?' [1992] JEL 1; Carnwath, 'Environmental Enforcement: the Need for a Specialist Court' [1992] JPL 799; and McAuslan, 'The Role of Courts and Other Judicial Type Bodies in Environmental Management' [1991] JEL 195.

Chapter 4

The basic materials on EC environmental law are to be found in Haigh, *Manual of Environmental Policy: The EC and Britain* (Longmans, 1992), an expensive loose leaf work that replaced the excellent Haigh, *EEC Environmental Policy and Britain* (2nd ed. Longmans, 1989). A major part of these works consists of an analysis of the history and scope of each Directive which could be said to be within the sphere of environmental policy.

For a more legalistic look at the legal basis of EC policy, a good book is Krämer, *EC Treaty and Environmental Law* (Sweet & Maxwell, 1995), written by the former Head of Application of Community Law in Directorate-General XI in the EC Commission. Also see Krämer, *Focus on European Environmental Law* (Sweet & Maxwell, 1992), which is a stimulating collection of essays on relevant topics and Krämer, *European Environmental Law Casebook* (Sweet & Maxwell, 1993).

There are a number of books on the general constitutional law of the EC. The easiest to read is Steiner, *Textbook on EEC Law*, 4th ed. (Blackstone Press, 1994), which is now supplemented by Steiner, *Enforcing EC Law* (Blackstone Press, 1995). These should be used to supplement any shortcomings in the explanations in this book on the general law of the EC.

Keeping up with changes in EC law is almost impossible. Very few people have the time to look through the pages of the *Official Journal or Europe*, though this is really the only way to do it. It is often a better bet to scan the reports of current events in the general environmental journals. There cannot really be any greater indictment of the secrecy that surrounds the decision-making processes in the EC! The only thing that makes this less disturbing is the fact that most pieces of environmental legislation take such a long time to get agreed that their import is known long before they are adopted.

Other recommended publications: Haigh and Baldock, *Environmental Policy and 1992* (European Cultural Foundation, 1989); Somsen, EC Water Directives [1990] 1 *Water Law* 93; the *European Environmental Law Review* (Graham & Trotman), a monthly journal combining news with articles; a set of essays, Somsen, *The Enforcement of EC Environmental Law* (Edward Elgar, forthcoming); and Stuart, 'Combating Non-Compliance with EC Environmental Directives' [1994] ELM 160.

Chapter 6

Anyone looking for some wider reading material on the enforcement of environmental law will find a number of extremely useful works. Most of these studies have tended to concentrate on the socio-legal aspects of empirical studies. Two seminal articles by Carson investigated the use of enforcement mechanisms in the Factory Inspectorate and described how the Factory Inspectorate first incorporated the idea of 'moral blame' in making any decision to prosecute for the breach of strict liability offences (see 'White Collar Crime and The Enforcement of Factory Legislation' (1970) 10 *British*

Journal of Criminology 383 and 'Some Sociological Aspects of Strict Liability' and 'The Enforcement of Factory Legislation' (1970) 33 MLR 39).

Following on from these and other works, a number of in-depth studies were carried out by the SSRC Centre for Socio-Legal Studies, Wolfson College, Oxford. Two further works were produced as a result, Richardson, Ogus and Burrows, *Policing Pollution — A Study of Regulation and Enforcement*, (Clarendon Press, 1982) and Hawkins *Environment and Enforcement: Regulation and the Social Definition of Pollution* (Clarendon Press, 1984). Both these studies examine the work of the water industry, the former looking specifically at the discharge of trade effluents into public sewers whereas the latter deals with the discharge of the trade effluents directly into watercourses. The final work in the series, Hutter, *The Reasonable Arm of the Law* (Clarendon Press, 1988) examines the enforcement processes of environmental health officers. All three works support the view that the enforcement of strict liability offences relies heavily upon the individual officers view of the offender and the offence.

For an up-to-date view of the enforcement of environmental regulations see Rowan-Robinson and Ross, The Enforcement of Environmental Regulation in Britain [1994] JPL 200. For a glimpse into the future and an explanation of some of the potential effects of the Government's deregulation initiative see Burton 'Environmental Aspects of Proposed Legislation on 'Cutting Red Tape" [1994] *Water Law* 93.

Chapter 7

The Royal Commission on Environmental Pollution has long campaigned for free access to environmental information. See generally: *Three Issues in Industrial Pollution* (The Second Report, Cmnd. 4894, 1972); *Pollution in Some British Estuaries and Coastal Waters* (The Third Report, Cmnd. 5054, 1972); *Air Pollution Control: An Integrated Approach* (The Fifth Report, Cmnd. 6371, 1976); *Agriculture and Pollution* (The Seventh Report, Cmnd. 7644, 1979). More specifically, however, *Tackling Pollution — Experience and Prospects* (The Tenth Report, Cmnd. 9149, 1984) gives a good introductory account of the arguments for and against disclosure. For a more informal essay *The Secrets File* ed. Wilson (Heinemann Educational Books, 1984) provides good anecdotal evidence of the use and abuse of secrecy. More particularly, Frankel, *How Secrecy Protects the Polluter*, Chapter 3, suggests that there are real benefits to be gained from a greater degree of openness. These works are largely made up of contributions from members of the Campaign for Freedom of Information in Britain whose periodical *Secrets* gives up-to-date briefings on access to official information of all types. Indeed, the success of the organisation is demonstrated by the two Acts of Parliament introduced by their lobbying — the Local Government (Access to Information) Act 1985 and the Environment and Safety Information Act 1988.

The Government replied to the criticisms contained in the Royal Commission's Tenth Report in Pollution Paper No. 23, which gives an overview of Government policy on access to environmental information. Other recommended reading: Birkenshaw, *Government and Information* (Butterworths, 1990); Birtles, 'A Right to Know; The Environmental Information Regulations 1992' [1993] JPL 615; Fairley, 'Integrated Pollution Control — Public Registers and Commercial Confidentiality' [1993] ELM 111; Jenn, 'Public Interest Litigation and Access to Environmental Information' [1993] *Water Law* 163; and *Environmental Information: Law, Policy and Experience* (Cameron May, 1993).

Chapter 8

This chapter looks at the law of tort from a single perspective and therefore does not attempt to cover all aspects of that particular field. More specialised works include Rogers, *Winfield and Jolowicz on Tort* (Sweet & Maxwell), Dias, *Clerk and Lindsell on Tort* (Sweet & Maxwell). For a more general survey of about the protection of private rights see Pugh-Smith, *Neighbours and the Law* (Sweet & Maxwell).

There are a number of articles dealing with the narrower area of the overlapping nature of the common law and the protection of the environment: McLaren, 'Nuisance-Law and the Industrial Revolution — Some Lessons from Social History' (1983) 3 OJLS 155; Ogus and Richardson, 'Economics and the Environment: A Study of Private Nuisance' [1977] CLJ 284. Both these deal with the socio-legal aspects of common law control. A thorough examination of the overlap can be found in Steele 'Private Law and the Environment: Nuisance in context' (1995) 15 LS 236.

Other recommended reading for those interested in the practical aspects of the common law include Croft, 'The Environmental Protection Act 1990 — Part III, Statutory Nuisance — Consolidation or Change?' [1991] LMELR 2, and Waite, 'Private Civil Litigation and the Environment', [1989] LMELR 113. The problem of historic liability for contamination in the wake of the *Cambridge Water* case (but pre-Environment Act) is discussed in Shelbourn, 'Historic Pollution — does the Polluter Pay?' [1994] JPL 703.

Chapter 9

There are many excellent books on the law relating to town and country planning which cover it in far greater detail than could be attempted in the confines of one chapter. They tend to vary between those which see the subject as a set of rules and those which put it in its policy context. Quite simply, the best book is Grant, *Urban Planning Law* (Sweet & Maxwell, 1982, supplement 1990), though it is now somewhat out of date. This large book combines clear explanations of the law with analysis of its difficulties, as well as providing coverage of the practical context and policy factors that are so important in planning law.

Those who wish to get an immediate impression of what planning law is all about would be best advised to supplement Grant by familiarising themselves with the Planning Policy Guidance Notes and Circulars and to ensure that they look at a few copies of development plans. In addition, some useful pieces on the direction of planning law are: Grant and McAuslan, 'The Scope of Planning: Back to the Future?', *Development & Planning* (editors Cross and Whitehead, Policy Journals, 1989); Garner, 'The Decline of Planning Control' [1985] JPL 756; McAuslan, 'Planning Law's Contribution to the Problems of an Urban Society' [1974] 37 MLR 134 and McAuslan, *Ideologies of Planning Law* (Pergamon Press) especially Chapters 1 and 6.

Other good textbooks on planning law are: Moore, *A Practical Approach to Planning Law*, 6th ed. (Blackstone Press, 1992). This is the clearest of the standard textbooks, but is rather too much orientated towards the exposition of principles through cases and hence fails fully to convey the central role that policy plays in the subject; Heap, *An Outline of Planning Law*, 10th ed. (Sweet & Maxwell, 1991) — a solid but a rather uncritical explanation of the law, though it is very full in its coverage; Telling and Duxbury, *Planning Law and Procedure*, 9th ed. (Butterworths, 1993), is more readable, but less complete than Heap. Purdue, Young and Rowan-Robinson, *Planning Law and Procedure* (Butterworths, 1990) is a very full practical guide to the area but is again somewhat out of date.

All of these books use the space available to explain the law on matters not covered in this book, such as advertisements, compensation, listed buildings and conservation areas, although a good introductory book on this last area is Ross, *Planning and the Heritage* (E & FN Spon, 1991).

An excellent and stimulating book which analyses the public law issues underlying the development control system is Alder, *Development Control*, 2nd ed. (Sweet & Maxwell, 1989).

Two good books on the relationship between planning and pollution control are: Miller and Wood, *Planning and Pollution* (Oxford University Press, 1983) and; Wood, *Planning Pollution Prevention* (Heinemann Newnes, 1989). Both include some interesting case studies of the application of the law in practice, and the second book also carries material on the USA by way of comparison.

The *Journal of Planning and Environment Law* (JPL), includes most important cases in the area. It has the advantage of having comments on the cases by Professor Purdue. It is, however, somewhat misnamed since in the past its contents almost exclusively related to the planning side of the title.

Keeping up-to-date is crucial in the planning area. *The Encyclopaedia of Planning Law* (Sweet & Maxwell), includes all the relevant statutory and non-statutory material and is updated each month. It also has the distinct advantage of Professor Grant's annotations and analysis.

Chapter 10

Most texts on planning law contain the basic information on environmental assessment. The best guide, however, is *Environmental Assessment — A Guide to the Procedures* (HMSO, 1989). This is a no-nonsense guide to the law and includes most of the basic points that would need to be covered. For a more critical view, see three articles by Salter: 'Environmental Assessment — The Challenge from Brussels' [1992] JPL 14; 'Environmental Assessment — The

Need for Transparency' [1992] JPL 214; and 'Environmental Assessment —
The Question of Implementation' [1992] JPL 313.

Chapter 11

For a critical evaluation of the historical development of environmental law
the Royal Commission on Environment Pollution Reports provide a good
background to the introduction of integrated pollution control. The Fifth
Report, *Air Pollution Control: An Integrated Approach* (HMSO, Cmnd. 6371,
1976), the Tenth Report, *Tackling Pollution — Experience and Prospects*
(HMSO, Cmnd. 9149, 1984) and the Twelfth Report, *Best Practicable
Environmental Option* (HMSO, Cmnd. 310, 1988) all trace the development
of the principles of integrated pollution control. Other works of interest
include UKELA's 'Best Practicable Environmental Option — A New
Jerusalem?' (1987). Also see 'Best Practicable Environmental Option and its
Antecedents' [1986] JPL 643.

For a more practical guide to the legal intricacies of the IPC system under
the EPA see Waite, 'Integrated Pollution Control and Local Authority Air
Pollution Control — The New Regime' [1991] LMELR 11. Also HMIP's
Integrated Pollution Control — A Practical Guide (HMSO, 1993) is helpful in
giving a view of the enforcement bodies thinking. For further information see
Purdue, 'Integrated Pollution Control and the Environmental Protection Act
1990: The Coming of Age of Environmental Law?' [1991] 54 MLR 534 and
Layfield, 'The Environmental Protection Act 1990 — The System of Integ-
rated Pollution Control' [1992] JPL 3.

For a view of how integrated pollution control systems have developed
elsewhere in the world see *Integrated Pollution Control in Europe and North
America* (edited by Haigh and Irwin, Institute for Environmental Policy,
1990).

Chapter 12

Good introductory background works on air pollution include Ashby and
Anderson, *The Politics of Clean Air* (Clarendon Press, 1981) and Elson,
Atmospheric Pollution (Basil Blackwell, 1987). The Royal Commission on
Environmental Pollution's Reports in 1976 and 1984 also provide a good
overview of the legislation historically.

Other areas which may be of interest include the overlap between planning
and environmental regulations (see Wood, *Planning Pollution Prevention*
(Heinemann Newnes, 1989) and Forster, 'Plugging the Gaps — The Revision of the Ozone Layer Protocol' [1990] 2 LMELR 74). Finally, for an
overview of the workings of the local authority air pollution control system
see Waite, 'Integrated Pollution Control and Local Authority Air Pollution
Control — The New Regime'[1991] LMELR 11.

Chapter 13

The starting point for any research on waste should be the Royal Commission on Environmental Pollution's Eleventh *Report — Managing Waste: The Duty of Care* (HMSO, Cmnd. 9675, 1985). This Report not only deals with waste management law and practice but also some of the wider issues surrounding the disposal of waste in Britain. Other helpful official publications include, House of Lords Select Committee on Science and Technology, Fourth Report, Session 1988–90, *Hazardous Waste Disposal* (HMSO, 1989); House of Lords Environment Committee Second Reports Session 1988/9, *Toxic Waste* (February 1989); House of Commons Environment Committee First Report Session 1988–90, *Contaminated Land* (January 1990).

For an excellent article dealing with the problems of defining waste see Purdue, 'Defining Waste', JEL (1990) 250. For a short discussion of the problems in the enforcement of the Control of Pollution Act 1974, see Hawke, *Waste Management Law and Enforcement* (Leicester Polytechnic Law Monographs, 1989). This contains a good overview of the old system and provides a quick guide to its defects. See also Ball, 'The Waste Management Licensing Regulations' [1994] Water Law 124.

There is now an excellent book on the law relating to waste in both the old and the new systems — Bates, *UK Waste Law* (Sweet & Maxwell, 1992), though it does not contain much by way of critical evaluation.

The clean-up of contaminated land has given rise to a host of articles and publications. The most comprehensive coverage of the law prior to the implementation of the Environment Act is to be found in Tromans and Turrell-Clarke, *Contaminated Land* (Sweet & Maxwell 1994).

For a stimulating examination of the problems of trying to regulate the clean-up of contaminated land whilst taking note of market effects (the stumbling block for the Contaminative Uses Register) see Steele, 'Remedies and Remediation: Issues in Environmental Liability' (1995) 58 MLR 615.

Chapters 14 and 15

There are good existing books on water pollution law. The best detailed coverage is Howarth, *Water Pollution Law* (Shaw and Sons, 1988, supplement 1990), though as the publication dates suggest, this is now somewhat out-of-date. Howarth, *The Law of Aquaculture* (Fishing News Books, 1991), though on a restricted subject matter, is also a most impressive book. Elworthy, *Farming for Drinking Water* (Avebury, 1994) is also worth reading on agricultural issues. Bates, *Water and Drainage Law* (loose-leaf, Sweet & Maxwell) provides a comprehensive survey of the law relating to the water industry for practitioners.

On the policy side, the National Rivers Authority has published strategy documents on each issue for which it has responsibility. It also produces an Annual Report and regular reports in its Water Quality Series, all of which are worth looking at. For a non-official view, see Birch, *Poison in the System* (Greenpeace, 1988). Up-to-date information is provided by *Water Law* (bi-monthly, Wiley Chancery) and, in news form, the NRA's monthly publication, *The Water Guardians*.

The history of the water industry from its early days to privatisation in 1989 is well covered in Kinnersley, *Troubled Water* (Hilary Shipman, 1988). Recommended writings on the current law are Wilkinson, 'The Re-determination of the K Factors', [1994] *Water Law* 153 (which covers the relationship between water prices and environmental protection); Waite, 'Water Pollution Law After the Water Act 1989' [1989] LMELR 146; Macrory, 'The Privatisation and Regulation of the Water Industry' [1990] 53 MLR 78; Wilkinson, 'Causing and Knowingly Permitting Pollution Offences: A Review' [1993] *Water Law* 25; Ball, 'Causing Water Pollution' [1993] JEL 128; Howarth, 'Poisonous, Noxious or Polluting' [1993] MLR 171; Ball, 'Cambridge Water; What Does it Decide?' [1994] *Water Law* 61; and McGillivray, 'Discharge Consents and the Unforeseen' [1995] *Water Law* 72 and 101, the titles of which are all fairly self-explanatory.

Chapters 16, 17 and 18

Reid, *Nature Conservation Law* (W. Green, 1994) provides a clear and full summary of nature conservation law (both north and south of the border). However, it is out-of-date in the sense that the Conservation (Natural Habitats &c) Regulations 1994 are not covered. Some thoughts on these and on nature conservation generally can be found in Ball, 'Reforming the Law of Habitat Protection' in a very useful set of essays, *Nature Conservation and Countryside Law*, ed. Rodgers (University of Wales Press, forthcoming). Another general book worth reading is Gregory, *Conservation Law in the Countryside* (Tolley, 1994).

However, there is a wealth of information on the state of our natural heritage and on nature conservation policy. As far as the former is concerned, the Annual Reports of the NCC (now English Nature) are of enormous interest. The NCC also publishes a wide range of literature on specific issues, and a general strategy is set out in *Nature Conservation in Great Britain* (NCC, 1984). The starting point for any reading on the shape of modern nature conservation must be the Huxley Report, *Conservation of Nature in England and Wales* (Cmd. 7122, 1947), which sets out all the arguments as to why nature conservation is important. There are many good books on the history of nature conservation (and also landscape protection). A stimulating introduction to the science of nature conservation is Moore, *Bird of Time: The Science and Politics of Nature Conservation* (Cambridge University Press, 1987), written by a former Chief Scientist at the NCC who had a special involvement in the drawing up of the current SSSI criteria. Adams, *Nature's Place: Conservation Sites and Countryside Change* (Allen and Unwin, 1986), provides another readable summary of conservation history.

Shoard, *The Theft of the Countryside* (Temple Smith, 1980), is a book which caused enormous controversy when it first appeared in the run-up to the Wildlife and Countryside Act 1981, and it provides a polemical view of what was (and arguably still is) happening in the countryside. The story is taken on further by Pye-Smith and Rose, *Crisis and Conservation Conflict in the British Countryside* (Penguin, 1984), and Lowe, Cox, MacEwen, O'Riordan and Winter, *Countryside Conflicts: The Politics of Farming, Forestry and Conservation* (Temple Smith Gower, 1986), which includes a number of case studies in the light of the Act. International instruments on wildlife protection are well explained in Lyster, *International Wildlife Law* (Grotius Publications Ltd, 1985). The law on species protection is well covered in a practical manner in Parkes and Thornley, *Fair Grant: The Law of Country Sports and the Protection of Wildlife* (Pelham Books, 1994).

A wide-ranging set of essays on the law and the countryside is *Agriculture, Conservation and Land Use* (ed. Howarth and Rodgers, University of Wales Press, 1992). More detailed information on landscape protection can be found in *Protected Landscapes in the UK* (Countryside Commission, 1987). As far as tree protection is concerned, many books on planning law include a brief chapter on this topic, though the best place for a review of the difficulties in the current law is the Department of the Environment consultation paper, *Review of Tree Preservation Policies and Legislation*, 1990.

Index

Abatement 192
  notice 197
Access to environmental information 14
  air pollution 142–3, 161, 343
  Britain's increasing acceptance 92
  chemical releases inventory 159–60
  commercial confidentiality 154–5
  decision making and 92
  EC Directives 78, 82, 86, 150
  as economic instrument 116
  Environmental Information Regulations
    1992 161–3
  integrated pollution control 156–9
  local government held information 161
  national security exemptions 154, 157,
    383
  necessary for public participation 139
  private prosecution limited by lack 120
  public registers 150–60
    access to 165–6
    atmospheric pollution 343
    awareness of public 164–5
    consents to discharge 150–2, 443–5
    contaminated land 155–6, 390–1
    drinking water quality 153
    interpretation of 166
    local authorities' 53–4
    sewerage undertaker registers 152
    utilisation 163–6
    waste management 382–3
    water pollution 150–2, 443–5
  secrecy policy
    administration costs 147
    air pollution 142–3
    commercial confidentiality 143–5
    development 141
    'green nutters' 145–7
    mechanisms 141–3
    miscellaneous controls 143

Access to environmental information –
    continued
    public environmental rights 149
    risk perception 148–9
    Royal Commission 147–8, 149–50
    water pollution 142
  trade secrets
    exclusions for 154–5, 157–8
    release of 158–9
Accumulation or deposit prejudicial to
    health 195
Acid rain 14, 38, 82, 325–6
Action Programmes (EC) 68, 77, 78, 83,
    290
Administrative regulation 86, 89–90
  British approach 90–2, 100–3
  delegation 103
  discretion 100–1
  eco-audit 117–18
  process of decision-making 90–2
    enforcement of permissions 92
    general policies established 90–1
    information provision 92
  standards
    application 91
    enforcement 92
    setting 91
  see also Regulation of environmental
    protection
Administrative sanctions 21
Adverse publicity 21
Advisory bodies 40
Agriculture
  nature conservation order restrictions
    482–4
  nitrates restriction 171–2
  silage effluence 114
  subsidies 114–15
  see also Countryside protection

Agriculture, Fisheries and Food, Ministry of
      (MAFF)
   countryside responsibilities   50
   environmentally sensitive areas   508–9
   influence of   37
   prior notification   507–8
Air, Noise and Wastes Directorate   38
Air pollution *see* Air pollution control
      system; Atmospheric pollution
Air pollution control system
   application for authorisation   341–2
      granting   342
   enforcement provisions   343
   framework of control   340–1
   guidance notes   342
   overlap with other controls   343–4
   public registers   343
   timetable for upgrading plant   342–3
Air Quality Standards Regulations   331
Alkali industry   322–4
Alkali Inspectorate   9, 10, 283, 324
Animals
   badgers   476
   conservation   470, 471, 473–4, 475–6
   foreign introductions   477
   as statutory nuisance   195–6
Areas of outstanding natural beauty   506
Assessment *see* Environmental assessment
Atmospheric pollution
   access to information   161
   acid rain   14, 38, 82, 325–6
   advisory bodies   328–9
   Air Quality Standards Regulations   331
   Alkali Act effect   323–4
   APC (air pollution control) system
      application for authorisation   341–2
         granting   342
      enforcement provisions   343
      framework of control   340–1
      guidance notes   342
      overlap with other controls   343–4
      public registers   343
      timetable for upgrading plant   342–3
   chimney height control   337–8
   dust control   335–7
   emissions *see* Emissions
   European Community and   330–2
      Directive   290–1, 330, 331
      future proposals   332
      worldwide basis for action   332
   fumes   195, 335–7
   furnaces   335–7
      monitoring   336–7
   global issues   326
   global warming   14, 38, 82, 115, 326
   grit control   335–7
   HMIP responsibilities   47

Atmospheric pollution – *continued*
   integrated pollution control   282–3
   local   322–5
   local air quality management areas
      328–9
   local authority responsibility   52
   market mechanism   332
   monitoring   329–30
   motor vehicles emission control   344–5
   National Strategy for Air Quality   327–8
   noxious emissions other than smoke
      340–4
   ozone depletion   14, 82, 326
   policy   327
   prescribed substances release   294–5,
      296–7
      secrecy surrounding   142–3
   product standards   331
   prohibition   332
   quality standards
      alert threshold   328
      guideline level   328
   set standards   91
   smoke *see* Smoke
   strategy   327–8
Auditing
   eco-audit   117–18
   environmental   21, 82

Badgers   476
Best available sources of information   272
Best available techniques not entailing
      excessive cost (BATNEEC)   107, 108
   air pollution control system   341–2
   definition   26
   HMIP guidance notes   308–12
   introduction of principle   291
Best practicable environmental option
      (BPEO)   289–90, 311–12
Best practicable means
   definition   26
   environmental assessment need   272
   introduction of concept   323
   principle applied   285
Birds, wild   474–5, 490–1, 493, 497
British approach to regulation   100–3
   centralisation   108
   context importance   106–7
   decentralisation   103–4
   discretion   22, 26–7, 105, 108
   flexibility   23, 27
   gradualism   105–6
   history   9–11
   market mechanisms *see* Economic
      mechanisms for regulation
   modern statutes   11–13
   new formalism   107–8

British approach to regulation – *continued*
  regulation 109–10
  scientific evidence, reliance on 105–6
Broads Authority 46
  see also Norfolk and Suffolk Broads
Brundtland Report 14
Business Deregulation Task Forces 138–9

Carbon dioxide *see* Emissions
Carbon tax 14, 82, 332
Central Directorate of Environmental
    Protection 38
Certiorari 31
Charging for pollution *see* Economic
    mechanisms for regulation
Chemical Industry Association 133
Chemical industry pollution control 295
Chemical releases inventory 159–60
'Chester Group' 60
CITES 470, 490
Civil liability
  damage caused by waste 82
  for environmental harm 17, 21
  environmental protection using 118–19
  statutory remedies 170–2
  see also Common law, civil remedies
Clean-up
  contaminated land 394–5, 396–7
  costs 21
  waste management 388–9
Common law
  civil remedies 190–2
    abatement 192
    damages 190–1, 457
    injunctions 191–2
    statutory 170–2
  development of protection 167
  private rights protection
    continuing control lack 170
    fault based system 169
    imprecise standards 168
    as primary role 167–70
    problems of proof 169
    reasonableness doctrine 168
    remedies ineffectual 170
    right of action limited 168–9
  public and private distinguished 167
  riparian rights protection 190
  tort *see* Negligence; Nuisance; Trespass
  water pollution 456–60
  weakness 170
  see also Statutes
Common Market *see* European Community
    (EC)
Compensation payments 115, 191
Competent authority 84
Conditions of planning 240–3

Conditions of planning – *continued*
  breach of condition notices 255
  development permitted, not related to
      240
  perverse 241
  planning purposes, not related to 240
  and policy 242
  pollution control 242–3
  tests for validity 240–2
  ultra vires 242
  uncertain 241
Confidentiality 143–5, 154–5, 157–9
  integrated pollution control 307
  public registers in waste management
      383
  release objection procedure 158–9
Consents to discharge
  acting within, nuisance claims and 460
  annual charges 437–8
  appeals 439
  conditions 134, 435–6
  consent system 434–5
  controlled waters 427–8
  NRA's discretion in setting 439–40, 443
  prohibition 427
  public registers 150–2, 443–5
  revocation 436–7
  secrecy surrounding 142
  Secretary of State's role 438–9
  trade effluent 462–5
  transitional provisions 437
  variation 436–7
  when required 426–8
Conservation areas, trees in 515
Conservation of nature
  1994 Regulations 493–5
  animals 470, 471, 473–4, 475–6
    badgers 476
    introduction of foreign 477
  current policy 470
  European marine sites 495
  European sites 493, 496, 497–8
  grants and incentives 471
  habitat protection 471, 477–8
    EC Directive 492–3
  history 468–9
    post-war period 469–70
  incidental protection 471
  international perspective 490
  internationally important sites 497–8
  limestone pavements 486
  management agreements 486–7
  Nature Conservancy Council (NCC) 12,
      50, 471–3
  nature conservancy orders 482–4
  nature reserves 471
    local 485

Conservation of nature – *continued*
  marine 485–6
  national 484–5
  planning permissions 487–9
  plants 470, 471, 473–4, 476–7
    introduction of foreign 477
  RAMSAR Convention on Wetlands
    496–7
  SSSIs 50, 373, 478–82, 486–9
    compensation 487
    duties on owners and occupiers 480–2
    government guidance note 488
    loss or damage to 489–90
    planning permissions 487–9
    'potentially damaging operations' 480
    waste management licensing 373
  types of protection 470–1
  wild birds 474–5, 490–1, 493, 497
Consultation
  environmental assessment 276–7
  waste management licensing 373–4
Contaminated land 389–99
  'appropriate person' 393, 394–5
  blight on land 390
  civil liabilities 398–9
  clean-up 394–5, 396–7
  Enforcement Agency 392
  Environmental Protection Act 398
  escapes of substances to other land 395
  identification of 393
  meaning 391–2
  nuisance 399
  reduction in value 390
  registers 155–6, 390–1
  remediation notices 393–4
    appeals 396
    non-compliance 396
    registers 396
  Rylands v *Fletcher* 395, 398–9
  statutory powers to remediate
    Environmental Protection Act 398
    planning authorities 397–8
    pollution of controlled waters 397
    statutory nuisance 397
Contracting out 109–10
  enforcement and 138–9
Controls *see* Enforcement procedures
Conventions 29
Countryside Commission 50, 502
Countryside Commission for Wales 46
Countryside Council for Wales 50, 472,
  504
Countryside protection 499–502
  agriculture and landscape
    environmentally sensitive areas 508–9
    prior notification 501–2, 507–8
    see also planning

Countryside protection – *continued*
  areas of outstanding natural beauty 506
  Countryside Commission 502, 504
  environmentally sensitive areas 508–9
  grant schemes under Agri-Environment
    Regulation 509
  heritage coasts 506
  landscape protection 502–3
    orders 506–7
  management agreements 114–15,
    502–3, 507
  moorland conservation orders 506
  national parks 214, 215, 226, 501, 502,
    503–6
    prior notification 507–8
  Norfolk and Suffolk Broads 501, 504
    prior notification 507
  planning 487–9, 499–502
    automatic permissions 500, 502
    change of use 500
    development control 499–500
    extra protections 501–2
    permitted development rights 500–1
    prior notification 501–2, 507–8
Criminal law in environmental protection
  16, 119–20
  British minimal use 102
  Crown Court trials 135
  decriminalisation 17
  identifying wrongs 119
  level of fines 135
  low sentences 120
  magistrates' powers 135
  prosecutions
    by NRA 132–3
    in cooperative approach 128
  subsidiary to regulatory process 120
  see also Enforcement procedures
Criminal liabilities 21
Crown Court trials 135
Crown immunity 10, 32, 318

Damages 190–1
Danish Bottle case 76–7, 115
Declarations 31
Decriminalisation of environmental law 17
Delegated legislation 24–5
Demolition 221
Department of the Environment
  appeals to Secretary of State 37–8
  Directorates 38
  integrated pollution control 293
  limited power 37
  regulatory agencies, accountability 36–7,
    38
  role 37–8
  see also Secretary of State

Deposit schemes   115
Deregulation   109–10
    enforcement and   138–9
Dioxins   347
Directive waste   364, 365–9
    exemptions   369–70
Discretion
    administrative   92
    improper exercise   30
    interpretation of EC law   55, 61
    legislative   26–7
Drinking water   423, 424–6
Dust, as statutory nuisance   195

Eco-labelling   116, 118
Economic growth   68
Economic mechanisms for regulation   14
    carbon tax   14, 82, 332
    charges
        levied on polluting materials or
            processes   113–14
        for operating regulatory system
            111–12
        reflecting full environmental cost of
            activity   112
        to finance control measures   113
    deposit schemes   115
    EC approach   116
    eco-auditing   82, 117–18
    future uses   115–16
    grants   114–15
    market mechanisms   110–15, 332
    'polluter pays' principle   14, 17, 182
        costs included   116
        EC principle   77
        establishment   7
        meaning   116–17
    pollution credits market   115
    refund schemes   115
    subsidies   114–15
Economic waste management instruments
    349–51
Edinburgh Summit 1992   83
Effluvia, as statutory nuisance   195
Emissions
    combination of substances   98
    diffuse   99, 100
    limits   331
    quotas   115
    smoke see Smoke
    standards   96, 97, 101, 289
        EC   290
    trading   115
    variable standards   99, 100
    see also Atmospheric pollution
Enforcement Agency, contaminated land
    392

Enforcement procedures
    administrative controls   92–4
        difficulties   130–1
        regulation   92
    aim of   123
    attitudes
        changes in   132
        towards offence   124–5
        towards offender   125–6
    British flexible strategy   102, 121
    capture theory   124–5
    confrontational approach   121
    cooperative approach   121
        increase in officer's visits   127
        presenting problem   126–7
        prosecution   128
        solving problem   127
        taking legal sample   127–8
    cost of control   17–18, 20–2
    costs of non-compliance   21
    differing levels   129–30
    discretion in interpreting regulations
        123, 124
    dual role of authorities   130–1
    EC law   82–3
    funding levels   131–2
    industry, enforcement agencies'
        relationship with   133–4
    informal tools   121, 123
    integrated pollution control   313–17
    legal context   122–4
    moral opprobrium   124
    nature of mechanisms   121–2
    non-statutory guidance   121
    prosecutions   128
        incidence of   122
        sanctions other than   126
    public bodies as enforcers   120
    public confidence in, lack of   128–9
    samples, number taken   131
    site visits, numbers of   131
    staffing levels   131
    strict liability   122
English Nature   46, 50, 472
Enhanced Urban Network (EUN)   329,
    330
Enterprise zones   212, 233
    environmental assessment   279
Environment agency   11, 12, 27, 36, 40–6,
    362
    composition   41–2
    cost-benefit duty   44–5
    enforcement and entry powers   45–6
    enforcement policy   138
    functions   42
    general powers and duties   42–3
    history   40–1

Environment agency – *continued*
  overlap with other agencies 46
  pollution control 42
  research and technical information 42
  water resources 42
Environment Department *see* Department of
  the Environment
Environmental assessment 82, 262–81
  alternative site selection 275
  appeals 273
  called-in application 273
  complexity 280
  consultation 276–7
  description 263–4
  determination of application 277–8
  Directive 262, 264–5
    direct effect 265–6
  enterprise zones 279
  lack of central guidance 280
  lack of consistent approach 280
  macro-siting process 276
  participants 263
  permitted development 269–70
  post-planning application determination
    of need 273
  in practice 279–80
  pre-application procedures
    best available sources of information
      272
    best practicable techniques 272
    directions of Secretary of State 270–2
    to establish need for assessment 270
  projects 263
    schedule 1, mandatory assessment 267
    schedule 2, discretionary assessment
      267–8
    significant effects 268
    thresholds 268, 271–2
  reform 281
  regulations 263, 266–7
  scoping 276
  screening process 276
  simplified planning zones 278–9
  statement *see* Environmental statement
  theory of stated objectives 264
  volunteering environment statement
    272–3
Environmental audits 21, 82
Environmental harm 119
  civil liability for 17, 21
  definition 22–3
Environmental Impact Assessment *see*
  Environmental assessment
Environmental Information Regulations
  1992 161–3
Environmental law
  definition 4

Environmental law – *continued*
  features 24
  future 16–20
  history 8–11
  modern developments 11–13
  policy and 22–3
  sources *see* Sources of environmental law
Environmental liabilities 21
Environmental policy future 13–16
Environmental Protection Agencies
  accountability 36–7, 38
  see also individual agencies eg National
    Rivers Authority
Environmental rights 113
  public interest 149
Environmental statement 263
  called-in application 273
  low quality 279
  objectivity lack 279–80
  specified information 273–4
  voluntary submission 272–3
Environmental taxes *see* Economic
  mechanisms for regulation
Environmentally sensitive areas
  (ESAs) 508–9
Environmentally significant discharges 134
European Commission 57
European Community (EC)
  Action Programmes 68, 77, 78, 83, 290
  atmospheric pollution 330–2
    Directive 290–1, 330, 331
    future proposals 332
    worldwide basis for action 332
  changing domestic law 13
  common market 67–8
  Council of Ministers 57–8
  Danish Bottles case 76–7
  environmental policy 68
    Article 235 73, 78
    Articles 100 and 100A 70, 73, 74, 75,
      76, 78
    Articles 130R, 130S and 130T 71–2,
      74, 77
    constitutional basis 69–77
    future of 81–3
    integration into other policies 78
    overriding free trade 76–7, 115
    qualified majority voting 73–4
    scope 77–9
  European Court of Justice 57, 59
  institutions 57–60
  motor vehicle pollution 345
  Single European Act 69, 73, 74
  transfrontier shipment of waste 357
  uniformity requirement 75–6
  waste management 356–7
  water pollution 418–24

European Community (EC) law 28–9
  compliance by member States 63–7
    British law 84–8
  compliance letter 64
  decisions 62–3
  direct effects 87
  Directives 55, 61–2, 79–80
    access to environmental information
      66, 78, 82, 86, 150
    air quality 330, 331
    assessment of the effects of certain
      private and public projects 262
    bathing water 84
    civil liability for damage caused by
      waste 409–10
    compliance 63–4
    drinking water 66, 85, 423, 424–6
    environmental 79–80
    environmental assessment 264–6
    framework 80–1
    habitats 492–3
    hazardous waste 356, 357, 407–8
    integrated pollution prevention and
      control 320–1
    landfills 357
    packaging and packaging wastes 75–6
    packaging waste 357
    sewage sludge 357
    urban waste water 20, 84, 422–3
    waste 356–7, 368, 369–70
    water pollution 418–20
    wild birds 490–1, 493, 497
  directly effective laws 62, 65–6, 87
  economic policies and environment 56
  enforcement 82–3
  European Court of Justice 57, 59
    direct effects 63, 65–6, 87
    indirect effect 65, 66
    rulings 64–5, 87–8
  infringement proceedings 64–7, 82–3,
    85–6
  monitoring powers 82
  parliamentary select committee 39
  Reasoned Opinions 64–5
  regulations 61
  sources 60–3
  supremacy 5, 19, 60, 65, 67, 80, 108
  treaties · 56, 61
  types of legislation 55–6
  UK environmental law, effect on 5, 13,
    28, 55–6, 84–8
  validity of legislation 63
European Court of Justice 57, 59
  direct effects 63, 65–6, 87
  indirect effect 65, 66
  rulings 64–5, 87–8

European Environment Agency 13, 59–60,
  83, 116
European Parliament 57, 58–9
  First Action programme 290
  single internal market 81–2
  see also European Community (EC)
Evidence, photography as 134
Expert Panel on Air Quality Standards
  (EPAQS) 329

Fact and degree test 26
Felling licences 516
Fertilisers
  diffuse emissions 99
  see also Agriculture; Nitrates
Fiscal instruments. 82
Fish poisoning 455
Fishing
  lead weights 456
  rights 457–8
Fly-tipping 403
Forestry
  subsidies 114–15
  trees and woodlands see Tree and
    woodland protection
  see also Countryside protection
Forestry Commission 50, 504, 514, 515,
  516
Fragmented control 284–8
Fuel and power industry 295
Fumes see Atmospheric pollution;
  Emissions; Smoke
Furnaces 335–7

Global warming 14, 38, 82
  definition 326
  emission quotas 115
  ozone depletion 14, 82, 326
'Going for Green' initiative 40
Government circulars 26, 27, 28
  setting standards 91
Government's Panel on Sustainable
  Development 40
Greenhouse effect see Global warming
Greenpeace 19
Guidance Notes 26, 27, 108, 310

Hazardous substance
  authorities 256–7
  consents
    application 257
    basis of giving 257–8
    deemed 260
    modification 259–60
  contravention notice 259
  enforcement 259
  extent of control 257

Hazardous substance – *continued*
  fees 261
  Health and Safety Executive role 258
  planning 256–61
  register 260–1
Hazardous waste 346, 356, 357
  see also Waste management, special waste
Health and Safety Executive 283
  hazardous substances 258
Hedgerow protection 517
Her Majesty's Inspectorate of Pollution 36,
    38
  advice to 133
  authorisations from 93
  divisions 47
  Environmental Agency and 41
  funding 131
  high profile enforcement 136–7
  integrated pollution control 133–134–4,
    291
    introduction 291–2
  public registers 156–9
  responsibilities 47–8
  role 46–8
  staffing levels 131, 136
  unifying body 133–4, 291
  see also Integrated pollution control
Heritage coast 506

Incineration 347, 388
  EC Directive 357
Industrial Air Pollution Inspectorate,
    registers 156
Industry
  chemical 133, 159–60, 295
  enforcement agencies' relationship with
    133–4
  integrated pollution control 292–6
Information *see* Access to environmental
    information
Injunctions 32, 191–2, 200–1, 459–60
  enforcement of planning law 254–5
Institute of Terrestrial Ecology 472
Integrated pollution control 26
  atmospheric pollution 282–3
  authorisation application 301–4
    additional information 302
    complex sites 303–4
    conditions 307–8
    determination 307–8
    envelope applications 303
    form 302
    guidance notes 310
    requirement 293–4
    special cases 302
    staged applications 302–3
    transfer 313

Integrated pollution control – *continued*
  best available techniques not entailing
    excessive cost (BATNEEC) 291,
    308–12
  best practicable environmental option
    289–90
  best practicable means 285–6
  call-in procedure 306
  commercial confidentiality 307
  consultation procedures 305–6
  determination of need for authorisation
    294
  development of 282
  discharge of effluent into sewers 299
  EC role 81, 290, 320–1
    Directive 320–1
  enforcement powers 313–17
    appeals 319–20
    corporate liability 318
    Crown immunity 318
    enforcement notices 315
    inspectors' powers 316–17
    offences 317–18
    prohibition notices 316
    remedies 317–18
    revocation notices 315
    variation notices 313–15
  fees and charges 304–5
    annual charges 304
    application fees 304
    levels 304–5
    OPRA ratings 305
    variation fee 304
  fragmented control 284–8
    cooperational approach 287
    discretionary decision-making 287
    failure to view whole environment
      286–7
    lack of public accountability 288
    overlapping controls 287–8
    Royal Commission Fifth Report 288
  HM Inspectorate of Pollution, role in
    133–4, 291
  implementation of system 313
  introduction 47, 292
  land, pollution on 283–4
    see also Waste disposal
  notes 312
  organisation and administration 292–3
  overlapping controls 298–9
  planning permission 299–300
  prescribed processes 294–5
  proportionality principle 290
  public participation 305–6
    registration 156–9
  release of prescribed substances 294–5,
    296–7

Integrated pollution control – *continued*
  transitional controls 300
  vorsorgeprinzip 290–1
  water pollution 284, 445–6
Interest groups
  locus standi in judicial reviews 32–4, 67
  see also Public participation
Internationalisation 14–15

Judicial review 19–20, 108
  abuse of statutory powers 141
  decision made when no power 30
  grounds 29
  planning matters, over 235–7, 247
  procedural unfairness 30–1
  procedure 32–4
  remedies 31–2
  restrictions 34–5
  standing (*locus standi*) of applicant 32–4,
    67
  sufficient interest 32–4
  ultra vires 30

Labelling of goods 116, 118
Land pollution *see* Landfill; Waste disposal
Landfill 346–7
  EC Directive 357
  levy 349, 350–1
  methane produced 346, 347
  tax 14, 113–14, 349, 350–1
Landscape protection 502–3
  orders 506–7
Law *see* Common law; European
    Community (EC) law; Statutes
Limestone pavements 486
Litter 119
Local authorities
  decision-making in 53–4
  enforcement action 53–4
  environmental roles 51–2
  planning authorities, as 94, 213–14
  public registers 156–9
  statutory nuisance responsibilities
    192–3, 196
    injunctions 200–1
  two-tier system 50–1
  waste disposal companies and 133
Local authority air pollution control (APC)
    guidance notes 26
Local environmental quality 100
Local Government Ombudsman 229
Local plans 217–18
Locality doctrine 168, 173–4
  planning permission 174

Maastricht treaty 70, 73, 77
Macro-siting process 276

Magistrates' powers 135
Management agreements 114–15
  countryside protection 502–3, 507
Mandamus 31
Marine nature reserves 485–6, 495
Market mechanisms 110–15, 332
  see also Economic mechanisms for
    regulation
Metals industry 295
Minerals industry 295
Ministry of Agriculture, Fisheries and Food
    (MAFF) 41
Monitoring pollution 168
Montreal Protocol 29
Moorland conservation orders 506–7
Motor vehicle emissions 344–5

National Environmental Technology Centre
    (NETCEN) 329
National Heritage Department 38
National parks 214, 215, 226
  planning protection 501, 502, 503–6
  prior notification 507–8
National Parks Authorities 46
National Rivers Authority (NRA) 36, 108
  discretion 27
  enforcement 131–4, 136, 137, 138
  Environmental Agency and 41
  environmentally significant discharges'
    134
  establishment 12
  general quality assessment 413
  prosecutions by 132–3
  public register of consents to discharge
    150–2, 443–5
  reasons for creation 84
  regulatory control 132–3
  responsibility 411–12
  role 48–9
  sewage disposal 20, 30
  waste plans 370–1
  see also Consents to discharge; Water
    pollution
National security 307
  waste management public register
    exemption 383
National Strategy for Air Quality 327–8
National Survey of Air Pollution 329
Nature *see* Conservation of nature
Nature Conservancy Council (NCC) 50,
    471–3
  dismantling 12, 472–3
Nature conservation orders 482–4
Nature reserves
  local 485
  marine 485–6
  national (NNRs) 484–5

Negligence 185–7
  defences
    act of God 189
    statutory authority 189
  duty of care 186
  escape of hazardous substances 187–9
  failure to warn of dangers 187
  fault based system 186
  limitations of, in pollution control 186
  non-natural user 187–8
  restrictions on 188–9
  Rylands v Fletcher rule 182–3, 187–9
Nitrates
  EC standards 422, 423
  restrictions 171–2
  sensitive areas 115, 453–4
Noise
  construction sites 198
  local authority responsibility to
      control 52
  as statutory nuisance 196
Norfolk and Suffolk Broads
  planning protection 501, 504
  prior notification 507
Nuclear incidents 171
Nuisance
  contaminated land 397, 399
  defences
    plaintiff came to nuisance 176–7
    prescription 176
    statutory authority 177–8
  definition 172
  duration 174–5
  expense of case 182
  locality doctrine 168, 173–4
  private 168
  public 183–4
  reasonableness doctrine 172
  role in regulating standards 9
  sensibility 175
    hyper-sensitive plaintiff 175–6
  standard of quality from 98
  statutory see Statutory nuisance
  vagueness of standards 91
  value in environmental protection 180–3
  water pollution cases 456

Official Secrets Acts 141
OFWAT 49
Ombudsman 35
  local government 229
Operator and Risk Appraisal (OPRA)
    scheme 305
Our Common Future (Brundtland
    Report) 14
Out of town superstores 213
Ozone depletion 14, 82, 326

Packaging waste 357
Pesticides
  diffuse emissions 99
  see also Agriculture; Nitrates
Planning
  agreements 171, 243, 246
  anticipatory control 94
  appeals 246–8
    number 247
    procedure 247–8
    public inquiry 247–8
    s.288 statutory appeals 249
    Secretary of State powers 206
    success rate 211
    see also Judicial review
  British aversion to long-term
      planning 102
  centralisation 108, 212
  change of use
    ancillary 222–3
    existing 225
      intensification 223
    incidental 222–3
    material 222–3
    planning units 223
    Use Classes Orders 223–5
  conservation of nature 487–9
  countryside protection 487–9, 499–502
    automatic permissions 500, 502
    change of use 500
    development control 499–500
    extra protections 501–2
    management agreements 502–3
    national parks 501, 502, 503–6
    Norfolk and Suffolk Broads 501, 504
    permitted development rights 500–1
    prior notification 501–2, 507–8
  creating permanent rights 93
  definition 209–10
  deregulation 212
  developer-led 209, 210
  development
    building operations 220–1
    change of use see change of use
    commencement 222
    control 219–20
    definition 219–20
    engineering operations 221
    mining operations 221–2
    waste disposal 222
  development plans 205–6
    development control and 218–19
    forward planning 214
    future 237
    influence 236
    non-statutory material 219

Planning – *continued*
  presumption in favour of following
    209, 237–8
  recent developments   215, 237–8
  setting standards   99–100
  enforcement of law
    breach of condition notice   255
    enforcement notices   249–51
      appeals against   252–3
      challenging validity   253–4
      procedure   251–2
    immunity from   251
    injunctions   254–5
    new powers   255
    planning contravention notices   255
    stop notices   254
  enterprise zones   212, 233
  environmental assessment *see*
    Environmental assessment
  environmental policy, and law   206–8
    conditions for continuing control   207
    mixed economy solution   207
    negotiated development   207
  fact and degree test   26
  gain   207, 243, 244–5
  General Development Order   225–7,
    229–30
  government role   210–11, 236–7
    policy decisions   242
  hazardous substances   256–61
    authorities   256–7
    consents
      application   257
      basis of giving   257–8
      deemed   260
      modification   259–60
    contravention notice   259
    enforcement   259
    extent of control   257
    fees   261
    Health and Safety Executive role   258
    other planning controls   258
    register   260–1
  legislation   208–9
  limited effect in control   207
  local authorities
    discretion   234–7
      judicial control of   234–7
    duties and responsibilities   51, 229–31
    permission to themselves   231
  local plans   217–18
  main features   205–6
  market forces   115–16
  material considerations   244, 245
  negative aspects   6
  obligations   243–6
    legitimacy   245–6

Planning – *continued*
  modification or discharge   246
  permissions *see* Planning permission
  policy   210–11
  political issues   207, 208
  positive aspects   6
  Private Bill procedures   212, 232
  Secretary of State's powers   234
    challenging under s.288   249
  simplified planning zones   212, 233
  special areas   232
  structure plans   215–17
  third party rights   234
  undertakings   243
  unitary development plans   218
  urban development corporations   212,
    214, 232–3
  urban problems   500
  waste disposal   207–8, 348–9
    areas of doubt   355
    development control   355
    planning conditions and obligations
      355–6
  waste local plans   354–5
  water pollution   454–5
  see also Local authorities
Planning permission   206
  alternative and special procedures   231–2
  applying for   227–30
  automatic   226–7
  certificate of lawfulness   227
  conditions   240–3
    breach of condition notices   255
    development permitted, not related to
      240
    perverse   241
    planning purposes, not related to   240
    policy, and   242
    pollution control   242–3
    tests for validity   240–2
    ultra vires   242
    uncertain   241
  Crown land   232
  decisions of local authority   230–1
  environmental control, and   94
  integrated pollution control   299–300
  local authorities granting to themselves
    231
  locality doctrine   174
  material considerations   238–40
  presumption in favour of   211
  private nuisance rights   173–4, 178–80
  requirement for   227
  Special Development Orders   232, 233
  trees   510–11
  types   227–8

Plants
  conservation 470, 471, 473–4, 476–7
  introduction of foreign 477
'Polluter pays' principle 14, 17, 182
  costs included 116
  EC principle 77
  establishment 7
  meaning 116–17
Pollution
  control 46–8
  critical levels 23
  HM Inspectorate see Her Majesty's
    Inspectorate of Pollution
  integrated control see Integrated pollution
    control
  limitations of statutory control 9–11
  relative concept 107
  sensitive areas 98
  statutory controls 11–12
  see also individual forms eg Emissions;
    Smoke
Precautionary principle 77
Private law remedies
  under Statutes 170–2
  see also Common law; Negligence;
    Nuisance
Private nuisance 168
Process standards 96–7, 99
Product standards
  EC Action Programme 78, 81
  as means of control 97, 98, 99
Prohibition 31
Proportionality concept 63
  see also Judicial review
Prosecutions see Criminal law in
  environmental protection
Protection of countryside see Countryside
  protection
Protection of environment
  enforcement and deregulation 138–9
  enforcement policy 136–8
  public perception of importance 134–5
  redefinition of importance 134–6
  regulation see Administrative regulation;
    Economic mechanisms for regulation;
    Regulation of environmental protection
  rights of its own 134
  see also individual aspects
Protection of trees and woodland see Tree
  and woodland protection
Public awareness 164–5
Public bodies, enforcing criminal sanctions
  120
Public health
  local authority responsibility 52
  statutory controls 9
  see also Statutory nuisance

Public inquiries 247–8
Public interest, release of confidential
  information in 158–9
Public nuisance see Nuisance
Public participation
  in development plans 205–6
  EC encouragement 82
  in enforcement process 139
  environmental rights 149
  evaluation of risks 148–9
  fisheries, compensation for loss 457
  in integrated pollution control 305–6
  judicial review see Judicial review
  statutory nuisance complaints 192–3,
    199–200, 456
  third party rights in planning matters
    234
  trade effluent system 465
  use of registers 163–6
  water quality, private prosecutions 444,
    456
  see also Access to environmental
    information; Common law
Public registers 150–60
  access to 165–6
  atmospheric pollution 343
  awareness of public 164–5
  consents to discharge 150–2, 443–5
  contaminated land 155–6, 390–1
  drinking water quality 153
  interpretation 166
  local authorities' 53–4
  sewerage undertaker registers 152
  utilisation 163–6
  waste management 382–3
  water pollution 150–2, 443–5
Publicity, adverse 21

Quality of Urban Air Review Group
  (QUARG) 329
Quotas
  emissions 115
  tradable 115

Radioactive discharges
  HMIP responsibilities 48
  water pollution and 447
RAMSAR Convention on Wetlands 496–7
Reasonableness doctrine 172
Recycling 348, 351–2, 365
Red List' substances 465–6
Refund schemes 76–7, 115
Registers see Access to environmental
  information, public registers; Water
  pollution
Regulation of environmental protection
  agencies, financial independence 38

Regulation of environmental protection –
    continued
  anticipatory controls   92–3
  authorities divorced from production   13
  British approach   90–2, 101–3
  changed emphasis   134–6
  charges for operating system   111–12
  continuing controls   93–4
  economic mechanisms, by   90
  planning   94
    see also Planning
  prevention   94
  public bodies   89
  voluntary approach   103
  see also Administrative regulation;
      Economic mechanisms for regulation;
      Standards of environmental quality
Regulations *see* Delegated legislation;
      European Community (EC) law
'Relator' action   34
Remediation notices, contaminated land
    393–4
Remedying Environmental Damage   18
Rio conference 1992   15
Riparian rights protection   190
River Quality Survey   413
Royal Commission on Environmental
    Pollution (RCEP)   39–40, 311
  access to environmental information, on
    147–8, 149–50
Rural Affairs Directorate   38
Rylands v *Fletcher* rule   182–3, 187–9, 395,
    398–9
  usefulness of   190

Sandford principle   503
SAVE programme   83
Scottish Natural Heritage   50, 472
Secrecy *see* Access to environmental
    information
Secretary of State
  challenging on planning matters   249
  default powers   193
  environmental assessment directions
    270–1
    challenges to   271–2
  waste management powers   383–4
  see also Department of the Environment
Select Committees, role   39
Self-regulation   102
Sellafield reprocessing plant   19
Sewage
  costs of disposal   20–1
  effluent defined   427
  sludge, EC Directive   357
Sewers
  consents required   446–7

Sewers – *continued*
  discharges
    domestic sewage   467
    enforcement   466
    Red List' substances   465–6
    sewage works, from   466
    trade effluent   462–4
      see also Trade effluent
  disposal
    cost of controls   20–1
    EC Directive   20–1
  effluent discharge into   299
  'look up' tables   446
  prosecutions over   447
  radioactive discharges   447
  sewerage undertakers   49
  split responsibilities   462
  waste discharged to   347
Shared responsibility   78
Shell (UK)   135
Silage effluent   114
Simplified planning zones   212, 233
  environmental assessment   278–9
Site licences   373
  surrender   377–9
Sites of special scientific interest
    (SSSIs)   50, 373, 478–82, 486–9
  compensation   487
  duties on owners and occupiers   480–2
  government guidance note   488
  loss or damage to   489–90
  management agreements   486–7
  planning permissions   487–9
  'potentially damaging operations'   480
  waste management licensing   373
Smoke
  Clean Air Acts   332–7
  control areas   339–40
  dark
    defences   334
    enforcement by local authorities   334
    exemptions   334, 336
    from chimneys, control   333–4
    from industrial plants   335
    inadvertent emission   335
    offences   334–5
    Ringlemann chart   333
    strict liability   334
  as statutory nuisance   194–5
Sources of environmental law
  European Community   28–9
  informal   27–8
  international law   29
  judicial review   29–35
    see also Judicial review
  Ombudsman   35
  statutes

Sources of environmental law – *continued*
  commencement 25
  definitions 26
  delegated legislation under 24–5
  discretions 26–7, 30
  features 24
  see also Statutes
Special Development Orders 232, 233
Special waste *see* Waste management, special
  waste
Standards of environmental quality
  Best Available Technique Not Entailing
    Excessive Cost 98
  Best Practicable Means 98
  British approach to regulation 101–3
  British and EC differences 100–1, 102–3
  'bubble' approach 99
  centrally set 100
  combinations of substances 98
  defining 95
  different types, strengths and weaknesses
    98–9
  emissions 96, 97, 101
    diffuse 99, 100
  identifying cause of failure to reach 98–9
  interrelationship of 97
  lack of incentive to better 99
  limit values (EC) 98, 101
  locally set 100
  monitoring 98, 168
  nuisance test 98
  objectives only 99
  precise 98
  process 96–7, 99
  product 97, 98, 99
  target standards 95–6
  variable 98
  see also Administrative regulation
Statutes
  environment defined 4
  environmental issues in 38–9
  planning legislation 208–9
  private remedies under 170–2
  reaction to circumstances 9–11
  statutory authority as defence in civil cases
    177–8, 189
  see also Sources of environmental law
Statutory nuisance 299
  abatement notice 197
    appeal against 199
    sentencing powers for contravention
      200
  categories 193–6
    accumulation or deposit 195
    animals 195–6
    effluvia 195
    fumes or gases 195

Statutory nuisance – *continued*
    noise 196
    nuisance 194–6
    prejudicial to health 193–4
    premises prejudicial to health 194
    smoke 194–5
  control 192–3
  defences 197–8
    best practicable means 198
    reasonable excuse 198
    special 198
  injunction use 200–1
  local authority responsibility 192–3
  person responsible 197
  prescribed process, in relation to 299
  water pollution 456
  see also Nuisance
Straw burning 12
Structure plans 215–17
Stubble burning 12
Subsidiarity 83–4
Subsidies 114–15
'Superfund' system 410
Sustainable development 14, 15–16, 78, 83
  Government's Panel 40
  UK Round Table 40

This Common Inheritance (White Paper) 3,
  12, 39, 88, 111, 348
This Common Inheritance: Second Year Report
  (1992) 14, 89
Tort *see* Common law; Negligence;
  Nuisance; Trespass
Towards Sustainability 14, 78
Town and country planning *see* Planning;
  Planning permission
Toxic torts 21
Trade effluent
  charges 464–5
  consents 49
  defined 427
  discharges 462
    consents for 124, 462–4
  objectives of control 462–4
  prescribed process, produced by 299
  public participation 465
  see also Sewers
Trade and Industry Department 38
Trade secrets 143–5, 154–5, 157–9
  integrated pollution control 307
  public registers in waste management
    383
  release objection procedure 158–9
Transfrontier contamination 171
Transport Department 38
Tree preservation orders
  compensation 515

Tree preservation orders – *continued*
  consent 514
  conservation areas 515
  defences to TPO offences 513–14
  enforcement notices 514
  felling licences 516
  making order 512–13
  offences 511–12
  proposals for change 516
  replacement trees 514
Tree and woodland protection 511–17
  compensation 515
  felling licences 516
  hedgerow protection 517
  planning permission 510–11
  tree definition 512–13
  woodlands, replacement trees 514
  see also Tree preservation orders
Trees *see* Forestry: Tree preservation orders;
    Tree and woodland protection
Trespass
  actionable *per se* 185
  definition 184
  direct interference 185
  inevitability 185
  intentional or negligent 184–5

UK Round Table on Sustainable
    Development 40
Unitary development plans 218
United Kingdom *see individual aspects and*
    British approach to regulation
United Nations Conference on Environment
    and Development (UNCED) 15
United States
  emissions trading 115
  regulation of environmental protection
    102
  'superfund' system 410
Urban development corporations 212,
    214, 232–3

Vehicle pollution 344–5
Voluntary methods of protection 116

Washington Convention on International
    Trade in Endangered Species
    (CITES) 470, 490
Waste collection authorities 363, 371
  clean-up powers 389
  public registers 382–3
Waste disposal
  authorities 283–4
  civil liability
    for damage caused 82
    for unlawful 408–10

Waste disposal – *continued*
  companies, arms length control by local
    authorities 133
  Control of Pollution Act 358–61
    controlled waste 358
    failings 359–61
    inability to control cowboys 360–1
    lack of central guidance 359–60
    lack of strategic plans 360
    licences *see* waste disposal licences
    need to prove deposit related offences
      360
    organisational problems 359
    surrender of licence 361
    waste disposal licences *see* Waste
      disposal licences
  controlled waste 298, 352–3
  development, as 222
  dumping at sea 347
  Environmental Protection Act 1990
    361–70
    main features 361–4
    management licensing system *see* Waste
      management licensing
    national Environment Agency creation
      362
    waste collection authority 363
    waste disposal authority 363
    waste regulation authority 363
  HMIP responsibilities 48
  incineration 347, 388
    EC Directive 357
  integrated pollution control 295
  landfill 346–7
    EC Directive 357
    levy 349, 350–1
    methane produced 346, 347
    tax 14, 113–14, 349, 350–1
  legislation 352–3
  licensing *see* Waste disposal licences; Waste
    management licensing
  local authority responsibility 51–2
  offences 384–6
    dangerous disposal 387
    defences 386–7
    penalties 385–6
  packaging waste 357
  planning and 207–8, 354–6
    areas of doubt 355
    development control 355
    planning conditions and obligations
      355–6
    waste local plans 354–5
  register of disposal licences 153–4
  release of prescribed substances 297
  to natural waters 347
  to sewers 347

Waste disposal – *continued*
  unlawful deposit   171
  waste disposal authority   358, 363
  waste plans   370–1
  waste regulation authorities (WRA)
    153–4
  see also Sewers
Waste disposal authority   358, 363
Waste disposal licences
  applications   358
  Control of Pollution Act   358, 361
  offences   359
  register   153–4
  surrender   361
  WDA duties   358
Waste management   346–410
  agricultural waste   346
  animal waste   369
  appeals to Secretary of State   383–4
  brokers   404–5
  carriage of waste   403–4
    cost-recovery charging system   408
    pre-notification procedure   408
    special waste   407
    transfrontier   357
  case law   367–8
  change from waste disposal to   352–3
  clean-up powers   389
  contaminated land *see* Contaminated land
  Control of Pollution Act
    authorities under   363
    definitions   364–8
    Environment Agency   362
  controlled waste   352–3
    definition   368–9
  deposit meaning   370
  directive waste   364, 365–9
    exemptions   369–70
  discard   365
  disposal *see* Waste disposal
  domestic waste   346
  duty of care   399–403
    description of waste   401–2
    enforcement of duty   402–3
    holders of waste   400–1
    prevention of escape   401
    transfer to authorised person   401
  EC Directives   356–7
  economic instruments   349–51
  Environmental Protection Act   387–8
  fly-tipping   403
  gaseous effluent   369
  hazardous waste   346, 356, 357
    see also special waste
  household waste, 'dump-it' sites   364
  industrial effluent   346
  legislation   352–3

Waste management – *continued*
  licensing *see* Waste management licensing
  mineral waste   346
  minimisation of waste   347, 348–9
  non-controlled waste   369–70
  offences   384–6
    dangerous disposal   387
    defences   386–7
    penalties   385–6
  policy   348–9
  potential waste   365
  powers of Secretary of State   383–4
  public registers   382–3
  radioactive waste   369
  recovery operations   366–7
  recycling   348, 351–2, 365
  seizure of vehicles   404
  sewage sludge   346
  solid industrial waste   346
  special waste
    advance notification   408
    carriage   407
    consignment notes   406–7
    definition   405–6
    mixing   408
    proposals for change   407–8
  toxic waste   346
  trade waste   346
  transfrontier shipment   357
  transport of waste   348
  US Superfund system   410
  waste collection authorities   371
  waste defined   364–8
  waste identification changes   367
  waste regulation authorities   372–6
    powers   405
Waste management licensing   371–9
  applications   373–4
  call-in powers   383
  certificate of completion   378
  clean-up powers   389
  conditions   376–7
  consultation   373–4
  Directive disposal operations   371
  Directive recovery operations   371
  enforcement   379–82
  exemptions   371–2
  fees and charges   382
  financial adequacy requirements   376
  lack of public participation   374
  modifications   379–80, 383, 384
  offences   384–6
  refusal   374–5
  registration   372–3
  revocations   381–2, 383, 384
  site licences   373, 377–9
  supervision of licence   379

Waste management licensing – *continued*
  surrender 377–9
  suspension 380–1, 383, 384
  technical competence 375
  transfer of licence 377
  WRA powers 374–6, 405
Waste regulation authority 363
  clean-up powers 389
  inspectors 405
  licensing powers 374–6, 405
  public registers 383
Water industry, SSSIs 482
Water pollution
  centralisation 108
  charges for application to discharge 48,
    111
  common law 456–7
  consents *see* Consents to discharge
  control 415–16
    EC Directive 84–5
  controlled waters 427–8
    washing or cleaning in 455
  criminal offences 119
  dangerous substances 419
  deposit of controlled waste 298
  discharge of effluent into sewers 299
  drinking water 423, 424–6
  easement to pollute 459
  EC and 84–5, 418–24
    Directive 419–22
    emission standards 290
  enforcement
    policy 449–50
    powers 447–9
    preventive powers 450–1
    remedial powers 450–1
  forms 412
  general environmental duties 49–50
  general pollution offences 428–34
    'cause or knowingly to permit' meaning
      430–4
    defences 429–30
    penalties 429
  general quality assessment 413
  groundwater pollution 458–9

Water pollution – *continued*
  HMIP responsibilities 47–8
  importing harmful substances 456
  industry, environmental duties 49–50
  injunctions 459–60
  inland waters, removing bed of 455
  integrated pollution control 284, 445–6
  National Water Council's classification
    441
  nitrates 171–2
    sensitive areas 115, 453–4
  'no appreciable effect' exemption 26
  planning controls 454–5
  poisoning fish 455
  policy 417–18
  precautions against 451–2
  public registers 150–2, 443–5
    drinking water quality 153
    sewerage undertaker registers 152
  quality approach 420–2
  release of prescribed substances 297
  remedies 459–60
  riparian rights 457–8
  River Quality Survey 413
  sampling powers 447–8
  Scotland 416–17
  secrecy surrounding consents 142
  set standards 91
  sources 412–13
  state subsidies for 114–15
  statutory controls 9
  statutory nuisances 456
  urban waste water treatment 422–3
  Water Act 1990 414–15
  water industry 413–14
    prosecution of companies 133
  water protection zones 452–3
  water quality standards 440–3
  Water Resources Act 1991 414–15
  water supply 423–366
  see also National Rivers Authority (NRA)
Water protection zones 452–3
Wetlands 496–7
Wild birds 474–5, 490–1, 493, 497
Woodlands *see* Forestry: Tree and woodland
  protection